A Centenary History of the Indian National Congress
(1885-1985)

ACADEMIC FOUNDATION

A Centenary History of the Indian National Congress

Volume I................................1885-1919

Volume II..............................1919-1935

Volume III.............................1935-1947

Volume IV.............................1947-1964

Volume V..............................1964-1984

A Centenary History of the Indian National Congress

(1885-1985)

Volume — I

This volume released by
Shri Rajiv Gandhi
at the Centenary Session
held at Bombay on 28th December 1985

INDIAN NATIONAL CONGRESS

ACADEMIC FOUNDATION

NEW DELHI

Published in 2011
by

ACADEMIC FOUNDATION
4772-73 / 23 Bharat Ram Road, (23 Ansari Road),
Darya Ganj, New Delhi - 110 002 (India).
Phones : +91-11-23245001 / 02 / 03 / 04.
Fax : +91-11-23245005.
E-mail : books@academicfoundation.com
www.academicfoundation.com

First published by
All India Congress Committee (I), 1985.

A Centenary History of the Indian National Congress—Vol. I
Indian National Congress

ISBN 10: 8171889158
ISBN 13: 9788171889150

Typeset by Italics India, New Delhi.
Printed and bound in India.

10 9 8 7 6 5 4 3 2 1

Congress History Centenary Committee

सत्यमेव जयते

PRIME MINISTER

Foreword

SINCE ITS INCEPTION the Indian National Congress has been the voice of resurgent India. Even before the days of a mass electorate, it spoke with authority on behalf of the people of India. Its founding fathers reflected Indian public opinion at its best. They represented all the geographical regions and ethnic and religious diversities of the country. The intellectual distinction and moral eminence of leaders of the Congress like Dadabhai Naoroji, Mahadev Govind Ranade, Badruddin Tyabji, Surendranath Banerjea and Subramania Iyer were such that the people looked upon the Congress as the Parliament of the emerging Indian nation. The Congress addressed itself to basic socio-political and economic issues. Its deliberations moulded a new national public. In the early years the Congress was still a reformist rather than a revolutionary organization. But the then foreign rulers had a healthy respect for it.

Like a mountain torrent that becomes a major river on entering the plains, the Indian National Congress received tributaries from all over the country and became the established political mainstream of the land. There were few persons of standing in any part of the country who did not owe allegiance to it. After the Swadeshi Movement, its mass base widened, under the impulse of men like Bal Gangadhar Tilak, Bipin Chandra Pal and Lala Lajpat Rai. With the end of World War I, the Rowlatt Act and Jallianwala Bagh, the pace of political change quickened. Mahatma Gandhi burst upon the nation. In Jawaharlal Nehru's words:

> He was like a powerful current of fresh air that made us stretch ourselves and take deep breaths, like a beam of light that pierced the darkness and removed the scales from our eyes, like the whirlwind that upset many things but most of all the working of people's minds . . . . He did not descend from the top; he seemed to emerge from the millions of Indians, speaking their language and incessantly drawing attention to them and their appalling condition.

The Congress came to be *of* the people not merely *for* the people. It placed the thunderbolt of non-violent action in the hands of the deprived. Satyagraha gave giants' strength to the weak. It marked India's mental liberation and undermined the rulers' moral authority. The law was no longer what the rulers laid down but what the people were ready to accept as just.

The manner in which Mahatma Gandhi was able to enlist the participation of the people of India in days before the mass media bespoke of his political genius. Every great leader is a great persuader. The Congress under Mahatma Gandhi welded the people of India into a political entity in spite of the multiplicity of languages, in spite of illiteracy, and in spite of the colonial Government's efforts to discredit it through its loyal cadres. But Gandhiji and the Congress succeeded because they knew what causes to take up and how to relate politics to the people's needs, and the nation's value system. Above all they succeeded because the people felt convinced that the Congress had righteousness on its side, while the ruling power only had brute force.

In party-building Mahatma Gandhi followed the simple but revolutionary expedient of considering every Indian a potential member of the Congress unless that person openly distanced himself from it. No priests or chamberlains guarded the entrance. While critics schooled in European political traditions, liberal or socialist, deplored the reluctance of the Congress to build up cadres and enforce doctrinal uniformity, it is evident today that the Congress could not have become an open, inclusive party that it is, if it had made membership selective and adopted a narrow and rigid credo. So many cadre-based parties have lost their elan and the capacity for self-correction but the Congress, although less than perfect and often criticized, has exhibited a remarkable capacity for self-renewal, and for deriving inspiration and sustenance from the people of India.

In drawing the masses in, the Congress attracted gifted personalities at the pinnacle of their professions, like Motilal Nehru and C.R. Das, men and women who had already made a mark, like Vallabhbhai Patel, Abul Kalam Azad, Rajagopalachari, Rajen Babu and Sarojini Naidu, and the most dynamic leaders of the younger generation, like Jawaharlal Nehru, Badshah Khan, Subhas Bose and Jayaprakash Narayan. Many humble workers came into the Congress who later became stalwarts, like Lal Bahadur Shastri and Kamaraj. Charisma called out to charisma and integrity attracted integrity. Thus it was that the people were convinced that the national movement could provide leaders superior to what the colonial system could.

At its very creation the Congress was democratic and secular. Under the influence of mass politics it also became socialist, pledged to promoting the interests of the vast millions of landless and propertyless. As Jawaharlal Nehru put it at the Lucknow Congress in 1936: 'I see no way of ending the poverty, the vast unemployment, the degradation and the subjection of the Indian people except through socialism. That involves vast and revolutionary changes in our political and social structure, the ending of vested interests in land and industry, as well as the feudal and autocratic Indian States systems.'

Fighting poverty, along with the abolition of untouchability, became the socio-economic programme of the Congress, even as winning freedom through non-violence was its political objective.

In the latter part of the twenties and throughout the thirties, Congressmen realized that they were fighting the battle not only of the people of India but of subject peoples all over the world. India had to win independence, and the entire edifice of colonialism would collapse. The Congress evolved a foreign policy which was based on our identification with the cause of freedom and equality everywhere. When World War II broke out, it was galling for India to be denied an opportunity to fight on behalf of the forces of freedom against fascism.

I am not going into the tortuous negotiations with the British and the circumstances leading to the end of imperial rule over India. I shall content myself with saying that when free India was born, it had a party with a large vision and lofty principles and a leadership of a calibre rarely seen in world history. It had an unparalleled hold on people's loyalties. Freedom could not have been consolidated and major programmes of social change through consent could not have been initiated if the Congress had thought that its work was over with the attainment of freedom. The Congress adopted a Constitution which reflected India's unity-in-diversity, and which provided for a strong Centre coexisting with thriving States. It undertook the grand task of national planning which, later under Indira Gandhi, enabled the nation to attain agricultural and industrial self-reliance.

At hundred, the Congress is young and vital. Its spirit of service and its sense of history are undimmed. Several groups have broken away from the Congress from time to time. But the Congress continues to be India's political mainstream. Freedom's battle has not ended. The causes of democracy, secularism and socialism, and of peace, coexistence and equality among the nations place continuing responsibilities on the Congress. It has to help the country to complete the unfinished revolution of technological modernization and eradication of poverty and thereby release the creative energies of India.

I think it most appropriate that as part of the Centenary celebrations, the Congress should place before the people of India, more particularly before the younger generations, a scholarly and comprehensive account of its role in the struggle for freedom and the social and economic reconstruction of India. Such an account has more than just antiquarian interest. The past offers no simple clues to the present or the future. But a scholarly work like the *Centenary History of the Indian National Congress* has much to offer to us by way of self-perception and poise as we face the new challenges. The Congress is grateful to Shri B.N. Pande and to the distinguished galaxy of scholars who have contributed to this collective endeavour.

(Rajiv Gandhi)

New Delhi
October 4, 1985

Preface

On 28 December 1985 the Indian National Congress, the party which won freedom for India and has shaped her fortunes since 1947, celebrates its centenary. The achievements of the Congress over the past century and its potential for the future have few parallels in the history of India. For the first sixty-two years of its existence, the Congress presided over a national movement of epic proportions, which sought to transform a civilization of antiquity into a modern nation, and inflicted a crushing defeat upon the greatest imperial power known to humankind. Moreover, the party which led the people of India to independence has, thereafter, played a decisive role in shaping their moral and material destiny. Indeed, under a youthful leader of distinguished stature, Shri Rajiv Gandhi, the Congress is today poised to lead the people of India into a new phase of national creativity in the 21st century.

As the centenary of the Congress drew near, the late Shrimati Indira Gandhi initiated a scholarly project with the objective of evaluating the party's contribution to the struggle for freedom as well as to the social and economic development of India in the decades since 1947. She believed that a proper appreciation of the Congress; of the great leaders who had shaped its politics; of their ideals and the movements which they initiated; and of the central place which the Congress held in the affections of the people; were vital to the task of building a resurgent India. Shrimati Gandhi also realized the colossal magnitude of such a scholarly endeavour. It was, therefore, her desire that a comprehensive history of the Congress be written through the participation of the community of historians which had grown in India over the past few decades. Shrimati Gandhi believed that this history of the Congress should be addressed to the people as a whole. But it was to be addressed in particular to the generations which had come of age after 1947, and could, therefore, profit enormously from a recapitulation of the ideals which sustained the freedom struggle; and the sacrifices of tens upon thousands which lay behind the emergence of India as a nation free to shape its destiny.

With this end in view the Congress (I) Working Committee appointed the Congress History Project Committee in April 1976, with Congress President as Chairman and B.N. Pande (myself) as Executive Director. It took many years in locating and collecting original documents and material. I was a bit apprehensive of the responsibility I had undertaken and of its successful execution. But with the inspiration and encouragement I received from Shrimati Gandhi and the co-operation from my distinguished colleagues and nearly fifty eminent scholars, I was able to fulfil this gigantic task of bringing out this Centenary History of the Indian National Congress, an organization with which I have had the honour and privilege of continuous association for the last 65 years, since 1920.

In planning *A Centenary History of the Indian National Congress*, we also received full support and encouragement from the Prime Minister and the President of the Congress, Shri Rajiv Gandhi, who took keen interest in the execution of this project. Shri Rajiv Gandhi's profound grasp of the ideals of Mahatma Gandhi, Jawaharlal Nehru and Indira Gandhi — ideals which underpinned the struggle for freedom and informed the reconstruction of India after 1947 — are a matter of public knowledge. Also important for us was his perception of what would interest and inform the younger generations, since our scholarly labour was specially directed towards placing before them a stimulating account of the past as a clue to the present and a guide to the future.

The task of writing a comprehensive history of the Congress turned out to be a colossal one. Perhaps it would be correct to state that rarely has a scholarly undertaking of such magnitude, drawing upon the labour of close upon fifty scholars, ever been attempted before. The results of this labour are now before you. It was my privilege to oversee their preparation in the capacity of its General Editor and Chairman of its Editorial Board. We trust that the people of India, more particularly the younger generations, will find in these volumes a stimulating account of the Congress; of the struggle which led to the liberation of our country; and also of the effort which went into the task of building a new nation on the foundations of an old civilization. Perhaps our account will also provide the people with the moral sustenance which they need for resolving the problems which they face today, and the challenges which they may encounter in the years which lie ahead.

I

While it would be difficult to portray in a brief account an overview of the Congress over the past century, more particularly because this task has been attempted by my scholarly colleagues in the accounts which follow, I would nevertheless like to highlight some of the seminal developments which constitute the substance of the *Centenary History*. It is well known that the Congress owes its genesis to the initiative of a British civilian, Allen Octavian Hume, who had over the years gained an understanding of the aspirations of the educated as well as of the popular classes. Hume posed before the intelligentsia the challenge of organizing an all-India forum, where matters of national concern could be debated, and the results of such deliberations communicated to the British Government for remedial action.

While Hume's role in organizing a national forum for the educated classes of India is well known, it would be simplistic to assume that his initiative was the solitary factor behind the genesis of the Congress. Indeed, there are two cores of political activity which need to be highlighted before we can appreciate the context in which the Congress came to life. At least half a century before Hume's initiative, the landed gentry, the commercial classes and the intelligentsia of Calcutta, Bombay and Madras had initiated a process which culminated in the birth of the Congress in 1885. The activities of these classes were reflected in the growth of the local and regional associations which mushroomed in the subcontinent in the decades under review. Even more important than this elite activity were stirrings within the popular classes — the peasantry, the tribal communities, and the working and artisan classes — some of which were articulated in the uprising of 1857. Here we touch upon social classes whose economic condition or political consciousness has been only partially explored, though their importance — they constituted the overwhelming majority of the Indian people — to the national movement hardly needs any emphasis. The aspirations of the popular classes are vividly reflected in the scholarly contributions to the *Centenary History*, since it is only through their participation in the freedom struggle that the Congress acquired the strength to dislodge British imperialism.

There is ample evidence in historical literature of the misery which the British Government inflicted upon the popular classes; and the manner in which this created in peasants, workers, artisans and tribals a sense of hostility towards the regime of imperialism. Indeed, throughout the decades under consideration, the popular classes rose repeatedly against the alien rulers, in movements of protest which are increasingly being drawn into the ambit of scholarly research. Perhaps the resistance of the peasantry to exploitation at the hands of the British Government is sensitively highlighted in numerous studies of agrarian nationalism. More dramatic were tribal uprisings against imperial exploitation, the most vivid example of which is the Santhal uprising of 1855. Within the cities of India, too, a working class had crystallized by the closing decades of the 19th century which erupted in movements of great strength against the colonial state. As already suggested, Hume was aware of these rumblings of disaffection within the womb of Indian society, just as he also realized that a nationalist alliance between the intelligentsia and the popular classes would seriously undermine British control over India.

The delegates who assembled in Bombay on 28 December 1885, at the first annual session of the Congress, were representative of all social classes and communities which subscribed to nationalism and sought to shape a new destiny for India. Most of the delegates were drawn from the local and regional associations which had sprung to life in the preceding decades in various parts of the country. Again, most of them were lawyers, or journalists, or scholars, or men of business, or members of the landed classes, and they represented an alliance of the intelligentsia with the professional and commercial classes, on the one hand, and the landed gentry, on the other. At first blush, therefore, it would appear that the organization which came into existence in 1885 spoke only for a small fragment of the Indian nation. Yet the modest base of the Congress, when it was born in 1885, did not exhaust the social vision of its members or preclude them from reaching out to the popular classes in subsequent decades.

That the Congress looked upon itself as a political movement destined to reach out to the nation as a whole, is demonstrated by its agenda of political action and the ideology which its leaders shaped out in the next two decades. While it is true that the Congress largely concerned itself with questions affecting the interests of the middle classes, such issues did not exhaust its social concerns. Thus, while among the issues taken up for deliberation were those pertaining to the creation of representative institutions within the country, and the increasing participation of Indians in the civil service, some leaders of the Congress, like Dadabhai Naoroji and R.C. Dutt, were equally concerned about relations between Great Britain and India and the manner in which these were articulated between different classes within Indian society. Thus, Naoroji elaborated the 'Drain Theory', which demonstrated how the wealth of India was siphoned off to Great Britain; and Dutt built up a critique of the manner in which this exploitation contributed to the impoverishment of the rural classes. The social vision of the leaders of the Congress, in the first two or three decades after its creation was, therefore, not limited to the interests of the classes which flocked to its annual sessions. Indeed, they assumed responsibility for the nation as a whole, more particularly for the peasantry, even at a juncture when they were not able to reach out to the popular classes.

The concern of the leaders of the Congress for the nation, for the rich as well as the poor, was by no means a purely abstract concern. Prominent among the youthful leaders who were drawn to the Congress at this juncture, in the first few years, were men like Bal Gangadhar Tilak, Gopal Krishna Gokhale, Badruddin Tyabji, Anand Charlu, Vijayaraghavachariar, Madan Mohan Malaviya, Lajpat Rai and Bipin Chandra Pal, all below 45 years of age, who were interested in reaching out to the popular classes, and who also believed that the idiom of nationalist policies would have to be indigenized, and given a structure appropriate to the cultural traditions of India, before such a consummation could be accomplished.

While the Congress was seeking to broaden its support, the British Government decided to strike a death-blow at the party as the embodiment of nationalism. The Viceroy, Lord Curzon, believed that the Congress enjoyed the support only of the educated classes, and could easily be wiped out of existence. Yet the educated classes were causing the British Government considerable disquiet, more particularly in the Presidency of Bengal. By partitioning the presidency into smaller territorial units, Curzon sought to fatally weaken the Bengali intelligentsia and dampen the fires of nationalism in the region. The partition of Bengal was ostensibly a measure of administrative rationalization. Actually, it sought to deliver the *coup de grace* to the nationalist classes of Bengal. Nor did the intelligentsia harbour any illusions about the motivations of Curzon. Indeed, the agitation against the partition of Bengal revealed the extent to which the political activity of men like Aurobindo in Bengal; Tilak in Maharashtra; and Lajpat Rai and Ajit Singh in the Punjab had disseminated nationalism among entirely new classes of Indian society. Even the moderate, Surendranath Banerjea, took offence at the insult hurled at Bengal. Needless to say, leaders like Aurobindo and Bipin Chandra Pal were much more effective than Banerjea in the anti-partition agitation, and they transformed the movement into something akin to a mass struggle in the region. Their efforts were augmented by the literary work of Rabindranath Tagore, the distinguished poet. The agitation against the partition of Bengal took the form of a movement, the so-called Swadeshi Movement, which attempted to bring about a far reaching transformation within Indian society. This movement shook the British Raj to its very foundations, and the populist support which it aggregated obliged the British Government to revoke the partition in 1911.

Beyond the 'Extremist', leaders of the Swadeshi Movement there emerged a number of revolutionary groups, whose members sought to liberate India through selective acts of violence. Such groups were often inspired by the writings of Aurobindo and Tilak, though their vision of liberation through violence differed from the vision of these two leaders. They believed that, through the assassination of key civil servants, they could inspire the people of India to rise against British imperialism and win freedom. Needless to say, the coercive resources available to the British Government outmatched the capacity for violence of the revolutionary nationalists, with the result that, within a decade, the British were able to break up the networks of such activities. Yet, while suppressing the revolutionaries, the British Government also devised a constitutional package — the so-called Minto-Morley reforms of 1909 — to secure the co-operation of Congress leaders, Moderates and Extremists, who fought for freedom without taking recourse to violence.

The Swadeshi Movement brought about seminal changes within the Congress. Two groups, to whom we have already referred as Moderates and Extremists, popularly called *Naram Dal* and *Garam Dal,* crystallized within the party in the course of the movement. The differences between these groups, which rested upon tactics rather than upon strategy, came to a head during the annual session of the Congress at Surat in 1907. However, the developments at Surat have not been properly interpreted by the historians of the national movement. It is significant that the Surat split came about at a time when a new generation of Indians had to be drawn into nationalist politics. Perhaps the extremist leaders, men like Tilak, Pal, Lajpat Rai and Aurobindo, represented as much the aspirations of a new generation in the country as they represented the aspirations of new classes within Indian society. Such changes in leadership, as a new generation attains maturity, characterize the history of the Congress over the past century; and they explain the remarkable capacity of this party to remain in the mainstream of politics for a century. Indeed, this process of renewal highlights a strange paradox: the Congress — the oldest party in India — is also the youngest party in the country in its leadership as well as in its support base.

II

The years of World War I (1914-18) mark a seminal transformation in the leadership and support base of the Congress. When hostilities broke out in 1914, the Congress had not recovered from the split of 1907. After Surat, there were a number of attempts at bringing together Moderates and Extremists, none of them very successful. Perhaps a more significant development was the alienation of Muslim opinion from the British Government, largely as a result of the growing tension in European politics between Great Britain and Turkey, the dominant Islamic state at this stage.

The outbreak of war, however, rallied nationalist opinion in India around the defence of the British Empire. The leaders of the Congress pledged their support to Great Britain, in the belief that their plea for political autonomy would be considered sympathetically by the British Government once hostilities come to an end. To reinforce this plea, these leaders were able to bring about substantial unity among different sections of opinion by 1916. Not only was the cleavage between Moderates and Extremists healed, but the Congress was able to persuade Muslim League leaders to jointly present to the British Government constitutional proposals seeking for India political autonomy within the British Empire.

At this juncture, a leader of epic stature staged his entry into nationalist politics in India. Mohandas Karamchand Gandhi had even prior to World War I attracted considerable attention through his struggle against racial bigotry in South Africa. More significantly, Gandhi had devised in the process a novel weapon of political agitation. The mahatma now sought to reshape the Congress in the image of his world-view. This is not the place to assess Satyagraha as a mode of political action and non-violence as the basis of the struggle for freedom in India. Such a task has been attempted elsewhere in the *Centenary History*. Yet a few salient facets of Gandhian ideology need to be highlighted here. Gandhi believed that all religions, shorn of ritual and cant, were capable of co-existing beneficially insofar as they sought to liberate humanity through truth and non-violence. He further believed that the social and the political domains were as valid arenas of religious activity as the spiritual domain. Indeed, the differentiation of the sacred from the profane, and the spiritual from the secular, had contributed substantively to the malaise which afflicted western society. Through equating the secular with the spiritual domain, it was possible to frame a strategy of political action which liberated the exploited at the same time as the exploiters. Within India, Gandhi believed that it was possible to conjure into existence a movement of national regeneration which would achieve the goal of swaraj at the same time as it revitalized the creative energy and reinforced the moral fibre of the people.

When Gandhi returned to India in 1915, he acquainted himself, as advised by Gopal Krishna Gokhale, with nationalist politics through a dialogue with the educated classes already active in the Congress and also by undertaking an extensive tour in the country. Gandhi had built an ashram at Ahmedabad to train a cadre of satyagrahis who would devote themselves to the reconstruction of Indian society on the basis of *satya* and *ahimsa*.

Notwithstanding his experiments in the revival of hand-spinning and weaving; the removal of untouchability; and national education; Gandhi was soon drawn into the vortex of Indian politics by events which constitute decisive landmarks in the history of our freedom struggle. Within the space of a few years, he led movements of the peasantry at Champaran and Kheda; and a strike of the textile workers of Ahmedabad. Gandhi's association with these agitations provided him with an insight into the political temper of the popular classes.

By the time the limited Satyagraha experiments of Gandhi came to a successful conclusion, World War I ended. Jawaharlal Nehru summing up the situation at the time wrote:

> And the peace, instead of bringing us relief and progress, brought us repressive legislation and martial law in the Punjab. A bitter sense of humiliation and a passionate anger filled our people. All the unending talk of constitutional reform and Indianization of the services was a mockery and an insult when the manhood of our country was crushed and the inexorable and continuous process of exploitation was deepening our poverty and sapping our vitality. We had become a derelict nation.[1]

At this juncture Gandhi appeared on the national scene. Describing the advent of Gandhi, Jawaharlal Nehru wrote:

> And then Gandhi came. He was like a powerful current of fresh air that made us stretch ourselves and take deep breaths; like a beam of light that pierced the darkness and removed the scales from our eyes; like a whirlwind that upset many things, but most of all the working of people's minds. He did not descend from the top; he seemed to emerge from the millions of India, speaking their language and incessantly drawing attention to them and their appalling condition. Get off the backs of these peasants and workers, he told us, all you who live by their exploitation; get rid of the system that produces this poverty and misery. Political freedom took new shape then and acquired a new content. . . . The essence of his teaching was fearlessness and truth, and action allied to these always keeping the welfare of the masses in view. The greatest gift for an individual or a nation, so we had been told in our ancient books, was *abhaya* (fearlessness), not merely bodily courage but the absence of fear from the mind. . . . But the dominant impulse in India under British rule was that of fear — pervasive, oppressing, strangling fear; fear of the army, the police, the widespread secret service; fear of the official class; fear of laws meant to suppress and of prison; fear of the landlord's agent; fear of the moneylender; fear of unemployment and starvation, which were always on the threshold. It was against this all-pervading fear that Gandhi's quiet and determined voice was raised: Be not afraid.
>
> So, suddenly as it were, that black pall of fear was lifted from the people's shoulders, not wholly of course, but to an amazing degree. . . . It was a psychological change, almost as if some expert in psycho-analytical methods had probed deep into the patient's past, found out the origins of his complexes, exposed them to his view, and thus rid him of that burden.

Regarding Gandhi's entry into the Congress, Jawaharlal said:

> Gandhi for the first time entered the Congress organization and immediately brought about a complete change in its constitution. He made it democratic and a mass organization. Democratic it had been previously also but it had so far been limited in franchise and restricted to the upper classes. Now the peasants rolled in and, in its new garb, it began to assume the look of a vast agrarian organization with a strong sprinkling of the middle classes. This agrarian character was to grow. Industrial workers also came in but as individuals and not in their separate organized capacity.[2]

The manner in which Gandhi was able to draw upon the aspirations of different communities and classes, Hindus, Muslims and Sikhs, the rich and the poor, capitalists and workers, zamindars and kisans, professional men and the intelligentsia, artisans and tribals, constitutes the theme of a number of contributions in the *Centenary History*. I do not propose to go over the ground already covered therein. However, it would be appropriate to focus upon some of the salient features of the anti-imperialist agitations organized by Gandhi in the first half of the 20th century. The most striking aspect of these agitations was the extent to which they succeeded in uniting different elements of Indian society. That these agitations rested upon non-violence; that as a result the sentiment of nationalism crystallized in new classes and communities; are some of the features of the Gandhian movements which need to be highlighted.

III

The transformation which Mahatma Gandhi brought about in the national movement was momentous in its implications for the relationship between British imperialism and Indian nationalism, on the one hand, and between different classes and communities within Indian society, on the other. Indeed, through the ideology of non-violence, Gandhi was able to change the very nature of the discourse between Great Britain and India as well as between different constituents of Indian society.

The changes which Gandhi wrought in nationalist politics were achieved without the loss of its former sources of support, namely, the intelligentsia, the gentry and the commercial classes. Nothing illustrates this better than the fiery enthusiasm with which Jawaharlal Nehru welcomed the advent of Gandhi and accepted satyagraha as the means of India's liberation. Nehru's stance reflected that of an entire generation of young Indians, who were deeply influenced by the liberal humanism of the West and ready to accept an ideology that would effect India's liberation through drawing the downtrodden classes into the struggle for freedom. Nehru saw in the mahatma a symbol of the rural classes and an assurance of their support for the freedom struggle. His political relationship with Gandhi was shaped most of all by the influence which the mahatma exercised over the poor and the deprived, at the same time as he stimulated the admiration of the middle classes. Gandhi's influence over the intelligentsia was inseparable from his influence over the peasantry; and this relationship constituted a crucial underpinning of the freedom struggle.

Nevertheless, in a country as large and complex as India, the non-violent agitation could not be sustained indefinitely. Thus it soon became clear that the Non-Cooperation Movement which was launched with conspicuous success in 1920-21 was running into serious trouble as a sequel to suspension of mass satyagraha followed by Gandhiji's arrest and subsequent incarceration. The Government of Turkey had already abolished the office of Khilafat leaving the Indian Muslims in a quandry. There were indications that the communities which had come together under the mahatma's leadership were finding it difficult to continue agitation against the British raj. Even more significant were the eruptions of Mopla violence in Kerala, at the same time as the peasantry fought British imperialism non-violently under the leadership of Gandhi. To the mahatma such violence was reflected most vividly in the incident at Chauri Chaura in February 1922, which prompted him to call off the planned mass Civil Disobedience. The Viceroy, Lord Reading, heaved a sigh of relief with the remark that, 'Gandhi's programme came within an inch of success.'

The suspension of mass Civil Disobedience and the arrest and imprisonment of the Mahatma in 1922 was as traumatic an experience for the leaders of the Congress as it was for the people of India. Small wonder, then, that some senior leaders, after their release from prison, put forward at this juncture an altogether new strategy for the attainment of swaraj. Prominent among them were C.R. Das, Motilal Nehru, and Hakim Ajmal Khan who sought to carry the battle of nationalism into the new legislatures which had been created by the Reforms of 1919. By breaking up the constitutional machinery devised by these reforms, the Swarajists sought to demonstrate the strength of nationalism in India.

A great battle was fought at the Gaya session of the Congress in December 1922, presided over by C.R. Das. But the resolution for council entry was lost by an overwhelming majority. The Congress was divided between 'No-changers and Pro-changers'.

When Gandhi was released in 1924, he persuaded Congressmen to give full freedom to Das and the elder Nehru to carry out their experiment. He himself decided to devote all his energies to organizing a 'Constructive Programme' in order to prepare the rural mass of the people for the next satyagraha struggle.

Mahatma Gandhi had virtually retired from active leadership of the

Congress in 1925 leaving the political field to the Swaraj Party led by C.R. Das and Motilal Nehru.

The AICC in its meeting held at Patna on 22 September 1925 resolved that, 'the work in connection with the Indian and Provincial Legislatures shall be carried on in accordance with the policy and programme laid down by the Swaraj Party.'

But there was already a significant body of opinion within the Swaraj Party which had always been opposed to the tactics of obstruction in the legislatures. The body was known as the Responsive Co-operation Party and included men like M.R. Jayakar, M.S. Aney, N.C. Kelkar, B.S. Moonje and others from Maharashtra.

The Swarajists succeeded for some time, in paralyzing the functioning of the legislatures. But before long the Swarajists' position, too, became untenable due to the success of the British Government in winning over individual members of the party to its standpoint, through the promise of office. Well before the erosion of Swarajist strength became an avalanche, however, Motilal Nehru and his followers walked out of the reformed legislatures to rejoin the mainstream within the Congress.

Perhaps a more enduring solution to the impasse was provided by Jawaharlal Nehru. Nehru discovered that socialism lent a novel meaning to the anti-imperialist struggle which Gandhi had initiated in 1920. A crucial question was whether the freedom movement was purely a political phenomenon; or whether it also involved a redistribution of social and economic power within Indian society. The socialist answer to this question was clear. The movement was as much concerned with social and economic objectives as with the attainment of freedom. For this reason, it was not only necessary to draw the masses into the struggle for freedom, but it was also necessary to assure them social equity when freedom was attained. Moreover, the national movement in India was not an isolated phenomenon; indeed, it was a part of the wider struggle which other colonial societies in Asia and Africa were also waging against European imperialism.

The dissemination of socialist ideas proceeded apace through the crusading zeal of Jawaharlal Nehru and other youthful leaders of the Congress, prominent among whom was Subhas Chandra Bose. These leaders were able to propagate a new consciousness among the intelligentsia, the working classes, and the peasantry as to how India could be liberated and Indian society reconstituted after liberation. Jawaharlal set out this vision with striking clarity in his writings after his return from Europe at the end of 1927, where, along with his father, he had paid a visit to Soviet Russia:

> What are we driving at? Freedom? Swaraj? Independence? Dominion Status? Words which may mean much or little or nothing at all? Again, . . .

> whose freedom are we particularly striving for, for nationalism covers many sins and includes many a conflicting element?
>
> Whither India? Surely to the great human goal of social and economic equality, to the ending of all exploitation of nation by nation and class by class, to national freedom within the framework of an international cooperative socialist world federation. This is not such an empty idealist dream as some people imagine. It is within the range of the practical politics of today and the near future. We may not have it within our grasp but those with vision can see it emerging on the horizon. And even if there be delay in the realization of our goal, what does it matter if our steps march in the right direction and our eyes look steadily in front. For in the pursuit itself of a mighty purpose there is joy and happiness and a measure of achievement. . . .[3]

The Madras Congress in 1927 authorized its President M.A. Ansari to appoint an All-Party Committee to draft a constitution for India. Ansari appointed this committee under the chairmanship of Motilal Nehru.

The report of the Nehru Committee was discussed at a conference in Lucknow in August 1928, and again in the All-Parties Convention in Calcutta in December 1928. In both places, it was evident that there were serious differences of opinion between different parties; yet all had tried to accommodate one another to the utmost in order to present an agreed solution.

Muslim separatism was by now firmly entrenched and cast its shadow over other sections of the population. Youth showed signs of drifting away, either to the Left or to a negation of non-violence, which was, with Gandhi, a creed, but with most Congressmen only a policy.

The first All-India Socialist Youth Congress was held in Calcutta on 27 December 1928 under the chairmanship of Jawaharlal Nehru. Several resolutions were passed, one of which is given below:

> In the opinion of this Congress complete Independence and not Dominion Status is the immediate political objective of India not as an ideal but as the necessary preliminary to a communistic society and rejects altogether the Nehru Committee Report for the following among other principles, viz.:
>
> That it allows the bourgeoisie to compromise with the British Imperialists by establishing the so-called Dominion Status which involves the safeguard of the vested interests, landowning, feudal and capitalist, and sacrifice the interests of the masses.[4]

Jawaharlal Nehru and Subhas Chandra Bose raised the demand of complete independence as the objective of the Congress. Gandhi, Motilal and other senior Congress leaders were sympathetic to this demand, but, for tactical reasons, they offered the British Government the space of a year to accept constitutional package which they had fashioned in 1928, and which called for Dominion Status as the basis of India's position within the British Empire. But when the British Government turned a deaf ear to this demand, the Congress, under the presidentship of Jawaharlal Nehru, at the historic session at Lahore in December 1929, approved of *purna swaraj* as the objective of a renewed struggle which was to be launched under the direction and leadership of Mahatma Gandhi.

As proposed by the Congress Working Committee, Mahatma Gandhi had met the viceroy on 23 December 1930, prior to the Lahore session of the Congress, with the object of giving him an ultimatum, calling for acceptance of the Calcutta Congress demand failing which civil disobedience would be launched. But a day earlier, an attempt was made to blow off the railway coach in which the viceroy was travelling to Delhi. Luckily he escaped. Earlier, a bomb had been thrown into the chamber of Central Assembly. In fact, since the arrival of Simon Commission and the death of Lala Lajpat Rai, as a result of police lathi blows, the political atmosphere was surcharged with violence.

Commenting on the series of violent events Mahatma Gandhi wrote:

> Take now the positive side of the argument. When, that is in 1920, non-violence came to be a part of the Congress creed the Congress became a transformed body as if by magic. Mass awakening came no one knows how. Even remote villages were stirred. Many abuses seemed to have been swept away. The people became conscious of their power. They ceased to fear authority. The system of *begar* (forced labour) vanished like mist in Almora and several other parts of India, wherever the people had become awakened to a sense of the power that lay within themselves. Such as it was, it was their freedom that they had attained by their own strength. . . . It was true Swaraj of the masses attained by the masses. If the march of non-violence had not been interrupted by events culminating in Chauri Chaura, I make bold to say that we would have been today in full possession of Swaraj.

Giving a warning against violence Mahatma said:

> We are now entering upon a new era. Our immediate objective and not our distant goal is complete independence. Is it not obvious that if we are to evolve the true spirit of independence amongst the millions, we shall only do so through non-violence and all it implies? It is not enough that we drive out Englishmen by making their lives insecure through secret violence. That would lead not to independence but to utter confusion. We can establish independence only by adjusting our differences through an appeal to the head and the heart, by evolving organic unity amongst ourselves, not by terrorizing or killing those who, we fancy, may impede our march, but by patient and gentle handling, by converting the oppo-

nent, we want to offer mass civil disobedience. Everybody owns that it is a certain remedy. Everybody understands that 'civil' here means strictly non-violent, and has it not often been demonstrated that mass civil disobedience is an impossibility without mass non-violence and without mass discipline? Surely it does not require an appeal to our religious faith to convince us that the necessity of our situation, if nothing else, demands non-violence of the limited type I have indicated. Let those who are not past reason then cease either secretly or openly to endorse activities such as this latest bomb outrage. Rather let them openly and heartily condemn these outrages, so that our deluded patriots may, for want of nourishment to their violent spirit, realize the futility of violence and the great harm that violent activity has every time done.[5]

For the attainment of *purna swaraj* Gandhi pointed out that:

The greatest and the most effective sanction, however, is civil disobedience including non-payment of taxes. Whilst the task of choosing the time and the method of it has been nominally and properly left to the All-India Congress Committee to decide, I know that it is a duty primarily devolving upon me. I must confess that I do not see the atmosphere for it today. I want to discover a formula whereby sufficient provision can be made for avoiding suspension by reason of Chauri Chaura. A time must come when there may be a fight to the finish with one's back to the wall. . . . I can only give the impatient patriot the assurance, that I am concentrating all my powers on discovering a workable formula. He can help me materially by assisting to promote a non-violent atmosphere and to push forward the constructive programme. I know that many have refused to see any connection between the constructive programme and civil disobedience. But for one who believes in non-violence it does not need hard thinking to realize the essential connection between the constructive programme and civil disobedience for Swaraj. . . . For such an indefinable thing as Swaraj people must have previous training in doing things of all-India interest. Such work must throw together the people and their leaders whom they would trust implicitly. Trust begotten in the pursuit of continuous constructive work becomes a tremendous asset at the critical moment. Constructive work, therefore, is for a non-violent army what drilling etc. is for an army designed for bloody warfare. Individual civil disobedience among an unprepared people and by leaders not known to or trusted by them is of no avail, and is an impossibility.[6]

The breaking of the Salt Law began on 12 March 1930, when Gandhi started on a 241-mile trek from Sabarmati towards the sea with a band of 79 associates. Careful preparations were made all over India for breach of this law, as well as of ordinances prohibiting peaceful processions and peaceful picketing of shops dealing in liquor or in foreign cloth. The whole of India watched with bated breath; and when the signal was given by Gandhi's symbolic breach of the Salt Law on the seashore on 6

April 1930, the whole country plunged into the campaign with unexampled enthusiasm.

The success was phenomenal. There was hardly any breach of non-violent discipline, and, altogether, during the duration of the campaign, nearly a hundred thousand of people suffered imprisonment, while during the Non-cooperation Movement the number had been of the order of 30,000.

An important feature of the Salt Satyagraha was an audacious step designed by Gandhi during the later stages of the campaign. When the government had almost settled down into the routine programme of imprisoning volunteers, or of manhandling them and a kind of stalemate seemed to have overtaken the campaign, Gandhi altered his tactics. In order to invite the government to do its worst, he designed 'non-violent raids' on the salt godowns of Dharasana and Wadala.[7] The invitation to the government was now, not merely to imprison, but also to shoot.

However, in the face of these tactics, the government did not actually shoot, but took measures to beat off the advancing satyagrahis. Shooting satyagrahis who were unarmed, and in the sight of numerous European and American newspapermen who had come to witness the strange scene, would have lowered their reputation considerably. And this is something they were anxious to avoid. But where conditions could be controlled by military censors, there was no dearth of situations where British soldiers did not hesitate to shoot straight with the intention to kill.[8]

The movement gained countrywide momentum and obliged the British Government to bring into full play the instruments of repression at its command. Yet a movement which defied the British raj non-violently seriously weakened the fabric of British rule over India, and undermined the morale of the civil services which were the instruments of this rule. Indeed, the British Government was under such enormous pressure that the Viceroy, Lord Irwin, invited Gandhi for negotiations in a bid to buy peace. The incorrigible Winston Churchill voiced the distress of an entire generation of Tory imperialists when he expressed his disgust at the spectacle of 'the half naked faqir' parleying with Irwin. These negotiations led to a truce, under which Irwin persuaded the Mahatma to participate in discussions in Great Britain designed to shape a new constitution for India.

As was expected, Gandhi was unable to gain much from the Round Table Conference held in London in 1931, and he landed back at Bombay empty-handed. His prominent colleagues Jawaharlal Nehru, Abdul Ghaffar Khan and others had already been arrested and imprisoned. The Congress Working Committee advised their countrymen to launch mass civil disobedience, including non-payment of taxes. Gandhi was arrested on 4 January 1932 and this was followed by countrywide resumption of mass civil disobedience. More than a hundred thousand satyagrahis were arrested. Lathi charges and firing became the order of the day. The non-violent struggle continued for over two years. In UP, Gujarat, Maharashtra and Andhra Pradesh it took the form of no-rent satyagraha where thousands of peasants were dispossessed of their land.

The British response to 1932-3 Civil Disobedience Movement was a new constitution which was adopted in 1935. This constitution marks an important stage in the growth of the national movement, although we are unable to endorse the view of some historians that the Act of 1935 was a statesmanlike initiative on the part of the British Government. According to these scholars, the constitution of 1935 reflected the recognition by the British Government of three articulate political forces in India; the great body of Hindu opinion organized under the aegis of the Congress; the minorities, more particularly the Muslim and the untouchable communities, which stood outside the framework of the Congress; and the Princely States, whose subjects were largely untouched by the leaven of nationalism. The Act of 1935, these historians further argue, brought together the three discordant forces into an effective polity. Our perception of the constitution of 1935 differs radically from that of such scholars. The federal polity envisaged by the constitution, so we believe, was an instrument designed to provide British control over India with a durable basis. It sought to do so through creating a federal government subject to imperial control, while nationalism expended itself in managing the autonomous provinces of British India.

Although the leaders of the Congress had serious reservations about the Act of 1935, they decided, after some initial hesitation, to contest the elections to the provincial legislatures held under its aegis, if only to demonstrate the support they enjoyed with the popular classes. Indeed, both the strength and the weaknesses of the Congress were fully demonstrated by the provincial elections of 1937. In six provinces of British India, which had a Hindu majority, Congress candidates won clear victories. In the rest, where the Muslims had a majority, or constituted a very substantial proportion of the population, the majority of votes went, not to the Muslim League but to regional parties which did not fully accept the policies of the Congress.

The problems facing the provincial Congress governments which came to power in 1937 were by no means easy of resolution. So far as the British Government was concerned, it welcomed official acceptance by the Congress as a means of persuading that body to expend its energies in the provincial arena, from where (so the British believed) it had little prospect of contesting the over-arching dominance of imperial power. For the principal leaders of the Congress — Mahatma Gandhi, Jawaharlal Nehru, Sardar Patel, Maulana Azad and Rajendra Prasad — the behaviour of the provincial Congress governments was a test of the ability of the provincial nationalist leaders to keep their strategic objectives firmly in focus while at the same time working to redeem their election pledges to the people.

The outbreak of war in 1939 did not catch the leaders of the Congress wholly unprepared. Since the time Jawaharlal Nehru had visited Europe in 1927, to attend an anti-imperialist conference, he had maintained contact with the socialist leaders of Europe as well as with the leaders of liberation movements elsewhere in Asia and Africa. He had also watched with concern the growth of fascism in Italy and in Germany. Repeatedly, in the course of the 1930s, the Congress adopted resolutions condemning the passivity of the capitalist democracies — particularly Great Britain and France — in the face of increasing fascist aggression in Europe and elsewhere. The Congress, as the representative of the people of India, not only distanced itself from the policy of appeasement pursued by Great Britain and France in the 1930s, but it also expressed sympathy for the victims of fascist terror. The leaders of the Congress believed, however, that the people of India could not participate in any war between the capitalist democracies and the fascist powers, until they were liberated, and joined an anti-fascist alliance as a *free* rather than as an *enslaved* people.

In view of the Congress stance upon the issue of war, the decision of the British Government to declare India a belligerent power in September 1939 was a serious mistake. To demonstrate their resentment of this step, the Congress ministries in the provinces where the party had won a majority in 1937 tendered their resignations. After this gesture of disapproval, the Congress leaders reviewed the national and the international scene, in order to devise an appropriate programme of political action. The situation was, of course, an exceedingly complex one. Prominent leaders like Jawaharlal Nehru looked upon Nazi Germany with extreme hostility; and they did not want to embark upon any step which would weaken the anti-fascist struggle in Europe. At the same time, Subhas Chandra Bose was aiming to liberate India with the help of the fascist powers. Besides, a majority within the Congress believed that popular sentiment for decisive action against British imperialism could not be lightly brushed aside. Above all others stood Mahatma Gandhi, second to none in his opposition to fascism, acutely sensitive to opinion within India, yet firmly opposed to wars, as wars failed to solve the problems which caused them.

The reconciliation of these differing viewpoints was no easy matter.

The Congress leadership decided to demand from the British Government a declaration of its war aims, more particularly as they applied to subject nations like India. When, in August 1940, the British Government replied through a statement which sought to exploit cleavages within Indian society, the leaders of the Congress realized that the time for action had arrived. In December 1940, therefore, they initiated yet another non-violent campaign against British imperialism; though in deference to the anti-fascist war in progress in Europe, this campaign was to be fought through individual rather than collective satyagraha.

In the meanwhile the fortunes of war turned increasingly against Great Britain in Europe as well as in Asia. After the fall of Poland, Nazi Germany turned westwards to vanquish France. Japan, too, took this opportunity to establish her supremacy over Southeast Asia. First Indo-China, then Indonesia and Malaysia, and finally Burma fell into the hands of the Japanese armies. By the spring of 1942, the Japanese stood on the frontiers of India, seemingly poised for an invasion of the subcontinent.

The prospect of a Japanese invasion obliged both the British Government and the Congress to reformulate their stances towards each other. Not surprisingly, there were some differences among the Congress leaders as to the manner in which the situation was to be handled. Gandhi, despite his opposition to Japanese fascism, was not willing to advocate violent methods to defend the integrity of India. So far as the mahatma was concerned, the country could best be defended through a scorched earth policy and mass non-cooperation against the Japanese invaders. On the other hand, Congress leaders like Jawaharlal Nehru and Maulana Azad wanted to actively organize the people for the armed defence of the country against a possible Japanese invasion. Notwithstanding these differences, all nationalist leaders wanted the British to leave India and thus enable her people to defend their country and contribute to the global struggle against fascism. The British Government, on its part, looked upon the prospect of a Japanese invasion of India with alarm, more particularly, if they had to contend simultaneously with a hostile population in the subcontinent. The British were also being urged by President Roosevelt to draw nationalist forces in India into the war effort against fascism through a policy of concessions. As a result of this, the Imperial Government sent Stafford Cripps to India in an attempt to persuade the leaders of the Congress to participate in the anti-fascist struggle, on the basis of an assurance that India would be granted freedom after the conclusion of hostilities. However, Cripps brought with him proposals which laid the door open for the balkanization of the subcontinent. The leaders of the Congress, therefore, treated these proposals as wholly unacceptable.

While the Cripps' proposals were rejected, popular sentiment for a determined assault upon British imperialism ran extremely high. As a result of this, the leaders of the Congress adopted, at a crucial session in Bombay in August 1942, a resolution demanding that the British quit India. The 'Quit India' resolution signified the grim determination of the Congress to embark upon a life and death struggle for the liberation of India. The British Government, however, was equally determined to be tough and ruthless. All the senior Congress leaders in Bombay were put under arrest, and similar arrests were carried out in the provincial cities and district towns.

Mahatma Gandhi had warned the people that Quit India Movement would be short and swift. There would be mass participation of the people. Each one would be his or her own guide. The government would resort to brutal and ruthless repression. People would have to face the challenge non-violently, in a spirit of 'Do or Die'.

The arrest of the Congress leaders triggered off a massive popular upsurge throughout India. In all the metropolitan cities, provincial capitals and district towns the people rose in revolt against the British Government. In large parts of India the centres of British administrative power were overthrown and, for the space of a few weeks, British rule ceased to exist. Indeed, non-violent means succeeded in establishing parallel administrations in some districts in Bengal, U.P., Orissa and Maharashtra. The British raj seemed to be in real danger of being overthrown.

Despite the initial success of the Quit India Movement, the British Government succeeded, through prompt use of the armed forces at its disposal in quelling the popular uprising. Just before this rising, the British had deployed substantial forces on the Indo-Burmese border to check a possible Japanese invasion. During August and September 1942, approximately ninety per cent of these forces were redeployed to quell the popular upsurge against the British raj. The suppression of the uprising of 1942 was as brutal an affair as the suppression of the uprising of 1857. Thousands of unarmed Satyagrahis were shot down and tens of thousands were incarcerated in British prisons. By the end of the year, the peace of the graveyard prevailed over India, bearing mute testimony to a mighty struggle for freedom on the part of the people, as well as to the ferocity with which the British Government had quelled it.

For the next two years, as all its leaders of any importance were in prison, there was no organized agitation on the part of the Congress. In the meanwhile, largely because of the reverses which the Nazi armies suffered in the Soviet Union, the fortunes of war tilted in favour of the Allied powers. On 6 June 1944, a joint US-British Expeditionary Force landed in Normandy, and gradually pushed back the Nazi armies.

Within a year, Germany faced an invasion by Soviet armies from the east and Anglo-American armies from the west. It was clear that the collapse of Hitler's Reich was merely a matter of time. One of the most horrifying wars in human history thus concluded in the west in victory for the forces of socialism and democracy in the world.

The triumph of socialism and democracy over fascism greatly strengthened the national movement in India. In the summer of 1945, the British people elected the Labour Party to power. The leaders of this party, men like Clement Attlee, Stafford Cripps and Lord Pethick Lawrence, were inclined to take a sympathetic view of Indian aspirations. Perhaps their altruism was also related to the strength of the national movement in India under the leadership of the Congress. Indeed, it was clear to the Labour government that it could hold on to India only through brute force, a prospect which was unlikely to be endorsed by the war-weary people of Great Britain.

However, the task of disengagement from India was one beset with serious difficulties. As suggested earlier, the British always sought to maintain overarching control, even after provincial autonomy had been conferred upon the country. To realise this objective, the British had extended support to the minorities as well as to the Princely States. When they surveyed the Indian scene in 1945 and 1946, they discovered that the support they had extended to the minorities, particularly to the Muslims, had created a powerful entity in the Muslim League under the leadership of Mohammad Ali Jinnah. The strength of this party lay in the religious passions which it stirred up in the country; and through exploiting the sentiment of communalism, the League was able to win a majority of Muslim seats in the election of 1946. Although the strength of the League rested upon a consciousness which held no place in a modern polity, it nevertheless conferred upon Jinnah a powerful position in the constitutional deliberations. Indeed, the elections of 1946 were a prelude to the partition of the country.

The British Government made one last bid through a Cabinet Mission to hammer out proposals seeking to create a three-tiered polity with a confederal centre at New Delhi. The details of this scheme and the reaction which it evoked in different circles constitute the subject of an important chapter in the *Centenary History*. Suffice it to mention here that the Cabinet Mission proposals satisfied neither the leaders of the Congress nor those of the League. Perhaps the Congress leaders, with their commitment to a centralized polity in India, feared that a confederal constitution would be merely a prelude to the balkanization of the subcontinent.

To resolve the dilemma, Clement Attlee appointed Lord Mountbatten as Viceroy of India with plenipotentiary powers to resolve the constitutional impasse. The new viceroy assumed office with a great reputation for dynamism and tact in negotiations. Moreover, during his tenure as the Supreme Commander of Allied forces in South-East Asia, he had gained a sensitive insight into the strength of Asian nationalism. In a short span of time, he was able to establish relations of confidence with the leaders of the Congress and other parties. Mountbatten put before the Indian leadership a plan for the partition of India and the creation of two autonomous dominions from the provinces of British India. The 563 Princely States, needless to say, were free to opt for union with either of these two dominions. The Mountbatten Plan, as it is popularly known, was a bitter pill for the Congress leaders to swallow; since from the very outset they fervently believed in the unity of the country. However, it became clear to Jawaharlal Nehru, Vallabhbhai Patel, Rajendra Prasad and others that the price of independence was the partition of the country. On 3 June 1947, therefore, the leaders of the Congress signalled their acceptance of the Mountbatten Plan, whereby two new dominions were to come into existence on 15 August 1947.

On the midnight of 14 August, Jawaharlal Nehru spoke in the Constituent Assembly of the prospect before the new nation: 'Long years ago', he stated, 'we made a tryst with destiny, and now the time comes when we shall redeem our pledge, not wholly or in full measure, but very substantially. At the stroke of the midnight hour, when the world sleeps, India will awake to life and freedom. A moment comes, which comes but rarely in history, when we step out from the old to the new, when an age ends, and when soul of a nation, long suppressed, finds utterance. It is fitting that at this solemn moment we take the pledge of dedication to the services of India and her people and to the still larger cause of humanity.'[9]

IV

15 August 1947 marked the culmination of one phase and the commencement of another in the history of modern India. After a long struggle against British imperialism, the leaders of the Congress had succeeded in creating an independent polity in India. The struggle for freedom was a popular movement, in which hundreds of thousands of men and women, drawn from different classes and communities, had fought for the liberation of the sub-continent. But the dawn of freedom also brought its share of tragedy. Since its genesis in 1885, the Congress had stood above all for the unity of India. Yet the full realization of this ideal eluded the Congress during the final years of the British raj. The provincial elections of 1946 had made it clear that, with some exceptions, Muslim communities in the north-west and north-east were unwilling to support the vision of a united India. As a result of this, two sovereign

dominions, India and Pakistan, emerged through the vivisection of British India in August 1947.

The historical literature on the national movement offers a number of explanations for the partition of the subcontinent. We do not propose to review this literature in the present context. Suffice it to mention here that the ethnic diversity of India, and the differing worldviews of the religious communities in the subcontinent, were among the factors which contributed to this phenomenon. Yet, any review of weaknesses in the social fabric of India does not fully explain the birth of Pakistan. Nor is partition to be explained wholly through the exploitation of such cleavages by the British. That the British Government exploited weaknesses in the social fabric to reinforce its position can be readily conceded. However, what the British desired above all was enduring economic and strategic control over the subcontinent, as a unified polity, rather than its break-up into two autonomous states. Nevertheless, the support which the British Government extended to the leaders of the Muslim League, with the objective of weakening nationalism, created a situation which resulted in the break-up of British India into the dominions of India and Pakistan in August 1947.

Whatever be the reasons behind the partition of India, Jawaharlal Nehru, as the Prime Minister of the Dominion of India, faced problems of terrifying magnitude as a result of it when he assumed office on 15 August. The most pressing of these was the problem of communal strife, resulting in the dislocation of tens of millions of people in the subcontinent. Even prior to August 1947, Jinnah had incidentally mentioned the possibility of exchange of populations between India and Pakistan. But the numbers that would be involved in such an exchange were so enormous that no one considered this possibility seriously.

However, there was such bitter hostility between Hindus and Muslims after August 1947, that Hindus trapped in the provinces of the Punjab and Bengal in Pakistan; and Muslims residing in the state of East Punjab (India); found it impossible to live with dignity in the new dominions where they constituted minorities. The bitter communal warfare forced millions of Hindus and Sikhs to migrate to India; and similarly, millions of Muslims left India to take shelter in the new dominion of Pakistan. The energies of the two infant states, India and Pakistan, in the first few months after their creation, were fully stretched in order to rehabilitate the refugees who sought shelter within their frontiers.

Perhaps nobody felt the tragedy of communal warfare more keenly than Mahatma Gandhi. Indeed, the last phase of his life was devoted wholly to the task of persuading Hindus and Muslims, in India and in Pakistan, to live peacefully with each other. The mahatma's martyrdom, on 30 January 1948, at the hands of a communal fanatic, was his last and greatest offering at the altar of communal harmony. Thus ended the epic life of the greatest Indian since the Buddha. We are so near to the mahatma in time, that it is not easy for us to assess his true stature; or to evaluate his place in history. Nevertheless, the leadership which he offered to the people of India, in their struggle against British imperialism, places him among the truly outstanding figures of the 20th century. Nor were his activities confined to the political domain. By articulating the traditional values of Indian civilization in the changing context of the 20th century, he provided the people of India with the moral and cultural resilience without which they would have found it difficult to acquire a new national identity. Small wonder, then, that he is widely regarded as the father of the Indian nation.

With the martyrdom of the mahatma, and the consequent stilling of communal passions, the way was open for the adoption of a new constitution by the people of India. Yet before this could be done, some crucial issues had to be resolved: What would be the structure of the polity in New Delhi? How would this be related to the provincial governments? What was the place which the erstwhile Princely States would occupy in the new order? How would rights of property and individual liberties be defined in the proposed constitution? How, once again, would the great minorities be drawn into a creative relationship with the major community in the subcontinent? These were some of the questions which were debated in the Constituent Assembly before it framed a new political system. India, it was decided, was to be a republic resting upon adult franchise; and the citizen would enjoy rights and bear responsibilities comparable to his rights and obligations under other liberal constitutions. The structure of governance in New Delhi was to be unitary. Yet the founding fathers recognized that a polity of India's complexity required centres of governance in the provinces (or the states, as they were now termed) no less powerful than the one envisaged in New Delhi. The new constitution, therefore, envisaged governments in the states which were endowed with substantial powers as well as considerable resources. The sagacity of the constitution framers is amply reflected in the fact that India is a functioning democracy in 1985, with a record of elections which have enabled the people to exercise free choice in determining who should preside over the government.

The constitution of India has many novel features, but the most striking feature is the right of franchise it bestows on every adult in the country. The first general elections held under the new constitution, in 1952, were to a great leap into the dark. Jawaharlal Nehru and the Congress leaders, although they presided over a party which had been the principal force behind the freedom struggle, had little indication of how they would fare electorally. A number of parties, ranging from the Hindu

Mahasabha to the Communist Party, had jumped into the fray. The leaders of the Congress were apprehensive that the parties of the right, which were inclined to appeal to the electorate on the basis of religious sentiment, would offer the most formidable challenge. However, the results of the election showed that, although communalism was far from dead, economic issues — the problems of poverty and social deprivation — would henceforth loom large upon the political horizon. The Congress secured 354 seats out of 469 in the Lok Sabha, and also won majorities in all the states. The most powerful opposition groups were the parties of the left, which offered radical (to the point of being impractical) solutions to the people's problems.

The results of the first general elections made it clear to Jawaharlal Nehru that the crucial issue before the country was the economic reconstruction of society along lines which would ensure a measure of material dignity and social equity to the humblest in the land.

The radical policies, which Jawaharlal Nehru now initiated, had been anticipated in the industrial policy resolution of 1948, wherein the state proclaimed its decision to control the 'commanding heights of the economy' through reserving for itself some of the seminal areas of economic activity, like the fabrication of steel, the generation of power, and the establishment of a machine tool industry. To give practical shape to this policy, Jawaharlal instituted a Planning Commission, which was vested with the responsibility of devising an overall economic strategy for India. The crux of planning, as it developed in India over the next few years, related to the creation of a publicly owned heavy industry sector, around which core the planners contemplated the growth of consumer industries, through the initiative of private capital; and the growth also of handicrafts, through the enterprise of small scale producers.

By the middle of the 1960s, Jawaharlal Nehru had brought about remarkable changes in the industrial and agrarian economy of India. Behind these changes stood a party which had been greatly strengthened as an instrument of social transformation.

The continuing popularity of the Congress was vividly reflected in the second general elections held in 1957. As before, the Congress secured a massive victory at the polls, winning 366 out of 483 seats in the Lok Sabha. Through the support which they extended to Jawaharlal Nehru and the Congress, the people of India firmly endorsed the progressive measures which had been initiated with the object of creating a modern industrial and agricultural economy. All this was reaffirmed at the Avadi session of the Congress, where a solemn decision was taken to build a socialist order in India.

Besides the social and economic reforms which he initiated within India, Jawaharlal Nehru also strove to place the country's relations with the world community on a durable basis. Even before 1947, he had attempted to establish a link between the liberation movement of India and those of other colonial societies in Asia and Africa. For what is now termed the Third World to take its rightful place in the international community, Jawaharlal Nehru believed that it needed a world-view of its own; and India, with her classical heritage so eloquently rearticulated in the 20th century by Mahatma Gandhi, could contribute substantially to the shaping of a distinctive ethos for the resurgent nations of Asia and Africa. The concept of non-alignment, the belief that it was incumbent upon developing countries to reflect their distinctive personality in a world polarized between the capitalist and the socialist blocs, grew out of such considerations. These ideas attracted wide support from the people of India; and they were destined to become a powerful force in international relations during the next few decades.

In reflecting upon the human condition in the 1950s, Jawaharlal Nehru felt that some of the perennial problems of war and peace had acquired a new urgency because of the existence of nuclear weapons. Wars had been accepted earlier as a legitimate means of resolving human problems. But it was no longer valid to do so. 'Thus, violence cannot possibly lead today to a solution of any major problem because violence has become much too terrible and destructive,' Jawaharlal Nehru observed. 'The moral approach to the question [of war or peace] has now been powerfully reinforced by the practical aspect.'[10] In this area, India had a special message for the rest of humanity. The Mahatma had initiated a great transformation within Indian society through non-violence; but there was reason to believe that problems between sovereign states, too, could be resolved through the ideology of non-violence.

The vision of the world community which Jawaharlal delineated with such sensitivity guided in particular India's relations with China. Like India, China had gone through the experience of exploitation by imperialism. Over and above this experience, there were longstanding ties which linked the civilization of India with that of China. For these reasons, Jawaharlal Nehru strove to establish relations of utmost cordiality with China. Perhaps the issue of Tibet was the first testing ground for the two great nations of Asia. Jawaharlal reacted to the assumption by China of control over Tibet with rare magnanimity. He also seized the opportunity to lay down the five principles of co-existence between sovereign states, which became the fundamental basis of the non-aligned movement.

Despite Jawaharlal Nehru's generosity towards China over Tibet, his gesture was probably interpreted as a sign of weakness, if not worse. For, soon afterwards, the Chinese Government started putting forward the most extraordinary claims upon Indian territories along the Himalayas. These claims were backed by the armed intervention of Chinese troops; and in Ladakh, the Chinese built a strategic highway which made a serious encroachment upon Indian territory. The earlier 'cartographic aggression' of China had dealt a blow to the friendly relations which Jawaharlal Nehru had tried to build with Peking over the years. Nevertheless, the government and the people of India took the view that the border problem could be resolved through peaceful negotiations. But the Chinese Government obviously thought otherwise. In the autumn of 1962, Chinese armies suddenly struck across the Himalayan border and seized hold of thousands of square kilometres of Indian territory.

The Chinese invasion of India was as humiliating as it was unexpected. Yet Jawaharlal Nehru, the Congress and the people of India emerged from the ordeal stronger than ever. This was largely due to the manner in which different classes and communities came together at their country's hour of peril. A united nation set about the task of repairing the damage wrought by the military reverses along the Himalaya; and in a matter of a few months, India had recovered fully from the shock which it sustained in the winter of 1962.

Jawaharlal Nehru's health was now well past its prime. Yet he turned to the task of revitalizing the Congress, and making it an instrument for the social transformation of India, with a zeal that would have done credit to a statesman half his age. During the last year of his life he held out once again the message of socialism before the people of India. Only through socialism could India realize material prosperity at the same time as she achieved equity for the poor and the deprived. Under his inspiring leadership, the Congress turned anew to the task of eradicating poverty and building a strong and self-reliant nation.

On 27 May 1964, Jawaharlal Nehru passed away, deeply mourned by the people of India and indeed by mankind as a whole. His achievements over a life of seven decades and more were truly remarkable. As a fiery young nationalist, he had joined the Congress and participated in the freedom struggle under the aegis of Mahatma Gandhi. Yet he soon outgrew the influence of the mahatma and, by disseminating socialism among the members of the Congress, he radically transformed the ideological climate of the national movement. Indeed, when India was liberated in 1947, Jawaharlal Nehru's socialist vision became the basis of a programme for transforming India into a modern industrial society, in which economic growth was married with social equity in finely balanced proportions. In the history of India, Jawaharlal Nehru stands among those rare statesmen who strove to bring about an epic change in the country. His commitment to the cause of peace, in a world threatened with nuclear devastation, was perhaps unrivalled among international statesmen who were his contemporaries.

V

The death of Jawaharlal Nehru removed a towering figure from the stage of Indian politics. Yet the Congress proved itself fully worthy of the trust which the nation reposed in it by electing Lal Bahadur Shastri, a politician with wide experience, as the new prime minister. The problem of succession rarely lends itself to easy resolution; and the manner in which the Congress tackled the issue demonstrated the maturity which it had attained within a brief span of time as a ruling party.

Nevertheless, the tasks which awaited resolution at the hands of Lal Bahadur Shastri were truly formidable, both in their magnitude and in their complexity. Within the country, the programmes of social and economic development initiated by his predecessor needed to be revitalized, if the dream of a self-sufficient India was to be realized. Outside the country, a hostile China and an unfriendly Pakistan promised turbulent weather ahead for the new prime minister. Yet the choice of Lal Bahadur Shastri was fully vindicated by the purposeful manner in which he tackled the problems facing the nation. At the outset, Shastri proclaimed his commitment to the principles of socialism which had informed the Congress since the 1930s; and which inspired the domestic as well as the foreign policies of Jawaharlal Nehru. Next, the prime minister turned to the vital task of generating a new vigour in rural society. It appeared that, despite the land reforms of the 1950s, the rural economy needed a new boost if agricultural production was to suffice for the growing population of the country. Shastri took the first tentative steps towards initiating a new strategy of rural development, which reached fruition under his successor, and became the basis of a regime of plenty in the land.

While Shastri was battling to resolve the economic problems which faced the country, Pakistan decided to strike a deadly blow at India. The rulers of Pakistan, taking their cue from China, advanced claims to Indian territory in Gujarat and initiated military action to realize these claims. However, it soon became clear that the manoeuvre in Gujarat was merely a diversionary tactic. In the autumn of 1965, Pakistan initiated military aggression against Kashmir with a view to conquering it. Shastri, with full support from the Congress and the people, demonstrated to all and sundry that India would fight with all the resources at its command to defend its territorial integrity. The Indian armies not only counter-attacked in Kashmir but, to seize the initiative from Pakistan, executed a limited military move across the Punjab border. This move succeeded in halting the aggression by Pakistan and, after a brief period of hostilities, both the countries agreed to a cease-fire.

The military action of 1965 was a great triumph for Shastri, for the Congress and for the people of India. Pakistan had struck at a moment when India appeared to be weak. Nevertheless, under the leadership of Shastri and the Congress, the people of India demonstrated their ability to withstand aggression, whatever be its point of origin. After the cessation of hostilities, a number of countries offered their good offices to India and Pakistan. But the leaders of the two countries considered it appropriate to accept Soviet mediation. The Tashkent conference flowed from this acceptance; and an agreement was worked out at this conference satisfactory to all concerned. While the people of India were preparing to extend a hero's welcome to Lal Bahadur Shastri, who had grown enormously in popular esteem, they learnt of his sudden demise at Tashkent on 10 January 1966.

VI

The death of Lal Bahadur Shastri once again posed before the Congress, and the people of India, the question of succession to the office of prime minister. Rarely had a party been called upon to resolve the leadership issue twice in so brief a span of time. Yet the leaders of the Congress proved themselves fully capable of handling this difficult situation. However, unlike in 1964, certain differences soon became evident in the party as to who should succeed Shastri. Some of the leaders of the Congress, particularly those inclined to a conservative view of politics, looked upon Morarji Desai as the most appropriate choice. As against this, a very large section of the radical leaders favoured the candidature of Indira Gandhi, who had demonstrated remarkable political skills as President of the Congress in 1959. The leadership of the Congress in 1966, therefore, was contested between Indira Gandhi and Morarji Desai, and the former won the election with a comfortable margin.

Although Indira Gandhi had a majority of the Congress behind her in 1966, the conservative leaders who had backed Morarji Desai did not give up the contest for supremacy. Between her election to supreme office in 1966 and the general elections of 1967, Indira Gandhi faced a number of challenges to her position as the leader of the party and the nation. The divided state in which the party went to the polls in 1967 was also reflected in the results of the election. In contrast to the comfortable majorities which the Congress had won in the first three elections held after independence, it secured only 280 out of 523 seats in the Lok Sabha in 1967.

The strength of the Congress in the post-1967 Lok Sabha enabled it to function as the party in power. Yet it was clear to Indira Gandhi and her supporters that the situation called for radical measures. A new bond of trust and confidence had to be forged between the people and the Congress if the country was to sustain the progress which it had achieved during the first decade and a half of independence. The forging of such a link called for a consummation which would carry the transformation of Indian society to a new qualitative level. Substantial sections of society — the tribal and Harijan communities; the poorer sections of the peasantry; the industrial working class and the artisan communities; and the minorities — had profited only marginally from the economic growth which the country had achieved since 1947. If the poor and the deprived could be persuaded that the Congress stood for their interests, then the party would once again acquire the popular support which it needed for eradicating poverty and stimulating progress. Needless to say, the crystallization of such radical policies meant a reactivation of the spirit of Mahatma Gandhi and Jawaharlal Nehru in the altered circumstances of the late 1960s.

The new mood of the Congress was reflected in a crucial session of AICC held in 1969. In voicing her views before the party, Indira Gandhi outlined a programme of social transformation which frontally attacked a wide range of vested interests within Indian society. She envisaged the abolition of princely privilege and the nationalization of banks as preliminary steps to an assault upon the sources of poverty and deprivation in the country. The radical leadership within the Congress immediately supported her programme, as one which would fortify the party in the eyes of the people, as the great instrument of social transformation in India. At the same time, the conservative leadership of the party broke away into a political formation which increasingly lost touch with the mood of the people.

The radical stance adopted by Indira Gandhi in 1969 became the basis of a series of policies seeking to stimulate the creative energy of the poor and the deprived and to introduce a new era of development in the country. Perhaps the most striking feature of these policies pertained to the rural economy, since the country had been facing actual shortages in food, partly due to failures of the harvest and partly also due to increase in population. Within the span of half a decade, Indira Gandhi's agrarian policies enabled the country to become self-sufficient in food production and even generate surpluses which were stocked in public granaries as a guarantee against future shortages.

With a series of remarkable successes to back her, Indira Gandhi went to the polls in 1971 on the slogan of 'Garibi Hatao' or 'Eradicate Poverty'. The people again demonstrated their confidence in her leadership, as well as in the party over which she presided, by extending enthusiastic support to the Congress. Out of a total of 525 seats in the Lok Sabha, the Congress secured 355. The electoral victory of 1971 was a clear indication that the country was fully behind Indira Gandhi in her efforts to improve the lot of the poor and the deprived; and that her policies, aimed at eradicating poverty, enjoyed the support of an over-whelming majority in the country.

The popularity which Indira Gandhi and the Congress enjoyed with the people was extended to the full in the crisis which soon erupted along the north-eastern frontiers of India. The province of East Pakistan (as it was called in 1971) was in a state of acute ferment for a number of reasons. Since its emergence in 1947, the rulers of Pakistan had treated the eastern wing very shabbily, concentrating all resources and development activity in the western wing. Over and above this, the people of the region had a number of grievances arising out of the cavalier fashion in which the regional language and culture were treated by the ruling classes of Pakistan. Altogether, a powerful movement for liberation grew up in East Pakistan under the leadership of Sheikh Mujibur Rahman. Yet the rulers of Pakistan were totally unwilling to recognize the legitimacy of this movement. Indeed, in 1971, as the demand for freedom gathered momentum, they unleashed a reign of terror in the eastern wing of Pakistan, literally forcing millions of Bengalis to seek shelter in India.

The crisis in East Pakistan posed Indira Gandhi a serious challenge. It was clear that India could not stand unconcerned while the aspirations of the East Bengalis were crushed under foot by the ruling establishment of Pakistan, which drew its strength from the western wing. This was all the more so because the millions of refugees who had poured into India literally threatened to wreck the economy, unless a way was found to repatriate them to their homeland.

The Bangladesh crisis evoked from Indira Gandhi statesmanship of a very high order. The strength of this statesmanship lay in the support which she received from the people. No less important was the support that the Soviet Union extended to India, through a treaty of friendship which henceforth became the cornerstone of Indian foreign policy. At the very moment when an army of liberation — the *Mukti Bahini* — initiated hostilities against Pakistani occupation forces in the eastern wing, the Indian Army also took upon itself the task of ending the tyranny of the rulers of Pakistan. A short military campaign brought Pakistan to its knees; and the new state of Bangladesh was born amidst universal rejoicing.

The liberation of Bangladesh, which followed closely upon the electoral victory of 1971, put Indira Gandhi and the Congress in a powerful position. The momentum for progress, which the prime minister had generated in 1969, was now augmented through a resounding victory at the polls and also through a magnificent success in restructuring the balance of power in South Asia in a manner very favourable to India. Indeed, Indira Gandhi rode a wave of popularity almost without parallel in Indian politics.

Yet there were conservative and communal interests which felt a sense of deep alarm at the changes which Indira Gandhi had already brought about; or planned to bring about in the future. Some of these interests were supported by the Congress leaders who had opposed Indira Gandhi in 1969; others drew upon communal ideology; others, yet again, indulged in the rhetoric of radical change without any understanding of what such change entailed. Altogether, these forces constituted a powerful coalition against Indira Gandhi and the Congress. However, although this alliance of reaction and irresponsibility had failed to muster any support in the national elections of 1971, or in the state elections of 1972, it nevertheless possessed the power to frustrate the progressive measures of Indira Gandhi. The reactionary circles got an opportunity for mischief when the states of Bihar and Gujarat erupted into crisis in the early 1970s. These circles were all too willing to throw their support behind leaders who sought to employ the weapon of 'satyagraha' in order to overthrow a legitimately elected government! The Bihar and Gujarat movements gained considerable strength in the next few years. On the surface, these agitations depended on moral persuasion; in reality, they rested upon techniques of intimidation which were as immoral as they were out of place in a democracy where legitimate power rests upon electoral support. The result of these movements, which were able to exploit the sentiments of sections of youth, was to paralyse the administration and create conditions of anarchy in Bihar and Gujarat.

At the same time as reaction and irresponsibility were launching an assault upon Indira Gandhi, an organized attempt was made to paralyse the railway system in India, which constitutes a crucial component of the economy. In 1974, some leaders of the opposition, who controlled the railway unions, called a strike which was a part of an overall plan of destabilization, although this objective was masked through presenting economic demands on behalf of the workers. Indira Gandhi read in the railway strike, as she also read in the agitations in Gujarat and Bihar, the clear intention of the leaders of the opposition, who had failed to secure popular support in the elections, to render the governance of the country an impossible business. She, therefore, took strong action against the railwaymen just as she also took strong action against those who attempted to disturb the peace of the realm in the northern and western states.

The attack on Indira Gandhi and on the Congress which was simultaneously an attack of the rich and the powerful upon the poor and the weak, also took the form of an attempt to unseat the Prime Minister from the Lok Sabha. At the same time, key members of the government and the judiciary were assassinated. Indira Gandhi reacted to all this by declaring a state of emergency, whereby the government could invigorate the administration and the economy. Her determination to set the wheels of progress in motion was expressed in a 20-point programme which, among other things, sought to reinforce the position of Harijans in society; distribute land to the landless; step up agricultural production; ensure a square deal to the industrial working class; and hold out encouragement to large and small scale industrial entrepreneurs. The 20-point programme was designed for the nation as a whole, but it reinforced in particular the position of the weaker sections of society.

The youth of India, under the leadership of Sanjay Gandhi, emerged at this juncture as a force of great potential and an instrument of social transformation. For the first time in its history, the Congress organized a wing devoted to the induction and education of youth; and this was put under the charge of Sanjay Gandhi. The Youth Congress built up a dedicated cadre, which served as a vibrant link between the party and the people; and it enabled Indira Gandhi to channelize popular enthusiasm into support of the policies of her government.

The years 1975-77 were fateful years in the history of India, when the Congress delivered a new message of striving and achievement to the popular classes. The period was marked by a far-reaching programme of land distribution to the tribals and Harijans; just as it was also marked by a new spurt of productive activity in the industrial and agrarian sectors. The results of all this were reflected in increases in the gross national product as well as in its equitable distribution between different classes and communities. The Congress became the party of the popular classes in a way it had never been so before. Indeed, its commitment to the principles of socialism, secularism and democracy acquired a sharpness of focus which made itself felt in all arenas of national endeavour.

Yet the radical policies adopted by Indira Gandhi also earned her the hostility of vested interests in Indian society. The upsurge of hope for a better future among the common people alarmed those classes which controlled a share of the national product out of proportion to their demographic strength. Such vested interests retaliated through a campaign of vilification against Indira Gandhi and the Congress. Their ability to mount such a campaign was considerable because of the control which they exercised over the levers of social and economic power. Small wonder, then, that when Indira Gandhi issued a call for general elections in 1977, an alliance of parties, which could come together only on a platform of hostility to progress, was able to inflict a defeat on the Congress at the polls. The reverses experienced by the Congress, in 1977 merely highlighted the formidable power of vested interests in the country; since, as subsequent events demonstrated, in reality the common people continued to support Indira Gandhi and her party.

A history of the Congress is no place for an evaluation of the Janata Party, which controlled power in New Delhi for a span of three years. Suffice it to mention here that the new ruling party, which elected as prime minister someone who had been rejected by the Congress earlier, failed to provide firm leadership to the country. As already indicated, the Janata Party was an alliance of political groups which were incapable of agreeing amongst themselves on the policies to be pursued with profit. As a result of the tensions which riddled this party, the economic strength of India as well as her ability to provide leadership to the Third World declined grievously.

The three years which Indira Gandhi spent in the wilderness were years of considerable distress for her and her political colleagues. The leaders of the Janata Party initiated a campaign of vilification against her and the machinery of the state was pressed into service in order to permanently undermine her position as a leader of the people. Yet in a democracy, it is impossible for a ruling party to hoodwink the people for long. The persecution of Indira Gandhi turned out to be wholly counter-productive and merely ensured for her the sympathy as well as the support of large sections of the people. On her part, Indira Gandhi battled fearlessly to clear herself of the charges levied against her by the Janata Party. Her opportunity for staging a comeback came when the leaders of the Janata Party turned a blind eye to the persecution of Harijans in the village of Belchi in Bihar. Indira Gandhi looked upon happenings at Belchi as reflective of what was happening to the deprived and the weak in the country as a whole under the new dispensation. She undertook a journey to Belchi in the summer of 1979 to demonstrate her deep concern for the poorest and the most helpless in the land. The pilgrimage to Belchi was a memorable journey, comparable in its symbolic and political significance to the mahatma's trek from Sabarmati Ashram in Ahmedabad to the remote village of Dandi, in 1930, to initiate the Civil Disobedience Movement.

VII

Belchi marks a decisive turning point in the political development of India. From the very outset, the strength of the Congress lay in the support of the popular classes for the party and its leaders. Indira

Gandhi's visit to a remote hamlet reaffirmed her concern for the socially deprived; and they responded to this gesture by showering their affection on her. The renewed popularity of Indira Gandhi and the Congress was reflected in the elections to the Lok Sabha held late in 1979. The Congress, which underwent a new schism during the years it spent in the political wilderness, went to the polls with a promise to the people of providing a government that would uphold their rights and protect their interests. The people responded by voting for Indira Gandhi in massive numbers and her party secured 351 seats out of a total of 544 in the Lok Sabha. Once again, the link between the Congress and the masses was reaffirmed through the electoral process.

When Indira Gandhi assumed power in 1980, she faced a number of problems arising out of the apathy of the Janata Party towards the welfare of the country. The policies which the Congress had initiated in the 1970s had been completely disowned by the conservative leaders who ruled between 1977 and 1979. To take one instance, land distributed to the Harijans prior to 1977 was taken away from them and restored to its erstwhile owners, the affluent rural classes, which constituted an important factor behind the Congress defeat in 1977. Similarly, other measures designed for progress, too, were repudiated by the Janata Party, whether they concerned the economy or the scientific and cultural development of the country. Typical of the retrogressive stance of the Janata were the attempts to undermine the principles of secularism which the Congress had espoused from the very outset. These principles were substituted by a worldview designed to place serious obstacles in the way of integration of different religious communities into a cohesive national polity.

Indira Gandhi's first task, after assuming office in 1980, was to redress the damage inflicted upon the fabric of society during three years of Janata rule. The machinery of economic growth was reactivated, through introducing a modified version of the 20-point programme, with special emphasis on the needs of the poor and the weak in rural and in urban society. At the same time, steps were taken to reverse cultural policies which had sharpened divisions between different communities. The secular spirit, which had guided the Congress since its inception, was rearticulated in the altered circumstances of 1980. This rearticulation highlighted treatment of strict equality to all classes and communities; just as it also highlighted the nurturing of the varied social traditions which underpinned the composite culture of India.

Perhaps the leadership which Indira Gandhi extended to the Third World stands as the most eloquent testimony to her towering stature in the 1980s. Here she had inherited from her father, Jawaharlal Nehru, a distinguished legacy, resting on the belief that the newly liberated countries of Asia, Africa and Latin America had political and economic interests which made them partners in a common endeavour, at the same time as it differentiated them from the superpowers. Whatever be the historical basis of non-alignment, Indira Gandhi discerned the substantive force behind it with unmistakable clarity during the course of events which led to the liberation of Bangladesh. Trends in international politics in the decade following the liberation of Bangladesh reinforced Indira Gandhi's conviction that the great issues of war and peace in the 20th century could only be resolved on the platform of the non-aligned movement. The growing economic anarchy in the world community constituted yet another problem which awaited resolution at the hands of the Third World. Throughout her tenure as Prime Minister, Indira Gandhi stressed the need for a more equitable economic relationship between the developing and the developed nations. All these issues were explored with great sensitivity in her speech before the Conference of the Non-Aligned Movement held in 1983. Never before had the Third World offered such perceptive leadership, on the question of peace in the nuclear age, and also that of equity in economic relation between nations, to mankind as a whole. Perhaps Indira Gandhi's chairmanship of the Non-Aligned Conference was her finest hour as the leader of the most populous democracy in the world. She had matured, by this time, into a political figure of epic stature; and the deep compassion as well as the subtle comprehension with which she reflected upon the problems facing humanity characterized her as one of the truly distinguished figures in world politics in the second half of the 20th century. Speaking before the leaders of Asia, Africa and Latin America, she stated:

> The Non-Aligned Movement has stood firmly for a thorough-going restructuring of international economic relations. We are against exploitation. We are for each nation's right to its resources and policies. We want an equal voice in the operation of international institution. We reiterate our commitment to the establishment of a New International Economic Order based on justice and equality. . . .
>
> Our plans for a better life for each of our peoples depend on world peace and the reversal of the arms race. Only general and complete disarmament can provide credible security. Negotiations confined to a closed circle of nuclear-weapon powers have made little progress. We are non-nuclear States, who want nuclear energy used only for peace. But we too have a right to live and be heard. In the name of humanity and on behalf of us all, I call upon nuclear-weapon powers to give up the use or threat to use of nuclear weapons in any circumstances; suspend all nuclear weapons' tests and the production and deployment of nuclear weapons; and resume disarmament negotiations with determination to reach agreement.[11]

If the tragic hand of fate had not intervened at this juncture, there is every reason to believe that Indira Gandhi would have contributed substantially to the resolution of the military and economic problems facing mankind. However, developments within India were soon to cut short a career so rich in achievement and varied in experience. These developments touched upon the relationship between the Congress and the Sikh community; and the principle of secularism as the basis of Indian unity. From the very outset, the Congress was a party to which many diverse classes and communities had extended their support for the fulfilment of their aspirations. Among those who did so were the Sikhs; a vigorous community of agriculturists whose enterprise had even before 1947 transformed the Punjab into the granary of the subcontinent. The Sikhs also made an outstanding contribution to the struggle for freedom; and since 1920, they had stood shoulder to shoulder with other communities in the anti-imperialist struggle.

Not long after Indira Gandhi returned to power in 1980, some members of the Sikh community, organized in the Akali Dal, presented to her government a series of demands on behalf of the entire community. Some of these demands pertained to the economic domain; others were linguistic in character; others yet touched upon religious freedom and cultural autonomy. Indira Gandhi admired the Sikh community and respected its legitimate leaders. She, therefore, entered into a dialogue with such leaders to ascertain what could be done to meet the grievances of the community.

However, there were small groups among the Sikhs, who attempted to use the grievances, real or imaginary, of the community to undermine the integrity of the Indian state. The leaders of such groups adopted a blatantly communal posture; and although they enjoyed little support from the majority of the Sikh community, they utilized the tactics of intimidation and terror to precipitate a very serious situation in the Punjab. The most serious facet of the Punjab crisis lay in the transformation of some Sikh shrines into centres of activity prejudicial to the security of India.

Indira Gandhi exhibited exemplary patience in her dialogue with the Sikh leaders stretching over a span of two years. However, it gradually dawned upon her, as it dawned upon the people of India, that a small section of the Sikh leadership was determined to challenge the integrity of the country. On 3 June 1984, therefore, Indira Gandhi entrusted to the army the task of liberating the holy shrines of Sikhism from the clutches of terrorists and secessionists. This task was carried out with the application of minimum force in a very short span of time.

The terrorists and secessionists in the Sikh community, who had held the Punjab to ransom for two years, tried to portray the liberation of the shrines as an attack on the Sikh religion. However, Indira Gandhi's commitment to secularism, and regard for Sikhism and the Sikh community, were too well known for these attempts to carry any credibility. Yet Sikh terrorists persisted in the tactics of terror; and on the 31 October 1985, Indira Gandhi was treacherously assassinated by two members of her security force who had been infected with the virus of communalism.

In the decade and a half during which Indira Gandhi led India with dedication and distinction, she had earned for herself a unique place in the hearts of her countrymen. During her tenure as prime minister, the economy was put firmly on the path to progress; and her conduct of foreign relations secured for India a place of distinction in the Third World, and a voice which commanded respect in the world community. Perhaps no other woman in history has shaped the destiny of a nation so decisively as Indira Gandhi shaped India's. Her assassination, therefore, was an act of brutality which affected the people most grievously; more particularly, it affected the poor and the deprived, who had looked upon her as their mentor and saviour.

Yet, in this moment of crisis, the Congress showed itself fully worthy of the confidence which the nation reposed in it. In a transition marked as much by promptness as it was by sagacity, the party elected Rajiv Gandhi as the new Prime Minister of India. This youthful member of the Congress had already revealed great promise as a leader. As prime minister, he turned to the nation, and gave voice to the belief that the removal of Indira Gandhi from the stage of politics conferred upon the people a sacred trust and a heavy responsibility: 'You and I have suffered a loss which can never be made good,' Rajiv Gandhi stated. 'You and I must work together to continue and complete the tasks which Indira Gandhi left unfinished. . . . With the scattering of her ashes in the Himalayas will end Indira Gandhi's earthly journey. But the nation's journey continues. Let us walk together, stout of heart and purpose, firm in step.'[12]

Although Rajiv Gandhi had been elected leader of the Congress without a single voice of dissent, it was nevertheless necessary for him to secure a mandate from the electorate. In December 1984, therefore, the Congress once again went to the polls to test its popularity with the people. The results of this election demonstrated the extent to which the people looked upon the Congress as the embodiment of national unity; and the party most likely to successfully accomplish the transformation of India into a modern industrial society. Out of 535 seats in the Lok Sabha, the Congress secured 400. Never before in its long history had the Congress ever scored so well at the polls. However, the greatest election victory ever won by the Congress was in reality a personal triumph for Rajiv Gandhi, whose vision of the future of India, and whose charisma, had captured the imagination of the people.

With the support of the people and the Congress, Rajiv Gandhi turned to the tasks which confronted him with rare determination and courage. Foremost on his agenda was the resolution of the Punjab problem, which had inflicted such grievous wounds on the body politic. However, equally significant was the call which the Prime Minister gave to the nation, to prepare itself for a technological revolution that would place it in the ranks of the foremost industrial nations of the world; and initiate a new era of prosperity in the country. As Rajiv Gandhi observed on the morrow of the election:

> You have given my party and me your confidence in overflowing measure. Who could ask for more? And how can we prove worthy of it? Only by working for you with unremitting faith and humility, summoning all our reserves of strength and energy, being as unsparing with ourselves as you have been generous with your trust. . . .
>
> In a few months we shall begin the Seventh Plan. The war against our old enemies — poverty, unemployment, disease, ignorance — continues. In the weeks ahead, we shall review our existing policies and programmes to ensure that our basic objectives of growth with justice are realised within the stipulated time-table.[13]

The people of India responded to the call given by Rajiv Gandhi with an enthusiasm rarely witnessed in the arena of national politics. The new Prime Minister cleared the decks by fashioning an accord with the leaders of the Punjab, which was sealed by the installation of a popularly elected government at Chandigarh. The path was thus opened for focussing attention upon the tasks of social and economic reconstruction through which alone can the people enjoy their rich cultural heritage.

What does the future hold for India? Obviously there is no simple answer to this question. The reconstruction of a nation inevitably involves ceaseless labour and toil over decades, before the results of such activity become manifest. But there is reason to believe that, under the leadership of Rajiv Gandhi, and that of the Congress, the people will prove themselves capable of transforming India into a creative society, dedicated to the ideal of generating peace and prosperity for itself, as well as for mankind as a whole. Perhaps the saga of struggle and achievement, spelt out in this *Centenary History,* will provide to the leaders and to the people, the poise and self-comprehension necessary for such an epic endeavour.

B.N. Pande
General Editor

Footnotes

1. Jawaharlal Nehru: *The Discovery of India*, p. 357.
2. Ibid., pp. 358-9.
3. *Whither India* by Jawaharlal Nehru, published as a series of articles on 9, 10 and 11 October 1933 in the Indian press: See *Selected Works of Jawaharlal Nehru*, Vol. VI, pp. 1-16.
4. Nirmal Kumar Bose: *Studies in Gandhism*, p. 171.
5. M.K. Gandhi: *Young India*, 2 January 1930.
6. M.K. Gandhi: *Young India*, 9 January 1930.
7. *Indian Annual Register*, I, pp. 112-9.
8. N.K. Bose: *Studies in Gandhism*, p. 178.
9. 'A tryst with Destiny', speech delivered by Jawaharlal Nehru at the Constituent Assembly, New Delhi, 14 August 1947.
10. Jawaharlal Nehru, 'The Basic Approach' *AICC Economic Review*, 15 August 1958.
11. Speech by Shrimati Indira Gandhi at the Inaugural Session of the 7th Non-Aligned Conference, *Seventh Non-Aligned Summit documents*.
12. Message to the People by Shri Rajiv Gandhi on 7 November 1984.
13. Speech by Shri Rajiv Gandhi on 5 January 1985, See *The Times of India*, 6 January 1985.

ACKNOWLEDGEMENTS

IN EMBARKING UPON a project of the scale of *A Centenary History of the Indian National Congress* (in five volumes), I have received support and encouragement from many quarters; and it gives me great pleasure to acknowledge such assistance as this colossal task stands completed.

The moral and material support which the project has received from the late Shrimati Indira Gandhi, and from the Prime Minister and President of the Congress, Shri Rajiv Gandhi, is acknowledged in the *Preface*. Over and above this, since the time when the *Centenary History* was conceived a decade ago, in November 1975, numerous colleagues and friends have extended invaluable assistance to me, among whom I would particularly like to mention Shri Devkant Barooah, Shri N.K. Sharma, and Sarvashri K.D. Malaviya and Triloki Singh, both of whom are no longer in our midst. However, most of all I would like to thank my friend and adviser, Shri H.Y. Sharada Prasad, without whose support it would have been impossible for me to fulfil these heavy responsibilities.

From April 1976 to March 1977, I took an extensive tour all over the country visiting National and State Archives, the National Library and the Asiatic Society at Calcutta, the Archives of All India Khilafat Committee Office at Bombay, the *Kesari* Office at Pune, the Headquarters Library of the Theosophical Society and the *Hindu* Office at Madras. I also paid a visit to Hyderabad and examined the records at the State Archives and the records of the Government of Nizam of Hyderabad. During my tour abroad, I spent nearly a week at the British Museum and India Office Library at London and Bibliopheque Nationale at Paris. Everywhere I received courteous treatment and promises of help. I express my gratefulness to all these authorities.

I was pleasantly surprised to discover nearly 20,000 pages of valuable material at the Bombay Archives on the events of Non-cooperation and Khilafat Movements which nobody had till then glanced at. I also located numerous citizens who had preserved in private collections valuable materials concerning the period from 1901 to 1919. The original records of the meetings of the Working Committee of the All India Khilafat Committee had been carefully preserved. They gave a fascinating account of the discussions on the Khilafat and Non-cooperation Movements. The signatures showed the presence of many stalwarts of Khilafat, and Congress leaders such as Hakim Ajmal Khan, M.A. Ansari, Maulana Mohammed Ali and Shaukat Ali, Maulana Abdul Bari of Firangi Mahal, Mufti Kifayatulla, Maulana Abul Kalam Azad and several others. I wish all this material is microfilmed and preserved for posterity in an appropriate repository.

After the Congress (I) returned to power in 1980, Shrimati Indira Gandhi constituted a Committee in 1982 with herself as Chairman and myself as Executive Director. Shri Rajiv Gandhi, when he became the General Secretary of the AICC(I), generously placed funds at my disposal and continued to remind me that the work had to be expedited.

I offer my thanks to my eminent colleagues of the Editorial Board and to the distinguished scholars who have contributed to the different volumes of the *Centenary History*. I offer my special thanks to Prof. Ravinder Kumar, Director, Nehru Memorial Museum and Library, who placed all the resources of the Library at the disposal of the contributors. Xerox copies of the documents were supplied to the contributors promptly and every possible effort was made to help them in collecting the materials from other sources. Prof. Kumar also took the arduous responsibility of guiding a team of proof readers and assisting in the preparation of index of each volume.

I offer my grateful thanks to Shri H.Y. Sharada Prasad, who took the responsibility of the production of the volumes and the selection of illustrations. I also acknowledge the valuable cooperation of Shri Samuel Israel, the literary and style editor.

But the publication of the volumes in time would not have been possible without the assistance of Shri G.U. Mehta and his colleagues of Vakil & Sons Ltd., Bombay, who took keen interest to ensure that no flaw remained in the production of these volumes.

I am also thankful to my staff who helped me in looking after the Central Office so efficiently for the last two years. I am particularly obliged to my daughter, Nandita Rao, who managed the Central Office of the Congress History Project as Office Executive during my long absence at Bhubaneswar.

With the help of so many eminent persons, agencies and organizations it had been possible for me to get these volumes ready to be released at the historic centenary session of the Congress at Bombay, in December 1985, by our beloved Prime Minister and Congress President, Shri Rajiv Gandhi.

B.N. PANDE
General Editor

A CENTENARY HISTORY OF THE INDIAN NATIONAL CONGRESS

VOLUME ONE

1885-1919

Edited by

N.R. Ray

Director, Institute of Historical Studies,
Calcutta.

Contents

About the Contributors

N.R. Ray is Director, Institute of Historical Studies, Calcutta.

Amitabha Mukherjee is Professor of History, Jadavpur University, Calcutta.

Sita Ram Singh was Professor & Head, Department of History and Dean of the Faculty of Social Sciences, University of Bihar, Muzaffarpur. He has now retired.

Sankari Prasad Basu is Reader, Department of Bengali, University of Calcutta.

B.N. Pande is Governor of Orissa, Bhubaneswar.

Santimay Ray was Head, Department of History, City College, Calcutta and Lecturer, Rabindra Bharati University, Calcutta. He has now retired.

Sunil Kumar Sen is Professor of History, Rabindra Bharati University, Calcutta.

S. Vijayalakshmi is Director, Centre for Social Research, Madras.

Tarasankar Banerjee is Professor & Head, Department of History, Visva Bharati, Santiniketan, West Bengal.

Ashim Kumar Datta is Principal, College of Arts, Jadavpur University, Calcutta.

Introduction

N. R. Ray

1. The Formative Years

AT MIDDAY ON Monday, 28 December 1885, 'very close to one hundred gentlemen' (actually 72) met in the hall of the Gokuldas Tejpal Sanskrit College and Boarding House in Bombay. They were attending the inaugural session of what was originally called the Indian National Union. This name was given up soon after in favour of a new one by which the historic body is known to this day — The Indian National Congress. This session thus marked the advent of a new era destined to see the fulfilment, in a little over sixty years, of the Indian nation's urge for liberation, sovereignty and self-reliance.

It is at best an interesting but, perhaps, not very important academic exercise to attempt to identify the particular circumstances, or the efforts of an individual or of individuals, as the principal immediate factor behind the event. Many scholars have made diligent attempts to do so, but evidences are conflicting. The decision to convene a conference of the Indian National Union at Pune in the Christmas week of 1885 had been taken nine months earlier, in March 1885. The main initiative in planning the conference was that of a recently retired senior member of the Indian Civil Service, Allan Octavian Hume. A decision had also been adopted by the Indian Association of Calcutta to hold the annual session of the Indian National Conference at Calcutta during the same Christmas vacation of 1885. Notices were accordingly sent out by the secretary of the Indian Association, Surendranath Banerjea, to its branches and other similar bodies, asking them to send delegates to the proposed session 'to discuss questions of national importance'. It is also believed by some scholars that the idea of holding a representative conference of Indians for the purpose of setting up a permanent political organization originated with 17 delegates who had earlier attended a Theosophical convention held at Adyar, Madras, in December 1884. Both these gave way to the Bombay meeting which united all three trends.

In attempting to analyse the factors which led to the calling of the first session of the Indian National Congress, Dr B. Pattabhi Sitaramayya, in his work, *The History of the Congress,* speaks at length on the role of Allan Octavian Hume and refers to the delegates at Adyar. He also dwells on the role of Surendranath Banerjea, in particular, and of the National Conference leaders, in general. He concludes thus:

> Whatever the origin and whoever the originator of the idea, we come to this conclusion that the idea was in the air that the need of such an organization was being felt, that Mr Allan Octavian Hume took the initiative and that it was in March 1885, when the first notice was issued convening the first Indian National Union to meet at Poona in the following December, that what had been a vague idea floating generally in the air and influencing simultaneously the thoughts of thoughtful Indians in the North and the South, the East and the West assumed a definite shape and became a practical programme of action.[1]

Viewed in a larger context, the founding of the Indian National Congress was a response to the political and socio-economic conditions confronting the country as the inevitable outcome of its long subjection to alien rule. Hopes entertained in some quarters that British rule would be productive of much that was good and wholesome were soon belied and there was growing discontent concerning the policy pursued by the government. That policy, enlightened public opinion held, was mainly responsible for the evils from which the country suffered. At the time, the thinking was not in terms of ending of foreign domination altogether. What was urged was only that government should desist from discriminatory legislation, discard racism; and, instead, undertake specific reforms in the administration, reconstitute the legislative councils on a wider and more liberal basis than was currently the case, increase opportunities for employment of Indians to posts commensurate with their qualifications, guarantee the rights and liberties of the Indian press, set up a consultative council for advising the government on matters relating to finance — in other words, government should adopt measures for the establishment of a responsible administration whose actions and policy would largely reflect the aspirations and interests of the Indian people.

The extent to which the political aspirations of the enlightened sections of the Indian people, emanating from the newly conceived concept of nationalism, had travelled and made their influence felt, will be evident from the number of associations which had been active since the 1830s, propagating the cause of reform in all spheres of administration. Apart from their number, the locations and composition of these associations testify to the extent and scope of their interest and activities in the promotion of political consciousness among various sections of the

Indian people. A mere recital of the names of the associations from the Landholders' Society (1837) to the Mahajan Sabha (1884) itself makes impressive reading. They were active throughout the country and were based not only in the presidency towns of Calcutta, Bombay and Madras, but also in towns and cities like Pune, Ahmedabad, Lucknow, Aligarh, Ghazipur, Lahore, Patna and Gauhati. There were also a number of associations pledged to serve the respective interests of particular communities or regions such as the Central Muhammadan Association, Anjuman-i-Islamia Association, Anjuman-i-Punjab, Mahomedan Literary Society and the National Mahommedan Association. Besides these, there were several other political organizations in different parts of India which acted as feeder institutions for the larger bodies and exerted considerable influence in local affairs — social and political.

Associations formed with the primary object of gaining civil and political rights for the Indians were not confined to India alone. They were organized in Britain too. Since the days of the East India Company's rule, independent and public-spirited individuals in Britain had been highly critical of British policy in India. The transfer of power to the Crown in 1858 did not diminish their number and influence. It was the prospect of winning their support and that of impartial and enlightened public opinion in England in general that led to the foundation of the East India Association in London on 1 December 1866. Its avowed objective was 'the independent and disinterested advocacy and promotion by all legitimate means of the interests and welfare of India generally'.

Though the membership of the East India Association included a fairly large number of Britishers and particularly the so-called Anglo-Indians, the brunt of the work in connection with the Association's activities was borne by Dadabhai Naoroji, whose faith in the sense of justice and righteousness of the British people remained unshaken throughout his life. The Association, however, did not fulfil the high hopes which greeted its advent and failed to secure for the Indians any tangible benefits. In an outspoken leader, the *Indian Mirror* expressed doubts about its efficacy:

> What has the East India Association done? It is a convenient platform from which ex-civilians now and then endeavour to enlighten the world with their exploded notions about Indian government. But certainly the East India Association does not represent the people of India.[2]

The period of half a century from the inception of the Landholders' Society in 1837 was no doubt a period more of aspirations than of achievements. It was also a period of preparation, setting the stage for the advent of the Indian National Congress in 1885, marking the culmination of the process initiated nearly fifty years earlier. Theodore Dickens, a practising lawyer in Calcutta and a person of liberal and enlightened views, expressed his great hopes for the future at the inauguration of the Landholders' Society in these words: 'I see in it the germ of great things and I am satisfied that the care and prudence which will be required to conduct these beginnings to fitting ends, will not be wanting.'[3] The emergence of the Indian National Congress was the vindication of the hopes Dickens had expressed and which were shared by the generation belonging to the age of what Dr S. R. Mehrotra, in his *The Emergence of the Indian National Congress,* aptly describes as 'the politics of the Associations'.

During the period under review the promotion of national interests and fostering of political consciousness was also championed by the Indian press which adopted the ideal set by Rammohun Roy in the prospectus of his paper, *Mirat-al Akhbar:*

> My only object is that I may lay before the public such articles of intelligence as may increase their experience, and tend to their social improvement; and that to that extent of my abilities I may indicate to the rulers a knowledge of the real situation of their subjects and make the subjects acquainted with the established laws and customs of their rulers; that the rulers may the more readily find an opportunity of granting relief to the people; and the people may be put in possession of the means of obtaining protection and redress from their rulers.[4]

The role of the Indian press, both English as managed by Indians, and vernacular, in propagating political consciousness among the literate sections of the Indian people, was creditable indeed. The newspapers and journals, irrespective of their place of publication, generally looked at problems and needs from the Indian or national, and not provincial or regional, point of view. The importance of their contribution to the building up of public opinion, on the basis of a pan-Indian background, cannot be overrated. There are instances when one or other newspaper came out in defence of governmental action not consistent with the national interest, but, on the whole, the columns of the press were utilized for the propagation of the nationalist point of view.

Legislation aimed at augmentation of government income through a Licence Tax on Trades and Professions and import duties on cotton roused vehement opposition, and this was voiced through the newspapers. The policy, or rather, the lack of it, in regard to cultivation of indigo which placed the poor cultivators at the mercy of the European planters, likewise, met with stubborn opposition at the national level. Incidents arising out of the deposition of Malhar Rao Gaekwad who had been charged with the attempted murder of the British Resident at

Baroda (1875) also did much to foster anti-government feelings, as voiced through the press.

In the formation of public opinion in defence of Indian national interests against the excesses and inequities inherent in colonial system of administration, the part played by Indian-owned journals, and specially the vernacular newspapers (some of which were bi-lingual and even tri-lingual), was bold and vigorous, though not uniformly consistent. The *Amrita Bazar Patrika, Hindoo Patriot, Som Prakas* and *Sadharani* of Calcutta, and the *Rast-Goftar, Indu Prakash* and *Native Opinion* of Bombay, and *The Hindu* of Madras were outspoken in ventilating the nation's grievances. While the *Hindustan, Bharat Mitra* and *Jagat Mitra,* among others, served the Hindi-speaking people of the north, *Jam-e-Jahan Nama,* and *Kushfil Akbhar* enjoyed wide circulation among Urdu-speaking readers. Ten years before the birth of the Indian National Congress, the *Hindoo Patriot* (1874) wrote: 'Home Rule for India ought to be our cry, and it ought to be based upon the same constitutional basis that is recognized in the colonies.'[5]

This was in sharp contrast to *The Times* (1886) which gave a stern warning to the Indian National Congress, within a few months of its foundation, as follows:

> It was by force that India was won, and it is by force that India must be governed, in whatever hands the government of the country may be vested. If we are to withdraw, it would be in favour not of the most fluent tongue or most ready pen, but the strongest arm and the sharpest sword.[6]

It should, however, be noted that political issues did not monopolize the attention of the vernacular press. They were also interested in social and economic problems. In South India, in particular, the newspapers were perhaps more concerned with religious and social issues like temple administration than with politics. Often considered to be as far greater importance than political demands was the issue of *swadeshi* or economic nationalism. It arose as a protest against the official policy which wantonly sacrificed the interests of Indian trade and manufactures for the benefit of British capitalists, the consequent unending drain of Indian wealth, and the mounting burden of economic disabilities imposed on India. Prominent Indians of the post-1857 era boldly expressed their resentment against economic exploitation and the industrial ruination of India, the two principal characteristics of colonial economy.

Examining the trend of events in the two and a half decades following the revolt of 1857, it appears that, outwardly, there was not much manifestation of discontent against alien rule, though there was an undercurrent of conviction that foreign domination was inherently opposed to the fulfilment of India's legitimate hopes and aspirations.

The first half of the 1870s, in particular, may strike an observer as a period of 'quiet, and by no means spectacular' years. But the lull was destined to be disturbed and challenged even before the opening of the next decade. Viewed in the context of what followed, since the late 1870s, the latter proved to be years of intense agitation and dynamic movements.

The advent of Lytton as Viceroy (1876) marked the beginning of a period of confrontation between the opposing forces of liberalism and reaction. The simmering discontent did not take long to assume tangible shape and reach the surface. The grandiose Durbar held at Delhi in 1858 to proclaim Queen Victoria of Britain, Empress of India, sought to impart to the British Empire in India a show of permanence, which proved to be illusory. The concept of paternalistic benevolence assiduously preached by the high priests of British imperialism failed to conceal its real character, based as it was on racial discrimination, economic exploitation, and wilfully imposed disparities in the administrative and judicial spheres. This was, no doubt, more true of the educated, elitist section of the Indian people, but this is not to say that the others had any love for or illusions concerning British rule. The two factors which, more than others, caused disillusionment in the minds of the Indian people were the dominance of the miniscule alien white minority with a racial-superiority complex and their utter indifference to the chronic economic distress to which the common man in India was subjected. The former gave birth to a rapidly growing conviction that British rule was designed essentially to serve British interests both in India and 'at home', to the utter disregard of those of the vast masses of the Indian people. The latter taught the people the lesson that their economic backwardness was the inevitable outcome of the policy pursued by the colonial power, in conformity with their traditional concept of colonialism. The famines of 1873 in northern India and Bengal, and again of 1877-8 in the North, did much to foster a growing loss of faith in British rule among nearly all classes of the Indian people.

The illusion of *Pax Britannica* received rude shocks from a series of movements which, strikingly enough, were organized from below and were in no way the work of elitist intellectuals, notwithstanding their growing disillusionment at the contradiction between the preachings of British political and social thinkers and the conduct, in practice, of their fellow countrymen in charge of the Indian administration. Such challenges, generally speaking, came from the lowest strata in the social and economic hierarchy, viz., the peasants and the tribal communities. These were sporadic but spontaneous, aimed more at the overthrow of the immediate sources of exploitation — the zamindars, moneylenders and tax-collectors, rather than that of the ultimate masters. Their objectives varied from region to region, and their plans of campaign exhibited no common pattern. Belief in a messiah, and the advent of a golden age, discernible in some of these movements, does not, however, detract from their relevance as movements of protest against the system built by the British over the years, following the passing of paramount power from the Mughals to their hands. The tribal and peasant uprisings of the period unmistakably demonstrate the spread and intensity of discontent against alien rule, and explode the myth of a period of *Pax Britannica* in India.

Thus, while persistent economic disparities and the resultant distress lay at the root of peasant and tribal insurrections, the growing disillusionment and alienation of the elitist intellectual combine was mainly the outcome of racial arrogance of the rulers. Its first manifestation occurred over discrimination in the administration of justice and in recruitment to public services, dating back to the 1820s and '30s. The struggles then waged by Indians related not so much to theoretical considerations concerning the evils of racism, as such, but to its implications in the actual working of the administration in British India. The press, in particular the vernacular press, acted as the principal media for exposing the anomalies inherent in the Acts governing justice and public administration. Anglo-Indian newspapers, owned or managed by Britishers, though at times critical, were not vocal and often underplayed the legitimate grievances of the people. The vernacular papers, on the other hand, not only reflected the growing resentment of the informed public but also collected, through extensive field-surveys, firsthand data illustrative of racism, in detail. As a result, while Indian public opinion was increasingly conscious of and resentful against discrimination in the eyes of law, the Europeans, acting under a sense of racial superiority, became increasingly aggressive in the post-mutiny years and came round to the view that a 'lordly air of supremacy in attitude towards the natives was necessary for maintaining the prestige of the Englishman'.

Here were materials enough for a confrontation. Whether it would surface immediately or lie dormant for some time depended on the attitude and action of the government. The government of Lytton, however, chose a policy which (as was foreseen by discerning observers) provoked further resentment among Indians. The atmosphere in which the Vernacular Press Act was passed is well illustrated by the attitude of one of the provincial satraps, the Lieutenant-Governor of the N.W. Province who, on being consulted by Lytton, wrote that the time had come when the British government should desist from

> putting its head in a bush and shouting that black is not white; and the sooner we plainly recognize and act upon that fact the better it will be for

> our influence and hold on the millions we govern. That there should be one law alike for the European and the Native is an excellent thing in theory, but if it could really be introduced in practice we shall have no business in the country.[7]

Lytton overrode the cautious pleadings of the Madras governor who thought that it would be unwise to shackle the vernacular press because it provided 'a useful barometer of Native feeling and sentiment; a barometer such as no menaced and sycophant press could possibly do'.[8] The law substantially restricting the freedom of the vernacular press was enacted in 1878.

This repressive measure came in the wake of growing discontent engendered by three other recent enactments. The first was the Dramatic Performance Act (1876), imposing strict censorship on public performances. The second was the Arms Act (1878) which deprived Indians of the right to bear arms. Even villagers could no longer use them to protect themselves against wild animals. The third was the amendment of the rules concerning recruitment to the Indian Civil Service to reduce the maximum age limit for the Civil Service Examination from 21 to 19. This was, not without reason, regarded as a wilful attempt to drastically restrict the prospects of Indian candidates. The diversion of the Famine Fund for the Afghan War (1878-9) also added fuel to the fire of discontent which was not confined merely to the so-called elitist-intellectual combine, but raged also among large sections of the public 'from Calcutta to Lahore and from Lahore to Madras', whose political consciousness had been greatly stirred by the activities of the Indian Association.

The forebodings of the *Bombay Gazette* that 'volcano-like passions lie hidden under the smooth words and mild exterior of the people of thé country' were re-echoed with greater precision as William Wedderburn wrote, 'The state of things at the end of Lord Lytton's regime was bordering upon a revolution.' Events proved that reactionary Lytton had been the unconscious initiator of public agitations destined to engulf India within three years of his departure. Surendranath Banerjea, whose role in public life had begun to unfold from about the second half of the 1870s, recalls: 'In the evolution of political progress, bad rulers are often a blessing in disguise. They help stir a community into life, a result that years of opposition would perhaps have failed to achieve.'[9]

'Liberal' Ripon succeeded 'Conservative' Lytton to the viceroyalty in 1880. This change appeared to some as the replacement of 'Conservative adventure' by 'Liberal experiment'. The author of *Indian National Evolution* deluded himself with the belief that 'the gathering clouds' under Lytton gave way to 'the dawning light' under Ripon. There was, no doubt, some indication that a change was at hand, since the new incumbent proclaimed his desire to widen the basis of Indian collaboration by winning over the support and goodwill of the educated middle class. His early actions in withdrawing the Arms and the Vernacular Press Acts were greeted with a promise of responsive co-operation. But hope was belied sooner than could be anticipated. The country was soon thrown into a convulsion which was more serious and more widespread than any Lytton had witnessed.

It was triggered off by an attempt by Ripon's administration to remove a glaringly discriminatory provision in the administration of criminal justice, based solely on 'race distinctions and the supposed personal privileges of a dominant caste'. The bill, named after the Law Member, C.P. Ilbert, sought to partially remove race disqualifications from Indian judges in the mofussil and reject the idea that an Indian, as such, was incapable of fairly trying a British-born subject. Unforeseen by Ripon, but not unexpected in the context of the long-cherished prejudice and racial arrogance of the average Briton-in-India ('The British Lion, a vulgar brute that wagged his tail and roared' — in the words of a contemporary English public servant, D. F. Carmichael, a member of the Madras Council), the entire white community rose up in violent protest against what they described as 'a scandalous bill'. What followed displayed all the symptoms of a mutiny. A vehement backlash from the Indians followed. It found expression in speeches at public meetings and in writings in the columns of the Indian-owned newspapers. Ridiculing the European reaction, *Rast Goftar* wrote: 'The conduct of the Englishmen in this matter lends colour to the story that they shake off their good traits of character at Suez.' The *Bengalee* congratulated the Indian public on launching a 'great agitation for a great principle at stake'. The *Indian Mirror* noted with appreciation 'the consensus of opinion and unity of action among our countrymen'. The action of the government in instituting a case against Surendranath Banerjea on a charge of contempt of court (since he had criticized, in the columns of the *Bengalee,* the action of one of the sitting judges in the Calcutta High Court in causing a *Saligram* to be brought to the Court), and his subsequent imprisonment caused an unprecedented stir. So intense and spontaneous was public resentment that, in Surendranath's own words, 'In the whole course of my public life, I have never witnessed except in connection with the agitation for the modification of the partition of Bengal, an upheaval of feeling so genuine and widespread as that what swept through Bengal in 1883'[10]. There were reactions outside Bengal also, only Madras remaining outwardly unperturbed.

Ripon, however, slowly began to deviate from his original position and yielded to the pressure of the European community. Eventually, he retraced his steps. A new bill followed in drastic modification of the original one. It restricted jurisdiction over Europeans only to Indian magistrates and sessions judges. It also conceded the European demand in respect of juries, half of which would have to be European or American in cases in which Europeans were being tried. It further stipulated that a district magistrate could sentence a European only to a maximum of six months' imprisonment or a maximum fine of Rs 2,000, or both.

For the Indian leaders who spearheaded the Ilbert Bill agitation in the hope of eliminating at least some of the prevailing racial disparities, Ripon's abject surrender to the protagonists of racial superiority came as a deep disappointment. But the racial pride of the Europeans was still not appeased. The extremists among them set up 'revenge parties' to deal with attempts at assertion of their rights by Indian victims of white insolence. In these circumstances, Indian opinion grew more restless. It was now evident to influential sections of Indian opinion that faith in British justice was ill-placed and that there would be no response from the authorities so long as their efforts were confined to mere meetings, petitions and resolutions. What was needed was self-reliance, determination, and national unity. A glance at articles and correspondence published in leading vernacular papers of 1883-4 will attest to the shift in Indian thinking *vis-a-vis* the British administrative system and the urgency felt for stronger and more organized efforts for the removal of Indian grievances.

'The evidence on the Ilbert Bill controversy and the aftermath', writes Dr N.S. Bose, 'leads to an almost indisputable conclusion that it was the early eighties and not the nineties of the last century that were the seed-time of extremism in the Indian national movement.'[11] He bases his conclusion on the widespread discontent among the various sections of India's population, irrespective of caste, creed and faith, who had grown impatient at the situation arising out of the racial discrimination practised by official and non-official Europeans alike. The virtual exclusion of Indians from higher avenues of livelihood, the close preserves of Europeans and Anglo-Indians for several categories of posts, the disparities between European and Indian members of the services, the inhuman treatment and physical assaults on peasants and workers and the utter helplessness of the administration to ensure security to Indians against usurpation of power by the white minority and outbursts of blatant racism — all these created in the minds of the average Indian a sense of frustration, anger and despair.

In this connection, reference is often made to William Wedderburn's statement that Allan Octavian Hume conceived of a permanent organization like the Indian National Congress as 'a safety-valve' against the dangerous prospect of an imminent 'terrible revolution' — the frightening vision of a massive outbreak of violence similar to that in 1857.

According to Wedderburn, Hume went through a mass of reports and recorded evidence,

> English abstracts or translations — longer or shorter — of vernacular reports or communications of one kind or another, all arranged according to districts, sub-districts, sub-divisions and the cities, towns and villages included in these. The number of these reports was enormous; there were said at the time to be communications from over thirty thousand different reporters. Many of the entries reported conversations between men of the lowest classes, all going to show that these poor men were pervaded with a sense of the hopelessness of the existing state of affairs, that they were convinced that they would starve and die, and they wanted to do something. They were going to do something, and stand by each other, and that something meant violence.[12]

The reports and evidences referred to have not been traced so far. In the circumstances, one is left wondering. Briton Martin attributes the apprehension of recurrence of the events of 1857 to Hume's obsession which 'prejudiced his assessment of Indian problems'.[13] Dr Bose, on the other hand, is inclined to the view that,

> Quite possibly, Hume had read the sort of material that was compiled by the Government of India to justify the enactment of the Vernacular Press Act in 1878. The issue, in his opinion, that was causing great concern to all sections of the people was the overbearing attitude and conduct of the Europeans, especially those living in the interior areas.[14]

This appears to be a plausible enough hypothesis, but one should perhaps find in the growing agrarian distress and economic discontent over extensive areas, yet another potential factor that held out the threat of 'a terrible revolution'. Years earlier the Indigo disturbances of 1859-62 had indicated in no uncertain manner the potentialities of a widespread agrarian uprising. These were intensified by the Pabna (1873) and Deccan (1875) Riots. Dr S.R. Mehrotra has rightly observed that 'there were many Britons who feared that both economically and politically India might go the way of Ireland.'[15]

Fear of a widespread agrarian uprising first manifested itself in the course of the Blue Mutiny. That fear did not subside. On the other hand, it grew increasingly acute in the 1870s and 80s. The series of famines that overwhelmed vast regions in India — Orissa and the eastern coast from Calcutta to Madras in 1866-7, the United Provinces, the Punjab and Rajputana in 1868-9, Bengal, Northern Bihar, Oudh and the North West Province in 1873, Madras, Mysore, Hyderabad, Bombay and again the N. W. Province in 1876-9, covering at its peak 257,000 square miles and a population of over 58 million — as well as the growing economic distress, had depressed the majority of people below subsistence level. Radical measures were urgently required, measures which the government was unable or unwilling to adopt or even plan.

The agrarian revolts, convulsing vast regions of India in the second half of the 19th century, were protests against the evils inherent in the system of land tenure and revenue in general, and the slump in the cotton market since 1865, restrictions on trade, the heavy burden of taxation and the exactions of moneylenders, in particular. Such spontaneous insurrections, unorganized though they were, were a pointer to even more serious risings to follow. The so-called Deccan Riots (1875) were an indication of the growingly militant nature of peasant uprisings. It has been observed that,

> The Deccan peasant risings of 1875 were the warning signal of the growing unrest and the anxiety of the government was revealed in the appointment of the Deccan Riots Commission in 1875. . . . By the last quarter of the nineteenth century the conditions were now present which had not existed in the first three quarters, for the beginning of the Indian national movement.[16]

As was only to be expected in the circumstances, the agrarian discontent prepared the ground for a new type of militant upsurge with unmistakable political overtones. Its first manifestation was the challenge thrown out by Vasudev Balwant Phadke (1845-83). His indignation against foreign rule and his determination to overthrow it by organized violent resistance was derived from his conviction that British rule was directly responsible for the terrible, insufferable economic distress to which the common man lay exposed. He launched a series of semi-military campaigns with the aid of armed followers recruited from among the Ramoshi tribals. There are indications that, at the beginning, at any rate, Phadke's movement was distinctly agrarian in character. But there was a difference between the Deccan Riots and the movement initiated by him four years later. The latter was more organized and better planned than the former which were wholly spontaneous and sporadic.

The gravity of Phadke's challenge was fully realized by Sir Richard Temple, the then Governor of Bombay, who wrote:

> The readiness with which they [peasants of humble caste but of hardihood and courage] . . . answered the mandate of their shadowy and half mysterious chief, like bees hiving, the apathetic and unsatisfactory behaviour of the people in many villages and the sympathy known to be felt, if not openly evinced, by many of the upper classes, were grave circumstances demanding reflection on our part.[17]

Also of interest in this connection are the contents of a letter written on 19 February 1881 by Karl Marx from London to N. F. Danielson, the first translator of the first volume of *Das Kapital* into Russian.[18] It records the writer's impression that 'in India serious complications, if not a general outbreak is in store for the British Government', by way of protest against the 'bleeding process' practised with a vengeance' by the alien rulers.

The conclusion thus appears irresistible that, apart from widely felt indignation against the racial arrogance of the rulers, there was also a growing agrarian discontent which tended to assume political overtones. These two forces worked simultaneously and created a situation which was politically volcanic and economically distressing beyond endurance. It is in this background that the genesis of the Indian National Congress has to be studied.

Apart from the reactions which the situation might have produced among the liberal section of Englishmen in India and in Britain, however genuine these might have been, what mattered more was the reaction among increasingly influential sections of enlightened Indians. 'The politics of the Associations' operating over nearly half a century since 1837 had no doubt caused some stir, but they did not go as far as the situation demanded. The Indian Association, founded in 1876, marked the culmination of a process initiated with the establishment of the Landholders' Society in 1837. The name 'Indian Association' was itself significant. So were its aims, viz., the creation of a strong body of public opinion in the country, the unification of Indian races and peoples on the basis of common political interests and aspirations, the promotion of friendly feeling between the Hindus and the Muslims, and the inclusion of the masses in the great political movements of the day. The Association had the distinction of being the first of such organizations, representing the educated middle classes, rather than the big landowning classes, to operate branches in several provinces. To this Association also belongs the credit for convening the first ever All India National Conference in 1883, attended by representatives from Bengal, Madras, Bombay and the United Provinces. Ananda Mohan Bose, one of the principal sponsors of the session, proclaimed that this conference was the first step towards a national parliament.

It is to be noted that Allan Octavian Hume, who fathered the concept of the Indian National Union, and the leaders of the Indian National Conference, were not the only persons to have given serious thought to the need for a permanent national organization, composed of as many elements of enlightened public opinion as possible. Mrs Annie Besant[19] wrote that the 17 'good men and true' who had attended the session of the Theosophical Convention at Adayar, Madras, in December 1884 had conceived the idea of forming a body to be known as the Indian National Congress. Dr R.C. Majumdar has made out a case which would cast doubts on the accuracy of Besant's claim.[20] It would, however, appear more reasonable to conclude, as Dr Pattabhi Sitaramayya does, 'the idea was in the air and the need for such an organization was being felt'.[21] Viewed in proper historical perspective, as stated earlier, the birth of the Indian National Congress was a response to the total situation prevalent in India, specially since the 1880s, and no single organization, not to speak of a single individual, can be given exclusive credit for its emergence. The Indian Association and Surendranath had shown the way by convening two successive sessions of the Indian National Conference in 1883 and 1885. It was certainly an act as much of supreme wisdom as of magnanimity when he decided in 1886 to merge the Conference in 'the Congress' which, in Surendranath's own words, 'was conceived on the same lines and had the same programme as the National Conference'.[22]

To attribute the foundation of the Indian National Congress to the initiative of a single individual is, therefore, an exercise in over-simplification. Yet, a consideration of the circumstances in which the first Congress met at Bombay on 28 December 1885 reveals that A.O. Hume has a large share in giving concrete shape to ideas that had been afloat for quite some time. A member of the Indian Civil Service, Hume resigned from service in January 1882, after having served for 32 years. From his father he inherited a radicalism to which he remained loyal throughout his service career. His sympathetic interest in India and her people was genuine. He felt unhappy at the rapidly deteriorating situation since the 1870s and was convinced that, unless some positive and immediate steps were taken, India would be thrown in the midst of 'a terrible revolution'. He felt uneasy about the trends of government policy and actions. In a letter to Northbrook, as early as 1 August 1872, he had expressed his fear that 'the fate of the Empire is trembling in the balance',[23] though he would not identify any particular situation which was responsible for this. What was a possibility in Hume's mind in 1872 became a near certainty in 1879. The attitude and the thinking that moulded it cannot be dismissed, as Briton Martin does, as a mere obsession with Hume. Hume was also convinced that the evil days could be tided over. He assiduously cultivated personal relations with Ripon and Dufferin, trying to win them over to his views on what government should aim at. He also kept himself in close contact with prominent leaders of public opinion, representatives of the press and of public associations. Nor did he neglect the rising generation. In a confidential letter addressed to the graduates of the Calcutta University (1 March 1883), he made a passionate appeal for setting up an association pledged to well-defined lines of action for achieving 'mental, moral, social and political progress in India.' The formation, at his initiative, of a permanent representative body of Indians, viz., the Indian National Union, presumably had Dufferin's approval.

While Hume's role in convening the first session of the Congress (and also a few succeeding ones) is unmistakable, controversy rages round the motives behind the action. One such controversial matter is the so-called 'safety-valve' against popular discontent theory. In Hume's opinion, as recorded by Wedderburn: 'A safety-valve for the escape of great and growing forces, generated by our own action, was urgently needed and no more efficacious safety-valve than our Congress movement could possibly be devised.'[24]

It is well known that Hume met Dufferin and placed before him his plan of setting up the new organization. Dufferin suggested some modifications which Hume readily accepted. The 'safety-valve theory' presupposes that Dufferin had a big hand to play, that he shared the views of Hume regarding the imminence of chaos and that he wished the Congress to act as a bulwark against forces of violence. But there is no evidence that either Dufferin or his two immediate predecessors in office shared Hume's fears concerning an imminent revolution. In seeking the origin of the Congress, it is far more fruitful to recall that the idea of a national Indian organization had been in the air for quite some time than to seek it solely in an individual's personal initiative, however well-intentioned and significant it might have been. Also, the conclusion seems inescapable that non-official circles had exaggerated ideas about Hume's influence over the makers of official policy.

The Report of the first Indian National Congress refers to a confidential circular issued by Hume which announced the plan for holding a conference of delegates from all parts of Bengal, Bombay and Madras Presidencies. The circular stated: 'This conference would form the germ of a Native Parliament which, if properly conducted, would constitute in a few years an unanswerable reply to the assertion that India is still wholly unfit for any representative institution.' It was further announced that the first conference would meet at Pune. Actually, however, the conference met at Bombay, the venue being changed, as there had been a few cases of cholera in Pune.

The first session met in Bombay on 28 December 1885 at 12 noon. It was an assembly of a modest size. Among the 'very close one hundred gentlemen' attending it, 28 were officials. The official Report of the First Indian National Congress gives full details on the participants and the proceedings. W.C. Bonnerjee from Calcutta, who presided, said, 'Surely never had so important and comprehensive an assemblage occurred within historical times on the soil of India,' and claimed for it an entirely representative character, notwithstanding the smallness of its size 'If community of sentiments, community of feelings and community of wants enabled any one to speak on behalf of others, then assuredly they might justly claim to be representatives of the people of India', he said.[25]

More revealing than the official Report is the reportage of the special correspondent of the Calcutta weekly, *Reis and Rayyet*. In its issue of 11 January 1886 he gave a vivid account of the atmosphere in which the delegates met:

> It seems to me that as if every member had inwardly resolved upon having less of words and more of work, every one of them inspired with an inward feeling that it was real work for his country which had called him to that hall, real work and no long or tall talk . . . a ring of true patriotic earnestness which thrilled through the sympathetic chords of all listeners every now and again.[26]

The resolutions adopted at the session related to the need for administrative reforms at several levels, curtailment of military expenditure and deprecation of the proposed annexation of Upper Burma — none of these suggestive of any radical change or transformation. A good government rather than self government was the desideratum of the hour. As Bonnerjee declared: 'All that they desired was that the basis of the government should be widened and that the people should have their proper and legitimate share in it.'

What would appear as strikingly peculiar to a modern critic is that the Congress at its birth should have professed its utmost loyalty to the throne and goodwill towards the British Empire. However strange this may seem, in the context of later developments, this position was an outcome of practical considerations which dominated the thinking of the educated middle-class in India in the 1880s. Bonnerjee did not see any contradiction between India's 'desire to be governed according to the ideas of government prevalent in Europe' and 'through loyalty to the British government'.

Yet the lesson and importance of the advent of the Indian National Congress was not lost upon the media of contemporary public opinion, viz., the press. Bonnerjee did not indulge in exaggeration when he described the assemblage of 1885 as 'the most important and comprehensive assemblage held within historical times on the soil of India', any more than another prominent participant, G. Subramanya Aiyar, did. In Aiyar's opinion

> the assemblage in Bombay of my chosen countrymen from Calcutta and Lahore, from Madras and Sind, from places wide apart and difficult of communication, indicates the beginning of a national political life, destined to produce a profound change in the immediate future.[27]

The Congress, as seen already, was a corollary and culmination of the 'politics of the Associations'. From the beginning it was clear that, though in respect of objectives, constitution and composition, it was similar to the associations which had preceded it, it was basically different from it in certain important ways. The pre-Congress associations, except the Indian Association, were local organizations, with headquarters in Presidency towns like Calcutta, Bombay and Madras and in some cases, Pune, Lahore and Aligarh. No doubt these bodies gave vent to some of the grievances common to the whole country, but their activities did not spread beyond their neighbourhoods. Besides, for many years, these older associations, generally speaking, derived their main support from the landed aristocracy and the affluent classes. The Congress, on the other hand, was promoted as a common platform for all sections of the Indian people, irrespective of the community and province to which they might belong. Its proclaimed object was 'the fuller development and consolidation of the sentiments of national unity' (Presidential Address by W.C. Bonnerjee). Even on the day the Congress held its first session, the *Indu Prakash* of Bombay saw in it 'the beginning of a new life and whatever traducers may say, it will greatly help in creating a national feeling and binding together distant people by common sympathies and common ends. The *Indian Mirror* of Calcutta made the prophecy that 28 December 1885 would become

> a red letter day in the annals of the national progress of Native races . . . If we were asked what was the proudest day in our life, we should unhesitatingly say it was the day on which we, for the first time, met all our brothers of Madras, Bombay, the North-Western Provinces and the Punjab under the roof of the Gokul Dass Tejpal Sanskrit College for the purpose of the National Congress. From the date of this Congress we may well count the more rapid development of national progress in India in future.

Similar sentiments were echoed in the columns of the *Hindoo Patriot* (Calcutta), *The Hindu* (Madras) and the *Hindustani* of Lucknow.

Future events confirmed the soundness of these prognostications. The foundation of the Indian National Congress marked, on the one hand, the culmination of the 'Era of Associations' and, on the other, the beginning of a movement aimed at engulfing the entire nation and securing for its people 'freedom and happiness' and destined to reach its goal within a little over sixty years (1885-1947) since its advent. The beginning was modest. As noted earlier, only 72 persons gathered at its first session; they were not elected by the people, the resolutions adopted were not radical or revolutionary by any standard. The president of the first session, W.C. Bonnerjee, while expressing the desire that 'the basis of the government should be widened and the people should have their proper and legitimate share in it', did not fail to give the assurance that 'our desire to be governed according to the ideas of government prevalent in Europe is in no way incompatible with our thorough loyalty to the British government.'[27a]

The second session which met at Calcutta in 1886 was better attended — 436 delegates 'elected either at public meetings or by Societies, Associations, and Sabhas', against the 72 of the previous year. Even an Anglo-Indian paper, *The Statesman* of Calcutta, not particularly known for its support to the legitimate aspirations of the Indian people, paid a handsome tribute to the historic session in the following words:

> We never remember to have seen the hall [of the British Indian Association] more densely packed, and what was more, a striking feature was its undoubtedly cosmopolitan character. It was, in short, a vast gathering of the Indian people. Every race and every sect was there represented.[28]

Dadabhai Naoroji who presided and Rajendra Lal Mitra who acted as Chairman of the Reception Committee were both outstanding personalities, commanding universal respect. What, however, imparted special importance to the session was that Surendranath Banerjea and the leaders of the Indian National Conference gave up their separate identity and merged with the Congress, to make it the sole spokesman of the entire Indian people.

Another remarkable feature of this session was its awareness of the need to end the growing impoverishment of the people. A resolution adopted at the session read:

> This Congress regards with deepest sympathies, and views with grave apprehension, the increasing poverty of vast numbers of the population of India (although aware that the government is not overlooking this matter and is contemplating certain palliatives) and desires to record its fixed conviction that the introduction of representative institutions will prove one of the most important practical steps towards the amelioration of the condition of the people.[29]

It is thus evident that, from the very beginning, the Congress had distinct aims in view. While demanding increasing association of Indians in the government of the country, it never lost sight of the other goal, viz. the eradication of poverty to which the mass of India's population lay exposed.

Till the end of the 19th century, the development of the Indian National Congress fell into a pattern. Political problems no doubt engaged its major attention, but economic problems were not matters of less concern. To meet the growing economic crisis through which the country passed during the 1880s and 90s (there were as many as 18 famines between 1876 and 1900 and W. Digby calculated that 'famines and scarcities have been four times as numerous during the last thirty years of the 19th century as they were one hundred years earlier'[30]), the Government took recourse to various measures, such as reimposition of income-tax and import duties and its extension to cotton goods, among others. These measures replenished the treasury (land revenue receipts alone increased from Rs 19.67 crores in 1881-2 to around Rs 24 crores in the 1890s), but intensified the people's distress. The situation worsened with the years. The concern of the Congress manifested itself in its resolutions, repeated year after year. The newly imposed countervailing excise duty of 5 per cent *ad valorem* on cotton piecegoods and yarns in particular (1894) evoked widespread resentment, since it was felt, not without reason, that the new duty would seriously cripple 'the infant Mill Industry of the country'. A resolution adopted at the 10th session of the Congress (1894) read:

> Resolved that:
>
> (a) This Congress respectfully enters its emphatic protest against the injustice and impolicy of imposing excise duty on cotton manufactured in India, as such excise is calculated to cripple seriously the infant Mill Industry of this country and
>
> (b) This Congress puts on record its firm conviction that in proposing this excise the interests of India have been sacrificed to those of Lancashire and it strongly deprecates any such surrender of Indian interests by the Secretary of State.[31]

This concern also found expression in the 1895 presidential address by Surendranath Banerjea:

> The present duties were not meant to be protective, but were levied only for revenue purposes, and . . . even Gladstone, the champion of the free-trade movement in England, had denounced the application of the free-trade doctrine to India as opposed to the needs of the people.[32]

The decision of the Government to lower the duty from 5 per cent to 3½ per cent together with the imposition of an excise duty on all Indian mill-made cloth failed to appease Indian opinion. As its spokesman, a former president of the Congress (1891), and then a member of the Legislative Council, P. Ananda Charlu, asked the government 'resolutely decline to submit to dictates either from their Lancashire compatriots or from such as care for Lancashire votes at the poll or Lancashire support in Parliament.'

The persistent refusal of the government to repeal the excise duty, besides others which had added to the people's distress, induced the Congress in 1902 to place the economic situation on a larger canvas and to attribute the distress to

> the decline of indigenous arts and manufactures and to the drain of wealth of the country which has gone on for years and to excessive taxation and over-assessment of land which have so far impoverished the people so that, at the first touch of scarcity, large numbers are forced to throw themselves on state help.

The military policy of the government, aimed at containing the 'enemies of England' on the frontiers, east and west of India, and the resultant burden on the exchequer also evoked criticism. At the 1895 session the president, Surendranath Banerjea, observed that the government's quest for a 'scientific frontier' had involved the state in extravagant expenditure. This, he warned, was responsible for 'alienating the sympathies of the people by wasting their resources'. The warning was repeated at the 19th session (Madras, 1903) when Lalmohan Ghose, the President of the Congress, questioned the propriety of maintaining an army in India much larger than actually required, and was outspoken enough to say that the British army was maintained not

> to defend the country against domestic enemies or against the invasion of warlike peoples of adjoining countries but to maintain the supremacy of the British power and the Government and on which millions of India's money have been spent.[33]

The problem of agriculture and land revenue was not less acute. That the leaders of the early Congress were aware of the intensity of the problem is borne out by the fact that, between 1888 and 1903, the matter came up for deliberation in all the Congress sessions. The land revenue administration, it was felt, should be so reorganized as to assure to the cultivators adequate income to face droughts and floods, often culminating in famines. What was immediately needed, in their opinion, was relaxation of revenue assessment in some form or other. The extension of the Permanent Settlement was considered by some, at the initial stage at least, as an answer to the problem. The efficacy of this step as a solution was questionable, but in government circles, at any rate, there was an apprehension that, unless the grievances were redressed soon, India might well be confronted with an explosive situation shaped by a combination of agrarian and political discontent.

The measures adopted by the government, like the Deccan Agriculturists' Relief Act (1879) and the Punjab Land Alienation Act (1900) seemed half-hearted and proved ineffective. The substantial increase in revenue, generally on account of excise duties, duties on liquor and forest produces and land revenue failed to counter the economic imbalance due to commitments of heavy expenditure in respect of the growing 'India Debt' to England, 'Home charges', war expenses and 'guaranteed interest' on railways, among others. The overall situation, the inevitable outcome of the colonial economy with its attendant evils of de-industrialization and a virtual British monopoly of exports of major agricultural products — tea, indigo, jute etc. — demanded an early reappraisal of state policy and programmes. As early as 1893, as President of the Congress, Dadabhai Naoroji described the poverty of the Indian people as 'the question of questions'. His immediate successor in office, Alfred Webb, shared this view and said, 'Nothing is more striking in considering the condition of India than its poverty.'

In 1901 the Congress resolved

> to call the attention of the Government to the deplorable condition of the poorest classes in India, full forty millions of whom, according to high official authority, drag out a miserable existence, on the verge of starvation even in normal years. . . .

The resolution urged, among other things, the establishment of agricultural banks; the adoption of a policy which would enforce economy, husband the resources of the state, improve the agriculture of the country, foster the revival and development of indigenous arts and manufactures, and help forward the introduction of new industries, with a view to stopping 'the drain of the wealth of the country, at least, in part, by the wider employment of the children of the soil in the public services.'[34]

It is thus evident that the Congress, from its inception, was alive to economic problems, which engaged its serious and constant attention, in a manner and to an extent which far exceeded the attention paid to them by the pre-Congress associations. In the opinion of the Congress leaders, political problems could be properly studied and analysed only in the context of the prevailing economic situation. As Banerjea observed (1902), 'the industrial and economic problems are indissolubly linked together'. The position was more explicitly stated by Lalmohan Ghose in the concluding portion of his presidential address (1903):

> May we not ask whether we are to believe that the policy which, many years ago, killed our indigenous industries, which even only the other day and under a liberal administration unblushingly imposed excise duties on our cotton manufactures, which steadily drains our national resources to

> the extent of something like twenty million sterling, and which, by imposing burdens on an agricultural population, increases the frequency and intensity of our famines to an extent unknown in former times — are we to believe that the various administrative acts which have led to these were directly inspired of a beneficent Providence?[35]

The answer was obvious.

As was only to be expected, however, politics claimed the largest share of the Congressmen's attention. Till 1892, the Congress had conformed to a set pattern; during these years it had struck roots; the number of members and delegates attending its deliberations increased steadily. It had outgrown the stage of being just an annual event and had become a full-fledged organization with a programme aimed at the fulfilment of the nation's aspiration, viz. a share in the conduct of the government.

The objective in view was modest. The steps to be taken for its attainment were cautious. With innate faith in England's commitment to democracy and liberalism, the leaders entertained the hope that the government in Britain would confer on the Indians the benefit of self-government with the attendant representative institutions. The hope grew into a conviction. The speeches of the leaders of the early Congress and the resolutions adopted invariably commenced with professions of 'deep loyalty' and 'profound devotion to the crown' and were replete with unqualified eulogies of the manifold benefits conferred by the government. A look into the resolutions adopted up to 1892 reveals that the objectives were limited to liberalization of the administrative pattern on a modest scale. These underscored the need for 'expansion of the Supreme and existing local Legislative Councils by the admission of a considerable proportion of elected members; the creation of similar councils for the North-Western Provinces and Oudh and also for Punjab'; simultaneous competitive examinations in England and India for 'appointments in various civil departments of the public service'; 'introduction of Representative Institutions . . . as one of the most important practical steps towards the amelioration of the condition of the people'; a material increase in the number of persons composing the Legislative Councils, both Provincial, and the Governor-General's; extension of the system of trial by jury; amendment of the Indian Code of Criminal Procedures; amenities for recruitment of Indians to higher grades of the military service; revision of the Income-Tax Act; introduction of Technical Education; relaxation of the Arms Act (X of 1878); extension of the right to vote; reduction in the 'extravagant cost of the present administration, military and civil, but especially the former'; establishment of military colleges; complete separation of executive and judicial functions; and 'fundamental reform of the Police Administration'.

From the above, it will be evident that what was in view was not a radical political or administrative restructuring, but only concessions in the form of, more or less, minor administrative adjustments. Even then, the government chose to remain, on the whole, unresponsive. The only concession was the announcement of an impending India Bill. P. Ananda Charlu who presided over the seventh session (1891) described this Bill as 'a confirmation of our views and a response — though a faltering response — to our chorus voice'. But he was not unduly elated. This appears from his candid admission that,

> Notwithstanding all these grounds for congratulating ourselves, the lamentable fact remains that in regard to our higher claims, little beyond lip-concession in this country and half-hearted and halting measures (now shelved) in the Imperial metropolis has as yet fallen to our lot.[36]

Cross's India Bill had already been enacted when the eighth Congress session met at Allahabad (1892). The Act fell short of the expectations of the Indian leaders and the Congress adopted a resolution expressing its 'regret that the Act itself does not, in terms, concede to the people, the right of electing their own representatives to the Council'. It disapproved of the official scheme of representation of 'races, classes and interests' provided for in the Act.

The year 1892 may be said to mark the end of the first period of Congress history. The period was one of slow growth. The object was the attainment of 'Responsible Government'. W. C. Bonnerjee asserted:

> What we want and have a right to get is that our countrymen should have the opportunity of fully representing to the Government the views of the people of this country in this country. What we want is that there should be Responsible Government in India.

The failure to attain this target emphasized the need for more concerted action. 'The Congress', as A. O. Hume said, 'had endeavoured to instruct the government, but the government had refused to be instructed.' Some amount of interest had, no doubt, been roused in favour of India's aspirations in non-official circles in Britain, but this by itself was not enough. The men who were at the helm of the Congress, products of western liberalism, honestly believed in the British sense of justice and regard for democracy. Over the years since the birth of the Congress, they met, discussed and adopted resolutions, embodying their views, and sent these over to the authorities, seeking their fulfilment. They sent petitions, appeals and deputations. These created some stir, but failed to achieve the results hoped for.

These limitations, inherent in this mode of functioning, do not, however, detract from the value of the work of the early Congress. The nationalist or 'Extremist' school, which came in the forefront soon after, expressed their grave dissatisfaction with this 'policy of mendicancy', prayers and petitions and 'a little too much talk about the blessings of British rule'. But to describe the leaders of the early Congress as 'a caucus' of individuals 'with an elitist life-style', a body of 'weak-kneed, woolly-headed politicians', 'a small urban educated minority fighting for their own interests', and to discover 'a link between early Congress professional intelligentsia and propertied groups' is to deny the positive and distinct services rendered at a formative stage by the founding fathers who were not indifferent to the woeful conditions in which the mass of their countrymen lived. Even within a couple of years of the foundation of the Congress, the importance of rallying the masses, especially the peasants, was realized. This is evident from the wide circulation of two pamphlets, *A Congress Catechism* and *A Conversation between Maulvi Furreduddin,* M.A., B.L., *Vaquil of the High Court, practising in this Zillah Court of Hakikatabad and one Ram Buksh, one of the Mukaddams of Kambakhtpur,* published in 12 regional languages, depicting the miserable poverty of the people, and exposing the evils of a despotic government and absentee landlordism. They stressed the nature of Britain's economic exploitation of India and the need of promoting the welfare of all sections of the people, and not merely of the sector to which the early Congress leaders belonged. Their actions reveal that they fully nourished the roots of nationalism and made the people of India conscious of the existence of the common enemy and the source of their political deprivation and economic distress. The changed attitude of Viceroy Dufferin and high government officials, who had at first expressed lip-sympathy for and goodwill towards the Congress and the directives to government officials banning contact with the Congress, attest to the sense of insecurity which the British Indian Government began to feel at the trend of affairs since 1885. This uneasy feeling among British officials in India is itself an index to the 'stir' that the Congress had created soon after it had come into being.

One area in which the Congress failed to win success was in its efforts to rally Indian Muslims who, by and large, were influenced by Sir Syed Ahmad Khan to believe that the Congress was a Hindu organization. Another sphere which proved contentious was that of social reform. Reforms were indeed needed, but the Congress leaders soon found that persistence in demanding legislation on the subject would only bring into sharp focus the divergence of opinions among its votaries, who were otherwise agreed on political and economic issues.

The period, 1892-1909, unlike the preceding eight years, was one of unrest and storm, in course of which the Congress itself underwent a metamorphosis.

In 1892 the Conservative government in England was replaced by that of the Liberals. This did not, however, bring about any change in the policy towards India. As a later British Prime Minister, Campbell-Bannerman, declared in 1905: 'It has been a pretty unbroken rule, a wise rule that we assuredly shall not be the first to break, to keep question of the internal administration of India outside the arena of party-politics.'

It was evident that though some constitutional reforms, however limited in nature, had been introduced, nothing had been done to remove or even mitigate the sufferings of the people on the economic front. This was likely to react unfavourably on the fortunes of the 'Moderates'. Gopal Krishna Gokhale no doubt tried to impart some sort of dynamism to their programme and activities, but there was no basic change, only one of degree, in their attitude towards the British government. As Gokhale declared from the presidential rostrum in 1905:

> The goal of the Congress is that India should be governed in the interests of the Indians themselves, and that in course of time a form of government should be attained in this country, similar to what exists in the self-governing colonies of the British Empire. For better or for worse, our destinies are now linked with those of England, and the Congress recognises that whatever advance we seek must be within the Empire itself.[37]

He warned the bureaucrats who, he thought, were primarily responsible for the inaction of the government, that the injustices committed by them would not be tolerated.

These warnings had no effect whatsoever either on the makers or implementers of British policy towards India. If there was a change at all in their attitude, it was increasingly towards reaction and even retrogression. The British premier, Salisbury (1886-92) was blunt enough to say that 'the principle of election of government by representation is not an eastern idea, it does not fit eastern tradition or eastern minds'. Curzon, who assumed the office of the Viceroy and Governor-General in 1899, regarded himself as the 'symbol of England's imperial mission to rule the lesser breeds without the law'. Within a few months of his assumption of office he wrote, 'In my belief the Congress is tottering to its fall and one of my great ambitions while in India is to assist it to a peaceful demise.'

The Congress, however, was in no mood to oblige the new viceroy. No doubt its leaders, to start with, eulogized the viceroy on 'the vigour and humanity' with which he dealt with the famine and passed a resolution to the effect

> that this Congress desires to record its gratitude to H.E. the Viceroy for the benevolence of his famine policy and for his firm resolution to uphold the

> interests of order and justice, as evidenced in the regulations recently issued regarding the grant of shooting passes to soldiers.[38]

But it was not long before the Indians, even the Moderates, were disillusioned. The Municipality Act (1899) imposing restrictions on the power of the elected commissioners of the Calcutta Municipality was a big jolt. A still bigger jolt came with the passing of the Indian Universities Act (1904) which aimed at curtailing nationalist trends by placing the universities under the wider and more effective control of the government. The climax was reached when the projected partition of Bengal was announced by Curzon. This plan of a redistribution of provinces had long been in the offing—since 1867-8, but it did not materialize before Curzon proclaimed the government's decision to give shape to it, though with some modifications (3 December 1903). The reaction of the Congress was quick and unmistakable. It met within a little over three weeks since Curzon made his first public announcement on the proposal, and adopted at its Madras Session (December 1903) the following resolution:

> This Congress views with deep concern the present policy of the Government of India in breaking up territorial divisions which have been of long standing and are closely united by ethnological, legislative, social and administrative relations, and deprecates the separation from Bengal of Dacca, Mymensingh and Chittagong Divisions of and portions of Chhota-Nagpur Division, and so the separation of the District of Ganjam and the agency tracts of the Ganjam and Vizagapatnam Districts from the Madras Presidency.[39]

Curzon not only stuck to his plan but even subjected the provinces to a larger and more drastic revision. He provided for severance of a much larger area of territory from Bengal, so as to justify the creation of 'a new province of sufficient size and importance' to be placed under a 'Lieutenant-Governor with a Legislative Council of its own'. The revised plan, providing for a new province of Eastern Bengal and Assam through partition of the erstwhile province of undivided Bengal, was made public on 19 July 1905. It was also proclaimed that the proposed partition would be made effective as from 16 October 1905.

The announcement caused a great and unprecedented stir, the like of which had till then rarely been witnessed. Sir Henry Cotton, who presided over the twentieth session of the Congress (1904), before the final decision of the government was announced, observed:

> To press on proposals such as these which have been put forward for the break-up of Bengal against the loudly expressed wishes and sentiments of the Bengali people can only be described as a most arbitrary and unsympathetic evidence of irresponsible and autocratic statesmanship.

The open session resolved to

> record its emphatic protest against the proposals of the Government of India, for the partition of Bengal in any manner whatsoever. The proposals are viewed with great alarm by the people, as the division of the Bengali nation into separate units will seriously interfere with its social, intellectual and material progress, involving the loss of various constitutional and other rights and privileges which the province has so long enjoyed and will burden the country with heavy expenditure which the Indian tax-payers cannot at all afford.[40]

Before the next session of the Congress met at Banaras (December 1905) much water had flown down the Ganga and the Brahmaputra. Protest meetings, observance of national mourning and fasting, signature campaigns, articles in the press condemning the proposed move, and other forms of popular disavowal notwithstanding, the government pressed ahead and made the partition effective on and from 16 October 1905 as scheduled. Within a couple of months, when the Congress met, with G.K. Gokhale as president, the situation had become so grave that in his Presidential speech Gokhale proclaimed that the Bengal partition was more than a mere provincial matter; that it was 'the uppermost question in the minds of us all at this moment'. He added:

> A cruel wrong has been inflicted on our Bengali brethren and the whole country has been stirred to the deepest depths of sorrow and resentment as has never been the case before. The scheme of partition, concocted in the dark and carried out in the face of the fiercest opposition that any government measure has encountered during the last half a century, will always stand as a complete illustration of the worst features of the present system of bureaucratic rule — its utter contempt for public opinion, its arrogant pretensions to superior wisdom, its reckless disregard of the most cherished feelings of the people, the mockery of our appeal to its sense of justice, its cool preference of service interest to those of the governed.[41]

The Congress followed with a resolution recording 'its emphatic protest against the partition of Bengal in the face of the strongest opposition on the part of the province' and appealing to the Government of India and the Secretary of State 'to reverse or modify the arrangements made, in such a manner as to conciliate public opinion and allay the excitement and unrest present among all classes of the people'. This was re-emphasized in Resolution XIII, voicing its

> earnest and emphatic protest against the repressive measures which have been adopted in Bengal after the people there had been compelled to resort to the boycott of foreign goods as a last protest, and perhaps the only constitutional and effective means left to them of drawing the attention of

the British public to the action of the Government of India in persisting in their determination to partition Bengal in utter disregard of the universal prayers and protests of the people.[42]

2. The Rise of Militant Nationalism

The anti-partition agitation was, in more than one sense, a turning point in the history of the Congress and indeed of the country. The events preceding the promulgation of the partition scheme had palpably demonstrated the hollowness and inefficacy of the policy of prayer, petition and deputation, so far followed by the leaders of the Congress with almost religious zeal. To this, attention was being drawn, for several years in the recent past, by a group of politicians whom it is customary to label 'Extremists' or 'Nationalists'. Apart from the rise of Extremism, the agitation also led to the great 'swadeshi' upsurge, destined to foster the movements for self-reliance and 'passive resistance' as new weapons to fight the government. It also placed the Indian National Congress in the forefront of Indian politics and enabled it to come in contact with the masses, imparting to the movement a new character and intensity unknown before. The year following the partition (1906) was also a landmark in that it witnessed the birth of the All India Muslim League, constituting a serious threat to the free growth and normal expansion of nationalism in a single indivisible stream for which the Congress had stood since its inception and of which it had become the embodiment.

The real weakness of the Moderates was derived from the contradictions in their own policy. Politically, their criticism of the existing British Indian administration was uniformly civil and constitutional, while their criticism of the economic policy of the Raj was vehement and devastating, the chief assailant being Dadabhai Naoroji. Their bona fides and particularly, those of Gokhale, were questioned by the British authorities, as is evident from despatches exchanged between Minto and Morley in July-August 1907. While Morley had 'half begun to wonder whether Gokhale was not at heart such a revolutionist as Pal' (Bipin Chandra), Minto expressed the view that 'he was thoroughly disappointed in him' and thought that it was a mistake on his part to have allowed his re-election to the Imperial Legislative Council. The British leaders, particularly those belonging to the Conservative Party, made no attempt to conceal their hostility to the demands of the Indian Moderates. The latter thus began to find themselves in an increasingly embarrassing situation. Their political rivals, the Extremists, began to make a dent in their monopoly as exponents of Indian demands. Aurobindo, for instance, criticized the leadership for keeping the proletariat 'off the board', since in his opinion, 'the proletariat was the real key of the situation'. With a view to spreading political consciousness among the masses, Tilak organized the Ganapati and Shivaji festivals. Even Poet

Rabindranath exposed the malaise of foreign rule and the progressively deteriorating relationship between the rulers and the ruled. His *Sadhana* (1893-4), it has been observed, 'was an articulate protest of a new generation against the moderate policy of mendicancy'.[43] He urged his countrymen to eschew 'old-style politics, trying in vain to placate the rulers and talking big in foreign tongue'.

The new school began to find enthusiastic acceptance among the youth of the country. It also derived much of its sustenance from its strong championship of Indian culture, ethics and religion, against the threat of westernization. While it is possible to discern some areas of difference in detail among the sections of the Extremists in Maharashtra led by Tilak, in Bengal under the leadership of Aurobindo and Bipin Chandra Pal, and in Punjab with Lajpat Rai at the forefront, it is also possible to identify some common features of their approach and policies. The chief of them was the basic fact that Extremism was essentially the revolt of the spirit of India against foreign domination and all its implications. Also it was largely shaped by the ideals of *swaraj* and *swadharma* associated with the revolt of 1857. The persistently unsympathetic attitude of the British authorities towards India's aspirations on the one hand, and the extremely limited success of the Moderates in inducing the British rulers to concede their demands, however modest, on the other, paved the way for the rise of the Extremists. Yet the difference between the two schools, Moderate and Extremist, was more a difference of degree than of kind. Professor S. R. Singh, in his contribution to this volume, has rightly emphasized the fact that

> though the Extremists used much stronger language, and Tilak and his followers had much more fight in them (though they had hardly any new ideas), they were not substantially different from the Moderates. . . . On critical occasions, such as during the partition of Bengal, their degree of alienation from the Raj was greater, and their language was stronger, but most of them did not think in terms radically different from those of the Moderates. Their attitude to the Empire was ambivalent, despite the indictment of British officials and administrators. They did not think of giving up constitutional methods or breaking all the ties with Britain. Tilak's approach to the Montford Reforms in their final stages bore a striking resemblance to those of Gokhale to Morley-Minto Reforms.[44]

Even so a trial of strength seemed inevitable. The Moderates attempted to postpone it by inducing the venerable Grand Old Man, Dadabhai Naoroji, then in his 82nd year, to accept the presidentship of the Calcutta Congress (1906). This was clever strategy, but it failed to bring the opposing parties together. The differences came to the surface over Resolutions XII and XIII relating to the partition of Bengal, swadeshi and boycott. A compromise was, no doubt, effected at the last moment and the resolutions were rephrased, but it was clear that this was only a truce and the fight was sure to be resumed. The differences cropped up again soon after, centred on the resolution on swadeshi. The Moderates looked upon swadeshism as a primarily economic weapon; the Extremists looked beyond and saw it as more than a measure of economic pressure; to them it was a spiritual as well as a political weapon, a sort of religious ritual, calculated to foster 'moral training in self-help, determination and sacrifice'. Dr A. Tripathi observes: 'The Moderates wished India to be a prototype of England of which they had read in Hallam, Burke and Macaulay. Aurobindo turned his face from this Anglo-Saxon model and went back to the Aryan mores of Indian civilization. . . .'[45]

Pal defined Passive Resistance as the only means and instrument for the attainment of swaraj. By passive resistance he meant 'not non-active but non-aggressive resistance . . . resistance offered by a people against laws which fail to respect our primary rights of all life and person, of property and similar primary rights.' The climax was reached early in 1907 when the Surat Congress ended in an imbroglio. Acrimonious arguments and open conflict took the place of 'quiet diplomacy and consensus through friendly negotiations' which had characterized the Congress sessions held till then.

The concept of swadeshi with its concomitant boycott of foreign goods was not a novel one. It had been propagated by Gopal Hari Deshmukh, alias Lokahitwadi, as early as 1848-9. Speaking about the miserable poverty of the average Indian, by way of remedy he gave a call for swadeshi and urged the need for a boycott of British goods. In Bengal, in the post-Mutiny days, Bholanath Chunder had drawn pointed attention to the abject poverty of the Indian people and came out with a programme of economic swadeshism. He did not use the word 'boycott' which was of much later origin, but stressed the need of production and consumption of countrymade goods and non-consumption of foreign manufactures. His exhortations came more than three decades ahead of the swadeshi days. About the same time (1874), Bharatendu Harischandra drafted a pledge which people could take undertaking to use only swadeshi goods and published it in the journal *Kavivachanasudha*. He called upon the people, in the name of Almighty God, to take a solemn vow to renounce foreign cloth and use only Indianmade cloth. This article has been described as 'a remarkable document in the history of the Swadeshi Movement in India. It anticipated the swadeshi agitation of Bengal more than three decades earlier.'[46]

The year 1905-6 saw the Swadeshi and Boycott Movements at their height, gathering momentum from the nationalist opposition to Curzon's ill-directed move of partition. The outcry was 'loud and fierce'.

Protest meetings and processions convulsed the whole of Bengal, all classes and communities participating in them. The Indian press was unanimous in condemning the move. Even some Anglo-Indian papers, usually playing the role of semi-official organs, joined the chorus of protest. *The Statesman* of Calcutta, for example, wrote:

> Our objections, and we believe the objections of all reasonable opponents of the scheme, are directed against the way in which the scheme has been formulated and put through, and against the objects of the Government which do not get stated in speeches and resolutions. These objects are briefly: first, to destroy the collective power of the Bengali people; secondly, to overthrow the political ascendancy of Calcutta, and thirdly, to foster in East Bengal the growth of a Mahomedan power which it is hoped will have the effect of keeping in check the rapidly growing strength of the educated Hindu community.

The writer quotes from the text of the official resolution underscoring its hope that

> the day is not far distant when not merely will the new province of Eastern Bengal and Assam have amply vindicated its creation as an administrative reform of the first importance, but when it will have acquired a character and influence not inferior to those of any of the older Indian provinces, and will have attracted to itself the spontaneous and devoted loyalty of its sons.

On these prognostications, *The Statesman* observed:

> It is perfectly possible that these words may be literally fulfilled. But — and this is the point — it is equally possible that the fulfilment may be the virtual defeat of the policy, to which, after so many delays and vicissitudes, the Government of India has now succeeded in giving shape.[47]

Considering the anti-partition agitation as a whole, one would be inclined to accept Dr R. C. Majmudar's assessment: 'It is difficult to conceive of a more unanimous and persistent opposition to a Governmental measure, there is certainly no precedent in the history of British rule in India.'[48]

Opinions differ on the extent and nature of the impact of the Boycott Movement on British trade. The effect, which was in reality marginal, has probably been exaggerated in nationalist circles. It is also true that a follow-up of the move in terms of sustained industrial enterprise was lacking. Also, it cannot be denied that the dream of national education remained largely unfulfilled. Yet another limitation it suffered from was the lack of response from the Muslim community, as a whole. No doubt a large number of Muslims had joined the movement but, by and large, the community stood aloof because of its fear of Hindu dominance assiduously fostered alike by mullah propagandists and British officials. Notwithstanding these limitations, viewed in a larger context, the Swadeshi Movement instilled among the people not only a sense of self-reliance, but also instilled in millions of them a passionate love for indigenous products. What was even more remarkable was that the movement, though started by the people of Bengal, soon spread to other regions like Maharashtra, the United Provinces, Central Provinces, Madras, Bihar and other places, taking the shape of a spontaneous mass movement. Nearly all the periodicals published from different regions during 1906-7 bear witness to the intense dissatisfaction with the policy of the government and the conduct of the bureaucracy on the one hand, and, on the other, the warm enthusiasm among the people in support of the Swadeshi and Boycott Movements. A significant feature of the movements was that they deeply influenced and reinforced the trend and technique of political movements on a national plane, lent them a greater dynamism and marked the advent of militant revolutionary nationalism. Even Gokhale, who disapproved of the Boycott Movement as too radical, regarded it as 'a landmark in the history of national progress'. Jawaharlal Nehru made a balanced appraisal: 'The nationalist movement in Bengal from 1906 onwards had, for the first time, shaken this [middle class life] up and infused a new life in the Bengali middle class and to a small extent even the masses.'[49] Its impact, one may add, spread over youthful middle-class minds in extensive areas beyond Bengal.

The Extremist challenge was not confined to the realm of ideology alone. While the Moderates pinned their faith on swaraj within the British Empire, the leaders of Extremism, at least a section among them, spoke in terms of severance of the British connection. This necessarily made it incumbent on them to prescribe new techniques. The ideal of passive resistance appealed to them only as one possible line of confrontation with the authorities. They were impatient with the techniques so far followed by the Moderates. But when they tried to come to grips with concrete problems and needs, they found themselves divided in their interpretation of passive resistance and its implications. One school was in favour of what Dr Sumit Sarkar describes as 'Constructive Swadeshi'. Its programme did not provide for intensive political action, but laid greater emphasis on the cult of self-reliance as a means of the ultimate realization of their objective, viz., the attainment of freedom. The other school, composed of activists, with no faith in any plan of slow regeneration such as the former school favoured, was bent on direct action with the sole purpose of gaining emancipation. They forthwith rejected the doctrines of prayer and petition, such as the Moderates (demoralized Anglicists' as they described them) advocated, and preferred to rely more on India's own cultural and religious heritage than on imported western ideas and ideals. Their preference for a revival of Indian religion and culture exposed them to the risk of being regarded as advocates of Hindu nationalism. But they did not find any element of contradiction between the two.

In the context of the Moderates' overemphasis on westernism, it is possible to understand, if not to justify, the attitude of the Extremists. Extremism, as conceived and practised, was, in a large measure, a blend of politics and religion. It is, however, possible to discern differences among the several schools of Extremism as it manifested itself in Maharashtra, Bengal and Punjab. In-depth analysis also reveals inconsistencies here and there. Aurobindo appears to have been most consistent in his ideas and preachings His articles entitled 'New Lamps for Old', published serially in 1893-4, marked the beginning of his crusade against Congress ideology and techniques, and the exposition of a new political creed and programme. He had already been deeply influenced by the secret revolutionary societies in Maharashtra, whose members had launched murderous assaults on oppressive bureaucrats as preliminaries to a full-fledged armed challenge. Complete severance of the British connection, and not merely piecemeal or progressive constitutional reforms, was their watchword. Aurobindo wrote:

> The new movement is not primarily a protest against bad government — it is a protest against the continuance of British control, whether that control is used well or ill, justly or unjustly, is a minor or unessential consideration.[50]

The origin of the new militant nationalism, miscalled 'terrorism', as a form of 'aggressive resistance', so far as the ideology or philosophy underlying it is concerned, is traceable to the same sources which helped the advent of the Extremist or Nationalist school. But a line of distinction needs to be drawn. History often offers examples of movements launched well beyond the limits of ideologies originally conceived and preached by the advocates of a particular school. The Extremists, for example, favoured direct action against the government, and accordingly drew up a programme of passive resistance. But they saw, before long, that the revolutionary urge that their preachings had generated gathered unforeseen momentum and found expression in new channels of 'aggressive resistance'.

This phase of militant nationalism working through secret societies and underground channels is described in official and administrative reports as 'terrorism' — a term which is more convenient than correct in the context of current usage of the term. From the activities of the secret societies, operating first in Maharashtra and in the area that is now Madhya Pradesh, and then in Bengal, it appears that, to start with, they had nothing to do with violent action. Their aim was to train youths in physical fitness, athletics, lathi, sword and dagger play, and inculcate in them a sense of dedicated discipline, a spirit of self-help and, above all, intense patriotic fervour. They learnt to look upon themselves as dedicated soldiers of liberation, for whom no sacrifice was too great, including the sacrifice of life in the struggle to overthrow alien rule. The rise of this type of neo-militants was not an unexpected or extraordinary phenomenon. As Professor R.C. Majumdar observed:

> History of all subject nations struggling for freedom shows that bands of young men, goaded by a spirit of frustration at the failure of all legitimate means to achieve their goal, or honestly convinced of their futility in advance, are lured by the prospect of gaining their end by armed resistance, and where it is not practicable to resort to it openly, naturally favour underground movements of secret organisations. The same thing happens in India.[51]

Not only the high priests of Extremism like Tilak and Aurobindo, but also some of the old guards of the Moderate school, like Surendranath Banerjea, are said to have cultivated contact with the newly rising generation of so-called terrorists. B.C. Pal, in his autobiography, informs us that Surendranath's lecture on Mazzini led to the formation of many secret societies on the model of the Carbonari organization in Italy with which Mazzini was associated at the beginning of his patriotic career and that the 'Calcutta student community was at that time almost honeycombed with these organisations', and what is more interesting still, 'Surendranath was himself, I think, the President of quite a number of these secret societies'.[52] This, however, does not prove that Surendranath or any of the Congress leaders continued their connection with these secret revolutionary societies when they took up programmes of direct action against the foreign rulers through organized murders and armed uprisings.

Though the secret societies in Maharashtra antedate similar societies in Bengal, it was in the latter province that the movement struck deeper roots and assumed a more serious character. From the turn of the century, events, both in India and abroad, moved at a rapid pace. Within India, the inadequacy of the technique followed by the Moderates and the need for a more dynamic programme, as publicized through the writings and speeches of the nationalist leaders, left an abiding impression on the minds of the youth. The Curzonian move of partitioning Bengal helped to intensify the opposition against the British administration. The policy of relentless repression resorted to by the bureaucracy, in vindication of so-called law and order, generated a feeling of widespread popular discontent. Abroad, the defeat of the Italian army in the Abyssinian War (1896) and the spectacular victory of Japan over the Russian high seas fleet at Tshushima (May 1905) symbolized the triumph of newly awakened Afro-Asian powers over western forces. The anarchist and socialist movements which had begun to convulse parts of Europe also made their impact felt on the minds of the Indian youths. The earlier British reverses in the Boer War (1899-1902) gave to the growing national consciousness of the Indians a new tone of strength and confidence. They felt inspired by the example of a minor people, then negligible from the military point of view, defying with success the mighty authority of superior western powers. Its lessons also left a deep impression on the minds of the younger section of the Indian people in particular. The example of the Irish fighters for independence also stimulated their imagination. Dr R.C. Majumdar has drawn attention to the close parallel which the struggle for freedom in Ireland offers to that in India:

> The constitutional agitation led by the Irish members of the British Parliament, the doctrine of Passive Resistance borrowed from Hungary, and adopted as a political programme by Arthur Griffith in 1900, the further development of it by the organisation known as Sinn Fein founded in 1905, and the underground government during the first quarter of the nineteenth century preceded by isolated acts of terrorism in the eighteenth — all have their exact counterparts in India. It is natural to imagine that two such closely parallel movements, both directed against the English and reaching their climax in the first quarter of the present century, were influenced by each other.[53]

The credit for crystallizing the amorphous revolutionary ideas of the time into an important element of contemporary Indian politics belongs to Aurobindo, though its psychological background had been earlier prepared by the intensely nationalist writings and utterances of Bankim Chandra and Swami Vivekananda. The cult of Sakti centred on Bhowani, Durga and Kali, as synonymous with the Motherland, and that of the Gita, with its emphasis on *dharmayuddha* evoked ready response and became cardinal tenets in the religio-revolutionary faith of a measurable section of Indians, particularly those belonging to the educated middle class.

At Aurobindo's instance, Jatindranath Bandopadhyay and Barindra Kumar (Aurobindo's younger brother) made efforts to bring the existing secret societies together. (The earliest and the most powerful among these was the Anushilan Samiti founded in 1899.) It was in the agitation against the partition of Bengal which began in 1903 that the revolutionary terrorists were first able to play a decisive role in the national struggle. Swadeshi was to the young revolutionaries not merely economic weapon or a political programme; it had for them a deeper significance, viz., that of national efflorescence in all walks of life — the arts, music, literature, economy, education and politics. The concept evoked in their minds a ready response. As a result, the movement, originally aimed at the regeneration of the youth — physical, moral and mental — left behind its early concern and moved on to a sustained armed struggle against alien rule.

The intensification of revolutionary terrorism, as observed earlier, was provoked to a large extent by the Curzonian move against the growing strength of nationalism. Its rise and spread was also helped by the growing lack of confidence in the policy and methods of the Moderates, the then spokesmen of the Congress. It is difficult to say which of these two factors contributed more to the growth of the revolutionary cult. But it is possible to suggest that even if the partition of Bengal (it did accelerate rather than create the process of national consciousness) had not roused the people to heights of feverish resentment, the growth of this new cult was inevitable. It was a protest against the programme of 'mendicancy' followed over the years by a band of 'demoralized Anglicists' and a bold assertion of the right to freedom. The partition agitation certainly intensified national resentment to foreign rule; but it did not create it.

The movement made considerable progress in Punjab too, in addition to Maharashtra, Central India and Bengal. Even Madras Presidency did not remain unaffected. It is not necessary here to give a detailed account of the activities of the revolutionary terrorism during the period under review. It is dealt with in detail in Chapter V of this volume. It is enough, for our immediate purpose, to indicate the main stages through which their activities passed, even though the various secret societies preferred to act through their separate units without losing their identity. The period 1906-10 saw the transition from the stage of preparation — propagation of revolutionary ideas; recruitment of youths through clubs and gymnasiums; and even robberies for raising funds — to the era dominated by the 'Cult of the Bomb'. Its most daring exploit was the bomb thrown at Muzaffarpur (30 April 1908) followed by the self-immolation of Prafullakumar, the arrest and execution of Khudiram (11 August 1908), the discovery of the site at a Calcutta suburb for the manufacture of bombs, the institution of the Alipore Bomb Case and the conviction of as many as fifteen of the undertrials to various terms of imprisonment and transportation.

The withdrawal of Aurobindo to Pondicherry in February 1910 witnessed the beginning of the next period, 1910-14. The efforts put in by the Yugantar group, the popularization of the Sivaji and Beerashtami festivals in Calcutta, and the propagation of revolutionary literature through *Bartaman Rananiti* and *Bhowani Mandir* (1906-8) were reinforced largely by the Dacca Anushilan Samiti which had, in the intervening years, set up connections with their revolutionary counterparts in the nothern provinces. The leading members of the Samiti brought on themselves the wrath of the government and were hauled up in the Dacca Conspiracy Case. The government's hope that Aurobindo's retirement from the scene of active politics would signal the suspension or weakening of revolutionary activities was belied.

The stress and tension caused by the inhuman tortures of arrested terrorists by the 'keepers of law and order' find expression in Sister Nivedita's letters to S.K. Ratcliffe from 1907 onward. In one of her letters dated 27 May 1907 she writes:

> The Government seems to have gone mad and is now trying to crush the National Movement by wholesale arrests, deportations etc. all because it dreads a repetition of '57. But this is of course the way to bring it about.

Another letter of 3 November 1909 reads:

> . . . only a few slaves continue to whine. Men of real independence are driven to silence. And the only movement that has room to grow is the secret propaganda of terrorism and revolution.[54]

The third period, 1914-9, saw a vigorous intensification of attempts towards revolutionary upheavals. This was rendered possible mainly by the prospect of international tension arising out of the First World War. The revolutionaries, in the meantime, had widened their activities not only over nearly the whole of India, north, south, east and west, but also had set up active centres in the UK, France, Germany, the USA, the Middle East and South East Asian countries. Within India, the most daring revolutionary projects were initiated by Rashbehari Bose in February 1915 and by Jatindranath Mukherji (popularly known as 'Bagha Jatin') in September of the same year. While the former aimed at an armed rising with the aid of defecting Indian troops, the latter worked on a plan of action based on arms and ammunition which authorized representatives of the German Government, then at war with England, had promised to supply. Both these attempts, daring in concept though they were, ended in failure. Even so, their importance cannot be denied. They opened new vistas of attack on the citadel of power, placed the question of India's liberation in the larger context of Asian liberation, pointed to new dimensions for the freedom struggle, forged closer ties between Indians in India and Indian communities abroad, and underscored the significant fact that what was aimed at was not swaraj within the Empire, but complete independence.

It would perhaps be interesting to enquire whether revolutionary terrorism had any repercussions on the Congress movement. Till 1917, the leadership of the Congress was in the hands of the Moderates, who rigidly followed their avowed policy of agitation on strictly constitutional lines — an idea which was formally proclaimed and embodied in the Congress Constitution in 1908. It was only towards the close of the last century that the section of the Congressites (and they were a minority till 1917) known as the Extremists, began to advocate new techniques of direct confrontation. But except for Aurobindo (whose direct contact presumably ended in 1909-10) there is no evidence to show that the Extremists, as a group, had any direct link with the activities of the revolutionaries. The involvement of Surendranath at the initial stage, as reported by Bipin Chandra Pal, perhaps relates to a period (viz., the 1870s) when the secret societies did not entertain ideas of 'secret assassination as the national salvation'. Tilak did not conceal his appreciation of the courage shown by the Chaphekar [Chapekar] brothers (1897) in Maharashtra and by Khudiram Bose (1908) in Bengal. His articles in *Kesari* entitled 'The Country's Misfortune' and 'These Remedies Are Not Lasting' brought on him a sentence of imprisonment in 1897 and of transportation in 1908. While it is possible that similar appreciation of the courage and self-sacrifice exhibited by the revolutionaries, was expressed by individuals in and outside of the Congress, the Congress as an organization as was only to be expected, did not approve of the activities of the revolutionaries. It remained wedded to its creed and techniques derived from the traditions of British liberalism. Consistently enough, the Congress at its Madras session adopted a Resolution recording its

> emphatic and unqualified condemnation of the detestable outrages and deeds of violence which have been committed recently in some parts of the country, and which are abhorrent to the loyal, humane and peace-loving nature of His Majesty's Indian subjects of every denomination.

Another resolution of 1912, placed on record 'its sense of horror and detestation of the dastardly attempt made on the life of Lord Hardinge', the then viceroy. Ideologies necessarily stood in the way of mutual understanding between the two camps, even though the revolutionary terrorists were convinced in their own minds that they were supplementing the work of liberation begun earlier under the auspices of the Indian National Congress. It is interesting to recall here Gandhiji's speech at the inauguration of the Banaras Hindu University which had grown out of Mrs Besant's Central Hindu College. The speech was delivered extempore and was more in the nature of thinking aloud.

> We may foam, we may fret [Gandhi said], but let us not forget that India of today in her impatience has produced an army of anarchists. I am myself an anarchist but of another type. But there is a class of anarchists amongst us, and if I was able to reach this class, I would say to them that their anarchism has no room in India if India is to conquer her conquerors. . . .*I honour the anarchist for the love of the country* [Italics added], but I ask him: Is killing honourable? Is the dagger of an assassin a fit precursor for such a death? I deny it.[55]

Later, in 1919, when the militant revolutionary movement was in a state of comparative lull, Motilal Nehru, while presiding at the Amritsar Session (1919) observed:

> No one can but deplore violence and political crime. But let us not forget that this is the direct outcome of continued repression. It is due to the perversity of the executive which blinds itself to the causes of the discontent and, like a mad bull, goes about attacking all who dare to stand against it.[56]

It was at a much later stage, when the Congress became involved, under Gandhiji's leadership, in a countrywide mass movement that the revolutionaries agreed to suspend their activities, for some time at any rate, to enable the 'apostle of peace and non-violence' to follow, undeterred, his own path of liberation.

3. The Congress, Communalism and Reformism

The emergence of communal politics was another development — one that was to have disastrous consequences for the country in the not too distant future. It was a curious coincidence that, just at the time when the ground was being steadily prepared for a showdown with the British, there should have appeared on the scene a political association avowedly pledged to safeguard the interests of a particular community exclusively. Thus was the All India Muslim League founded at Dacca on 30 December 1906. Historically viewed, this was no sudden phenomenon. It owed its origin to the days shortly after the Indian National Congress had been launched on the historic journey towards its 'Manifest Destiny'. Since its birth, the Congress had time and again declared its aims and objectives in unequivocal terms, and made it clear beyond any possible scope for misunderstanding that it stood for the betterment of the nation as a whole, irrespective of creeds, races, castes and languages. Even a cursory examination of the resolutions adopted at succeeding sessions of the early Congress sessions reveals that its objects, by nature modest enough, were reform and expansion of the Supreme and Provincial Legislative Councils for the N.W. Provinces and Oudh and the Punjab, enlargement of the powers of the Councils, and extension of the franchise. Recommendations such as these were intended to serve the interests of all sections of the Indian people. Even so, the leaders of the Congress were not indifferent to the special interests of the minority communities. Section 5 of Resolution II adopted at the fifth Congress session held at Bombay in 1889 clearly expresses the concern for minority interests. It emphasized the need for election of representatives to the Provincial Legislative Councils in such a manner that

> whenever the Parsees, Christians, Mahommedans or Hindus are in a minority, the total number of Parsees, Christians, Mahommedans or Hindus, as the case may be, elected to the Legislature, shall not, so far as may be possible, bear a less proportion to the total number of members elected thereto, than the total number of Parsees, Christians, Hindus or Mahommedans, as the case may be, in such electoral jurisdiction, bears to its total population.

The principle of election by the people and the representation of the minorities were the two main principles which governed the views of the Congress regarding the future constitution of the country.

Even so, right from the start, the Congress failed to enlist the support and goodwill of the Muslims to the extent its leaders desired. The general indifference of the Muslims to the Congress and its activities is attested by the insignificant number of Muslim delegates to its early sessions, even though there was a steady increase in their numbers year by year — 2 in 1885, 33 in 1886, 83 in 1887, 222 in 1888, and 254 in 1889. This failure was sought to be explained by Rahmatullah M. Muhammad Sayani, President of the twelfth Congress session held in Calcutta (1896) on the plea that the Muslims were lacking in education and hence ignorant about the Congress and its ideals. He observed:

> Indeed by far the largest part do not know what the Congress movement is. Education of any sort or kind is conspicuous by its absence among them and their habitual apathy has kept them from understanding the movement at all. In fact they are blissfully ignorant.[57]

What started as ignorance or apathy before long turned to distrust and hostility. This change was markedly noticed in an article contributed by Sir Syed Ahmad to the *Aligarh Institute Gazette* (23 November 1886) in which he blatantly described the Congress movement as 'seditious'. This was done when the Congress had yet to complete the first year of its existence. When invitations were issued asking for names of delegates proposed to be deputed to the second Congress session, the Mohammedan Literary Society (founded in 1863) and the Central Mohammedan Association (founded in 1877) hesitated to comply. As the years passed, Sir Syed Ahmad's opposition to Muslim participation in Congress sessions became more pronounced. Within less than a year of the establishment of the Congress, he founded the Muhammedan Educational Congress as a parallel organization, especially in the field of education. The arguments on which he sought to build up a case for Muslim abstension from Congress sessions varied from time to time: 'the seditious character' of the Congress movement, the danger of perpetuating Bengali rule, the risk of 'grievous injury' to the Muslim community in case Congress demands were conceded, the danger of Hindu domination, and even just expediency. Congress spokesmen did their best to counteract this propaganda in the hope of preventing a deterioration in Hindu-Muslim relations, on whose cordiality it placed the greatest value. This is revealed in a resolution adopted as early as in 1888, at the fourth session of the Congress which resolved:

> That no subject shall be passed for discussion by the subjects committee, or allowed to be discussed at any Congress by the President thereof, to the introduction of which the Hindu or Mohammedan Delegates, as a body, object unanimously or nearly unanimously; and that if, after the discussion of any subject which has been admitted for discussion, it shall appear that all the Hindu or all the Mohammedan delegates as a body are unanimously or nearly unanimously opposed to the Resolution which it is proposed to pass thereon, such Resolution shall be dropped; provided that this rule shall refer only to subjects in regard to which the Congress has not already definitely pronounced an opinion. (Resolution XIII)[58]

Reviewing the attitude of the Indian National Congress at a later date, Abbas S. Tyabji asked the pertinent question: 'Has the Congress pressed for any rights during the last 25 years which would have specially benefitted the Hindus at the expense of the Mohammedans?'[59] It is interesting to note that M.A. Jinnah fully supported the 'secular, liberal, modernist' view expressed in Badruddin Tyabji's presidential address at the Congress session of 1887.[60]

It will be proper at this stage to probe into the peculiar situation in which, notwithstanding the appreciable growth in political consciousness of the Indians and the increasing urge for efforts towards responsible and representative co-ordinated government, the Indian Muslims or, at any rate, a large section of them, could be persuaded to support Sir Syed Ahmad, who advocated that they should stay away from the mainstream of the rejuvenating national life. Was it an inferiority complex which the Muslims might have developed owing to their failure to take advantage of western education? Or was it ignorance as Sayani suggested? Or could it be a sense of frustration arising out of the loss of a privileged position, 'all the good things of the world', which the community had enjoyed till the decades immediately preceding the transfer of power from the Mughals to the British? To this phenomenon of

Muslim ascendancy in pre-British days, pointed attention was drawn by Sayani in his presidential address at the Congress session in 1896. Or again, could this phenomenon be explained in terms of British support, born of a desire to keep the two great communities as far apart as possible, in consonance with the proverbial practice of empire-builders? Could it be the outcome, as suggested by some, of the British dread of a possible recrudescence of anti-British Muslim fanaticism and, hence the need felt in official circles to win over the Muslims through emphasizing the urgency of an identity of their own, as a distinct community? Or again, was the Muslim stance the outcome of a sense of social discontent generated by the poverty of the general masses of the Muslim population, the decline of the feudal aristocracy, lack of industrial enterprise, exclusion from services, and the burden of ruinous taxation? The identity crisis, it was thought, could be best exploited by inducting religion into politics. Whatever might be the reasons, the fact remains that the Indian Muslims, by and large, grew at first suspicious and distrustful and then hostile to the Hindus, who, in their view, were well on the way to establish their exclusive right to speak for the nation.

The phobia of Hindu domination which gained fresh and stronger expression on the formation of the Congress has been formulated earlier by the reformist movement initiated by Saiyid Ahmed Barelwi (1786-1831), the Waahabis and the Faraizis, in spite of their anti-British overtones. To these were added the impact of Sir Syed Ahmad's Aligarh Movement. These developments constituted a serious obstacle to the fulfilment of the ideals for which the Indian National Congress stood. As was only to be expected, the ruling power sought to utilize the situation to its advantage.

This unfortunate situation cannot be explained just in terms of a conflict of outlook between the two communities. For one thing, there was a number of Muslims who wholeheartedly joined the Congress. Their number, small though it was in comparison with the total number of Indian Muslims, was by no means negligible. For another, there were distinct groups among the Muslims themselves who, as a matter of principle, preferred to be anti-British. The pan-Islamic section among the Indian Muslims, led by Jamal al-Din Afghani (1839-97) was convinced that the interests of the Muslims would be best served by maintaining an anti-British stance. They felt alarmed at the anti-Muslim activities of the Western powers in the various parts of the Muslim world — Tunisia, Egypt, Eritrea, Sudan and Turkey.

That there was a genuine desire for amelioration of the condition of the Muslims in India, especially in regard to education, is attested by the establishment of several voluntary organizations like the Muhammedan Literary Society (1863) and the Central National Muhammedan Association (1877), both of which antedate the Congress. The contemporary Indian papers like the *Hindoo Patriot*, the *Indian Mirror* and *The Bengalee* welcomed their advent and gave full support to their efforts for advancement of education among the Muslims.

Such gestures, as also those of the Congress, however, failed to evoke response from the general mass of Muslims. Urdu as well as Bengali Muslim periodicals preferred to ventilate Muslim grievances against the existing system not so much as caused by alien rule as by so-called Hindu dominance.

A notable exception to the Muslim organizations with a strong anti-Congress bias was the movement named after its headquarters, Deoband, located ninety miles north-east of Delhi. Its nucleus was the Dar-ul-illam (seminary) founded in 1867 by Maulana Muhammad Qasim Nanotawi (1832-80) and Maulana Rashid Ahmed Gangoni (1829-1905). Both of them had been actively involved in the rebellion of 1857. When they decided to found this seminary it was in the spirit of that uprising. Unlike the Aligarh School, the Deoband Seminary aimed at the rehabilitation of Muslim socio-religious identity and the rediscovery of their 'original' cultural and religious distinctiveness for the Indian Muslims, in a spirit of co-operation with the Indian National Congress, in total rejection of collaboration with the ruling power. The seminary flourished as a remarkably active centre of Islamic theology, with students joining it (and its branches) not only from different parts of India but also from countries like Afghanistan, China, Malaysia, Siam, Iraq, Iran, Kuwait, Saudi Arabia, South Africa and Russia. Deoband thus attained an international status as a centre of Sunni Islam, promoting 'a sense of cultural continuity in a period of alien rule'.[61]

The motivation behind the Deoband organization was no doubt religious, viz. the resuscitation of Islam through a lifting the dead weight of legalistic dogma and the vindication of the true teachings of the Koran. Its programme was intensely pragmatic. Its fundamental creed was 'to regard any co-operation with the government as injurious' and to convince the world that it is possible for 'the 'edifice of faith to remain standing without the support of the state'. The Deobandis considered it incumbent upon the Muslims to challenge, to curb and even to overthrow foreign rule, which was a serious hindrance to the free development of their own culture and religion. It is thus not surprising that Rashid Ahmad Gangoni made the bold announcement that 'it was possible according to the *Shariat* for the Muslims to enter into agreement with the Hindus'. This prepared the ground for collaboration between the Deoband School and the Indian National Congress. 'The decision of the learned head of the Deoband School,' writes Dr Tarachand, 'was an unambiguous declaration that the concept of nationality based upon the unity of all religious groups did not contravene any Islamic principle.... The Deobandi Ulema in times of great communal dissensions continued to uphold the cause of national solidarity and Indian Independence.[62] Shibli Numani (1857-1914) of the School yielded to none in his devotion to Islam but he felt that, as citizens of India, it was the bounden duty of the Muslims to join the Congress movement so as to free themselves from the deprivation which British rule had imposed.

It is of interest to note that in their zeal to overthrow alien rule, some Deobandis went to the length of joining the revoluntionary movement working towards armed insurrections, with the aid of foreign military powers, if necessary. In the wake of the First World War, Maulana Obaidullah Sindhi (1872-1944), a product of the Dar-ul-illam at Deoband and associated with it as a teacher till 1913, took a leading part in proclaiming the 'Provisional Government of India' on 1 December 1915 at Kabul and also in organizing a branch of the Indian National Congress in the Afghan capital with himself as its president. Maula Muhammad Hasan (1851-1920), the Head Maulvi of the Deoband Madrasa, who made strenuous efforts to organize anti-British activities in the N.W. Frontier Province in 1915, went to Hejaz and campaigned for the launching of a *jihad* against the British. For this, he hoped to enlist the support of Turkey and Afghanistan. The 'Silk Letter Plot' is testimony to the efforts made to raise an 'Army of God' at Medina with branches at Constantinople, Teheran and Kabul. The efforts failed, but they illustrate the extent to which a section of Deoband mullahs were prepared to push their anti-British activities.

Apart from those of the Deoband School, there were nationalists among other Muslims who were convinced that there was no conflict between their obligations to Islam and their love for and duty towards India. The first Muslim to have presided over a Congress session (the third, in 1887 at Madras) was Badruddin Tyabji (1844-1906), who commanded universal respect as one of the foremost nationalist leaders. He was fully aware that 'each one of our great Indian communities has its own peculiar, social, moral, educational and even political difficulties to surmount', but he also stressed that

> so far as general political questions affecting the whole of India — such as these which alone are discussed by this Congress — are concerned, I for one, am utterly at a loss to understand why Mussalmans should not work shoulder to shoulder with their fellow countrymen, of other races and creeds, for the common benefit of all.[63]

Nine years later Rahmatullah M. Mohammed Sayani, the second Muslim to preside over the Congress (twelfth session, Calcutta, 1896) urged the Muslims to join the Congress which he regarded as representing 'all that is loyal and patriotic, enlightened and influential, progressive and disinterested'.

At a later stage, the younger generation of western-educated Muslims ranged themselves in opposition against the Aligarh Movement. They were distrustful of British policy towards the nascent nationalist movements in Turkey, Iran and Egypt. Apart from the pan-Islamic sympathies, they were influenced by a sense of moral indignation against British imperial domination for whose overthrow they joined the Indian nationalist movement led by the Congress. Besides Abul Kalam Azad, trained in traditional Muslim theology, the group consisted of promising youths like Fazli Husain and Saifuddin Kitchlew of Punjab, Muhammad Ali, Syed Mahmud, Abdul Rahman Bijnori, T.A.K. Sherwani (of U.P.), Fazlul Haq (Bengal), Mazharul Haq (Bihar), Yakub Hasan (Madras) and Abdul Rehiman (Kerala). They were intensely nationalist in outlook and their allegiance to Islam did not interfere with their commitment to a struggle against the British.

But Sayani's appeal, like that of the nationalist Muslim leaders, failed to strike a chord in the hearts of most Muslims. By and large, they chose not only not to join the Congress but even to oppose it, taking positions that were communal rather than national.

The formation of the All India Muslim League in 1906 was the greatest jolt that the resurgent nationalist movement had received. Till 1908, the Congress had deluded itself into believing that the government was intent on introducing constitutional reforms on the lines of the demands consistently made in successive Congress sessions, since 1904 in particular. The Secretary of State's announcement on impending reforms in the House of Lords on 17 December 1908 was warmly welcomed in Congress circles. The Congress at its open session adopted a Resolution welcoming the move and expressed the opinion that

> the proposed expansion of the Legislative Councils and the enlargement of their powers and functions, in the appointment of Indian members to the Executive Councils with the creation of such councils where they do not exist and the further development of Local Self-Government, constitute a large and liberal instalment of the reforms needed to give the people of the country a substantial share in the management of their affairs and to bring the administration into closer touch with their wants and feelings.[64]

The Muslim League, however, had reservations on several issues, particularly the non-inclusion of any guarantee of separate electorates and representation to minorities in excess of their numerical strength. Strangely enough, these were ultimately conceded. The Rules and Regulations under the Reform Act published on 15 November 1909 caused bitter disappointment in the Congress fold. The president of the 1909 session of the Congress dwelt on 'the just grounds of complaint' concerning the drastic modification of the reforms as originally announced. The Congress adopted a resolution placing on record 'its strong sense of disapproval of the creation of separate electorates on the basis of religion'. The Muslim League, on the other hand, welcomed the final shape in which the reforms were enacted as they fulfilled 'to a material extent the pledges given to Indian Mussalmans by His Excellency the Viceroy and the Right Honourable the Secretary of State'.

What is perhaps more important than a recital of facts relating to the Great Divide is an enquiry into the causes for it. British officials had, of course, a major role in encouraging the separatist move spearheaded by an organization, the Muslim League, whose membership did not at that time exceed even four hundred. This was admitted by Minto in his letter to Morley dated 15 August 1906 and is corroborated by the private papers of Dunlop Smith, the viceroy's private secretary. Even though the deputation of the Muslim League to the viceroy and the League itself might not have been 'a command performance' as suggested by some, the fact of motivated encouragement by the British cannot be ruled out. The problem, it appears more reasonable to suppose, can be properly studied only in the context of some basic factors which governed and even became a part and parcel of the Muslim mind — factors which the Congress, with membership and support naturally drawn dominantly from the largest single community in the country, was unable to anticipate and comprehend. Muslim sentiment sensed some contradictions between the professed Congress ideology and its actual performance. While it unambiguously proclaimed its 'non-sectarian character', some of its prominent members openly acknowledged their identification of nationalism with Hinduism. 'The alliance with Orthodox Hinduism and revivalism', it has been observed, 'inevitably weakened the Congress claim of being a "non-sectarian" organization. Indeed, Muslims continually harped on this fact to justify their aloofness from the Congress and began to search for ways to counter what they perceived as a threat to their religion.[65]

Dr Hossainur Rahmen, in a contribution on this theme, observes in elucidation the roots of this phenomenon:

> The Hindu-Muslim conflict was not merely a religious one in the western sense of the word; it was cultural as well, the protest of an alien civilization which could only be reconciled by a new synthesis. But the reverse happened: all their antagonistic characteristics, dormant for generations, were quickened to new life by Hindu and Muslim political leaders. Among these characteristics, the concept of national allegiance was one of the most important. A genuine Muslim nationalism arose among Muslim communities in India, which was still rooted in the old concept of Islamic civilization:

> a nation is equated with a community of the faithful, with a consensus (*ijma*) of faith irrespective of geographical location or spatial boundaries. In the traditional Islamic view, states are always multi-racial, religious communities could co-exist in the same space and yet be entitled to the principle of autonomous nationhood. And while the Hindus and Sikhs felt that their nationalism was rooted in the soil of India, irrespective of their religious creeds, the Muslims clung tenuously to that old concept but eventually modernized it so as to include a definite geographical formation carved out of India; that was the origin of the modern state of Pakistan. Yet as this galvanising of Muslims proceeded the issue deepened, namely, the joint Hindu Muslim action. Clearly they were natural allies in the pursuit of political independence, yet their instinctive repulsions, religious, social, personal and even culinary, made for the paradox of co-activity in mutual avoidance. And Gandhi once declared that to make the situation triangular there was the overall fact of British government.[66]

To pursue the story to its tragic climax, the principle of communal representation which the Act of 1909 provided for was basically opposed to the ideals of a democratic government. It was natural enough for the Congress, which stood for the fulfilment of the interests of all communities comprising the Indian nation, to oppose and condemn it. But the ruling power was adamant. The Act remained in force for only about ten years, till its supersession by the Government of India Act, 1919. During the decade of its operation, efforts were, no doubt, made to achieve an understanding between the two major communities. The outcome was the Lucknow Pact of 1916. Though bitterly opposed, in principle, to communal electorates, the Congress, in its anxiety to forge a united front with the League, agreed to a plan of constitutional reform acceptable to both parties, which provided for the distribution of seats in the legislatures on the basis that each community should elect its representatives in separate constituencies. Thus, in effect, the Congress accepted communal electorates for the Punjab and Central Provinces. The Muslim League reciprocated by giving up the privilege of voting with the general electorates which the Morley-Minto Reforms had secured for them. This change, in so far as the Muslim attitude was concerned, was mainly due, as observed earlier, to the initiative of the U.P. based Young Party, led by persons who believed that the Muslims should not remain subservient to the British government, should participate in the mainstream of the struggle for freedom and, accordingly, reach an agreement with the Indian National Congress.

The Khilafat–Non-Cooperation Movement of the twenties brought the two communities, at least the large bulk of them, closer together. The Congress, now under the leadership of Gandhiji, with the loyal, enthusiastic and consistent support of the Muslim nationalists headed by Maulana Abul Kalam Azad, was unremitting in its efforts to foster and build up a national, as distinct from regional or sectarian, consciousness. But, as everybody knows, the efforts failed, after initial success, and by 1947 the partition of the country was an accomplished fact. The unity of the country was the price for its freedom. Medievalism triumphed over the demands of the modern concept of one indivisible nationhood.

One of the oft-repeated criticisms of the early Congress by some later historians is that it was dominated by an elitist group, obsessed with the idea that they were the sole custodians of India's interest and her accredited spokesmen. They lived, it has been said, in a world of their own, without any contact with the toiling millions of the people and with little knowledge about or even interest in their problems. A critic reminds his readers that many top Congressmen had developed 'a highly elitist life-style'.[67] To drive the point home he recalls the example of 'Mehta travelling in a special railway saloon' or that 'Ranade visited Simla in 1886 with 25 servants'. The information recorded may be factually unassailable, but one is likely to err if one judges an individual wholly in terms of his way of living. The leaders of the early Congress, as observed before, were mainly a group of affluent persons, westernized in their ideas and outlook. But they were not indifferent to the sufferings of their countrymen. They knew that the people were a disorganized mass, mostly unlettered and utterly incapable of giving expression to their feelings. However acute their discontent might have been against alien rule, left to themselves, they were unable to articulate their grievances or to formulate any positive plan of action for their remedy. The series of anti-British and anti-Establishment plots and civil disturbances in the past, for nearly a century and a half, had invariably turned out to be abortive. Even the later cult of the bomb had not achieved the objective aimed at. The prospect of an armed insurrection on any appreciable scale was then a very remote possibility. To the men at the helm of the Congress in its early years, the programme of constitutional progress was not as much dictated by expediency as by conviction. To their innate faith in the tradition of British liberalism and democracy was added their deep-rooted conviction that they alone were the rightful spokesmen of the nation; and that if their demands for additional rights and responsibilities, such as they felt would be conducive to the good of the people and the advancement of the country, there would be an end to the evils of the existing regime. Pherozeshah Mehta, in his presidential address at the Sixth Congress Session (1890) met the criticism that 'the united voice of the Congress is the voice only of a certain portion of the people and not of the masses' and that 'it is even the voice of indifference and not of urgency or excitement' in these words:

> These remarks are intended to be cast as matters of reproach against the Congress; properly understood they constitute its chief glory. If the masses were capable of giving articulate expression to definite political demands, then the time would have arrived, not for Consultative Councils but for representative institutions. It is because they are still unable to do so that the function and the duty devolve upon their educated and enlightened compatriots to feel, to understand, and to interpret their grievances and requirements, and to suggest and indicate how these can best be redressed and met. History teaches us that such has been the law of widening progress in all ages and all countries, notably in England itself. That function and that duty, which thus devolve upon us, is best discharged, not in times of alarm and uneasiness, of anger and excitement, but when the heart is loyal and clear and reason unclouded. It is, I repeat, the glory of the Congress that the educated and enlightened people of the country seek to repay the debt of gratitude, which they owe for the priceless boon of education by pleading and pleading temperately for timely and provident statesmanship.[68]

In this statement, is it possible to discern misplaced loyalty and the excessive and unjustified confidence placed by the Moderates in the British sense of justice; in other words, it is possible to criticize the background of Moderates thinking and hence also their technique and their policy. But to do so does not entitle one to question their solicitude for the welfare of the people and their earnestness to ameliorate their condition.

In this context, it is relevant to examine the composition of the Congress and its organization as a party during the early years of its existence and to evaluate its claim to represent the nation. The official *Report of the First Indian National Congress* does not indicate clearly the principle followed in inviting the participants who were described as 'representatives' in preference to the more commonly used 'delegates'. The latter appellation was applied to the members of the recent deputation sent to the United Kingdom. It is not known which organizations or individuals had been contacted by Hume prior to the first session. It is permissible to presume that, in course of his extensive tours, Hume approached persons who were expected to be like-minded. W.C. Bonnerjee, in his presidential address admitted, as mentioned earlier, that 'judged by the standard of the House of Commons, they were not representatives of the people of India in the sense the members of the House were representatives of the constituencies'. Nevertheless he claimed 'if community of sentiments, community of feelings and community of wants enabled any one to speak on behalf of others, then assuredly they might justly claim to be representatives of the people of India.'

Reviewing the composition of the second session and analysing the occupations of the participants attending it with the aid of statistics, it was claimed that

> not only were all parts of India thus represented, but also most classes; there were barristers, solicitors, pleaders, merchants, landowners, bankers, medical men, newspaper editors and proprietors; principals and professors of independent colleges, head-masters of schools, religious leaders and reformers.

It is on evidence that 69 associations sent representatives to the second session. Among these were obscure local organizations like the Habiganj Peoples Association, Silchar (Assam), and the Khirpai Association, Midnapore (Bengal). A patent indication of growth is the fact that the number of representatives attending each successive session steadily increased. Needless to say, educated people constituted the bulk of the representatives at the sessions. In this connection Hume remarked:

> The Congress of 1886 may be said to have grown, almost spontaneously, out of the unanimous resolve of the educated and semi-educated classes, throughout the Empire, to take a decisive step towards the attainment of that political enfranchisement to which they have come of late years, to attach so much importance.

In his report as General Secretary, Hume admitted, by implication, the absence of money-lenders and shop-keepers and inadequate representation of *ryots* and the Muslims.

The *Report of the Fifth Congress* (1889) refers to election by different bodies of delegates to the Congress. The only guideline laid down was that no province, other than the one in which the Congress was held, should send more than two delegates per million of its total population. At that teething time it was thought that in matters of election no guidelines in detail were called for. It was thought proper 'to let the thing develop in its own fashion for a year or two before attempting to lay down any fixed rules'. The number of editors or proprietors of newspapers increased from 24 in 1886 to 47 in 1887 and the number of delegates from different associations from 69 in 1886 to 106 in the following year.

The first session was not a costly affair. It cost only about Rs 3,000. A large number of the representatives who gathered declined reimbursement of travel expenses. Wealthy rajas, maharajas and zamindars offered donations, though some of them preferred to remain anonymous.

No doubt, the number of zamindars, jagirdars and talukdars attending the early Congress sessions exceeded the number of *ryots*, the inadequacy of whose representation was commented upon in 1886. Even though the number of *ryots* increased soon after, it is not clear whether they were peasants, peasant-proprietors or landlords and well-to-do men holding prestigious positions in local government bodies. The criticism in official circles, headed by the Viceroy, Lord Dufferin, who described the educated class represented in the Congress as 'a microscopic minority', was met by the Congress spokesman, Manmohan Ghosh at the 1890 Calcutta Session of the Congress:

> It is asked whom does the National Congress represent? What right has it to speak on behalf of the masses of the people who knew nothing about the Congress? My answer is, the National Congress represents the thinking portion of the people of India.

This was by no means an extraordinary situation. It is a well-established fact in history that the struggle for liberty, in any country, where it had been denied, always starts under the leadership of an enlightened, educated class who form a minority among communities held in surveillance, but invariably ends in a mass insurgence. The message of the Congress similarly reached an increasingly larger circle of literate people through the medium of the press on the one hand, and the propagation of Congress ideals and resolutions through pamphlets and manifestoes on the other. The section of the people who had been denied literacy did not remain unaffected either. They responded to calls for public meetings organized from time to time and thus quickened their political consciousness. Dr Ashim K. Datta has rightly observed:

> That common people who could read their own language were supporters of the Congress aims is beyond doubt. It is they who read the thousands of pamphlets that we are told were printed in the different Indian languages by and for the Congress at this time. It is they who were behind the increase in the circulation of the newspapers printed in the Indian languages. Their contribution to the debates of the Congress was nil though a few of them are found as delegates in the different sessions, but neither their support of the ideology of the Congress nor their admiration for the top leaders can be doubted.[69]

With the passing of the years the Congress machinery tended to improve and grow. The first session was 'little more than an experiment'. By the time the Congress met at the Madras Session (1887) 'it bore every appearance of becoming a permanent institution'. It saw the formation of Subjects Committee for the first time. These were authorized to 'set on foot the necessary elections in their several jurisdictions and to ascertain and communicate . . . the subjects that their people desired to be brought forward at the coming Congress.'

A list of subjects thus collected was processed through electoral committees and then circulated in the provinces. This enabled the delegates to become acquainted, well in advance of the session, with the questions that were to be discussed. The selection of items for discussion was then finalized by the Congress sub-committees, composed of representatives from every province. A sub-committee was empowered to draft resolutions on such of the subjects as were agreed upon unanimously or with near-unanimity. This procedure, on the one hand, enabled the leaders to understand the trend of public thinking and, on the other, to give their deliberations at the open session a businesslike shape. What is even more important, it helped the Congress to press upon the attention of Government of India and the people and the British Government only those reforms in regard to which the whole country had come to a substantial agreement; in regard to which the people of all provinces, of all races, castes and creeds, were of practically one mind.

With the growing strength and popularity of the Congress, the need for expanding its organizational wing was increasingly felt. The Congress was, before long, more than an annual conference. It adopted for itself a programme whose execution necessarily involved a central secretariat and a corresponding organizational network. From the report of the proceedings of the Third Congress (1887) it appears that a committee was set up with authority to draw up a constitution for the Congress. From the commencement, Hume served as General Secretary. He held that office even after he had gone back to England in 1892. This was not considered extraordinary, since a good deal of work had to be attended to in England also. No doubt, he came back every year in the winter months when the Congress was in session. To give some relief to the General Secretary who was over-burdened, from 1889 onward the office of a Joint General Secretary was provided for. Pandit Ajodhya Nath Kunzru of U.P. was called upon to hold the office. It was not till 1903 that an Additional Joint Secretary was appointed in the person of Gopal Krishna Gokhale. In 1908 it was resolved to have two General Secretaries, D.E. Wacha and Daji Abaji Khare. Nine years later the number was raised to three.

To facilitate the election of delegates, the country was divided into electoral divisions. The report of the proceedings of 1888 session mentions 12 such divisions or circles. By 1893, the number of circles rose to 29.

The activities of the Congress were not restricted to India alone. From the moment of its birth, Hume had been laying utmost importance on systematic propaganda among the British public as a counterpoise to the obstructionist tactics of the British officials in India. In consequence, a permanent committee, known as the British Committee of the Indian National Congress, was set up in London in July 1889 which, in the words of the then President of the Congress, 'was needed like a telephone to carry the voice of the people of India to the ear of the people of England'. At his suggestion it was resolved to raise 'a sum of Rs 45,000 for the expenses of the Congress work in this country and in England'. Its work was largely supplemented by the Indian Parliamentary Committee. By 1893 it was able to enlist the support of 154 members of the House of Commons. The British Committee's journal *India* was a powerful vehicle for propagation of India's demand for constitutional rights. Dadabhai Naoroji, one of its principal sponsors, paid it eloquent tribute as 'an absolute necessity, as an instrument and part of the organization' and wished that it could be made a weekly instead of a monthly organ.

Such efforts were in line with the conviction of the Moderates that enlightened public opinion in England would assert itself in the formulation of governmental policy, a belief which turned out to be chimerical in the end.

Coming back to activities in India, it appears that the Congress leaders, for over twenty years since the foundation of this great national organization, were unwilling to adopt any written constitution. In fact, no attempt was made to adopt a comprehensive constitution for the Congress till 1908. This lapse, if it can be so described at all, was deliberate, and instead of weakening the Congress it did much to strengthen it and widen its base. The lack of a well-defined constitution is an unusual phenomenon for a political party, but the promoters of the Congress felt from the beginning, the need for 'linking in' all the progressive forces in the country and preferred to keep its doors as wide open as possible, without insisting on any rigid rules regarding membership, etc.

The Congress was thus conceived as a national platform rather than as a party. It was felt that its role as a national platform could be more effective if it refused to bind itself within the narrow constraints of an exclusive party. Herein lay its strength, for it enabled the Congress to enlist the support and goodwill of heterogenous organizations and of newspapers, by and large, representing various views on matters of public interest. The strength of the Congress lay in the fact that it was not just one more addition to the numerous political organizations then in existence. It has thus been truly observed that

> the message of the Congress percolated down to the common man's level, because to the extent the common man understood politics, he found that the Congress was speaking out his mind and more so, when the Congress leaders addressed public meetings, in his own language.[70]

4. Peasants' and Workers' Movements

It has been observed earlier that from the very beginning the leaders of the Indian National Congress were deeply concerned about the abject poverty in which their countrymen lived and were keen to end it. In fact, an analysis of the resolutions adopted at succeeding sessions of the Congress reveals that these indicated a more radical attitude towards economic problems than toward political ones. The leaders were well aware of the basic problems created by the socio-economic impact of colonial rule. Agrarian distress had been steadily on the increase. The lack of any programme for the mobilization of Indian industry left to the people no alternative but to resort to agriculture as the principal means of their livelihood. At the time of the emergence of the Indian National Congress and for years after that, India was a backward agrarian country, with more than 80 per cent of its population living in villages; and, of them, 70 per cent were engaged in agriculture. Apart from the incidence of excessive land tax, the neglect of irrigation, recurring famine conditions and the overall denial of tenancy rights accounted for the progressive deterioration in the condition of the peasant-cultivators. At the beginning, the leaders of the early Congress took the view that the extension of the Permanent Settlement would ensure security of tenure and bring some improvement in the condition of the landlords as well as the cultivators. It was at their suggestion that the Congress in its fifth session (1889) resolved that

> the question of the introduction of a permanent settlement of the land revenue demand into the Madras and Bombay Presidencies and other provinces be referred to the several standing Congress committees, with instructions to report upon the same, in so far as it affects their respective circles. *(Resolution XIV)*

At its next session (1890) the Congress decided to urge the Government

> to take up this question of Permanent Settlement without further delay, with a view to practical action thereon such that fixity and permanency may be given to the Government Land Revenue demand, as explicitly promised by Her Majesty's Secretary of State more than a quarter of a century ago. *(Resolution VI)*

One member from Bengal went to the length of claiming that 'this Permanent Settlement must be considered as the very best manure you can give to the land'. Resolutions in support of the extension of the Permanent Settlement featured in successive Congress sessions till 1898. In 1902, G.K. Gokhale, then a member of the Viceroy's Legislative Council, pressed the urgency of the extension of the Settlement of 1793. The demand was repeated in 1913.

Economists of today will, however, judge the recommendation as fallacious. The poverty of the people was undoubtedly there, the agriculturists being the worst victims. But it was due more to other factors than the non-permanent settlement of land revenue. The problem of poverty in permanently settled areas was no less acute than in areas not covered by it. The Settlement of 1793, instead of containing land-transfer, had intensified it. The urban middle classes and traders found in land an attractive field of investment. This resulted in the growth of a class of non-productive rent-receivers on the one hand, and on the other, the disappearance of small peasants in increasingly large numbers. By and large, a process of de-peasantizing followed, in consequence of which the one-time owners were reduced to the position of agricultural labourers. Rent legislations gave little or no relief to the under-*ryots* or *bargadars* who continued to remain at the mercy of the landlords.

The condition of the peasants in tribal areas was even worse. Deprived of the right to enjoy the fruits of their labour and constantly harassed by the greedy money-lenders and rent-receivers, they rose in periodical armed revolts, but without success.

The Congress remedy, i.e. the extension of the Permanent Settlement, was not an effective remedy, but the concern of the Congress leaders at the growing poverty of the agricultural classes was genuine. This is evidenced by resolutions adopted in Congress sessions between 1891 and 1895 which underscored the need for remedial measures against a state in which 'fully fifty millions of the population, a number yearly increasing, are dragging a miserable existence on the verge of starvation and in every decade several millions actually perish by starvation.' The remedies, they said, lay in drastic reduction of military expenditure, abolition of home charges, establishment of Agricultural Banks, opportunities for larger employment, relief against agricultural indebtedness, withdrawal of the restriction of the right of private alienation of land, relaxation of the rigidity of the existing system of revenue collection, effective famine relief measures and amendment of the forest laws, among others. From a review of the relevant Congress resolutions and the programme of work in subsequent years in pursuance thereto, Dr S.K. Sen concludes: 'It seems that the interest shown by the early Congress in the tribal peasants survived, and the Congressmen working at the grass roots became involved in Forest Satyagraha in Madras in 1920-21 and again in Central Provinces in 1930-32.'[71]

In regard to the working classes, the problem was less acute at the time the Congress was born. Industry then was not widespread and the number of workers in factories was small and they were organizationally weak. Even then they had reasons to feel aggrieved — low wages, excessive hours of work, indiscriminate employment of child and woman labour, and insanitary conditions of living, among others. In fact, the first Indian Factory Act was not passed till 1881. Its provisions were far from adequate.

The development of industry was a 19th-century phenomenon in which both Indian and British capitalists played their roles. The first railways and coal mines had their beginning between 1857 and 1859, while jute factories in Bengal and textile mills in Bombay were set up in the 1850s by British and Indian capitalists respectively. Light industry had a predominant share in manufacturing industries. It has been calculated that 80 per cent of factory workers in India were then engaged in light industry. 'The proportion in the Indian economy of the highest form of capitalist industry (the manufacturing industry),' it has been said, 'was exceedingly small at the beginning of the First World War although India was that time industrially the most developed of the colonies.[72]

In the days following the birth of the Congress the workers had become slightly better organized. In fulfilment of their demands, from time to time, they took recourse to strikes. Between 1892 and 1908 there had been a number of strikes in jute and cotton mills and in the railways. The labour movement made a notable advance in eastern India. In the days of the swadeshi upsurge, the workers came increasingly under the influence of the nationalists. The most conspicuous among the nationalists who made sustained efforts to mobilize the working people was B.G. Tilak. His arrest in 1908 evoked a spontaneous strike among the mill workers of Bombay, the dock workers making common cause with them. But these actions did not lead very far. The reason is not far to seek. As Nehru observed:

> An industrial proletariat was growing up in India, it was unorganized and helpless, and the terribly low standards of the peasantry, from which it came, prevented wage increases and improvement. So far as unskilled labour was concerned, there were millions of unemployed persons who could be drawn upon and no strike could succeed in these conditions. The first Trade Union Congress was organized round about 1920. The numbers of this new proletariat were not sufficient to make any difference to the Indian political scene; they were a bucketful in a sea of peasants and workers on the land. In the 'twenties the voice of industrial labour began to be heard, but it was feeble. It might have been ignored but for the fact that the Russian Revolution had forced people to attach importance to the industrial proletariat. Some big and well-organized strikes also compelled attention.[73]

It was only on the eve of the 1920s that the problems of peasants and workers began to attract serious attention. It was calculated that at the end of the First World War there were 27.8 million agricultural workers constituting 26 per cent of the independent rural population.[74] There was also a considerable increase in the volume of industrial output. The conditions of workers showed no sign of improvement. They lived, as Nehru wrote, 'at an incredibly low level of existence in filthy disease ridden hovels, with no window or chimney, no light or water supply, no sanitary arrangements.'[75]

It was under Gandhiji's leadership that the Congress embarked upon peasant mobilization and thus forged the link between the Congress and the peasant masses. The first area chosen by Gandhiji for peasant mobilization was Champaran in Bihar where in 1921-2 a struggle was waged against British indigo planters. The government, which sided with the foreign investors, was eventually compelled to adopt some reforms such as the abolition of the *tinkathia* which had gone on for over a century. As Gandhiji wrote: 'The ryots who had all along remained crushed, now somewhat came to their own.'[76] Next came the turn of Kaira (Kheda) in Gujarat (1918). There the struggle took the character of a mass no-revenue movement. It was a protest against government's refusal to suspend assessment of land revenue in consideration of the famine conditions prevailing there. The government replied with the usual methods of repression — heavy penalties, threats of confiscation of property and attachment of cattle. But the spirit of resistance could not be overcome. Ultimately, the government partly yielded. Gandhiji described the Kheda movement as 'the beginning of an awakening among the peasants of Gujarat, the beginning of their true political education'.

The next theatre of Gandhiji's activities was Ahmedabad. The textile workers resented the decision of the mill-owners, on grounds of coal shortage and increased cost of production, to withdraw some extra emoluments granted earlier. In February 1918 the workers went on strike. This was Gandhi's first intervention in an industrial dispute. The risks were high. The workers were poor and could not be expected to continue the strike for long. Also, by nature, they were volatile, and generally lacking discipline. But once Gandhiji was convinced of the genuineness of their demand, he stood by them, raised funds and distributed leaflets among them asking them to remain peaceful and shun violence at all costs. Later, he took a vow not to touch food unless the strikers rallied and continued the strike till a settlement was reached. The impact of his action was instantaneous; the mill-owners were compelled to announce an overall 35 per cent increase in pay.

Gandhiji's objectives were limited and his achievements in this action were not spectacular. But the movement was important, for it involved issues and groups which had till then been beyond the range of institutional politics.

Four years later (1922), a bigger no-tax campaign was organized in Bardoli, also in Gujarat. The *ryots* resented the imposition of an enhanced rate of tax. When all attempts on their part to persuade the government to at least review the assessment failed to evoke a response, the peasants started a no-tax movement, under the leadership of Vallabhbhai Patel. In Nehru's assessment:

> The Bardoli peasantry met with a considerable measure of success; the real success of their campaign, however, lay in the effect it produced amongst the peasantry all over India. Bardoli became a sign and symbol of hope and strength and victory to the Indian peasant.[77]

The growing impoverishment of the peasantry, the deepening unrest among the industrial workers, the imbalance arising out of monopolistic capital and the conflicting interests of labour and capital created a situation which called for urgent remedies. As noted earlier, trade unions had already begun their activities. While Gandhiji had formulated his own plans and experiments in regard to local issues, it was a healthy sign that some Congressmen, already prominent or about to attain prominence, became actively interested in the trade union movement. Among them were Motilal Nehru, Vithalbhai Patel, K.F. Nariman and N.M. Joshi. They attended the first session of the Trade Union Congress presided over by Lala Lajpat Rai (1920).

In referring to Bardoli we have strayed beyond the limits set for this volume, but the increasing number of strikes among the industrial workers and the peasant movements from 1917 onward stressed the need for a reorientation of Congress policy. The Moderates had begun to feel that leadership was slipping out of their grasp and the way was being prepared for a new and more dynamic group of leaders. It was widely felt that the time had come for the Congress to discard its upper-urban-middle-class-minded ideas and actions and take on the role of a full-fledged national organization bringing together all sections constituting the Indian nation. The leaders saw more and more clearly the need for bringing the growing labour movement under its influence. The Amritsar Session of the Congress (1919) registered this new realization when it adopted a resolution urging

> its Provincial committees and other affiliated associations to promote labour unions throughout the country with a view to improving social and economic conditions and securing for them a fair standard of living and a proper place in the body politic of India. *(Resolution XX)*

5. Early Congress Foreign Policy

The British Empire in India was at its zenith when the Congress was born. Barely eight years earlier, its splendour had been loudly proclaimed at a spectacular display of pomp in Delhi. Ironically, at that time vast areas of India were suffering the consequences of a devastating famine.

On the transfer of power from the Company Bahadur to the British Raj in 1858, the Queen proclaimed, *inter alia*: 'We desire no extension of our present territorial possessions.' But the desire to strengthen and consolidate British dominions in India showed no signs of waning. Rather, it became more assertive. By 1896, the British Sovereign was proclaimed suzerain of the Indian States, seriously modifying the previous position in which the Indian States had been recognized as independent and sovereign allies and not subjects of the British Government.

The British appetite for territories was easily not satisfied. There was no question of open grabbing of territories any more, in the crude old fashion. But the old theory of 'scientific frontier' had not lost its appeal. Nor did the equally old Russophobia cease to provide a convenient pretext for aggression on India's frontiers. The despatch of British expeditionary forces was not confined to areas contiguous to Afghanistan alone; it extended to the north-eastern region as well. In the very year of the foundation of the Indian National Congress, Upper Burma was added to the British Indian Empire, thus completing the subjugation of the whole of Burma. Here, the fear of France's designs, instead of those of the proverbial Russians, was a good enough pretext for Britain's armed intervention. Another source of injury to Indian sentiment in the same year was the enactment of legislation (Law 3 of 1885) by the Transvaal Government, setting serious restrictions on the Indian settlers there. It laid down that 'the aboriginal races of Asia' would not be permitted to acquire the rights of citizenship, own landed property or live in apartments located in streets, wards and localities not specifically notified for them.

The policy aimed at expansion of the British sphere of influence, if not territories, in countries immediately beyond the frontiers of India, found a resolute exponent in Lord Curzon. The policy underlying the Younghusband Mission to Tibet (1904) was largely an outcome of British concern at the prospect of Russian infiltration into Tibet as a sequel to successive Tibetan Missions to Russia between 1898 and 1901. This was but a phase in the long-drawn-out rivalry between Britain and Russia in Central Asia. The upshot was a Convention concluded between Tibet and British India (1904) by which the former agreed to open three trade marts in Tibet and to allow the English to occupy the Chumbi Valley for three years.

Another area which caused some concern among the British Indian authorities was the Assam border. Hostile action by the Abors provided a pretext for armed intervention in the Dihang Valley of the Abor country on the north-eastern frontier (1911). The unmarked boundary of the Chinese province of Yunan, located on the frontier of Burma, also caused some concern to the British authorities. In the end, a mutually acceptable settlement of the frontier issue was arrived at through negotiations.

Apart from its frontiers, the situation within Afghanistan proper, following the accession of Amir Amanullah in February 1919, led to a deterioration in Anglo-Afghan relations. The stage for an armed conflict was largely set by the breakdown of the Anglo-Russian *entente* following the advent of the new socialist regime in Russia on the one hand and the growing unrest in India on the other. The new Amir, partly under pressure of internal troubles and partly under the influence of the war party in the kingdom, embarked on a war with England (April-May 1919). However short and uneven the war might have been, it contributed substantially to the growing destabilisation across India's north-western frontier.

While there was no major armed conflict in Europe between 1878, the year of the conclusion of the Russo-Turkish war by the Treaty of Berlin, and the commencement of the Balkan wars of 1912-13, stirring events were taking place in the Afro-Asian world. In Africa, the balance of peace and also of power was disturbed by a series of European colonial adventures of a blatant nature, and rivalries among the big powers, each eager to outdo the other in its bid for spoil. The 'Dark Continent' had become an arena for military exercises for European armies.

The Middle East too was a happy hunting ground for the competing western powers whose activities there also gave rise to serious tensions. Central Asia offered the same uneasy spectacle. In the Far East, China and Japan chose different ways to safeguard their interests and integrity against the threat of western penetration. While China found in the U.S.-sponsored 'Open Door Policy' a convenient but temporary device for containing western dominance in a limited way, Japan underwent a military transformation and met the challenge with far more success. South East Asia lay dormant under the shackles of colonial rule, waiting for an opportunity to assert their right to self-determination.

The tensions and stresses in the colonial world, however disturbing, were relegated to the background when 1914 threw Europe and the world into the cauldron of an unprecedented and all-engulfing armed conflict. It easily surpassed, by far, in terms of death and destruction, all wars that had hitherto been waged in the entire course of human history.

The period from 1885 to 1914, the first thirty years of the Indian National Congress, was one of 'armed peace' (so far as Europe was concerned), a period which saw a mad rush for armament, colonial aggrandisement and preparation for a titanic military clash at the first opportune moment. That a World War flared up in 1914 is no surprise. What is surprising is that it did not break out earlier.

Few people, here or elsewhere, could remain indifferent to the explosive situation which held out a serious threat to the security of all mankind. The Indian press and individual Indian leaders analysed the nature and implications of the tension and gave vent to their reactions on the steadily deteriorating situation. However, unlike the movements towards nationalism and democracy which convulsed vast regions in Europe from the 1830s onward, and which were hailed by eminent leaders like Rammohun and his followers, the post-1885 movements, except in Afro-Asian countries, were mainly the outcome of aggressive nationalism and military chauvinism. In the circumstances, the Indian National Congress, did not feel called upon to record its reactions, except in general terms and in platitudes. The Indian press and academics were the only sections which reviewed and analysed the fast-changing situation.

That, at the beginning, at any rate, the Congress refrained from recording its opinion in official resolutions is not surprising. Looking back on the early days when the Congress, Nehru wrote, was passing through the early phase of its life,

> the National Congress, like all other political organizations in India, was for long entirely engrossed in internal politics and paid little attention to foreign developments. In the nineteen-twenties it began to take some interest in foreign affairs. No other organizations did so except the small groups of socialists and communists. Moslem organizations were interested in Palestine and occasionally passed resolutions of sympathy for the Moslem Arabs there. The intense nationalism of Turkey, Egypt, and Iran was watched by them but not without some apprehension, as it was secular, and was leading to reforms which were not wholly in keeping with their ideas of Islamic traditions. The Congress gradually developed a foreign policy which was based on the elimination of political and economic imperialism everywhere and the co-operation of free nations. This fitted in with the demand for Indian independence. As early as 1920 a resolution on foreign policy was passed by the Congress in which our desire to co-operate with all neighbouring countries, was emphasized. The possibility of another large-scale war was later considered, and in 1927, twelve years

> before World War II actually started, the Congress first declared its policy in regard to it.[78]

It is true that the nationalist and democratic movements all over the world entered into a period of fresh and renewed activity in the post-war years. These were also the years which saw the emergence of the world's first socialist republic in Russia. The Indian Congress, as was to be expected, formulated during the same period, clear-cut policies on matters affecting India's foreign policy and international relations.

So far as the pre-1919 period is concerned, the attitude of the Congress to the foreign policy pursued by the British Indian government was intensely pragmatic. The two main principles that governed and shaped it were (1) consideration of India's strategic security, and (2) concern for Indians settled abroad, specially in the British colonies in Africa.

The proceedings of the first session of the Congress were far from elaborate. The resolutions betrayed a note of excessive but not wholly unexpected caution and restraint. But they did not hesitate to convey in unequivocal terms its sharp reactions to two current incidents, viz., the Third Burmese War, and the Transvaal Act denying to the Indian settlers some fundamental rights. In Resolution VII (1885) the Congress announced its deprecation of the annexation of Burma and recommended that, 'if the Government unfortunately decide on annexation, the entire country of Burma should be separated from the Indian Viceroyalty and constituted a Crown Colony, as distinct in all matters from the Government of the country as is Ceylon.'[79] In this connection, the related question of mounting military expenditure also came up for criticism (Resolution V). The Congress, in fact, went on repeating from time to time its disapproval of the expenditures incurred on this item. In 1891, Dinshaw Edulji Wacha drew pointed attention to the urgency for a change in the military policy of the government:

> It is time for us all by our persistent agitation to bring about a healthy and wholesome change in the military policy of the Government. The military activity, which has been unceasing and restless since 1885, will never cease until we make it clear to the British electors at home that it needs to be altered. If we are only true to ourselves, we ought from this time forward to take every legitimate and constitutional means in our power to expose the utter wickedness, the absolute madness, of the course on which the Government are embarked. We must din it, not only into the ears of our rulers, for they seem to be those who having ears hear not, but into the ears of the public of Great Britain, that this growing military expenditure is eating away the vitals of the people, and can only lead to the ruin alike of India and of England.[80]

Similarly, the punitive expeditions sent to the north-west frontier and also military occupation of some areas were subjects of trenchant criticism in the session of 1892. In proposing Resolution VII in protest against the abnormal increase in the annual military expenditure of the empire since 1885/6, the same member (D.E. Wacha) invited attention to the fact in these words:

> Apart from the long-standing scandal of the charges in connexion with Home depots . . . and apart from other unjust charges such as those of transport, arrears of pensions, and so forth . . . the Imperial policy of Great Britain in its relations with Russia, and its attitude towards the whole question have foisted on India the annual permanent charge of 2 crores on account of the 30,000 additional troops maintained since the acquisition of Upper Burmah and the Panjdeh incident.

The speaker also held the view that 'the sole object of Russian advance nearer the confines of India is the logical sequence of Britain's imperial policy'.[81]

The humiliating conditions to which the Indian settlers in Africa were compelled to submit came up for discussion in detail in the eleventh session of the Congress in 1895. In support of Resolution IX, registering 'its solemn protest against the disabilities sought to be imposed on Indian settlers in South Africa' attention was also drawn to the 'immorality' of the action against Chitral. The President of the session, Surendranath Banerjea placed his considered views before the open session:

> Taking every view, then of this great question — the progress of Russia in Central Asia, the effect it will, in course of time, have upon India, the arrangements which we should have to make to meet — I am firmly of opinion that our proper course is not to advance our troops beyond our present border, not to send English officers into the different states of Central Asia, but to put our own house in order by giving the people of India the best form of government in our power, by conciliating as far as practicable, all classes and by consolidating our resources.[82]

The question of the Indian Settlers in South Africa again came up for discussion at the 1896 session. It adopted a resolution (Resolution IX) recording its 'solemn protest against the disabilities imposed on Indian settlers and the invidious and humiliating distinctions made between them and European settlers' and appealing to the governments of England and of India 'to guard the interests of the Indian settlers and to relieve them of the disabilities to which they are subject.'[83]

At the thirteenth Congress (1897) G. Subramania Iyer criticized the 'Forward Policy' of the government and referred to the emerging British Asiatic Empire:

> What 20 or 25 years ago was an Indian appendage, an Indian Empire has ceased to be an Indian Empire: it is an Asiatic Empire. Burma and further border lands beyond the Himalayas no more form a portion of India than Kamschatka. The thrifty and half-starved peasants of India are virtually paying for the Asiatic Empire. It is high time that this Congress entered its emphatic protest against this frontier policy which has cost not only millions of money but is sure to cost much more in future and entirely absorb all the resources available for the good progress and advancement of the people.[84]

So far as the other major problem, viz. the problem of Indians settled in South Africa was concerned, it commanded the largest attention at succeeding Congress sessions from 1901 to 1913. The question had received additional significance from the fact that a little-known Indian barrister-at-law, Mohandas Karamchand Gandhi, then temporarily living in South Africa on a professional mission, had decided to champion it with consequences which could be hardly foreseen in the late nineties of the last century. South Africa saw the beginning of his experiment with satyagraha, a technique and a creed, a vehicle which, on being developed later, imparted to the Congress movement for India's freedom a unique character in the history of the world's liberation struggles, and to Gandhi the appellation of *Mahatma*, the apostle of peace and non-violence.

6. The Decline of the Moderates and the Advent of Gandhi

The challenge to the Moderates at the Surat session (1907) had its origin in 'the logic of history'. Twenty-two years had elapsed since the Congress was born. Those who had steered it were convinced that the British authorities could be persuaded to institute, by stages, reforms from above, thus enabling the Indians to take their due share in the country's administration. They relied on appealing to Britain's conscience. The response was, however, far from satisfactory. Even the Moderates themselves admitted that what Britain had conceded fell far short of their reasonable expectations. But they clung to their old policy of prayer and petition. This persistent faith in British justice was not their only weakness. They did not do much to educate and involve the general mass of the people, or at least a big section of it, in their efforts. The Congress organization, as such, largely remained a close preserve of the educated middle-class. When they saw that the British authorities in England were irresponsive to their demands they held the bureaucracy, rather than the makers of the policy, responsible. It would be unfair to question their sincerity, but there can be little doubt that both in regard to their policy and their ways of implementing it, they were grievously mistaken. To start with, the Swadeshi and Boycott Movements had opened up new possibilities and held the promise of a sustained mass-oriented movement in Bengal. The Congress leaders applauded the movement but did not adopt it for the rest of India. The revolutionaries, miscalled terrorists, with their faith pinned on armed challenges against alien rule had created a legend and won the admiration of the country by their acts of singular courage and self-sacrifice. In contrast to their activities, the programme of the Congress appeared insipid and halting to a large section of the people. The Congress condemned economic exploitation, but failed to evolve any well-defined programme for curbing it. The repeated proclamation of their 'deep loyalty' and 'profound allegiance to the British Crown' exasperated a growing number of people. Even when there were spontaneous mass meetings and riotous demonstrations in protest against Tilak's transportation, the Moderates remained silent. Commenting on this indifference, the *Bande Mataram* wrote:

> It has reduced the Government to a state of moral helplessness on the one side, it has also revealed the want of any living hold of the pretensious moderate Bombay leaders upon the general population of their city on the others. It has burst, we think, the Mehta-Gokhale bubble completely. The events of the last two weeks in Bombay have completely shown up the claims of the Bombay Moderates to the real leadership of the people.[85]

The inaction of the Moderates in practice and the insufficiency of their programme in theory, encouraged their opponents to make a bid for the leadership of the Congress. The senior Moderate leaders were getting too old for active leadership and appeared to be nearly spent. Their opponents, by contrast, had in their forefront persons endowed with youthful vigour and dynamic energy. But the conflict was not one of personalities; its roots lay deeper. It was more a conflict of ideologies. In 1907, the Extremists, as events soon proved, took a miscalculated step when they openly directed their whole effort to wrest the leadership from their opponents. The Moderates who had been in control of the organization could not be dislodged. Surat ended in an imbroglio.

The Moderates survived the challenge, at least for some time. To forestall loss of command they adopted at the next session in Madras (1908) constitutional safeguards for keeping out of power those who would rely on extraconstitutional means to achieve their end. The amendment redefined the Congress creed as follows:

> The objects of the Indian National Congress are the attainment by the people of India of a system of Government similar to that enjoyed by the self-governing members of the British Empire, and a participation by them in the rights and responsibilities of the Empire on equal terms with those members. These objects are to be achieved by constitutional means, by bringing about a steady reform of the existing system of administration and

> by promoting national unity, fostering public spirit and developing and organizing the intellectual, moral, economic and industrial resources of the country.[86]

Thus, constitutional agitation was specified as the only approved means for attaining the objective of the Congress. The attendance at the Madras session (1908) showed a substantial fall in attendance — from 1,663 in 1906 to 626 (of whom as many as 404 were from Madras Presidency alone). The next year (1909) it reached its lowest ebb since 1886, the number of delegates being as low as 243. For the next few years the Congress Session was an annual ritual and more or less a tame affair, harping on pious resolutions, not forgetting, however, to condemn 'the detestable outrages and deeds of violence which have been committed recently in some parts of the country, and which are abhorrent to the loyal, humane and peace-loving nature of His Majesty's Indian subjects of every denomination.' (Resolution III, Madras Congress Session, 1908).

For a few months before as well as following the Surat split, the government, in pursuance of a policy of ruthless repression in dealing with growing nationalism, had striven to destabilize the nationalist front. Lala Lajpat Rai's political creed was akin to that of the Extremists, but with a difference. He did not support the extravagant attacks on the old leadership. Nor did he approve of the unpleasant controversy in Bengal on the issue of the presidentship of the ensuing Calcutta session. He regarded the proposed election of the Grand Old Man, Dadabhai Naoroji, as a wise decision. He had equal regard for Tilak and Gokhale. It was due to his moderating influence that the Calcutta session ended without an open rupture.

The government, however, felt panicky at the growing unrest in Punjab, arising mainly out of administrative lapses and an ill-conceived decision in favour of enhanced land revenue. Their panic led them to believe that preparations had been afoot for a mass upsurge in 1907, which happened to be the fiftieth anniversary of the Revolt of 1857. So panicky were the rulers that they came down with a heavy hand in May 1907 and deported Lala Lajpat Rai and Ajit Singh to distant Mandalay under Regulation III of 1818. This high-handed act was resented by the Moderates and Extremists alike. Tilak wrote in *Kesari*: 'If the rulers adopted this Russian method then the subjects in India will imitate the subjects in Russia.'[87]

The force of repression did not exhaust itself with the deportation of Lajpat Rai and Ajit Singh. Bipin Chandra Pal was imprisoned for six months for his refusal to give evidence in the *Bande Mataram* case (September 1907). Soon after came the turn of Aurobindo and Tilak.

While the former was prosecuted for conspiracy to wage war against the King (May 1908), Tilak was sentenced to six years transportation in Mandalay (July 1908).

Thus, by the time the Madras Congress met, the Extremist leaders had been out of action. It was not possible for them to make their influence felt in the deliberations of the Congress. But their influence on the larger community of the people went on growing.

Viewed from a larger perspective, not only from the general trends of Indian politics but also from the point of view of the Indian National Congress, the ultimate result of the Surat split turned out to be just the reverse of what many placed high in official and non-official circles expected. The Congress is doomed to die, they had prophesied. The divergence of opinions which lay at its root was, in a sense, desirable. But, as the *Madras Standard*[88] wrote, 'It [the split] showed that the Congress was not a moribund mass, but full of vitality and brimful of energy, an augury of a long life of splendour and sure sign of ultimate triumph.'

A review of Congress history over the years shows that, whenever there was a split, the Congress came out stronger, the forces of progress getting the better of their opponents. It is worthwhile recalling the inimitable words of Rabindranath Tagore while presiding over the Bengal Provincial Congress Conference at Pabna in 1908:

> When the dead wood breaks, it breaks for ever, but the cut limb of a living tree blossoms forth with all the greater vigour. Let us, therefore, put into the duty of avoiding partition from *within* the same wholehearted devotion with which we have been resisting partition from *without*.

The 'triumph' referred to in the *Madras Standard,* however, was not immediately in sight. The determination of the Moderates to hold on, on the one hand, and on the other, the enforced removal of the prominent Extremist leaders from the scene (the only exception being Aurobindo who voluntarily retired from active politics in quest of spiritual fulfilment in distant Pondicherry), postponed the coming into power of the Extremists till 1918.

While the Congress was unable to end the differences in its rank, the militant nationalists went ahead with their programme of direct confrontation. The Swadeshi Movement spread to wide areas comprising the N.W. Frontier, Bengal, Western India, the United Provinces and the Madras Presidency. This brought on rigorous measures of repression. A series of 'lawless laws' were passed and deportations and imprisonments followed. The press was heavily gagged. Police raids, house searches and indiscriminate arrests became the order of the day. Not content with these measures of direct repression, the Government took recourse to indirect methods of weakening the growing nationalist movement. They tried to keep the Moderates in 'a state of contentment' by holding out to them the bait of a 'liberal dose' of constitutional reform on the one hand, and on the other, by winning over the Muslims through a promise of constitutional safeguards for their special interests. The Moderates responded to Viceroy Minto's gesture with alacrity and adopted a Resolution (No. II) in the Madras session, welcoming the Reform Proposals as announced by Secretary Morley in the House of Lords (December 1908). The only items which came in for criticism at that session were the continuous failure of the government to redress the mounting grievances of the Indians in South Africa and repressive legislation within India such that providing for deportation and arbitrary imprisonment. The Congress warned that 'such a policy would never succeed except to help the Government to convert the prison houses into martyrdom.'[89]

The Moderates and the Muslims were the only sections who welcomed the reforms of 1909. The Extremists, having abstained from the Congress, the session at Lahore in 1909 was an unimpressive show, with a poor attendance of 243 delegates. Among the notable absentees was Lala Lajpat Rai, who had in the meanwhile been released. Gokhale, in a mood of despair, described the Lahore Congress as 'the poorest gathering on record'. Efforts made at the succeeding session at Allahabad to bring the two wings together proved abortive. This division among the Congressites encouraged the government to administer yet another dose of repression, viz. the enactment of the Press Law of 1910 and the extension of the Seditious Meetings Act (August 1910).

In 1911 the government announced through the King Emperor its decision to annul the partition of Bengal in the hope of appeasing public sentiment. The Moderates hailed it as a 'remedy of a great wrong'. But the Congress failed to retrieve its pre-1907 position. Its session at Bankipur (1912) and Karachi (1913) were attended by no more than 207 and 349 delegates respectively. The only redeeming feature was an appreciable rise in the number of Muslim delegates attending these sessions. Indeed, the president of the Karachi session claimed that the differences between the Congress and the Muslim League had lessened to such an extent as to enable the Muslim League to announce its acceptance of the Congress ideal of self-government. This Congress was thus the seed-time of the celebrated Lucknow Pact of 1916.

The absence of senior Moderate leaders like Mehta, Gokhale and Malaviya at the Madras session (1914) was unfortunate and the session made a poor show of depleted strength. 'But the absence of these stalwarts at what was certainly an important session of the Congress', writes Dr S. Vijayalakshmi, 'was amply compensated by the presence of Mrs Besant.'[90]

Mrs Besant had already made known her ideas through incessant writings in the *New India* which she edited. The outbreak of the First World War (August 1914) raised new and vital issues which brought into prominence the position of India *vis-á-vis* other constituents of the British Empire. While the other colonies were ethnically and culturally bound to England by close ties, India had reasons to feel estranged because of the severe restrictions under which her people had to live, not only in their own country but also in other British colonies like South Africa, Australia and Canada. Notwithstanding these and other grievances the Madras Congress reaffirmed 'unswerving allegiance to the British Government' and 'welcomed' the despatch of Indian troops to various theatres of war. Apart from the Moderates, even an Extremist like Tilak (who had been released in June 1914) expressed the opinion in the *Maharatta* that 'the duty of every Indian, be he great or small, rich or poor, is to support and assist His Majesty's Government, to the best of his ability.' But his ideas went further. Since his release he had studied the Indian political situation thoroughly and was convinced that the Congress should re-unify, the Muslims should be befriended, and a united national front should be built up without further loss of time. Tilak, it has been suggested, defined the goal of India as Home Rule instead of Swaraj to which the British had developed an allergy.[91] This is at best a hypothesis. In reality, for Tilak, home rule and swaraj were synonymous terms. He made this clear:

> I said that it was our right to have Home Rule but that is a historical and European way of putting it; I go further and say that it is our *Dharma;* you cannot separate Home Rule from us, as you cannot separate the quality of heat from fire; both are inseparably bound up.[92]

His idea was to press for the grant of self-rule at a time when India was rendering splendid service to the British Empire, engaged in a war 'to make the world safe for democracy'.

Mrs Besant too saw in the war situation an opportunity to reemphasize India's right to self-rule. Like Tilak, she felt that, for the attainment of this objective, a union of the two wings of the Congress was a vital necessity, as much as a closer link, if not identification of Hindu and Muslim interests. Tilak had, however, one advantage over Mrs Besant. He did not have to wait for formal admission to or approval of the Congress, which he had left in protest in 1907. Once he had made up his mind, he lost no time in inaugurating the Home Rule for India League on 28 April 1916.

Mrs Besant thought it expedient to wait till she was able to win over the All India Congress Committee, of which she was a member, to her views. She got the green signal, and the formation of the much-awaited All India Home Rule League was announced in September 1916. The Moderates' hesitation was voiced by Surendranath Banerjea who wrote that an organization like the Home Rule League 'would serve to overlap and perhaps weaken the Congress'.[93]

Tilak and Besant agreed that the two Home Rule Leagues would work in clearly demarcated areas. In explaining the objects of her League Mrs Besant wrote in words similar to those of Tilak below:

> The cry for Home Rule, Swaraj (Self-Rule) ringing from all parts of India, is really a cry for that which is most priceless in a Nation's life, for the life of its very soul, for its right to grow, to evolve, on its own National lines.[94]

The initiation of the Home Rule League movements eroded the last remnants of the Moderates' power. They still retained control of the Congress machine, but from now on it was a question of how soon they would have to abdicate rather than how long they would servive. By 1916, Mrs Besant was able to prepare the ground for the re-entry of the nationalists into the Congress.

At the Lucknow Congress (1916), Mrs Besant made her influence felt as the most dominating and popular leader. This session owes its significance to two developments of supreme importance, viz. the re-entry of the Extremists, or Nationalists, and the rapprochement between the two great communities, the Hindus and the Muslims, both accepting self-rule as their ultimate political goal. The outcome of the latter was the Lucknow Pact of 1916. It raised hopes which were ultimately destined to involve the country in a situation not visualised at the time when the pact was concluded.

1917 saw the Home Rule Movement at its height. The government was at first non-plussed and did not know how to meet the challenge. Soon after, however, they overcame their hesitancy and fell back on the old policy of repression. Mrs Besant and her close colleagues were put under arrest. This, instead of weakening the movement, made it stronger still. The British government at home felt that some steps were called for, for appeasement of the Indian sentiment. Accordingly, the Secretary of State, Edwin Montagu, was sent to India with instructions to explore possibilities of introducing a major programme of constitutional reform. For the purpose of creating a favourable atmosphere for conciliatory talks, Mrs Besant and her co-workers were released. Besant whose popularity then stood high, was elected president of the Congress in 1917. In her presidential address, regarded as 'one of the great documents of the Independence movement', she emphasized India's birthright to freedom. She ended her passionate appeal with these stirring words:

> To see India free, to see her hold up her head among the Nations, to see her sons and daughters respected everywhere, to see her worthy of her mighty past, engaged in building a yet mightier Future — is not this worth working for, worth suffering for, worth living and dying for?[95]

The growing and spontaneous response with which the Home Rule League activities were greeted made it quite clear that the old Moderate-dominated Congress had outlived its utility and the way was now clear for its transformation into a radical structure with its strength derived from mass support. It has always been characteristic of the Congress, and its evolution over the years, that a new and vigorous leadership had always emerged from within, whenever its organizational pattern or composition seemed to be threatened, either with an irrevocable split or the prospect of the rise of an organization distinct from the Congress, with an ideology and programme of its own. Alarmist forebodings in such situations have always proved to be baseless. So also at this juncture, purged of old and worn-out forces, the Congress emerged stronger and more vigorous than ever before. The explanation for this remarkable phenomenon lies in the fact that, at moments of crisis, the leadership which failed to respond to the people's wishes had to make way for a new one capable of voicing the people's demands and channelizing their struggles into the mainstream of the larger national struggle. It is no surprise that the Moderates parted company with their opponents and, in doing so, greatly helped the Congress to rejuvenate itself.

The emergence of a new leadership was mainly occasioned by the Moderates' unqualified support of the constitutional reforms envisaged by the British Government on the basis of the Montford proposals, which were totally opposed by the Nationalists. While the Moderates welcomed the proposals as 'a definite stage in the progressive realisation of responsible government', their opponents were clearly of the view that the responsible government as envisaged in 1919 was not even a close approximation to their concept of swaraj. 'The Scheme', as Tilak observed, 'is ungenerous for England to offer and unworthy for India to accept.' A special session of the Congress was convened at Delhi in August 1918 to consider the reforms of which the outlines had already been announced. The Moderates not only stayed away from the session but met at a convention of their own (March 1918) under the auspices of a new body, christened the Indian National Liberal Federation. This marked the final exit of the Moderates. Andrews and Mookerjee rightly observed:

> It can hardly be questioned that the Moderates failed to give to the nation the lead which it so badly needed. The fact was that it did not reflect national opinion, but represented only a group of older men, desperately sincere and earnest, but too conservative in their view to reflect the rising in the spirit of the country as a whole.[96]

With the Moderates out of the way, the Congress Session at Delhi in December 1918 adopted a resolution condemning the reforms as 'inadequate, unsatisfactory and disappointing'. For the Moderates this marked a point of no return.

The end of the Moderate regime was not a sudden phenomenon; it was the culmination of a process which had been at work since 1907, if not earlier. The 'Nationalists' were now at the forefront. But within less than a year, it was evident that, contrary to reasonable calculations concerning trends in Indian politics, the Congress and the country found a new leader and a new technique of national struggle. The new leader was Mohandas Karamchand Gandhi. The new technique was *satyagraha*, on which he had experimented with appreciable success in South Africa.

Gandhiji's entry into Indian politics was at first little noticed. On his final return to the country in 1915, after twenty years of activity in South Africa, he contacted prominent Indian personalities like Mehta, Gokhale and Tilak. He recorded his impressions as follows:

> Sir Pherozeshah had seemed to me like the Himalaya, and Lokamanya like the Ocean. But Gokhale was like the Ganges. One could have a refreshing bath in the holy river. The Himalaya was unscaleable, and one could not easily launch forth on the sea, but the Ganges invited one to its bosom.[97]

Gandhiji was so impressed by Gokhale that he described him as his mentor, his political guru. Gokhale, on his part, had seen the potentialities of Gandhi in his movement of satyagraha in South Africa. In 1912, when the struggle against the racist South African Government was at its peak, Gokhale wrote that Gandhi was, 'without doubt made of the stuff of which heroes and martyrs are made. Nay more. He has in him marvellous spiritual power to turn ordinary men around him into heroes and martyrs.'[98] How prophetic were these words!

Gokhale's premature death at the age of 49 was a great national calamity and to Gandhi a grave personal loss. It was in accordance with Gokhale's advice that Gandhi had resolved to minutely study the trends of the Indian political situation for at least a year before initiating or participating in any direct political action. True, he attended the Congress session in 1915 and was even nominated by the president of the session as a member of the Subjects Committee. He was also present, four months later, at the Belgaum Conference. There he supported the move for the reunification of two wings of the Congress, but 'insisted that he himself was an outsider who did not belong to any party, and was merely present because he thought it was his duty as a servant of his country.'[99] He maintained the same stance in the Lucknow session of the Congress in 1916 and abstained from speaking on any resolution, except the one condemning the recruitment of indentured labour. He was also consistent in his refusal to join the Home Rule Movement, on being invited to do so by Besant and Tilak.

In 1917, Gandhi emerged from his self-imposed seclusion. He chose local areas of disaffection — Champaran, Kaira (Kheda) and Ahmedabad — to which reference has been made earlier. About the Champaran struggle Robert Payne observes that 'the experiment in Champaran was not, strictly speaking, based on satyagraha principles; the battle was won by compiling voluminous reports and by demonstrating to the government that these reports described an intolerable condition.'[100] Judith Brown looks upon the Kaira Satyagraha as a failure since 'it led neither to an independent enquiry nor to the suspension of revenue he [Gandhi] had first demanded.'[101] The importance of Gandhi's first experiments in India, however, lies in what these were rather than what they achieved. The success was indeed limited; but these brought Gandhi in contact with areas and communities not reached before, not only by the Moderates but also by the Home Rule Leagues — in other words, areas and communities beyond the range of normal institutionalized politics. Gandhi's experiments were still more important for another reason, viz. the technique adopted by Gandhi and the philosophy underlying it, *satyagraha*. This was basically different from the concept of 'passive resistance' which had gained currency from 1906 onward. As Gandhi himself explained:

> Satyagraha differs from Passive Resistance as the North Pole from the South. The latter has been conceived as the weapon of the weak, and does not exclude the use of physical force or violence for the purpose of gaining one's end; whereas the former has been conceived as a weapon of the strongest, and excludes the use of violence in any shape or form.[102]

Elaborating on this Gandhiji wrote: 'Satyagraha is the vindication of truth not by infliction of suffering on the opponent but on one's own self.' He laid down, in detail, the duties of a satyagrahi in three situations, viz. as an individual, as a prisoner, and as a member of a group. Below are some of his injunctions:

1. A Satyagrahi, i.e. a civil resister, will harbour no anger.
2. He will suffer the anger of an opponent.

3. In doing so he will put up with assaults from the opponent, never retaliate, but he will not submit, out of fear of punishment or the like, to any order given in anger.
4. A civil resister will not salute the Union Jack, nor will he insult it or officials, English or Indian.
5. As a prisoner, a civil resister will behave courteously towards prison officials and will observe all such discipline of the prison as is not contrary to self-respect; as for instance, whilst he will *salaam* the officials in the usual manner, he will not permit any humiliating gyrations and will refuse to shout 'Victory to Sarkar' or the like.
6. A civil resister will make no distinction between an ordinary prisoner and himself, will in no way regard himself as superior to the rest; nor will he ask for any conveniences that may not be necessary for keeping his body in good health and condition. He is entitled to ask for such conveniences as may be required for his physical and spiritual well being.
7. A civil resister will joyfully obey all the orders issued by the leader of the corps, whether they please him or not.
8. He will carry out orders in the first instance even though they appear to him to be insulting inimical or foolish, and then appeal to higher authorities. . . If the sum total of the energy for the corps appears to a member to be improper or immoral, he has a right to sever his connection: but being within, he has no right to commit a breach of its discipline.
9. No civil resister is to expect maintenance for his dependents. It would be an accident if any such provision is made. A civil resister entrusts his dependents to the care of God. Even in ordinary warfare wherein hundreds of thousands give themselves up to it, they are able to make no previous provisions. How much more, then should such be the case in Satyagraha? It is the universal experience that in such times hardly anybody is left to starve.

Judith Brown remarks:

> Satyagraha was peculiar to Gandhi's total religious vision, although forms of self-suffering to convert an opponent had long been known in Gujarat just as passive resistance was well established in western political thinking. But Gandhi seems to have come to it without any conscious reflection on either tradition. For him Satyagraha was the last resort of those strong enough in their commitment to truth to undergo suffering in its cause.[103]

There were a number of prominent public leaders in India who had their reservations on the efficacy or adequacy of the technique. But Gandhi stuck to his plan. How soon the plan of campaign would be initiated depended largely on the action of the British Indian Government. Gandhi wrote in *My Experiments with Truth:*

> Upto this time my share in the annual proceedings of the Congress was confined only to the constructive advocacy of Hindi by making my speech in the national language and to presenting in that speech the case of the Indians overseas. Nor did I expect to be called upon to do anything more this year. But as has happened on many a previous occasion responsible work came to me all of a sudden.

Gandhiji's rise in 1919, however meteoric, was a response to the situation India faced at the end of the First World War; it proved to be an effective and practical answer to the needs of the national movement.

The situation in 1919 was alarming indeed. According to Nehru,

> The end of the World War found India in a state of suppressed excitement. Industrialization had spread and the capitalist class had grown in wealth and power. The handful at the top had prospered and were greedy for more power and opportunity to invest their savings and add to their wealth. The great majority, however, were not so fortunate and looked forward to a lightening of the burdens that crushed them. Among the middle classes there was everywhere an expectation of great constitutional changes which would bring a large measure of self-rule and thus better their lot by opening out many fresh avenues of growth to them. Political agitation, peaceful and wholly constitutional as it was, seemed to be working itself to a head and people talked with assurance of self-determination and self-government. Some of this unrest was visible also among the masses, especially the peasantry. In the rural areas of the Punjab the forcible methods of recruitment were still bitterly remembered, and the fierce suppression of the 'Komagata Maru' people and others by conspiracy trials added to the widespread resentment. The soldiers back from active service on distant fronts were no longer the subservient robots that they used to be. They had grown mentally and there was much discontent among them.[104]

To the dissatisfaction, in general, caused by the inadequacy of the constitutional reforms of 1919 was added a strong national reaction against detention of the Ali Brothers for participation in the Khilafatist agitation and the repressive nature of the so-called Rowlatt Act rushed through the Imperial Legislative Council (February-March 1919). It incorporated some of the recommendations of the Sedition Committee headed by Sir Sidney Rowlatt, in utter disregard of unanimous non-official opposition. It invested magistrates with drastic powers to arrest and detain persons after summary trial and placed the liberties of the people at the tender mercy of the bureaucracy. Gandhi criticized the provisions of the Act as 'unjust, subversive of the principles of liberty and destructive of the elementary rights of the individual.' When his repeated efforts to persuade the government to repeal the Act failed, he decided upon an all-India agitation on the issue. He founded the

Satyagraha Sabha whose members took a solemn vow to disobey the Act and court arrest.

The reaction of the people, and specially of the youth finds expression in Nehru's writings:

> When I first read about this proposal [Rowlatt Satyagraha] in the newspapers my reaction was one of tremendous relief. Here at last was a way out of the tangle, a method of action which was straight and open and possibly effective.[105]

The resentment spread in extent and intensity soon after, when the Government of Punjab perpetrated one of the worst crimes against humanity by ordering the indiscriminate massacre of innocent people at Jallianwala Bagh (13 April 1919). Not content with this act of barbarous cruelty, the government proclaimed martial law and let loose a veritable reign of terror in Punjab. The shocking news of these atrocities gave rise to a nationwide sense of righteous indignation. C. Sankaran Nair, then a member of the Viceroy's Council, who had already written two famous minutes of Dissent in the Despatches on Indian Constitutional Reforms, pointing out the defects inherent in them, announced his resignation from the Council in protest against the atrocities of the British rulers in Punjab. Tagore, who did not receive the news of atrocities in Punjab till the end of May owing to strict press censorship, wrote to the viceroy his historic letter, renouncing his knighthood in order to 'give voice to the dumb anguish of terror as the time has come when badges of honour make our shame glaring in the incongruous context of humiliation.'

The British Committee of the Indian National Congress in London issued a statement recounting the events in India so as to provide the British public with 'a clear vision regarding India where through the folly of the government a cloud bigger than a man's hand has already gathered, threatening to break into a storm, the dimensions of which no one can foresee.' It recalled the unfortunate fact that notwithstanding the remarkable contribution of India to the British triumph in the war and added:

> So far as 'a new claim' is concerned, the Government of India since the Armistice has requited India's glorious services by legislative and administrative repression, depriving India of freedom of press, freedom of speech, freedom of the person, provoking public protest and riots, particularly in the Punjab, with Martial Law, deportation of leaders beloved by the people, confiscation of property, suppression of newspapers, execution, public flogging, imprisonment of prominent and patriotic citizens on fantastic charges, refusal of permission to choose counsel for their defence before Military Tribunals, shooting by machine-guns and bombing by military planes of defenceless men and women, a regime of blood and iron which, if

practised by Germans, would have filled Englishmen with horror and indignation.[106]

It was in the midst of such unprecedented stress and tensions that the Congress met at Amritsar, where only a few months earlier the grim tragedy had been enacted. Pandit Motilal Nehru was elected president. There was some disagreement among the delegates on the Resolution on the Reforms of 1919, one section being in favour of giving these a trial, notwithstanding their inadequacies, another favouring total rejection. There was also some dubiety in regard to Gandhi's resolution condemning the incidents of mob violence in Punjab and Gujarat provoked by the acts of senseless repression committed by the government. But, on the whole, Gandhi made his influence felt as the nation's new leader. Whatever the verdict of posterity be on the Resolution on the Reforms (Resolution XIV), Sitaramayya observed, 'There is no manner of doubt whatever that, it was a triumph for Gandhi'.[107]

Pandit Motilal Nehru in his presidential address painted a picture of India's aspirations:

> It may be that when we get the power to mould our institutions, we shall evolve a system of Government which will blend all that is best in the east and the west. Meanwhile let us beware of the errors of the West and at the same time cast out the evil customs and traditions which have clung to us. We must aim at an India where all are free and have the fullest opportunities of development; where women have ceased to be in bondage; and the rigours of the caste system have disappeared; where there are no privileged classes or communities; where education is free and open to all; where the capitalist and the landlord do not oppress the labourers and the ryots; where labour is respected and well paid, and poverty, the nightmare of the present generation, is a thing of the past. Life will then be worth living in this country, it will be interspersed by joy and hope, and the terrible misery which we see around us, will become a bad dream which has faded away from our memory, on our awakening to welcome the morning sun.

Motilal ended with these inspiring words:

> We shall have a difficult path, full of obstacles and pitfalls before us. Let us march ahead with Truth for our guide and Courage as our watchword, and before long, we shall reach the Promised Land.[108]

India was destined to reach the 'Promised Land' within twenty-eight years of Motilal's prophecy. 'Truth' and 'Courage' to which he referred, found their greatest apostle in Mohandas Karamchand Gandhi whose leadership of the greatest national organization in India dates from 1919, a year which draws the curtain on one era, only to open out a new one, dominated by a novel technique and inspiring ideology, and destined to ensure and accelerate not only India's march to freedom, but also to influence profoundly and mould the course of liberation of underdeveloped countries the world over. At the conclusion of the Amritsar session Gandhi is reported to have said to the press reporters, 'Plassey laid the foundation of the British Empire, Amritsar has shaken it.'[109]

Notes and References

1. Pattabhi Sitaramayya, *The History of the Indian National Congress*, 1885-1935, Bombay, 1935, pp. 16-17.
2. 8 May 1878.
3. *Bengal Hurkaru*, 21 March 1883. Quoted in S.R. Mehrotra, *The Emergence of the Indian National Congress*, Delhi, 1971, p. 1.
4. Quoted in Hemendra Prasad Ghose, *The Newspaper in India*, Calcutta, 1952, pp. 25-6.
5. Ibid., p. 33.
6. Ibid., p. 39.
7. See N.S. Bose, *Racism, Equality and Indian Nationalism*, Calcutta, 1981, p. 142.
8. *Parliamentary Papers*, Vol. IX, 1884, p. 13.
9. Surendranath Banerjea, *A Nation in Making*, Calcutta, 1963, p. 59.
10. Ibid., pp. 73-4.
11. N.S. Bose, op. cit., 217.
12. R.P. Dutt, *India Today*, Calcutta, 1970, pp. 313-14.
13. *New India*, 1885, Berkley, 1969, p. 54, n. 3.
14. N.S. Bose, op. cit., pp. 219-21.
15. S.R. Mehrotra, op. cit., p. 239.
16. R.P. Dutt, op. cit., pp. 308-39.
17. R.C. Temple, *Men and Events of My Time in India*, 1882, p. 470.
18. Partly quoted in C. Sehanavis in his paper on Phadke contributed to *Challenge — A Saga of India's Struggle for Freedom*, New Delhi, 1984.
19. A. Besant, *How India Wrought for Freedom*, Adyar, 1915, pp. 1 ff.
20. R.C. Majmudar (ed.), The British Paramountcy and Indian Renaissances, Vol. C, Part II in *History and Culture of the Indian People*, Bombay, 1965, pp. 525-6.
21. Pattabhi Sitaramayya, op. cit., p. 16.
22. Ibid., p. 98.
23. Quoted in S.R. Mehrotra, op. cit., p. 311.
24. W. Wedderburn, *Allan Octavian Hume, Father of the Indian National Congress, 1829 to 1912*, London, 1913, p. 77.
25. See A.M. Zaidi & S. Zaidi, *The Encyclopaedia of the Indian National Congress*, Vol. I, Delhi, 1976, pp. 44-5.
26. Quoted in S.R. Mehrotra, op. cit., p. 415.
27. *Report of the Indian National Congress, 1885.*

27a. Ibid.

28. 28 December 1886.
29. *Report of the Indian National Congress, 1886*, Resolution II.
30. See R.P. Dutt, op. cit., p. 125.

31. Resolution I(a) and (b), 1894.
32. *Report of the Indian National Congress, 1895,* Presidential Address, p. 33.
33. *Report of the Indian National Congress, 1903,* Vol. VII.
34. K. Iswara Dutt, *Congress Encyclopaedia, The Indian National Congress,* 1885-1920, n.d., p. 155.
35. *Report of the Indian National Congress,* 1903, Presidential Address, p. 18.
36. A.M. Zaidi & S. Zaidi, op. cit., Vol. II, p. 59.
37. *Report of the Indian National Congress, 1905,* Presidential Address, pp.10-13.
38. *Report of the Indian National Congress, 1900,* Resolution VII.
39. *Report of the Indian National Congress, 1903,* Resolution IX.
40. *Report of the Indian National Congress, 1904,* Resolution XIV.
41. *Report of the Indian National Congress, 1905,* Resolution XII.
42. Ibid., Resolution XIII.
43. A. Tripathi, *The Extremist Challenge,* Calcutta, 1967, p. 59.
44. S.R. Singh, *A Centenary History of the Indian National Congress,* Vol. I, Chapter II, New Delhi, 1985.
45. A. Tripathi, op. cit., p. 71.
46. B.B. Majumdar, *History of the Indian Social and Political Ideas,* Calcutta, 1967, p. 229.
47. 21 July 1905.
48. R.C. Majumdar, *History of the Freedom Movement in India,* Vol. II, pp. 7-8.
49. Jawaharlal Nehru, *An Autobiography with Musings on Recent Events in India,* London, 1936, p. 29.
50. *Bande Mataram,* 26 April 1907.
51. R.C. Majumdar, 'The Genesis of Extremism', *Studies in the Bengal Renaissance,* Jadavpur, 1977, p. 198.
52. B.C. Pal, *Memories of My Life and Times,* Calcutta, 1973, p. 200.
53. Ibid., p. 202.
54. See Sankariprasad Basu, Chapter III of this volume.
55. See Robert Payne, *The Life and Death of Mahatma Gandhi,* London, 1969, p. 298.
56. A.M. Zaidi & S. Zaidi, op. cit., Vol. VII, Presidential Address, p. 475.
57. *Report of the Indian National Congress, 1896,* Presidential Address.
58. *Report of the Indian National Congress, 1888.*
59. A.S. Tyabji, *Muslim League,* pp. 25-6.
60. C.S. Wolpert, *Jinnah of Pakistan,* New York, 1984, p. 18.
61. See Barbara Daly Metcalf, *Islamic Revival in British India: Deoband, 1860-1900,* Princeton, 1982. Map showing schools having ties with Deoband, p. 126.
62. Tarachand, *History of the Freedom Movement in India,* Vol. II, p. 385.
63. Quoted in A.M. Zaidi & S. Zaidi, op. cit., Vol. VII, p. 218.
64. *Report of the Indian National Congress, 1908,* Resolution II.
65. Mushirul Hasan, *Nationalism and Communal Politics in India,* Columbia, 1979, pp. 30-1.
66. Hossainur Rahman, 'The Congress and the Muslims', manuscript essay, 1985.
67. Sumit Sarkar, *Modern India,* Delhi, 1984, pp. 91-2.
68. *Report of the Indian National Congress, 1890.*
69. Dr Ashim K. Datta's contribution to this volume.

70. Ibid.
71. S.K. Sen, Chapter VI, *A Centenary History of the Indian National Congress,* 1985.
72. V.V. Balabushevich and A.M. Dyakov (eds.), *A Contemporary History of India,* Moscow, 1959, p. 3.
73. Jawaharlal Nehru, *The Discovery of India,* 1956, p. 356.
74. *Royal Commission on Agriculture in India,* London, 1972.
75. Nehru, *The Discovery of India,* p. 359.
76. M.K. Gandhi, *The Story of My Experiments with Truth,* p. 443.
77. Nehru, *Autobiography,* p. 171.
78. Nehru, *The Discovery of India,* p. 423.
79. *Report of the Indian National Congress, 1885.*
80. *Report of the Indian National Congress, 1891.*
81. A.M. Zaidi & S. Zaidi, op. cit., Vol. II, p. 150.
82. Ibid., Vol. II, p. 636.
83. *Report of the Indian National Congress, 1896.*
84. *Report of the Indian National Congress, 1897.*
85. 9 August 1908.
86. *Report of the Indian National Congress, 1908.*
87. See V.C. Joshi (ed.), *Lala Lajpat Rai : Writings and Speeches,* Vol. I, New Delhi, 1966, p. xxxiv.
88. 29 December 1908. Quoted in S. Vijayalakshmi, Chapter VII of this volume.
89. *Report of the Indian National Congress, 1908.*
90. See Chapter VII of this volume.
91. See T.L. Shay, *The Legacy of the Lokamanya,* Oxford, 1956, p. 130.
92. Ibid., p. 131.
93. S.N. Banerjea, op. cit., p. 237.
94. *Bal Gangadhar Tilak : His Writings and Speeches,* Madras, 1922, p. 186.
95. S. Vijayalakshmi, Chapter VII of this volume.
96. C.F. Andrews and G. Mukherji, *The Rise and Growth of the Congress in India,* London, 1938, p. 232.
97. M.K. Gandhi, op. cit., p. 415-16.
98. See Dr T.S. Banerjee, Chapter VIII of this volume.
99. Bombay Police Abstract, 1916, par. 757, quoted in Judith Brown, *Gandhi's Rise to Power : Indian Politics,* 1915-1922, Cambridge, 1972, p. 48.
100. Robert Payne, op. cit., p. 324.
101. Judith Brown, op. cit., p. 105.
102. P. Sitaramayya, *Gandhi and Gandhism,* p. 101, quoted in Chapter VIII of this volume.
103. Judith Brown, *Modern India : The Origins of an Asian Democracy,* N. Y., 1984, pp. 205-6.
104. J. Nehru, *Autobiography,* p. 40.
105. Ibid., p. 41.
106. P. Sitaramayya, *The History of the Indian National Congress,* pp. 301-2.
107. Ibid., p. 306.
108. A.M. Zaidi & S. Zaidi, op. cit., Vol. VII, p. 525.
109. Durga Das, *India from Curzon to Nehru and After,* London, 1969, p. 71.

Chapter I

Genesis of the Indian National Congress

Amitabha Mukherjee

1. The Pioneers

28 December 1885 is a red-letter day in the history of Indian nationalism; it is the birthday of the Indian National Congress. But every birth is preceded by conception, a period of gestation, and the birth of the Congress was preceded by a fairly long period of evolution of Indian national consciousness. The development of national consciousness in the 19th century was almost exclusively the work of the new middle class created by the impact of British rule. Even before this class, inspired by a national consciousness and a pride in the glory of their past, started their constitutional agitation for political rights, the masses, groaning under the oppressive British rule, had risen in sporadic rebellions in different parts of the country. Thus, for example, there were the Sannyasi rebellion in Bengal (immortalized in Bankim Chandra's famous novel, *Anandamath*), the Wahhabi and Faraizi movements in Northern India (finally crushed in the early 1870s), the Moplah risings in the south (1849-55), the Santal rebellion in Chhotanagpur (1855-6) and the famous Indigo Agitation (1859-60) which drew the attention of the educated middle class to the sufferings of the masses and made them understand the oppressive character of British rule in India. The Great Rebellion of 1857-8 also saw an outburst of the accumulated discontent of the masses in different parts of this country. But, on the whole, the sporadic mass movements had no great sequel, except perhaps an intensification of the racial animosity between the Indian subjects on the one hand and their British masters on the other.

The middle class agitation, which began in the third decade of the 19th century, had, however, a completely different character and significance, and was the product of an entirely different set of circumstances. English education began to spread rapidly among the upper and middle classes in the Indian cities from the 1830s. Through a study of English literature and European history and philosophy, educated

Indians came to imbibe the spirit of liberalism, social equality and national patriotism which England at that time unequivocally declared to be her political ideals. A tremendous wave of liberalism was passing over English politics and literature during the 19th century, and this could not but influence the Indian mind. Western education expanded not only Indian capacities but also Indian desires. The various public pronouncements of the British Government, from the days of the Charter Act of 1813, to the effect that its great object in India was to promote the interests and happiness of the Indian people also created new aspirations in the minds of educated Indians.

One great aspiration of the English-educated Indians was to have a greater share in the government of their country. This was to be achieved through the development of representative institutions and the appointment of Indians to the higher ranks of government service. During the greater part of the 19th century educated Indians had immense faith in the benevolent character of British rule in this country. They were not merely impressed by the superior culture and strength of the British people but also felt grateful to the latter for various reasons. The British Government, they believed, had united the whole country under one political banner, restored peace and order throughout the land after a long period of anarchy and chaos, introduced a uniform system of law and government, facilitated trade and commerce within the country and secured to the Indians the benefits of modern methods of communication. It was again the British Indologists who had unveiled the records of India's glorious past and thus greatly stimulated the national pride of our people. Educated Indians like Raja Rammohun Roy (1774-1833) therefore believed that the process of modernization of the Indian society would be completed under British rule, and that it would be entirely for our benefit. The Indian people had, of course, numerous grievances, political and economic, but these would be redressed by our benevolent rulers only if we could draw the attention of the British Government and Parliament to these through timely prayers and petitions. In the beginning, therefore, the middle class agitation in our country consisted only in the ventilation of some specific political and economic demands. The movement had no definite political programme, but only some vague nationalist ideas.

The beginning of modern political agitation in India may be traced back to the days of Raja Rammohun Roy. The latter believed that India's political emancipation would come only after a long period of British tutelage, and that her political and economic progress would be accelerated if, in the meanwhile, England's relations with India were strengthened through colonization. But, though a collaborator with the British Raj in this sense, the Raja was keen to defend the rights and interests of his countrymen as he understood them. In 1823 he championed the liberty of the press and boldly protested against the censorship measures of the government. In 1827 he drew up a petition against the Jury Act which exempted all Christians in this country, including Indian converts, from the degradation of being tried by either a Hindu or a Muslim juror. In 1830 he protested against the resumption by the government of all rent-free tenures. On the eve of the renewal of the East India Company's Charter in 1833, Rammohun demanded the abolition of the Company's trading rights and the removal of heavy export duties on Indian manufactures. In 1831, while in England, he suggested to a Parliamentary Committee various measures of reform in the Indian administration like Indianization of the army, introduction of trial by jury, separation of the offices of judge and magistrate, codification of criminal laws and substitution of English for Persian as the language of the law courts. It may be said that, in general, Rammohun laid down the lines for organized political agitation in a constitutional manner which were followed later by the Indian National Congress. At the same time, the Raja had very liberal international sympathies and contacts, and took a keen interest in current international affairs, particularly in progressive political movements, wherever these might occur.[1]

A continuation of this trend of agitation was noticed in Bengal during the two decades following the death of Rammohun, and gradually it spread over other parts of British Indian territory. The Landholders' Society was established at Calcutta in July 1838, with Dwarkanath Tagore as its principal leader, for keeping a watch on the activities of government officials and voicing the grievances of the landlord class in particular. Though designed primarily to protect the class interests of the zamindars of Bengal, Bihar and Orissa, it claimed also to protect the interests of the *ryots*, and aimed at setting up branch societies in all the districts of the British Indian Empire.[2] Thus, the very first political association started in this country in the 19th century sought to place political activities on an all-India footing, though the success achieved by it was really meagre.

In 1839 George Thompson, a well-known British philanthropist and orator, established in London the British Indian Society in collaboration with Rammohun's friend, William Adam. This organization established contacts with the Landholders' Society of Calcutta and sought to carry on the agitation in England. Thompson came to Calcutta in 1842 along with Dwarkanath Tagore (who was then returning from his first visit to England) and created a new enthusiasm among the educated public of Calcutta by his political lectures. The Young Bengal group, consisting of men like Ramgopal Ghosh, Pearychand Mitra and Tarachand

Chakravarty, felt particularly attracted to him, and they started the Bengal British India Society in April 1843, with the object of protecting the rights of the subject people by concerted activity. Collecting information about the true condition of the common people of our country and striving in a constitutional and peaceful manner for the improvement of different classes and sections of Indians were among the declared objects of this association. While the Landholders' Society represented the 'aristocracy of wealth', the Bengal British India Society represented the 'aristocracy of intelligence', but neither association could achieve any great popularity.[3]

Indians and Europeans in this country had collaborated in organizing the Landholders' Society as well as the Bengal British India Society; but the agitation which began in 1849 over the question of the European British subjects' privileges in criminal trials created a racial cleavage which had its impact on Indian politics. The so-called Black Act, drafted by J.E.D. Bethune, proposed to bring the British residents in India living in the mofussil under the jurisdiction of the ordinary district courts. The proposed piece of legislation was very much resented by the European community because it hurt their racial pride and arrogance, and they started an agitation against it. To counteract this European agitation and to defend Indian interests and rights, all groups of Bengali politicians, radical as well as moderate, combined to form a new political organization, composed of Indians only, called the British Indian Association (1851). It was, in effect, an aristocratic body dominated by landed interests. Raja Radhakanta Deb was its first President and Debendranath Tagore its first Secretary. The *Hindoo Patriot*, edited by the talented journalist, Harishchandra Mukherjee, became practically its official organ. The British Indian Association had an all-India outlook from the very beginning, and in 1852, on the eve of the renewal of the East India Company's Charter, it presented a general petition to the British Parliament, demanding the abolition of the Company's monopoly in salt and indigo, state aid for Indian industry, admission of Indians to the higher government services, and the creation of an Indian legislature. These demands naturally went unheeded, but the association went on clamouring for the admission of Indians to the Legislative Councils and the holding of the Civil Service Examination simultaneously in India and England for the convenience of the educated and talented youths of this country. In 1856 the British Indian Association supported a missionary memorial for enquiry into the conditions of the tenants in the Permanent Settlement areas.[4]

Associations of a similar character were established in different Indian cities during the 1850s. The most important of these were the Madras Native Association and the Bombay Association, both established in

1852. Petitions were sent to the British Parliament from both these associations on the eve of the renewal of the Company's Charter (1853). The Deccan Association founded at Pune in 1852 did not, however, show much activity. All these political bodies — clubs, societies and associations — were dominated by the English-educated, wealthy commercial and landed interests, and had only a regional character. They demanded mainly administrative reforms, more employment of Indians in administrative services, spread of English education, association of Indians with legislative councils, and encouragement of Indian trade and industry. Many of these demands were later also voiced by the Indian National Congress.[5]

The conflict between the British Government in India and the English-educated upper and middle classes gradually intensified after the failure of the Revolt of 1857. The latter now began to grasp more clearly the exploitative character of British rule in India. The series of devastating famines which occurred in India between 1866 and 1901 brought home to the educated Indians the stark poverty of the people and the economic decline of the country, brought about by a huge drainage of wealth and the decay of indigenous trade and industry. The Indian intelligentsia did not fail to notice that the British Government in this country spent less than three per cent of its budget on education and had abandoned all attempts at social reform after 1858.[6] The growth of Indian industries was hampered by an enforced free trade policy, implemented on the insistent orders of the Secretary of State for India. The incidence of unemployment was also on the increase, because the government services failed to absorb the growing number of graduates produced by the Indian universities and also because there was no proper industrial growth in the country. Freedom of the press had been curtailed and so was the right to hold public meetings. Above all, there was great racial discrimination against the Indians, and even the judicial machinery was perverted in the interest of the members of the ruling race. European offenders escaped with small fines, even in cases of murder or grievous assault. Planters and soldiers were perhaps the worst offenders in this respect, but some of the most highly placed government officials also exhibited a racial arrogance which was bound to offend educated Indians.[7] All these factors contributed to the growth of a powerful nationalist political movement directed against British imperialism.

Though the Bengali intelligentsia had taken no significant part in the Great Revolt of 1857, they came forward two years later to protest vigorously against oppression by the European indigo-planters. Bengali journalists like Harishchandra Mukherjee became directly connected with the movement of the indigo-cultivators, and Bengali literary figures like Dinabandhu Mitra, Madhusudan Datta and Kaliprasanna Sinha also indirectly encouraged it.[8] A group of Bengali leaders, comprising men like Rajnarayan Bose, Nebagopal Mitra, Bhudev Mukherjee and Jyotirindra Nath Tagore tried to stimulate Hindu nationalist sentiment in the post-1857 period. The Hindu Mela was organized for the first time in 1867 for cultivating national sentiment and promoting the growth of indigenous art and craft in a spirit of self-help.[9] Bhudev Mukherjee, it may be noted, was the first Bengali writer to suggest the adoption of Hindi as India's national language. Some of the earliest Bengali patriotic songs were composed at this time by Satyendra Nath Tagore, the first Indian member of the I.C.S. Bankim Chandra Chatterji's famous novel *Anandamath,* which later served as a great source of inspiration to the Bengali revolutionaries was published in 1882, but his immortal song *Bande Mataram,* which became our national anthem during the freedom struggle, had been composed a few years earlier (1875). The tempo of political agitation increased in the seventies of the century when Sisir Kumar Ghose, the celebrated editor of the *Amrita Bazar Patrika,* openly demanded western parliamentary institutions for India (1870) and tried to link up the various political associations that had meanwhile been established in different parts of Bengal.

In Western India, the Bombay Association, founded in 1852, ceased to be an effective political body after the Great Revolt of 1857. The great Maharashtrian political thinker, Gopal Hari Deshmukh, better known as 'Lokahitawadi' (1823-92) demanded for India 'a Parliament like that of England', and also recommended the revival of village communities. The Poona Sarvajanik Sabha was established in 1870 by M.G. Ranade, G.V. Joshi, S.H. Chiplunkar and others to represent the wants and wishes of the inhabitants of the Deccan. It published a quarterly journal from 1878 onwards and did much for awakening the political consciousness of the people of Maharashtra.[10] To carry on political propaganda in England, some Indian students like Pherozeshah Mehta and Badruddin Tayabji from Bombay and W.C. Bonnerjee and Manmohan Ghose from Calcutta set up the London Indian Society in 1865 under the guidance of the great Parsi leader, Dadabhai Naoroji, who later became famous as the 'Grand Old Man of India'. Within a year, this society was amalgamated with the East India Association (December 1866), founded in collaboration with a committee of retired English officials. Members of the latter association were drawn from different Indian provinces, and it counted among its patrons and sympathizers a large number of Englishmen who had distinguished themselves in different walks of life. Branches of the East India Association were established in Bombay, Madras and Calcutta in 1869, and by 1871 the number of its members ran into four figures. The association, however, never won effective support in Bengal or Madras, and it slowly lost its popularity during the 1880s.[11]

The work of creating a public opinion in India by direct appeal to the people was first undertaken by the Indian Association of Calcutta and its great leader, Surendranath Banerjea. After his dismissal from the 'heaven-born service', Surendranath took to teaching and became closely associated with political activities in Bengal. He and his friends like Ananda Mohan Bose and Sivanath Sastri soon broke away from Sisir Kumar Ghose and his India League (1875) and founded the Indian Association in July 1876. Unlike the British Indian Association which was a conservative and pro-zamindar body, the Indian Association was dominated by the new middle class and the intelligentsia, and it claimed to speak for the common people. The new association was based, in the words of Surendranath on 'the conception of a United India, derived from the inspiration of Mazzini'. The objects of the Indian Association were (1) to create a strong body of public opinion in the country, (2) to achieve the unification of the Indian races on the basis of common political interests and aspirations, (3) to promote the ideal of Hindu-Muslim unity, and (4) to enlist the support of the masses for the public agitations of the day. The association soon established branches in different districts of Bengal and formed links with popular organizations outside the province.[12]

The openly reactionary and anti-Indian measures adopted by Lord Lytton's government between 1876 and 1880 afforded the Indian Association an excellent opportunity to organize a number of all-India political agitations. The removal of import duties on British textiles to benefit the Lancashire manufacturers at the cost of the nascent Indian textile industry and the aggressive warfare in Afghanistan, the burden of the expense on which was thrown on the Indian exchequer, were resented by many politically conscious Indians. But, it was the government's decision to reduce the maximum age for competing in the I.C.S. examination from 21 to 19 which provoked the Indian Association to launch its first political campaign of an all-India character. The obvious motive behind government's decision was to strictly limit the access of qualified Indians to higher appointments. In a public meeting held in Calcutta under the auspices of the Indian Association it was decided to send a memorial to the Secretary of State for India, requesting him to raise the age limit to 22 and to arrange for simultaneous examinations in India and England. Surendranath himself toured different provinces during 1877-8 and tried to create an all-India public opinion on the civil service issue. A deputation led by the well-known Bengali barrister, Lal Mohan Ghose, was sent to England to present the memorial of the Indian Association. The agitation was successful and, in the end, the Civil Service Regulations were modified to some extent.[13]

The civil service agitation was followed within a year by the Arms Act agitation and the Vernacular Press Act agitation. The Arms Act of 1878 prohibited the keeping of arms by Indians, while the Vernacular Press Act passed in the same year sought to muzzle newspapers in Indian languages which preached the message of nationalism and strove to make the common people politically conscious. The agitation against the Arms Act was not successful, though Gladstone himself took up the Indian cause in his Midlothian campaign. But the agitation against the Vernacular Press Act was crowned with success in 1882 when Lord Ripon repealed the Act. To put itself out of the purview of this repressive measure, the *Amrita Bazar Patrika* in Bengali turned itself overnight into an English journal, while a new nationalist journal in the English language, *The Hindu*, was born in Madras (1878).[14] The Indian Association also championed in some instances the cause of the common people. On the Bengal Tenancy Bill of 1883 it favoured the cause of the tenants and organized peasant demonstrations. The association also concerned itself with the grievances of the tea-garden labourers in Assam. As a result of all these agitations, a strong public opinion gradually began to take shape in Bengal. Huge mass meetings were organized in district towns, attended at some places by ten to twenty thousand people.[15] Some of the leaders of the Indian Association also earned recognition outside Bengal. Surendranath Banerjea was perhaps the first political leader in modern Indian history to gain all-India popularity. When Lal Mohan Ghose returned from England after his successful deputation, he was first accorded a public reception in Bombay.[16] The Muslims, however, did not join the Indian Association in large numbers. The Muslim educated classes got their own organization in 1877 when Syed Ameer Ali founded the National Mohammedan Association.

The efforts of the Indian Association to stimulate the political consciousness of the Indian people were aided by two important events in 1883; the first was the Ilbert Bill controversy and the second, the imprisonment of Surendranath in a contempt of court case. Under the existing Criminal Procedure Code, European British subjects in India were subject to the criminal jurisdiction only of European district magistrates and sessions judges. Indian members of the Indian Civil Service working as district magistrates and sessions judges could not try them. Sir Courtenay Ilbert, Law Member in Lord Ripon's Council, prepared a bill to remove this invidious distinction between European and Indian members of the same Civil Service which was based solely on racial considerations. The European community in Bengal and also in other parts of India at once raised a hue and cry against this simple administrative measure, just as they had done during the Black Act days. Bureaucrats, merchants, lawyers and planters belonging to this community formed a Defence Association with branches all over the country and collected nearly one and a half lakh of rupees to conduct a virulent anti-Indian campaign. The Indian Association organized a counter-agitation, various public associations of Bengal and Bombay fought hard for the bill and a joint representation was made by them to the Viceroy. But nothing availed. Ripon had ultimately to yield to the violence of his own countrymen and accept a compromise which frustrated the original purpose of this measure. In its final form, the bill provided that every European British subject brought for trial before a district magistrate or sessions judge would have the right to claim trial by a jury of which no less than half the number must be Europeans or Americans. The Ilbert Bill agitation 'left behind it a rankling sense of defeat, disgrace and humiliation in the hearts of the Indians'; but, at the same time, they 'learnt the value of combination and organization in political struggle', and their eyes were opened to their ignoble status in their own country. The lessons which they now learnt helped their political advance in subsequent years.[17]

The other notable event of 1883 to which reference has already been made was the imprisonment of Surendranath himself (May 1883). Chief Justice Norris of the Calcutta High Court had ordered a Hindu litigant to produce the image of his deity in the court. Surendranath made some adverse comments on the conduct of the Chief Justice in the pages of the *Bengalee*, and at once a charge for contempt of court was brought against him. The case created a great sensation because Norris had already made himself very unpopular by taking a prominent part in the Ilbert Bill agitation. The majority of the judges in this contempt of court case held Surendranath guilty and sentenced him to two months imprisonment, but the only Indian judge on the Bench dissented from this verdict. Surendranath's imprisonment, however, served only to make him a martyr in the eyes of his countrymen and to strengthen the bond of unity and fellow-feeling among different sections of Indians. The court's verdict evoked a spontaneous protest not only from all sections of people in Bengal, the educated classes as well as the masses, but also from people in other Indian provinces. Protest meetings were held in such remote places as Agra, Amritsar, Fyzabad, Lahore and Pune, and even a pandit of Kashmir, completely ignorant of English, is reported to have burst into tears on hearing the news of Surendranath's imprisonment.[18]

After Surendranath's release from jail in July 1883 it was decided at a largely attended public meeting in Calcutta to raise a National Fund for securing 'the political advancement of the country by means of constitutional agitation in India and in England'. The promoters of this Fund wanted to secure wider employment of Indians in all branches of administration, reform in the system of local self-government, introduction of representative institutions and maintain a permanent delegate in the U.K. In spite of the opposition of the British Indian Association, nearly twenty thousand rupees were soon collected, mostly from Bengal, and placed at the disposal of the Indian Association for the promotion of its political activities.[19]

The year 1883 saw several other significant developments in Indian politics. Early in 1883, K.T. Telang, a nationalist leader of Bombay, came to Calcutta to establish contacts with the leaders of the Indian Association. In January 1883, Dadabhai Naoroji started the *Voice of India* to publish extracts from the Indian press. There was also a proposal to set up a national federation of Indian editors, but it did not produce any tangible result.[20] On 4 February 1883, an Irish member of the House of Commons, O'Donnell, published a letter, in the Bombay *Native Opinion*, suggesting the establishment of a national association. Many Indian newspapers reproduced the letter in their columns and welcomed O'Donnell's proposal.[21] Tarapada Banerjee, a young lawyer of Krishnanagar (in the district of Nadia, Bengal), also suggested the foundation of a national assembly to agitate for the introduction of representative institutions in India. His proposal was published in the *Indian Mirror* of Calcutta on 4 July 1883.[22]

It was, however, left to the Indian Association to organize the first All-India National Conference in Calcutta in December 1883. An international exhibition was scheduled to be held in Calcutta in December 1883, and visitors were expected to come from all over the country. The Indian Association therefore decided to hold their conference at the same time. Ananda Mohan Bose hoped that it would be the first step towards a national parliament. Surendranath wrote in his book, *A Nation In Making* (1925), that it was 'the reply of educated India to the Ilbert Bill agitation'.[23] But the National Conference which met at the Albert Hall in Calcutta from 28 to 30 December 1883, with the eminent educationist Ramtanu Lahiry in the chair, was attended by hardly one hundred persons. A handful of delegates came from Bombay, Madras, Ahmedabad and Upper India, but the rest were all local men. The British Indian Association of Calcutta held aloof, and outside Bengal the local newspapers gave it scant attention. Yet, as Dr Anil Seal has observed, the first National Conference was, in its programme and proceedings, 'a dress-rehearsal' for the Indian National Congress. The subjects discussed at this conference were essentially the same as those which were later discussed in the National Congress session, e.g., representative councils, education — general and technical, separation of the judiciary from the executive in the administration of criminal justice, and under-employment of Indians in the public services. The proceedings of the National Conference were conducted in English because that was the only language which educated people from all over India understood. Wilfrid Blunt, the author of *India Under Ripon,* saw the conference as 'evidence that India was ready for self-government'.[24]

In 1884 Surendranath Banerjea, undertook a propaganda tour in Northern India. The Indian Association gradually expanded, establishing its branches in different parts of the country. A new organization called the Indian Union also came into existence in Calcutta (March 1884) with the Maharaja of Darbhanga as its President and W.C. Bonnerjee as its Secretary. It consisted mainly of Hindu lawyers but also had some Muslim members.[25] In May 1884, the Mahajana Sabha was established in Madras with Rangiah Naidu as its President and Veeraraghavachariar and Ananda Charlu as its Secretaries. Its first conference, held in December 1884, was attended by about seventy delegates representing both the Tamil and Telugu districts of the Madras Presidency. The main subjects discussed at this conference were reform of the legislative councils, separation of the executive from the judiciary, changes desired in the structure of the Indian Government and the condition of the agricultural classes. The programme put forward by the Sabha in December 1884 was very similar to the proposals adopted by the National Conference a year earlier.[26]

The first conference of the Mahajana Sabha in December 1884 almost coincided with the annual convention of the Theosophical Society at Adyar, near Madras. Taking advantage of the latter convention, Dewan Bahadur Raghunath Rao, an ardent Theosophist, privately collected at his residence in Madras city a dozen or so of the delegates to this convention, and a few other Hindu gentlemen of Madras, and drew up a blueprint for an all-India political organization. Narendra Nath Sen, editor of the *Indian Mirror,* who was also a Theosophist, attended this private meeting, and, on his return to Calcutta, wrote a series of articles in his paper during January-February 1885, urging the desirability of establishing a national organization in India on the lines agreed to at Madras. A circular containing the resolutions adopted at the Madras meeting is also reported to have been issued in the beginning of 1885. When the Indian National Congress was born in December 1885, the Theosophists began to claim it as their child. Colonel Olcott, one of the founders of the Theosophical Society of India, asserted in 1886 that his society was the parent of the Indian National Congress. Raghunath Rao in 1888 and N.N. Sen in 1889 reiterated this claim and virtually accused Hume of having stolen their thunder. Even Mrs Annie Besant, who later became Congress President, wrote in 1914 that the decision to convene the Congress was first taken in Madras by seventeen leading members of the Theosophical Society at the house of Raghunath Rao towards the end of December 1884. But this claim need not be taken very seriously.

As S.R. Mehrotra has pointed out, the idea of holding annual conferences of representatives from different parts of the country in order to promote national objectives had been current in India long before the founders of the Theosophical Society landed in Bombay in February 1879. Moreover, the deliberations at Raghunath Rao's residence in Madras in December 1884 were not followed by any political action, a fact which has been indirectly admitted by Mrs Besant herself. Dr Mehrotra therefore rightly concludes that the organization of the First Indian National Congress was the result of developments which had nothing to do with the Theosophical Society and was on lines very different from those suggested at the Madras meeting.[27]

Towards the end of 1884, Lord Ripon, a popular Viceroy, returned to England on the expiry of his term of office. On this occasion farewell demonstrations were arranged in different important cities between Calcutta and Bombay (November-December 1884). The spontaneity of these popular demonstrations took the bureaucracy by surprise. 'If it be real, what does it mean?' Sir Auckland Colvin, the Indian Finance Minister, asked in great bewilderment in a pamphlet of that title. These demonstrations also revealed a spirit of organization hardly ever seen in the country earlier.[28]

In January 1885, three prominent leaders of Bombay, Pherozeshah Mehta, K.T. Telang and Badruddin Tayabji, set up the Bombay Presidency Association. The association had, from the beginning, very cordial relations with the Poona Sarvajanik Sabha and, by April 1885, it took up the project for a National Telegraph Union. In September 1885, the Bombay Presidency Association, the Poona Sarvajanik Sabha, the Mahajana Sabha of Madras and the Indian Association of Calcutta sent a joint deputation to England to present India's case before the British electorate. The deputation was led by N. Chandavarkar of Bombay, Ramaswami Mudaliar of Madras, and Manmohan Ghose of Calcutta. Three months later, it was the Bombay Presidency Association which played host to the first Congress.[29]

It is clear from the foregoing review that the emergence of the Congress was not a sudden or unexpected development. It was really the culmination of a long process of evolution of political ideas and organizations which had started during the thirties of the 19th century. Politically conscious Indians were becoming increasingly aware of the necessity for an all-India political organization to ventilate their grievances and voice their demands, and some of their leaders in different parts of the country, particularly Calcutta, Bombay, Pune and Madras, had almost simultaneously begun to plan the setting up of such an organization. It was, however, left to an Englishman and retired civil servant, Allan Octavian Hume, to give a concrete shape to their ideas in collaboration with some of them.

Son of the British Radical leader Joseph Hume, Allan inherited his father's political views and in his early days took interest in European revolutionary associations. He joined the East India Company's Civil Service in 1849, served in the North-Western Provinces and became a Secretary to the Government of India in 1870. But he was looked upon as an eccentric and renegade by his official contemporaries, was superseded by juniors like Ashley Eden and threatened by Viceroy Lord Northbrook with dismissal from service. He also failed to get on with Lord Lytton, suffered demotion in 1879 and retired from service in 1882. Instead of returning to England like his fellow civilians, Hume settled down in Simla and began to take an active interest in Indian politics. He had access to many Indian political leaders of his time, and became increasingly absorbed in Indian philosophy and Theosophy. He was, however, more in sympathy with the Bombay and Pune groups than with Calcutta leaders like Surendranath Banerjea and Narendra Nath Sen. Hume also came into contact with Viceroy Lord Ripon, became enthusiastic about the latter's scheme of local self-government and, by late 1883, began to advise the viceroy unofficially on Indian public opinion and politics.[30]

In spite of all his eccentricity and conceit, Hume had a genuine sympathy for the interests and welfare of India, combined with a faith in the basic goodness and wisdom of British rule. After retiring from service he addressed an open letter to the graduates of the Calcutta University on 1 March 1883, appealing to them to take the initiative in establishing an association which would promote the mental, moral, social and political regeneration of the people of India. Strangely enough, we find no allusion to this letter in the contemporary Indian press, and most probably it was circulated privately amongst the small circle of Hume's trusted friends. We have no way to measure precisely their response to it.[31] The Ilbert Bill agitation extended Hume's contacts throughout India. Ripon's compromise over the bill created a bitter feeling of disappointment and disillusionment among the politically conscious Indians. Hume, however, defended Ripon's compromise and also organized the initial farewell demonstrations for Ripon.[32]

Between December 1884 and March 1885, Hume had prolonged talks with eminent Indian nationalist leaders in Calcutta, Bombay, Pune and Madras. It was, however, on the Bombay leaders like William Wedderburn, Dadabhai Naoroji, M.G. Ranade, Pherozeshah Mehta and D.E. Wacha that Hume relied most for launching his new political movement in India. He discussed with them his plans for holding an annual conference of representative men from all parts of India, organizing a central national association for directing political activity throughout the country, preparing a charter of demands to be presented to the British Parliament and also forming an Indian party among the members of that Parliament.[33] In March 1885, Hume and his friends from Bombay and Pune drew up a plan for an Indian National Union. The Union was to take the form of an annual conference to be attended by leaders of various provincial associations. It would decide upon different types of reforms — political, economic, social and educational — which would be undertaken during the ensuing year. The conference was to be associated with the government and used as a sounding board for enlightened Indian public opinion. Officials would be encouraged to participate in this annual conference, and the Governor or Lieutenant Governor of the province where it would be held would be requested to preside over it. 'The key to the entire plan,' B. Martin (Jr) aptly remarks, 'rested upon official sanction and participation', and after his return to Simla in May 1885, Hume placed it before the new Viceroy, Lord Dufferin, for his support.[34]

Dufferin showed considerable interest in Hume's plan of an Indian National Union, and (if Hume is to be believed) warmly approved of the proposal because it would at least furnish the government with something like an authoritative statement of the views and wishes of educated and intelligent Indians throughout the country. But he objected immediately to the idea of having any official link with the Union, because he thought that 'the functions of such an assembly must of necessity consist in criticizing the acts or policy of the Government and in formulating demands which probably it would be impossible to grant'. In a letter to Lord Reay, Governor of Bombay, on 17 May 1884, Dufferin advised him not to serve as chairman of the conference of representatives which Hume was going to hold at Pune in the coming winter. 'I am sure', Dufferin wrote, 'it would be a mistake if we identified ourselves personally with either the reforming or the reactionary enthusiasts.'[35]

Hume's plan of summoning a representative gathering of Indian political leaders with the approval of the viceroy has given rise to much controversy regarding his real intentions and also the original character of the Congress organization. William Wedderburn in his biography of Hume, tells us that the latter was deeply alarmed at the growing discontent of the Indian people and believed that it threatened an imminent danger to the government. About a year before the end of Lord Lytton's Viceroyalty, Hume got very definite information about the explosive situation in India, created by the economic sufferings of the masses and the alienation of the educated classes. This information was contained in seven large volumes of communications, mostly in the form of reports received by different religious gurus from their disciples. These communications referred to the concealing of old swords, spears and matchlocks which would be made available to the rebels when required. Not that an organized rising was imminent, but the people, pervaded with a sense of hopelessness, wanted to do something to register their protest. The whole thing might start with a sudden outbreak of sporadic crimes like murder of obnoxious persons, robbing of bankers and looting of bazars. This would probably be followed by a general development of lawlessness, paralysing the government and the respectable classes. Small bands of rebels would begin to coalesce into large ones, and then a small section of the educated classes, bitter against the government, would join the movement, assume its leadership and give it the character of a national revolt against the British rulers.[36]

The condition of India in the 1880s was indeed deplorable. The peasantry had been impoverished by famines and there was widespread dissatisfaction about the costly and unsuitable civil courts set up by the British Government, the corrupt and oppressive police, the rigid revenue system and the galling administration of the Arms and the Forest Acts. The bureaucracy had not only done their best to block new concessions; they had also sometimes taken away privileges inherited from a former generation of reformers such as the liberty of the press, the right to hold public meetings and the autonomy of the universities. 'These ill-starred measures of reaction, combined with Russian methods of police repression brought India under Lord Lytton within a measurable distance of revolutionary outbreak.'[37] The Faraizi movement, the Pabna disturbances in Bengal, the Deccan riots in Pune and Ahmadnagar districts (1875) and the armed rising of Vasudeo Balwant Phadke in Maharashtra (1879) clearly showed the temper of the people. Vernacular newspapers were also rapidly growing in number and influence, and to restrain them the government of Lord Lytton had passed the Vernacular Press Act in 1878. Hume therefore came to the conclusion that it was high time to take some definite action to counteract the growing unrest. He conceived of the Congress as a sort of safety valve to be used for preventing a violent explosion of the people's discontent. As Hume himself candidly confessed, 'a safety valve for the escape of great and growing forces, generated by our own action, was urgently needed', and the purpose would be served best by providing for the leaders of the educated classes a constitutional channel for their political activities.[38]

From what has been narrated above, Dr R.C. Majumdar has come to the conclusion that the Congress was originally intended not to secure representative government for India or to train the educated Indians in the parliamentary form of government, but 'to arrest the progress of a revolutionary outbreak'.[39] Its real purpose was to hold back the Indian intelligentsia from joining an apprehended mass uprising against the British Government. R.P. Dutt, a Marxist writer, also observes that the Congress was brought into being 'through the initiative and under the guidance of direct British governmental policy, on a plan secretly pre-arranged with the Viceroy, as an intended weapon for safeguarding British rule against the rising forces of popular unrest and anti-British feeling'.[40]

It would, however, be rather unhistorical to regard Hume as a conspirator whose sole object was to perpetuate British rule in India at any cost. Eccentric as he was, Hume was always obsessed by the fear that the British Raj in India was on the brink of destruction. In a letter to Viceroy Northbrook dated 1 August 1872, Hume wrote, 'I am strongly impressed with the conviction that the fate of the empire is trembling in the balance'.[41] But, as Dr Anil Seal has pointed out, Hume was also one of the fiercest critics of the British bureaucracy in India, and his sympathy for India was also real, like that of William Wedderburn, Henry Cotton, Henry Beveridge and men of their ilk. He was one of the few British administrators who retained faith in collaboration with educated Indians and wanted to act as a link between Viceregal Lodge and the educated and politically conscious section of the Indian people.[42] Dr R.C. Majumdar also admits that Hume was inspired by a genuine sympathy for the interest and welfare of India, though he did not certainly have the same national sentiment and patriotic yearning for the freedom of India which characterized the advanced political thinkers of the country.[43]

Moreover, we should draw a clear line of distinction between Hume's intentions and the forces which made possible the foundation of the Congress. Professor Bipan Chandra rightly observes that, whatever might have been Hume's real purpose, the safety valve theory is 'totally inadequate and misleading as an explanation of the foundation of the National Congress. This at the most explains to a limited extent Hume's role in the episode'.[44] As we have already explained in the foregoing pages, the Congress was not the work of Hume alone, though he played a very important role in bringing it into existence. Hume's Indian collaborators who actively worked for the creation of this all-India political organization represented new social forces which were opposed to the exploitation of India for British interests. 'They were patriotic men of high character and were in no way stooges of the foreign government.' They needed Hume's support because they did not want to arouse official hostility to their early political endeavours. As Gopal Krishna Gokhale pointed out in 1913, 'no Indian could have started the Indian National Congress. . . . If the founder of the Congress had not been a great Englishman and a distinguished ex-official, such was the distrust of political agitation in those days that the authorities would have at once found some way or the other of suppressing the movement'. Professor Bipan Chandra therefore aptly remarks that, 'if Hume wanted to use Congress as a "safety valve", the early Congress leaders hoped to use him as a lightning conductor'.[45]

The role played by Viceroy Dufferin in founding the Congress has also been misinterpreted by some contemporary writers. W.C. Bonnerjee, the first President of the Congress, tells us in his Introduction to Natesan's *Indian Politics* (1898) that Hume originally intended to begin his reform propaganda on the social side only and did not desire to dabble in politics. His idea was to allow provincial organizations like the Indian Association of Calcutta, the Presidency Association of Bombay and the Mahajana Sabha of Madras to take up political questions. But, when Dufferin came to be acquainted with this plan, he sent for Hume and told him that there ought to be a body of persons in this country who would perform the function of Her Majesty's Opposition in England, point out to the government the defects in the existing system of administration and also suggest remedies. Hume had also wanted the provincial governors to preside over the annual conferences of the Indian National Union. But Dufferin told him that they should be held under the chairmanship of some respectable Indian, because in the presence of the provincial governor the participants might not like to speak out their minds. Hume was ultimately convinced by Dufferin's arguments, and the Indian leaders whom he consulted about his scheme endorsed Dufferin's stand. Dufferin, however, made it a condition that his name should not be divulged so long as he remained in India as Governor-General.[46]

This account by W.C. Bonnerjee and corroborated by W. Wedderburn makes Dufferin almost a co-founder of the Congress along with Hume and his Indian friends. But it is very difficult to reconcile this story with Hume's own confession that he wanted the Congress to serve as a 'safety valve' against a possible outbreak of mass violence in the country. The Congress certainly could not serve this purpose by eschewing politics altogether. Moreover, early in 1885, Hume told B.M. Malabari, who was trying to enlist his support for a programme of social reform, that a national organization would have to leave such matters strictly alone. On the other hand, Dufferin in his speech delivered at the St Andrews Day Dinner in Calcutta in November 1888, advised the Congress to direct its attention only to social questions.[47] It is true, however, that Dufferin was acquainted with Hume's plan and acquiesced in the project, though he did not want high officials like provincial governors to have any direct connection with the Congress for reasons already stated.

In March 1885, a circular was issued by Hume and his friends stating that the first conference of the Indian National Union would be held at Pune in the last week of December 1885. This conference would be attended by delegates chosen from among leading politicians, well acquainted with the English language, from the Bengal, Bombay and Madras Presidencies. The circular boldly declared that 'Indirectly this conference will form the germ of a Native Parliament, and if properly conducted, will constitute in a few years an unanswerable reply to the assertion that India is still wholly unfit for any form of representative institutions'.[48] The Poona Sarvajanik Sabha, under Chiplunkar and his friends, agreed to form a reception committee for hosting this first conference of the Indian National Union. A reception fund was also started for this purpose, and it was decided that the delegates would be free to contribute to it, if they so desired. Some time later, K.T. Telang, one of the sponsors of the conference, wrote to Surendranath Banerjea from Bombay, requesting him to send some notes about the First National Conference held in Calcutta in 1883.[49] This clearly shows that the founders of the Congress were inspired, at least partially, by the example set by the Indian Association of Calcutta two years earlier.

Between August and November 1885, Hume was in England and had consultation with leading Liberals there. Among the eminent politicians he consulted were Lord Ripon, Lord Dalhousie, Sir James Caird and John Bright. Under their advice he organized what later became the nucleus of the Indian Parliamentary Committee in England, whose members promised to take an active interest in Indian affairs. He also set up an Indian Telegraph Union which would arrange for quick publication of Indian news in the leading newspapers of England.[50] The results of the English parliamentary elections held at that time were, however, very disappointing to the Indian leaders. Almost all their friends, including the Calcutta barrister Lalmohan Ghose who tried to enter Parliament as a Liberal candidate from Deptford, were badly defeated.[51]

It is indeed surprising that Surendranath Banerjea, the most well-known Indian political leader of the time, and his friends in the Indian Association remaind completely in the dark about Hume's move to hold the first conference of the Indian National Union at Pune in December 1885. In late November 1885, Surendranath issued a circular calling the Second National Conference in Calcutta during the Christmas week of 1885 (25 to 27 December 1885). Leaders of the Poona Sarvajanik Sabha and the Bombay Presidency Association now changed the name of their conference to 'Congress', and shifted the date of their meeting from 25 to 28 December 1885, in order to avoid confusion. An attempt was also made later to persuade Surendranath to attend the Congress, but he declined because of his preoccupation with the Second National Conference in Calcutta.[52] It is very likely, as Dr R.C. Majumdar has suggested, that Hume and his friends did not like the politics of agitation in which Surendranath and other leaders of the Indian Association believed at that time. Surendranath's dismissal from the Indian Civil Service and his imprisonment in 1883 also made him a suspect in their eyes. That is why they chose the Calcutta barrister, W.C. Bonnerjee, who virtually lived the life of an Englishman and ridiculed all sorts of political agitation, as the first President of the Congress. Surendranath whose reputation had spread all over India by this time was naturally hurt by this deliberate neglect, and therefore might have hesitated at first to associate himself with the moderate leaders of Bombay.[53] In his autobiographical work, *A Nation In Making*, Surendranath, however, categorically states that it was not possible for him to cancel at this stage the Second National Conference in Calcutta and then rush to Bombay.[54]

The Second National Conference which met shortly before the first Congress was also 'largely a Bengali affair', but it was perhaps not less representative than the conference which had met in Calcutta two years earlier. It was convened jointly by the British Indian Association, the Indian Association and the Central Mohammedan Association of Calcutta. Participants came from Assam, Tripura, Orissa and the North-West Provinces (cities like Allahabad, Banaras and Meerut), and a single member, V.N. Mandlik, from the city of Bombay. The largest number of participants naturally came from Calcutta itself. The Second National Conference and the First National Congress were organized on similar lines and they adopted resolutions on almost the same subjects. Both planned to hold annual conferences in different Indian cities. A certain amount of jealousy and rivalry might have initially existed between the organizers of the two national assemblies; but they were magnanimous enough to exchange telegrams of greetings, and when the Second National Congress met in Calcutta in December 1886, Surendranath and his friends joined this body without reservation.[55] The latter perhaps calculated, as Dr R.C. Majumdar has pointed out, that an organization sponsored by a British civilian and Indian leaders of different provinces was more likely to command respect as an independent all-India organization than a body which was largely Bengali in character and liable to be represented by the British Government as the handiwork of the Bengali agitators. It must be said to the credit of Surendranath and other leaders of the Indian Association that they did not allow their pique and Bengali pride to get the better of their patriotism.[56]

2. The First Congress

Besides the Second National Conference in Calcutta, several other conferences were held in different parts of India during the latter half of December 1885 to promote almost identical causes. These included the

Eurasians' Conference at Jabalpur, the conference of the Prayag Central Hindu Samaj at Allahabad and the second annual conference of the Mahajana Sabha at Madras.[57] But, by far, the most important conference which met during this fortnight was the First Indian National Congress (28 to 30 December 1885). The venue of the Congress was shifted from Pune to Bombay in the third week of December on account of an outbreak of a cholera epidemic in Pune. The Congress began its session at 12 noon on 28 December 1885, in the hall of the Gokuldas Tejpal Sanskrit College, Bombay. It was a very colourful gathering, delegates from different regions appearing in their respective regional or communal dresses and some in European dress. Seventy-two delegates actually registered their names as 'representatives' and about thirty attended as observers. The latter were mostly government servants who could not officially join any political gathering. Among the participants were Dadabhai Naoroji, K.T. Telang, Pherozeshah Mehta, D.E. Wacha, B.M. Malabari, and N.G. Chandavarkar from Bombay; M.G. Ranade and G.G. Agarkar from Pune; Dewan Raghunath Rao, P. Rangiah Naidu, P. Ananda Charlu and S. Subramania Iyer from Madras; W.C. Bonnerjee and Narendra Nath Sen from Calcutta; Lala Baijnath from Agra; and last, but not least, Allan Octavian Hume from Simla. Editors of many well-known Indian newspapers like the *Dnyan Prakash, Indian Mirror, Hindu, Tribune, Crescent* and *Hindusthan* attended the session. The largest number of representatives, thirty-eight, naturally came from the Bombay Presidency, while the smallest number, just three, came from Bengal. The Congress met in camera and only a brief report of its proceedings was supplied to the press each day. The detailed report of the session was published only in late 1886.[58]

Though Bengal sent the smallest number of delegates to the first Congress, it was a Bengali barrister and Standing Counsel to the Government, W.C. Bonnerjee, who was chosen as the president of this session. His name was proposed by Hume and seconded by S. Subramania Iyer and K.T. Telang.[59] In his presidential address W.C. Bonnerjee emphasized the representative and constitutional character of the Congress. Surely never, Bonnerjee asserted, had so important and comprehensive an assemblage occurred within historical times on the soil of India. It was true that the members of the Congress were not representatives of the Indian people in the sense the members of the House of Commons were representatives of the people of England. But, if community of sentiments, community of feelings and community of wants enabled any one to speak on behalf of others, then the Congress, according to Bonnerjee, might justly claim to be the representative of the people of India. The presidential address was extremely loyal in its tone. It referred pointedly to the blessings of British rule in India — law and order, railways, post and telegraph, western education, and so on, and declared that without these there would have existed no national unity in India and no feeling of progress. But this thorough loyalty to the British Government was not in any way incompatible with the desire for political reform. In fact, Bonnerjee asserted that 'the more progress a people made in education and material prosperity, the greater would be their insight into political matters and the keener their desire for political advancement'. Bonnerjee then laid down four main objects of the Congress which were: (1) promotion of personal intimacy and friendship among the persons working in the country's cause; (2) eradication by direct intercourse of all possible racial, communal and provincial prejudices amongst all lovers of our country and development of the sentiment of national unity; (3) recording of the matured opinions of the educated classes in India on the more important and pressing social questions of the day; and finally, (4) determination of the line of action to be followed by Indian politicians during the following year. The first three objects were well worked out, but the fourth one was given little importance in subsequent years.[60]

The speeches of the delegates which followed were characterized by moderation and extreme effusion of loyalty to the British Crown. According to the correspondent of the Calcutta weekly *Rais and Rayyet*, the most remarkable things about the first Congress session were the moderation, earnestness, practicality and loyalty of its representatives. Almost every member tried to be brief, concise and to the point, and the moderation which they displayed in their tone and language might have put to shame the most moderate Anglo-Indian.[61] The proceedings of this Congress were conducted in a very orderly and efficient manner, and in spite of some differences of opinion among the representatives, all the resolutions were adopted in perfect harmony. Some government officials also took part in drafting the resolutions, and Justice Mahadev Govind Ranade even spoke at the open session of the Congress.[62]

The first Congress adopted nine resolutions, which 'marked the beginning of the formulation of India's political demands'. The first resolution demanded the appointment of a Royal Commission to inquire into the working of the Indian administration. Indians were to be represented adequately on this commission and evidence was to be taken both in India and in England. The second resolution demanded the abolition of the Council of the Secretary of State for India. Full responsibility for the Indian administration was to be entrusted to the House of Commons and the Secretary of State was to be made directly responsible to Parliament. This would provide a parliamentary safeguard against bureaucratic actions. The third resolution demanded the creation of Legislative Councils for the North-West Provinces and Avadh and for the Punjab. Another resolution demanded the reform and expansion of the supreme and local legislative councils by the admission of a considerable proportion of elected members. These members would have the right to discuss budgets and also the right of interpellation. A standing committee was to be constituted by the House of Commons to receive and consider formal protests from majorities in the Councils against the flouting of their decisions by the Executive authorities. All the resolutions mentioned above were related to changes in the framework of government. There was a resolution relating to administrative reform which demanded that competitive examinations should be held simultaneously in India and England for appointments in various civil departments of the public service, and that the maximum age of candidates for entrance into the covenanted civil service should be raised to 23. The resolution relating to finance protested against the proposed increase in the military expenditure of the Empire. It demanded that military expenditure should be reduced and the budget balanced by reducing top official salaries and imposing customs duties on imported goods. It called for exemption from income tax of all annual incomes up to Rs 1,000. There was also a resolution on foreign policy. The Congress condemned the war in Upper Burma and opposed its annexation to the Indian Empire of Great Britain. The resolution further demanded that the new territory, if annexed, should be kept separate from India as a crown colony. Finally, the Congress resolved to hold its next session in Calcutta on 28 December 1886.[63]

A few pertinent observations may be recorded here about the composition and character of the first Congress. Regarding its composition, it may be said that the members of the Congress belonged mostly to the new English-educated professional middle class, composed of lawyers, doctors, journalists and teachers, many of whom also held some land. It was this class of people who had taken the initiative in establishing local political associations before the birth of the Congress, and they had common interests, values and aspirations. Among them again lawyers formed the predominant group. Dr Anil Seal has pointed out that over half of the delegates at the first Congress, 39 out of 72, were lawyers, and that for decades to come more than one-third of the delegates at every Congress, belonged to the legal profession. The old aristocracy, people like rajas, maharajas, big zamindars and very wealthy merchants, were conspicuous by their absence in the Congress organization. Nor did the peasants and artisans feel attracted to it.[64] Though a very restricted gathering, the first Congress was representative of different sections of the educated people of this country. Almost all leading Indian political associations were represented in it, and so were the principal Indian-owned newspapers, members of legislative councils and presidents and members of municipal committees and local boards. Hindus of different castes. Christians (native, European and Eurasian), Parsis, Jains and Muslims took part in the first Congress session. The number of Muslims was, however, only two, and both of them, R.M. Sayani and A.M. Dharamsi, came from Bombay. The Muslim representation substantially increased later; it was 33 out of a total of 434 in 1886 and 116 out of 677 in 1890.[65] But the Congress could never claim to represent the majority of the Indian Muslims. At the initial stage, this Muslim abstention was due largely to the opposition of Sir Syed Ahmad Khan of Aligarh who launched an open attack on the Congress in December 1887.[66]

The Congress at this initial stage was, however, far from being a well-knit political organization. It had no regular paying membership, no central office, no official other than a general secretary (a post occupied by Hume himself) and no regular funds. Members of the first Congress were not elected but chosen. They became delegates by paying a small fee. In the following year, however, the delegates were elected at public meetings held for this purpose in different provinces. For quite a number of years the Congress did not have any written constitution. Every year its session was held in a different Indian city under a different president, and it was managed by a local reception committee with locally collected funds. After the session was over this committee remained in existence for a few months to arrange the printing and distribution of the Congress Proceedings. 'As far as its organization and finances were concerned, each session was a separate and independent undertaking.'[67] Yet, as Dr A.C. Banerjee has aptly remarked, 'the Congress grew from strength to strength because it made itself the mouthpiece of national aspirations and attracted the support of thousands who did not attend its sessions'.[68]

Analysing the political views of the Congress, we find in the first place that it was thoroughly loyal to the British Government. Percival Spear has rightly pointed out that the members of the first Congress were 'almost more concerned with insisting on their loyalty and the blessings of British rule than calling for progress and reforms'.[69] W.C. Bonnerjee, in his presidential address, referred to the various blessings of British rule in India. Dadabhai Naoroji, speaking at this Congress, observed, 'Britain is the parent of free and representative Government and . . . we, as her subjects and children, are entitled to inherit the great blessing of freedom and representation'.[70] Subramania Iyer, the first speaker on the first resolution, also declared that 'by a merciful dispensation of Providence India . . . has been brought under the dominion of the great British power. . . . The rule of Great Britain has, on the whole, been better in its results and direction than any former rule'.[71] The very growth of a feeling of national unity among the Indian people was, according to this speaker, a result of British domination over India. At the concluding session of this Congress Hume proposed three cheers for Her Majesty the Queen Empress, and the whole house applauded him.[72]

In the second place, the Congress emphasized from the very beginning the unity of the Indian nation. The first Congress was certainly not 'thoroughly representative of the entire nation', as Hume claimed; the old aristocracy as well as the masses of peasants and artisans remained outside its pale. But, the new professional middle class which constituted the great bulk of the Congress delegates believed that 'they were representing the best interests of the Indian people'. In fact, 'no aspiration was more warmly felt or keenly expressed during the Congress than that for national unity'.[73] The Bombay correspondent of the London *Times* reported (weekly edition, 5 February 1886): 'For the first time, perhaps, . . . India as a nation met together. Its congeries of races, its diversity of castes, all seemed to find common ground in their political aspirations'.[74] Though the Muslims did not join the Congress in large numbers, it cannot be said that the Congress made any discrimination against them or against the followers of any other religion or sect. The second annual session of the Congress (1886) was presided over by a Parsi, Dadabhai Naoroji; the third (1887) by a Muslim, Badruddin Tyabji; and the fourth (1888) by a Christian, George Yule. Social questions and regional issues were intentionally excluded from the deliberations of the Congress because this might lead to serious differences amongst members of different castes, sects and religious communities, ultimately resulting in a schism within the national organization. Dadabhai Naoroji emphasized in his presidential address of 1886 that the Congress must confine itself to questions in which the entire nation had a direct interest.[75]

In the third place, though not aspiring for the country's freedom and cherishing a firm faith in the British sense of justice, the leaders of the Indian National Congress demanded political reforms and stood for orderly political progress along constitutional lines. They were not lacking in patriotism but being realists, they felt that a direct challenge to the British rule was bound to meet with failure at that time. Therefore they concentrated their energies on building up a strong public opinion in India, arousing the political consciousness and national spirit of the people and educating and uniting them on political and economic questions.[76] While professing loudly their loyalty to the British Crown, they claimed a share in the government of the country. That is why their programme centred on the reform of the legislative councils. They demanded expansion of these councils by the introduction of an elective element into their composition and the enlargement of their functions.

True, the leaders of the Congress did not demand voting rights for all Indian citizens; but universal adult suffrage was unknown even to England at that time. It is generally admitted that the Congress demand for the introduction of representative institutions had some influence on the making of the Indian Councils Act of 1892, though, unfortunately, this Act did not contain any provision for direct election.[77]

With regard to the Indian administration, the Congress wanted the British Parliament to take a more keen and lively interest in Indian affairs. That is why they demanded the abolition of the Council of the Secretary of State for India and making the Secretary of State directly responsible to Parliament. This demand was based upon the idea that the English people were essentially just and fair, and if properly informed, would never deviate from the right path. It was in this belief that the Congress later decided to carry on political propaganda in England. The British Committee of the Indian National Congress was formed in July 1889, and a sum of Rs 45,000 per annum was voted for its support. Later the journal *India* was launched in England for the same purpose.[78]

The Congress laid special stress on the civil services for two reasons. In the first place, the posts in the Indian Civil Service carried very high salaries and pensions in those days, and monopolization of these posts by Englishmen would mean a heavy drain of wealth from this country. Secondly, it was morally degrading for educated and talented Indians to take their orders always from their English superiors and to lose, in course of time, all their administrative talents. It was to enable educated Indian youths to enter the Indian Civil Service in larger numbers that the Congress demanded simultaneous competitive examinations in India and England and also a higher age limit for these examinations. This was, of course, a repetition of the demand made earlier by the Indian Association and other local political bodies.[79]

The economic demands of the Congress naturally reflected the interests and aspirations of the educated professional middle class which constituted the bulk of this national organization. The demand for raising the taxable minimum on incomes was designed to benefit primarily this section of people. The fact that landed incomes were sought to be exempted from taxation bears striking evidence to the influence of the landed gentry on the Congress.[80] But the Congress was not oblivious of the misery of the Indian masses. Dadabhai Naoroji in his presidential address at the Congress felt a deep sympathy for the poor people of this country,[81] and the Congress soon demanded a permanent settlement with the ryots, relaxation of the rigidity of forest laws and lowering of the salt tax which was a great burden on the poorer classes. The Congress also believed that the introduction of representative institutions would prove 'one of the most important practical steps towards the amelioration of the condition of the people'.[82]

It is interesting to note that from its very inception the Congress took an interest in India's foreign policy. Its condemnation of the aggressive war in Upper Burma and opposition to the annexation of that country clearly showed that the Congress leaders were quite conscious of the dangers to which India was exposed on account of her imperialist connection. Significantly enough, the Congress also opposed the proposed rise in the military expenditure of the Empire. Probably, it apprehended that the British Government might involve India in still more wars during the years to come.

Though the Congress demands were rather mild and moderate in character at this initial stage, the leaders of the national organization wanted to create a strong public opinion in the country in their favour. One of the resolutions which the first Congress adopted on the closing day provided for the ratification of the decisions of the Congress by political associations all over the country. This resolution also clearly showed, as S.R. Mehrotra has observed, that the national leaders wanted the Congress to be 'no isolated demonstration, but the beginning of a movement'.[83]

The reaction of the British Government and the British people to the establishment of the Congress was not very favourable, if we leave aside some honourable exceptions. *The Times* of London seized upon the weaknesses of the Congress, namely the absence of adequate Muslim representation, the preponderance of lawyers, teachers and journalists in the organization, the neglect of social reform and so on. It then reminded the Congress leaders in a blatant manner that India was won by force and must be governed by force. 'If we were to withdraw, it would be in favour not of the most fluent tongue or of the most ready pen, but of the strongest arm and the sharpest sword.'[84] It is evident that the editor of this very influential English newspaper looked upon the Congress as the greatest enemy of British rule in India, in spite of its leaders' repeated and loud profession of loyalty. The Anglo-Indian newspapers of this country showed little interest in the Congress.

The attitude of the Viceroy, Lord Dufferin, was somewhat ambiguous. There is no doubt that, initially, he was not hostile to Hume's idea of holding a yearly conference of the Indian National Union. As Professor B.B. Misra has observed, the viceroy most probably wanted the Congress to act as 'a barometer of public opinion'.[85] He was also not opposed to all constitutional demands of the Congress. In a speech delivered in 1886 he declared:

> My own ambition would be to examine carefully and seriously the demands which are the outcome of these various movements, to give quickly and with a good grace whatever it may be possible or desirable to accord, to announce that these concessions must be accepted as a final settlement . . . for the next ten or fifteen years, and to forbid mass meetings and incendiary speechifying.

Evidently, the viceroy's intention was to separate the loyalist elements among the educated classes from the extremists. Dufferin even admitted that 'Putting aside the demands of the extremists . . . the objects even of the more advanced party are neither very dangerous nor very extravagant', and that he had met a considerable number of able and sensible Indians upon whose loyal co-operation he could undoubtedly rely.[86] Although, for political reasons, no government servant could take an active part in the work of the Congress, the viceroy himself invited to a garden party some of the leading Congress delegates who had assembled at Calcutta in December 1886.[87] He, however, made it quite clear that by doing so he was not according the Congress any official recognition. By 1888, however, Dufferin's attitude completely changed. In November 1888, he wrote a minute on the Congress, pointing out clearly its narrow social base, its preoccupation with constitutional questions and lack of concern for the real grievances of the masses. A single piece of legislation such as the Bengal Tenancy Act or the Oudh Rent Bill, he wrote, would bring greater happiness to thousands of peasant homes in India than the acceptance of all the constitutional demands of the Congress.[88] About a month later, the viceroy made a scathing attack on the Congress in the course of his speech at the St Andrews' Day Dinner in Calcutta. He plainly told his audience that the British Government would never allow the Congress which represented 'a microscopic minority' of the population of India to control her administration.[89] Taking his cue from the viceroy, Sir Auckland Colvin, Governor of the North-West Provinces, tried to put many obstacles in the way of holding the Congress session at Allahabad in December 1888.[90] Yet, Dufferin was far too astute a statesman to disregard totally the constitutional demands of the Congress, and very soon he wrote a confidential despatch to the Home Government, putting forward some proposals for liberalizing the composition of the legislative councils. These proposals, first published in the *Bengalee* in March 1889, later formed the basis of the Indian Councils Act of 1892.[91] Dufferin also appointed a commission of inquiry to consider the demand for more general and higher employment of Indians in the public services.[92]

Taking everything into consideration, the first Congress session at Bombay in December 1885 was a unique and historic occasion. As Professor S.R. Mehrotra has pointed out, the 'representatives' who attended this Congress session were quite conscious that they were making history. 'Surely never has so important and comprehensive an assemblage occurred within historical times on the soil of India,' claimed W.C. Bonnerjee in his presidential address. The establishment of the Congress quickened the growth of political consciousness of the Indian people. The Congress itself was a visible symbol of their growing unity as a nation. Its Bombay session demonstrated that united action in India was not completely impossible, that educated Indians could meet and deliberate successfully on a common political platform and dare to criticize the actions of the British Government in India while proclaiming their loyalty to the British Crown. The resolutions adopted at this session were widely circulated in the country and discussed by local political associations. Indian newspapers like the *Indian Mirror, Hindoo Patriot, Hindu, Indu Prakash, Hindusthani* and others heartily welcomed this new organization and put forward various suggestions for the consideration of the next Congress.[93] True, the Congress was still a very weak organization, its views were rather mild and moderate and the obstacles in its way numerous. But, as Pattabhi Sitaramayya, the first official historian of the Congress, has observed:

> Great institutions have always had small beginnings, even as the great rivers of the world start as thin streams. . . . It [the Congress] had to cut its way through mighty obstacles and therefore entertained modest ideals. . . . From an attitude of prayerfulness and importunity, it developed self-consciousness and self-assertion.[94]

Notes and References

1. S.D. Collet, *Life And Letters of Raja Rammohun Roy,* edited by P.C. Ganguly and D.K. Biswas (Calcutta, 1962), Chapter VIII.
2. R.C. Majumdar, *History of the Freedom Movement in India,* Vol. I (Calcutta, 1962), pp. 315-16.
3. Ibid., pp. 316-17.
4. Ibid., pp. 318-19; A.C. Banerjee, *The New History of Modern India* (Calcutta, 1983), p. 351.
5. B. Chandra, A. Tripathi and B. De, *Freedom Struggle* (New Delhi, 1983), pp. 52-3.
6. Ibid., pp. 36-7.
7. R.C. Majumdar, op. cit., pp. 352-54.
8. Ibid., pp. 354-55.
9. Ibid., pp. 329-34.
10. Ibid., pp. 381-83.
11. Ibid., p. 385; Anil Seal, *The Emergence of Indian Nationalism* (Cambridge, 1968), pp. 246-48.
12. R.C. Majumdar, op. cit., pp. 367-68.
13. Ibid., pp. 368-70.

14. Ibid., pp. 370-72.
15. B. Chandra, A. Tripathi and B. De, op. cit., p. 55.
16. Ibid., also R.C. Majumdar, op. cit., pp. 372-73.
17. Ibid., pp. 373-75; A.C. Banerjee, op. cit., p. 443.
18. R.C. Majumdar, op. cit., pp. 375-76.
19. Ibid., p. 377; S.R. Mehrotra, *The Emergence of the Indian National Congress* (Delhi, 1971), pp. 361-62.
20. Anil Seal, op. cit., pp. 256-57.
21. N.S. Bose, *The Indian National Movement — An Outline* (Calcutta, 1982), p. 51.
22. Ibid., p. 52.
23. S.N. Banerjea, *A Nation In Making* (*Oxford University Press*, 1963. First published in 1925), p. 80.
24. R.C. Majumdar, op. cit., pp. 378-79; Anil Seal, op. cit., pp. 261-62.
25. S.R. Mehrotra, op. cit., p. 394; Anil Seal, op. cit., p. 263.
26. Ibid., p. 264; S.R. Mehrotra, op. cit., pp. 387-89.
27. Ibid., pp. 390-92; Annie Besant, *How India Wrought For Freedom* (New Delhi, 1975, originally published in 1915), pp. 1-3.
28. Anil Seal, op. cit., p. 265; S.N. Banerjea, op. cit., pp. 81-2.
29. Anil Seal, op. cit., p. 264.
30. B. Martin (Jr), *New India, 1885* (*Oxford University Press*, 1970), pp. 53-56.
31. R.C. Majumdar, op. cit., p. 391; S.R. Mehrotra, op. cit., pp. 354-55.
32. B. Martin (Jr), op. cit., p. 70.
33. S.R. Mehrotra, op. cit., pp. 382-88, 393-95.
34. B. Martin (Jr), op. cit., pp. 77-8.
35. Ibid., p. 118, and S.R. Mehrotra, op. cit., pp. 395-98.
36. W. Wedderburn, *Allan Octavian Hume, Father of the Indian National Congress* (London, 1913), pp. 80-1.
37. Ibid., p. 101.
38. Ibid., p. 77.
39. R.C. Majumdar, op. cit., p. 392.
40. R.P. Dutt, *India Today* (Calcutta, 1979), p. 309.
41. Quoted in Anil Seal, op. cit., p. 269.
42. Ibid., pp. 270-71.
43. R.C. Majumdar, op. cit., p. 389.
44. B. Chandra, A. Tripathi and B. De, op. cit., p. 57.
45. Ibid.
46. W.C. Bonnerjee, Introduction to *Indian Politics*, edited by G.A. Natesan (Madras, 1898), pp. vii-viii.
47. Anil Seal, op. cit., p. 276.
48. B. Pattabhi Sitaramayya, *The History of the Indian National Congress*, Vol. I (Bombay, 1946), p. 16.
49. S.N. Banerjea, op. cit., p. 92.
50. S.R. Mehrotra, op. cit., pp. 402-03; B. Pattabhi Sitaramayya, op. cit., p. 17.
51. S.R. Mehrotra, op. cit., pp. 404-05.
52. Ibid., pp. 406-07.
53. R.C. Majumdar, op. cit., pp. 394-95; Daniel Argov, *Moderates And Extremists In the Indian National Movement, 1883-1920* (Bombay, 1967), pp. 30-1.

54. S.N. Banerjea, op. cit., p. 91.
55. Ibid., p. 91; Daniel Argov, op. cit., p. 30; Anil Seal, op. cit., pp. 266-67; S.R. Mehrotra, op. cit., p. 409.
56. R.C. Majumdar, op. cit., pp. 395-96.
57. S.R. Mehrotra, op. cit., pp. 408-10.
58. Ibid., pp. 410-13; Sitaramayya, op. cit., pp. 18-9; Annie Besant, op. cit., pp. 5-6.
59. Besant, Ibid., p. 6.
60. *Congress Presidential Addresses,* published by G. Natesan & Co., pp. 3-4; *Proceedings of the Indian National Congress, Report of the First Congress,* p. 15.
61. *Reis And Rayyet,* 16 January 1886, quoted in S.R. Mehrotra, op. cit., p. 415.
62. B. Martin (Jr), op. cit., p. 306; R.C. Majumdar, op. cit., p. 400.
63. C.H. Philips (ed.), *The Evolution of India and Pakistan, 1858 to 1947, Select Documents* (London, 1962), pp. 151-52; B. Pattabhi Sitaramayya, op. cit., p. 18; R.C. Majumdar, op. cit., p. 399.
64. Anil Seal, op. cit., pp. 278-79.
65. B. Martin (Jr), op. cit., pp. 293-95; *Proceedings of the Indian National Congress, Report of the First Congress,* pp. 11-2; *Report of the Second Congress,* p. 6.
66. D. Williams and E. Daniel Potts (eds.), *Essays in Indian History* (Bombay, 1973); M. Chughtai, *The Indian National Congress and the Muslims, 1885-1896,* pp. 94-5.
67. Anil Seal, op. cit., pp. 277-78.
68. A.C. Banerjee, op. cit., p. 561.
69. Quoted in N.S. Bose, op. cit., p. 56.
70. Quoted in B. Martin (Jr), op. cit., p. 298.
71. Verney Lovett, *A History of the Indian Nationalist Movement* (London, 1968), p. 36.
72. R.P. Dutt, op. cit., p. 317.
73. B. Martin (Jr), op. cit., p. 297.
74. *Proceedings of the Indian National Congress, Report of the First Congress,* p. 153.
75. C.H. Philips (ed.), op. cit., p. 140.
76. B. Chandra, A. Tripathi and B. De, op. cit., p. 59; A.C. Banerjee, op. cit., pp. 562-64.
77. Ibid., p. 563.
78. B. Pattabhi Sitaramayya, op. cit., p. 60; Anil Seal, op. cit., p. 285.
79. A.C. Banerjee, op. cit., p. 564.
80. B. Martin (Jr), op. cit., p. 303.
81. C.H. Philips (ed.), op. cit., p. 140.
82. Ibid., pp. 152-4; A.C. Banerjee, op. cit., pp. 565-66.
83. S.R. Mehrotra, op. cit., p. 414.
84. Quoted in the *Proceedings of the Indian National Congress, Report of the First Congress,* pp. 160-61.
85. B.B. Misra, *Indian Political Parties (Oxford University Press,* 1978), p. 46.
86. Sir Alfred Lyall, *Life of the Marquis of Dufferin and Ava* (London, 1905), Vol. II, pp. 151-52.
87. B.B. Misra, op. cit., p. 47.
88. C.H. Philips (ed.), op. cit., pp. 143-45.

89. Lord Dufferin, *Speeches Delivered in India, 1884-1888* (London, 1890), pp. 237-44.
90. S.N. Banerjea, op. cit., p. 101.
91. Ibid., p. 86.
92. Verney Lovett, op. cit., p. 42.
93. S.R. Mehrotra, op. cit., pp. 417-19; R.C. Majumdar, op. cit., p. 400.
94. B. Pattabhi Sitaramayya, op. cit., p. 19.

APPENDIX 1.1

A.O. Hume's Letter to the Graduates of the Calcutta University dated 1 March 1883*

Hume's memorable letter begins with the following passage:

'Constituting, as you do, a large body of the most highly educated Indians, you should, in the natural order of things, constitute also the most important source of all mental, moral, social, and political progress in India. Whether in the individual or the nation, all vital progress must spring from within, and it is to you, her most cultured and enlightened minds, her most favoured sons, that your country must look for the initiative. In vain may aliens, like myself, love India and her children, as well as the most loving of these; in vain may they, for her and their good, give time and trouble, money and thought; in vain may they struggle and sacrifice; they may assist with advice and suggestions; they may place their experience, abilities, and knowledge at the disposal of the workers, but they lack the essential of nationality, and the real work must ever be done by the people of the country themselves.'

Hume then tries to emphasize that scattered individuals, however capable and however well-meaning, are powerless singly. What is really needed is union, organization, and well defined lines of action; and to secure these an association is required, armed and organized with unusual care, having for its object to promote the mental, moral, social and political regeneration of the people of India. 'Our little army must be *sui generis* in discipline and equipment, and the question simply is, how many of you will prove to possess, in addition to your high scholastic attainments, the unselfishness, moral courage, self control, and active spirit of benevolence essential in all who should enlist.'

Hume next proposes that a commencement should be made with a body of fifty 'founders', to be the mustardseed of future growth. 'If only fifty men, good and true, can be found to join as founders, the thing can be established, and the further development will be comparatively easy.' The details of the organization will have to be decided by the members themselves. But Hume makes some suggestions as to the personnel, discipline, and working methods of the association; and specially he insists on its constitution being democratic, and free from personal ambitions. The head should merely be the chief servant, and his council, assistant servants.

---

* Taken from Sir William Wedderburn's *Allan Octavian Hume, C.B., "Father of the Indian National Congress"* (London, 1913), pp. 50-3.

Hume's long letter ends with a stirring appeal: 'As I said before, you are the salt of the land. And if amongst even you, the elite, fifty men cannot be found with sufficient power of self-sacrifice, sufficient love for and pride in their country, sufficient genuine and unselfish heartfelt patriotism to take the initiative, and if needs be, devote the rest of their lives to the Cause — then there is no hope for India. Her sons must and will remain mere humble and hopeless instruments in the hands of foreign rulers for "they who would be free, *themselves* must strike the blow". And even if the leaders of thought, wedded to personal concerns, . . . dare not or will not strike a blow for their country's sake, then justly and rightly are they kept down and trampled on, for they deserve nothing better. Every nation secures precisely as good a government as it merits. If you, the picked men, the most highly educated of the nation, cannot, scorning personal ease and selfish objects, make a resolute struggle to secure greater freedom for yourselves and your country, a more impartial administration, a larger share in the management of your own affairs, then we your friends are wrong, and our adversaries right; then are Lord Ripon's noble aspirations for your good fruitless and visionary; then, at present, at any rate, all hopes of progress are at an end, and India truly neither lacks nor deserves any better government than she now enjoys. Only, if this be so, let us hear no more fractious, peevish complaints that you are kept in leading strings, and treated like children, for you will have proved yourselves such. Men know how to act. Let there be no more complaints of Englishmen being preferred to you in all important offices, for if you lack that public spirit, that highest form of altruistic devotion that leads men to subordinate private ease to the public weal, that true patriotism that has made Englishmen what they are, — then rightly are these preferred to you, and rightly and inevitably have they become your rulers. And rulers and taskmasters they must continue, let the yoke gall your shoulders never so sorely, until you realize and stand prepared to act upon the eternal truth that, whether in the case of individuals or nations, self-sacrifice and unselfishness are the only unfailing guides to freedom and happiness.'

APPENDIX II

Resolutions adopted at the First Congress, Bombay, December, 1885†

Royal Commission

I. That this Congress earnestly recommends that the promised enquiry into the working of Indian Administration, here and in England, should be entrusted to a Royal Commission, the people of India being adequately represented thereon, and evidence taken both in India and in England.

Abolition of India Council

II. That this Congress considers the abolition of the Council of the Secretary of State for India, as at present constituted, the necessary preliminary to all other reforms.

Expansion of Legislative Councils

III. That this Congress considers the reform and expansion of the Supreme and existing Local Legislative Councils by the admission of a considerable proportion of elected members (and the creation of similar Councils for the N.W. Provinces and Oudh, and also for the Punjab) essential; and holds that all Budgets should be referred to these Councils for consideration, their members being moreover empowered to interpellate the Executive in regard to all branches of the administration; and that a Standing Committee of the House of Commons should be constituted to receive and consider any formal protests that may be recorded by majorities of such Councils against the exercise by the Executive of the power, which would be vested in it, of overruling the decision of such majorities.

Simultaneous Examinations in England and India

IV. That in the opinion of the Congress the competitive examinations now held in England, for first appointments in various civil departments of the public service, should, henceforth, in accordance with the views of the India Office Committee of 1860, be held simultaneously, one in England and one in India, both being as far as practicable identical in their nature, and those who compete in both countries being finally classified in one list according to merit, and that the successful candi-

---

† Taken from *The Indian National Congress*, published by G.A. Natesan & Co., Madras, 1917, Part II, pp. 1-2.

dates in India should be sent to England for further study, and subjected there to such further examinations as may seem needful. Further that all other first appointments (excluding peonships, and the like), should be filled by competitive examinations held in India, under conditions calculated to secure such intellectual, moral, and physical qualifications as may be decided by Government to be necessary. Lastly, that the maximum age of candidates for entrance into the Covenanted Civil Service be raised to not less than 23 years.

Military Expenditure

V. That in the opinion of this Congress the proposed increase in the military expenditure of the Empire is unnecessary, and regard being had to the revenue of the Empire and the existing circumstances of the country, excessive.

VI. That in the opinion of this Congress if the increased demands for military expenditure are not to be, as they ought to be, met by retrenchment, they ought to be met, firstly, by the reimposition of the customs duties; and secondly, by the extension of the license tax to those classes of the community, official and non-official, at present exempted from it, care being taken that in the case of all classes a sufficiently high taxable minimum be maintained. And further, that this Congress is of opinion that Great Britain should extend an imperial guarantee to the Indian debt.

Annexation of Upper Burma

VII. That this Congress deprecates the annexation of Upper Burma and considers that if the Government unfortunately decide on annexation, the entire country of Burma should be separated from the Indian Viceroyalty and constituted a Crown Colony, as distinct in all matters from the Government of this country as is Ceylon.

Congress Resolution

VIII. That the resolutions passed by this Congress be communicated to the Political Associations in each province, and that these Associations be requested with the help of similar bodies and other agencies within their respective provinces to adopt such measures as they may consider calculated to advance the settlement of the various questions dealt with in these resolutions.

Next Congress

IX. That the Indian National Congress re-assemble next year in Calcutta, and sit on Tuesday, the 28th of December, 1886, and the next succeeding days.

Chapter II

Moderates and Extremists
The Congress till the Surat Split

S.R. Singh

1. The Early Congress — Organization of the Educated Urban Middle Classes

THE ORIGIN OF the Congress as recounted in Chapter I is a matter of some controversy with regard to the respective roles of Hume and Dufferin[1] in its inception, the nature of the Congress,[2] and its achievements.[3] A careful scrutiny,[4] however, will show that the history of the Indian National Congress is the story of the birth, teething troubles, infancy, childhood, adolescence and maturity of the Indian nation. The scholar will have to take into consideration all factors animating its life, and not only one which suits his particular point of view.

During the fourth quarter of the 19th century there was a general atmosphere encouraging the growth of all-India associations which might seek to fulfil the rising aspirations of the thinking section of the Indian people. Of all the attempts made, that of Hume was the most successful. The seed of the Congress is to be largely found in Hume's stirring letter[5] to the graduates of Calcutta University dated 1 March 1883. This letter was responded to by men who came forward from all parts of India to form the 'Indian National Union.' A preliminary report was prepared and issued to members, containing suggestions and conclusions. The Union appeared to be absolutely unanimous in insisting that universal loyalty to the British Crown would be the keynote of the institution. The union would also be prepared to oppose, when necessary, by constitutional means, all authorities in India or in England, high or low, whose acts or omissions were opposed to the principles of the Government of India as laid down from time to time by the British Parliament and endorsed by the British sovereign. But continued affiliation of India to Great Britain was thought to be absolutely essential to the interests of Indian national development.[6]

The following qualifications for membership were most commonly insisted on: (1) an unblemished record, public and private; (2) an earnest or unwavering desire to improve the status, either material, mental, moral, or political of the people of India; (3) marked natural intelligence, adequately developed by education; (4) a willingness to sink, when occasion demanded this sacrifice, selfish and personal, in altruistic and public considerations; and (5) independence of character, coupled with sobriety of judgment.[7] Accordingly, local select committees were formed at Karachi, Ahmedabad, Surat, Bombay, Pune, Madras, Calcutta, Banaras, Allahabad, Lucknow, Agra and Lahore, all of which promised to attend the Conference at Pune.[8] It was proposed that until the formation of a Central Committee, there should be a General Secretary to the whole Union whose duty should be not only to activize the select committees, but also to look after the practical details connected with the conference, receive all communications from the various committees and circulate these to others, and generally supervise the office work of the Union. This tiresome duty fell to the lot of Hume. Having thus laid the foundations of a national organization to voice the aspirations of the Indian people, Hume proceeded to England to influence the British Parliament and British public.[9]

Hume came back to India in early December 1885. At the last moment the venue was shifted from Pune to Bombay, the session to meet on 28-30 December 1885. This meeting of the Congress marked a red-letter day in the life of the Indian nation. The detailed report of the first Congress does not give that vivid picture of the scene as has been given in the account of the 'Special Correspondent' (pseudonym, Chiel) of the *Reis and Rayyet* (a Calcutta Weekly) which can help us recapture even today something of the spirit of the occasion and of the distinguished men there.[10] The adjectives used to describe the first Congress were, 'historic,' 'unique,' 'colourful,' 'national,' and 'thoroughly representative.'[11] Drawing a graphic picture of the growth of Indian national consciousness, Briton Martin talks of Dufferin's lost opportunity. By July 1885, the warm rapport between Dufferin and Young India began to cool. Dufferin gradually moved away from liberalism.[12] The maturing of the forces that would give birth to the Congress was taking place first. According to Martin, 'At the beginning of 1885, the educated Indian leaders were still searching for their role and purpose in British Indian society. By the end of the year, they had found both. "New India" stood forth "unveiled". It stood in opposition to official policy.'[13]

The core resolution adopted at the first session of the Congress was a prayer for substantial popular representation on the Indian Legislative Council and ran as follows: 'Resolved — that this Congress considers the reform and expansion of the supreme and existing Local Legislative Councils, by the admission of a considerable proportion of elected members (and the creation of similar Councils for the North-West

Provinces and Oudh, and also for the Punjab) essential; and holds that all Budgets should be referred to those Councils for consideration, their members being moreover empowered to interpellate the Executive in regard to all branches of the administration; and that a Standing Committee of the House of Commons should be constituted to receive and consider any formal protest that may be recorded by majorities of such Councils against the exercise by the Executive of the power which would be vested in it, of over-ruling the decisions of such majorities.' This was moved by K.T. Telang, seconded by Subramania Iyer and supported by Dadabhai Naoroji. This is the resolution of which Mr Hume said that it 'indicated the very essence of the great task which the people of India, at last a nation, one and indivisible henceforth, and for ever, was solely and deliberately girding up their loins to undertake.'[14]

Much has been made of the Congress being a political organization as against a social body. This arose from the statements of early Congress leaders like Bonnerjee[15] and Dadabhai Naoroji. The former claimed that it was on his advice that the Congress leaders agreed to leave out social questions from the Congress movement and make it a purely political one.[16] The latter also declared the Congress a political body.[17] A number of Congress presidents affirmed this opinion.[18] In 1888, at the instance of Badruddin Tyabji, president of the third Congress, a resolution, providing that the Congress would not discuss any subject to which Hindu or Muslim delegates were in each group opposed, or nearly unanimously opposed, the object being to remove the apprehensions of the Muslim minority community.[19] It was not that Congress leaders were not for social change. Rather they wanted to avoid such problems as might create dissensions in the Congress. There were different social problems among different communities, castes, creeds and races in different parts of the country and at various stages of development. These problems could be tackled at their own levels. In their own way, Congress leaders were working for social amelioration. Dadabhai Naoroji, for example, the son of a Parsi priest, had started a journal, *Rast Goftar*, for social reform. But they wanted to avoid any matter which might be detrimental to united political action.

Already, certain Muslim detractors of the Congress, egged on by their British supporters, were spitting venom against the Congress. Sir Syed Ahmad Khan and many other opponents had already started calling the Congress a Hindu body. Even in the political sphere of its activity, the Congress had to face strong Muslim opposition. Two of its main demands — reform of the Council on an elective basis and simultaneous examinations for recruitment to the Indian Civil Service — were considered by Syed and his party as harmful to the Muslims.[20] The Congress could not convince him that the demands served the common interests of Hindus and the Muslims alike. So it had to agree in 1889 to Bradlaugh's proposal that the total number of seats for the minority community to be filled by election, should not be less than the proportion of their population in a province.[21]

Even among the Hindus there was difference of opinion among the Conservatives and the Progressives with regard to certain matters. For example, while all agreed that simultaneous examinations should be held in India, many, including Rajendralal Mitra, Chairman of the Reception Committee of Calcutta Congress (1886), was opposed, mainly on religious grounds,[22] to the idea of candidates selected in India having a compulsory training in England.

As a result, the Congress resolution of 1886 omitted this point, which had been included in a resolution of 1885. In 1888, John Adam again demanded that the Congress give a clear lead.[23] In view of strong opposition encountered, the resolution of 1886 was retained.

So also there was a sharp division of opinion even on an innocuous matter like the Age of Consent Bill in 1891 (which sought to mitigate the evil of child marriage by providing that marriage should not be consummated before the age of 12). Hume favoured the Bill. R.C. Mitter, a former High Court Judge, was opposed to it. Tilak was still more strongly opposed to it. He was absolutely against using the Congress platform for any social work. In 1895, his group objected to the Congress pandal being used by the National Social Conference. The controversy became very bitter and the use of the pandal was denied. Only the sagacity of Ranade, who withdrew his claim to hold the session of the National Social Conference in the Congress pavilion, saved the situation.[24] In consideration of this tendency to keep social matters distinct from the political ones, it is argued by some scholars that it is not proper to connect the national movement with the social and religious movements which are supposed to have created an atmosphere of national consciousness from which the Indian National Congress derived much inspiration.[25] This conclusion, however, is not warranted by facts. It is true that, for the sake of avoiding controversy, the leaders wanted to keep the social and political platforms apart, but the movement in 19th century India was for the total emancipation of the people and the reconstruction of different aspects of life could only be interdependent.[26]

As the representative of the entire nation, the Congress could be only 'a compendium of all the races, castes, creeds, professions, trades and occupations',[27] as well as of provinces. But this broad sweeping description does not give a correct idea of the then situation. Actually, there was a great disparity in the representation of various castes, creeds, races, professions, trades and provinces. Among the classes, the educated middle class had the largest share. The legal profession was most heavily represented among the professions. The Brahmins among the castes, were comparatively larger in number. Among the provinces, Bombay, Bengal and Madras took the lead. The masses were conspicuous by their absence. For fear of the authorities, the landed classes also stayed aloof. So the Congress was, by and large, an entirely middle-class affair.[28]

A look at the figures of the members who attended the early sessions of the Congress will bear out this statement. The total number of members attending the Congress in 1885 was 72, of which 39 were lawyers, 1 a doctor, and 14 journalists; in 1886, the total was 434, lawyers 166, doctors 16, journalists 40; in 1887, the total was 607, lawyers 206, doctors 8, journalists 43; in 1888, the total was 1,248, lawyers 435, doctors 42, journalists 73.[29] Over half the delegates at the first Congress were lawyers, and for decades to come more than a third of the delegates at every Congress belonged to that profession. There were also doctors, journalists and teachers. But there were only 2 teachers at the first Congress and 59 at the fourth. Many more, however, sympathized with the movement. Though the old aristocracy was not interested in public affairs,[30] the Congress tried to enlist its sympathy as well. Support from the princes and the aristocrats would demonstrate the unity of all India, native and British; would impress the Conservatives in Britain and would help to finance the movement. Dadabhai had been handsomely helped by the Maratha chiefs.[31] But it was not certain how long they would continue to help the Congress financially. Any frown from the Government would browbeat them into hasty retreat.

The faith of early Congressmen in the efficacy of peaceful and constitutional agitation was implicit. The press, the platform and annual sessions were their agencies. The press was the only agency through which the Congress propaganda was carried out through the year. In fact, many Congress leaders were editors of either English or Indian language newspapers[32] and wielded their pens powerfully. Among the methods of Congress propaganda, the holding of the annual session was by far the most important. At these meetings the government policy was discussed and demands were made. Only in connection with these annual meetings would Congress machinery be fully in action. The sessions attracted the attention of both the educated classes and the government. But the greatest drawback[33] was that the Congress functioned fully for only three days in the year. It had no machinery set up to carry on the work in the interval between two sessions. At the root of this neglect of organization was the strong belief of early Congressmen in the essential sense of justice and goodness of the British nation. The British people needed only to be told about the true state of affairs in

India for justice to be done. It was only the British bureaucracy that stood between the people and their rights.[34]

The Congress continued to make the same set of demands year after year. The more important of these was the reorganization of the Councils, simultaneous civil service examinations in India and Britain, the abolition or reconstitution of the India Council, the separation of the judiciary from the executive, the repeal of the Arms Act, the enlistment of Indians as volunteers in the auxiliary armed forces, the appointment of Indians to the commissioned ranks in the army, the reduction of military expenditure and the expansion of the Permanent Settlement to other parts of India. The Congress expressed opinions on all the important measures of the government and protested against the unpopular ones. The Congress was confirmed in its conviction that only by conceding these demands could the government be made popular. In spite of the annual repetition of the demands, there was no response from the government.

During the first twenty years of Congress, there was practically no change in its programme. The major demands had more or less, all been formulated at the first two or three sessions. This is borne out by a perusal of the Congress resolutions. The demand for the reform of the legislative councils and representative institutions was made by Resolution III in 1885, III and IV in 1886, II in 1887 and I in 1888. The demand for simultaneous examinations and raising of the age limit for the covenanted service examination was made through Resolution IV in 1885, VI in 1886, and II in 1888. The demand for a Royal Commission or Parliamentary Committee on India was made through Resolution I in 1885, V in 1886 and XI in 1888. Abolition of the India Council was asserted through Resolution XII in 1886, and V in 1887, and reaffirmed in 1888. Separation of judicial and executive functions and trial by jury were demanded by Resolutions IX and XI in 1886, III in 1887, and reaffirmed in 1888. Raising the taxable minimum for income tax was voiced by Resolution VI in 1887 and VIII in 1888. Careers for Indians as army officers was demanded by Resolution IV in 1887 and reaffirmed in 1888. The need for a system of technical education was put forward by Resolution VII in 1887 and Resolution IX and X in 1888. Repeal of the Arms Act was demanded by Resolution VIII in 1887 and reaffirmed in 1888. Extension of Permanent Settlement of land revenue was put forward in Resolution XIV in 1888. Investigation into police administration and setting up a commission for the purpose were requested through Resolution V in 1888.[35]

However, despite these limitations, the Congress was a national body in the true sense of the term, from the very outset. There was nothing in its programme to which any class might take exception. Its doors were open to all classes and communities. It supported the interests of the landed class and was friendly to the Indian chiefs. Charles Bradlaugh, a supporter of the Congress, took up in Parliament the case of the deposed Maharaja of Kashmir.[36] Later, the Congress passed a resolution that no Prince should be deposed on the ground of maladministration or misconduct until the charge was established to the satisfaction of a public tribunal enjoying the confidence alike of the Government and the Princes.[37] Similarly, the Congress was sympathetic to the landed aristocracy also. The Congress demanded extension of the Permanent Settlement, so favourable to the zamindars and of little benefit to the ryots and the government, though Hume opposed it.[38] The Congress did not enjoy any wide, active co-operation of the aristocracy, but it did have their sympathy. Its programme was broad enough to accommodate all interests. It may be said that it was not a party but a movement.[39] Though the leadership and, for the most part, the following, were supplied by the middle class, and the aristocracy and the masses, by and large, kept aloof, the movement was national because it generally transcended all local and executive interests.[40]

This point has been well brought out by Dr Bipan Chandra.[41] The most important problem that faced the people of India in the eyes of Indian nationalist leaders during 1880-1905 was one of their increasing impoverishment, affecting the interests of all sections of the people. The alien rulers rather than Nature were, in their opinion, to blame for this condition of the country. As their suggestions for improving conditions were not accepted, many of them began to doubt the bona fides of the rulers and to feel that the country was stagnating economically because of foreign rule and its exploitative policies, and that there could be no national economic regeneration without first getting rid of foreign rule.[42] The Indian leaders advocated economic policies which were basically anti-imperialist. They advocated basic changes in the existing economic relations between India and Britain. Even though their political demands were moderate, their economic demands were radically nationalist.[43] They vehemently opposed the attempt of alien rulers to convert India into suppliers of raw materials, a market for British manufacturers and a field for investment of foreign capital. They criticized the official policies on tariff, trade, transport and taxation as obstructing rather than helping the growth of industry, as bringing about the increasing de-industrialization of the country. Most of them opposed, on grounds both economic and political, the large-scale import of foreign capital in railways, plantations, and other industries and the facilities accorded to it by the government. By attacking expenditure on the army and the civil service, they challenged the very basis of British supremacy. By attacking the land revenue and taxation policies, they sought to undermine the financial bases of British rule. By condemning the use of the Indian army and revenue for British imperial purposes in Asia and Africa, they spotted another form of economic exploitation. Some of them even questioned the propriety of placing on Indian revenues the entire burden of British rule itself. In the form of the *drain theory,* they impressed upon the popular mind a potent symbol of foreign economic exploitation of India.

Indian leaders were concerned with the problem of economic development as a whole rather than with economic advance in isolated sectors. They wanted to examine the central question of economic growth. Developments in different fields were to be viewed in the context of their contribution to the economic development of the country. Even the problem of poverty was seen to be one of lack of production and of economic development, which again stressed, for them, the necessity of all-out industrial development. They, therefore, set rapid industrialization as their main economic goal, and they were loyal to the cause of industry and not of commerce.[44] In keeping with this national approach towards economic development, their total concern was with the welfare of the community, and as such they tried to represent the interests of all sections of society. They pleaded for an equitable system of taxation in which the burden of public revenues would be borne by those who could pay. Particularly, they consistently agitated for reduction of land revenue and sales tax. They pressed for rapid industrialization so that the sources of national income might be enlarged. They pleaded for expenditure of public revenue in such a manner as to lead to the greatest good of the greatest number. It is true, however, that they did not take up the class demands of the peasantry or the working class; they neither asked for a reform of the existing systems of land tenure nor espoused the cause of factory labour. But then theirs was a consciously national approach since they believed that all classes of Indians suffered economically under British rule and that all of them stood to gain under the programme of national economic regulation for which they were agitating. They felt that while they were engaged in the struggle for the entire nation, they should not take up the fight for justice and equality between classes. Within these limits they actively worked for the particular welfare of the peasantry and working class. They campaigned to protect the true interests of plantation labour because there was no clash in their case with any other Indian interest since their employers were foreigners. It is also a fact that, by the end of the 19th century, there were signs of new pro-labour attitudes among nationalist leaders in general. In the case of peasantry Congressmen agitated for the lowering of land revenue and for its permanent settlement. Many of them also pleaded for safeguards against tenants being rack-rented by landlords.[45]

It must be said to the credit of the nationalist leaders that, though they belonged to the urban educated middle class, they were too broad-minded and magnanimous to espouse only their particular class interest, overlooking the larger interests of the people in general. They were objective enough not to allow their economic policies to be unduly influenced by the interests of a job-hungry middle class, and on occasion, went against them when larger considerations were involved. Thus, they opposed the removal of cotton import duties, though the middle class was the chief consumer of foreign cloth; they supported protection for industries, even though the cost would ultimately have to be borne by this class; they preached swadeshi, though foreign goods were cheaper; they supported the falling rupee, even though it meant that, as buyers of imported goods, the members of this class had to pay more for them, and, as earners of fixed incomes, the educated employed stood to gain from any increase in the purchasing power of the rupee and to lose by a decrease in it; most of them supported income tax and opposed the salt tax; they wanted reduction of high salaries and increase in the salaries of chaprasis; for the promotion of industries and welfare activities, they were willing to advocate higher taxation; they criticized the development of railways which increased the comfort of the middle class and favoured expenditure on irrigation and industrial development instead; many of the nationalists also opposed the development of the country by foreign capital, even though such development would open out new avenues of employment for educated Indians; they actively agitated for the replacement of the British-created courts, which made for the ruin of the ryots through litigation, by conciliation courts or by a revival of the old panchayat system. While they took up some of the demands of the urban lower, middle and upper classes, this was done as part of the all-round agitation around the economic demands of all sections of the Indian society.[46]

Bipan Chandra does not regard the early Indian nationalists as representatives of the middle class alone and rightly views them as intellectual spokesmen of nationalism and all the new Indian classes whose outlook was guided by their solicitude for the cause of the nation as a whole rather than by the interests of their class, whatever it might have been. Even if they reflected the interests of a class or group, they did so through the prism of ideology and not directly as members or the obedient servants of that class or group.[47] Even if their outlook was capitalist, it was not out of any narrow-minded desire or prejudice to promote the interests of that class, that they stressed industrialization, but out of the conviction that industrial development along capitalist lines was the only way for the economic regeneration of the nation.[48] It was during this period that the roots of Indian nationalism were fully nourished as the nationalist leaders made the people of India conscious of the bond of common economic interests and of the existence of the common enemy, and thus helped to unite them in a common nationalism. They gave a precise nationalist form to the inchoate and incoherent economic aspirations of the people and propagated economic development.

This was a major contribution by early Congress leadership to the national cause. In this light it is difficult to agree with those who hold that the then Congress leadership was in the hands of those who barked well but shrank from biting. Perhaps the time was not appropriate for biting. The advantage of this method was that the movement went on without any serious opposition from the government; the disadvantage was that it lacked the necessary strength which alone could make the ruling authority part with some of its powers and privileges.[49]

In this context, it seems strange that Seal should say that

> . . . India was not only an agglomeration of regions in uneven stages of development; it was also a league of submerged nations, a chaos of overlapping castes, a cockpit of rival religions. Between their tongues, sects and communities there were intense competitions which under the circumstances of foreign rule mainly took the form of struggles for status.[50]

This line of thought is not new. Seal and his ilk are only repeating in more sophisticated terms, with a plethora of facts and figures, what was asserted even when the Congress was struggling for recognition. W.S. Lilly (who was for some time in the Indian Civil Service), for example, asserted that there were no political lines among the inhabitants of India; that there was no national feeling; that Indians as a rule cared for nothing outside their own family or caste; that the slogan 'India for the Indians' was meaningless; that there were no entities like Indians; that there were only Pathans or Tamils, Sikhs or Burmese, Rajputs or Marathas, Bengalis or Jats; that treating the population of India as a homogeneous people was an absurdity; that even this absurdity was surpassed when the Congress, assembling from time to time to discuss Indian affairs, pretended to be representative of races existing in such great variety and in such different psychological and moral conditions.[51] Other of Lilly's sentiments are also echoed in Anil Seal's work.[52]

Whatever detractors might say against the early Congress, it marched on from strength to strength, albeit haltingly and through trials and tribulations. The third Congress marked an important turning point in the development of the organization and refuted the numerous criticisms that Anglo-Indian editors and officials had levelled at the first and second Congresses. From the moment Hume ceased to be an intermediary between the Viceroy and the educated Indians, he directed all his efforts towards making the Congress a political success.[53] Genuine changes took place in the structure of Congress politics. The annual session now became the high point of the political year as also an outstanding social event. Attending the Congress session marked a man's political stature in his district, and to propose or second a resolution or to be on any Congress committee became highly prestigious. The local associations that had been very helpful in the formative stages, now tended to fall more and more under central direction by the Congress. The annual meeting amplified their political demands and their task was to reiterate these demands when the Congress was not in session. Many of the associations merged into the local committees of the Congress, and henceforth their initiative was restricted more and more to provincial matters. Another feature, in imitation of the Congress, was that provincial conferences were held at Pune, Calcutta and Madras in 1888, where local matters, outside the ken of the all-India body, were discussed in addition to extending support to the National Congress and thus strengthening its hands.[54]

Some other changes were also taking place. Hume's dominance over the early Congress, because of the feeble nature of its organization, was very great. The vagueness of the Congress constitution at the first and second sessions was obvious. At the Calcutta session (1886), Rajendralal Mitra insisted on the Bengalis being given a proper share in its direction; 'we cannot join the Congress to play the role of the bearer of the hubble-bubble *[hukkabardar]* of anybody else,'[55] he declared. A decision was taken to accelerate local activities through the formation of Standing Congress Committees at all important centres.[56] Bombay and Calcutta promptly followed the directive and formed local committees and sent out circulars about the need for better organization before the 1887 session. But even so, the working of the Congress at Madras was still deficient. No one was told what the agenda was, or how it would be drawn up. There was still no constitution, laying down rules for electing delegates or conducting the sessions. The arrangements for publicity were also poor. These weaknesses were too glaring to be ignored and the Madras Congress set up a representative committee to draft the new rules. These were intended to give the Congress a definite institutional form which would keep it active between its annual sessions. Its local standing committees were to meet regularly, and they were to be composed of all the delegates who had attended the previous annual Congress. Under their auspices, sub-committees were to be formed to meet once a week at important centres. A change was to take place in the Central organization as well. Hitherto, the general secretary had held office at the pleasure of the different Congress Committees;[57] from now on, he was to be elected by each Congress for the ensuing year. There was, however, not much support for the clear-cut provisions of the draft rules presented at the Congress. They were never adopted and organization remained as flaccid as ever until it adopted a Constitution in 1899.[58]

The early Congress was faced with many difficulties, internal and external, organizational and financial, and, above all, born out of inexperience. But the greatest handicap of all was the apathy, ridicule and active hostility of the authorities, both high and low, which was only to be expected. The Congress was the embodiment of the aspirations of nascent Indian nationalism. The British Government in India was, at best, a benevolent, paternalistic despotism; and, at worst, a callous alien bureaucracy interested only in advancing British imperial interests. The then Congress wanted Indians to accept the sovereignty of the British monarchy, conditional on their enjoying the rights and privileges of British citizens. This the authorities could never stomach. As B.R. Nanda points out:

> The demand for holding the entrance examination to the I.C.S. simultaneously in India and England, and for the grant of commissions to Indians in the army directly threatened the British monopoly of higher ranks of civil and military services. The separation of the judicial from the executive functions was seen as an attempt to weaken the authority of the district officer — the kingpin of the administration. The call for larger and more powerful legislative councils was seen as an inroad into the functions of the Government of India and the British Parliament. The insistence on a lower duty on salt, a higher minimum for income tax, and the repeal of the Arms Act seemed sheer political demagogy. The demands for the enforcement of prohibition, a ban on prostitution, and police reform may have seemed innocent, but even their acceptance was not without its hazards to the prestige of the government.[59]

And this 'prestige' (*izzat*) was the cornerstone of British rule in India about which the Anglo-Indians were very sensitive. To most Britons in India, men like Hume and Wedderburn were, at best, cranks, and, at worst, traitors. To the official world even moderate Indian leaders like Dadabhai Naoroji, W.C. Bonnerjee, Ranade and Mehta seemed irresponsible firebrands or scheming politicians who were out to undermine the Raj.[60]

In fact, the British official class had come to nurse a deep hatred for the enlightened Indian middle class. Gone were the days when a Macaulay could glory in raising a class of Indians who would be educationally and culturally in every respect Englishmen except in their colour. After 1857, owing to the growing mutiny-phobia, lessening social contact between Europeans and Indians, easy communications between

England and India, and the rise of the ideals of neo-imperialism, there was a widening racial gulf between the Europeans and the Indians,[61] and the worst target of this racial hatred was the educated middle class, which, though small and scattered, was able and vocal, and was bidding fair to be the leader of the Indian masses.[62] The British masters could no longer afford to be indulgent towards them.

This is amply borne out by the comments of a contemporary Briton, Sir Henry J.S. Cotton, whose family had, for three generations, served in the Bengal Civil Service:

> The more Anglicised a native is, the more he is disliked by Englishmen. The sense of jealousy becomes greater. Whatever may be professed, Englishmen are ready to encourage the natives who speak broken English, those who are subject to Hindu prejudices more than those who have renounced them; and generally those who are far removed from English habits of thought and life more than those who have made a very close approach to them. They are more pleased with the backward Hindu than with his advanced compatriot, because the former has made no attempt to attain equality with themselves.[63]

Against this psychological background, it is easy to understand the official response to the Congress.

To begin with, it was cautious. Steering clear of the controversy, Dufferin was not opposed to the Congress in 1885. At Calcutta in 1886, he even entertained the delegates to a garden party at Government House as 'distinguished visitors'. This honeymoon lingered up to the third Congress (1887) at Madras where a similar compliment was paid to them by Lord Connemara, Governor of Madras.[64] But the officials were becoming wary; it was becoming dangerous to play with this toy — it was a living organism and promised to turn against its master. Years had passed and yet there were no signs of any concessions being granted. Platonic expression of sympathy was mere mockery. Hume was obsessed by the misery of the masses and the belief that most of it was preventible. In a pamphlet, *The Old Man's Hope,* he drew a pathetic picture of the condition of the peasantry. Drawing inspiration from Cobden's Anti-Corn Law League, Hume declaimed with a new militancy:

> So has it fared with us; our educated men singly, our press far and wide, our representatives at the National Congress — one and all — have endeavoured to instruct the Government, but the Government, like all autocratic governments has refused to be instructed, it will now be for us to instruct the nations, the great English nation in its island home, and the far greater nation of this vast continent, so that every Indian that breathes upon the sacred soil of this our Motherland may become our comrade and

> adjutor, our supporter, and, if need be, our soldier in the great war that we, like Cobden and his noble band, will wage for justice, for our liberties and rights.[65]

So intensive propaganda was carried in India; an appeal for funds was made to all classes of the Indian community. Tracts, pamphlets and leaflets were distributed and everywhere meetings were called. Over a thousand meetings were called, at many of which over five thousand persons were present. Arrangements were made for the distribution of half a million pamphlets. Translations into twelve Indian languages of two remarkable pamphlets, *A Tamil Congress Catechism* by Veraraghava Chariar of Madras, and *A Conversation between Moulvi Furreduddin and one Rambuksh of Kambakhtpur*, were issued. The former explained in simple language the aims of the Congress, its demands for representative councils, and the need for organizing affiliates in town and village and for contributing funds to the Congress. The latter showed through a parable the necessary evils of absentee state landlordism, however benevolent the intention might be.[66]

Once the propaganda began to be addressed to the masses, the official attitude, which till then had been one of more or less friendly neutrality, became distinctly antagonistic.[67] Hume delivered a speech at Allahabad on the 30 April 1888, which was published under the title 'A Speech on the Indian National Congress, its Origin, Aims and Objects.'[68] But the officials continued to be critical and Dufferin's image of the Congress, its leaders and its principal mentor was that they were 'unrepresentative, misguided and disloyal.'[69] Needless to say, Indians continued to hold Hume in the highest esteem. Speaking at the Hume Memorial Meeting in London on 6 August 1912, Gokhale said, 'No Indian could have started the Indian National Congress. . . . If the founder of the Congress had not been a great Englishman and a distinguished ex-official, such was the distrust of political agitation in those days that the authorities would have at once found some way or other to suppress the movement.'[70] Bhupendranath Basu was more eloquent when he said that Hume had the courage

> to conceive and carry out what great Emperors and Empires in the past had failed to do. He conceived the great idea of binding together the different people and nationalities and communities and creeds of India into one common nation. . . . Who do you think had the power in the early days of the eighties, to bring together men unknown to each other, from Bombay, from Madras, from the Punjab, from Bengal, from the United Provinces?[71]

Certain indiscretions he might have committed, but Hume was irrevocably wedded to inculcating the parliamentary spirit in India.

Speaking of the spirit which it was desired to inculcate among the people, he quoted the record on the inception of the Congress which was intended

> to foster a wider altruism and a more genuine public spirit, by concentrating the most strenuous efforts on great national problems, and diminishing the absorption in local or purely selfish interests; to educate all who took part in it, not only in the art of public speaking and debate, developing the faculty of thinking out clearly opinions, and expressing them lucidly to others, not merely in habits of accuracy and research, but also in the practice of self-control, moderation and willingness to give and take — to educate them in fact into what has been described as a genuinely parliamentary frame of mind — to familiarise the country with the methods and working of representative institutions on a large scale, and thus, as this familiarity grew, to demonstrate to the Government and people of England that India was already ripe for some measure of those institutions to which the entire intelligence of the country so earnestly aspires.[72]

Having thus made clear the spirit of the movement, Hume asserted that there was no cause to fear political danger from the Congress:

> The people are taught to recognise the many benefits they owe to British rule, as also the fact that on the peaceful continuance of that rule depend all hopes for the peace and prosperity of the country. They are taught that the many hardships and disabilities of which they complain are after all, though real enough, small in comparison with the blessings they enjoy, but all these grievances may be and will be redressed if they all join to press their views and wishes unanimously, but temperately, on Government here and on the Government and people of England. The sin of illegal or anarchical proceedings is brought home to them, and the conviction is engendered that by united, patient constitutional agitation they are certain ultimately to obtain all they can reasonably or justly ask for, while by any recourse to hasty or violent action they must inevitably ruin their cause and entail endless misery on themselves.[73]

Thus Hume pleaded for the logical continuity, on the part of the British nation, of the humane and enlightened educational policy of 1833 and 1854:

> It is the British Government in their noble enthusiasm for the emancipation of this great people — God's trust to them — from the fetters of ignorance, who by the broadcast dissemination of western education and western ideas of liberty, the rights of subjects, public spirit and patriotism, have let lose forces which, unless wisely guided and controlled, might, nay sooner or later certainly must, involve consequences, which are too disastrous to contemplate. And it is precisely to limit and control these forces and direct them, while there is yet time, into channels along which they can flow auspiciously, bearing safely the argosies of progress and prosperity on their

> heaving waves, that this Congress movement was designed. The Government has, broadly speaking, never realised the vast proportions of the coming flood which is being engendered by the noble policy of which in 1833 Lord Macaulay was so prominent an exponent; and it is we of the Congress, who through good repute and ill-repute, careless of what men say of us if only haply God may bless our efforts, who standing between the country and the coming development, are labouring — labouring almost frantically — to provide in time channels through which this surging tide may flow, not to ravage and destroy but to fertilize and regenerate.[74]

This speech caused some genuine alarm among the authorities. Needless to say, Hume was working for genuine understanding between England and India.

But Dufferin had been already incensed. He had received a shock when he had been accused by Hume of inspiring a strong article in the *Pioneer* and of sending a despatch recommending restrictions on the press. When Hume had met Dufferin, the latter had charged him with spreading falsehoods and told him that he had never tried to influence a newspaper article.[75] The Governor of Bombay, Lord Reay, however, followed a policy of 'benevolent neutrality' towards the Congress. He considered it wrong policy to call Congressmen disloyal or dangerous. His policy was not to exclude from appointments those who did not belong to the Congress, nor to appoint those who were strong advocates of its policy.[76]

Not to speak of high functionaries who had always put their trust in espionage, encouraged Muslim hostility to the movement, and sought to suppress the Congress, even recommending that Hume should be deported, even a person like Sir Auckland Colvin, the Lt Governor of North-West Provinces, belonging to the liberal official camp, a distinguished member of the Civil Service who, until the new departure which followed the third Congress at Madras, was distinctly friendly to the Congress, turned hostile. His letter (8 October 1888), written in calm and courteous language, gave Hume an opportunity to clear his position. Colvin's letter covered twenty printed pages and Hume's reply (13 October 1888) was in sixty printed pages. The two letters were published as *Audi Alterum Partem* (1888). Hume wrote therein, 'You are personally hostile to the Congress . . . you desire to ruin all who take a prominent part in it . . . you will favour and reward all who oppose it. . . .'[77]

Auckland Colvin had written in his letter that he was in sympathy with the principle and general objects of the Congress; he was especially in favour of the expansion of the legislative councils. He had no objection to the proceedings of the Congress of 1885 and 1886, but the propaganda on the Anti-Corn Law pattern after 1887, aggressive and assertive, was, he felt, premature and likely to defeat the objects in view. Mischief might follow from the aggressive and denunciatory propaganda. It might produce counter-agitation and divide the country into strongly hostile camps. Colvin also took exception to the tone and substance of the pamphlets recently published. He objected to the supporters of the Congress unfairly claiming to represent the whole Indian population. He suggested that the reformers should occupy themselves with social welfare rather than political reform.[78]

Hume's reply was that, far from being premature, the fear was that the action of the Congress might be too late. Instead of being inflammatory, the pamphlets depicted the real grievances of the rural people. They were suffering because of costly and unsuitable civil courts, the corrupt and oppressive police, the rigid revenue system, and the galling administration of the Arms Act and the Forest Act. They needed cheap, sure and speedy justice; police as friends and protectors of the people; a more elastic and sympathetic land revenue system; and a less harsh administration of the Arms and Forest Laws. In this situation, the pamphlets and his speech could not 'blink or pretend to ignore the grave evils that exist,' and, as such, the pamphlets might serve as an eye-opener to the Government. Hume asserted that there was no risk of counter-agitation. In spite of Sir Syed Ahmad[79] and his friends, the whole culture and intelligence of the country was favourable to the Congress. The anti-Congress platform consisted of a small knot of 'Anglo-Indians,' mostly officials, supported by a section of the 'Anglo-Indian' press; 'a few Indian fossils, honest, but wanting in understanding; a few men who in their hearts hate British rule or are secretly in the employ of England's enemies;' and a certain number of 'time-servers,' men not really in their hearts opposed to the Congress, but who have taken up the work of opposition to it, because it has seemed to them that it will "pay." In fact, the Congress instead of dividing, was uniting, was binding in harmonious co-operation, men who previously scarcely met, except to quarrel or even to fight. The Muslims, in Hume's opinion, were a fine people, never opposed to unity, and they would gain most from united action, which would bring them into the main current of modern life. If there was any hostility, the hostile stimulus came from outside, from a few ill-advised officials, the proponents of *divide et impera* and from the 'unfriends' of the British.[80]

As to the objection that the Congress had no right to claim that it represented the people of India, Hume pointed out that in Great Britain the Mother of Parliaments represented directly only a small fraction of the people, and that less than 10 per cent of the population took part in parliamentary elections. There was no doubt that 'the Congress represented the culture and intelligence of the country', a claim later confirmed by Lansdowne when he said that the Congress represented 'the more advanced Liberal Party.' As to the advice that the Congress should devote itself only to social work, Hume's reply was that the great movement sought the regeneration of India on all lines, spiritual, moral, social and political, and that the Congress, a part of that movement, was directed to national and political objects desired by all classes in India.[81] The Government was by then very actively working against the Congress. A circular of 29 October 1888 prohibited government servants from collecting subscriptions for political purposes.[82]

A much harder blow was struck at the Congress by Lord Dufferin in his speech at a St Andrew's Day dinner on 30 November 1888. He emphasized the division of India into two major communities, and a number of minor nationalities, and criticized the Congress for seeking the introduction of a parliamentary system which England herself had evolved only by slow degrees. Dufferin believed that the institution of a democratic system in India would be a risky plunge into the unknown. According to him, no effective representation of the people was possible. He decried the Congress as a 'microscopic minority' not fit to control the administration. He branded the Congress demand for raising the income-tax exemption limit as selfish.[83] He too emphasized that the Congress should have taken up social reform.[84] It is a remarkable coincidence that the objections raised by Dufferin were very similar to those raised by Auckland Colvin.

As noted earlier (perhaps encouraged by Colvin and others), Sir Syed Ahmad mounted his opposition against the Congress and delivered militant and provocative speeches on 28 December 1887 and 4 March 1888.[85] In August 1888, the United Patriotic Association was formed which was joined by both Hindus and Muslims. Its aim was to counteract the Congress agitation and to strengthen British rule. In 1893, a new organization, called the Muhammadan Anglo-Oriental Defence Association was set up to protect Muslim interests, to prevent political agitation from spreading among Muslims and to strengthen British rule. Syed remained hostile to the Congress to the end of his life, and in this work he was helped by Theodore Beck, Principal of the college at Aligarh.[86] Some members of the aristocracy also were set up against the Congress in 1888. Raja Udai Pratap Singh of Bhinga denounced the programme and denied the representative character of the Congress.[87] The Maharaja of Banaras declared that if the Government did not put down the mischievous movement and writings, the minds of the masses might be prejudiced against it. He also said that representative institutions were not suited to India.[88] The Raja of Bhinga went to the length of accusing the Congress of fomenting communal riots, an absurd proposition. The Raja also criticized the British Government for showering honours on those who were trying to subvert it, and urged the government firmly to determine the line on which India was to be governed.[89]

The government now went to the length of putting obstructions in the path of the Congress in holding its annual session. Difficulties faced by the Congress in holding its session at Allahabad (1888) were enumerated by Ajodhyanath, the Chairman of the Reception Committee. The authorities gave and then cancelled permission for holding the session, first, at Khusro Bagh, then on a plot of waste land lying between the Fort railway station and the Fort itself. Then the Reception Committee managed to secure a group of houses belonging to the members of the Reception Committee and other friends. Some of the houses were within the cantonment limits and the military authorities raised obstacles.[90] But the Congress session was held at Allahabad in spite of these obstructions. Lowther Castle, soon after its purchase by the Maharaja of Darbhanga, was made available for Congress use. According to Ajodhyanath the people were warned in many districts by officials that they would come to grief if they joined or helped the Congress. A number of subscribers wanted to keep the fact of their aid secret. Money also came from princes and chiefs and even from men whose names appeared among the leaders of two or three anti-Congress associations sponsored by government officials.[91]

The Government's attitude during Lansdowne's viceroyalty was neither friendly nor hostile. In reply to a question, John Gorst said that Dufferin and Colvin had not objected to the Congress but to the action of some of its supporters, to the language of some of the newspapers and the character of the pamphlets.[92] Even among the Liberals the language of the pamphlets caused some flutter. Speaking on the Indian Councils Bill, Lord Northbrook said that the pamphlets had been couched in a language which, if read by any larger number of Indians, might be decidedly dangerous.[93] At the time of the Calcutta session (1890), the Bengal Government issued a circular which said that the Government of India's orders definitely prohibited the presence of government officials at such meetings. The seven admission cards to the visitors' enclosure of the Congress pavilion which had been sent to the Lieutenant Governor and the members of his household, were returned. When the attention of the Governor-General was drawn to this fact, he at once clarified that the orders had no special reference to the Congress movement which was perfectly legitimate and which private persons were free to promote. The government would respect the constitutional rights of the Congress. Government servants were to abstain from active participation in political or quasi-political movements of all kinds, and were prohibited from using their influence upon others to join or not to join them. The orders did not apply to pensioners.[94]

In 1893, the Government of India showed great concern over the widespread activities of the cow-protection societies and the outbreak of Hindu-Muslim riots in the North-Western provinces and Bombay. The cow-protection agitation spread in different provinces, but its stronghold was Bombay Presidency. The government suspected that the advanced wing of the Congress had a hand in it, and that it had been organized by men disloyal to the government. C.J. Lyall was of the opinion that the movement had been fostered from political motives.[95] Lansdowne's view was that the more advanced wing of the Congress saw in this movement a means of establishing connection between itself and the great mass of the Hindu population. 'The subterranean connection,' he wrote, 'which has now been established between the Congress and the cow will, unless I am mistaken, convert the former from a foolish debating society into a real political power, backed by the most dangerous elements in native society.'[96] Ostensibly it might be directed against the Muslims, but it might turn against the British as well. The note of the Thagi and Dacoity Department described the agitation as 'part of the Hindu revival of which the National Congress is another manifestation, the aspiration at the root of both being directed to the formation of an Indian nation and the displacement from power, place and emolument of the ruling race.'[97]

In spite of these suspicions, the government did not change its attitude towards the Congress and allowed it to hold its annual sessions. Lansdowne turned down Crosthwaite's suggestion that the situation called for an amendment of the law of conspiracy.[98] He considered the Congress a political group and showed its leaders courtesy. His attitude towards the Congress was one of 'good-humoured indifference.' When Dadabhai Naoroji, the President of the Congress in 1893, returned to England, Lansdowne said in an interview to Reuter that the government 'shows no hostility nor opposition to the movement. Of course, it is being closely watched.'[99] Opponents of the Congress were at pains to show that it represented only a very small minority. In 1892, Curzon, then Under-Secretary of State for India, said in Parliament that the Congress represented a minute and microscopic minority whose plans and policy left the 'vast amorphous residuum' absolutely untouched.[100] According to Fitzpatrick, Lieutenant Governor of the Punjab, the Congress represented an infinitesimal fraction of the population, and its demand of larger admission of Indians in the higher services could be considered only if it represented the great mass of the population.[101] George Chesney, formerly Military Member in India, was extremely hostile to the Congress, saying that it was representative only of that small and special class which wanted a larger share of the official loaves and fishes. He criticized it for demanding lowering of the income-tax exemption level since income-tax was the only one the middle class paid.[102] The Congress resolutions, he said, if taken seriously, were very vehemently condemnatory of the government, and, if implemented, would make all government impossible. In his opinion, 'the holders of these Congresses are a set of inept, blundering political charlatans. They have never made one useful or practical suggestion, but their proceedings, when not merely silly, are undoubtedly mischievous.'[103]

But these prejudices notwithstanding, there were also more sober assessments of the character of the Congress. Sir Richard Garth, for example, the former Chief Justice of Calcutta High Court and a Tory in his personal views, regarded the Congress as a large and influential association of patriotic men, who were bold enough to think for themselves and their ignorant countrymen, and had the conviction to condemn abuses and demand important reforms, such as the reduction of extravagant expenditure, the reform of the police administration, an enquiry into the Home Charges, a council for the Punjab, and the establishment of colleges. He was also of the view that many worthy persons had been deterred from taking a more direct and open part in the movement by the open hostility of the authorities towards the Congress.[104]

During the first two years of Elgin's viceroyalty there was no change in the government's attitude, and in June 1896 *India* wrote that there was good reason to believe that the Government of India was adopting a more sensible and friendly attitude.[105] But this optimism was shortlived and there ensued a long period during which the Congress could expect no sympathy from the government. In fact, in Curzon's time the Congress had only contempt and hostility in store for it. Lord George Hamilton, Secretary of State for India, remained suspicious and unsympathetic throughout. Elgin was more sympathetic, but he was too weak-willed to take any effective action. Owing to a number of events — the incidence of famines, the unpopularity of the plague operations (resulting in the assassination of Rand and Ayrst, the arrests of the Natu brothers, the imprisonment of Tilak; and the enactment of sedition laws), and the North-West Frontier expeditions, which led to strong resentment in Congress circles — the attitude of the Government stiffened during the last years of the Elgin's administration.

Government tried to stop the flow of funds to the Congress from the rich and felt very satisfied when it learnt that, in spite of his repeated requests, Wedderburn was short of funds to meet the expenses of Congress propaganda in England.[106] Congressmen were, in fact, in financial difficulty. Until 1887, members of the aristocracy sympathetic to the Congress made contributions to its fund. The Congress Report of 1886, for example, mentioned that the Maharajas of Cooch Behar, Darbhanga, Hathwa and Dumraon made contributions. The Maharaja of Darbhanga contributed Rs 2,500.[107] As reported in 1887, the Maharajas of Mysore, Vizianagram, and Travancore contributed Rs 1,000, Rs 1,000 and Rs 500 respectively. The Rajas of Cochin and Venkatgiri donated Rs 500 each. Raja Ganpati Rao and the Raja of Bobili gave Rs 325 and Rs 200 respectively.[108] When the displeasure of the authorities against the Congress became known, only a few had the courage to make donations. No doubt, a few continued to do so secretly, but, as the years rolled by, the number of princely helpers dwindled fast. In 1895, however, the Maharaja of Ramnad contributed Rs 10,000. It is mentioned in the Report of 1898 that the Reception Committee at Madras received no donation from the Native Princes or the rich classes and the funds were raised by house to house collections.[109] When the session of the Congress was held at Lucknow in 1899, the moneyed class and the landed aristocracy made no contributions for fear of government displeasure.[110]

In 1899, the Secretary of State for India (Hamilton) asked the Government of India to find out the names of the persons who financed the Congress. From 1888 onwards, Congressmen tried to keep the names of their sympathizers secret for fear of exposing them to government disapproval. Among the early supporters of the Congress, the name of Maharaja Lakshmishwar Singh of Darbhanga is well-known. The Government was also aware of this fact, but had no precise information. A contemporary report of the Intelligence Department, though not wholly reliable, supplies some revealing details. It has already been mentioned that the Maharaja had donated Rs 2,500 in 1886 and purchased the Lowther Castle in 1888, which enabled the Congress to hold its session at Allahabad. He also contributed liberally to the publication of *India,* the organ of the British Committee of the Congress, and it was the surmise of the government that it was through his munificence that the paper became a weekly one in 1898, and that he also donated Rs 1,000 each year to the Congress. But according to the Note of C.S. Bayle (the General Superintendent for the Suppression of Thugi and Dakaiti) there was no evidence to prove that the Maharaja gave any particular amount. The note, however, states that, in 1888, it was rumoured that he was going to be nominated as Congress president. In 1890 he and the Raja of Vizianagram donated Rs 5,000 each to meet the cost of Surendranath's deputation to England, and the same year he is reported to have given Rs 2,000 to W.C. Bonnerjee as a first instalment towards expenses of the next Congress session.[111] Many other donations to the Congress are said to have been made by the Maharaja.

The private letters of Hamilton to Elgin and Curzon are very revealing of his attitude towards the Congress. He was deeply hurt by the criticisms of his policy in the Indian press and in Parliament. He felt, 'They are all of them a thankless, ungrateful, venomous crew and Wedderburn ought to know better than head the gang.'[112] After the murder of Rand and Ayerst at Pune he wrote to Elgin that the more he heard of the National Congress, the more he was impressed with the seditious and double-sided character of the prime movers of the organization.[113] Pune was to him the centre of seditious propaganda and the headquarters of the more violent section of the Congress and he described the Maratha Brahmans as the ablest and the most determined of the opponents of British rule.[114]

This attitude of the authorities towards the Congress notwithstanding, the government appointed Congressmen to high offices during 1885-1900. A number were appointed as high court judges,[115] and many were appointed members of the legislative councils.[116] The appointments were made purely on the grounds of merit, but at least they signified that the Congress was not regarded as a seditious body and that its membership was not a bar to one's elevation to higher posts. The Government's policy was neither to show favours to Congressmen, nor to penalize them. The appointment of N.G. Chandavarkar as a judge of the Bombay High Court is a fact which illustrates this point. He presided over the Congress session of 1900 and was appointed judge a few weeks later. His nomination to the Bench was known before he presided over the Congress.[117] Congressmen were also selected as members of certain commissions. In 1895 Wedderburn, Naoroji and Caine, who were all members of the British Committee of the Congress, were appointed members of the Welby Commission. The Indian witnesses, namely, Banerjea, Gokhale, Wacha, G. Subramanya Iyer and K.N. Bahadurji, were all associated with the Congress. It was indeed a great achievement for the Congress. 'Though the Government sneered at the Congress claim to represent Indian opinion, it did realise that the Congress was the only body, which with all its imperfections, gave expression to the views of the educated classes.'[118]

But the Congress was being tolerated because there was no way out. The government had no means of suppressing the Congress so long as it remained wedded to constitutional means. Curzon, an imperialist to the marrow, was in search of an opportunity to destroy the Congress. He wrote to Hamilton thus: 'My own belief is that the Congress is tottering to its fall, and one of my greatest ambitions while in India is to assist it to a peaceful demise.'[119]

It has been noted earlier that the authorities were out to use any stick to beat the Congress with. They had encouraged the Muslim opposition, goaded the aristocracy to work against the Congress, pressurized all who were likely to make donations to the Congress Fund to withhold them, and to foment dissensions in Congress ranks in whatever way they could. There was also another method by which a portion of the supporters of the Congress could have been weaned away. It was the acceptance of some of the demands which had been made by the movement from time to time. Dufferin's minute of 1888, which denounced the Congress movement so strongly, also contained a plan of council reform designed to give 'full play to the legitimate and praiseworthy ambition of the loyal patriotic, and educated class'. The advantage of such a reform would be, Dufferin asserted, to shift the centre of gravity of Indian political activity 'from the self-constituted associations and the little knot of politicians and newspaper writers' to 'the really responsible classes.'[120] The Act of 1892 was regarded by the opponents of the Congress as a concession to political agitation though it fell far short of Congress demands. It would be wrong to say that the grant of demands, even in a large measure, would have meant the end of the Congress demands. It can, however, be said that the Congress would have been satisfied during the period 1885-1905 with even modest concessions.

2. Dufferin, Lansdowne and Council Reform

A close study of the initiation, the enactment, the provisions and the enforcement of the Act of 1892 will reveal the motives behind it and how far its provisions satisfied the Congress and what were its shortcomings.

Dufferin had always been in favour of reform of the councils. Accordingly, he formed a committee for this purpose which submitted its recommendations on 10 October 1888, the main ones being (1) the expansion of the Madras, Bombay and Bengal Councils with enlarged functions; (2) the establishment of an executive council in Bengal as a condition precedent to the recognition of its legislative council; (3) the reorganization of the councils with reference to the representation of the more important interests; (4) provision for direct election to the First Division of the Council, consisting of representatives of the hereditary nobility and landed classes, and for indirect election to the Second Division, consisting of the trading, professional and agricultural classes, and the European planting and commercial community; (5) the representation of the Muslims in proportion to their population; (6) the reservation of a few seats to be filled by nomination as a safeguard against any inequality in the results of elections; (7) and the division of provincial administration into two branches, general and local, and the council to be invested with larger powers over the latter.

The recommendations of the committee were limited to the reconstitution of the Councils of Madras, Bombay and Bengal. Even the reorganization of the Central Legislature was left for future consideration. The size of the provincial councils was to be decided on the advice of the provincial governments. The Committee suggested that the First

Division of Bengal Council should consist of 7 officials and 6 elected members, and the Second Division of 12 officials, 7 elected and 4 nominated members. In each division and officials were to have a majority of one.

The most important recommendations of the Committee were concerned with the enlargement of the functions of the councils. It recommended that they should have the power to originate discussion, and make suggestions on any subject connected with internal civil administration; to ask questions and, subject to certain restrictions, call for papers. It further proposed that provincial finance should be divided into general and local branches, the first relating to the subjects classified as belonging to general administration and the second to such expenditure as was incurred on schools, hospitals, sanitation, communications, town police, etc. Over the local part of the budget the council was to exercise the same control as the district boards under the local self-government acts in their own areas. In regard to the general branch of provincial finance, the council was to have less powers, but the budget was to be laid before it for discussions.

Lord Dufferin characterized the scheme 'as a plan for the enlargement of our Provincial Councils, for the enhancement of their status, the multiplication of their functions, the partial introduction into them of the elective principle, and the liberalisation of their general character as political institutions.' He thought that these proposals would place the government in contact with a large section of Indian public opinion and that the association of the 'loyal, patriotic and educated classes' with the councils would shift the centre of political gravity from the 'self-constituted associations and the little knot of politicians and newspaper writers' to the 'really responsible classes.' He characterized the proposals as a fresh advance on the road to reasonable political progress. But he stressed that there was no intention on the part of the government to bring about any radical change or to introduce a parliamentary system. He pointed out that the provision of a nominated majority in the councils and the governor's power to overrule them left no room for an approximation to the English constitutional pattern. The Committee too had emphasized that 'the only possible way of proceeding is to develop established methods and not to introduce new and untried ones.'

The Dufferin minute, in one respect, went beyond the recommendations of the Committee, which had limited its scheme of reform to the provincial councils. Dufferin suggested that the Central Council also should be vested with power to undertake a full, free and thorough examination of the policy of the government. His other proposal was to invest the Central Council with power to ask questions on matters of domestic interest. In his view, it was through these two methods that the government would be able to explain its policy and neutralize the effects of misrepresentation of its measures. He limited his suggestions to the functions of the Central Council and did not refer to the enlargement of its size.

Even to these mild proposals, there were adverse reactions. Lord Salisbury, the Prime Minister, for example, regarded the introduction of the elective system as dangerous. He said, 'we shall in no way please the classes on whose goodwill the submission of India depends; we shall not reconcile our enemies; but we shall give them arms against ourselves.'[121]

Lord Lansdowne, Dufferin's successor, was very anxious that the reforms should be expedited. He wanted to see the reformed councils functioning before he retired. He was supported in this by the Secretary of State for India. Lansdowne also made it known that the Government of India was in favour of a moderate recognition of the elective principle.[122] Cross, the Secretary of State for India, was willing to enlarge the councils and confer upon them the right of interpellation and general discussion of the budget, but, he said, the real difficulty lay in the elective principle, which would not secure the representation of the ryot 'whose sole protector is the British Government,' nor would the Muslims consent to the principle of election. He invited Lansdowne's views on the Government of India's constitutional proposals of 1888.

Lansdowne wrote back that there was a general consensus of official and non-official opinion that the existing councils lacked local knowledge and authority, that they should possess a more representative character, and that opinion was generally in favour of a part of the provincial councils being elected. Nomination, however, was considered necessary for the representation of different classes and communities like the Muslims. Lansdowne was against a uniform system for all the provinces. He was of the opinion that the number of elected members should not be more than those nominated. He rejected the argument that the territorial areas which formed the constituencies had no common interests. The matters of general interest were sanitation, schools, communications, hospitals, and the administration of the police. Adequate representation of the aristocracy was stressed by Lansdowne, which would add to the weight of the councils as well as act as a counterpoise to the influence of the elected members. He thought that the reformed councils would also counteract the activity of the 'self-constituted bodies' and conciliate the 'more reasonable' section of the educated people.[123] His other recommendations included a considerable increase in the strength of the councils and giving them the right of interpellation. Lansdowne had also suggested that there were two ways in which the exercise of the right of interpellation could be restricted:

first, by excluding *en bloc* certain classes of subjects, such as military and foreign affairs; second, not by forbidding by rule the asking of questions on certain subjects, but by empowering the president to disallow any question, which, in his view, could not be answered consistent with public interest.

But Lord Cross, the Secretary of State for India, in his despatch of 1 August 1889, made clear that he was opposed to the principle of election because it was, Cross thought, foreign to oriental institutions and, its application to the local bodies being still in the experimental stage, its extension to the provincial bodies would not be desirable.[124] In a despatch of the same date accompanying the draft bill, Cross suggested that the representation of a considerable section of the community might be best effected by a 'simple extension of the existing system.' He indicated that, at a suitable opportunity, he would submit to Parliament the proposal for the reconstitution of the Councils.[125] It is pertinent to mention here that the provisions in the draft bill did not undergo any material alterations during its passage through Parliament.[126]

The Government of India was in complete agreement with the draft scheme except in one respect. The Secretary of State had rejected its proposal concerning elections. The Government of India suggested that it might be introduced in a modified form. The Bill was finally introduced in the House of Lords in February 1892. G.N. Curzon, then Under Secretary of State, introduced it in the House of Commons on 28 March 1892.[127] The Bill was passed by both Houses of Parliament and received royal assent on 20 June 1892.

In August 1892, the Conservative government was replaced by a Liberal one. Thus, while the Indian Councils Act of 1892[128] was passed by a Conservative Government, the rules and regulations regarding the appointment of non-official members, the asking of questions and financial discussions, were sanctioned by a Liberal government. What had been in the making for quite some time ultimately took shape in 1892.

Both Lord Dufferin and Lord Lansdowne had been anxious to implement the reorganization of the councils. Early in 1886, the former had urged that whatever concessions were possible should be granted early and with good grace.[129] Lansdowne also, soon after his arrival in India, pursued this matter. In 1889, the Government of India expressed itself in favour of introducing the Indian Councils Bill into Parliament without delay.[130] But the matter was much delayed due to several factors: (1) the comparative unimportance of the subject in the eyes of the British Government, (2) general indifference towards Indian affairs, (3) the shaky position of the Conservative Party which was tending towards disintegration, (4) the anticipated difficulty in piloting the Indian Bill, which had a few enemies and no supporters, through Parliament, and

(5) Salisbury's fear that the passage of the Bill in the Commons would lead to a series of inflammatory speeches by the votaries of popular government in India, and specially by Gladstone.

The last reason seems fantastic. The real reason, it seems, was that Salisbury was not a believer in the policy of political concessions for India. Liberal members like Northbrook and Kimberley were in favour of some system of election, though they were decidedly opposed to any scheme of parliamentary government for India. Kimberley said that the notion of a parliamentary system for a vast country like India was 'one of the wildest imaginations that ever entered the minds of men'. In the view of Lord Salisbury, the prime minister, 'the principle of election or government by representation is not an eastern idea, it does not fit eastern tradition or eastern minds.'[131] He urged the House not to slip into that great innovation which, once accepted, would not admit of being confined to a restricted area.[132] Salisbury emphasized that the introduction of occidental institutions into India would bring into power not the strong and natural elements of Indian society, but its 'artificial and weakly' parts.[133]

There was little difference between the Conservatives and the Liberals on the Indian Councils Bill. It was passed by the House of Commons exactly as it had been passed by the House of Lords. On all important provisions, such as the size of the councils and their functions, both parties in Parliament were unanimous. Opposition members like Gladstone, Kimberley and Northbrook were all satisfied with the measure of advance the bill made on the existing system. In Northbrook's opinion, the bill 'provided fully for all present needs in respect of the increase of numbers'.[134] The only change in which the opposition was keenly interested was with regard to provision for some sort of election, but the Act very scrupulously avoided this term.

The act did not meet the demands of the Indian politicians. The government scheme of representation of 'races, classes and interests' provoked particular criticism. The Poona Sarvajanik Sabha criticized it as wrong in principle. In its opinion, according races and creeds separate representation would harm the country.[135] The Governor of Bombay in his reply to the Poona Sarvajanik Sabha and others justified the stand of the Government.[136]

Nobody expected much to follow from the Indian Councils Bill of 1892. According to Gladstone, it was not expected to produce 'large and imposing results.'[137] Curzon said, 'This Bill is not, perhaps, a great, or heroic measure; but, at the same time, it does mark a decisive step, and a step in advance.'[138] For Lansdowne, the provisions of the Bill marked 'substantial steps' in advance.[139] Surendranath Banerjea's interpretation of the Act of 1892 was that there were no special electorates or representation of class or commercial interests. The constituencies were the district boards and the municipalities, the former representing the rural areas and the latter the urban interests. The middle class had not received the measure of prominence to which they were entitled.[140]

There was, however, nothing substantial in the Act. As we have seen when discussing its genesis, the sole purpose of the Act was to steal the thunder from the demands of the Congress, not to set India on the way to Parliamentary government. A contemporary scholar is of the view that, possibly, the 1892 reforms did help to reduce the tempo of Congress agitation for a few years, with a number of prominent leaders finding their way into the provincial or imperial councils. He further asserts that general demands for council reform were not very prominent in the agenda of the Congress sessions between 1894 and 1900. But this effect was very shortlived, and the same years saw the first stirrings of Extremism and, by 1904, the Congress was again demanding a further big dose of legislative reform.[141]

This process of so-called constitutional reform, was, however, associated throughout with two other major strands of official policy: periodic attempts to rally the Moderates and skilful use of divide-and-rule techniques. Whether the British followed this policy consciously or unconsciously is not the point at issue; the fact is that conflicts over scarce resources in education, administrative jobs and, later, political spoils, lay in the very logic of colonial underdevelopment. Political reforms consistently extended and sharpened such rivalries right through this period.[142]

And this was the dilemma of the Moderates. They had implicit faith in orderly progress as part of the British Empire, but the Raj by its very nature, was bound to breed dissensions in India's body-politic. Being caught between the two grinding-stones of growing official indifference, ridicule and even active hostility on the one hand and the rising tempo of the militant spirit of a renascent nationalism, on the other, the Moderates in Indian politics had to face a very rough weather.

It was very unfortunate for the Moderates that the sudden radical turn which Indian politics took in the wake of the partition of Bengal, and the advent of Gandhi on the political scene, helped to foster the widespread belief that they (the Moderates) were political mendicants, weak-kneed, woolly-headed politicians, only petitioning and praying to the British Government for petty concessions instead of demanding swaraj. It was also the common view that the Moderates were a small, urban, educated minority which had been fighting only for their own interests. These estimates of the Moderates are readily believed because later generations find it difficult to appreciate the heavy odds against which the

Founding Fathers of the Congress had to contend. The evolution of the Indian nationality was not as simple a phenomenon as it might seem to later generations. But for the wisdom and sagacity of a few Indians and Britons, it might have been delayed, if not arrested altogether. It is true that by the middle of the 19th century the Bengalis had taken to British administration, the Parsis and Gujaratis to British commerce and the Punjabis to the British-Indian army; but the fusion of these diverse elements into an organic whole was a difficult task.[143] In spite of changing material conditions, national unity was the dream of a very small minority; most of even the educated Indians habitually thought in terms of their castes[144] and localities, and in this their rulers encouraged them. That, in these adverse circumstances, the Congress was founded in 1885 and survived into the 20th century may seem to some a miracle.[145]

But this flowering of Moderate thought was the culmination of a tradition which can be traced back to Raja Rammohun Roy,[146] who stood for the rational, individualistic tradition of contemporary Europe. His demands for political reforms ultimately reappeared as the demands of the early Congress.

As with Rammohun, so with the early Congress leaders, the presence of the British administration was a *sine qua non* for continued political progress. Their language was cautious and their expectation very moderate. To Romesh Dutt, no class of officials in the world were more careful, and able, and desirous to be just than high British-Indian officials, from the members of the Provincial and Viceregal Executive Councils to the members of the India Council; and yet the people were unrepresented in the offices which ultimately shaped their destinies. So, Dutt believed, in the interest of good administration, some means should be provided, not for transferring to Indian hands the ultimate decisions on Indian questions, but for securing some representation of Indian opinion in those executive councils in England and in India which decided on great Indian questions. This would improve and strengthen Indian administration and not weaken it, and it would improve British administration in India if each Indian province sent one member to the Viceroy's Executive Council and one member to the Council of the Secretary of State for India. This aspiration, Dutt thought, was not unreasonable. He advocated a corresponding reform of the legislative councils. Each district should be allowed to send one representative to the provincial legislative council. The number of nominated or official members might also be increased if necessary, and the new councils thus constituted should meet three or four days in a week to discuss questions relating to laws and administration, and to represent fully and adequately the wishes and sentiments and views of the people. Dutt believed, 'such really Representative Councils would bring the

Government of India in real touch with the people, and would popularise and strengthen and consolidate British rule in India.'[147]

Further, Dutt believed, it would help the Viceroy and the Secretary of State to understand better the feelings, wishes and interests of the people, and would create a bond of sympathy between the administration and the people. This would strengthen the councils in local knowledge and experience, and, to some extent, make them broad-based, on the people's will. It would remove that worst defect of British rule in India — the utter lack of touch between the people and their rulers. 'And it would substitute an intelligent and rational method of dealing with the great, loyal, and civilized population of India for a method which regards human beings as livestock, good for milking and shearing, but incapable of understanding their own interests or promoting their own well-being.'[148]

Dadabhai Naoroji was equally enamoured of the benefits of British rule. Political conditions in India before the British came were deplorable. There was, he added, the usual oriental despotism, disorder, want of law, want of security of property and life, and general ignorance. The moral condition was similarly hopeless. There was the influence of an ignorant priesthood, superstition and some unfortunate institutions, such as *sati*, life-long widowhood, and female infanticide. Materially, India was at a standstill. There was utter stagnation and even gradual retrogression. All desire to progress and improve, to develop the resources of the country had completely died out. On the intellect, all these baneful factors had their full effect. But British rule, Dadabhai stressed, brought law and order, security of life and property, assured justice between man and man, and laid down that law and not the despot's will would prevail. Enlightenment spread because of the universities and educational establishments. Owing to the development of railways, canals and public roads, the exploitation of India's natural resources, and, above all, English enterprise generally, there was material progress. Because of this all-round progress, there was also social elevation and Indians were inspired with new political life.[149]

Naturally, when these Moderate leaders assembled in the Indian National Congress, they developed identity of opinion. They realized that, after centuries of political disunity, social stagnation and economic backwardness, they had now an opportunity to imbibe from the West the spirit of reform and progress and of winning India her proper place in the comity of nations. In this great adventure, they looked for guidance to the English nation, a nation not only one of the greatest on earth, but also one of the most progressive.[150] They had the Whig view of English history as a continual upholding of constitutional liberty and individual freedom, broadening from precedent to precedent.

The Moderate leaders, to begin with, were very modest in their political outlook. They wanted to confine their attention to certain reforms and did not advocate democratic or full parliamentary government for India. K.T. Telang, for example, clarified, 'we have not asked for parliamentary institutions which England has got after many centuries of discipline; we have not asked for the power of the purse; and we have not asked that the British Executive should be brought under subjection to us.'[151] Surendranath Banerjea was more emphatic in asserting that theirs was not a claim to democratic government: 'We do not think India is ripe for it yet nor do we want Home Rule . . . We [only] press the reform of the Legislative Councils which impose taxes and make the laws.'[152] Such 'sweet reasonableness' was expected to reassure English public opinion which, it was thought, would be very effective in getting Indian demands accepted. Dadabhai Naoroji observed in 1886, 'If we honestly expect the English nation will do its duty towards us, we must prove ourselves worthy by showing that we are never unreasonable, never violent, never uncharitable. We must show that we are earnest, but temperate, cognizant of our rights, but respectful of those of others. . .'[153]

As time passed, the Moderate demand became more comprehensive and definite. By 1905, Gokhale was asserting that the evils of a bureaucratic government could no longer be tolerated. In the earlier days, he would add, when English rule had to be consolidated, and Western standards had to be introduced into the country, English work was done in a manner which secured the gratitude of the people; but that gratitude was no longer there. The new generation was not aware of what was done two generations ago. They were aware now only of what the officials were doing with their monopoly of power and resisting all the legitimate efforts of the people to participate in that power. Thus the new generations were growing up full of bitterness at the exclusion about which they had every right to complain.[154] So Gokhale affirmed that the goal of the Congress was that India should be governed in the interests of the Indians themselves and that, in course of time, a form of government should be attained in India similar to that which existed in the self-governing colonies of the British Empire; that, for better, for worse, the destinies of India were now linked up with those of England and the Congress party was bound to seek all advance within the empire itself; that that advance could be only gradual as at each stage of the progress it might be necessary for the Indians to pass through a brief course of apprenticeship before they could go to the next one; and that it was a reasonable proposition that the sense of responsibility required for the proper exercise of the political institutions of the West, could be acquired by an Eastern people through practical training and experience only.[155]

Gokhale explained the policy and programme of the Moderates in his lecture, 'The work before us,' at a meeting in Allahabad presided over by Motilal Nehru in early 1907. He remarked that the middle class had to find its path between the British bureaucracy, holding the monopoly of power, with the backing of a firmly entrenched, mighty empire, on the one hand, and the vast mass of India, inert and apathetic, except when under the sway of a religious impulse, deplorably divided and subdivided, with hardly any sense of true discipline, plunged in abject poverty and ignorance, on the other. This middle class, at one time so well disposed to British rule, was daily growing more sullen and disgruntled, resenting the non-fulfilment of solemn promises, feeling keenly the humiliation of its subject position and determined to attain for itself a political status worthy of the self-respect of civilized people.[156] Gokhale wanted his country to take its proper place among the great nations of the world in every walk of life, which was possible, he believed, within the British Empire, as the French in Canada and the Boers in South Africa had done. There had been, he added, most lamentable lapses on the part of the British, but the genius of the British people, as revealed in history, had been, on the whole, for political freedom and constitutional liberty.[157]

Self-government, Gokhale went on, was the goal; and constitutional agitation was the means of its achievement. In his opinion, constitutional agitation, not narrowly construed, embraced even passive resistance and the non-payment of taxes. Only violence and revolution fell outside its ambit. But, Gokhale added, everything that was constitutional was not necessarily wise or expedient.[158] This lecture immensely appealed to Motilal who in his letter to Jawaharlal in England described it as a 'masterpiece of close reasoning and sound commonsense expressed in the best and purest English.'[159]

Gokhale was of the view that Tilak and his supporters were wrong in suggesting that constitutional agitation had failed in India. In fact, he added, the people of India had not exhausted even a thousandth part of the possibilities of real constitutional agitation. The Congress could have achieved much more if it had been able to enthuse its followers more intensively. Political privileges could not be had for the asking. They had cost other peoples prolonged struggles. The British bureaucracy was, Gokhale conceded, impervious to constitutional agitation in India, but British democracy might pressurize it.[160] That was why work in England was an integral part of the Congress programme. But, Gokhale remarked, nine-tenths of the work lay in India — much remained to be done to bridge the gulf between the Hindus and the Muslims, and between the different sections of the Hindu community, and to develop a strong and highly principled character and discipline, and finally, to cultivate an intense feeling of nationality above caste, creed and class.[161]

After explaining the Moderate creed and strategy, Gokhale exposed the weakness of the Extremist doctrine. The Extremists held that there should be universal boycott, the real significance of which they only vaguely understood. Gokhale added that the implications of an industrial boycott were grave enough, that it entailed a deliberate sacrifice on the part of the people in buying indigenous articles which were of poorer quality and priced higher than imported goods, that there was also the stupendous problem of setting up new industries to dispense with imports, and that, therefore, the talk of a general or political strike was sheer madness. He further remarked that it was impossible within a measurable time to set up national schools and colleges on a scale sufficient to replace institutions aided or run by the government. The boycott of local bodies, legislative councils, and government, was likewise, in his opinion, simply suicidal. The object of the Indian people should be, Gokhale said, to seek steadily to increase what little power of administration and control they possessed, rather than risk losing what they had secured after years of agitation and struggle.[162]

But the difficulty with the Moderates was that they were victims of inner contradictions. While politically their criticism of British administration was very civil, their economic analysis of the Raj was scathing, devastating, and striking at the very root of the Empire.[163] Dadabhai Naoroji, who was never tired of singing paeons in praise of the Raj,[164] was very bitter about the economic devastation it had brought about. Speaking on the great drain of India's wealth, he said that there was security of life and property only in one sense, i.e., it was secure from violence among Indians or from native despots, and India was grateful; but from England's own grasp, there was no security of property at all, and consequently no security of life. England was perfectly free to carry away from or consume in India, India's wealth and was doing so at the rate of some £30 or 40 million Sterling a year. Thus British rule was an unceasing and increasing encroachment on India's resources, progressively and utterly ruining the country. Former foreign invaders, Dadabhai remarked, came and plundered and went away or settled in the country, but England, which did not come with the intention of plundering, had become under the force of circumstances, the worst foreign invader India had the misfortune to know, an invader that did not give her even a moment to breathe, to recover from the depredations, to rebuild. He deplored that the cry always was more and more Europeans. With the deprivation of the vital, material life-blood of the country, the whole higher 'wisdom' of the country was also carried away. So India did not enjoy the security of her property, or her life, or knowledge or 'wisdom.' To millions in India, life was simply 'half-feeding' or starvation, or famines and disease.[165]

There could not be a greater condemnation of British rule in India than this. Other members of the party agreed with Dadabhai.[166] It may be pointed out that Dadabhai Naoroji tried to resolve this inner contradiction in his stand by describing what obtained in India as 'un-British.'[167] It may be said in defence of the Moderates that they were rendering a great service to the cause of Indian nationalism by exposing the exploitative material basis of the British rule.

By 1907, the Moderate Party was almost utterly exhausted. The veteran leaders were getting old and growing inactive. The government was not conceding their demands. The imperious Pherozeshah was too aloof to attract a warm and enthusiastic following; the comparatively younger and gentle Gokhale was the only hope of the Moderates. But even he was intensely distrusted and disliked by the British authorities. When, after Lajpat Rai's deportation, Gokhale became very active to get him (Rai) freed, Morley wrote to Minto, 'I half begin to wonder whether Gokhale is not at heart such a revolutionist as Pal, etc., and as determined to discount sensible and steady reforms as Tilak or Lajpat.'[168] Minto was not prepared to allow Gokhale to play with fire and tamper with the army. He held Gokhale responsible for the unrest in the Punjab and was 'thoroughly disappointed in him.'[169] Minto was thoroughly worked up and he felt sorry that he had allowed Gokhale to be re-elected to the Imperial Legislative Council.[170] He decided not to include Gokhale in the Factories Commission because, with his ability and eloquence, he would exert great influence upon his colleagues and his appointment would be strongly disapproved and misunderstood by many of the most loyal Indian supporters of the British. They looked upon Gokhale as an arch-traitor.[171]

The Moderates thus found themselves in a tight corner, with the political temperature rising up and the British authorities doubting their bona fides. The ground was slipping from under their feet. The Extremists were attracting the more youthful sections of society. Already, Motilal was apprehensive of the impatient student community and he wrote to his son that no sober or serious leader could expect a patient hearing from them.[172] Chintamani also at the time complained to Gokhale that the student leaders of the United Provinces were inviting people from outside to address them, advocating boycott, insulting the local leaders, and doing other reprehensible things.[173] This was not a congenial atmosphere for the Moderates to work in.

The Moderate image of British democracy as opposed to British bureaucracy was too romantic to stand the test of reason. The Liberal leaders in England took little interest in Indian affairs. They did not want to make India a party issue. Immediately after taking office, Prime Minister Henry Campbell-Bannerman had declared, 'It has been a pretty unbroken rule, a wise rule that we assuredly shall not be the first to break, to keep questions of the internal administration of India outside the arena of party politics.'[174] Thus, between the aspirations of the Moderate leadership in India and the objectives of the Liberal statesmen in Britain, there was a wide gulf which could not be bridged by courteous phrases. The Liberal leaders in England might be more willing than the Conservatives to widen the base of the legislatures, or to appoint Indians to a few high executive posts; but their object was not to transfer authority to Indian hands, but only to provide safety-valves for political discontent. Even this limited objective was vitiated by the self-righteousness of the cadre of professional civil servants. 'Men on the spot' in India who were, by and large, opposed to any constitutional reform in India on parliamentary lines.[175]

As against the lofty idealism of the Moderate leaders in India, the British were practising Machiavellianism to thwart the dream of a united and prosperous India. Minto, for example, saw the safety of the Raj in the 'allegiance of conservative forces . . . the Indian princes, the commercial community, the Mohammedans, and the Indian staff of public services.'[176] Harcourt Butler, one of the knights-errant of the Raj, depended upon different elements in different parts of the country for support. In the Deccan and South India, he was to help in breaking the power of the Brahmins. In Bengal, he was to watch and counter the influence of the religious ascetics. In the Punjab, the divisions in the Arya Samaj were to be utilized. In the United Provinces, the loyalty of orthodox Hinduism centred at Banaras, Ayodhya, Allahabad, Mathura and Hardwar was to be retained and built up. And, generally, the landowning and agricultural classes were to be assisted to hold their own. 'There will always be a certain movement against the aliens,' Butler wrote, 'We require all our strength and prudence. We must make friends. We must reward loyalty and make it pay.'[177]

Little wonder that the well-meaning, 'loyal', but patriotic, Indian Moderates could not stand before this Machiavellianism and the Extremists won the heart of Aryavarta.

3. The 'Extremist' Challenge

Extremism in the Indian National Congress did not spring up all of a sudden in the first decade of the 20th century. It had been in incubation at least since the revolt of 1857. The nationalist ideas behind that revolt, according to the Extremists, were swadharma and swaraj.[178] Attachment to pan-Indian nationalism and Western ideals had alienated the Liberal school in India from the masses. That is why, despite their high idealism, they failed to make any effective impact on the people. In due time there was bound to come a reaction, with a sudden rush. And from the adoration of all things Western, there was a movement by the 1890s calling people back to their ancient civilization. There had always been an undercurrent of this trend, and even during the revolt of 1857 it had manifested itself. But the English-educated community had kept itself generally aloof from the main current of Indian life. The historic task of bridging the gulf between the educated few and the people in general was accomplished by the almost illiterate Paramahansa Ram Krishnadeo and his English-educated disciple, Swami Vivekananda; by Swami Dayananda, who was well-versed in the Vedic literature, and his Arya Samaj; and by the eclectic Theosophical Society and Annie Besant. Because they shed every vestige of inferiority complex *vis-a-vis* the West, their belief in the spiritual heritage and mission of India, their emphasis on self-assertion, these people have been misunderstood by certain writers as having encouraged social conservatism, though they were politically radical.[179] While among the political Radicals, there was instinctive attachment to native culture, native religion and native policy,[180] they were not social conservatives. Rather, they were ardent nationalists who wanted to deal with other countries and cultures on terms of equality and self-respect.[181] They would not be docile pupils at the feet of the West. Naturally, they turned their backs on such a servile position and got their impetus from a desire to get from shams to realities, and the necessity of suffering and self-sacrifice for the achievement of national salvation. This being their outlook, it was natural that they were antipathetic to the Moderates.[182] To the Extremists, emancipation meant something much deeper and wider than politics. To them it was a matter of building up a national character, of reinvigorating all departments of national life. They thought that a trial of strength between the two peoples was inevitable, and so they argued that a new Indian people must be made.[183]

Thus Extremism was an idea at once religious and political which gripped the mind of a number of Indian leaders in the last decade of the 19th century and the first of the 20th. The contradictions between the two trends were further complicated by economic factors.[184] Extremism was a response to the challenge of haphazard and superficial westernization of Indian life, thought and politics. Spiritually it countered the threat to traditional Hindu religion, ethics and social values posed by Christianity, Utilitarianism and Brahmoism; culturally it stood against a mechanistic, materialistic and individualistic civilization; and politically it was opposed to a slow merger of Indian national identity in the 'vast and inchoate British Empire.' In all the Extremist leaders, the same appeal to Indian history, the same pride in India's spiritual heritage, and the same desire to escape from the snares of the Circe[185] of westernism is to be found.[186]

There were three schools of Extremists — the Maharashtra school, headed by B.G. Tilak; the Bengal school represented by B.C. Pal and Aurobindo; and the Punjab school led by Lala Lajpat Rai. The Bengal Extremists were very much influenced by the ideas of Bankim Chandra, a liberal conservative (like Burke), who wanted no break with the past which, he thought, might create more problems than it would solve. He was opposed to thoughtless and precipitate reforms imposed from above, out of turn. In his view, reforms should wait on moral and religious regeneration, which again should be based on *dharmatattwa* (the fundamental of religion).[187] Bankim's daring and cogent utilization of weapons from the arsenal of the West surprised the anglicized sceptics and agnostics, while his rational, humane and universal exposition of the Hindu view cowed the obscurantist into silence.[188] 'He laid down the strategic bridge-head across which Vivekananda would march to invade the West in its own citadel. At home, Arjunas, perplexed by the confrontation of the East and the West, enervated by an alien rule and economy, emasculated by an education which caused disharmonious development of personality and bred indecision and doubt, took heart.'[189] Bankim blazed the trail for the Extremists with contemptuous criticism of the Moderates.[190] But, for Bankim, patriotism was at best only a means to an end which was the welfare of all mankind.[191]

This nationalism of the Extremists was highly charged emotionally. It was a gospel. The civic, economic, and political ideals were all blended in this inspiring central conception of nationalism, which was a religion for new India. In the words of Pal, 'The eternal problem of Nationalism is how to preserve, to develop, to perfect those elements in the consciousness and character of the nation which constitute its essential note, and contribute to its specific functions in the universal life of Humanity.'[192] Carrying this message of universal life to the West, Vivekananda generated tremendous self-confidence and will-power.[193] Aurobindo even raised patriotism to the pedestal of mother-worship.[194] He said in a letter, 'I know my country as my mother. I adore her. I worship her.'

Aurobindo was very much attracted by the ideas of Dayananda, which were little influenced by the ideas of the West. He credited Dayananda with outstanding work for the nation.[195] Bankim Chandra, Dayananda and Vivekananda thus prepared the ideological background against which the Extremists drew up their political programme.

It is not easy to trace the growth of the political programme of the Extremists. It has been already remarked that it can be traced back to the slogans of swadharma and swadesh in the revolt of 1857. Definite rumblings of it can be heard in the early 1890s, its seed-time. Tilak resented any interference by an alien government in the domestic and private life of the people. He quarrelled with the reformers over the Age of Consent Bill in 1891. He introduced the Ganpati festival in 1893. Aurobindo published 'New Lamps for Old' in the *Indu Prakash* between 1893 and 1894. Tilak threw a challenge to the National Social Conference in 1895 by not allowing it to hold its session in the Congress pavilion in Pune.[196] Needless to say, the National Social Conference was sponsored by the Moderates. The Poona Sarvajanik Sabha was captured by the Extremists from the Moderates in the same year. The Shivaji festival[197] was first celebrated on 15 April 1896. With the foundation of the Deccan Sabha on 4 November 1896, the break between the Extremists and Moderates in Maharashtra was complete. But it was not so all over India. Pal, for example, the leader of the Bengal Extremists was still a Moderate. He wrote in 1897: 'I am loyal to the British Government, because with me loyalty to the British Government is identical with loyalty to my own people and my own country; because I believe that God has placed this Government over us for our salvation.'[198] Only in 1902, could he write: 'The Congress here and its British Committee in London, are both begging institutions.'[199]

Rabindranath Tagore exposed the inhumanity of the bureaucracy and gave a sound analysis of the worsening relations between the rulers and the ruled in *Sadhana* (1893-4), which gave voice to the protest of the young generation against the mendicancy of the old.[200]

Because of the mild policy of the Congress, Lajpat Rai also lost interest in Congress matters. Between 1893 and 1900, he did not attend a single Congress meeting. He felt during this period that Congress leaders cared more for fame and pomp than for the interests of the country. He had no love for 'holiday patriots who uttered plausibly-worded platitudes and well-disguised commonplaces.'[201]

The foregoing shows that Extremism was an expression of the revolt of the spirit of India against foreign domination in every walk of life. But Seal sees in this revolt of the spirit also an example of uneven growth and competition. In his opinion, many of the developments inside Congress between 1888 and 1907 should be interpreted in terms of unevenness and competition. The disputes between the leaders of the educated still turned on the issue of how best to conserve their own positions. The innovation of the period was that these disputes now drove the movement into regions whose backwardness would otherwise have still left them politically inert. For all the disputes over tactics or over the issue of social reform, Extremism was less an ideology than a technique. Its most conspicuous form was an all-India coalition of dissidents who, having been outmanoeuvred in their own provinces, tried to reverse at the top the defeat they had suffered in the localities. Their organization was another skin-deep affair. It fell to pieces after Tilak was transferred to Mandalay gaol.[202] It will be enough to quote the opinion of another scholar in whose opinion the so-called 'Indian radicals' of Dufferin's time had become 'moderates' by Elgin's time and a new group of leaders had emerged — Bal Gangadhar Tilak, Lala Lajpat Rai and the Bengali Extremists, and these and other men were destined to give to the terms 'radical' and 'extremist' true meaning for the Congress and the Government of India.[203]

The changing spirit of the time and the diehard policy of the British authorities had made the position of the Moderates very critical. Even though the Moderates had full faith in the British sense of justice, Hamilton had conceded that, 'Just now India is exploited for the benefit of the Civil Service', and that the Congress movement was 'an uprising of Indian native opinion against, not British rule, but Anglo-Indian bureaucracy.'[204] The general Anglo-Indian view was that India could be well governed only by despotic benevolence. 'A benevolent despotism suits Asiatics best . . . what India wants is a modern Akbar.'[205]

The Moderates, with all their sweet reasonableness had not been able to show any worthwhile results. The India Council was not abolished. Lord Cross's Act (the Act of 1892) was a half-hearted measure which had not gone as far as even the Government of India desired.[206] To quote Gokhale's phrase, the Government had set 'minorities above the general public.'

The simultaneous civil service examinations demanded by the Congress and even granted in a resolution by the Gladstonian House of Commons (2 June 1893) were disallowed by Kimberley for fear that it would imperil the predominance of the European element.[207] The score of Indians in the I.C.S. were already too many competitionwallas for Curzon who was vexed to see the covenanted posts being filched away by the superior wit of the natives. The Conservatives were stoutly opposed to any extension of representative institutions or diminution of any European establishment as endangering the Raj. A decade of Moderate agitation (the Extremists would have called it 'mendicancy') failed to make any dent in the Conservative fortress of reaction. The Whigs were ridiculed for their romantic hopes about India. A free press, civil courts, literary education and competitive examination, which had once been paraded as the blessing of British rule, were now regarded as evil portents of disintegration.[208] Other demands of the Congress also had not been heeded. Protests against the increase in military expenditure had been turned down by Kimberley. The policy of defraying the expenses of Indian contingents outside India from Indian revenues had been opposed by Elgin in vain. There were also other burdens on Indian revenues. Curzon warned that such arbitrary and unfair treatment 'does quite as much to shake the moral basis of our domination in India, as does any unrighteous or tyrannical conduct of our officials on the spot.'[209] While Elgin's countervailing excise duties still rankled, Joseph Chamberlain's fiscal policy completely ignored India. The Tariff and Cotton Duties Acts of 1894 and 1896 were an important spur to the growth of Extremism.[210]

The leaders of all shades of opinion and the newspapers of both the Moderates and the Extremists unanimously criticized the inroads into the economic interests of the Indian people. The *Maharatta* of Tilak and the *Bengalee* of Surendranath both condemned this policy. R.C. Dutt and Gokhale both denounced it as extremely harmful to Indian interests. Tilak wrote in the *Kesari:* 'Surely India is treated as a vast pasture reserved solely for the Europeans to feed upon.'[211] Curzon's politics, more than his economics, alienated India. 'He was the Old Testament Prophet, the Divine Right King and the Enlightened Despot rolled into one.'[212] Curzon never vacillated in his opposition to the Congress. He queered the pitch for the Moderates as no one else could have. 'By repudiating the Western-educated intelligentsia he was repudiating the tenuous link of loyalty that still bound India to Britain.'[213]

Curzon's educational reforms too alienated the intelligentsia. He made the Moderates look foolish and their failure undermined the assumptions of their faith in British rule and brought grist to the Extremist mill. The idea of national education, so long confined to a few, caught the popular imagination. While disillusionment after disillusionment enervated the Moderates and weakened their cause, the victories of Japan over Russia (1904-5) sent a thrill of enthusiasm through Asia. Now the tones of Dadabhai and Digby changed. Henceforth British rule began to be referred to as dishonourable, hypocritical and destructive. Hamilton, the Secretary of State for India, and Curzon, the Viceroy, were specially responsible for taking matters from bad to worse. Indians were now urged to claim unceasingly their birthright and pledged rights of British citizenship, of self-government.[214] Curzon's plan for the partition of Bengal ensured the emergence of the Extremists as a national party. The aim was no longer colonial self-government, swaraj was now the goal.

It would be appropriate at this point to analyse the credo of the Extremists and seek the common points between them and the Moderates. Tilak wrote, on 2 January 1907, that the British Government in India did not suit the people, that a government of one country by another could never be a successful and permanent government, that there was no difference of opinion on this fundamental proposition between the old and the new schools and that it was certain that the alien government had ruined India. In the beginning, Tilak added, the Indians were taken by surprise and were made to believe that the British government descended from the clouds to save the Indians from internecine warfare and internal and external invasions. It was, Tilak went on, English education, growing poverty and closer familiarity with the English rulers that opened the eyes of the people of India and their leaders. Dadabhai Naoroji, at 82, Tilak said, was a bitterly disappointed man. The old and the new parties both now agreed that appeals to the bureaucracy were fruitless. Like the Moderates, Tilak believed that under British rule Indian industries had been ruined and wealth drained out of the country, reducing India to the lowest depths of poverty. But the way out was not, Tilak affirmed, through petitioning, but boycott. No palliatives would work. Indians should have the key of their house, and not merely one stranger turned out of it. Self-government was the goal and the 'New Party' wanted the Indians to realize the fact that their future rested entirely in their own hands, that they could be free if they meant to be free. Tilak was of the opinion that the way to win swaraj was not through resort to arms, but through developing the power of self-denial and self-abstinence in such a way as would enable Indians to withhold co-operation from the foreign power ruling over them, e.g. in collecting revenue, policing the country, fighting aggressive wars with Indian blood and money, and in the functioning of the law courts. Tilak advised his countrymen to set up their own courts, to stop paying taxes, and thus they could be free the very next day.[215] The philosophical radicalism of Aurobindo went even further. He wrote in *Bande Mataram* on 14 April 1908 that the alien government carried the germs of an occidental malady which was injecting all aspects of life in India. To present the destruction of all that was valuable in the Indian way of life it was urgently necessary to get rid of foreign rule and seek refuge in India's own superior civilization. Naturally, Aurobindo added, the work of nationalism was (1) to win swaraj for India so that the existing unhealthy conditions of political life, full of the germs of the social and political ptosis which was overtaking Europe, might be entirely and radically eliminated and (2) to ensure that the swaraj achieved would be a swadeshi swaraj and not an importation of the European article. This was why, he went on, the movement for swaraj found its first expression in an outburst for swadeshi sentiment directed not merely against foreign goods, but against foreign habits, dress, manners and education, and which sought to bring back the people to their own civilization. It was an instinctive protest of Nature against the malady eating into the national system and threatening to corrupt its blood and disturb the soundness of its organs. Any irrational features in the revolt of the people against foreign things were the violence of the reaction necessitated by the violence of the malady. 'India must remain India if she is to fulfil her destiny.'[216] Earlier, on 26 April 1907, Aurobindo had declared in *Bande Mataram* that Extremism had been born of a conviction that the time had come when India could, should and would, become a great, free and united nation; and that Indian nationalism was not a negative current of destruction, but a positive, constructive impulse towards the making of modern India. 'It is not a cry of revolt of despair, but a gospel of national faith and hope. Its true description is not Extremism, but Democratic Nationalism.'[217]

From the foregoing it may appear that, though the Extremists used much stronger language, and Tilak and his followers had much more fight in them (though they had hardly any new ideas), substantially, they were not very different from the Moderates. Gokhale in his presidential speech (Banaras, 1905) and Dadabhai Naoroji in his presidential speech (Calcutta, 1906) had both advocated self-government and swaraj as the goal of the Congress.[218] Almost all the Extremist leaders had grown under the shadow of the founding fathers of the Congress. On critical occasions, such as during the partition of Bengal, their degree of alienation from the Raj was greater, and their language was stronger, but most of them did not think in terms radically different from those of the Moderates. Their attitude to the Empire was ambivalent, despite their indictment of British officials and administrators. They did not really think of giving up constitutional methods for breaking all ties with Britain. Tilak's approach to the Montford reforms in their final stages bore a striking resemblance to that of Gokhale to the Morley-Minto reforms.[219]

It need not be emphasized that just as there were different shades of opinion among the Moderates — from the imperious Pherozeshah Mehta to the gentle Gokhale — so were there different shades of thought among the Extremists. On the extreme 'left' was Aurobindo, and on the extreme 'right' Lajpat Rai. In between, stood Tilak. It is strange that the controversy between the Moderates and the Extremists raged mainly round the personality of Tilak.

The clash of personalities at Pune from the beginning of the 1890s had been intense. There had been serious differences between Tilak and Agarkar (though they had been co-workers in the Deccan Education Society) and, ultimately, Tilak was pushed out of the society. Thereafter, there had been a constant tussle between the followers of Tilak and his opponents. The opponents rallied round Mahadev Govind Ranade and Gokhale, backed in Congress affairs by Pherozeshah Mehta from Bombay. We have already earlier mentioned these differences. Gokhale enjoyed the support of the Congress establishment. As the Moderates were losing their *elan vital* and the Extremists were capturing the imagination of the country, the conflict in Maharashtra in general and in Pune in particular became sharper.

There was ferment, more or less, all over India. The *Bande Mataram* under Aurobindo was not only challenging the right of the British Government to rule India, but also the right of the veteran leaders to speak for the country. Outside Bengal, Tilak was the first to recognize the potential of the ferment in Bengal. The partition of Bengal was to him not so much a British blunder as an Indian opportunity. He extended support to the anti-partition movement and encouraged the emerging Extremist leaders in Bengal. Gokhale had seen this Tilak-Pal alliance gaining strength since the Banaras Congress (1905) and this caused deep concern not only in the Government, but also among Congress leaders. Tilak was regarded as a dissident, if not a rebel. P. Mehta, D.E. Wacha and the whole Bombay group had distrusted him since the controversies that had raged in the 1890s. The differences were partly ideological and partly temperamental. For at least fifteen years there had been a cold war between the Congress establishment headed by Mehta on the one hand and Tilak on the other.[220]

Tilak was *persona non grata* with the Moderate group in Bombay. But he was a shrewd tactician waiting for his opportunity. The unity forged at the Banaras Congress (1905) with the Bengal Extremists proved advantageous to Tilak at the Calcutta Congress (1906).[221]

Before we discuss the Calcutta Congress, it would be useful to consider Gokhale's low estimate of the Extremist stalwarts. In a letter to a personal friend, he wrote:

> I do not think that two at least of the three [Tilak and Pal] would ever have been really conciliated by any compromise on the subject of a constitution. Mr Pal[222] has never worked for the Congress in the past. He is a very unscrupulous man and inordinately ambitious. Being a very powerful speaker, he does not see why he should not have the same influence in the country as Mr Surendranath [Banerjea] and he is determined to play the role of a leader at all costs. He uses brave words, but behind these words, there is neither courage nor character and, of course, there is no judgement, and I have little doubt that in a year or two, we shall see this man's collapse, whatever noise he may succeed in making temporarily. . . .
>
> Mr Tilak[223] is, of course, in many respects a wholly different kind of man, but he too, I am sorry to say, is afflicted with an ambition to which there are no limits. . . .
>
> Mr Tilak has a matchless capacity for intrigue and he is not burdened with an exacting conscience. As a result, he is often about to play for his own hand when to all appearances, he is fighting for a principle only. His great talents, his simple habits, his sturdy and dauntless spirit and above all the cruel persecution which he has had to bear at the hands of the

Government have won for him the hearts of the millions in all parts of the country. And this general affection and admiration make it comparatively easy for him to play his game.

I think you will agree with me when I say that no man of our time was ever more pure-minded or more humble, more entirely devoted to national welfare and more anxious for conciliation all round than the late Mr Ranade,[224] and yet Mr Ranade in spite of his utmost efforts failed to conciliate Mr Tilak, not only in matters of social reform but in regard to political work also. While therefore Sir Pherozeshah Mehta's unyielding and dictatorial attitude may be justly deplored, I do not think a greater conciliation on his part would have made any difference as regards Mr Tilak's ambition and his methods. . . .[225]

Gokhale did not only have his own estimate of the Extremist leaders, he had also premonitions about the Calcutta Congress (1906). He wrote to Krishnaswami Aiyer:

Even if all arrangements for the next Congress are completed in time and the Congress does meet in Calcutta during next Christmas, there will be great trouble about the programme of work. Bipin Chandra Pal and his party are working hard to get a large contingent of delegates on their side and they want to sweep the present programme of the Congress clean off the board and substitute in its place only three resolutions, the first declaring our inherent right to govern ourselves and demanding autonomy, absolute and immediate, free from foreign control; the second calling upon all Congressmen to withdraw their sons and wards from all government institutions and make independent provision for their education so that the rising generation should grow up full of a determination to wrest complete autonomy from England; and the third advocating not only Swadeshism in the industrial field but a comprehensive boycott against everything English . . . so that the only points of contact between the Government and the people should be those of violent hatred. This is the programme of the new Bengal Party and they profess they will make no compromise with any one who proposes to agitate for mere reforms, as the success of such agitation would mean an improved and therefore a prolonged foreign rule. They are claiming Mr Tilak as their leader, though we all know that he does not believe in the practicability of their programme; only as is his wont, he will do nothing to discourage their belief that he is their leader.

When the Congress meets, if it meets at all in Calcutta, we must be prepared for violent scenes and disorderly attempts to make its work on old lines impossible . . . It may be that we are, after all . . . 'the mere sport of an aimless destiny'.[226]

This suspicion did not augur well for the Congress. To begin with, there was controversy over the presidentship. Pal and Aurobindo wanted Tilak to be the president, but the Moderates were in no mood to accept him. To have their way, the latter resorted to an unscrupulous manoeuvre, and, without consulting the Reception Committee, wired Dadabhai Naoroji to accept it. After the latter's acceptance, the Extremists were presented with a *fait accompli*. Thus, having been foiled in their attempt to get Tilak installed as president, the Extremists — Tilak, Aurobindo, Pal, Aswini Kumar Dutt, Khaparde, etc. — formed themselves into a pressure group to press their points. Khaparde wrote in his diary: 'We have a clear majority here and a great deal of local support.'[227]

The air was thick with animosity. On the initiative of Dadabhai, preliminary discussions between the two groups took place at the house of the Maharaja of Darbhanga, Dadabhai's host. There were heated exchanges between Tilak, Pal and Khaparde on the one hand and Mehta, Malaviya and Gokhale on the other. The meeting of the subjects Committee was stormy. Resolutions were discussed and amended as the Extremists wanted. Motilal wrote to Jawaharlal, 'The Extremists are in the ascendant and they outnumber the Moderates.'[228]

Pherozeshah Mehta was the special target of the Extremists' fury. They objected to his sitting next to the president and shouted, 'Down with Mehta!' and 'kick him off'. Mehta, Malaviya and Gokhale were heckled and booed. Debate on the swadeshi and boycott resolutions was extremely acrimonious. The Extremists acted as a solid block. Dadabhai refused to put the disputed resolutions to the vote. Thereupon, the Extremists walked out in protest and threatened to challenge the resolutions in the plenary session. Then a compromise was hurriedly made, and the resolutions on the partition of Bengal, swadeshi and boycott were re-phrased and secured a smooth passage in the open session. But there was no union of the minds and hearts of the antagonists. Dadabhai's presidentship staved off the danger for the time being, but a festering sore was left. He was too old and too committed to the Moderate cause to effect a real compromise.

Even though Dadabhai's presidential address was not too revolutionary and tried only feebly to accommodate the New Spirit, it shocked the Anglo-Indian Press. *The Civil and Military Gazette* concluded that 'the veteran agitator in his old days had gone over to the Extremists.'[229] *The Englishman* commented that Dadabhai, who had been called in by the Moderates to quench the flames of hatred against British rule in India, had used kerosene for the purpose.[230] Dadabhai's address, despite the mention of the magic word 'swaraj' was, in fact, not a revolutionary statement. It was full of contradictions.[231]

Dadabhai commanded reverence, but he was no longer effective in controlling the New Party. The mouthpiece of the New Spirit, the *Bande Mataram,* published an article entitled 'The Man of the Present and the Man of the Future' on the opening day of the Congress session, which presented a comparison between Dadabhai and Tilak which was unflattering to the former, who was described as 'worn and aged, bowed down with the burden of half a century of toils and labour, a man of the past, reminding us of a generation that is passing away, ideals that have lost their charm, methods that have been found to be futile, and energy and hope once buoyant and full of life, which now live on only a wearied and decrepit old age, phantom-like, still babbling exploded generalities and dead formulas.'[232] The Calcutta Congress revealed that the old leaders no longer commanded the respect and awe they used to evoke earlier. Clearly the ground was being prepared for a head-on clash.

Though the Extremists had failed to get Tilak elected the President of the Calcutta Congress (1906), they were satisfied with what they achieved there. The *Maharatta* wrote on 6 January 1907; 'The Congress has emerged triumphant and rejuvenated.'[233] Even the *Bande Mataram* recognized that 'all that the forward party has fought for has in substance been conceded.'[234] The Extremists had emerged as a strong, coherent and powerful force; they had thwarted what they believed to be determined attempts to water down the Congress programme and had kept the Moderates at bay. The Moderates left Calcutta with mixed feelings of bewilderment, humiliation and dismay. What they were worried about was not the resolution passed on swadeshi and boycott, but the way in which the resolutions were pushed through. 'Gone was the genteel decorum of a gathering which had hitherto conducted itself as if it was an unofficial Parliament of India. Acrimonious argument and open conflict had replaced quiet diplomacy and consensus through friendly negotiations.'[235]

We have seen that the resolution on swadeshi had been a bone of contention between the two groups. Though both the factions had participated in the swadeshi movement,[236] there was a good deal of difference between the views of the Moderates and the Extremists on swadeshism. For Tilak, Pal and Aurobindo, boycott had double implications. Materially it was to be economic pressure on Manchester which would by a chain reaction, hit the Indian Government. Spiritually, it was a means of destroying *maya* or the illusion of British power and a necessary sacrifice for swaraj. Tilak called it 'the yoga of *bahishkar*,' a religious ritual of self-punishment. Swadeshi had primarily an economic message for Gokhale — the message of industrial regeneration imparted to him by M.G. Ranade. 'The Swadeshi Movement,' according to Surendranath, 'was in spirit a protectionist movement.' It appealed to the masses because they had the sense to perceive that it would 'herald the dawn of a new era of material prosperity for them.' To Tilak and Rai it was a moral training in self-help, determination and sacrifice, as well as a weapon of 'political agitation'. To Aurobindo, swadeshism was not 'the mere secularity of autonomy and wealth', but a return to a faith in India's destiny as the world-saviour. Thus swadeshism had a far richer content for the Extremists than for the Moderates.

Difference of temperament and ideology and the clash of personalities were to accentuate the feelings among the rival factions. Persistent criticism and ridicule by the Extremists alarmed the Moderates, who were afraid that the Extremists had already captured Bengal, Maharashtra, Berar and the Punjab, and there was danger of the rest of the country also being lost to them. It was not a simple question of which party would be predominant in the Congress; the stakes were much higher. Mudholkar warned Gokhale that the prevailing struggle was no simple fight for titular leadership, that it was fight for the establishment of certain principles, for the organization of certain definite methods of work. He added that the Extremists believed in and preached 'revolutionary' methods for driving the foreign devils from India, who had usurped sway there. Mr Khaparde, he went on, almost semi-publicly talked of a war and an insurrection which might be expected in a couple of years and the year 1913 was confidently predicted by him as the year which would see the end of British power in India. Mudholkar's final advice was that it was the duty of the Moderates to themselves, to the country and to God, to expose the true character, aim and object of the new school and to protect the Indian people from the wild and fanatical teachings of those dangerous lunatics.[237] So the students' hearts and minds must be captured, and the United Provinces and Madras, yet out of the clutches of the Extremists, must be saved. To fulfil this, Gokhale took a tour of the U.P. and Punjab early in 1907 to explain the liberal creed.[238]

Clearly, the road to Surat had been firmly laid out. While Gokhale was busy with the case of Lala Lajpat Rai (who had been deported), another crisis was deepening in the Congress. At the Calcutta session (1906), it had been decided that the next session of the Congress would be held at Nagpur where G.M. Chitnavis (a Moderate leader) thought that he had a majority. This was a clever device to prevent the holding of the session at Lahore which had of late grown to be an Extremist centre. In February 1907, the Provincial Congress Committee and the Reception Committee both met at Nagpur to elect the office bearers. Chitnavis was elected president of both the committees and B.S. Moonje (an Extremist leader) was elected joint general secretary of the Reception Committee. The two factions failed to work together. The Extremists led a propaganda campaign against the Moderate leaders, controlled a local Hindi paper [239] and also decided to publish a Hindi edition of the *Kesari* from Nagpur. The Moderates also decided to start an Anglo-Marathi paper of their own from Nagpur. There was unseemly competition in enrolling new members and raising funds. The Extremists wanted to elect Tilak, president of the session, the Moderates were against this. In spite of their numerical majority in the local Congress, the Moderates had a disadvantage in that Chitnavis was not assertive in a crisis. The election of the Congress president for the ensuing session (1907) developed into trial of strength between the Moderates and the Extremists. The Moderates were determined not to allow Tilak to hold the presidential chair:

> We say it clearly Mr Tilak has made himself impossible for a position of so much responsibility as the Presidentship of the Congress at a grave crisis such as the country is passing through at present, and that his election may mean nothing less than the secession of the most experienced, most trusted and most competent leaders of the movement in every part of the country.[240]

This attitude was an ominous sign and betrayed the determination of the Moderates to wreck the Congress if Tilak got elected president, and the Extremists had an upper hand.

The Moderates were unanimous on the exclusion of Tilak, but not on who should take the chair. Pherozeshah might have been an ideal choice for a session which promised to be stormy, but he had already presided thrice over the Congress. So his choice was Nawab Syed Muhammad Bahadur of Madras, both as a gesture to the South and the Muslim community.[241] Gokhale had his eyes fixed on Rash Behari Ghose, a renowned lawyer and an eloquent orator, who might also draw a large number of Bengali delegates on the side of the Moderates and otherwise who might vote with the Extremists.[242] The meeting of the Reception Committee to elect the President took place in the Town Hall at Nagpur on 22 September 1907. The Moderate leaders who had come for the meeting were jeered at by a crowd of the local mob and students. The Extremists who were in minority bullied the 500-odd Moderates and prevented Chitnavis from taking the chair and pushed through the election of their own members to the executive committee. Chitnavis was unnerved by this unprecedented situation and he washed his hands of the Congress session. R.N. Mudholkar, one of the Moderate leaders from Central Provinces and Berar, acquainted Pherozeshah Mehta with the Moderate predicament, and informed him that there was rumour that there was great jubilation among the European officers over the internal bickerings among Congressmen and some people feared that order under Section 144 Cr. P.C. might be suddenly issued to put a stop to the meeting of the Congress.[243] Needless to say that these forebodings came true even after the venue of the session was changed from Nagpur to Surat. But of that later.

Attempts were made to settle the matter. The Extremists came to the negotiating table when emissaries came from Bombay for effecting a compromise. They agreed that both the parties should be represented on the executive committee and the choice of the president should be left to the Standing Committee of the Congress. But the negotiations broke down on the somewhat complicated and sordid question of how to dispose of the funds collected for the Congress session. The contention of the Nagpur Extremists was that only the 'Rashtra Mandal', which had raised the fund, could take a decision on its disposal. They however, agreed to recommend to that body that it should hand over the fund to the Reception Committee on the condition that it was to be ultimately refunded out of any savings that might be left at the end of the session. The Extremists were ready to waive refund if Tilak was elected president. In a way, the Extremists offered a financial bait to the Moderates to get Tilak elected.[244]

The happenings at Nagpur set the Moderates thinking. They now thought that this was the 'New Spirit' of which the Extremists had been talking of late so loudly. It was felt that the indiscipline, violence and intimidation exhibited at the meeting of the Reception Committee at Nagpur might shatter the fabric of the Congress built so laboriously over the last 25 years. The Moderates attributed the Hindu-Muslim tension in East Bengal, the divisions in the ranks of the educated class all over the country, the stiffening of the attitude of the bureaucracy as evident from the deportation of Lala Lajpat Rai, and the consequent setback to constitutional reforms, to the tactics of the Extremists.

Advocating strong and energetic action against the Extremists, H.A. Wadya, a confidant of Pherozeshah Mehta, wrote a letter to a Bombay paper, *Jame-Jamshed,* in which, among other things, he said:

> The only discipline these men have known and shown is to proceed from abuse to assault, and to impose by brute force the policy they cannot enforce by argument. The union of these men with the Congress is the union of a diseased limb to a healthy body, and the only remedy is a surgical severance, if the Congress is to be saved from death by blood poisoning.[245]

The vehemence of the language of this letter need not be commented upon. Its impact on the Extremists can better be imagined than described.

Under adverse conditions the Moderates would look up to Pherozeshah, the sledge-hammer, the oracle, for guidance. But this time the oracle was dumb. The oracle spoke a month later with his usual firmness. Mehta called a meeting of the Central Standing Committee on 10 November in his palatial house in Bombay. Among those present were

Gokhale and Wacha, the two Joint General Secretaries, Vijayaraghavachariar from Madras, Daji Abaji Khare, M.A. Jinnah, G.D. Parekh and Ambalal Sakerlal from Bombay, Tilak and Khaparde. The last two were the only representatives of the Extremists; B.S. Moonje, A.B. Kolhatkar and N.R. Alekar were with Tilak, but Pherozeshah did not allow them to attend the meeting saying that they were not members of the Central Standing Committee. The committee was informed that it was not possible to hold the meeting at Nagpur. Vijayaraghavachariar tried to effect a compromise to make the two parties work together at Nagpur. When his proposal for compromise was opposed by Khaparde on behalf of the Extremists, Pherozeshah sent for a deputation of Gujarati gentlemen who were waiting in an adjacent room. They offered to hold the Congress session at Surat. The offer was accepted by all those who were present, excepting, of course, Tilak and Khaparde, who did not vote.

On second thought, Tilak persuaded Khaparde and other Nagpur Extremists to accept the offer of Vijayaraghavachariar.[246] Next morning, two emissaries from Tilak met Wacha, the Joint General Secretary of the Congress, on behalf of the Nagpur Extremists, and agreed to the reconstitution of the executive committee and to leaving the choice of the Congress president to the Central Standing Committee. But now it was too late. Wacha consulted Pherozeshah who refused to reopen the matter. Wacha wrote to Gokhale: 'It is too late now and the irreconcilables must repent of their extreme folly and obstinacy. I think they have been excellently served. I am not sorry for what has happened. It is a stern lesson [to the Extremists].'[247]

Aurobindo's reaction was that Pherozeshah Mehta had 'juggled the Congress into Surat'.[248] The former had earlier led the Extremist group against Surendranath at the Provincial Conference at Midnapore and rehearsal of Surat was enacted there. Surendranath accused Aurobindo of forcing a split in the Bengal Congress and of an attempt on Sir Andrew Fraser's life.[249]

Kesari reacted to the shifting of the venue from Nagpur to Surat thus: 'Gujarat is a private street of Mehta and Co. and according to the adage which says that every contemptible dog becomes important in his own street . . . the Moderates will preponderate in the Surat Congress.'[250]

The tense atmosphere and the intemperate language used by both sides pointed to the inevitability of the coming crisis at Surat. The meeting of the Reception Committee was held at Surat. Gokhale attended. The Extremists proposed the name of Lala Lajpat Rai, just released from Mandalay, for the presidentship. He had great admiration for Tilak and was sceptical about the strategy of the Moderates, but he did not want to become a pawn in factional politics and so declined to be presidential candidate of a faction and also discouraged the idea of an exclusively Extremist Congress at Nagpur.[251] Aurobindo called Rai's refusal of the offer 'a fatal blunder'.[252] Rash Behari Ghose, whose name had been supported by all the provincial Congress committees, except that of Berar, was elected the Congress president.

Relations between the two groups were to worsen still further. B.R. Nanda described the situation thus: 'Persistent denunciations of the Moderate leadership and politics in press and on the platform, frantic competition with the Moderates in the enrolment of delegates, and the allegations of an imminent betrayal of the nationalist cause by the Moderate leadership could hardly create a climate for the compromise.'[253]

The change of the venue of session did not avert the showdown. No doubt, Surat was a Moderate stronghold, but nothing could prevent the Extremists from collecting their followers from other places. Gokhale was warned on 23 November that the Extremists were planning to take hundreds of rowdies there from Nagpur.[254] It was suggested that, to maintain their supremacy, the Moderates also should recruit a thousand delegates of the 'right stuff and mettle' from Gujarat, besides having sizeable contingents from the Deccan and other places. There was great tension in the air at Surat. Several days before the commencement of the session, Khaparde was in Surat addressing public meetings and explaining the creed of his party to the people. One of the secretaries of the Reception Committee wrote to Gokhale: 'Mr Khaparde is daily preaching here. The mob only attended these lectures. No people of higher rank go there.'[255] The Extremists' meetings were well attended and their camp in the Congress was fast filling up. Khaparde noted, 'We number over 600.'[256]

The Extremist orators condemned the 'mendicancy' of their Moderate opponents and declared their determination not to allow any backsliding from the resolutions passed by the Calcutta Congress (1906). At a meeting at Gheekantawadi, with Aurobindo in the chair, the Extremist speakers condemned the idea of any truck with the Moderates and pleaded for a purely Extremist Congress. But it must be said to the credit of Tilak that he did not approve these utterances. He is reported to have said, 'Now I feel I shall bring round this very Congress to my way of thinking. As we do not have a majority today, we must compromise with the Moderates and keep ourselves in the Congress itself.'[257]

But events were shaping themselves otherwise. The Congress session was to commence on 26 December 1907, but two days earlier had come the news of the attempt on the life of Allen, the Collector of Dacca. The Moderates were deeply disturbed by the news. History was to repeat itself in 1907. As in 1897, the country was confronted with a vicious circle of repression, terrorism and counter-terrorism. The Moderate leaders saw a logical connection between the reckless propaganda of the Extremists and the wild aberrations of impressionable youth. The Dacca outrage steeled them in their resolve to stand no further nonsense from their political opponents.

About 1,600 delegates and 800 visitors assembled on the bank of the Tapti on 26 December 1907. The atmosphere was tense, but nobody could predict the course of events. A tumultuous ovation was given to Lala Lajpat Rai who had just returned from a six-month deportation to Burma and Dr Rutherford, a fraternal Liberal delegate, who had specially come from England to attend the session as a friendly observer. Then came the presidential procession, including Dr Rash Behari Ghose, the president-elect, Pherozeshah Mehta, Wacha, Gokhale and other leaders. After T.N. Malvi had read his welcome address, Ambalal Sakerlal Desai proposed formally that Rash Behari Ghose should take his chair. Tilak and Khaparde had promised not to oppose the election of Rash Behari Ghose if the resolutions on swaraj, swadeshi, boycott and national education, passed at the Calcutta Congress (1906), were kept unchanged. The Moderates did not play their cards honestly — they had changed the venue, they had outmanoeuvred the Extremists in the selection of the president, and now they put forward vitally altered resolutions on these subjects, hoping to pass them by a contrived majority. The comprehensiveness and the force of the original Calcutta resolutions were deliberately restricted by rewording them.[258]

So cries of protest were raised by a section of the audience against Ghose being elected president. When Surendranath, who rose to second the proposal was shouted down, the meeting was postponed to the next day. As the attitude of Mehta, Gokhale and Malvi hardened, the next day (27 December 1907) Tilak resolved on moving an amendment to the presidential election. Meanwhile, Aurobindo had been vilified in vulgar language and his group was spoiling for a fight.

Tilak's request for time to speak, after the nomination for president had been seconded, was not heeded. After waiting vainly to be called by the chairman, Tilak rushed to the dais and insisted on his right to move the amendment. Neither Malvi, the chairman of the Reception Committee, nor Ghose, the president-elect, allowed him to speak, Tilak refused to be ruled out of order and insisted that Ghose had not yet been elected president, and that he had right to appeal for a decision to the delegates. Now pandemonium broke out and the lifting of a Gujarati chair was the signal to send a Maharashtrian shoe flying and Nevinson witnessed the Indian National Congress 'dissolving in chaos'.[259] There were shouts and counter-shouts, brandishing of sticks and the unrolling of turbans and the breaking of chairs and the bruising of heads.

The responsibility for what happened at Surat continued to be debated for long. The Moderates published their version of the incident on the evening of 27 December 1907. The Extremist version came out four days later. In the eyes of the Moderates, Tilak was the villain of the piece. As a matter of fact, Tilak was most unhappy over the incident. At the instance of Motilal Ghose of the *Amrita Bazar Patrika*, on 28 December 1907, he tried to appease his opponents by writing what amounted to a letter of regret, waiving his opposition to the election of Rash Behari Ghose, pleading for 'forgetting and forgiving', and offering his co-operation in preserving the unity of the party. But Motilal, the bearer of the letter, was howled out by the Moderate leaders, headed by no less a person than Pherozeshah Mehta himself.[260] Aurobindo who was in the thick of the fight at Surat wrote many years later: '. . . to no one was the catastrophe so great a blow as to Mr Tilak. He did not love the "do-nothingness" of that assembly, but he valued it both as a great national fact and for its unrealised possibilities.'[261]

What Lala Lajpat Rai wrote 18 months after the events at Surat seems to be a correct appraisal of the situation:

> . . . instead of leading his party, Tilak had allowed himself to be led by some of its wild spirits. Twice on my request at Surat he agreed to waive his opposition to the election of Rash Behari Ghose and leave the matter of the four Calcutta resolutions to the subjects Committee, but the moment I left him he found himself helpless before the volume of public opinion that surrounded him.[262]

Rai's impression was confirmed by Aurobindo, one of the most uncompromising Extremists at Surat: 'Very few people know that it was I (without consulting Tilak) who gave the order that led to the breaking of the Congress and was responsible for the refusal to join the new-fangled Moderate convention.'[263] Aurobindo wanted deliberately to 'mend or end' the Congress. It was no sacrilege for him. He wanted an inner struggle, and not a fictitious unity. He was certain from his study of revolutions that in any contest between the Moderates and the Extremists, one or the other must be crushed or prevail before the unity of a regenerated nation could replace the false unity of acquiescence in servitude.[264]

It is not easy to establish responsibility for the Surat split. But from a close study of the events between the Banaras Congress (1905) and the Surat Congress (1907), certain facts are obvious: that the tone of the letters of Wadya, Wacha and Mudholkar were very offensive; that the Extremists were writing very strongly; that Mehta broke his silence after a month (was he confabulating with the Surat people?); and that Tilak was denied the Congress presidential chair while others had occupied the gaddi, twice or thrice (even Gokhale, junior to Tilak, had become Congress president in 1905). Why was Tilak, the idol of the people, the Lokmanya, the model of self-sacrifice and the ardent patriot, not selected Congress president? Partly the clash of personalities and partly the conflict of ideologies, led to the inevitable split at Surat.

After Surat, the Extremist mood was one of righteous indignation; so also was the mood of the Moderates, but tinged with a sense of relief, because they thought that the diseased limb had been amputated. Pherozeshah Mehta was of the opinion that the separation between the two parties was inevitable if the Congress was not to submit itself to the rule of the Extremists whose dreams were unreasonable and unrealizable and such as would not be acceptable to the majority of Congressmen.[265] He was particularly annoyed with Tilak whose biting sarcasm in the *Kesari* and the *Maharatta* had deeply wounded him and whose influence among reputable people in India was due to his place in the Congress. Now, after the split, he would be exposed.[266] Other Moderates also thought similarly.

But whoever might have been more responsible for the split and whatever its cause, it was a great national calamity. Gokhale was aware of the magnitude of the disaster and its impact on the nationalist movement and organization. About two months before the split at Surat, he had written to Wedderburn; 'If a split does come it means a disaster, for the Bureaucracy will then put down both sections without much difficulty.'[267] The first British official reaction to the split was a telegram from the District Magistrate of Surat to the Governor of Bombay: 'Indian National Congress Meeting today became disorderly blows being exchanged. President called on police to clear assembly room and grounds. Order now restored. None reported seriously hurt. No further disturbance anticipated.'[268] Minto exultingly told Morley that the 'Congress collapse' was a 'great triumph for us'.[269] But Morley knew better. Almost prophetically he told the Viceroy that, their immediate collapse notwithstanding, the Extremists would eventually capture the Congress.[270]

Gokhale felt very much depressed by the Surat episode. He felt 'like one who has been blown up into high air with the fort he was guarding and who descends on earth to find himself surrounded only by ruins . . . meanwhile there is so much to do if only to gather ruins before the others, better equipped for the task, begin the work of reconstruction.'[271]

From the jubilation in the official circle and the despondency in the Congress camp (both among Moderates, such as Gokhale, and among Extremists, such as Tilak and Lajpat Rai) we can well measure the harm that was done to the Congress in particular and the Indian nation in general. It can be said that the Moderates were the brain of the Congress and the nation, and the Extremists were its heart; the former were the 'law' and the latter the 'impulse'. The united action of both was absolutely necessary for the proper functioning of the body-politic of the nation. With the Extremists in the wilderness, the Moderates were to achieve little. The British understood only the language of strength. Unfortunately the Moderates were not in a position to show that strength for about a decade after 1907. It was only after 1916, with the re-entry of the Extremists into the Congress and the exit of the Moderates (1918) that the Congress could be re-activized. But then it was a new story. Gandhi, Gokhale's political disciple,[272] with his emphasis on the synthesis of reason and faith, law and impulse, representing the eternal and immortal spirit of India, was to activize and rejuvenate the Congress and the nation into an altogether new life. But we must not anticipate events.

Notes

1. *Indian Politics,* with an Introduction by W.C. Bonnerjee, Madras, 1898, pp. vii, viii. For a detailed discussion of Hume, cf. Briton Martin (Jr.), *New India, 1885* (British Official Policy and the Emergence of the Indian National Congress), Bombay, 1970, pp. 53-77.
2. Anil Seal, *The Emergence of Indian Nationalism; Competition and Collaboration in the Late 19th Century,* Cambridge, 1968.
3. John R. McLane, *Indian Nationalism and the Early Congress,* Princeton, 1977.
4. Ibid. McLane has given a very balanced account of the achievements of the early Congress.
5. W. Wedderburn, *Allan Octavian Hume C.B., Father of the Indian National Congress,* London, 1913, gives extracts from the letter on pp. 50-3. See Appendix I, to Chapter I above.
6. Ibid., p. 53.
7. Ibid., pp. 53-4.
8. Ibid., p. 54.
9. Ibid. For a critical estimate of Hume's role in the establishment of the Congress, cf. Seal, op. cit., p. 272, and also pp. 276-80. How some people were biased against Hume can be inferred from the following: 'Hume was said in my time to be the greatest liar who ever came to India' (Maine to Dufferin, 2 June 1886, quoted in Briton Martin, op. cit., p. 61).
10. Quoted in S.R. Mehrotra, *The Emergence of the Indian National Congress,* Delhi, 1971, pp. 415-17.
11. Briton Martin (Jr.), op. cit., p. 292.
12. Ibid., p. 133.
13. Ibid., p. 311.
14. W. Wedderburn, op. cit., pp. 58-9. See also *Report, First I.N.C.* (1885), Resolution III.
15. Bonnerjee, op. cit., p. vii. See also Hiralal Singh, *Problems and Policies of the British in India, 1885-1898,* Bombay, 1963, pp. 210-11.

16. *The Hindustan Review*, December 1903, p. 478.
17. *Report, Second I.N.C.*, (1886), p. 54.
18. Badruddin Tyabji, *Report, Third I.N.C.*, (1887), p. 75. W.C. Bonnerjee, *Report, Seventh I.N.C.*, 1892, pp. 11-12.
19. Resolution XIII, *Report, Fourth I.N.C.*, (1888).
20. Cf. the Syed's letter to Badruddin Tyabji, 24 January 1888; speech at Lucknow, 28 December 1887; speech at Meerut, 14 March 1886. S.V. Desika Char (ed.) *Readings in Indian Constitutional History, 1757-1947*, Delhi, 1983, pp. 310-2.
21. Resolution II, *Report, Fifth I.N.C.*, 1889.
22. *Report, Second I.N.C.*, 1886, p. 34.
23. *Report, Fourth I.N.C.*, 1888, p. 33.
24. *Report, Eleventh I.N.C.*, 1895, Introduction. For details see Sita Ram Singh, *Nationalism and Social Reform in India (1885-1920)*, Delhi, 1968, pp. 41-3.
25. Hiralal Singh, op. cit., p. 214.
26. For the interdependence of nationalism and social reform, see Sita Ram Singh, op. cit. Also see B. Pattabhi Sitaramayya, *History of the Congress*, Delhi, 1969. pp. 8-9.
27. *Report, Fifth I.N.C.*, 1889, Introduction iv.
28. Hira Lal Singh, op. cit., pp. 214-5.
29. *Reports, First-Fourth I.N.C.*, 1885, 1886, 1887, 1888.
30. *Report, Second I.N.C.*, 1886, p. 5.
31. Naoroji to Mansukhram, 7 November 1885, N.P.
32. For example Surendranath Banerjea *(Bengalee)*, G. Subramania *(The Hindu)*, Tilak (*Kesari* and *Maharatta*), the *Indu Prakash* (first edited by Telang and then by Chandavarkar) and N.N. Sen *(Indian Mirror)*.
33. Seal is very harsh on this point. According to him, the Congress might have seemed to be India's national party, but during its early years it was hardly that. In his opinion it was more of a ramshackle set of local linkages whose task was to organize an annual tamasha. There were no paying members, no permanent organization, no officials other than a general secretary, no central offices and no funds. Each year the annual conference was held in a different city, where a reception committee, locally recruited and locally financed, collected funds, hired lodgings and generally prepared for the winter meetings. When the session was over, this committee remained in being for a few weeks to arrange the printing and distribution of the Congress reports. Then there would be an interregnum for some months until another reception committee would be organized in the city where the Congress session was to be held next. As far as its finances and organization were concerned, each session was thus a separate and independent undertaking. (Anil Seal, op. cit., p. 278).
34. Samuel Smith, *India Revisited*, 1886, pp. 28-9.
35. *Reports, I.N.C.*, 1885, 1886, 1887, 1888.
36. *Hansard's Indian Debates*, 20 June 1889, pp. 330-1.
37. Resolution XVIII, *Report, Twelfth I.N.C.*, 1896.
38. *Report, Second I.N.C.*, 1886, p. 68.
39. Hira Lal Singh, op. cit., p. 217.

40. Ibid., pp. 217-8.
41. Bipan Chandra, *Rise of Economic Nationalism in India (Economic Policies of Indian National Leaders, 1880 to 1905)*, New Delhi, 1966.
42. Ibid., p. 746.
43. Ibid.
44. Ibid., p. 748.
45. Ibid., pp. 751-2.
46. Ibid., pp. 751-2.
47. Ibid., p. 752.
48. Ibid., pp. 753-4.
49. Hira Lal Singh, op. cit., p. 218.
50. Anil Seal, op. cit., p. 11. See also Gallagher, Johnson, Seal (eds.), *Locality, Province and Nation*, Cambridge, 1973.
51. W.S. Lilly, *India and its Problems*, London, 1902, p. 242.
52. Ibid., pp. 243-8.
53. Briton Martin (Jr.), op. cit., p. 324. For details see ibid., pp. 326-9.
54. Anil Seal, op. cit., pp. 285-6.
55. B.C. Pal, *Memories of My Life and Times*, Vol. II, p. 16.
56. Ibid., pp. 31-5. Also Report of the I.N.C., 1887, Resolution I, p. 63.
57. *Report, First I.N.C.*, 1885, pp. 94-5. At the fourth Congress Hume was reappointed according to the new procedure. He continued to be General Secretary till 1892 when he left India.
58. N.V. Raj Kumar, *Development of the Congress Constitution*, New Delhi, 1949, pp. 1-5.
59. B.R. Nanda, *Gokhale — The Indian Moderates and the British Raj*, Delhi, 1977, p. 482.
60. Ibid.
61. See for details, Percival Griffiths, *The British Impact on India*, London, 1952.
62. See S.R. Singh's article, 'Indo-British Antagonism in the 19th Century', *Proceedings Volume of the Indian History Congress*, 19th Session, Agra, 1956, pp. 372-9.
63. H.J.S. Cotton, *New India or India in Transition*, London, 1885, pp. 40-1.
64. W. Wedderburn, op. cit., p. 60.
65. Ibid., pp. 60-3. Martin says that during 1886 Hume played a most critical, but unfortunate, role in worsening relations between Dufferin and the educated Indian leaders. *The Rising Tide* and *The Star in the East*, two pamphlets, played a major role in embittering the relations between the viceroy and Hume. The relation finally became so bitter that in Hume's own words, 'I never wrote to him or saw him again.' (Briton Martin (Jr.), op. cit., pp. 320-3.
66. W. Wedderburn, op. cit., p. 63. (See also Briton Martin, op. cit., p. 325).
67. Wedderburn, Ibid., p. 64.
68. Ibid.
69. Briton Martin, op. cit., p. 334.
70. W. Wedderburn, op. cit., pp. 63-4.
71. *Report, Twenty-seventh I.N.C.*, 1912, p. 50.
72. W. Wedderburn, op. cit., pp. 64-5.
73. Ibid., pp. 65-6.

74. Ibid., p. 66.
75. Dufferin to Kimberley, 11 June 1886 'Kimberley Papers', PC/D/22d.
76. Reay to Kimberley, 5 March 1886, 'Kimberley Papers', PC/D/26b.
77. *Audi Alterum Partem,* p. 5.
78. W. Wedderburn, op. cit., pp. 68-9.
79. Sir Syed Ahmad was an enlightened Muslim who wanted his community to take to English education. It was no accident that Syed became particularly bitter against the Congress at this time and organized a front against the Congress.
80. W. Wedderburn, op. cit., pp. 70-2.
81. Ibid., pp. 70-80.
82. To Provincial Governments, 29 October 1888, Public Proceedings No. 54, April 1890.
83. It must be said in defence of the Congress that its demand was to raise the limit to Rs 1,000 per month, whereas most of the delegates had incomes above that level.
84. Dufferin, *Speeches, 1884-1888, 1890,* pp. 237-44.
85. See n. 79, *supra.*
86. Rajendra Prasad, *India Divided,* Bombay, 1946, pp. 98-101.
87. Raja of Bhinga, *Democracy not suited to India,* p. 90. According to *The Hindu,* he got the book written under the dictation of Colvin. (The *Hindu* quoted in *India,* May 1893, p. 156.
88. *The Times,* 13 August 1888, p. 5.
89. 'Cow Agitation', *The Nineteenth Century,* April 1894.
90. Pandit Ajodhyanath's speech, *Report, Fourth I.N.C.,* 1883.
91. *Report, Fourth I.N.C.,* 1888, p. vii.
92. *Hansard's Indian Debates,* 22 February 1889, p. 16.
93. Ibid., 6 March 1890, pp. 54-5.
94. *Report, Sixth I.N.C.,* 1890, Introduction, XXXIV; Pub. Progs. Nos. 1-4, January 1891.
95. C.J. Lyall's Note of 16 August 1893, 'Kimberley Papers', PG/E/18d.
96. Lansdowne to Kimberley, No. 52, 22 August 1893 'Lansdowne Papers, Correspondence with Secretary of State, 1893'.
97. Note of 9 August 1893 by D.E. McCrackew, encl. to Lansdowne's letter to Kimberley, 22 August 1893, 'Kimberley Papers', PC/E/18d.
98. Lansdowne to Kimberley, 7 November 1893, Ibid., PC/E/18e.
99. Ibid., 1 March 1894, p. 89.
100. Indian Parliamentary Debates, 28 March 1892, pp. 131-2.
101. Note of 23 September 1893, Pub. Progs. No. 67, November 1893.
102. *Indian Parliamentary Debates,* 21 September 1893, p. 675.
103. 'India — the Political Outlook' in *The Nineteenth Century,* June 1894, pp. 897, 901; *Indian Polity* (1894), pp. 385-7.
104. *India,* April 1895, p. 122.
105. Ibid., January 1896, p. 1.
106. Enclosure to Curzon's letter to Hamilton, 28 December 1899, 'Hamilton Papers', XV, 395-401.
107. *Report, Second I.N.C.,* 1886, Introduction, p. 10.
108. *Report, Third I.N.C.,* 1887, Introduction, p. 13.

109. *Report, Fourteenth I.N.C.*, 1898, Introduction, iii.
110. *Report, Fifteenth I.N.C.*, 1899, Introduction, v.
111. Enclosure to Curzon's letter to Hamilton, 28 June 1899, 'Hamilton Papers', XIV, pp. 63-5.
112. Hamilton to Elgin, 5 February 1897, 'Hamilton Papers', II, 29.
113. Hamilton to Elgin, 24 June 1897, ibid., II, 295.
114. Hamilton to Elgin, 16 November 1898, ibid., III, 486; 20 October 1899, ibid., IV, p. 363.
115. K.T. Telang, Badruddin Tyabji and S. Subramania Iyer. Tyabji was the president of the Third Congress (1887, Madras) and became a High Court Judge in 1895.
116. Some of the important Congressmen who were appointed members of the central or provincial legislatures were Pherozeshah Mehta, Telang, Naoroji, Tyabji, Tilak, R.M. Sayani, Gokhale, W.C. Bonnerjee, Surendranath Banerjea, A.M. Bose, Rampal Singh, Ananda Charlu, C. Sankaran Nair, and C. Vijayaraghavachariar.
117. Hira Lal Singh, op. cit., p. 249.
118. Ibid., p. 249-50.
119. Curzon to Hamilton, 18 November 1900, 'Hamilton Papers', XVIII, pp. 293-4.
120. Dufferin's Minute enclosed with 'Pub. Des. from India', No. 67, 6 November 1888.
121. Lady G. Cecil, *Salisbury*, IV, pp. 194-6.
122. Lansdowne to Cross, No. 8, 11 February 1891, 'Lansdowne Papers', Correspondence with Secretary of State (1891).
123. Lansdowne's Minute of 4 May 1889, 'Lansdowne Papers', Notes and Minutes (1889-94), pp. 31-2.
124. Cross to Lansdowne, No. 33, 28 June 1889, 'Lansdowne Papers', Correspondence with Secretary of State (1889), 'Pub. Des. to India', No. 80, 1 August 1889.
125. 'Pub. Des. to India', No. 81, 1 August 1889.
126. For Draft Bill, see 'Pub. Progs.', No. 151, May 1890.
127. For Curzon's speech introducing the Bill, see S.V. Desika Char, op. cit., pp. 415-9.
128. For the full text of the Act, see S.V. Desika Char, op. cit., pp. 419-21.
129. A.C. Lyall, *Life of Lord Dufferin*, Vol. II, p. 151.
130. 'Pub. Des. from India', No. 75, 24 December 1889.
131. *Hansard's Indian Debates* (1890), p. 84.
132. Ibid., p. 86.
133. *Indian Parliamentary Debates*, 15 February 1894, p. 33.
134. *Hansard's Indian Debates*, 1890, p. 55.
135. From Sarvajanik Sabha to Government of India, 3 June 1893, *Pub Progs.*, No. 137, July 1893.
136. *Pub. Progs.*, No. 193, July 1893.
137. *Indian Parliamentary Debates*, 1892, p. 147.
138. Ibid., p. 134.
139. Progs. of the Leg. Council of the Governor-General, 16 March 1892, XXXII, p. 111.

140. S.N. Banerjea, *A Nation in Making,* Calcutta, 1963, p. 115.
141. Sumit Sarkar, *Modern India, 1885-1947,* Delhi, 1983, pp. 19-20.
142. Ibid., p. 20.
143. B.R. Nanda, op. cit., p. 480.
144. For a fuller discussion of this aspect, see Sita Ram Singh, op. cit., pp. 151-60.
145. B.R. Nanda, op. cit., p. 481.
146. M.A. Buch in his, *Rise of Indian Liberalism,* discusses social liberalism and then shows that political liberalism was an adjunct of that social liberalism. In list of liberals, he gives prominent place to Rammohan Roy, Mahadev Govind Ranade, Dadabhai Naoroji and Gopal Krishna Gokhale.
147. S.V. Desika Char, op. cit., p. 313.
148. Ibid., p. 314.
149. Dadabhai Naoroji on 2 May 1867, ibid., pp. 301-2.
150. R.C. Dutt, *England and India,* London, 1897, p. 121.
151. C.L. Parekh, *Eminent Indians of Indian Politics,* Bombay, 1892, p. 275.
152. Ibid., p. 96.
153. *Report, Second I.N.C.,* Calcutta (1886), p. 112.
154. S.V. Desika Char, op. cit., Gokhale on the limitations of the bureaucratic government, 14 November 1905, pp. 315-6.
155. Ibid., p. 319.
156. Karve and Ambekar (eds.), *Gokhale's Speeches and Writings,* Vol. II, p. 216.
157. Ibid., p. 217.
158. Ibid., p. 218.
159. Motilal to Jawaharlal, 7 February 1907, Nehru Papers.
160. The Moderates had a pathetic faith in appealing to the conscience of the British public though India counted for little in British public life.
161. Among the Moderate leaders it was Gokhale who laid the greatest stress on character-building and it was with this end in view that he established the Servants of India Society.
162. Karve and Ambekar, op. cit., p. 221.
163. See Bipan Chandra, op. cit.
164. *Supra.*
165. S.V. Desika Char, op. cit., Dadabhai Naoroji on 4 January 1881, pp. 303-4.
166. For example, R.C. Dutt, Ranade and Gokhale also criticized the British for the economic ruination of India.
167. See his *Poverty and Un-British Rule In India,* London, 1901.
168. Morley to Minto, 18 July 1907 (M.P.).
169. Minto to Morley, 7 August 1907 (M.P.).
170. Minto to Morley, 10 July 1907 (M.P.).
171. Minto to Morley, 12 September 1907 (M.P.).
172. Motilal to Jawaharlal, 24 January 1907 (Nehru P.).
173. C.Y. Chintamani to Gokhale, 15 March 1907 (G.P.).
174. *India,* 29 December 1905.
175. B.R. Nanda, op. cit., p. 487.
176. Minto to Morley, 27 May 1908 (M.P.). These four elements continued to be the pillars of the Raj to its last days.

177. Note on political discontent enclosed with Minto to Morley, 28 April 1910 (M.P.). It is remarkable that the British continued to play this role to the end of the Raj.
178. M.A. Buch, *Rise and Growth of Indian Militant Nationalism,* Baroda, 1940, p. 2.
179. M.A. Buch, for example, regarding the Tilak school as a good running commentary on the limitations of the earlier Liberal school, considers it a bridge between the earlier school of cultural nationalism of Dayananda Saraswati and Swami Vivekananda and the later Gandhi school of Indian politics, Ibid., Preface.

    Buch says further:

    In India political radicalism and social conservatism have gone, to some extent, hand in hand. The school of new nationalism which rears its head prominently from 1905, is a mixture of this type. It connects itself on the one hand with the forces which expressed themselves in the Mutiny of 1857 against British Government, and on the other hand with movements of religious and social revival started by Swami Dayananda and Swami Vivekananda. Ibid., p. 1.
180. Ibid., p. 16.
181. Dayananda had realized the utter futility of making any progress under foreign rule:

    When a country falls on evil days, the natives have to bear untold misery and suffering. Say what you will, the Swadeshiya Rajya is by far the best. A foreign Government, perfectly free from religious prejudices, impartial towards all the native and foreigners alike, kind, beneficent and just to the natives alike their parents though it may be, can never render the people perfectly happy.

    Satyarth Prakash, Chapter VIII, quoted in Swami Sharaddhananda's *Inside Congress.*
182. Edwin Bevan, *Indian Nationalism: An Independent Estimate,* London, 1913, p. 99.
183. Ibid., p. 112.
184. Amles Tripathi, *The Extremist Challenge,* Calcutta, 1967, p. vii.
185. Strangely enough, Nirad Chaudhuri wants us to be free from the snares of this Continent of Circe today.
186. Amles Tripathi, op. cit., p. 1.
187. Ibid., p. 10.
188. Ibid., pp. 14-5.
189. Ibid., p. 15.
190. Ibid., p. 15.
191. Ibid., p. 17.
192. B.C. Pal, *The New Spirit,* Calcutta, 1907, pp. 74-5.
193. Amles Tripathi, op. cit., p. 24.
194. Aurobindo to Mrinalini Devi, 30 August 1905.
195. Amles Tripathi, op. cit., p. 34.
196. For details of this incident, see Sita Ram Singh, op. cit., Chapter II.
197. For details of Durga Puja and Shivaji Festival, see Ibid., pp. 108-110.
198. B.C. Pal, *The National Congress,* 1897, p. 9.

199. B.C. Pal, 'The Test of Patriotism', *New India,* 17 July 1902.
200. Amles Tripathi, op. cit., p. 59.
201. V.C. Joshi (ed.), *Autobiographical Writings of Lajpat Rai,* Delhi, 1965, pp. 86-91. Also Lajpat Rai, 'The Coming Indian National Congress — Some Suggestions', *Kayastha Samachar,* November 1901. Rai himself refers to the safety-valve function of the early Congress. V.C. Joshi (ed.), *Lala Lajpat Rai, Writings and Speeches,* Introduction, pp. xxi-xxii.
202. Anil Seal, op. cit., p. 347.
203. Briton Martin (Jr.), op. cit., p. 336.
204. Quoted in Amles Tripathi, op. cit., p. 46.
205. Samuel Smith, *My Life-Work,* pp. 442-3.
206. See *supra,* the passing of the Indian Council's Act of 1892.
207. Kimberley to Lansdowne, 9 June 1893, quoted in Amles Tripathi, op. cit., p. 48.
208. Hamilton to Curzon, 9 January 1901, 'Hamilton Papers', Vol. 3, p. 9.
209. Curzon to Hamilton, 22 July 1903, quoted in Amles Tripathi, op. cit., p. 49.
210. Amles Tripathi, op. cit., p. 49.
211. Quoted, ibid., p. 50.
212. Ibid., p. 52.
213. Ibid., p. 55.
214. *India,* 10 June 1904, pp. 281-2.
215. S.V. Desika Char, op. cit., pp. 323-5.
216. Ibid., pp. 325-6.
217. Ibid., p. 326. From the writings of both Tilak and Aurobindo it appears that they were anticipating Gandhi.
218. *Congress Presidential Addresses,* 1885-1910, Madras, 1935.
219. B.R. Nanda, op. cit., pp. 490-1.
220. B.R. Nanda, op. cit., pp. 245-6.
221. Ibid., p. 252.
222. Bipin Chandra Pal, leader of the Bengal Extremists.
223. Bal Gangadhar Tilak, the most popular Extremist leader.
224. Mahadev Govind Ranade, the soul of the National Social Conference, the power behind the Congress and the spiritual and political mentor of Gokhale.
225. Gokhale to Natesan, 2 October 1906 (G.P.).
226. Gokhale to Krishnaswami Aiyer, 29 September 1906 (G.P.)
227. Khaparde Diary, 31 December 1906.
228. Motilal to Jawaharlal, 27 December 1906 (Nehru P.).
229. Quoted in B.R. Nanda, op. cit., p. 258.
230. Quoted ibid., pp. 258-9.
231. *Congress Presidential Address, First Series, 1885-1910,* Madras, 1935.
232. *Bande Mataram,* 26 December 1906.
233. Quoted in B.R. Nanda, op. cit., p. 260.
234. *Bande Mataram,* 31 December 1906.
235. B.R. Nanda, op. cit., pp. 260-1.
236. For a detailed, critical and comprehensive study of the movement, see Sumit Sarkar, *The Swadeshi Movement in Bengal (1903-1908),* New Delhi, 1973.

237. Mudholkar to Gokhale, January 1907 (G.P.)
238. *Supra.* Needless to say, Gokhale's personality won laurels, but his teachings found little support.
239. *The Desh Sewak.*
240. *Hindustan Review,* April 1907.
241. H.S. Dikshit to Gokhale, 10 September 1907 (G.P.)
242. Gokhale to H.N. Apte, 11 September 1907 (G.P.)
243. R.N. Mudholkar to Pherozeshah Mehta, 2 October 1907 (G.P.) A copy of the letter was sent to Gokhale.
244. Chintamani to Gokhale, 20 October 1907 (G.P.).
245. Copy enclosed with H.A. Wadya to Gokhale, 20 October 1907 (G.P.).
246. *Khaparde Diary,* 10 and 11 November 1907.
247. Quoted in B.R. Nanda, op. cit., p. 284.
248. *Bande Mataram,* 17 December 1907.
249. S.N. Banerjea, op. cit., p. 235.
250. Quoted in B.R. Nanda, op. cit., p. 284.
251. Lala Lajpat Rai to Gokhale, 3 November 1907 (G.P.).
252. *Bande Mataram,* 20 December 1907.
253. B.R. Nanda, op. cit., pp. 285-6.
254. Mudholkar to Gokhale, 23 November 1907 (G.P.).
255. Nanabhai to Gokhale, 20 December 1907 (G.P.).
256. *Khaparde Diary,* 24 December 1907.
257. S.L. Karandikar, *Lokmanya Bal Gangadhar Tilak,* Poona, 1957, pp. 261-2.
258. Amles Tripathi, op. cit., p. 131.
259. For Surat Congress, see M.R. Jayakar, *The Story of My Life,* Vol. I, Bombay, 1958, pp. 78-84; Nevinson, *The New Spirit in India, 1908,* pp. 247-8; A.C. Majumdar, *The Indian National Evolution,* Madras, 1917, pp. 104-13.
260. P. Dutt, *Memories of Motilal Ghose,* Calcutta, 1935, p. 173.
261. S.B. Bapat, *The Reminiscences and Anecdotes of Lokmanya Tilak,* Poona, 1925, p. 18.
262. V.C. Joshi (ed.) *Lajpat Rai, Writings and Speeches,* Vol. I, p. 180.
263. *Sri Aurobindo on Himself and on the Mother,* Pondicherry, 1953, p. 82.
264. *Bande Mataram,* 27 October 1907.
265. J.R.B. Jeejeebhoy, *Some Unpublished and Later Speeches and Writings of the Hon'ble Sir Pherozeshah Mehta,* Bombay, 1918.
266. Ibid.
267. Gokhale to Wedderburn, 11 October 1907, in Morley to Minto, 31 October 1907 (M.P.).
268. Telegram from District Magistrate, Surat, to Secretary, Judicial Department, Bombay Government, 27 December 1907. 'Report of the Disturbances at the Indian National Congress Meeting at Surat', Bombay Government Judicial Department 1908, (1) Vol. 98.
269. Minto to Morley, 5 January 1908 (M.P.)
270. Morley to Minto, 27 December 1907 (M.P.).
271. Gokhale to Ray, 23 January 1908 (Ray P.).
272. M.K. Gandhi, *Gokhale — My Political Guru,* Ahmedabad, 1955, p. 47.

Chapter III

The Swadeshi Upsurge

Sankari Prasad Basu

1. Historical Background

THE SWADESHI MOVEMENT (1905-11), though initiated by the people of Bengal in protest against the partition of the province, soon extended its area of activities, influencing, to a great extent, the growth of Indian nationalism and the freedom struggle. It led to the formulation of a new British policy towards India, a policy that prevailed for more than two decades and which culminated in basic changes in the Congress ideology. The movement can therefore claim a place of honour in the history of modern India. It has been established by in-depth researches that one of the main reasons behind the partition was Lord Curzon's desire to curb and, if possible, crush the Indian National Congress. It is thus also a very important chapter in the history of the Congress. There is no other example of any other movement, primarily concerning a particular province, spilling over and influencing national life in so many ways and to such a degree.

The movement exposed the ineffectiveness of the erstwhile Congress policy of petitions and appeals and led the party and the nation to a head-on collision with the rulers, seriously undermining the influence of the Moderates in the Congress and leading ultimately to their withdrawal from it.

By adopting boycott and passive resistance as methods of agitating the movement was able, for the first time, to give the struggle a mass character. These methods, with some adaptation, were adopted later in Gandhian non-cooperation. It also opened the way for more militant forms of struggle, underground and open, and attracted the youth to the movement. The Swadeshi Movement was largely a youth movement. It showed, by example, that the fight for freedom was no part-time occupation but called for a total commitment to the cause. It gave to the nation an articulated philosophy of nationalism, a national anthem, a national war cry, and the blazing ideal of *Purna Swaraj* (complete independence). It also stimulated the creative impulse which fostered the fine arts, literature and science, and also economic researches and educational reforms, thus leading to a total national awakening on all fronts. In the face of this mass confrontation, the British rulers launched their policy of 'repression and reform' and 'divide and rule'.

For historical reasons, which were not all necessarily deplorable, the movement displayed some Hindu overtones which led to some misgivings among Muslims. These, fanned by the imperialists, strained relations between the two communities, leading to successive bitter clashes.

To understand how, what started as a regional protest developed into the all-India Swadeshi Movement and accomplished so much, it is necessary to examine the situation in Bengal at that time. Geographically, Bengal Presidency then included not only the whole of Bengal (West Bengal and East Bengal), but also Bihar and Orissa, covering an area of 189,900 square miles, with a population of 78.5 million (more than a quarter of the then total population of India), its gross revenue being Rs 11 crore. It was administered by a lieutenant governor ('always chosen from the senior ranks of the Indian Civil Service'), assisted by a legislative council. Its capital, Calcutta, was India's capital too. The jurisdiction of the Calcutta High Court and Calcutta University stretched even beyond the border of the presidency. With three major modern Indian languages (Bengali, Hindi and Oriya) and a number of dialects being spoken in the presidency, and two major religions, Hinduism and Islam, the behavioural pattern of the population was complex. The languages crossed the bar of religion, and religions the bar of language.

This presidency, with so much diversity and such manifold interests, had, due to historical circumstances, come to be largely dominated by the Bengali Hindus in both the political and the cultural spheres.

British rule being first firmly established in Bengal, Calcutta being the centre of British commercial enterprises, and also the capital of India, British influence was markedly dominant here and the bureaucracy spread its wide network. For administrative reasons, the Britishers encouraged the spread of English education. The idea was to produce a number of English-knowing 'babus' in order to facilitate the smooth running of the administrative machinery. The spread of English education, initially among the upper strata of the Bengali society, opened a new horizon to the progressive section of Bengal with their genius for assimilation and adaptation. It was hailed not only because it paid dividends in the material sense — people with a working knowledge of English had an opening to minor jobs in commercial firms — but also because it opened a window to Western culture and humanism. It also served as a catalyst for the growth of political consciousness and the urge to search for a national identity. It brought Bengal to the threshold of a new era of intellectual ferment which the rulers did not visualize and bargain for.

Thus East and West met and reacted in the Bengali mind to stimulate an unprecedented surge of creative consciousness in 19th century Bengal, variously called an Awakening, Regeneration, or even a Renaissance. 'At the inrolling wash of the first wave of modern consciousness on the ancient shores of Hindu culture', wrote Vivekananda, 'appeared great humanizing lives like Raja Rammohun Roy ('the first man of the regenerated India'), and others.'[1]

Here we may recall William Carey and the pundits of the Fort William College for their contribution towards an early development of Bengali prose; the Hindu College and its untiring zeal for the promotion of English education, and David Hare, again to quote Vivekananda, 'one of the educators of Bengal, the old Scotsman and atheist to whom the clergy of Calcutta refused Christian burial, . . . so his own boys carried his dead body and buried it in a swamp and made the grave a place of pilgrimage'.[2] Then there was the fiery young teacher of Hindu College, Henry Louis Vivian Derozio, and his radical students dubbed Young Bengal; Devendra Nath Tagore, Keshub Chander Sen and the great Brahmo Movement and various activities relating to religious and social reforms.

In conflict with radical materialistic thought and also with Christian missionary preachings, Hindu self-assertion became manifest, first through revivalistic tendencies, led by Raja Radhakanta Deb, in whom a peculiar combination of both progressive and the reactionary elements existed, and then through rationalistic interpretations of Hinduism, mostly by Bankim Chandra Chatterjee.

A great literature was born through the genius of Madhu Sudan Dutt, the epic poet, Bankim Chandra Chatterjee, the great novelist and essayist, Giris Chandra Ghose, dramatist (popularly known as the Father of the Bengali Stage), Dinabandhu Mitra, also a dramatist, whose drama *Nildarpan* depicted vividly the white indigo-planters' brutal atrocities and created a great stir, Vidyasagar and Akahaykumar Dutta, both essayists, and no less a poet than Rabindranath Tagore, who, by the end of the century, was recognized as a writer of genius.

There was also a great advance in political consciousness — 'one of the striking trends of the Indian awakening . . . leading to the beginning of the national movement for independence'.[3] Contacts with European literature and history aroused ideas of rationalism, individualism, democracy, liberalism and nationalism. Not only the philosophical ideas of Comte, Mill and Bentham, but also the radical socio-political views of

Montesquieu, Voltaire and Rousseau, powerfully influenced educated Bengal. Inspiring accounts of struggles for emancipation and revolutions stirred their souls, as they came to know and appreciate the lives of Mazzini and Garibaldi. English education in the universities produced hundreds of young men who could not secure appropriate jobs. Though by the Act of 1833 and the Proclamation of 1858, the principle of gradual Indianization was accepted, 'these declarations practically remained dead letters'. Naked racial discrimination and the aggresive arrogance of the Europeans in India showed elite Indians what foreign rule meant. This factor and the harrowing conditions of the people — ravaged by famine, flood and epidemic — described day by day by the Indian press (vernacular and English), made the people increasingly conscious of their helplessness. The intelligentsia became painfully aware that the mean and cruel economic policy of the British, with its steady drain of wealth to England through various channels, meant ruin to Indian industry and trade.

In the half a century before the advent of the Indian National Congress, the movement for constitutional reform under the auspices of several organizations like the Landholders' Society, the Bengal British Indian Society, the British Indian Association, and, above all, the Indian Association, had roused popular feeling against the injustices of alien rule. The most galling among these were racial discrimination and exploitation of the cultivators by the planters and zamindars. Two associations with moorings in the Bengal Presidency deserve special mention. These were the National Society and the Students Association founded at the initiative of Nabagopal Mitra and Ananda Mohan Bose respectively. Their contribution to national awakening was of inestimable value. The Blue (indigo) Mutiny of the late 1850s and early 1860s, followed by protest movements against the Vernacular Press and Arms Acts, and the white frenzy against the Ilbert Bill to partly remove judicial discrimination between Indians and Europeans, had done much to quicken political consciousness and to impress on them the urgency of setting up an all-India organization capable of providing leadership to a movement aimed at self-rule. The Indian Association, which had convened the first representative all-India assembly in 1883, willingly merged with the Indian National Congress when it was established on 28 December 1885.

When George Nathaniel Curzon (First Baron Curzon of Kedleston, later First Marquess Curzon of Kedleston) came to India as Viceroy in January 1899, he had some very definite ideas as to how to rule the country. One of the most important of his objectives was to crush the influence of the Bengali 'babus' in the Congress and even the Congress itself. He was fully aware of the Indian situation since he had served as

Under Secretary of State for India in 1891-2 and also as Under Secretary for Foreign Affairs from 1895 to 1898.

Curzon was most knowledgeable and was remarkably efficient, and always boasted about it. 'So able and so self-satisfied and so ambitious', Sir William Wedderburn once said of him to Sister Nivedita, who agreed, adding a dubious compliment to Curzon's 'strict sense of justice in administering the law that is created on the basis of injustice'.[4] Efficiency he had, but no insight. He knew politics well enough, also how to run bureaucratic machinery, but the realm of the spirit was beyond his area of comprehension. As such, it is doubtful whether he was conscious of the new spirit that had awakened in Indian national life at the time.

Bengal and India as a whole progressed through different stages of political consciousness to reach the period of organized constitutional agitation in the eighties of the 19th century. But the belief in the beneficence of British rule persisted. Many believed it to be Divine dispensation. Thus a sense of inferiority prevailed. The rich literature that sprang up in Bengal from the middle of the 19th century and the expression of national ideas therein, the glories of ancient Indian civilization discovered through the researches of the Orientalists and archaeologists, European and Indian, which created a sense of national pride, could not, as yet, give the nation the confidence that it could face the onslaught of alien culture and preserve its own with courage and determination. This diffidence to a great extent suddenly disappeared at the wondrous advent of the young Swami Vivekananda. A disciple of Sri Ramakrishna, this young sannyasi of thirty appeared at the Parliament of Religions at Chicago in September 1893, and presented the greatness of Indian religion and culture in such a masterly way that he attained glory both for himself and his native land. Annie Besant who witnessed the scene wrote:

> A striking figure . . . Monk, they called him, not unwarrantably, but warrior-monk was he, . . . his figure instinct with pride of country, pride of race. . . . All was subdued to the exquisite beauty of the spiritual message which he had brought . . . the wondrous teaching of the self. Enraptured, the huge multitude hung upon his words; not a syllable must be lost, not a cadence missed.[5]

The American newspapers (also later the English newspapers, but to a lesser degree) showered heaps of praise on him. The Indian newspapers quoted them extensively,[6] creating unprecedented enthusiasm throughout the land. This, with Annie Besant's extensive lecture tour in India in 1894, glorifying Indian religion and culture, made the Indians understand for the first time in the century and a half long period of British domination that they were still a people to be reckoned with, that their civilization had that strength within it which could raise itself up against the assertive West. India got then the most needed thing for the growth of aggressive nationalism — a sense of identity and self-confidence. This is what came to be called the *New Spirit*.

Vivekananda did not rest content with this triumph. After his return to India in 1897, he received tremendous ovations while lecturing from Rameswar to Almora and fire flowed from his lips. He made his countrymen conscious of their degradation, mercilessly exposed their social and religious bigotry, and condemned the unpardonable sin of untouchability and narrow regionalism. He called on the youth to rise up and 'shake off the delusion that you are sheep'. 'Strength, strength is what I want', he cried. He called upon his countrymen to be strong, vigorous and sincere to the core as this could revolutionize the world.[7] He further said:

> For the next fifty years this alone shall be our keynote — this, our great Mother India. Let other vain gods disappear for the time from our minds. This is the only god that is awake, our own race, everywhere his hands, everywhere his feet, everywhere his ears, he covers everything.[8]

Thus was created not only pride in heritage, a sense of self-reliance, but also a tremendous urge for a life of struggle and dedication, to sacrifice everything at the altar of the Motherland. Appeals and prayers were replaced by the audacious declaration of the spirit of revolt. 'Liberty is the first condition of growth' — these words of Vivekananda permeated Young India. Consciousness of one's identity, self-confidence, longing for liberation, readiness for sacrifice, adoration of the motherland as a goddess, belief in its unity, fraternal feeling for fellow-countrymen, recognition of the truth in all the religions — all these were the characteristics of the New Spirit, and Vivekananda offered these to his countrymen. Contemporary sources confirm this and even Anglo-Indian and missionary journals acknowledged the role of Vivekananda in initiating a pervasive national consciousness. The *Madras Christian College Magazine* quoted Rev. Slater in its March 1897 issue: 'A wave of restlessness and of religious revival is passing over it [India] and the present time may not be ineptly described as the renaissance period in the history of the Hindus.' The *Madras Times*, a well-known Anglo-Indian newspaper, wrote on 2 March 1895:

> The present revival of Hinduism [appears] . . . to one who looks calmly on from outside . . . as hardly other than a national uprising . . . . The movement is indeed a national fact. North, South, East and West, it is occurring and a crowded audience can everywhere be electrified to enthusiasm with the name of a national missionary or a national saint.

The whole thing was so very sudden and unexpected that the bluenosed imperialist daily *Pioneer* of Allahabad, wrote facetiously, but not without mixed apprehension: 'Do I sleep? Do I dream? Do I wonder or doubt? Are things what they seem? Or is vision about?' (9 March 1894).

That Vivekananda inspired this national regeneration was recognized not only by practically all Indian nationalist leaders of India[9] but also by savants abroad. Thus Romain Rolland, after referring to Vivekananda's thunderous call to the nation in his Madras lectures, wrote:

> From that day the awakening of the torpid colossus began. If the generation that followed, saw, three years after Vivekananda's death, the revolt in Bengal, the prelude to the great movement of Tilak and Gandhi, if India today has definitely taken part in the collective action of organised masses, it is due to the initial shock of the mighty 'Lazarus, come forth' of the message from Madras.[10]

Between Vivekananda's death in July 1902 and the beginning of the Swadeshi Movement in August 1905, Sister Nivedita, Vivekananda's Irish disciple, did much to spread the New Spirit, particularly among the youth. She was involved in revolutionary activities even before Vivekananda's death, in league with Kakasu Okakura, a Japanese art critic who came to India ostensibly to take Vivekananda to Japan, but also with some hidden design. Aurobindo confirmed that Nivedita was a member of the Revolutionary Council formed by him (in 1904?). She supplied revolutionary literature to the secret group then formed in Bengal under Aurobindo's younger brother, Barindra Ghose's leadership. But her public role as speaker and writer, as propagator of Vivekananda's philosophy of nationalism, was more important and fruitful. In 1900, she wrote a booklet, *Kali the Mother,* which Sri Aurobindo described as being, 'inspiring' and 'full of rebel spirit [with] no semblance of non-violence'.[11] 'I was very much enamoured at the time [when in Baroda] of her book *Kali the Mother*', he wrote.[12] That this book influenced Aurobindo when he wrote his revolutionary pamphlet, *Bhavani Mandir,* is acknowledged by historians. Barindrakumar also spoke of the influence of this book on the revolutionaries. Nivedita helped Okakura to write *Ideals of the East* (1903) which cast a spell on the minds of educated Indians. Nivedita contributed an introduction, in which she dealt with the theme, 'Asia is One', and made it the proclamation of the newly risen Orient.

With this may be mentioned Nivedita's great book, *The Web of Indian Life* (1904), which was recognized at the time as the best interpretation of Indian cultural life. It contained a marvellous exposition of the philosophy of nationalism. Nivedita asserted 'This book is not a mere rhapsody on the customs of the Orient', '. . . . Custom is interpreted in consonance with self-respect. Religions are described in demonstration of unity.' The real gist of the book lay in the passages that discussed 'the process of creating a great nation' and 'nation-making consciousness of nationality'. The message of the book was, according to the author, 'Believe in your organic relatedness. Imagine a life in which all have common interests, common needs and mutually complimentary duties.'[13] In innumerable lectures and talks Nivedita preached this philosophy. Listening to her famous lecture, 'Dynamic Religion', Bipin Chandra Pal remarked that it was not dynamic but dynamite. She wrote a number of articles expounding the same philosophy. When she initiated the All-India Vivekananda Gold Medal essay competition, she chose the following topics on which competitors were invited to write: (1) That the work of Indian Religious Teachers has always been more or less fruitful in some awakening of the national sense; (2) That great men have a passionate love for the common people; (3) That his country has a greater claim on a man than his family; (4) That all the Indian peoples together form an organic unity; (5) That Hindu and Muhammadan life and thought are alike in many important characteristics, which distinguish them both from Western thought; (6) That the lives of Asoka and Akbar, taken together, prove that in India the idea of democracy is essential to Nationality.[14]

The young men who came in contact with Nivedita felt inspired. Parmeshwar Lall, a noted public man of Bihar, wrote feelingly: 'In those days of despair in the opening years of the new century and even before the victories of Japan had given an impetus to Indian nationalism . . . as we went away from her Bagh Bazar house one felt elated with the new sense of nationalism and pride in having been born in India.'[15] Nivedita's contribution to the Awakening had been recognized with glowing tributes by extremists like Bipin Chandra Pal, Moderates like Rash Behari Ghose and Gokhale, scientists like Sir J.C. Bose, writers like Rabindranath Tagore, and artists like Abanindranath Tagore. Nivedita herself was conscious of her role in rousing nationalism before the Swadeshi Movement started. 'My time came before the awakening,' she wrote in a letter on 2 May 1906. Thus S.K. Ratcliffe (one time editor of *The Statesman*) did not exaggerate when he wrote: 'The influences that have gone to the shaping of the New India are still obscure; but this may be said with complete assurance that among them all there has been no single factor that has surpassed, or equalled the character, and life and words of Sister Nivedita.'[16]

When Curzon assumed the viceroyalty of India he faced the growing political unrest caused by a series of stirring events, the havoc of the plague epidemic, the barbarity of the British soldiers in Pune in enforcing plague regulations, the Rand (the plague officer) and Ayerst murder, and, for that, the death sentence on the Chapekar brothers, imprisonment of Tilak on the charge of preaching sedition, and long prison sentences on several journalists of Maharashtra on the same charge. The harrowing tale of British oppression was commented on by Vivekananda in his letter to Mary Hale of 30 October 1899:

> No good can be done when the main idea is blood-sucking . . . . Centuries of anarchy that reigned during the struggles of the English to conquer, the terrible massacre the English perpetrated in 1857 and 1858 and the still more famines that have become the inevitable consequence of British rule . . . [that] take off millions . . . [Now] education will no more be permitted to spread; freedom of the Press stopped already (of course we have disarmed long ago), the bit of self-Government granted for some years is being quickly taken off. . . . For writing a few words of innocent criticism men are being hurried to *transportation for life,* others imprisoned without *any trial;* and nobody knows when his head will be off. There has been a reign of terror for some years, English soldiers are killing our men and outraging our women — only to be sent home with passage and pension at our expense.

Swamiji in this letter referred to the 1897 incidents in Maharashtra and also to the first eighteen months of the Curzon regime. During this period, the Viceroy curtailed the powers of the elected municipal commissioners of Calcutta by enacting the Calcutta Municipal Act (1899). This effort to 'officialize the Calcutta Corporation', wrote Surendranath Banerjea, had thrown Calcutta 'in the vortex of an agitation that was only surpassed by the anti-Partition demonstration'.[17] Curzon who believed seriously that 'the British Empire is, under Providence, the greatest instrument for good that the world has ever seen',[18] next directed his efforts to curbing the growing trend of nationalism by officialization of education. This was done through the Indian Universities Act of 1904. Nivedita described it as an attempt 'to kill all education'[19] and observed that Curzon did not stop only in making 'The Indian Universities . . . the most completely Governmental Universities of the World', but had decided to 'stand in history as the most anti-British influence that India ever saw'.[20] Curzon grievously offended Indian sentiment when he claimed in his Calcutta University convocation address (11 February 1905) that 'the highest ideal of Truth is to a large extent a Western conception' and that 'Truth took a higher place in the moral codes of the West before it had been similarly honoured in the East'. This preposterous claim evoked strong protests through articles, letters, and public meetings. Nivedita cited an instance from Curzon's own book, *Problems of the Far East* to show that the author admitted therein that he had told a lie and misrepresented his age while presenting himself before the President of the Korean Foreign Office. The public resentment found bold expression in the speech delivered by Dr Rash Behari Ghose in one of the public meetings held in the Calcutta Town Hall:

> The truth was the Viceroy attached no importance to the desire of the people but was determined to carry out his own will, and almost all the measures [the moves to officialize the Calcutta Corporation and the universities] tended to strengthen the Simla Bureaucracy and to 'Russianise' the administration.[21]

But the greatest challenge to the growing nationalism was yet to come in the shape of the project to partition Bengal. Reviewing Curzon's administration Nivedita wrote: 'The constant aggression upon liberty goes on, grows worse and worse — and more and more despairful.' In her letter of 5 March 1905 she wrote: 'This man Curzon seems the incarnation of insolence and evil.'[22]

2. The Bengal Partition

The huge size and the large population of the Bengal Presidency made it really difficult for a lieutenant governor to manage. This was a 'burden more than mortal man can fitly bear', Lord Dalhousie said even in 1853.[23] Schemes of partitioning the province therefore came up from time to time, and for one reason or another they were rejected or shelved. The proposal first came as early as 1867-8, that this province be placed like the Presidency of Bombay or Madras under a full-fledged governor with an executive council but was rejected by Sir John Lawrence on the ground that 'some kind of despotism' was essential 'to give unity, force and consistence to Government'. Lawrence favoured separation of Assam and the addition to it of some adjoining Bengali districts, and also the placing of Bengal under a Chief Commissioner, dividing the province into three commissionerships. The position of Bihar and Orissa were to remain unchanged. 'Thus was laid', writes Dr Amales Tripathi, 'the genesis of the Partition of Bengal.'[24] From then to 3 December 1903, when the Risley paper was published as the Government of India's awowed scheme for partitioning Bengal, many proposals were considered at the government level. Of them, the following were comparatively important: Sir George Campbell suggested in 1872 the separation of the Hindi-speaking areas (population 20 million). Instead of accepting this suggestion, Assam was separated in 1874 (population 2 million), enlarged by three Bengali-speaking districts — Sylhet, Cachar and Goalpara. More than two decades later, in 1896, Sir William Ward proposed a comprehensive scheme which could not be executed due to opposition from various quarters, but it is interesting to note that the scheme formed the basis on which the Bengal Partition was finally executed.

Ward proposed that the whole of Chittagong Division and the districts of Dacca and Mymensingh should go to Assam, to form a lieutenant governor's province. Curzon toured Assam in 1900 where the tea planters made a strong plea for a nearby port which would reduce the prohibitive freight charged by the Assam-Bengal Railway for carrying goods to Calcutta port. This necessitated the formation of a new province, about which Curzon remained at that time undecided as he did not favour a piecemeal solution and would not be content before he could devise something that would last through the 'next generation'. For this reason, Sir Andrew Fraser's suggestion that Orissa be immediately separated was not accepted. Curzon wanted a comprehensive redistribution of provincial boundaries, and at his instance Fraser hurriedly presented Ward's old scheme with very little modification and that was published as the Risley paper, mentioned earlier. According to the scheme, Chittagong Division and the districts of Hill Tippara, Dacca and Mymensingh would go to new Assam; Chhota Nagpur to the Central Provinces against which Bengal would get Sambalpur from C.P. and Ganjam from Madras. The new province of Assam, thus created, would be placed under a chief commissioner without any legislative council, and would remain beyond the jurisdiction of the Calcutta High Court.

The whole of Bengal burst out in protest. Sir Henry Cotton (dubbed the 'White Babu') made a more considerate proposal, viz., the separation of Hindi- and Oriya-speaking areas from Bengal, thereby reducing the size of the province, but maintaining the integrity of the Bengali-speaking people. The Congress (1903) vehemently protested against the 'preposterous' government scheme and suggested that Bengal be placed under a governor with an executive council.

The government remained silent for some time, thereby rousing in the hearts of the 'loyal' Indians justification of their belief in the British sense of justice. But all the time the bureaucracy was scheming. Curzon convinced himself that there was not an iota of reason in any of the hundreds of letters and articles sent to the government or published in the newspapers or journals in protest against the partition proposal, and the pundit in him was not ready to be taught by the 'untaught or unteachable' Congress leaders. On the contrary, the very intensity of the agitation confirmed, in Curzon's view, the wisdom of the proposed partition.

In this self-righteous frame of mind, Curzon's answer to the 'hysteria' was further provocation. While on tour in East Bengal in 1904, he suggested that the new province should comprise Dacca Division, Chittagong Division, and Rajasahi Division excluding Darjeeling but adding Malda to it. He assured his Muslim audience there that his idea of

Partition was 'to invest the Mohamedans in Eastern Bengal with a unity which they have not enjoyed since the days of the old Musalman viceroys and kings'. [25] In this design Curzon received enthusiastic support from Andrew Fraser (Lieutenant Governor of Bengal), Bampfylde Fuller (Chief Commissioner of Assam) and Sir Herbert Risley (Home Secretary, Government of India), with additional proposals for including some more districts to the proposed new province.

The Congress again protested; its President for the 1904 Session, Sir Henry Cotton, tried to convince Curzon of the impracticability of the scheme. But the viceroy was determined. To his thinking, everyone other than the Bengalis had accepted the proposal. When Bombay was silent, Madras mute, the Bengalis were vociferous, Curzon said. On 2 February 1905, he sent a final despatch to John Brodrick, the Secretary of State for India. It reached him on 18 February and he placed it before the India Council, where Sir Alfred Lyall, along with some others disagreed:

> That large and upon the whole homogeneous community of 41½ millions, with Calcutta as their centre of culture and political and commercial life, should object to the transfer of ⅗th of their number to a new administration with a distant capital, involving the severance of old and historic ties and the breaking up of racial unity [seems] . . . in no way surprising.

Brodrick had his reservations too. But he bowed 'before a more forceful personality'. 'He really abdicated his duty,' Tripathi writes with obvious distaste, 'though his Councillors made him amply aware of it.'

Curzon with his watchword, 'efficiency' showed how quickly he could act. On 6 July 1905, the Government of India officially announced from Simla its decision to constitute the new province. On 19 July, the government resolution on the subject was published. On 10 October, the British Government published partition papers and requested Curzon to postpone the promulgation for three weeks. But the viceroy did not comply with the request as that would have shaken the prestige of the government. On 16 October, Bengal was partitioned, with Bampfylde Fuller as the Lieutenant Governor of the new province of Eastern Bengal and Assam. It was a day of deep satisfaction for some Anglo-Indian officials and a dark day of mourning for millions of Bengalis.

How Curzon unscrupulously manoeuvred the British Government into a position in which they were compelled to accept his plan had been described by the British observer, S.K. Ratcliffe: 'It was carried through when Parliament was not sitting, when Lord Curzon was on the eve of leaving India and despite Mr Brodrick's promise to furnish the House with further information before the Bill became law.'[26]

Acceptance of Partition by the British Government was offered like a healing balm to Curzon's wounded feelings (Curzon had to quit his post on being defeated in a power tussle with the C-in-C, Lord Kitchener) by grievously wounding the feelings of millions of the subject people. Nevertheless, 'it was undoubtedly a master plan' to divide the Bengali Hindus, 'hated and dreaded by Curzon for their advanced political ideas', and to make them minority in both the newly demarcated provinces, observed Dr R.C. Majumdar.[27] But long before him, S.K. Ratcliffe had exposed the true purpose in a brief but masterly analysis:

> It meant a splitting up, under two separate and self-contained administrations, of the Bengali Hindus, the creation of a new province in which the Mohamedan population would predominate, and the balancing, in Bengal proper, of the intelligent and educated Hindu community by large numbers of aboriginal and otherwise backward tribes. The province thus carved out — known as Eastern Bengal and Assam — is 106,540 square miles in extent, and has a population of 31 million — of whom 18 million are Mohamedans and 12 million Hindus. Bengal proper has an area of 141,580 square miles, and a population of 54 million — 42 million Hindus and 9 million Mohamedans.[28] Calculated differently, in Bengal proper Bengali-speaking population would be 17 million and Hindi-speaking population 20 million, and the rest — 17 million — speaking Oriya and many other tribal dialects.[29]

Curzon was thus successful in striking at the solidarity of the Bengalis and at the Congress. He had Fraser and Risley as enthusiastic adherents. Modern historians like Dr Amales Tripathi and Dr Sumit Sarkar have cited many instances of Anglo-Indian official distrust and consequent bitterness against the 'Bengali babus', which led to the partition plan. W.B. Oldham thought, as early as February 1896, that the formation of the new province would weaken the 'politically threatening' position of the Hindus. Fraser convinced the already convinced Curzon of 'the advantage of severing these eastern districts of Bengal, which are hotbeds of the purely Bengali movement, unfriendly if not seditious in character, and dominating the whole tone of administration' (1 June 1903). Risley put across the idea saying, 'Bengal united is a power; Bengal divided will pull in different ways. That is perfectly true and is one of the merits of the scheme' (7 February 1904). J.R. Mclane assured that the scheme was not aimed at 'communal disruption', but admitted that it intended 'a division of Bengali Hindu politicians' (3 December 1903). Risley had put forward his argument against the counter-proposal of placing Bengal under a governor with an executive council, saying, in that case the governor would come directly from Britain and 'would care very little for the prejudices and interests of the I.C.S.', and also, no less important, the Bengalis would then enter the executive council and 'with their genius for intrigue . . . would find their own advantage and indulge their ruling instinct in stirring up strife and paralysing the Executive.'

But, as has been hinted earlier, here Curzon needed no schooling, rather he surpassed everyone. He certainly could not allow the 'Bengali babu' to fulfil his cherished dream of entering Government House as Lieutenant Governor. Curzon reacted sharply against Sir Alfred Lyall's suggestion of separating only Chhota Nagpur and Orissa as 'It would tend to consolidate the Bengali element by detaching it from outside factors and would produce the very effect that we desire to avoid. The best guarantee of the political advantage of our proposal is its dislike by the Congress Party' (24 May 1905). Curzon opened up his mind in a remarkably candid letter written to Brodrick on 2 February 1905, saying, 'Calcutta is the centre from which the Congress Party is manipulated throughout the whole of Bengal, and indeed the whole of India. Its best wirepullers and its most frothy orators all reside here. The perfection of their machinery, and the tyranny which it enables them to exercise are truly remarkable.' Curzon went on undaunted (and paying tributes though left-handed to the Bengali babus):

> They dominate public opinion in Calcutta; they affect the High Court; they frighten the local Government of India. The whole of their activity is directed to creating an agency so powerful that they may one day be able to force a weak Government to give them what they desire. Any measure in consequence that would dethrone Calcutta from its place as the centre of successful intrigue, or that would weaken the influence of the lawyer class, who have the entire organisation in their hands, is intensely and hotly resented by them.

While Curzon had anticipated that 'the outcry [would] be loud and very fierce', he had at the same time, assured himself that Bengalis 'howl until a thing is settled and then they accept it'. Lord Hardinge, who later annulled the Partition, was made wiser by events. Recognizing the reality that the partition scheme was intended 'to aim a blow at the Bengalis', he accepted also the fact, as late as 13 July 1911, 'the political power of the Bengalis has not been broken. . . . The Bengalis are born agitators and there is no doubt . . . that they will never cease to agitate until they have attained a modification of the Partition.'[30] Through the viceroyalties of Curzon and Hardinge, the great Swadeshi Movement gathered strength, spread wide, diminished outwardly after 1909, but went underground to burst out at times with bloody fury.

The movement had started as a constitutional agitation in December 1903, when the government first openly declared its intention to partition Bengal. The memorial submitted to the Secretary of State for India in July 1905, mentioned that, after the publication of the Risley paper on 3 December 1903, no less than 500 protest meetings were held in East Bengal alone within a period of two months. From the annual report of the Indian Association for 1911, we learn that:

> From December 1903 to October 1905 more than 2000 public meetings attended by 500 to 50,000 people both Hindus and Mussalmans, were held in different parts of East Bengal and West Bengal to protest against the Partition. The resolutions unanimously adopted at these meetings were regularly submitted to the Government of India as well as the Secretary of State. The people of united Bengal, both Hindus and Mussalmans, Maharajas, Nawabs, Rajas, the educated community and the masses met five times at the Calcutta Town Hall to give expression to their feeling and protest against the ill-advised measure. Memorials were submitted by the British Indian Association, the Bengal Landholders' Association, as well as from nearly all the important and recognized public bodies and associations in either part of the province, and in July 1905, when the public mind was in a state of feverish anxiety, a mammoth representation over the signature about 70,000 people of all classes and communities was submitted to the Secretary of State from East Bengal. The Indian Press, both in Bengal, as well as in other provinces, were unanimous in their condemnation of the proposed dismemberment of Bengal, and even a large section of the Anglo-Indian Press, some of which are recognised as semi-official organs, joined in protest.

'Indeed', as Dr R.C. Majumdar rightly observed, 'it is difficult to conceive of a more unanimous and persistent opposition to a government measure; there is certainly no precedent in the history of British rule in India.'[31]

Why did so many people with varied interests — social, religious, political and economic — come forward to oppose the scheme? Certainly there was something in it which injured all of them in one way or another. Ratcliffe briefly presented the case of the anti-partitionists thus:

> That the line of division between the two provinces was arbitrary, and could only be explained on a political hypothesis; that it took little or no account of ethnic, linguistic or geographical conditions but drove straight through the community which was at once the strongest and the most homogeneous, creating a social and economic gulf between the two halves of the Bengali-speaking people; that it joined advanced and long-settled districts with others of a more primitive character; that it duplicated a form of administration which was already too costly and was becoming obsolete; that it imperilled the power of the Calcutta High Court, which to Indian and European alike is the only effective bulwark against an all-powerful Executive; that it was calculated to revive between Hindu and Mohamedan a religious antagonism which was rapidly disappearing under present-day influence.[32]

Thus we see that every interest group was affected — politicians, zamindars, businessmen, lawyers, government employees of the lower and upper cadre. There was also the element of emotional attachment to a united Bengal which this measure sought to destroy. For hundreds of years, the Hindus and Muslims of Bengal were nourished by a common culture, a rich heritage. Calcutta under British rule had grown not only as a centre of administrative and political activities but much more — as the cultural capital of Bengal and India. The two major communities could hardly reconcile themselves to the thought of separation from it. Partition struck direct at this sense of identity.

3. Swadeshi and Boycott

When speeches and writings were of no avail, the people decided to act. Their action took the form of the Swadeshi and Boycott Movements. The boycott of British goods was meant 'to call attention to the wrongs done' by the rulers, by attacking their commercial interests. The other side of the coin, swadeshi, pledged the people to the use of indigenous products exclusively, whatever their quality. Both these were obviously related to the economic regeneration of the country, but the immediate motivation and objective was essentially political.

It is said that it was Krishna Kumar Mitra who suggested in his paper, *Sanjivani,* of 13 July 1905, that people should boycott all British goods, observe mourning, and shun all contacts with officials and official bodies. The suggestion was accepted in a meeting at Bagerhat, Khulna, on 16 July ('all British and foreign goods should be boycotted until Partition orders were withdrawn'), also at a meeting at Dinajpur on 21 July (Lal Mohan Ghose proposed the 'resignation in a body of all Honorary Magistrates, members of the District Boards, Municipalities') and many other places in East Bengal. The first boycott meeting in Calcutta was organized by students at the Ripon College, followed by other students' meetings enthusiastically supporting the boycott proposal. Calcutta leaders met and held conferences and discussed it a number of times. Then at a great public meeting held in the Town Hall on 7 August 1905, the Swadeshi Movement was formally inaugurated and the boycott proposal finally accepted as a national mode of struggle. This very important meeting, attended by thousands, including delegates from the districts, was addressed by well-known leaders. So huge was the assembly that three meetings had to be arranged simultaneously, two in the Hall and a third on the Maidan nearby. At the main meeting, at the Town Hall, presided over by Maharaja Mahindra Chandra Nandy of Cossimbazar, where 'Rajas and pleaders and babus jostled with each other and the gathering shaded off into the poorest class', Narendra Nath Sen, editor, *Indian Mirror,* moved the boycott resolution, which ran:

> That this meeting fully sympathises with the resolution adopted at many meetings held in the mofussil, to abstain from the purchase of British Manufactures so long as the Partition Resolution is not withdrawn, as a protest against the indifference of the British public in regard to Indian affairs and the consequent disregard of Indian public opinion by the present Government.

The boycott decision spread like wildfire all through Bengal. It created tremendous enthusiasm, particularly amongst students and youth. An example of how they were roused into action is the lecture delivered by Sister Nivedita at the Dawn Society on 20 August 1905. She urged the students to devote themselves entirely to the country's cause, leaving, for the time being the 'old beaten family track'. She extolled the example of Kunwar Singh, the hero of Bihar, 'who would not die until he had news from his brother that all the female members of his family have [had] been put to death — not by the cruel hand of the enemy, but by the loving hands of their own husbands and fathers, by their own brothers and uncles'. 'It is not the truth to say that India has always, under every circumstances, put the family before the country,' Nivedita asserted. She warned against 'sham spirituality that dreads trouble and hankers after safety', also 'sham patriotism that harbours thoughts of ignoble ease under the garb of spirituality, that seeks safety by a cowardly retreat from the battle-field of life'. And then she gave the call for boycott, which certainly was not just an inoffensive call to abstain from purchasing foreign goods, but much more:

> The first advice to young men . . . should be . . . at all costs shun Government service. Government service has the baneful effect of degrading the national character and sowing seeds of dissension among brothers — among the Hindus and Mohamedans for instance. It fetters our activity. It makes us in many cases dishonest men, acting against the dictates of our moral sense. . . . Let us make it a point not to voluntarily put chains on ourselves by accepting Government service and thus to make ourselves slaves morally as we are physically.[33]

Three days before this speech, Nivedita wrote in a letter: 'Did I tell you of the great Swadeshi Movement here and the sudden resolve to *Boycott* English goods?'[34] Again, on 13 September, she wrote: 'India appears to be waking up in these days. The incubus of Curzon is off and of course you have heard of the *Boycott*. . . . The people are feeling their power. I think Curzon has broken the British Empire.'[35] Nivedita informed Gokhale in a letter of 20 September 1905 (i.e. before partition was implemented), '300 clerks in one house of business here have struck work' (the Burn Co. incident), and expressed her wish for unionized movements. ('If all the graduates in India could be registered in a union, for instance, or all the Hindu and Mohamedan clerks in Calcutta! Before the latter no union of employers could stand.') She was hopefully seeking the 'spontaneous loyalty of the Indian people, utterly unpractised and inexperienced in these matters, as they were, to their brothers. They say that even in Madras this particular firm (Burn Co.) has advertised for clerks and none will come forward'. In the trade union movement she found an extension of boycott. 'The Boycott meanwhile', she wrote with the great enthusiasm with which the air was surcharged at the time, 'is spreading even to women and priests — and the amount of sacrifice that has been made is extraordinary. . . . Even petty shopkeepers are found to remonstrate with Indian customers who ask for a *Videshi* commodity.' 'By this particular power of unknown people to perform obscure acts of sacrifice', she proceeded, 'under a dominating idea of the community, you can exactly measure the national potentiality. It was by this power in the Russian people that Napoleon's march on Moscow was turned into disaster. It was by the same power in the French that Napoleon's armies were raised. By this, America won freedom and so on and so on.'

The fateful day, 16 October 1905, was observed as a day of mourning and of remembrance. Programmes to observe the day were fixed in advance. A day of fasting, purification of body and mind by taking a dip in the holy water, and taking a vow of struggle and sacrifice. Rabindranath Tagore put forward his suggestion concerning the observance of Rakhi Bandhan to demonstrate the indelible unity of the Bengali people at two meetings held in the last week of September 1905. The proposal was readily accepted. He also wrote an inspiring song for the occasion. At a Town Hall meeting on 22 September, plans to erect a Federation Hall were also approved. The proposed hall 'was to be a symbol of the indissoluble union between the two provinces, a meeting ground of Eastern and Western Bengal'. This idea, Surendranath Banerjea recorded, was inspired by what he saw 'at the Hotel des Invalides in Paris, where round the tomb of the great Napoleon are laurelled statues, representatives of the different provinces'. Surendranath further wrote that the proposal was warmly supported by Sir Taraknath Palit and Sister Nivedita.[36] It was also decided that shops would be closed, business suspended and funds raised for helping the handloom industry on 16 October 1905. Surendranath described the response:

> The day dawned; the streets of Calcutta re-echoed from the early hours of the morning with the cry of *Bande Mataram*, as band after band of men,

> young and old, paraded the streets on their way to bathe in the river, stopping at intervals to tie the Rakhi round the wrists of passers-by. They were often accompanied by *Sankirtan* parties singing the *Bande Mataram* and patriotic songs. The bathing-ghats were crammed with a surging mass of men and women, all furnished with quantities of *rakhis,* which they tied round the wrists of friends and acquaintances, and even of strangers. . . . It was a day worth living for — a day of inspiration that perhaps comes only once in a life time.[37]

The Federation Hall foundation stone-laying function on Circular Road at 3.30 p.m. on that day, before a vast gathering of 50,000 people, with Ananda Mohan Bose, then bed-ridden with a mortal illness, carried in an invalid chair to inaugurate the ceremony, was indeed memorable. Surendranath read Ananda Mohan's written English speech; Sir Ashutosh Chaudhuri read the Proclamation; Tagore made and read their Bengali versions. After the function, the crowd walked more than two miles, all barefooted, in company with the leaders, to reach Pashupatinath Bose's house at Baghbazar where again a mammoth meeting was held and Rs 70,000 collected on the spot for the National Fund.

The tremendous excitement and exuberance visible on 16 October (the day was declared as a National Day) did not peter out as the rulers prophesied. Sir Bampfylde Fuller, the new Lieutenant Governor of the province of Eastern Bengal and Assam, in justification of partition and the subsequent repressive measures wrote, 'Enthusiasms in the East are short-lived'.[38] But he was wrong, at least to a degree, as we see that even in the third year of the movement, enthusiasm persisted. W. Nevinson, noted humanist and writer of repute, stated from personal experience:

> October 16 is becoming the Ash Wednesday of India. On that day thousands on thousands, probably millions, of Indians rub dust or ashes on their foreheads; they bathe as at a sacred fast; no meals are eaten; the shops in cities and the village bazaars are shut; women refuse to cook; they lay aside their ornaments; men bind each others' wrists with a yellow string as a sign of remembrance; the whole day is in resentment, mourning and the hunger of humiliation. In Calcutta vast meetings are held, and the errors of Government are exposed with eloquent patriotism. This is now the third year that it has been celebrated as a day of calamity, and the indignant protest shows no sign of growing weaker. The crowds are bigger, the ceremonial is more widely spread, the fast more rigorous.[39]

Scholars remind us that the Swadeshi Movement for the regeneration of Indian industries was not a new concept. Gopal Hari Deshmukh ('Lokahitawadi') of Bombay urged it in the middle of the 19th century. Bholanath Chunder of Bengal presented in 1873 a well-written comprehensive scheme in which he called on patriots to work for

> the founding of independent Native banks, Native companies and Corporations, Native mills and factories and Native Chambers of Commerce in the province. . . . They should collect and compile details of Indian urban life to draw public attention to the helpless condition of our weavers, blacksmiths and mechanics. They should point out the enormous and unceasing drain upon the profits of Indian labour, to show that the country is growing poorer day by day and thoroughly expose the statistical delusion of the authorities.

He strongly denounced the industrial slavery of the country, and emphasized that foreign capital should not be used for the development of Indian industires.[40]

Instances are not wanting to show how propaganda was carried on in Bengal and the rest of India for promoting the use of articles of Indian origin instead of foreign goods. Even Swami Dayananda had pleaded for it. The *Hindu Mela* also carried on vigorous propaganda in this matter. Swadeshi ideology and enterprise were stimulated by the writings of Dadabhai Naoroji, M.G. Ranade and, particularly, Romesh Chandra Dutta. About Dutta's great work, *The Economic History of India Under Early British Rule,* Aurobindo wrote in an article: 'Without *Economic History* and its damning story of England's commercial and fiscal dealings with India we doubt whether the public mind would have been ready for the Boycott. In this one instance it may be said that he not only wrote history but created it.'[41] At this time, Indian papers were publishing articles on the subject with obvious political overtones. In Bengal, Sakharam Ganesh Deuskar (a Maharashtrian by birth but a recognized writer in Bengali) in his Bengali book, *Desher Katha,* presented the facts of England's economic exploitation of India in a lucid and dramatic way. The book ran into several editions in a short time and became a must for the revolutionaries. Indian leaders harped on this topic whenever they got a chance to. Nevinson had recorded what Tilak said to him during an interview:

> Mr Tilak briefly referred to the well-known complaints so often brought against our Administration by students of Indian economics — the drain of £ 30,000,000 a year to England from an impoverished country, the ruin of old Indian trades and manufactures for the advantage of English, Austrian and American firms, the reduction of the whole population to a starving agriculture, and the unexplained increase of famine and plague.[42]

The expounding of this 'Drain Theory' influenced the public mind so much that the government became irritated to the extreme and did its best to restrict its propagation. Deuskar's *Desher Katha* was proscribed.[43]

Ideological disputes arose amongst the leaders and intellectuals as to the real nature of swadeshi. One school of opinion held that it implied only restoration of the 'ancient Indian industries which were driven out of existence by European and specially English machine-made productions . . . . The populations which had lived on handicraft of one kind or another . . . being forced into agriculture, already overcrowded and hazardous with recurring famines'.[44] But was it only the restoration of the old Indian industries that the Swadeshi Movement aimed at, as would have been acceptable to officials like Sir George Birdwood? What about mechanized industrialization? The large-scale industries of the West and the materialism and evils that went with it, made thoughtful Indians wonder about the desired nature of the industrial revival. This question was raised and discussed in a number of issues of the *Dawn*. The journal, Sumit Sarkar reminds us, 'repeatedly warned against the uncritical transplantation of Western industrialization'.[45] This was but natural because this journal and the National College had in later years fallen into the hands of the not-very-progressive N.N. Ghose and others. Nivedita wrote thus about the situation in a letter:

> Everyone knows that Boycott and Science are the determinants of the future. The National College is abandoned to forces of reaction. The thing was founded in a blaze of excitement — and its nationalism was a *word*, not a *thing* — not an idea. . . . But genuine public effort goes forward in things like the Technical Institution at the Parsee Bagan — in the little Swadeshi Enterprises and in the crowding-out of the Science departments at Presidency and Scottish Mission Colleges — for B.Sc. and M.Sc.[46]

During the days of the Swadeshi Movement, Nivedita lent her weight in favour of science and industry (she helped Dr J.C. Bose in his scientific work) because her Master, Swami Vivekananda, took great interest in science and industry. This helped to create a favourable background for swadeshi enterprises. Vivekananda, who was a friend of Dr J.C. Bose, urged him to express his nationalism only in scientific discoveries. He also encouraged Jamsetji Tata to set up industries and not merely profit-making trading business by dealing only in foreign goods. Tata in 1898 offered property worth Rs. 30 lakhs for a Post-Graduate Science University and sought Vivekananda's support when confronted by an unfavourable government reaction. 'I know not who would make a more fitting general of such a campaign than Vivekananda', wrote Tata feelingly. Vivekananda warmly welcomed the project, as is evident from his article in *Prabuddha Bharata* (April 1899), which read in part:

> In these days of keen competition it [the 'food question'] can only be solved by letting the light of modern science penetrate every pore of the two giant feeders of mankind — Agriculture and Commerce. . . . We are not aware if any project at once so opportune and so far-reaching in its beneficent effects was ever mooted as that of the Post-Graduate Research University of Mr Tata.

Nivedita took a leading part in mobilizing support for the project from Indian and European intellectuals.[47]

Here we should not fail to mention the geologist, Pramatha Nath Bose, at whose suggestion Tata established his workshop at Garumahisani in Bihar, whose pamphlet (1886) pleaded for a proper science curriculum in the university syllabus and a separate science and technological institute, and who lent his support in the establishment of the Indian Industrial Association. We must mention also Jogendra Chandra Ghose's Association for the Scientific and Industrial Education of India (1904), and its scholarships for foreign training. Thanks to all these efforts and the supporting intellectual background it became possible to include projects for technological institutes in the National Education Scheme,[48] though apprehension concerning the evils of industrial materialism persisted amongst some intellectuals, including Tagore and Gandhiji.[49]

Swadeshi, as an endeavour for the restoration and expansion of home industries, thus started long before the Partition, but it took the shape of a widespread movement only as part of the anti-Partition movement. The political emphasis was unmistakable. But there were also non-political promoters of swadeshi, its best exponent being Rabindranath Tagore. In his scheme of *Swadeshi Samaj* (1904) he underscored the supreme necessity of village reconstruction. He urged the revival of traditional village society with a new awareness, to be achieved by spreading enlightenment in village homes, by organizing lectures, etc. in the village *melas,* through magic lanterns and other media (Vivekananda's similar ideas preceded Tagore's). This has been described as Constructive Swadeshi based on the gospel of *atmashakti.* Tagore urged people to eschew the 'old-style politics, trying in vain to placate the foreign rulers and talking big in a foreign tongue', and to immerse themselves in the real life of the people. Tagore had his critics here even among his ardent admirers. He soon parted company with the Swadeshi Movement, as perhaps politics did not suit his poetic sensibilities, or he was disappointed at seeing the shift of emphasis of the movement to the political rather than to the constructive programmes. He went on, in his own way, with constructive village works in his zamindari. At the same time, he did not refrain from drawing attention to the hollowness of the methods adopted by others, and projecting his own views. This he did particularly in his Pabna Conference Address. He did not like boycott because, to him, it was negative, coercive and charged with hatred. The nationalists, engaged in frontal struggle with the imperialists, could not forget the stark reality of partition and did not relish Tagore's call to switch over from political to non-political swadeshi. Aurobindo in seven brilliant articles on passive resistance *(Bande Mataram,* 11-23 April 1907) took issue with Tagore on many points. Boycott was not a gospel of hatred, he emphasized, it sought independence, to be achieved through resistance. The New Party certainly believed in self-help, no less than others. But Aurobindo raised the pertinent question: Would the rulers allow self-development of the subject people? Aurobindo warned that repression would not end in Fullerism only, it might go on to terrible Tsarism. Thus, 'to attempt social reform, educational reform, industrial expansion, the moral improvement of the race without aiming first and foremost at political freedom, is the very height of ignorance and futility.'

But Tagore was uncompromising in his attitude. Not only in many of his essays at the time, but in novels too, he expressed himself. He was so bitter about Boycott and the revolutionary movement, that in his novel, *Ghara Baire,* the picture presented of the boycotters and the militants displeased many, and many voices were raised in protest.

These ideological conflicts, which led ultimately to a parting of ways, not only among the intellectuals but also among the politicians in Congress, brought into focus the deep intensity of the movement. Let us therefore examine the viewpoints of the leaders and sympathizers of the Boycott and subsequent Passive Resistance Movements, specially of Nivedita, Bipin Pal and Aurobindo.

As mentioned earlier, Nivedita wrote mostly on the philosophy of nationalism, its sociological aspects and emotional creativity. In the article 'The Task of the National Movement in India' (*Indian Review,* July 1906) she warned young India not to be fascinated by the political spectacle in European countries and indulge in petty party disputes. To her, Congress was important, but more important was the nation. She expressed this beautifully: 'Thus the Congress represents, not a political or partisan movement, but the political side of a national movement. . . . 'The real task of the Congress is that of an educational body, educating its own members in that new mode of thinking and feeling which constitutes a sense of nationality.' The 'cry of Home-land' must be there but that 'cry' could reach 'the inarticulate, uneducated helpless masses' only 'by means of the industrial reconstruction which the Swadeshi vow has necessitated'. Women and the peasant should be the main concern, to whom the national missionaries should reach with magic lantern, map of India, etc., and with 'head and heart full of ballads, stories and geographical descriptions'.

But Nivedita was not only an idealogue, she wanted 'a little of the venom of the cobra in undertaking and financing national self-defence associations, farmers' aid organizations, co-operative credit enterprises'. In the Swadeshi days Nivedita certainly did not preach anarchist philosophy, but emphasized the need of boycott to enhance and protect swadeshi. In her well-known arrticle, 'The Swadeshi Movement', in *Indian Review* (March 1906), quoted extensively and appreciatively by *Review of Reviews* of London (May 1906) she greeted the Indian people for starting the movement which expressed 'manliness' and thus earned respect from the whole world. 'The world respects that which shows that it is to be feared and the one thing that is feared by all is strong, intelligent and united action.' She tried to refute the argument that, without high protective tariff, the Swadeshi Movement could not succeed. She said 'Western people . . . are educated in a system of co-operation for self-interest . . . [while] Indian nations [are] educated in a system of co-operation for self-sacrifice.' She was not interested in presenting statistical data to demonstrate the success of the movement but mentioned the gratifying fact that 'in all directions small industries have sprung up like flowers'. She raised the question not only of production but also of distribution. The small shops, as they were the real distribution centres, had to be captured; Swadeshi Committees should be formed in each town 'to keep a register of all industrial undertakings'; commercial credits should be distributed. But Nivedita's emotional involvement was with the hopes and aspirations 'of the downtrodden . . . ignorant and helpless'. She was overwhelmed when listening to a Bengali Muslim, addressing his fellows, on 16 October, National Day, who told how, since they could not earn even four annas a day, some were compelled to steal and spent eight months of every year in prison, while the womenfolk ate outside their homes, 'but now, how everything is changed. Ten annas a day, with comfort and decency.'

Nivedita emphatically supported Boycott in an unsigned article in the *Modern Review*,[50] stating categorically that 'Swadeshi and Boycott are the two necessary aspects of one and the same thing. One cannot flourish and strive without the help of the other'. She quoted extensively from historians to show boycott to be a legitimate weapon of any nation for fostering their economic growth. 'That it [The Boycott Movement] has succeeded is proved by the fact of the closure for a time of over 500 cotton mills of Lancashire.' To the Moderates, Nivedita suggested enthusiastically, after citing examples of England's policy of protection for the benefit of their own industries, 'Imitation is the most sincere form of flattery. Those who think that everything English is good should take a leaf out of the political-economical philosophy of the English and practise what they do to encourage their home industries.'

Boycott culminated in passive resistance. Here we have two great intellectuals as exponents, Bipin Chandra Pal and Aurobindo Ghose. Bipin Pal, the great orator and distinguished writer, editor of *New India*, also for some time of *Bande Mataram*, become the acknowledged spokesman for extremism in the 1905-6 period. Aurobindo considered him a man with original political thoughts. Pal, he said, was 'the prophet and first preacher of Passive Resistance'.[51] Aurobindo spoke highly of Pal's 'triumphant oratory . . . the Pythian inspiration of his matchless eloquence'.[52]

It must be noted that earlier Pal was not an extremist, but partition made him one. He was a champion of 'absolute political independence',[53] and as early as 1902 attacked petitioning agitation ('we have given a new name to begging; we call it agitation') and declared in *Bande Mataram* in 1906: 'Our ideal is freedom, which means absence of all foreign control. Our method is passive resistance, which means organized determination to refuse, to render any voluntary or honorary service to the government.'[54]

Pal undertook all-India tours to preach the ideas of nationalism and passive resistance, and his Madras lectures in April-May 1907 were so volcanic that the Rowlatt Committee Report said that 'An outburst of seditious activity followed upon the visit of Bipin Chandra had resulted in various trials.' The report also referred to Pal's lecture at Calcutta on 25 May in which he recommended the worship of Raksha Kali, before whom 'white goats' were to be sacrificed. One Madrasi gentleman, according to the Report, followed Pal in declaring that they ought to go abroad to learn the manufacture of explosives and return to the country to sacrifice at every *amavasya* night 108 whites, who were their enemies.[55]

But Pal was no revolutionary. He abhorred violence, and was dead against political murders. He soon parted company with the extremists, one of whose pioneer leaders he had been. Even his interpretation of passive resistance differed from that of Aurobindo on vital points. In fact, it was Aurobindo and not Pal who, in a clear masterly style, enunciated the doctrine of passive resistance, particularly in the series of seven articles mentioned earlier. Aurobindo listed three types of resistance: (1) passive resistance, (2) active or aggressive resistance, and (3) open armed revolt. In the prevailing Indian conditions he recommended passive resistance as the 'most natural weapon', but added, 'There is a limit, however, to Passive Resistance. . . . To break an unjust coercive law is not only justifiable, but under given circumstances, a duty.' He went on to say, 'Passive resistance cannot build up a strong and great nation unless it is ready at any moment and at the slightest notice to supplement itself with active resistance.'

Pal never wanted to move that far. Instead he moved back in a short time.[56] Aurobindo, on the other hand did not rest only with the exposition of boycott or passive resistance, but defended the cult fiercely. When Gokhale tried to prove the economic 'impossibility' of 'graduated boycott', Aurobindo took up the challenge and pointed out how it could be made possible and was made possible in Bengal regarding cloth, sugar and salt.

The Swadeshi Movement gradually extended itself in two ways. First, anti-Partition agitations, centering on protest meetings, the cry of *Bande Mataram* (by then accepted as the national slogan) and the singing of *Bande Mataram* (accepted as the national anthem); secondly, setting up of swadeshi enterprise and boycott efforts. In the beginning, all sections of the people and practically all shades of opinion supported the anti-Partition movement, including the merchants, zamindars, professionals, Muslims and even the British commercial community, besides the Anglo-Indian press. But gradually a section of the zamindars withdrew their support because of government pressure, as did a large number of Muslims, for various reasons. The British commercial community withdrew its support when the boycott was actually implemented as it endangered their material interests. The movement then turned largely into one of middle-class and lower-middle-class Bengalis, and professional men, and of course the students. The peasants and workers were also partially involved. On the whole, it took the shape of a genuine national movement.

Innumerable samitis sprang up, some of them well-organized, which helped the movement for some time. Special mention must be made, however, of the Anushilan Samiti, with branches spread all over Bengal; in West Bengal through the efforts of Satish Basu, and the Barindra group (which originally belonged to Anushilan Party led by P. Mitra); and in East Bengal through Pulin Das and his associates. Other important societies, political and non-political, were the Dawn Society, Anti-Circular Society, Chhatra Bhandar, Bande Mataram Sampradaya (all in West Bengal), and the Brati Samiti, Suhrid Samiti, Sadhana Samaj and Swadesh Bandhab Samiti in East Bengal. Boycott and Swadeshi became effective in many of the districts of East Bengal, largely through the sustained efforts of these samitis. Among the latter, one organization claims special mention: the Swadesh Bandhab Samiti of Barisal. They permeated distant villages and were taken up by both Hindus and Muslims. Thanks to the efforts of this Samiti and its undisputed leader, Aswini Kumar Dutta, a man of unimpeachable character, with great organizational abilities and a heart full of love for the land and the people, Swadeshi and Boycott were most successful in this district. Though moderate in political views, Dutta was greatly respected by the Extremists. Nivedita knew him personally, and worked with him for some time in the famine and flood-devastated villages of East Bengal, particularly in Barisal.

Aswini Kumar Dutta had started social service long before the Partition, mostly with the help of the students and teachers of the

Brojomohan School and College which he had started. In 1897 he had a long talk with Vivekananda at Almora, mostly on national problems. When asked about the Congress, Vivekananda said, 'of course something is better than nothing'. Then he sharply put the counter question: 'Can you tell me what the Congress has been doing for the masses? Do you think merely passing a few resolutions will bring you freedom?' The Swami then elaborated his ideas about religion ('Strength is religion, and nothing is greater than strength'), and pointed to the right way for national regeneration. Knowing that Aswini Kumar was engaged in educational work, Swamiji urged him to spread 'man-making education among the masses', and to build up the students as 'the thunderbolts'. 'Out of the bones of the Bengali youths shall be made the thunderbolt that shall destroy India's thraldom', he prophesied. Swamiji's final advice to Aswini Kumar was: 'Go to the untouchables, the cobblers, the sweepers and others of their kind, and tell them, "You are the soul of the Nation, and in you lies infinite energy which can revolutionise the world. Stand up, shake off your shackless.". . . . Go and found schools among them.'[57]

The reason for the success of swadeshi and boycott in Barisal was that the volunteers were close to the peasants, both Hindus and Muslims, and won their confidence. Dr Sumit Sarkar has quoted government records which show how alarmed the officials were at Dutta's influence with the Muslims. On 20 June 1907, the district magistrate wrote with apprehension that Aswini Kumar, when on tour, was 'associating closely with low class Mussalmans'. 'In two years' endeavour,' another report of the same period stated, 'Babu Aswini Kumar Datta and his band of agitators have succeeded in instilling a spirit of hostility to government and hatred of the Europeans into the great majority of the Hindus, and they are now making deliberate efforts to excite similar feelings among the ignorant and turbulent Mohamedan peasantry.'[58] The Muslim peasants had great respect for Dutta and refused to be instigated into disruption by the agents of the Dacca Nawab, as the 'Babu' had helped them in all possible ways during times of distress. It is, therefore, not surprising that Aswini Kumar was deported without trial, and Barisal suffered most brutally at the hands of the imperial government.

The term 'National Volunteers' which 'alarmed the sensationalists' in England was the 'sole invention' of a Calcutta journalist 'to make the flesh of the India Office creep, . . . and [which] succeeded'. Nevinson traced the history of the volunteer movement and its role in swadeshi and boycott. The volunteers, mostly students of schools and colleges, participated not only in political agitations but also performed commendable social work. Physical exercises were part of their programmes. In times of social disturbance, they stood for the protection of the weak, particularly the weaker sex. About their role in boycott, Nevinson wrote:

> The young men of towns and villages formed themselves into associations to preach the boycott. Shops that continued the sale were surrounded by groups that implored customers for the sake of their country to go away. Boys threw themselves prostrate in supplication, as is the Indian way. This was the only form of persuasion used. [There were exceptions.] Sometimes the boycott took the further form of destroying British goods. Usually the goods were first paid for, but in some cases payment was not made.[59]

Keir Hardie, M.P., and leader of the Labour Party in England, toured India in 1907, and from personal experience related the extent and magnitude of the movement. His observation was that in Mymensingh and Barisal 'Boycott has been conducted on strictly constitutional lines', though, he admitted, here and there 'zealous youths' overstepped. 'Be that as it may, the fact remains that Swadeshi has a strong hold in the district [of Barisal], and in some of the villages no *Bilati* goods are sold.'[60] Keir Hardie had been informed about the coercive methods of the boycotters, particularly against the Muslims, who preferred cheaper and durable *'Bilati'* cloth, and that police were employed to protect their interests. Keir Hardie visited some villages to see for himself and found, to his surprise, that the villagers, the majority of them Muslims, wore 'native goods, because they lasted longer and gave better value'. He could not accept the story about police protection for the Muslims, saying, 'It has to be borne in mind that 75 per cent of the people of East Bengal are Mohamedans, that the entire forces of the government are behind them if they prefer foreign goods, and to speak of these fighting men thus situated as being intimidated into supporting Swadeshi is grotesque in its absurdity.'[61] Nevinson also could not accept the government version that the Muslims insisted on having Manchester goods, because they, Nevinson wrote, 'have most to gain by the Swadeshi Movement, for they form the great majority of the hand-loom weavers, and owing to Swadeshi that industry for which Dacca was long famous over the world, has in the last two years not only revived but redoubled'.[62]

Social boycott was used to pressurize reluctant individuals. We have it that

> the cobblers in Mymensingh refused in a body to mend English shoes. The Oriya cooks and servants in Barisal . . . [decided] that they would not serve masters using foreign goods. The washermen of Kalighat . . . [agreed on] boycotting the washing of foreign clothes. . . . The priests refused to officiate in marriage ceremonies where foreign cloths were used. . . . The

> orthodox pundits lent their support to the movement and laid down that the use of foreign salt and sugar was not sanctioned by Hindu religion.[63]

Social boycott affected most Indian dealers in foreign cloth. While Nevinson was travelling on a river steamer in East Bengal, 'five or six dark forms gathered round him' with 'gestures of secrecy'. They were none other than the big merchants who had large dealings in Manchester cottons, and in consequence were generally shunned. Barbers would not shave them, milkmen would not sell them milk, friends would not come to their daughter's marriages'. Spiteful pity was their natural due. 'They were martyrs to the cause of British commerce', Nevinson wrote.[64]

It is a moot point among historians how far Swadeshi and Boycott were successful on the economic front. Contemporary accounts differed, according to the different affiliations of the commentators. The Indian nationalist press naturally published enthusiastic accounts of success; Anglo-Indian journals tried to play them down. *The Statesman* was an exception among the Anglo-Indian journals. Till the middle of 1907 it was edited by Nivedita's friend, S.K. Ratcliffe. But no paper owned and managed by Englishmen could go completely the Indian way and rigid objectivity was maintained in reports of this period at least. By September 1905, one of its representatives wrote, after surveying the market, that 'for Manchester *dhotis* there was practically no demand'. One big merchant conveyed to the representative that, in the first half of September 1904 'he had sold 5000 bales of stuff, but in the first two weeks of that month in 1905 he had only succeeded in clearing 125 bales, and even that at reduced prices'. *The Statesman* published tables to show the sharp fall in the sale of English goods. It reported on the pitiable plight of dealers in foreign salt. Cigarette dealers were still worse off. Dr R.C. Majumdar quotes a *London Evening News* report, of early October 1905, which told of the 'dreadful reaction that the Boycott Movement produced on British import cargo'. Official reports also acknowledged the grim situation. One European firm in Bengal cabled to England: 'Boycott result is disastrous. Books are not saleable; the busy season has closed; hosiery, hats and wrist-bangles are also affected.' And on 1 September 1905, the Marwari Chamber of Commerce (Marwaris were denounced by the *Bengalee* of 22 May 1906, as 'the greatest enemies of the Swadeshi Movement',[65] sent a frantic cable to the Manchester Chamber of Commerce with an appeal to persuade the Secretary of State to prevent partition: 'The sale of Manchester goods has been practically stopped. We shall be ruined and shall not be able to make future contracts. . . . The matter is very urgent.'

Critical accounts of latter-day historians, however, point out that the total effect of the movement on British commerce for the period 1905-10 was marginal. 'The effect of boycott on British imports has been inflated', writes Dr Amales Tripathi, and to prove his point he refers to the *Annual Reports on the Maritime Trade of Bengal 1903-8*. He also ascribes other reasons for the fall of British imports into India, depending on Frederic Noel-Paton's *Review of the Trade of India in 1908-9*, which explained 'the decline by over-trading and over-production of the previous quinquennium and the stringency of world trade in 1908'.[66] Dr Sumit Sarkar, depending on the same reports and other sources, especially official records, came to the conclusion that though, over the whole period, the impact on imports was marginal, 'sharp dips are noticeable in cotton goods, apparel, tobacco and liquor for the years 1906-7 and 1908-9, while the fall in the import of cigarettes proved to be a permanent trend'. Also, it has been said that, 1907 onwards, the boycott was not particularly successful in West Bengal, but that the picture was different in East Bengal. By the middle of May 1907 it became evident, the business of foreign goods there was 'heavily damaged by agitation'.[67]

The overall picture was that, while there was enthusiasm in plenty in Bengal, sustained industrial enterprise was not visible. This was partly due to the Bengali people's admittedly unpractical nature, but more to lack of capital. The enthusiasts were mostly middle-class Bengalis, not as much interested in business as in intellectual pursuits. And, it must be admitted that whatever success the Swadeshi Movement achieved had been made possible by the Indian cloth mills of Bombay and Ahmedabad. They met, as far as possible, the huge demand from Bengal for Indian cloth and, in the process, made huge profits out of what was described as 'Bengali sentimentalism'. Nevinson reported,

> here in Bombay the old Swadeshi Movement and its extreme form of boycott between them have raised the demand for Indian cottons to such an extent that 80 or 90 mills in the city and the 300 more in the Presidency simply cannot supply it, going as hard as they may. Nearly all this extra demand comes from Calcutta. . . . The supply cannot keep pace with what Bengal wants, and Bengal will have no other. The most significant thing is that the Bengalis will pay a little more for a rather inferior stuff if it is genuine Swadeshi.[68]

The irony of the situation was that the millowners of Bombay, making profits to the utmost, and not sharing the benefits with the workers,[69] 'helped Bengali Swadeshism to fight Manchester'.

In fine, it should be emphasized that though the Swadeshi Movement did not match the high expectations it generated, its achievement was quite considerable. It not only gave the people a sense of self-confidence and faith in self-reliance but also charged the national mind with passionate love for indigenous goods. This feeling was voiced in the memorable song, *Mayer deoya mota kapar mathaya tule ne re bhai* (O brothers, accept with bowed heads the coarse cloths that your mother can offer). The movement provided the nation with an example and experience that paved the way for the more successful and widespread Gandhian Khadi movement.

The effects of Swadeshi and Boycott extended over a sphere which, with greater success, could have made the situation difficult, if not critical, for the rulers. The industrial unrest during 1905-7 also had its effects. As has been mentioned before, Bengal was the centre of British commerce in India. To paralyze British industrial concerns in India by boycott should have been one of the objectives of the agitators. For several reasons, this was not pursued. First, the economic condition of the workers was so lamentable that long strikes would spell certain starvation for the concerned families. So, on a wide national level, a call for boycott of industries could not be given. Secondly, the European concerns could not be made the sole target of attack, because the conditions of workers in Indian-owned factories was even worse than in British-owned ones. Considering the unfair competition Indian entrepreneurs had to face against the Europeans, and the need for sustaining their existence by any means whatsoever, the Indian nationalists were hesitant to call for a general industrial boycott. Thus, only British-owned enterprises became targets of attack. The irrefutable logic of the poverty of the workers and rising prices was a factor; the shameless display of racial discrimination on the part of the British owners certainly aggravated the situation; and these, at the same time, were responsible for the growth of political consciousness in this country and were naturally relevant for the Swadeshi Movement. The Swadeshi Movement did therefore play a part in the strikes. Its organizing leaders were intimately connected with the movement. Most prominent among them, Aswini Kumar Banerjee, barrister, public speaker, conspicuous for his defence for the political agitators, had actively participated in the anti-partition movement in its early stage. There is no doubt that he changed his course in a short time, moved to co-operation from passive resistance, and this change was sharply criticized; but the reason behind this criticism was aggrieved shock, because 'this Aswini . . . one day went like a beggar from door to door asking for help for the printers who had gone on strike'. With this comment, *Nabasakti* (an extremist journal) of 12 November 1907, added, 'but we knew that his nature had become polluted with *bilati* ideas when he accepted a commissionership in the Calcutta Corporation'.[70] Prabhatkusum Roychaudhuri, also a barrister, and supporter of the Movement, was moderate in outlook but a genuine activist on the labour front. The third labour leader Premtosh Bose, was an extremist with alleged revolutionary connections. He tried to infuse some of his ideas into the labour field. The fourth, again a barrister, Apurbakumar Ghose, had socialist leanings and taught socialism to the Anushilan boys. Prominent nationalist leaders like Brahmabandhab Upadhyay, Bipin Chandra Pal, Liakat Hussain, Shyamsunder Chakrabarti, more or less actively supported the strikes. Brahmabandhab's *Sandhya* of 24 July 1906 called on everyone to do 'everything . . . to make the [Railway] strike successful', and suggested consultation with the nationalist leaders on this account.

Bande Mataram (7 September 1907) visualized the hand of God working behind the campaign for national education, the volunteers and the strikes. A contributor to *Prabasi* (November 1905) supporting the cause of nearly 300 retrenched Burn Co. strikers wrote that, 'if the three hundred heroes of Burn Company die of hunger, it would show that we deserve nothing better than kicks and blows'. Thus the strikes got adequate coverage in the nationalist press and the necessary sympathy and support from the Movement and the public.

The news of the strike of some three hundred clerks at the Burn Iron Works at Howrah (mentioned by Nivedita) created so much 'enthusiasm and admiration' at a Swadeshi meeting at College Square (2 September 1905) that it defied 'all attempts at description'. The strike, though it failed ultimately, was considered an outcome of Swadeshi inspiration. At Gloster Jute Mill (at Bauria) a strike was sparked off when the European manager objected to 'Bengali clerks and Muslim mill-hands exchanging rakhis'. Twelve hundred workers struck work at the Burn Company Shipyard 'on being refused leave to attend the Federation Hall meeting'. In 1905-8 there were numerous other strikes in British and government concerns. The politically important among them were the Press strike (Government of India Press and Bengal Secretariat Press), the East India Railway strike and the jute workers' strike 'affecting at different times 18 out of 37 mills in the province'. These strikes were the outcome of indirect political incitement and were inspired by nationalist leaders, and showed, to an extent, the involvement of labour in the national agitation. At the same time, it had also been asserted that the strikers were mostly clerks having some political consciousness and not 'proletariat' workers. The strike wave of this period inspired some to seek comparison with parallel Russian strikes. Dr Amales Tripathi thinks this comparison is 'superficial' as these strikes were nothing but explosions of 'anti-imperialist hatred, not the awakening of class consciousness'.[71] Yet it is doubtful whether the existence of some sort of class consciousness could be denied. We see that, about seven years earlier, Vivekananda visualized in contemporary Indian strikes early signs of a proletarian rising.[72]

Anyway, the British imperialists became apprehensive of a simultaneous explosion of the Swadeshi Movement and labour unrest. The *Pioneer,* on 21 July 1906, commented on the 'more mischievous turn' of the Swadeshi Movement 'in forming trade unions amongst employees in large concerns managed by the Europeans'. Dr Sumit Sarkar has quoted from *Administration of Bengal Under Andrew Fraser (1903-8)* which pointed to the power of organization of the 'professional agitators' in the trade union movement also. 'Briefless Bengali Hindu barristers' formed these unions amongst Indian press employees, mill-hands and railway servants , 'strikes were started or encouraged, and the strikers were backed up' by them.[73] These 'briefless barristers' did one necessary thing, they allied labour with the national struggle, though to a restricted degree.

4. Swadeshi and Cultural Renaissance

That the Swadeshi Movement ushered in a genuine national awakening was proved by the fact that it flowered in many-sided creativity of the national genius in the areas of education, literature, science and the fine arts.

The urge for education on national lines was deeply felt by patriots even prior to the swadeshi days and isolated efforts had been made to provide it. Two efforts need special mention: one, by Sister Nivedita; the other by Rabindranath Tagore. The institutions they founded flourished to become great national centres of learning and culture. Nivedita's efforts not only culminated in the present well-known Nivedita Girls' School at Calcutta but also paved the way for the foundation of a number of other educational institutions, including a first-grade college run by the Ramakrishna Sarada Mission, Dakshineswar. Nivedita's school was established in November 1898 with the encouragement of Swami Vivekananda and the blessings of Sarada Devi, consort of Sri Ramakrishna. It aimed at, and to some extent succeeded in, providing instruction in 'English and Bengali languages and literature, elementary mathematics very thoroughly taught, some elementary science very thoroughly taught and handicrafts with a special bearing on the revival of the old Indian industries'. The object of including handicrafts was to enable 'every pupil to earn her own living, without leaving her home, by a pursuit which should be wholly ennobling'.[74]

In the Swadeshi days Nivedita was helped to run the school by two ardent nationalists, Sister Christine, a disciple of Vivekananda, who had made India her home, and Sudhira Bose, sister of the well-known revolutionary writer, Debabrata Bose. Nivedita constantly tried to infuse love for India and its heritage in the minds of her pupils by taking them to museums and places of historical interest and narrating to them the glorious Indian saga of heroic sacrifice. With great emotion she would say, 'My children, daughters of the Ind, let you constantly utter this mantra, Bharata-Varsha! Bharata-Varsha! Bharata-Varsha!' By way of change, she would take her girls to the Brahmo Girls' School and give them a chance to listen to swadeshi lectures in the adjoining park. She introduced spinning in her school curriculum; made the 'prohibited' *Bande Mataram* the daily morning prayer. When in January 1910, the deported national leaders, Aswini Kumar Dutta, Krishnakumar Mitra and others, were released, 'her school was decorated with auspicious banana leaves and festoons and it was closed for the day'.[75]

In 1901 Rabindranath started his 'Boarding School' at Santiniketan, which flourished and developed to become the Visvabharati of today. At the initial stage the school was organized by Brahmabandhab Upadhayay in the form of a *brahmacharyashrama*, after the ancient Indian tradition. Teachers were to be taken as *gurus*, students to follow a disciplined, austere life, and instruction was to be given under trees, in the open air, beginning with prayers. Tagore wrote in a letter at the time (28 Chaitra 1308 BS) that he wanted the students to absorb knowledge in a tension-free, serene and pure atmosphere, following the old Indian ideal of *brahmacharyashrama*, away from the allurement of Western luxuries.[76] The poet, charged with emotion and imagination asked in an earnest voice, 'If in the Vedic times there could be *Tapobana* Ashramas, if in the Buddhistic era Nalanda could flourish, then why in modern times should high and noble ideals be treated with ridicule as unattainable millennium?'[77] After two years of experimentation, he again wrote in a letter (2 Aswin 1310 BS) to say how wonderful it was to realize every day the revolutionary process through which the school proceeded and gained more and more energy and strength. He prophesied that a day would come when doubts would disappear and the morning glow of new advent would shine in sureness in the minds of the sceptics.[78]

Tagore tirelessly went on expressing his ideas about education on national lines in private letters and articles, experimenting and gaining experience through conducting his own school and thereby became the leading figure in the National Education Scheme, which became an urgent necessity in October 1905, in view of the call to boycott government and government-aided institutions.

The idea of national education was not new, but now, for political reasons, the immediate setting up of national schools became an unavoidable obligation. Students whose leading role in the Swadeshi Movement was apparent became targets of attack from the government. They were warned, chased, lathi-charged, and even flogged, but were undaunted. It was they who took out processions, sang national songs in chorus, shouted *Bande Mataram*, crowded to the meetings, took part in picketing, carried and supplied swadeshi goods to village shops, and did all they could to annoy the government. To restrict them, R.W. Carlyle, officiating Chief Secretary to the Government of Bengal, sent a secret circular on 10 October 1905 to magistrates and collectors, which instructed, 'If any attempt is made by boys attending any school or college in your district to take any public action in connection with boycotting, picketing and other abuses, associated with the so-called Swadeshi Movement, you will at once take cognizance of that action.' Heads of institutions were asked to take action against these boys, failing which all government aid would be withdrawn and the university be asked to disaffiliate them. A most ignoble suggestion was made, viz., that teachers might be asked to act as 'special constables', i.e., as government agents, in detecting offenders. A similar circular was issued by P.C. Lyon, Chief Secretary to the Government of Eastern Bengal and Assam (16 October 1905) with more vicious implications: 'If any institution disregards your [commissioners' and district officers'] advice, the case should be reported to me without delay.'

Similar other circulars were issued in rapid succession. All these circulars had given uninhibited power to the officials to interfere with the internal matters of educational institutions. The official instructions were ruthlessly carried out; but voices of protest could nevertheless be heard. While the residents of Rangpur decided to set up a National School of their own, the teachers of eleven schools in Madripur subdivision of Faridpur District refused to be brow-beaten by the officials. In a body, they defended the action of the Headmaster of Madripur School, Kali Prasanna Dasgupta, in refusing to punish one of his students with flogging for his refusal to furl an umbrella in the presence of a local 'sahib'. In these circumstances it became obligatory for the leaders to find means of accommodating expelled school-boys and dismissed teachers. National schools was the only alternative.

Boycott of the prevalent educational institutions also featured along with other boycotts prior to the Carlyle Circular. On 5 August 1905, Bipin Pal, C.R. Das, P. Mitra and others met at the Albert Hall, Calcutta, and proposed to raise a fund for the students who would leave European-managed institutions to join Indian ones. About the same time, papers like *Sandhya* called for a national university. After the Carlyle Circular, within a span of three months, many meetings and conferences were held to adopt the national education proposal and to formulate programmes for its implementation. Not only political but intellectual leaders like Rabindranath, Surendranath, Rashbehari Ghose, Tarak Nath Palit, Nilratan Sarkar, Satischandra Mukherjee, Sister Nivedita, Bipin Pal, Abdul Rasul, Hirendranath Dutta, Shyamsundar Chakravarti and Krishnakumar Mitra took part in the deliberation. On 24 October

1905, at a crowded meeting at the Field and Academy Club ground, the establishment of a National University was proposed to counteract the Carlyle offensive. On 4 November, the Anti-Circular Society was formed under the energetic leadership of a young man, Sachindraprasad Bose. This society of the students played an active part in organizing national schools. The 9 November meeting at Panti's *math* was notable for the munificent offer of a lakh of rupees by Subodh Chandra Mallik for promoting national education. As a token of gratitude, the people bestowed on him the title Raja. This was followed by another offer of Rs 5 lakhs the very next day by Brojendra Kishore Roychaudhury, zamindar of Gouripur, Mymensingh. The meeting on 16 November, marked as 'historic', was attended by a large number of eminent persons, political and intellectual, who decided to set up a National Council of Education which would organize a system of education — literary, scientific and technical — on national lines and under national control.

But all was not well with the scheme and its implementation. A section of people was not altogether ready for complete disassociation with the Calcutta University; some objected to the ambitious three-dimensional scheme; some felt that emphasis on tradition was not desirable and so on. Anyway, two institutions were finally formed, the National Council of Education (registered on 1 June 1906) and the Society for the Promotion of Technical Education. The promoter of the second organization was Tarak Nath Palit; its first Secretary and the first Principal were Pramatha Nath Bose and Dr Nilratan Sarkar respectively. Leading scientists like Dr J.C. Bose and P.C. Ray joined its committee as advisors. It was the National Council, however, that caught the imagination of the people. Its comprehensive approach towards education, and its link with radical political elements, at least in the first stage, drew many to it. The Council founded the National College at Bowbazar Street, Calcutta, with Aurobindo Ghose, the brilliant scholar, as its first Principal. Aurobindo had resigned from lucrative Baroda State Service (his pay there being Rs 750 per month) to join his new post at a monthly salary of Rs 75. Another person who needs a special mention was Satischandra Mukherjee. He was a man of exceptional qualities — educationist and idealist to the bone, but at the same time imbued with a strong practical sense. Satischandra had been Secretary of the famous Dawn Society before taking over as Superintendent of this National College.

The *Dawn* magazine (founded in 1897) and the Dawn Society must be mentioned in any history of national education in Bengal. Satischandra, with another idealist, Ajayhari Banerjee, started the magazine. (Later, Banerjee became Swami Swarupananda, a disciple of Vivekananda and the second editor of the famous journal of the Ramkrishna Mission,

Prabuddha Bharata.) *Dawn* had been launched to propagate moral and spiritual ideals to the rising generations. Satischandra attracted brilliant boys, inspired them to develop the power of original thinking and a sense of nationalism because, for him, 'intense nationalism was the basis and foundation of society'. The Dawn Society had its industrial section also, with a Swadeshi Store, to produce and sell indigenous articles. *Dawn* magazine regularly published articles on Indian economy. On 5 November 1906 a large meeting of students was held at the Dawn Society where Satischandra 'exhorted the students to sever all connections with the officialized University and boycott its examinations'. For the next few months he devoted himself entirely to organizing the National Education programme and the Bengal National College. Though Aurobindo Ghose was the principal of the college during its first year (August 1906 to August 1907) he could not spare much time for the college because his main concern was the extremist daily *Bande Mataram*, and underground revolutionary activities. He involved himself in Congress politics also. Thus Satischandra became the heart and soul of the college and its council. After Aurobindo's resignation, he bore the extra burden of principalship, till his own resignation at the end of 1908.

The National Council worked vigorously for some time and created an atmosphere of hope and purpose. Many national schools of East and West Bengal were affiliated to it, received financial assistance, though meagre, from the council. Its initial success was appreciated by the Indian National Congress in its 1906 Session. Tagore at the Pabna Education Conference congratulated the people for accepting responsibility of public instruction; they 'had already given a proof of their earnestness by establishing on a firm footing the National Council of Education'.[79] Aurobindo however was more interested in this institution as a training ground for would-be national workers, while the officialized university education tended to create 'machines for administrative and professional work, and not men'.

However, Aurobindo could not spare time for national education as he became immersed in politics up to the eyes. Tagore soon realized that he could not go hand in hand with either the national movement or the national education movement. It was not long before it became evident that the control of the National Education Council had gone out of the hands of the radical nationalists. In the council Aurobindo represented the radicals, but he left. Another school in the council, dominated by the Brahmos, moderate in political ideas but modern in social outlook, parted company with it to form the Technical Institute. The third school, led by the Moderate politician, Surendranath Banerjea, never seriously wanted to boycott Calcutta University (Banerjea owned Ripon College, Calcutta), not even Aswini Kumar Dutta wanted this. As a result, control shifted to persons who were moderate in political outlook (Satis-chandra was even a loyalist), were deeply attached to traditional ideas, and had a pious interest in indigenous industries. They wanted the National Schools to have no connection with politics. But as the East Bengal National Schools, having originated from political stirrings, could not totally eschew politics, they lost favour with the council.

Government officials had at first become panicky at the rapid growth of National Schools in different parts of East Bengal. Lord Minto, in his note of 7 December 1908, commented that 'it is out of the question that we should tolerate the national schools as they are'. He was ready to introduce new legislation for controlling these schools, but soon found, with satisfaction, that the National Council, led by Ashutosh Choudhuri and Hirendranath Dutta, had taken on their shoulders the distasteful responsibility that was his. On 26 August 1909, Minto wrote to Morley: 'It is very satisfactory that the National Council of Education has been doing much to keep the students of the national schools under control.'[80]

Nivedita's position was interesting and unique here. Certainly she was a great supporter of the National Education Movement, but it took no time for her to understand that nothing tangible would emerge from the National Council's efforts. She had great faith in India's dynamic past, but her eyes were always fixed to the future. So when she, the extremist and the revolutionary that she was, saw to her dismay, the controlling authority of the council had backed out from national struggle and were indulging in traditionalism she knew that the council was doomed. The only hope lay at the Technical Institute, she thought. She was up against 'sham spirituality'. She found that the council had no real interest in higher science, without which intellectual advancement was impossible in modern times. She called for boycott of government services and British goods, but it is doubtful whether she approved boycott of university-affiliated schools and colleges, as they were the only existing venues for scientific knowledge. She wanted to fight for de-officializing of the educational institutions. (Ashutosh Mukherjee succeeded in some measure in extending Indian control over the Calcutta University.) The National Council resources were too meagre to run a parallel stream of education, suited to modern conditions. At the same time, Nivedita knew and admired the great cause the National Council represented. As its respected though unofficial advisor, she did her best to secure the services of a great intellectual to rescue the National College from its reactionary degradation. He was no other than Patrick Geddes, recognized in the contemporary West as a leading sociologist, possessing encyclopaedic knowledge (he was a biologist, physicist, botanist, economist, educationist, town-planner and what not). Nivedita had made him take interest in the Tata Postgraduate

Science University Scheme. Now she wanted Geddes to take charge as principal of the National College. That was the only way, she believed, to save the institution from disaster. The National Council had offered Dr Ananda Coomaraswamy the principalship at an annual salary of Rs 10,000. But Nivedita was not happy. Coomaraswamy, though brilliant, was an 'incorrigible reactionary'. 'With his intolerance of the present . . . [he was not] altogether sufficient as a guide.'[81] Coomaraswamy too suggested Geddes as the 'right man', and Nivedita wrote on 2 September 1909: 'I made the hot suggestion.' But she added, 'I fear £ 1,000 a year would not be enough to offer him.'[82] In other letters also, she expressed her intense desire to get Geddes for the National College, because 'apart from P.G. it is bound to fall back upon a narrow orthodoxy'.[83] Nivedita's efforts did not succeed, Geddes did not join the college at that time, though afterwards he did come to India, and served as a professor at the Bombay University. He wrote the well-known biography of Dr J.C. Bose.

The National Education Scheme did not succeed. It was a part of the Swadeshi Movement, and when the movement died down, this scheme also met its natural death. From the very beginning, it had to fight against heavy odds. The very urgent question was of future employment of its students. Government offices and the foreign business enterprises would not entertain National School products. University-affiliated schools or colleges would not accept them as teachers; the quality of scientific training in these institutions did not reach the necessary standard due to lack of resources and even the few Indian-owned industrial concerns therefore hesitated to employ their products; commercial possibilities were extremely limited; to say nothing of the hostility of the government. Even an eminent Indian like Dr Ashutosh Mukherjee was antagonistic to the National System as this rival educational system harmed the interests of Calcutta University, then more or less controlled by him. He even went so far as to instigate Lord Minto to take actions against National Schools and Colleges.[84]

But the Scheme of National Education should be judged, not by the measure of its material success, but by the stimulation to the national consciousness that it provided. In a limited sense, National Education achieved material success too. In 1910, the Technical Institute was amalgamated with the National Council. The Technical Institute survived to become Jadavpur Engineering College, and then to prosper after independence as Jadavpur University, mainly owing to the efforts of Dr Bidhan Chandra Roy.

Higher scientific discoveries cannot directly come out of a movement. But a movement can and does generate spirit which might move a man to deep longing for artistic creations or scientific discovery. More, a movement can claim and fight for better and congenial working conditions for its talented persons, and itself be, at the same time, stimulated by their achievements. All these things happened in the Swadeshi days, centering on Dr J.C. Bose's scientific work and his 'world-shaking' discoveries.

Jagadis Chandra Bose (1858-1938) was the first man to place India on the scientific map of the world in modern times. His discoveries started pouring in from 1895. By 1899, he was a recognized world scientist. Praises were heaped on him by Western scientists and scientific papers, and the Indian papers enthusiastically quoted them. His advent coincided with Vivekananda's, and together they symbolized Indian awakening. Nivedita had said, 'In religion Vivekananda and in science Bose have made offerings to the World.'[85]

But Bose was soon under attack. The petty, scheming Anglo-Indian officials of the education department in Bengal (Bose was a professor in Presidency College, Calcutta) could not stomach with grace the world-wide fame of a native. The same feeling prevailed in a section of British scientists. They had put forward all mischievous devices possible to thwart Bose's progress. Thus the 'Bose War' started, which could well be regarded a part of the national struggle. Indian papers and intelligentsia came forward to support Bose's case; R.C. Dutta, Rabindranath and Nivedita, joined hands to mobilize opinions and resources in favour of Bose, who 'lifted her [India] in the comity of nations' by 'his services to science'.[86] 'Dr Bose's discovery is in some special sense the contribution of his whole race.'[87] In Bose the Indian 'Sannyasi mind' worked for science and vindicated the great theory of Advaita by scientific methods. Vivekananda saw for himself the glorious spectacle — among the white galaxy of geniuses' of the Paris Scientific Congress of 1900, 'stepped forth one distinguished youthful hero to proclaim the name of our motherland . . . Dr J.C. Bose.' Vivekananda was besides himself with joy. 'At the top of all physicists — Jagadis Chandra Bose — an Indian, a Bengali.'[88] And how great was his anguish on knowing about the bitter antagonism of the officialdom to Dr Bose. 'The English rulers want to push him into a corner,' he wrote to Mary Hale on 17 June 1900, 'they don't of course like that sort of development in the Indian race.'[88]

Thus it was natural that the Indian nationalists would launch a 'Bose War' as part of a bigger war. They were encouraged in doing so because Bose was an ardent nationalist. Bose in so many of his letters written to Rabindranath from England in 1900 had repeatedly said that his heart of hearts remained in India and India alone. If he could do anything for India, he said, he would feel blessed. Bose was a devout swadeshist. On 16 October 1905 (partition day), he had sent a *rakhi* to Mrs Ole Bull and had written: 'They had divided us by law but we all over India bid ourselves by this symbolic tie to stand by each other for all time and stand and face everything.'[90] After three years, on the same date, he wrote to Nivedita, 'This is the great day of consecration for the Motherland. May we all be consecrated to her service.'[91]

Nationalist leaders knew Bose and his feelings; they knew also that Bose, by working in the scientific field, would push forward the movement more than by indulging in active politics. The same was the case with Rabindranath, who helped the movement not so much by his active participation as with his inspiring songs. So Gokhale, Bhupendranath Basu and others took up Bose's case as a national cause and protested against government's obstructionist policy. The government, on the plea of encouraging technical education, curtailed funds for higher science. Bose's great scientific works, published at the time when the Swadeshi Movement was at its highest pitch, were regarded as an extension of India's national genius to hitherto uncharted areas. Bose's two great works, *Plant Response as a Means of Physiological Investigation* (1906) and *Comparative Electro-Physiology: A Physico-Physiological Study* (1907), were published at the time of the Swadeshi Movement and hailed by Patrick Geddes as works for which 'there can be few parallels in science'. And all the time, when engaged in science, Bose did not for a moment forget that he was working for his motherland. When he was preparing the schemes for his own laboratory, Basu Bijnan Mandir, his comprehensive mind placed science in a wider intellectual perspective. 'He wanted History, Archaeology, Art, and Women's Education there [in his laboratory]. All this is the outcome of that wonderful personal quality . . . that makes him at home with all greatness of every kind, instinctively welcoming and becoming comrade to it.'[92]

But Bose was not alone in the field of science in the Swadeshi days. At the Presidency College was Prafulla Chandra Ray, the great chemist, who, by his discovery of new mercury compounds in 1896, won wide recognition. Such was his love for his motherland that, instead of publishing his papers in foreign journals, he published them in the Calcutta Asiatic Society journal, from which translations were made in Germany's *Journal of Inorganic Chemistry*. The *Amrita Bazar Patrika* congratulated Bose and Ray for their simultaneous achievements in its issue of 30 May 1896. But the great P.C. Ray was greater as guru of young scientists in the ensuing years. His disciples included Satyendranath Bose, Meghnad Saha, J.C. Ghose, and others. The laboratory was his home, students the heart, and the motherland the object of worship for this real *acharya*.

The need for books and articles on science in the mother tongue was also keenly felt. Here must be mentioned the works of Jagadananda Roy who, inspired by Tagore, wrote in lucid Bengali about Bose's discoveries. But most important among such writers was Ramchandrasundar Trivedi, a dedicated science professor and a distinguished writer of Bengali prose. His scientific and philosophical writings were greatly admired. Nivedita in a letter urged him to devote himself wholeheartedly to this work: 'How I wish you would be free of affairs and profession and devote yourself altogether to the great task of writing Science in Bengali, in which direction I am told that your personal work will leave a permanent impress on the mother tongue.'[93]

The Swadeshi Movement, more than any other national upsurge, either before or after it, found a profound reflection in Bengali literature which rose to great heights under its inspiration. When a genius like Rabindranath Tagore took the lead, the quality was assured. The bulk of Tagore's national songs were written in this period. It is significant to note here that Tagore was now very much charged with the spirit of Bankim Chandra's *Bande Mataram*. In most of his swadeshi songs he hailed the country as the Mother. But he was not alone in the field. There were others too, perhaps a little less inspired in poetic quality, but nevertheless matching the needs and emotions of the time and therefore quite popular. Dwijendralal Ray, Rajanikanta Sen, Kaliprasanna Kavya Visharad, Debabrata Basu, Satyendranath Dutta and a host of others kept up a steady flow of patriotic verse. Swadeshi songs were so much in demand, and were written in such numbers that at least nine collections of them were published in 1905-8.

The wide appeal of the movement was also reflected in the innumerable folk-songs that were composed and sung in the villages by beggars and *bairagis*, village minstrels. And finally, but not the least, was the glorious *Jatrawala*, Mukunda Das. *Jatra*, a popular form of village drama, immensely attractive to village people for its direct appeal, was taken up by this courageous man as a medium of preaching swadeshism. Mukunda Das himself wrote jatra plays, and composed songs for them. With his imposing figure, and a voice at once deep and resounding, he could carry thousands with him. He moved from village to village, creating so much enthusiasm among them that the authorities saw in him a grave danger. After the Regulation of Meetings Ordinance was promulgated, the district magistrate of Bakaragunge wrote that the jatras were effective substitutes for swadeshi meetings. Jatra 'reaches all classes and spreads seditious doctrines among them', he wrote.[94] Aswini Kumar Dutta was a great patron of these jatras. Mukunda Das became so very offensive in the eyes of the government that his jatra was prohibited and he was 'sentenced to a year's rigorous imprisonment on 23 January 1909.'

It is interesting to note that the Swadeshi spirit found no particular expression in short stories and novels. Songs and plays are directly communicative and immediately effective. That is why a good number of dramas were written and staged with great success at the time. Because of legal prohibitions, these plays could not openly preach against British rule, but they took the cover of history to achieve the same end. Thus the heroic tales of the Rajputs and the Marathas fighting against the then aggressor, the Mughals, were used to show what patriots should do when confronted with foreign invaders. It must be stressed that the playwrights had no intention of creating ill-feeling against the Muslims when they depicted Hindu heroism against the Mughals; it was just a question of fighting foreign invaders. Thus, when Bengal was attacked by the Mughals, a Bengali Hindu feudal chief Pratapaditya Roy joined hands with the Pathan Mussalman chiefs (who had made Bengal their homes) to fight against them. Not only that, in these plays, Siraj-ud-daulla was presented a great nationalist ruler, who saw through the cunning game of the British and fought them to the last. Mir Kasim was also made a national hero of the same type. The aim of the dramatists was to show Hindu-Muslim comradeship and how they made common cause against usurpers. Long patriotic speeches and songs were inserted in these patriotic-cum-historical plays. All the noted dramatists of the period came forward to write them. Girish Chandra Ghose, actor and dramatist, the undisputed leader of the Bengali stage of his times, wrote and staged *Siraj-ud-Daulla* (1905), *Mir Kasim* (1906) and *Chhatrapati Shivaji* (1907). D.L. Roy wrote *Rana Pratap* (1905), *Durgadas* (1906), *Mebarpatan* (1908). Another popular dramatist, Kshirodprasad Vidyabinod, wrote *Chand Bibi* (1907), *Palasir Prayaschitta* (1907) and *Nandakumar* (1908). That Girish Chandra's objective was to promote Hindu-Muslim fraternity, is amply expressed in Siraj-ud-Daulla's stirring call in the play: 'O Hindu, O Mussalman, forget the past bitterness, forgive each other, come and join hands to do good to Bengal so that your descendants cease to be the servants of the whites.' About the political significance of Girish Chandra's *Mir Kasim*, Surendranath Banerjea's *Bengalee* wrote on 23 June 1906:

> The tumultuous period that followed the accession of Mir Kasim to the throne, the strenuous fight that the ruler had with the East India Company for the protection of the indigenous industries and the various stratagems resorted to by both sides to win their points, have with remarkable fidelity and consummate art, been portrayed by Bengal's greatest play-wright.

The Statesman of 17 November 1907, appreciatively wrote about the 'high watermark of excellence' of acting and testified to the unmistakable acclaim of the 'huge audience'.[95]

Not only historical dramas but historical accounts were written in abundance at this period in book form or in exhaustive articles in journals. Subjects were chosen with an eye to rouse patriotic feelings. Thus was written Akshay Kumar Maitra's *Mir Kasim*. (Ten years earlier, in 1897, he had written *Siraj-ud-daulla* in the same strain.) Nikhil Nath Roy's *Pratapaditya* belonged to the same genre. Though latter-day historians like Dr R.C. Majumdar have been a bit harsh on these historical writings, specially on the dramas based on them, as 'perversion of history' and deliberate attempts 'to support prevailing political conceptions' through misrepresentation of 'the relation between Hindus and Muslims, during the medieval period of Indian history, as much more favourable or friendly than it actually was', or lifting the 'Sepoy Mutiny' to the 'level of a War of Independence' — it is possible that these interpretive histories and historical dramas will find favour with historians who see merit in a subjective, ideological interpretation of history. Anyway, important is the acknowledgement by Dr Majumdar, that 'It is hardly possible to exaggerate the importance of the role it [the dramas and historical works] played in the new era that this movement had ushered in. For, whatever we may think of the real character of the literary productions of the age from a historical point of view, they were taken as genuine, and produced immense effects.'[96]

Though written long before the Swadeshi Movement, Bankim Chandra's novel *Ananda Math* and the immortal song it contains, *Bande Mataram*, exerted more influence on the movement than any other literary work. The song became something of a *Vedamantra* to the nationalists; and the rulers tried to throttle those who uttered the *mantra*. *Bande Mataram* become a most seditious phrase. *The Indian Review* of Madras, while giving a translation of the song in its issue of December 1905, stated that 'it is now the shibboleth of the Bengal Swadeshis and the horror of the Bengal Civilians'.[97] The same journal, in its issue of May 1907, quoted from the daily *Bande Mataram*, in which had been related 'the services rendered to politics by the writings of this great man', Bankim Chandra. Referring to the 'great song which had become the national anthem of United India', it said:

> It was thirty-two years ago that Bankim wrote his great song and few listened; but in a sudden moment of awakening from long delusions the people of Bengal looked round for the truth and in a fated moment somebody sang *Bande Mataram*. The *mantra* had been converted to the religion of patriotism.[98]

The resounding *Bande Mataram* reached the 'Albion shore' and disturbed many. The *Morning Leader* of England, while reviewing the English translation of *Ananda Math* by Naresh Chandra Sengupta, referred to 'the interest attaching to the so-called seditious cry of Bande Mataram, which has sprung into prominence as the rallying call of the

Bengal nationalists.'[99] Tagore paid high compliments to this song to proclaim what literature can do. At the Literary Conference, organized during the Congress Session of 1906 at Calcutta, he emphasized that 'the Bengalis considered themselves to be Bengalis, not because of any geographical boundary, but because of the Bengali language and literature, which bind them. We should remember that the great mantra *Bande Mataram,* is a gift of the Bengali literature',[100] the poet stressed.

The importance of the Indian art movement in Bengal, which began in the Swadeshi days, was highlighted by Aurobindo. This movement was typically a swadeshi product. It is true that Abanindra Nath Tagore, the artist-leader of this movement, had started painting in Indian style prior to the partition, but that was only a feeble, exclusively personal venture. It took the shape of a movement only after 1905. But nor should it be assumed that it blossomed suddenly. A decade of preparation lay behind it. The organizing leadership was that of E.B. Havell, who joined the Government Art School, Calcutta, as principal in 1896. Havell, who till recently had been the principal of the Madras Government Art School, was struck with the beauty of ancient Indian art and felt the necessity of Indianizing art education in India. He therefore removed the low grade specimens of European art from the Calcutta Art School and began collecting Indian art treasures, thereby creating a commotion in art circles all over the country. Momentous was his meeting with Sister Nivedita in 1902. Nivedita had got her Indian art education from Swami Vivekananda. She had learnt that Indian art did not seek to imitate nature but to depict the ideal behind the form, that it was spiritual in essence, a creation by the people and for the people and that it could not seek inspiration from ancient Greece. She was also aware of the Swami's attitude towards the then tremendously popular paintings of mythological subjects by Ravi Varma, which were superficial and blindly imitative of the Western painting, devoid of any real Indian sense. Imbued with these ideas, when she met Havell at the Art School and was confronted with his sad lamentation, 'I can teach a man to draw and paint, but I cannot make him an artist, or a genius,' her instant reaction was, 'But I can. . . . Love of country — love of fellows — pride of birth — hope for the future — dauntless passion for INDIA — and there will be such a tide of Art, of Science, of Religion, of Energy, as no man can keep back. Instead of dolts — heroes; instead of copyists — original geniuses.'[101] Comradeship between these two talented persons in the field of art, produced tremendous positive results.

Another happy occurrence followed: the publication of Okakura's, *Ideals of the East,* with an introduction by Nivedita. The book traced the history and extent of Indian influence on Chinese and Japanese art. It informed educated Indians about their country's glorious art heritage.

But the most important event was Abanindra Nath Tagore's joining the Art School, as vice-principal. Abanindra Nath had been introduced to the wider art world by Havell's appreciative writing on his works in the famous British art journal, *Studio*. Havell, in an article in the same journal in 1908, narrated the progress of Abanindra Nath under his guidance:

> The reorganisation of the Calcutta Art Gallery was the starting point in Mr Tagore's career as an artist of New India: for the masterpieces of Moghul painting which I discovered in Calcutta were as much a revelation to Mr Tagore, as they were to the great majority of Anglo-Indians. Up to that time he, like all other Indian art students, had looked to Europe for guidance in technique, and followed purely European ideals of artistic expression. Henceforth, all his efforts were directed towards the endeavour to pick up the lost threads of Indian tradition.

After joining the Art School, he 'not only made much progress in his own work', Havell added, 'but under his inspiring teaching, several of the advanced students of the School now bid fair to rival their master'.[102] Thus was born the New Bengal, rather the New Indian Art Movement, in the heyday of the Swadeshi Movement.

Within two years of its inception, the New Art Movement got welcome support from a great lover of art and noted editor, Ramananda Chatterjee. His famous monthly, *Modern Review*, was started in January 1907. It regularly carried reproductions of paintings in colour with excellent interpretations by Nivedita. Ramananda had already started his Bengali monthly *Prabasi* in 1901, and had been regularly publishing art plates in it, but mostly of European masterpieces and paintings by Ravi Varma. Nivedita wrote appreciations of the European paintings, but was not satisfied with this. It was she, who, Ramananda acknowledged in writing, attracted him to the art creations of the New Indian School, and thus gave it most valuable support and wide publicity. She encouraged educated Indians in the recognition and appreciation of genuine art and also introduced the new school of Indian Art to the people of Bengal through her wise criticism of the paintings of this school. This became the special feature of *Modern Review*.[103] Ramananda secured for his magazine another art critic, later recognized as the greatest writer on the philosophy of Indian art, Ananda Coomaraswamy, whose contributions, particularly those pertaining to the relation between the national heritage and art, gave a fillip to the movement. In November 1908 came Havell's epoch-making book, *Indian Sculpture and Painting*, 'a readable authoritative account, well illustrated, on the psychological attitude in which competent persons might approach Indian art'. All these developments worked successfully to uphold the glory that was Indian art, and heralded a new age of artistic achievement. Taking the cue from Vivekananda, Nivedita with Okakura, Havell, Coomaraswamy and Aurobindo, thoroughly analysed the European theory concerning the supposed Greek influence in the origin of Indian art and discarded it with forceful logic. The symbolism in Indian art was discussed; and it was explained that the seemingly grotesque nature of some of its images was an expression of symbols of deep spiritual significance, beyond the reach of the nature-imitating European art. From Nivedita came high and mighty pronouncements on the true ideals of art and the newly born art-impulse in India. She was nevertheless conscious of the universality of art. 'The appeal of the highest poetry is universal,' she wrote; 'One of the supreme blossoms of culture is taste.' She urged time and again the importance of civic ideals in art. That was indeed a necessity in India. She visualized an art-school as a University where the common talk would cover 'all the burning questions of the day', and the reading of the students would 'be marked by an insatiable curiosity for all the noble secrets of the world'.[104] In letters and articles of this period, she strongly stressed the necessity of civic ideals in art, because the Swadeshi Movement needed this. She wanted the proposed Federation Hall at Calcutta to be decorated with civic and historic mural paintings.[105] Art is the 'great common speech', she said, which crosses barriers of language. She went so far as to write, 'I sometimes think that our greatest work in modernizing India might be done through Art, instead of through the Press or the Universities.' The first full-blown expression of this type of art she had found in Abanindra Nath's *Bharat Mata*. On this picture she wrote exuberantly at least twice. In August 1905, she wrote both in *Prabasi* and the *Indian World* on this picture, describing the technical skill it displayed and the symbolic idea it represented. The *Prabasi* note started with this sentence: 'We have here a picture which bids fair to prove the beginning of a new age in Indian art.' The *Indian World* note declared:

> It is the first masterpiece, in which an Indian artist has actually succeeded in disengaging, as it were, the spirit of the motherland — giver of Faith and Learning, of Clothing and Food — and portraying Her, as she appears to the eyes of Her Children . . . From beginning to end the picture is an appeal, in the Indian language to the Indian heart.

With deep emotion she wrote, 'I would reprint it, if I could, by tens of thousands, and scatter it overcast over the land, till there was not a peasant's cottage, or a craftsman's hut, between Kedarnath and Cape Comorin, that had not this presentment of Bharat-Mata, somewhere on its walls.'[106] That the new Art Movement was not unrelated to the Swadeshi Movement was clear from the writings of its philosopher-guides. Collections of Coomaraswamy's contemporary articles in book form were given the titles, *Essays in National Idealism* and *Art and Swadeshi*. In the very first two issues of *Modern Review* (January and February 1907) was published Nivedita's brilliant essay, 'The Function of Art in Shaping Nationality.' The title itself suggested the aim and attitude of the writer. 'Its [Art's] rebirth in India today can only take place, if it be consciously made the servant and poet of the mighty dream of an Indian Nationality,' she wrote.

The New Indian Art Movement was attacked from many quarters. Not only the imperialist Europeans and the Europeanized Indians criticized it, but even the orthodox Indian school did not relish the delicacy and exquisiteness of this form of art. They preferred healthy, robust anatomical realism, strangely forgetting the symbolical element in the paintings of Ajanta and the sculptures of Ellora and elsewhere. But the regeneration of Indian art in swadeshi Bengal was an accomplished fact, acclaimed by contemporary authorities. Abanindra Nath was fortunate in having a number of talented disciples, including the great Nandalal Bose, whose paintings were not only printed in important journals but were also exhibited in different parts of India. Such was the excellence of these pictures that even the imperialist Anglo-Indian daily *Pioneer* of Allahabad made this favourable comment in 1909, in connection with an exhibition at Simla: 'The paintings of Mr Abanindra Nath Tagore and his students have already become famous in the domain of artistic beauties, having attracted the admiring attention of artists of both East and West. . . . Mr Tagore's labour and works to the cause of revival of Oriental arts to its ancient glory are a matter of pride to his countrymen.'[107] The London Correspondent of *Pioneer*, while reviewing some pictures of Abanindra Nath and Nandalal, bestowed high praise on them, and then went on to say, 'The Indian artist is wise in seeking to build upon the art traditions of his own country, which are different from, but not inferior to, our own. As long as Indian artists worshipped at the shrine of South Kensington they were doomed to be banal, insincere, commonplace.' Mr Justice Woodroffe contributed to the Japanese art journal *Kokka*, an article on the pictures of the New Indian School in which he wrote that in those pictures could be seen 'a true expression of the spirit of Indian nationality'.[108]

Within a decade after the Art Movement had got under way, the worth and usefulness of it was so widely recognized all over India that Lionel Heath, the Principal of the Mayo School of Art, Lahore (the Assistant Principal there was S.N. Gupta, one of the pupils of Abanindra Nath Tagore) wrote: 'We want work of this kind in Punjab,' which would train the students' minds about 'appreciation for beauty and power of expressing Indian thought and subjects'. The Lieutenant governor of the Province was so pleased to see the art products of the New School, that he remarked the 'works of the Bengal School would lead the students of art in Punjab . . . to draw inspiration from their achievements'. *The Punjabee* (edited by Lajpat Rai) wrote on the same occasion, 'its advent marks an epoch in the history of the Indian paintings'.[109] During an 'Exhibition in Indian Paintings in Madras' in 1916, J.H. Cousins said that 'The first quality of the modern Indian painters . . . was their *Indianness*. . . . The Indian artists only found themselves when they gave up imitating poor Western copies.' W.S. Hadaway, the Superintendent of the Madras School of Arts admitted, 'The best work in painting and drawing which India has produced in modern times is undoubtedly the work of this group of Bengali artists.'[110]

It should be pointed out that to some foreign observers the importance of the literary and artistic productions of the Swadeshi Movement was greater than the political ones. After going back to England on completion of his Indian tour, Ramsay MacDonald, M.P., said in a speech at Leicester on 29 May 1910, 'The modern revival of poetry, of music, of art in India was of Bengal. The modern folk-song of India, the modern Indian novel were Bengali productions. There one got the spirit of Bengal — High Church in its expressions, revolutionary in its sentiments, and literary in its mode of action and thought'.[111] H.E.A. Cotton, L.C.C., while reviewing Ramsay MacDonald's book, *The Awakening of India,* written on the experiences of his Indian tour, quoted a portion which spoke of Bengal politics in oblique terms ('Its politics must be for some time an uncertain mingling of extremist impossibilism and moderate opportunism, of religious yearning and artistic idealism', 'Bengal politics are too volatile, too philosophical, too nervous'), but recognized at the same time that 'the Bengali inspires the Indian Nationalist Movement. . . . In Bengal he (the nationalist) is a person of lively imagination who thinks of India.'[112] Even Ramsay MacDonald who did not hold a favourable impression of Bengali politics, admitted, 'Bengal is perhaps doing better than political agitation. It is idealising India. It is translating nationalism into religion, into music and poetry, into painting and literature. . . . It is creating India by song and worship, it is clothing her in queenly garments.'[113] Rev. Professor C.F. Andrews (then still a missionary and not connected with the Indian freedom struggle) in an article in the *Modern Review,* November 1908, tried to trace 'the correspondence between literature and art and national life'. He proceeded to say that no one 'who has studied closely the remarkable history of Art, Music and Literature in Bengal . . . can fail to notice that in that province it is an awakening not merely of a class but of the people.' He claimed that 'as a student of history and nationality' he closely followed the 'National Movement, which has sprung up today in India with such remarkable force'. He concluded 'that the awakening . . . is no artificial or galvanised movement, manufactured by busy enthusiasts, . . . but a genuine uprising.'[114]

5. The Government and Congress Response

The first Congress session after the announcement of the partition was held at Banaras in the last week of December 1905. It was a momentous session in which a definite decision had to be taken regarding boycott. Congress, in its two preceding sessions, had adopted resolutions condemning the proposed partition proposals but without commitment to any action. It was willing to criticize the measure in the strongest terms and lend support to swadeshi as this did not demand any confrontation with the government. But boycott was something different. It was an open challenge, something like a declaration of war, though within a limited sphere. The very word boycott sounded sinister to the Moderates. 'It is bound to rouse angry passions on the other side,' Gokhale said, '. . . as it has got unsavoury associations and conveyed a vindictive desire to injure.' Tilak's views were diametrically the opposite, and the two leaders clashed at the ensuing Congress session and the two subsequent sessions, ending in a parting of ways.

The Banaras Congress was of great importance for the Bengali Swadeshists and radical groups outside Bengal. For Bengal, the importance lay in the fact that, to transform Bengal's movement into an all-India movement, acceptance of boycott by the Congress was absolutely essential. The movement needed not only vocal but active support from this all-India organization for sustenance and growth. The radical leaders outside Bengal, like Tilak and Lajpat Rai, wanted to push forward the newly awakened national spirit to a confrontation through the boycott proposal. But for die-hard moderates like Pherozeshah Mehta, or for patriotic yet cautious moderates like G.K. Gokhale, boycott posed an insoluble dilemma. Open confrontation with the rulers was out of the question. Of course, it was not an acute problem for men like Pherozeshah Mehta who were ready with an emphatic 'No' to any boycott, but to the flexible Gokhale, the solution was not so easy, particularly when awakened national feeling urged effective action and pressure was mounting on the Congress. On finding an acceptable solution to this dilemma depended the continuance of moderate control of the Congress. Gokhale knew this; and Pherozeshah no less.

Contemporary official and unofficial sources confirm that over a year or two, the Swadeshi Movement became an all-India national movement. Tilak's two weeklies, the *Maharatta* and the *Kesari*, extended wholehearted support to it. In a series of articles the *Maharatta* laid bare the inherent limitations of constitutional agitation,[115] warmly supported the boycott proposal and congratulated Bengal for adopting boycott as the only retaliation open to her' against 'the viceroy's open demonstration of unstinted contempt for India and the Indian people'. It also declared 16 October as 'Indian Day or the Day of the United India',[116] and expressed satisfaction with the 'Rakhi Bandhan ceremony'.[117] It recalled the revolutionary uprising in Russia (1905) and warned that 'this should serve as a warning to the bureaucracy in India'. It quoted extensively from an article by Lala Lajpat Rai in the August number of the *Hindustan Review* in which he wrote: 'What Bengal has done should be done by every province in ventilating its grievances. The whole country ought to do [it] simultaneously . . . giving effect to the Bengal resolutions regarding the boycotting of English goods.'[118]

Tilak was the main leader of the radical element in the Congress. He was ably supported by Lajpat Rai. The third important radical was Bipin Chandra Pal, who represented Bengal's uncompromising spirit. Certainly Pal and his colleagues were glad at the apparent success of Swadeshi and Boycott in East Bengal. From the confidential government reports of the time we find that the officials had admitted, though grudgingly, the movement's rapid expansion outside Bengal. 'The Boycott-Swadeshi Movements assumed [the character of] an all-India event towards the end of 1905,' a report stated. It then went on narrating the names of places in Bombay and Madras Presidency and in Punjab where the movement was strong as also names of the leaders or organizations involved.[119] Well-known Madras editor and Congress leader, G. Subramania Iyer, openly confessed that 'The Congress has inspired the educated classes with the lofty sentiment of patriotism; . . . but in the minds of the great masses it is the Swadeshi Movement that is planting the seeds of National self-consciousness.'[120]

Now the president-elect of the Banaras Congress, Gokhale ('the prince of moderates'), was in two minds when he left to attend the session. Boycott was 'sinister', but, at the same time, how could it be ignored that a 'cruel wrong' had been done against Bengal? Bengal he loved, there was no doubt about that. He openly acknowledged India's debt to Bengal in his presidential speech at Banaras:

> The tremendous upheaval of popular feeling . . . in Bengal in consequence of the Partition, will constitute a landmark in the history of our national progress. For the first time since British rule began, all sections of the Indian community . . . have been moved by a common impulse . . . to act together in offering resistance to a common wrong. . . . Bengal's heroic stand . . . has astonished and gratified all India, and her sufferings . . . have helped to draw closer all parts of India in sympathy and in aspiration.

This was not the first or last example of Gokhale's exuberance about the Bengalis. While speaking on the Seditious Meetings Act (which of course he supported), he made it clear that he was not a Bengali and that, as such, he could speak without reserve. He then continued:

> The Bengalis are in many respects the most remarkable people in all India. . . . In almost all the walks of life open to Indians the Bengalis are among the most distinguished. Some of the greatest social and religious reformers of recent times have come from their ranks. Of orators, journalists, politicians, Bengal possesses some of the most brilliant. . . . Take science or law or literature. Where will you find another scientist in all India to place by the side of Dr J.C. Bose or Dr P.C. Roy, or a jurist like Dr Ghose, or a poet like Rabindranath Tagore? . . . . A race of such capability cannot be put down by coercion.

Gokhale appealed to the viceroy and warned him at the same time: 'Conciliate Bengal. There is the root of trouble. With Bengal unconciliated in the matter of Partition there will be no real peace, not only in Bengal but in any other province in India.'[121]

Despite all this, Gokhale's inherent belief in the British sense of justice, his attitude of helpless surrender to imperialist force as apparently unconquerable, led him only to petitioning and speech-making. In September 1905, Gokhale, as representative of the Congress, left for England to ascertain the British Government's real attitude towards the partition question. His friends were not sure about what his position on the question would be under pressure from the government. Nivedita, in a letter of 20 September 1905, while congratulating him for being elected as the next Congress President, cautioned him saying, 'A rumour has been started here, it is said by the authorities that you gave your opinion in favour of Partition.' His friends knew 'that this is not true', but, if that be true, to undo the misdeed, Nivedita suggested, 'it would still be open to you to write asserting that the will of the people shall be supreme with regard to their own interests in this matter.'[122]

Anyway, in England, Gokhale could secure nothing but cold shrugs or pious advice and he returned home somewhat disillusioned. Even then with the help of other Moderates (the Bengal Moderates too did not press hard enough for boycott), he tried his best to block the boycott resolution and succeeded partially, as Congress did not approve of boycott for the whole of India, but could not prevent it being sanctioned for Bengal. Gokhale, of course, did not mince words in condemning the Partition, which, he said was 'concocted in the dark and carried out in the face of the fiercest opposition that any government has encountered during the last half a century'. But he approved of the limited boycott not out of moral obligation, nor even on account of Nivedita's influence on him, which was at that time considerable indeed, but because of the threat by Tilak and Bipin Pal that they would oppose the Congress resolution welcoming the Prince of Wales. Minto was not happy with Gokhale's performance. He wanted total surrender of the Congress led by Gokhale.

The extremists in the Congress were not happy either, as all their hopes had not been fulfilled. For the next twelve months, bitter attacks and counter-attacks followed. The Extremists had by now been strengthened by Aurobindo's joining them. Aurobindo, through his famous journal *Bande Mataram* (started in early August 1906), along with Bipin Chandra Pal, vehemently preached passive resistance, and pleaded for complete independence (which, according to Gokhale, no one outside the lunatic asylum in India could aspire for) and mercilessly attacked and exposed the 'mendicant' Moderate policy. His revolutionary group had already been formed. They openly advocated violent methods through their Bengali mouthpiece *Jugantar* (started in March or April 1906). The Bengali journal *Sandhya,* edited and controlled by the fiery sannyasin, Brahmabandhab Upadhyay, also erupted with fire and brimstone. In Madras also, an extremist group was formed, their mouthpiece being the English-language journal *Bala Bharata.* This group accepted Nivedita as their philosopher and guide. With this group was connected the Tamil poet Subramania Bharati (Bharati accepted Nivedita as his *Guru,* and dedicated his first two books of poems to her), who among the great poets of Indian nationalism suffered most at the hands of the rulers. Besides editing *Bala Bharata,* Bharati took over as editor of the Tamil journal, *India,* under instruction from Alasinga Perumal, an ardent disciple of Vivekananda. Bharati's first poem in *Swadesh Mitram,* in which he was working, was 'Hail Bengal', welcoming Bengal's heroic struggle,[123] published on 15 September 1905. He attended the Banaras Congress of 1905, (and again the Calcutta Congress of 1906) and went on writing noble and inspiring poems, preaching the glory of freedom and the cult of Shakti, and created a tremendous national spirit in the south.

The story of the Great Divide between the Moderates and the Extremists ending in the Surat Split has been dealt with in Chapters II and VII of this volume. The Bengal scene,however, calls for a fuller study, and this is undertaken here.

Confronted with a massive upsurge, the bureaucracy resorted to a three-pronged strategy: 'Repression' for coercion, 'Division' for weakening, and 'Reform' for conciliation, a strategy that paid them a good dividend at the time.

In answer to boycott in East Bengal, particularly in Barisal, Lieutenant Governor Fuller arrived there with Gurkha troops on 5 November 1905. The ferocious Gurkhas went on the rampage in the town, insulting, assaulting, trespassing, looting. This reign of terror supplemented repressive measures like the dismissal of nationalist teachers and rustication of 'swadeshi' boys from schools which have been referred to earlier. Many clerks were also dismissed for their alleged connection with the Swadeshi Movement. Elderly and respected gentlemen humiliated in all possible ways, including being forced to 'drill with belt and baton' as 'special constables', for no other offence than joining in the cry of *Bande Mataram*.

The atrocities reached an ugly peak at the time of the Provincial Conference at Barisal, in April 1906. Well-known all-India leaders, headed by Surendranath Banerjea, reached Barisal, by steamer on the evening of 13 April. The cry of *Bande Mataram* had been forbidden on the streets of Barisal, which, the leaders held, could not be done under the law. However, to avoid an immediate confrontation with the authorities, the *Bande Mataram* slogan was not raised when the first batch of Calcutta delegates were welcomed on arrival at Barisal. Then, on 14 April, around 2.30 p.m., when the president-elect, Abdul Rasul, with his English wife, and Surendranath, Motilal Ghose and Bhupendra Nath Bose entered the pandal in procession, a big contingent of police was present armed with regulation lathis ('fairly thick sticks, six feet long'). The leaders were 'allowed to pass unmolested', but just after that the police party went into action, mercilessly beating the younger delegates. When Surendranath protested, he was arrested by the Superintendent of Police, and was taken to the house of the magistrate. There the magistrate insulted him with angry shouts and then fined him for contempt. Surendranath paid the fine and returned to the conference to witness a memorable scene there which he described thus:

> Presently there appeared on the platform Babu Manoranjan Guha, accompanied by his son, Chittaranjan Guha, with a bandage round his forehead, to tell the delegates the story of the assault. . . . Chittaranjan had been attacked by the police with their regulation *lathis* and thrown into a tank full of water. The assault continued, notwithstanding the helpless condition of the boy, who offered no resistance of any kind, but shouted *Bande Mataram* with every stroke of the *lathi*. . . . The spectacle of father and son, standing side by side on the platform, the father relating the story, the son bearing witness to it by the marks of violence on his person, was a sight ever to be remembered.[124]

The next day the Conference was banned by the authorities.

Bad as it was, this Barisal incident was nothing compared to the atrocities which followed, but it showed to what lengths the authorities could go even with and in presence of the all-India leaders. Just before the Barisal incident, Nivedita wrote in *Indian Review* of March 1906:

> All India is watching today the struggle that is going on in Eastern Bengal. Scarcely a word appears in the papers, yet the knowledge is everywhere.

> The air is tense with expectation, with sympathy, with pride, in those grim heroic people and their silent struggle to the death, for their Swadeshi trade.

Nivedita warned the tyrants: 'Beware! In all history there comes an hour when the merciless man trembles, and cries out himself on the mercy of God, to find it gone.'[125]

Curzon, with the help of bureaucrats like Risley and Fuller started this game. It was disturbing for them to see a large number of Muslims, with some of their important leaders, joining the Hindus in anti-partition demonstrations with cries of *Bande Mataram* and *Allah-ho Akbar*. Notable Muslim leaders who supported the movement were A. Rasul, Abdul Halim Ghaznavi (Mymensingh) and Abul Kasem (Burdwan). And there was the indubitable Liakat Hossain, 'a simple bearded old Mohamedan with a fez . . . upright, incorruptible, like an old Biblical character, . . . selling his little wares, buttons and keys and stone cups to make ends meet, but always the apostle of a cause.'[126]

But the day was not of the Liakat Hossains but of the Salimullas. Curzon was able to win over Salimulla, Nawab of Dacca, with the argument that the newly created province of East Bengal would end Hindu dominance there and would thus serve Muslim interests. This 'logic' of Curzon's, supported by his monetary 'logic' — lending Rs 14 lakhs to Salimullah at a very low interest — won over the Nawab and he, with the help of fanatic mullahs, loosened the hell hounds of communal hatred. The fact that Muslim ryots were often oppressed by the Hindu zamindars, no doubt helped them to carry conviction. The mullahs succeeded in hiding from the ordinary Muslims the fact that the Salimullahs were no better than their Hindu counterparts, if not worse. Riots broke out in Comilla on 4 March 1907, continuing for four days, and subsequently, in Jamalpur in Mymensingh, on a more serious scale. Thus the dark shadow of dissension was cast on the renascent nationalism, built on Hindu-Muslim unity. Earlier, in December 1906, the Muslim League had also been founded. Thus, as the newly awakened nationalism devised the means to strike at British imperialism, so did the powerful and cunning imperialist rulers devised ways of hitting back.

The reign of terror and the oppression of those times was fully described by many contemporary Indian papers. But it is better to depend on foreign observers like Keir-Hardic and Nevinson's eye-witness accounts. Keir-Hardie found the town of Mymensingh

> like a place in a state of siege. Every twenty yards or so two armed constables were posted, whilst the ordinary policemen were also a good deal in evidence. These armed and other police had been imported from a distance to preserve order in the village. . . . These special men are called

> the Punitive Force, and are quartered on villages, which are saddled with the cost, as a punishment for some offence real or imaginary.

Then, after visiting Barisal, Keir-Hardie made the remark that these things 'savoured more of Russian than of British methods'.[127] After describing how the educational institutions were interfered with by stringent government circulars, he went on to say:

> Not content with Public Meetings Ordinance which expired on November 10, the Government enacted a new law by which the ordinance has been perpetuated, and so the educated and enlightened portion of the people in Eastern Bengal — the most enlightened and educated people I have yet met in India — are gagged and bound and practically at the mercy of the police. The bill has been so drawn that if twenty people assemble at a funeral or marriage or any other light function, the police may charge them with holding a seditious meeting.[128]

Keir-Hardie did not find any trace of sedition in India. He wondered, why 'there was no sedition' when 'according to the official returns in the last 40 years of the last century . . . 15 millions of the people of India were certified to have died of hunger, . . . 40 millions of people always hungry after 150 years of British rule, and in the brightest jewel of the Crown of England'.[129] Referring to the deportations of leaders from Bengal and other parts of India (on 16 December 1908, from Bengal alone, nine eminent persons were deported, including Aswini Kumar Dutta, Krishna Kumar Mitra, Subodh Chandra Mallik, Manoranjan Guha Thakuratha, Shyamsundar Chakrabarti, Pulin Behari Das) he wrote of those who were in active sympathy with Reform movement that 'their footsteps are dogged by corrupt secret police agents, their homes broken into and ransacked, and when no evidence is found upon which a prosecution will lie, they are apprehended, and without being told of what they are accused, without trial of any kind, are deported as exiles.' Keir-Hardie cited eleven such cases of deportation in two years; since 1 January 1907, 63 cases of prosecution of newspaper editors and others; 132 cases of imprisonment following convictions, and fines, in addition to imprisonment, amounting to Rs 15,300. He cited examples: One of the *criminals* got seven years for sending a 'seditious' telegram, another five years for 'exhibiting seditious photographs', a third, a Mohamedan, two years for a 'seditious' article. . . . 'In many cases the printing plant has, in addition to fine and imprisonment of the editors been confiscated.' Keir-Hardie complimented the British Government for 'rapidly qualifying for a place in the gallery in which the autocratic governments of the Czar of Russia and the despised Sultan of Turkey occupy such prominent positions'.[130] Keir-Hardie had complained, 'that he was shadowed by detectives, that telegrams were held back, letters torn up'.[131]

Nevinson also compared the Indian situation with that of Russia and ended one of his despatches with wondering whether 'the whole movement will . . . gradually be driven underground by repression'.[132]

Before he became Secretary of State for India, Lord Morley was widely known as a radical journalist, critic, biographer, and a humanist who championed the cause of the oppressed. He was affectionately called the 'Honest John'. He had to work mostly with Lord Minto who became Viceroy of India in August 1905, which post he held till 1910. Before coming over to India, Lord Minto was well known as a 'British soldier and administrator'. The last post he had held was that of Governor-General of Canada. During Minto's tenure as Viceroy, the Swadeshi Movement developed into an all-India movement for swaraj. Minto truly attributed this widening to the misdeed of Curzon. The demand for reprisals from his infuriated conservative countrymen was already pressing. In spite of this, Minto, at the early stage, took a balanced view of the situation. Amales Tripathi quoted a witty civilian of Calcutta on this: 'Minto's Sense and Sensibility replaced the Pride and Prejudice of Lord Curzon.'

Though Morley was a Liberal, his liberalism stopped short for India. He thought 'the Parliament or Parliamentary Committees are quite useless and helpless in doing good to India'.[133] Nivedita, who knew Morley better than the Indian Moderate enthusiasts, wrote on 28 December 1904: 'I remember . . . someone had told me that in matters Indian he [Morley] is utterly reactionary — and would make as bad a secretary as Llyod George or Hamilton or even worse.'[134] It is thus hardly a surprise that, notwithstanding the loud promises of Morley and Minto, the Indian Councils Act, 1909, in its final shape, was a large concession to the bureaucrats in India and the Conservatives in England. Its reactionary character stood exposed, fanning animosities between the two great Indian communities — the Hindus and the Muslims. A bomb attack was made on Minto at Ahmedabad in November 1909, from which the viceroy barely escaped, 'frightened to death'. These were the net results of repression and reaction.

6. Revolutionary Extremism and the British Response

That was not of course the first bomb in India. It had appeared a year and a half earlier as one of the results of the swadeshi upsurge. Bhupendranath Dutta, one of the earlier revolutionaries, connected with Barindra group, has positively contradicted the assertion that the revolutionary movement in Bengal was an outcome of the Swadeshi Movement. On the contrary, he said, the Swadeshi Movement was strengthened by the active participation of revolutionary workers in it. Partially agreeing with this view, we must say that the revolutionary movement would not have been so wide and powerful had there not been the tremendous aggressive nationalism created by the Swadeshi Movement.

Revolutionary ideas had permeated educated Bengali minds long before partition. Some inconsequential societies were formed which indulged in amateurish discussions only. The first really important person in this field was Pramatha Nath Mitra, a barrister by profession, widely known as P. Mitra, who organized groups and encouraged physical culture amongst young men. In early 1902, a group was formed by Okakura and Nivedita to which we have referred before. Sarala Ghosal and Surendranath Tagore joined this group and also some Calcutta notables, including Chittaranjan Das. Nivedita informed Aurobindo of this group while she was in Baroda on a lecture tour in October 1902. It did not make much headway.

The really important revolutionary party which was to play a great and glorious role had been formed in March 1902. It was the Anushilan Samiti of Calcutta. This samiti was initiated by Satis Chandra Bose, who came directly under the influence of Swami Vivekananda and Sister Nivedita. P. Mitra became its supreme leader. Probably by the end of 1902, Aurobindo sent his emissary, Jatindra Nath Banerjee, to Bengal, who joined this group and started organizing gymnasium training for revolutionary boys. Some time later, Aurobindo himself came to Bengal, studied the situation (he had already opted for revolutionary activities) and formed a committee of five to accelerate action. His brother Barindra came to join the Jatindra's group. Barindra soon formed a group within the group and his intimates were sent to different parts of Bengal and India to preach revolutionary ideas. Nivedita had lent a lot of revolutionary literature to this group. In the first phase, this particular group and other groups too did not make much progress, but then partition came and the atmosphere changed, became ripe for a daring thrust. This time, Barindra, under the direct guidance of Aurobindo, succeeded in forming a genuinely revolutionary group whose secret activities first came to light in April 1908, when Khudiram Bose and Prafulla Chaki's bomb killed Mrs and Miss Kennedy at Muzaffarpur.

Various reasons had been cited as causes of the revolutionary upsurge. The more cynical assessment of some present-day writers, that it was nothing but the outburst of some angry and hungry young men, prey to unemployment, cannot be sustained since it denies the heroism and total dedication of the many thousands who participated in it. But the factor of hunger, not of the revolutionaries but of the millions of Indians who fell prey to British imperialism, certainly was a motivating factor. The racial arrogance of the whites, insults, abuse of justice, denial of human rights — all combined to make the load of subjugation unbearable. Also important was the awakening of the self-reliance and self-confidence brought about by the achievements, exhortations and burning eloquence of Vivekananda, referred to earlier. His influence on Indian nationalism in all its aspects was tremendous. But the revolutionaries were more particularly inspired by his example and teachings.

Aurobindo himself said that the Swadeshi Movement became so potent and pervasive because Ramakrishna and Vivekananda had inspired it.[135] In a number of articles of this period he spoke in glowing terms about the tremendous role of Ramakrishna and Vivekananda in moulding India's destiny. In his revolutionary pamphlet, *Bhawani Mandir* (about whose 'evil' power government reports expressed concern), he described these two personalities as human idols. Many of the revolutionary followers of Aurobindo, like Barindra, Debabrata Bose (who later joined the Ramakrishna Mission to become Swami Praganananda), and others, closely adhered to Vivekananda's ideals.* Vivekananda's youngest brother, Bhupendra Nath, who was never interested in religion, and afterwards turned a Marxist, nevertheless confessed that Vivekananda's *Lectures from Colombo to Almora* and Mazzini's autobiography had made him a revolutionary.[136]

Most of the important revolutionary groups that sprang up between 1902 and 1910 owed allegiance to Vivekananda's teachings. Satis Bose of the Calcutta Anushilan Samiti, and the top leaders of the Dacca Anushilan Samiti, started by Pulin Das, under the inspiration of P. Mitra, were devout Vivekanandites. A large number of organizations came up as Ramakrishna Ashramas, outwardly doing commendable social service, but were actually revolutionary bases. After the deportation of Pulin Das, those who combined to lead the Dacca Anushilan Samiti like Makhanlal Sen, Naren Sen, Pratul Ganguly, Trailakya Chakravarti, were all ardent followers of Vivekananda. This was also true of the leader of another Dacca Group headed by Hemchandra Ghose and his co-workers. Hemchandra always claimed that he had been directly led to the revolutionary path by Vivekananda's exhortations. Other great revolutionaries, including Jatindra Nath Mukherjee (Bagha Jatin) and his associates (Jadugopal Mukherjee, M.N. Ray, Hari Kumar Chakravarti), and also Motilal Roy, Rashbehari Bose, Sachin Sanyal — all acknowledged Swamiji's influence on them. Almost all the secret government reports confirm this. 'Do you ask about the influence of Vivekananda on the revolutionary movement? One sentence is sufficient as answer, his inspiration was the greatest,' wrote Hari Kumar

* For an examination of Swami Vivekananda's influence on Indian nationalism and an account of the activities of the revolutionaries see Chapter V of this volume — Editor.

Chakravarti. 'What really was the revolutionary movement in Bengal?' he continued. 'It was nothing but some young men's determination for death — if by dying they could show others how to live. They jumped on the death-pyre. Vivekananda pulled them out from their homes. His words were nothing but leaping flames.'[137]

The literature of Bankim Chandra, particularly his *Ananda Math*, fascinated the Extremists. The very name, *Bande Mataram*, given to the chief organ of the Extremists in Bengal, amply shows Bankim's influence. The revolutionaries took up as model the organizational structure as described in *Ananda Math*, and could be seen reflected in the Aurobindo group's Bhawani Mandir scheme. And the name of the biggest revolutionary organization, Anushilan Samiti, was taken from Bankim's literature.

Japan's victory over Russia, symbolizing Asia's newly awakened power, shattering Western forces, created a tremendous impact on the Indian mind. Anarchist and socialist movements in Europe too made their impressions. The Bengali journal *Jugantar* of the Barindra group openly preached sedition. Sir Lawrence Jenkins was not far from the truth when he said that 'They exhibit a burning hatred of the British race [the word 'race' should be replaced by 'Raj'], they breathe revolution in every line, they point out how revolution is to be effected.'[138] The government prosecuted the paper and arrested Bhupendra Nath Dutta on 5 July 1907, as he took full responsibility for the publication at Aurobindo's instance. He was sentenced to one year's rigorous imprisonment on 24 July. Bhupendra Nath made history by refusing to submit any written statement in British Court. 'I have done what I thought to be my duty to my country. You may mete out any punishment you like. I will bear it cheerfully', he said. Aurobindo paid handsome tribute to this heroic stance in an editorial in *Bande Mataram* of 25 July 1907. Recalling Bhupendra's performance in court, he wrote: 'It is a mistake to whine when we are smitten, as if we had hoped to achieve liberty without suffering. To meet persecution with indifference, to take punishment quietly as a matter of course, with erect heads and undimmed eyes, this is the spirit in which we must conquer.'

The prosecution of *Sandhya* and the arrest of its editor, Brahmabandhab Upadhyay, on 13 August 1907; his declaration in court that he did not want to take part in the trial which sought to condemn him for carrying out his 'God-appointed mission of Swaraj', and his assertion that he was not 'in any way accountable to alien people' also created a great sensation. But the *Bande Mataram* case had a wider impact as it brought Aurobindo fully to the public eye. The government registered a case against the paper for seditious writing. An arrest warrant was issued against Aurobindo on 16 August 1907. He surrendered and was released on bail. But the government could not punish him as editor, for at that time the declaration of the editor's name was not obligatory. Bipin Pal refused to give evidence about who was really the editor. Bipin Pal got six months' simple imprisonment for contempt. The printer was also convicted, but Aurobindo was acquitted. Aurobindo's arrest so deeply affected Rabindranath Tagore that he wrote an inspiring poem on Aurobindo, beginning, 'Aurobindo, take Rabindra's salutations'. Severe action was taken against many more mofussil papers, and to strengthen its control over the press, the government passed The Newspapers (Incitement to Offences) Act in 1908.

The incident that suddenly drew public attention to underground activities and brought Aurobindo and his revolutionary followers into the limelight occurred at Majaffarpur on the night of 30 April 1907 when Khudiram Bose and Prafulla Chaki made a bomb attack on a horse carriage, mistakenly taking it to be that of the notorious Chief Presidency Magistrate of Calcutta, Kingsford. The bomb killed Mrs and Miss Kennedy who were in the carriage. The government instantly acted with surprising promptness, combed revolutionary hideouts at Maniktalla Garden House and other places, arrested in a day or two the whole Barindra group and also Aurobindo. Barindra and many of his comrades made confessional statements, but with meticulous care avoided any information about Aurobindo's connections with them. Unfortunately, they implicated Narendra Gossain as an accomplice without Gossain's permission, and Gossain retaliated (many suspected Gossain to be a government spy) by implicating Aurobindo in turn. Kanailal Dutta and Satyendranath Bose, then in jail custody, and belonging to this group, hatched a plan and succeeded in killing their co-prisoner Gossain in the police hospital. They were hanged after trial. But Aurobindo was saved, thanks mainly to the legal acumen of Chittaranjan Das.

Among the great Indian leaders, Tilak suffered most for openly supporting Bengal's Swadeshi Movement with its subsequent extension in revolutionary terrorism. Tilak courageously wrote five lengthy articles in the *Kesari* on the Bengal revolutionaries. When Tilak wrote them he was fully conscious of the consequences. The articles gave the government their much-desired opportunity to take penal measures against a man who was primarily responsible for rallying support for the Swadeshi Movement outside Bengal. He was arrested on 24 June and his bail application was rejected. During the trial he defended himself with the sole object of expressing India's national aspirations and exposing at the same time the autocratic rule of the alien government. He was awarded six years' imprisonment after a farce of a trial. Defiantly he told the court:

> I have not come here to ask you any grace. . . . I am not going to tell you that I wrote those articles in a fit of madness. I am not a lunatic. I have written them believing it my duty to write in the interest of the public in this way, believing that that was the view of the community.

After the judgement was announced, Tilak calmly expressed his confidence that 'There are higher powers that rule the destiny of things and it may be the Will of Providence that the cause which I represent may prosper more by my suffering than by my remaining free.'[139]

Tilak was grateful to Bengal for the warm support it extended to the Shivaji festival. When he arrived in Calcutta accompanied by Khaparde in June 1906 to participate in the Shivaji festival, he was given a rousing welcome at the station platform and in the streets by Hindus and Muslims alike. The Anushilan Samiti, Sanatan Sampraday, Bande Mataram Sampraday, anti-Partition Party, Swadeshi Procession Party, all joined the grand procession. On 9 June Tilak said, at the Beadon Square Utsab Mandir, that the cry of Bande Mataram had been taken up by the Maharashtrians 'and the words could now be found inscribed on the temple of the great Shivaji at Raigar'. The next day, at a mammoth meeting, Tilak tried to dissipate Muslim apprehensions about the festival. 'Shivaji did not fight the Mohamedans but against the tyrannical power that existed at the time,' he said. He cited instances of Shivaji's respect for and understanding of the Muslims and also Muslim allegiance to him: 'History tells us that in the worst days of Mohamedan rulers, Mohamedans worshipped Shivaji with the same enthusiasm as the Hindus.' Tilak also spoke about the spiritual affinities between the Bengalis and the Maharashtrians saying that, 'The Goddess Kali is the presiding deity in Bengal. The same Goddess was the protectress of Shivaji.' Aswini Kumar Dutta, who presided over the meeting, and was known to have attracted most of the Muslim support to the Swadeshi Movement, dealt also with the Muslim feelings about it. 'Like the great Akbar himself,' he said, 'Shivaji might have endeared himself both to the Hindus and the Mussalmans alike if our Mussalman brethren of the period had been as liberal towards a Hindu sovereign as the Hindus had been towards the Mughal emperors.' He enunciated the object of the festival as being 'to awaken a feeling of respect for the noble', and also 'the union of the Bengalis with the Mahrattas'.[140]

In 1905-6 there was a revolutionary upsurge in Russia. The *Maharatta,* appreciating the logic behind such actions, wrote that when 'an entire generation was mown down by Despotism, one must act, and not speak'. Terrorism, the paper reminded, was 'conceived in hatred, nurtured in patriotism and by hope it grew up in the electrical atmosphere'.[141]

After the prosecution of Bhupendra Nath Dutta in the *Jugantar* case, the paper, in great enthusiasm, described the 'defence' of Bhupendra Nath as 'perhaps the first of its kind in India'.[142] It quoted from the London *Spectator* which asserted that, 'If the Bengalis of today had no heritage of martial traditions, they will at least leave such traditions as a legacy behind.'[143]

Tilak denied the charge that the Bengal revolutionaries used the bomb out of hatred for particular individuals; theirs was not the action of some 'roguish mad-cap'. The organizers of the secret societies knew perfectly well that, through such sporadic bomb-attacks, British rule would not be overthrown. They just wanted to register their protests. Tilak then compared the situation of Czarist Russia with that of India, and said that the similarity of situation caused similar outbursts in both the places. He warned that 'there is also a limit to the patience of humanity'. He said that, in the face of all sorts of oppression, 'the desire of the people to obtain the rights of *Swarajya* is growing stronger'. Tilak had pointed out at the time of the deportation of Lala Lajpat Rai that 'if the rulers resort to oppressive Russian methods then the Indian subjects too, would be compelled to imitate the methods of the Russian people'. The course of events in Bengal had proved him right. Defending the Bengali revolutionaries he wrote: 'There is an excess of patriotism at the root of the bombs in Bengal.' He severely criticized the policy of disarming of Indians, comparing their condition with that of caged parrots. They had not only been caged, the government had 'also commenced to pluck the wings and break the legs in order that they should not go out of the cage. . . . The manhood of the nation was slain by the Arms Act.' Tilak pointed out the significance of the bomb in the political life of India. It had made clear to the government 'that the tyranny of its acts has become unbearable to its subjects'. 'The bomb has reduced the importance of military strength,' because, like muskets or guns, bombs could not be taken away from the subjects by means of the Arms Act. Knowledge of how to make them had come to the Indians; Barindra's factory had produced 'faultless' bombs. 'The bomb . . . is a kind of witchcraft, it is a charm, an amulet.' If the policy of repression went on unabated, 'what time will it take for the charms and the magical lore of Bengal to spread throughout India?' The real and lasting means to stop bombs consists in making a beginning 'to grant the important right of *Swaraj* to the people,' Tilak concluded.

Maharashtra rose in violent protest against Tilak's imprisonment. Strikes and riots followed with killings by police firing. Bureaucratic machinery was also active in other ways. To justify the government action, competent imperialist writers like Valentine Chirol came out with the thesis of 'brahmin and babu conspiracy'. Chirol in a series of articles in the London *Times* (which in 1910 came out in book form as *Indian Unrest*) projected the theory that the Swadeshi Movement and the national movement were 'an organised scheme for recovery of Brahmin ascendancy', helped by the Bengali babus. Chirol admitted a 'deep stirring of the waters amongst a people endowed with no mean gifts of head and heart'. It took no time for him to understand that Tilak was 'one of the most dangerous pioneers of disaffection'. Chirol even went so far as to say that Tilak was the 'father of Indian unrest'. He argued that Tilak was opposed to Western modernism, and was determined to establish a 'priestly aristocracy', was a 'triumphant champion of Hindu orthodoxy', and a 'revivalist' to the backbone. But Chirol was fully aware of the potentiality of Tilak as a militant national leader. He wrote: 'The great development of the cotton industry during the last ten years . . . *had given Tilak an opportunity of establishing contact with a class of population hitherto outside the purview of Indian politics.*'[144]

Nivedita's letters to Ratcliffe, then in England, are invaluable as primary sources of information about the national struggle in the period 1907-11. These, sent mostly through agents to avoid interception, give valuable information and provide an insight into the existing state of affairs. One such letter reads: 'The government seems to have gone mad and is now trying to crush the national movement by wholesale arrests, deportations etc., all because it dreads a repetition of '57. But this is of course the way to bring it about' (27 May 1907). In several letters Nivedita refers to the inhuman torture of those held in police and jail custody. 'You can see,' she wrote, 'the government has thrown the country into a very pretty state of war. We all laugh when we meet but we all know that no man can tell whose turn will be next. Of course I trust we shall continue to laugh even then' (19-20 July 1910). She also refers to the arrest of a hundred weavers in the district of Midnapore for weaving a certain song into the borders of dhotis. In another letter dated 22 September 1907 she wrote:

> I suppose there have been few moments in the world's history and few places where as little was thought of Freedom and the Rights of Man as guiding principles — as here, now. I doubt that Spain, Venice, England under Mary, or the Papal States before 1860 — have been much worse.

Strangely, the historians of the Swadeshi Movement have so far paid scant attention to the warm support given by a section of British Liberals and Labourites to India's political aspirations. It is difficult to assess the effects of this support on the formulation of British Government policy towards India. The British public were either generally apathetic to Indian questions or were largely influenced by bitterly anti-Indian Tory propaganda. The Government of India needed support from 'Home' for their policy of repression and the Tory was there amply to supply it. Nevertheless, historically it is important to assess the quantum of liberal response to the Indian problem and its effects. It must first be said with due emphasis that the police atrocities were somewhat mitigated by liberal protest in England, and the vicious Conservative propaganda that cried for blood, was somewhat restrained by it.

Facing for the first time a widespread resistance movement from a nation considered docile and submissive, many Englishmen in England and India were unnerved. Was it the beginning of the end of the British Raj in India? Time and again hovered the spectre of another Mutiny. A.J. Fraser Blair, Editor of *Empire,* and sympathetic to Indian aspirations, dismissed the Mutiny possibility, but stated in clear terms that a 'political portent' like this had 'never [before] appeared in India' and 'the movement is . . . for the most part intensely . . . anti-British; not even at the time of the Mutiny was the anti-British feeling so strong and so widespread.' He pointed to the growing pan-Asian feelings: 'The Indians feel that they are in line with a gigantic continental movement. . . . [for] the removal of Western predominance from Eastern politics.'[145] Dr S.K. Mallik in a letter to the *Daily News* (8 July 1907) protested against Reuter's continuously alarming telegrams about the 'babu seditionists' and the 'campaign of sedition directed from Calcutta'. A Reuter representative had taken 'three tours' in East Bengal and produced reports about the nature of which the *Morning Leader* commented: 'They were undertaken with a distinct view to the discovery of evidence of sedition, which has then been judiciously collected and compressed into an effective and ever terror-striking whole.'[146]

Sir Charles Eliot (not to be confused with Sir Charles Elliot, the Lieutenant Governor of Bengal, 1891-8), in an article in the *Westminster Gazette* (2 December 1907) rejected the predictions of mutiny because the army was under the full control of the government ('the control of the artillery is exclusively in the hands of the European troops'), but he nevertheless did not underestimate the extent of the real danger that the government faced. The very nature of the government was such that it depended heavily on Indians, and if they ceased working it would be a hopeless situation for the English officials in India. Sir Charles mentioned the 'hysterical sentiment' in India, and the telegrams that appeared in English newspapers stating that 'on certain railway lines Europeans dared not travel without carrying loaded rifles as a protection'. He wholeheartedly supported Lajpat Rai's deportation without trial, as he himself resorted to deportations for 'which no reason was assigned'.[147]

Sir Macworth Young, an ex-Lieutenant-Governor of Punjab, on the other hand, at the Pan-Anglican Conference, very sympathetically presented examples of the wide extent of the movement. 'What is happening is a development, not a phase, a new birth, not a sickness,' Sir Macworth said. '. . . It is not merely the Bengalee agitator or the Maharatta plotter, the Mohamedan student in London or Aligarh, and the educated Jat of the Punjab, but every intelligent person who has a new idea of nationality, a new vision of liberty.'[148] Naturally this could not be the view of the ex-Lieutenant-Governor of East Bengal, Sir Bampfylde Fuller, who in an article in the *Nineteenth Century* supported all the ruthless measures taken to tackle the volcanic Indian situation. These, he asserted, were adopted for 'the protection of the young'.[149]

Alexander Ular in *La Revue* (June 1908) identified the real source of the 'hysteria'. 'The oligarchy of 2,000 British civil and military officials who constitute the Empire of India had no real foundation', Ular wrote. 'The English only go to India in official capacities to enrich themselves and to remain as short a time as possible in the country' and 'it is impossible to rule a world for any length of time under the pretext of mercantile advantages'. He very rightly brought out the significance of the Swadeshi Movement: 'England has long feared the loss of India by the invasion of a powerful enemy, but now she is beginning to realise that India may be lost by the fact of India itself.'[150] A Conservative paper, *Quarterly Review,* not subscribing to these liberal views, analysed, in a 'very gloomy vein', the causes of the unrest, and sharply reacted to 'the caricature of the Anglo-Indian as a hectoring, domineering, swaggering overlord'. It saw in the 'aloofness' of the English in India 'one of the secrets of their strength', and strongly recommended that, if there be any Indian civilian in receipt of a government pension preaching sedition (obviously pointing to R.C. Dutt), his pension should immediately be stopped. 'The Government of India should not be expected continually to subsidise their own foes.' The paper warned about the grave danger the situation posed in case of war with another great power: 'A spark then may set the whole country ablaze. . . . It will probably take the form of series of murderous riots spreading from city to city; . . . [and] . . . means of communication may be interrupted.' After referring to the series of railway and telegraph and postal strikes, the writer particularly called attention to the enormous coast-line of India which would make it impossible wholly to prevent entry of foreign arms into India.[151] The writer no doubt anticipated future activities of the Indian revolutionaries during the next two Great Wars.

Blackwood's Magazine (September 1908) published a 'mournful' article, 'The Writing on the Wall,' in which it described the widespread hatred for and unrest against the English in India: 'It exists and extends beyond the limits of one province and beyond the members of any one class. . . . Men spit as the Englishman passes and do not disguise their contempt.'[152]

That the Swadeshi Movement spirit charged not only men but women too, had been stated by an Anglo-Indian correspondent of the *Morning Leader*, 'The Swadeshi boycott movement was begun three years ago,' the article stated, 'by the political leaders, but its continuance was due to the Hindu women, commonly supposed in this country to be 'half chattel and half toy' with no intelligence and little influence.'[153] C.J. O'Donnell, M.P., in a letter to the *Westminster Gazette* (17 November 1908) wrote about the extraordinary 'demonstration at the funeral of the murdered Kanai [lal Dutta]', in which 'the active part taken by zenana ladies is perhaps the most noticeable feature'.[154]

Naturally, these events infuriated the Anglo-Indian officials. Col. H.S. Massy, C.B., sent a letter to the *Daily Telegraph* (17 November 1908) roundly criticizing the 'mild' government policy in dealing with the unrest: 'When the Babu editor incites to murder and outrage, instead of simply hanging him . . . we treat him as a kind of first-class misdemeanant — in fact a good deal better than our own suffragists in London.'[155] Sir Edmond C. Cox, late police D.I.G. of Bombay, in a 'very gloomy article' in the *Nineteenth Century*, criticized the Indians for their 'one and only cry, India for the Indians'. 'Agitation is in the air,' he went on, 'Agitate, Agitate and Agitate.' He stated candidly: 'The fact remains indisputable that Europeans will not accept Indians on equal terms in society, and equally the fact remains that to the Indians this constitutes an intolerable slur.'[156]

Yes, the Indians could not be accepted as equals because Curzon and his spirit were very much alive at the time. Curzon wrote an article in the *North American Review* on the manifold virtues of British rule in India. Only a person of Curzon's tribe could boast of this 'virtue': that he, as viceroy, 'was able to send out to South Africa in the Boer Campaign 13,200 British officers and men from the British army in India, and 9,000 natives, principally followers. To China we dispatched from India 1,300 British officers and men, 20,000 native troops, and 17,500 native followers.' Curzon claimed for the glory of the British rule that thousands and thousands of native Indians could be sent as labourers to Africa: 'Indian coolies have penetrated to the remote Pacific.' And India offered British youth service with the Indian Civil Service, a most useful and lucrative training ground. The young English men, so trained, had become the 'administrative pioneers of the Empire'. For these virtues India must be retained for England.[157]

But there were others in Britain who overcame their petty personal and narrow national interests. Sister Nivedita disagreed with Aurobindo's criticism that the pro-Indian Britishers services to India were valueless or even derogatory to the interests of Indian movement, because, by advising moderation, they were ultimately serving British interests. In an article in the *Modern Review* (April 1909) entitled 'Our Friends in Parliament and Outside', she vigorously defended the British Committee of the Indian National Congress. Her political sagacity made her aware of the value of foreign propaganda. That the journal *India* was publishing abundant information regarding Indian political affairs, collecting it from different sources; that the office of the British Committee preserved valuable records which were used by the pro-Indian members of the British Parliament, all these were sufficient reasons in favour of its existence.[158] She reminded readers that the British Committee's opinions were at times even 'bolder' than those of the Moderate Congress leaders. The members of the committee were 'sufficiently broad-minded to feel and say that no nation has a right to rule another. They recognize the dangers of Empire and their patriotism requires of them to agitate against the risks to which an all-absorbing Imperialism exposes their own liberties'. Those who supported in the British Parliament the demand for India's self-government, did so 'on higher grounds of humanity and political morality', and 'by doing so they incur great risks and sometimes jeopardise even their seats'. Their liberalism, Nivedita pointed out, might result in losing even a cabinet seat or the viceroyalty of India or Canada. She made special mention of some supporters of the Indian cause as Sir Henry Cotton, Frederic Mackerness, Dr V.H. Rutherford, Keir-Hardie, J. Hart-Davis, James O'Gardy, C.J. O'Donnel, William Redmond; and journalists like H.W. Nevinson, S.K. Ratcliffe, and Hyndaman: and papers like the *Morning Leader, Manchester Guardian, Daily News, Star, New Age, Labour Leader,* and *Justice.*

Nevinson visited India in October 1907, and his series of articles were published in the *Manchester Guardian, Daily Chronicle* and *Glasgow Herald.* He was a very powerful writer, widely known as a progressive humanist, a warm-hearted friend of India and a friend of the 'cause of liberty in all lands and climes and for all men and women'. His articles in three influential British newspapers therefore created substantial reactions. Keir-Hardie's reports did the same, and also the articles of Ramsay MacDonald. Nivedita wrote with satisfaction on 28 April 1910: 'It's just splendid to read how K.H. [Keir-Hardie] and he [Ramsay MacDonald] go on bombarding.'[159] The idea circulated at the time that, but for the uneasy conscience of Lord Morley, nine deported nationalists of Bengal (Aswini Kumar Dutt and others) would not have been released. No doubt Morley urged their release. But at the time he seemed so weak and vacillating that outward pressure on him became the determining factor. 'The release of the deportees is said to be due not to Morley's conscience but to Keir-Hardie and Ramsay MacDonald,' Nivedita wrote.[160] She criticized the young Maharaja of Burdwan who at the instigation of the Anglo-Indian bureaucrats had described Kier-Hardie as 'The White Sirdar Coolie'. The impertinent Maharaja, was also rebuked by the *Modern Review* (July 1910).

Special mention should be made here of the invaluable services rendered by S.K. Ratcliffe. While in India, editing *The Statesman,* he presented the Indian cause in such an objective and sympathetic way that it irked the government as well as the proprietor of the paper. Eventually, he had to resign and return to England. Back home, he became 'a constant contributor' to the *Daily News,* the *Manchester Guardian* and the *Nation*. He also organized the Indian Civil Rights Committee in England. Along with Mackerness he made strenuous efforts to counteract the 'Home' Government's intention to deport Aurobindo, even after he published an Open Letter in the *Karmayogin* (30 July 1909), declaring his abandonment of violent means of political struggle and his adoption of constitutional methods. Nivedita thanked Ratcliffe and Mackerness for their fruitful efforts.[161] But the attitude of the Government in India remained unchanged. In the circumstances, at Nivedita's insistence, Aurobindo absconded to avoid arrest.

Another friend of the Indian movement was William Stead, a venerated journalist. He worked as assistant editor with John (later Viscount) Morley in the *Pall Mall Gazette* and then became its editor. During the days of the Swadeshi Movement, he was editing the famous *Review of Reviews*. This journal regularly published news of the Indian movement, culled from various sources. Stead courageously took up the cause of the freedom of press in India. In the October 1909 number of the journal, he condemned the action of A.H.S. Aston, Chief Presidency Magistrate of Bombay, in ordering the arrest of the Bombay agent of *Swaraj*, edited by Bipin Chandra Pal. Pal had written an article, 'The Aetiology of the Bomb,' in which he criticized the bomb as 'the worst and the most diabolical form of assassination', but also the government largely responsible for its policy of partition and repression which was the root cause of the evil of the bomb. Stead not only attacked Aston but also the Secretary of State. He threw out a challenge: 'Mr A.H.S. Aston can apply to the *Review of Reviews,* if he pleases, Article 124 A of the Indian Penal Code,' and warned, 'If this is the way India is to be governed, the Astons will succeed in making Englishmen as disaffected as the Indian nationalists.' The Government of India promptly reacted by ordering the confiscation of the said issue of the *Review of Reviews*. Stead threw up a counter-challenge: 'If such an article be seditious under the English law, then the *Pall Mall Gazette* under Mr Morley's editorship was full of sedition from first to last.'

A man who created a great commotion in England by agitating against the police atrocities in the Swadeshi Movement days and thereby suffered most was Frederic Mackerness, M.P. He was a radical liberal of the old school. Though an M.P. of the Liberal Party, he did not shrink from attacking the 'great liberal', Lord Morley's repressive Indian policy. He accepted the Chairmanship of the

> India Civil Rights Committee, and raised a storm of protest in and outside Parliament against police torture in India. The *Christian Commonwealth*, recalling his services to India, wrote, 'No voice was raised more powerfully in the last Parliament on behalf of the native peoples than that of Frederic Mackerness, member for Newbury. He did run the risk of the displeasure of his party whips and leaders. . . . The arbitrary acts of the present administration in India especially aroused his indignation, and since the notorious deportations of untried British subjects during the last two years he has used every opportunity of educating public opinion.[162]

The same sentiment was expressed in a letter to *The Times* (3 August 1910) by W.P. Byles, M.P.[163]

For two years, Mackerness fought a hard relentless battle on the issue. In a letter to the *Morning Leader* (5 January 1909), he wrote against the enactment of repressive measures by the Government of India. Ratcliffe also wrote fearlessly on the same topic in the *Daily News* (5 January 1909), in which he described India as 'the policemen's kingdom'. Mackerness also raised questions in the House of Commons about police methods in India, but failing to secure any answer to these 'grave questions' he again wrote a letter in the *Daily News* on 23 January 1909. He also wrote a letter in *The Times* (29 January 1909) in which he protested against the deportation of nine prominent nationalists of Bengal, including Aswini Kumar Dutt, who were men of 'high character' and had rendered 'long service to the cause of education and social reform'. Wedderburn supported Mackerness in the *Westminster Gazette* (2 February 1909).

Curiously enough, Mrs Besant had extended her full support to the Viceroy who, in her words, was 'immensely popular with the best Indians'. She harshly criticized Aurobindo who 'would use any methods which would upset British rule.'[164] The British Government at the same time had put pressures on the outspoken Liberal members against their anti-Government moves. The *Outlook* reported how Lord Morley forced Lord MacDonald 'into silence' regarding his opposition to partition. A similar attempt to 'dragon the Liberal Party into silence is in progress over these deportations'.[165] In this connection Mackerness again wrote a letter to the *Daily News* stating that 'all we know is that they [the deportees] have committed no crime which can be formulated, that there is no evidence against them which can be even submitted to a court of law, and the informants against them are persons whose names cannot be disclosed'.[166]

Morley reacted to the criticisms by asserting that he suspected the existence of a great conspiracy in India against law and order, and that the deported Indian leaders were connected with it. But he admitted that there was no direct evidence and that the nature and the source of such evidence as there was could not be disclosed to Parliament or even to the victims themselves. Morley's statement provoked a sharp rejoinder from Mackerness, who regretted 'that "reasons of state" are being set up as rivals to the old Liberal concepts of justice and personal rights'.[167] Exchanges between Morley and Mackerness followed. In a series of articles contributed to the *Nation*, the latter cited various recent incidents of police atrocity. The *Nation* wrote long editorials in his support, Keir-Hardie and Ramsay MacDonald joined hands with Mackerness. In the House of Commons they 'called attention to the prevalence in India of the practice of torturing under-trial untried prisoners for the purpose of extorting evidence.' Under the circumstances, the Under Secretary of State, E.S. Montagu, had to come forward with some sort of explanation. Mackerness gave a sizzling reply to all the points in his letters to the *Daily News* and the *Morning Leader*.[168]

In April 1910, Mackerness published a pamphlet, *The Methods of Indian Police in the Twentieth Century*. The pamphlet was proscribed first in the province of East Bengal and subsequently in Punjab, Bengal and other provinces. What Mackerness could not do by his previous articles and agitation, was now achieved by this act of the government. 'Where, before the proscription one person had been interested, now ten thousand. . . . Everybody was asking, what is this pamphlet? And what is the dangerous matter contained in it?'[169] The British Liberal Press came forward in a body to support Mackerness. Initially, some of them were lukewarm, perhaps because of their reluctance to court the displeasure of Lord Morley.[170]

On the other side, there was the jubilant yellow press, like the *Standard, Daily Express*, vociferous in their support for the government. The Under Secretary of State, Montagu, made the sweeping remark that the pamphlet contained 'an enormous number of inaccuracies on every page', and Mackerness's attacks on the police methods were 'wholly unsubstantiated by evidence'. Mackerness on his part wrote a number of letters in *The Times, Daily News* and other papers, and there he cut to pieces all of Montagu's irresponsible assertions. The case became hopeless for Montagu. The Liberal press, in the meantime, could secure nothing from Montagu but sweeping allegations against Mackerness. The *Morning Leader* sarcastically wrote: 'There may be excuses for the notorious fact that the Indian police system is a crying scandal and a cesspool of corruption. There can be none for pretending at this time of day that it is not.'

Harsh and hard was the attack of the *Nation:* 'Mr Montagu defended with a violence of language singularly unbecoming in a young Minister almost absurdly new to his task, the suppression of a pamphlet on the Indian Police by a veteran whose services to a fearless liberalism he is never likely to emulate.' Even the *Manchester Guardian,* then the most important supporter of government policy, warned Montagu, saying that this type of irresponsible behaviour could affect the career of a young politician like him. Montagu made a lengthy speech in self-defence in his constituency at Newton, and expressed himself eloquently in torrents of half-truths and untruths. Mackerness immediately exposed him in his true colours, in a letter to *The Times* (15 August 1910):

> His vehemence grows apace and from the comparatively mild charge that my pamphlet contained 'enormous inaccuracies on every page', he has now advanced to the more highly coloured picture of it as 'horrible and mischievous', and 'as deserving the strongest condemnation from every patriotic Indian and Englishmen.[171]

This time the entire Liberal press condemned Montagu. Severest was the *Manchester Guardian:*

> Mr Montagu's speech seems to have consisted largely of rhetorical attempts to represent his conduct towards Mr Mackerness as a piece of gallantry displayed in defence of the Indian Civil Service. Such heroics should be left to the minor theatres. The Indian Civil Service has no need that politicians at home should either forget good manners or lose their sense of evidence on its account.

Because of press censorship the people of India knew little about what Mackerness was doing for the Indian nationalists in England. But Indians in England acknowledged his role and gave him a 'complimentary luncheon' in which noted Indians like Sir M. Bhownaggree, Lajpat Rai, Bipin Chandra Pal, G.S. Khaparde, M.K. Tyabji, and sympathetic Englishmen like H.W. Nevinson, G.P. Gooch and L.W. Ritch were present. The Chairman of the meeting, J.M. Parik, voiced the common sentiment when he said:

> Mr Mackerness was one of the old order of Liberals, always ready to champion the cause of the weak against the strong, and more specially the cause of those who, like the Indians, were misrepresented and muzzled. He had been influential in founding the Indian Civil Rights Committee, which had done yeoman service in the cause of freedom in India.[172]

7. Partition Annulled

When Charles Hardinge succeeded Minto as the Viceroy of India there was apprehension in Indian circles that a die-hard Conservative like him, with 'an iron-set, coach and four physiognomy' would let lose a reign of terror immediately after assuming office. 'That steeltrap looking face, and familiarity with Russia,' Nivedita gasped, seeing his picture in the newspapers. But she had to revise her opinion in a short time. She found Hardinge to be that iron man who did not spare corrupt high officials, including a police chief and even a lieutenant governor.[173] His stern anti-corruption measures, even against high officials, earned him much respect.[174]

Hardinge soon understood what unrestricted power had done to degrade the administration. He also realized that the root cause of the unrest was the Partition. As a chain reaction it had brought unlimited power to the bureaucrats, resulting in unthinkable corruption. The then Secretary of State, Lord Crewe, shared his views. Having made up his mind, Hardinge 'carried his whole Council with him' in the decision to annul partition. Certainly it was by no means an easy task — to make the 'settled fact unsettled', and thereby to displease the so-far-wooed and privileged separatist Muslim elements. The prestige of the Raj was a formidable bar. But he surmounted everything to achieve his goal. 'Advantage was taken of the King's Coronation celebrations in India to annul the Partition and to shift the metropolis of India from Calcutta to Delhi.' The announcement was at the close of the Coronation ceremony, on 12 December 1911. It read thus in part:

> We are pleased to announce to our people that . . . the creation at as early a date as possible of a Governorship-in-Council for the Presidency of Bengal, of a new Lieutenant-Governorship-in-Council administering the areas of Bihar, Chota Nagpur and Orissa, and of a Chief Commissionership of Assam, with . . . administrative changes and redistribution of boundaries. . . .

Thus ended, at least formally, that part of the Swadeshi Movement which had been unleashed by the Partition. But the upsurge continued with a new dimension and in a new direction.

Remembering the glory that was the Swadeshi Movement, historians at the same time have pointed out its limitations. Dr Nemai Sadhan Bose has listed some of them. An all-round industrial regeneration did not materialize, nor was the desired success of the national education scheme achieved. Boycott had but little impact on the national economy. Industrial unrest was short-lived, and the peasantry mostly remained out of its fold. And 'the movement failed to achieve Hindu-Muslim unity and could not offer any powerful resistance to the communal riots which continued to remain a dark feature of Indian politics.'[175] Tripathi holds a similar view when writing about the Extremists of the swadeshi era. But on one point he seems more severe. 'Instead of uniting the country,' he wrote, 'Hindu fanfare alienated the most substantial minority.'[176] But he and also Sumit Sarkar objected to the simplistic version of the Marxian class approach in analysing the trends of the movement. Sarkar distinctly refuses to over-emphasize the economic motivation to political action and ideals.

The Bengali middle class were not the counterpart of the European middle class. They were 'virtually unconnected with capitalist forms of trade, industry or agriculture'. Here we should state that the Bengali middle class were prone to emotional exuberance, and were the backbone of the movement. Because of their emotional sensitivity, religion played a dominant role in motivating them and in determining their subsequent actions. This was but natural in a country where religion for thousands of years came to be regarded as its life blood.

It should also be borne in mind that the movement was sparked off when the country was quite unprepared for a sustained struggle. Enough time was not granted for solid preparation. There was only an indomitable will and an inner spirit of confidence which only the traditional culture content could bring out. The culture-base was overwhelmingly religious, and the agitation, because the persons involved were mostly Hindus, seemingly took on a Hindu tone and colour in some respects. This explains the predominance of the Mother cult in most of Tagore's national songs of this period, though it is well known that Tagore was generally a believer in the Father cult, because of his adherence to the Brahmo ideology. And, as the movement started on a specific issue, the Partition of Bengal, Tagore's songs appealed specially to Bengal's heart for unity and sacrifice. Yet Tagore was in no way provincial.

It is well to remember, as this was the first national upsurge, with no wealth of experience behind it, that all the expectations could not possibly be fulfilled. Again, this movement was actually an integral part of the overall freedom movement, embracing all classes of the peoples of the land. If only the economic grievances of the working class were to be made a base for the movement, then a clash of interests between the different sections of the agitators would be inevitable, for the movement had in its fold numerous big Indian businessmen and zamindars. The dilemma of choosing the target of attack, of clubbing together the British imperialists and the Indian feudals and capitalists, continued not only during the swadeshi years, but till the end of the freedom movement. That is why, even the Extremists within the Congress prescribed a two-phased revolutionary process, first against the imperialistic British, then against the capitalistic Indian. The case of pre-revolution Russia and pre-independence India was not the same because the Russian revolutionaries had to fight only against their own countrymen, whereas the Indians had to fight firstly against the most powerful foreign imperialist power of the day, and then, if possible, against their native exploiters. Realizing the impossibility of this two-way struggle, the revolutionaries-turned-Marxists mostly moved away from the freedom movement in the thirties.

Those who over-emphasize the Hindu religious content in the Swadeshi Movement, and search there for the causes of Muslim separatism, tend to forget the enormous strength of the imperialist power and its ability successfully to apply a divide and rule policy. The adoption of some Hindu religious symbols or rituals by the Hindu agitators could not have been powerful enough to be the main cause of the alienation of the Muslims from the national struggle. If the Hindu nationalists and the militants adopted some Hindu rituals, like oath-taking or pujas at the temple or holy bath, it was done to rouse the latent energy of the masses and to accumulate the necessary strength. In short, it was a character-building process. For the Hindus it was easier to draw inspiration from their own cultural sources, as it was so for the Muslims. We do not know of any case where a Muslim nationalist fell from favour with his Hindu comrades for being a devout Muslim and praying in the mosque and taking an oath in the name of Allah. Critics should remember that dedicating one's life to a cause is not an easy thing, and he who dedicated himself to the freedom struggle had to be prepared to face all sorts of eventualities — confinements, physical torture and even death. This needed mental preparation, and the mind grows in strength and draws sustenance from its natural surroundings. Thus, after considering all the avoidable and unavoidable limitations, we had better turn to the all-comprehensive greatness of this national movement which was 'co-extensive with the entire circle of our national life', and which, as Dr Nemai Sadhan Bose has said, 'occupies a unique place in the history of the Indian national struggle for independence.' Here, it is apt to remember the oft-quoted words of Mahatma Gandhi, 'The real awakening [of India] took place after the Partition of Bengal.' He considered the partition day as 'the day of the partition of the British Empire'.

Closing our panoramic view of the many-splendoured Swadeshi Movement we can aptly conclude with the great words of Vivekananda:

> The lion when stricken to the heart, gives out his mightiest roar. When smitten on the head, the cobra lifts its hood. And the majesty of the soul comes forth, only when a man is wounded to his depths.[17]

Notes and References

1. Sister Nivedita, *The Complete Works of Sister Nivedita* (Sister Nivedita Girls' School, 1967), (henceforth, *Nivedita Works*), Vol. I, p. 298.
2. *Nivedita Works*, Vol. I, p. 298.
3. Nemai Sadhan Bose, *Indian Awakening and Bengal* (Firma K.L. Mukhopadhyay, Calcutta, 1976), (henceforth, Nemai Sadhan), p. 235.
4. Sister Nivedita, *Letters of Sister Nivedita*, edited with introduction by Sankari Prasad Basu (Nababharat Publishers, Calcutta, 1982), (henceforth, *Nivedita Letters*), Vol. II, p. 540. Nivedita to Alberta Sturges and Hollister Sturges, 20 September 1903.
5. Annie Besant, *Brahmavadin*, March-April 1914.
6. For detailed reports see *Vivekananda in Indian Newspapers, 1893-1902*, edited by Sankari Prasad Basu and Sunil Behari Ghose (Modern Book Agency, Calcutta, 1967).
7. Swami Vivekananda, *The Complete Works of Swami Vivekananda* (Advaita Ashrama, Calcutta), (henceforth, *Vivekananda Works*), Vol. III (1960), pp. 223-4, 225-6.
8. *Vivekananda Works*, Vol. III, pp. 300-1.
9. Surendranath Banerjea: 'The history of a nation is the history of its great men . . . Ramakrishna and Vivekananda were shining spiritual guides to influence aspirations of the educated India. . . . Vivekananda was a patriot in the truest sense of the term.' Annie Besant: 'Vivekananda roused the strongest feeling of Nationality.' According to Bipin Chandra Pal, 'In some respects, Vivekananda may well claim to be the greatest preacher and prophet of our modern nationalism.' Tilak thought that Vivekananda's historical role was comparable to that of the great Sankaracharya. Tilak's paper, *Maharatta*, wrote on 14 June 1912: 'Swami Vivekananda is the real father of Indian nationalism.' Aurobindo, in the Swadeshi days, perceived Vivekananda's 'influence working gigantically . . . Vivekananda lives in the soul of his Mother, and in the soul of her children.' Gandhi said that, 'after having gone through them [Vivekananda works] the love that I had for my country became a thousand fold.' Chakravarti Rajagopalachari categorically stated that 'But for him . . . we would not have gained our freedom.' Jawaharlal Nehru pointed out that, 'Directly or indirectly he has profoundly influenced the India of today.' And to Subhas Chandra Bose, Vivekananda was the guru who moulded him and was his mentor in all walks of life.
10. Romain Rolland, *The Life of Vivekananda*, (Advaita Ashrama, Calcutta, 1960), pp. 113-4.
11. Niradbaran, *Sri Aurobinder Sange Kathabarta* (Sri Aurobindo Ashrama, Pondicherry, 1961), (henceforth, Niradbarana), p. 268.
12. *Sri Aurobindo on Himself and on the Mother*, p. 97.
13. *Nivedita Letters*, Vol. II, pp. 663-4. Nivedita to Mrs Ole Bull, 28 July 1904.
14. *The Dawn*, November 1905.
15. *Hindustan Review*, October-November 1916.
16. Nivedita, *Studies From an Eastern Home*, Appendix.

17. Surendranath Banerjea, *A Nation in Making* (Humphrey Milford, 1927), (henceforth, Surendranath), p. 164.
18. Amales Tripathi, *The Extremist Challenge*, Calcutta, 1967 (henceforth Tripathi), p. 90.
19. *Nivedita Letters*, Vol. II, p. 540. Nivedita to Alberta Sturges and Hollister Sturges, 28 January 1903.
20. *Nivedita Letters*, Vol. II, p. 654. Nivedita to Miss MacLeod, 4 July 1904.
21. *India* (organ of the Indian National Congress, published by the British Committee, from England), 17 March 1905.
22. *Nivedita Letters*, Vol. II, p. 726. Nivedita to Mrs Ole Bull, 5 March 1905.
23. S.K. Ratcliffe, 'The Story of the Bengal Partition', *New Age* (*India*, 3 April 1908).
24. Tripathi, pp. 91-2.
25. Ibid., p. 97.
26. *India*, 3 April 1908.
27. R.C. Majumdar, *History of the Freedom Movement in India* (Firma K.L. Mukhopadhyay, Calcutta, 1963), (henceforth, Majumdar), Vol. II, p. 5.
28. *India*, 3 April 1908.
29. Majumdar, Vol. II, p. 9.
30. Tripathi, p. 102.
31. Majumdar, Vol. II, pp. 7-8.
32. S.K. Ratcliffe, 'The Story of Bengal Partition,' *New Age* (*India*, 3 April 1908).
33. Nivedita, *The Dawn*, 20 August 1905, 'Family or Country'.
34. *Nivedita Letters*, Vol. II, p. 753. Nivedita to Mrs Ole Bull, 17 August 1905.
35. *Nivedita Letters*, Vol. II, p. 755. Nivedita to Miss MacLeod, 13 September 1905.
36. Surendranath, p. 212.
37. Surendranath, pp. 213-4.
38. Bampfylde Fuller, *Review of Reviews*, July 1908, 'The Vision Splendid of Indian Youth'.
39. W. Nevinson, *Manchester Guardian*, 10 January 1908, (*India*, 17 January 1908).
40. Majumdar, Vol. II, pp. 31-2.
41. Sri Aurobindo, *Bankim-Tilak-Dayananda* (Sri Aurobindo Ashrama, Pondicherry, 1955), p. 65.
42. Nevinson, *Daily News*, 28 November 1907 (*India*, 6 December 1908).
43. By 1910, Surendranath Banerjea, now a confirmed loyalist, had to back-track on things for which he had stood for so many years. About his unenviable position, Nivedita wrote to Ratcliffe on 14 September 1910: 'Sir G.B. [George Birdwood] has presided over something at Ripon College, I understand, and poor old S.N.B. [Surendranath] is understood to be up to the chin in pledges that his boys shall not even learn to spell the word politics'. Then about the Drain Theory: 'A circular has been issued to the Education Department calling upon officers to combat the *mischievous doctrine* of *The Drain to England* of all things. Do they want people to believe that it is *drain* from England?' (*Nivedita Letters*, Vol. II, p. 1146).
44. Nevinson, *Daily Chronicle*, 25 November 1908 (*India*, 29 November 1908).

45. Sumit Sarkar, *The Swadeshi Movement in Bengal 1903-8* (People's Publishing House, New Delhi, 1973), (henceforth, Sarkar), p. 105.
46. *Nivedita Letters*, Vol. II, p. 1033, Nivedita to S.K. Ratcliffe, 25 November 1909.
N.N. Ghose, a well-known professor of history and English literature, editor of *Indian Nation*, nevertheless harboured backward ideas about science and industry. In the Bengal Provincial Conference in 1901, he made this astounding declaration that science was not necessary for industry, as ancient India had shown remarkable skill in paper, leather and cotton industries without knowledge of science. A correspondent vehemently protested against these unreasoned utterances in a lengthy letter to the *Bengalee* of 22 May 1901.
47. For a detailed account see *Prabuddha Bharata* (October and November issues, 1978), for an article by the present writer, 'Vivekananda, Nivedita and Tata Research Scheme.'
Vivekananda was attracted to pure science by philosophic bent of mind and to applied science by his humanitarian outlook. He favoured material civilization for India's material prosperity. Louise Burke in her well-known work, *Vivekananda in America: New Discoveries*, has presented the revealing fact that one of the major reasons for Vivekananda's visit to America was to secure funds 'to organize monks for industrial purposes, that they might give the people the benefit of this industrial education and thus elevate them to improve their conditions'. (Burke, quoted from the *Salem Evening News*, 29 August 1893, and also the *Daily Gazette* of the same date). That Vivekananda really had that intention can be found from the rules and regulations that he framed for the new monastic order, in May 1897. 'Now the aim is to develop this Math into a full-fledged university. In that, along with the study of philosophy and religion, a complete technical institute has to be created. The latter is the first responsibility.' (Saralabala Sarkar, *Swami Vivekananda O Sri Sri Ramakrishna Sangha* (1954, p. 118). Swamiji urged his disciples to acquire a big plot of land, healthy and fertile,' in Hazaribag or in adjoining areas (rich in minerals) and establish there a big-scale industrial institute and also workshop'.
48. Nivedita did her best for technological training for the Indians. She wrote a pamphlet on the subject also (published by S.S. Setlur, a friend of both Vivekananda and Tilak) from which lengthy extracts were published in the *Prabuddha Bharata*, May 1905, under the title, 'Manual Training as a Part of General Education in India', now included in *Nivedita Works*, Vol. IV, pp. 415-43.
49. Though Subhas Chandra Bose was aware of Tagore's support for his National Planning programme based on mechanized industrialization, as late as 1945, in a lecture at Tokyo University, he bracketed Tagore and Gandhi as having similar attitude towards industrialization and its necessary evil. He no doubt took Tagore's total attitude into consideration.
50. *Modern Review*, August 1909, 'The Swadeshi and Boycott Movement.'
51. *Karma Yogin*, 22 January 1910.

52. Aurobindo, *Bande Mataram*, 10 March 1908. Quoted in *Sri Aurobindo and the New Thought in Indian Politics*, edited by Haridas Mukherjee and Uma Mukherjee, p. 284.
53. *Bande Mataram* (weekly edition) 14 June 1908. Compiled in *Bande Mataram and Indian Nationalism* (1957) edited by Haridas Mukherjee and Uma Mukherjee.
54. Girijasankar Raichoudhury, *Sri Aurobindo O Banglay Swadeshi Jug* (Nababharat Publishers, Calcutta, 1956), (henceforth, Girijasankar), p. 543.
55. *Sedition Committee Report, 1918* (New Age Publishers, Calcutta edition, 1973), pp. 162-3.
56. Girijasankar, pp. 575-91.
57. *Life of Swami Vivekananda*, by His Eastern and Western Disciples (Advaita Ashrama, 1960), pp. 575-6.
58. Sarkar, pp. 387-8.
59. W. Nevinson, *Manchester Guardian*, 3 January 1908 (*India*, 10 January 1908), 'The National Volunteers in Bengal'.
60. Keir-Hardie, *Labour Leader*, 27 December 1908 (*India*, 3 January 1908).
61. Keir-Hardie, *Labour Leader*, 3 January 1908 (*India*, 10 January 1908).
62. W. Nevinson, *Manchester Guardian*, 3 December 1908 (*India*, 10 January 1908).
63. Majumdar, Vol. II, p. 19.
64. W. Nevinson, *Manchester Guardian*, 3 January 1908 (*India*, 10 January 1908).
65. Sarkar, p. 143
66. Tripathi, pp. 139-40.
67. Sarkar, pp. 137-40, 146.
68. W. Nevinson, *Daily Chronicle*, 25 November 1907 (*India*, 29 November 1907).
69. Nevinson described the dire poverty of the mill workers, and their appalling living conditions: 'I have lately spent many sweating hours in the fluffy atmosphere of the mills, where there are no fans to disturb the dust, the heat or the smell. Little boys and girls, who are legally over nine years old, but are often less, were doing half-time or six hours, at 2¾ d. a day (4 rupees a month). Over 14, boys and girls were working the full time of 13 hours, with half-an-hour's rest, for 8 rupees a month. The highest woman's wage is 10 rupees a month and the average for man is 18 rupees a month.' Then after presenting a picture of the harrowing condition of the bustees and the base quality of the food consumed, Nevinson wrote bitterly but with deep sympathy: 'An all night long, under the waning moon, the mill hands have sat under the verandahs of these wretched homes, beating tin drums and chanting their barbaric scales — "praising God" — as they said, though what form of God, or for what reason of praise they did not explain.' (*Daily Chronicle*, 25 November 1907.)
70. Sarkar, p. 210. Sarkar has complained that historians did not pay due attention to the labour unrest of the period. To undo the wrong he zealously wrote a lengthy chapter (pp. 182-251) on the subject from which I have used relevant material.

71. Tripathi, p. 118.
72. Vivekananda had said this to his 'disciple', Sarat Chandra Chakrabarti, some time in 1898 at Belur: 'They [the "lower class"] have worked so long uniformly like machines . . . and the clever educated section have taken the substantial part of the fruits of their labour. . . . But times have changed. The lower classes are . . . determined to exact their legitimate dues. The masses of Europe and America have been the first to awaken. . . . Signs of this awakening have shown themselves in India too, as is evident from the number of strikes among the lower classes nowadays. The upper classes will no longer be able to repress the lower, try they ever so much.' (*Vivekananda Works,* Vol. VII, p. 149.)
73. Sarkar, pp. 183-4.
74. Pravarjika Atmaprana, *Sister Nivedita of Ramakrishna-Vivekananda* (Nivedita Girls' School, Calcutta, 1967), p. 107.
75. *Atmaprana,* p. 221.
76. Prabhatkumar Mukhopadhyay, *Rabindra Jibani* (Viswabharati Granthalaya, Calcutta, 1355 BS), (henceforth, Prabhatkumar), Vol. II, p. 31.
77. Prabhatkumar, p. 32
78. Prabhatkumar, pp. 85-6.
79. Majumdar, Vol. II, p. 83.
80. Sarkar, pp. 172, 176-7.
81. *Nivedita Letters,* Vol. II, pp. 1116-7. Nivedita to Ratcliffe, 19-20 July 1910.
82. *Nivedita Letters,* Vol. II, p.1001. Nivedita to Miss MacLeod, 2 September 1909.
83. *Nivedita Letters,* Vol. II, p. 1033. Nivedita to Ratcliffe, 25 November 1909.
84. Sarkar has quoted (p. 170) Minto's letter to Morley of 3 November 1908, which, I fear, is not complimentary to Sir Ashutosh's memory. Minto wrote: 'Dr A. Mukherjee tells me that the national schools and private colleges are hotbeds of sedition, and that till we deal with them we can have no permanent peace.'
85. *Nivedita Letters,* Vol. II, p. 1236, Nivedita to Miss MacLeod, 13 September 1911.
86. *Bengalee,* 31 July 1901, 'London Letter'.
87. Nivedita, *Review of Reviews,* October 1902, 'Is Matter Alive? by Professor Bose'.
88. *Vivekananda Works,* Vol. VII, pp. 379-80.
89. *Vivekananda Works,* Vol. VIII, p. 523.
90. *Nivedita Letters,* Vol. II, p. 778. Dr J.C. Bose to Mrs Ole Bull, 16 October 1905.
91. *Nivedita Letters,* Vol. II, p. 941. Dr J.C. Bose to Nivedita, 16 October 1908.
92. *Nivedita Letters,* Vol. II, p. 1158-9. Nivedita to Mrs Ole Bull, 29 September 1910.
93. *Nivedita Letters,* Vol. II, p. 1145. Nivedita to Ramendrasundar Trivedi, 10 September 1910.
94. Sarkar, p. 302.
95. *Girish Rachanabali,* Vol. II (Sahitya Samsad, Calcutta 1971, edited with introduction by Dr Debipada Bhattacharya), pp. 37-8 (Introduction).
96. Majumdar, Vol. II, pp. 146-7.

97. *Indian Review,* December 1905, 'Bande Mataram'.
98. *Indian Review,* May 1907, 'Rishi Bankimchandra'.
99. *India,* 22 February 1907, 'Bande Mataram: The Story of India's Rule Britannia'.
100. Prabhatkumar, Vol. II, p. 154.
101. *Nivedita Letters,* Vol. I, pp. 456-7. Nivedita to Miss MacLeod, 28 February 1902.
102. *Indian Review,* August 1908, 'The New Indian School of Painting'.
103. Sir Jadunath Sarkar, *Amrita Bazar Patrika,* 31 May 1965, 'Ramananda Chatterjee: India's Ambassador to the Nations'.
104. *Nivedita Works,* Vol. III, p. 12.
105. *Nivedita Works,* Vol. III, p. 87.
106. *Nivedita Works,* Vol. III, pp. 58-9.
107. *Modern Review,* September 1909, '*The Pioneer* on Indian Pictures'.
108. *Indian Review,* May 1909, 'A Modern School of Indian Painting'.
109. *Modern Review,* March 1915, 'Lahore Art and Crafts Exhibition'.
110. *Modern Review,* March 1916, 'Exhibition of Indian Paintings in Madras'.
111. *India,* 3 June 1910.
112. *India,* 14 October 1910.
113. *Modern Review,* October 1910.
114. C.F. Andrews, *Modern Review,* November 1908, 'National Literature and Art'.
115. *Maharatta,* 13 August 1905.
116. *Maharatta,* 20 August 1905, 'The Partition of Bengal'.
117. *Maharatta,* 22 October 1902, 'Rakhi Bandhan'.
118. *Maharatta,* 26 November 1905, 'Our Struggle for Freedom'.
119. Majumdar, Vol. II, pp. 88-9.
120. Majumdar, Vol. II, p. 133.
121. *India,* 6 December 1907, 'Conciliate Bengal: Mr Gokhale's Appeal to the Viceroy'.
122. *Nivedita Letters,* Vol. II, p. 757, Nivedita to Gokhale, 20 September 1905.
123. Prema Nandakumar, *Subramania Bharati* (National Book Trust, New Delhi, 1968), p. 15.
124. Surendranath, p. 225.
125. *Nivedita Works,* Vol. IV, p. 274.
126. *Nivedita Letters,* Vol. II, p. 1214, Nivedita to Ratcliffe, 20 July 1911.
127. Keir-Hardie, *Labour Leader,* 27 December 1907 (*India,* 3 January 1908).
128. Keir-Hardie, *Labour Leader,* 10 January, 1908 (*India,* 17 January 1908).
129. *India,* 17 April 1908. 'Keir-Hardie at the Caxton Hall, Westminster' (9 April 1908).
130. Keir-Hardie, *Labour Leader (India,* 28 May 1909).
131. *Tribune,* quoted by *India,* 27 December 1907.
132. W. Nevinson, *Manchester Guardian,* 15 January 1907. (*India,* 17 January 1907).
133. *Modern Review,* June 1908, 'The Present Situation'. (An unsigned article, presumably written by Nivedita.)
134. *Nivedita Letters,* Vol. II, p. 704. Nivedita to Miss MacLeod, 28 December 1904.

135. Niradharan, p. 40.
136. Bhupendra Nath Datta, *Bharater Dvitiwa Swadhinatar Sangram* (Nababharat, 1983), p. 91.
137. Harikumar Chakravarti, *Viswabibek* (Vak-Sahitya, Calcutta, 1963), 'Biplab Andolane Swamijir Prabhab', p. 246.
138. *Sedition Committee Report*, p. 22.
139. G.P. Pradhan, A.K. Bhagwat, *Lokamanya Tilak* (Jaico Publishing House, Bombay, 1959), pp. 228, 230-1.
140. *Maharatta*, 10 June 1906, 'The Shivaji Festival of Calcutta: Reception to Messrs Tilak and Khaparde'.
141. *Maharatta*, 2 September 1906, 'Terrorism in Russia'.
142. *Maharatta*, 28 July 1907.
143. *Maharatta*, 24 November 1907.
144. *Indian World*, July 1910, 'Mr. Valentine Chirol Again.' (Quoted from the *Times*.)
145. A.J. Fraser Blair, *Hindustan Review*, March 1907 (*Review of Reviews*, May 1907).
146. *India*, 12 July 1907, 'The Best Reply', and 'Morning Leader's Comment'.
147. *India*, 6 December 1907, 'Blowing Hot and Cold: Sir Charles Eliot on the Unrest'.
148. *Review of Reviews*, September 1908, 'The Birth Pangs of the Indian Nation'.
149. *Review of Reviews*, July 1908, 'Sir Bampfylde Fuller's Views'.
150. *Review of Reviews*, July 1908, 'Shall We Lose India?'
151. *Review of Reviews*, August 1908, 'The Unrest in India'.
152. *Review of Reviews*, September 1908, 'The Situation in India'.
153. *India*, 20 November 1908.
154. *India*, 20 November 1908, 'Mr O'Donnell, M.P., Points the Moral'.
155. *India*, 20 November 1908, 'An Anglo-Indian on the "Practical Issue".
156. *Review of Reviews*, December 1908, 'India Seething in Sedition'.
157. *Review of Reviews*, August 1910, 'British Rule in India'.
158. Much later, at the instance of Mahatma Gandhi, the British Committee and the paper *India* were abolished. Subhas Chandra Bose doubted the wisdom of the decision. He wrote: 'There was one resolution [passed at the Nagpur Congress in December 1920] which must be regarded as a great blunder. That was the decision to wind up the British Branch of the Indian National Congress and stop publication of its organ, the paper *India*. With the carrying into effect of this resolution, the only centre of propaganda which the Congress had outside India was shut down.' (Subhas Chandra Bose, *Indian Struggle*, 1948 edition, p. 69.)
159. *Nivedita Letters*, Vol. II, p. 1093; Nivedita to Ratcliffe, 28 April 1910.
160. *Nivedita Letters*, Vol. II, p. 1066, Nivedita to Ratcliffe, 17 February 1910.
161. *Nivedita Letters*, Vol. II, p. 1031. Nivedita to Ratcliffe, 21 November 1909.
162. *Christian Commonwealth*, 'Is Britain Just to India: An Interview with Mr Mackerness', (*India*, 10 June 1910).
163. *The Times*, 3 August 1910. Letter from W.P. Byles, M.P. (*India*, 5 August 1910).
164. *Daily Chronicle*, 12 May 1909, 'An Interview with Mrs Annie Besant', (*India*, 14 May 1909).

165. *India,* 14 May 1909, 'A Polite Evasion'.
166. *Daily News,* 25 May 1909 (*India,* 28 May 1909).
167. *Nation,* quoted by *India,* 25 June 1909.
168. *India,* 6 May 1910.
169. *India,* 12 August 1910.
170. *India,* 1 July 1910, 'Silence and Slander'. 'The Government Press has preserved a significant silence on the subject. . . . Not one line has been published in the editorial columns of the *Manchester Guardian* or of the London Liberal newspapers. Even the *Nation* has found it politic to forget that Mr Mackerness' pamphlet is nothing more than a reproduction of letters which appeared, without protest or proscription, in its own columns. As Lord Morley is understood nowadays to look upon criticism of his Indian policy as a personal attack upon himself, they are no doubt wise in their forbearance. But their reticence is thrown into stately relief by the braying trumpets of the Yellow Press, which has once more overwhelmed the Secretary of State with praise.'
171. *India,* 19 August 1910.
172. *India,* 12 August 1910, 'Mr Mackerness and the London Indians: Complimentary Luncheon'.
173. *Nivedita Letters,* Vol. II, p. 1211, Nivedita to Ratcliffe, 6 July 1911.
174. *Nivedita Letters,* Vol. II, pp. 1211-2, Nivedita to Ratcliffe, 8 July 1911.
175. Nemai Sadhan, pp. 305-6.
176. Tripathi, p. 145.
177. *Nivedita Works,* Vol. I, p. 124.

Chapter IV

Trends in Muslim Indian Politics, 1857-1918 The Role of Aligarh and Deoband

B.N. Pande

1. Repression to Reconciliation

WHEN THE FOLLOWERS OF ISLAM came to India they must have been struck by the high level of religious tolerance that prevailed there, perhaps the highest among all countries for those times. They must also have wondered how people who were so tolerant of outsiders and so free from all racial and political bias, were at the same time so rigidly exclusive in their social habits and customs. The mosaic of their caste system with its political reflection as independent and conflicting social segments required to be built up anew into a harmonious structure. The people had to be welded into a common brotherhood, and corresponding political unity had to be evolved to serve their common needs and save them from unending conflicts. The need of the hour was religious tolerance, social and cultural synthesis, political integration and a secular outlook. Destiny had ordained that the Mughals would play this unifying role. So strong was this tradition among the Mughals that even Aurangzeb could play the bigot only half-heartedly, and with considerable self-restraint. And in spite of the disruption which followed at the end of his rule, the convulsions of politics could not overwhelm the synthesis of social life that had been achieved.

The feeling of harmony remained dominant in the minds of the two communities up to the uprising of 1857. This is clear from the attitude of Muslim divines towards the Hindu rulers. W.W. Hunter, in his book, *Indian Musalmans*, quotes a *fatwa* of the Qazi of Jaunpur in which he declares that the Muslims should regard regions under the Maratha rule as *Dar-ul-Islam*, on the ground that the rulers permit the Muslims to say their Friday and Id festival prayers and maintain the laws of Islam, although they have to ask the rulers to appoint their *qazis* and governors.

Nor, in spite of the existence of two different religions, were there any deep cultural differences between the two communities. Hindus and

Muslims contributed equally to the development of Hindi and Urdu and took pleasure in the study of one another's religion, philosophy and science. Their arts were common. There were no prejudices regarding participation in each others fairs and festivals. They spoke the same language; wore similar clothes; furnished their houses in the same style; had similar outlook upon the life of this world — if not also of the next; their industry and commerce, urban and rural occupations, were parts of one economic system. The universal surge of loyalty and devotion to Bahadur Shah, the symbol of political revolution in 1857, conclusively showed, for the first time in history, that India had become politically self-conscious and that the foundations of Indian nationalism had been truly and deeply laid.

The War of 1857 was a widespread movement in which all sections of the people participated. There was no trace of communal motives. Its flag was the green Mughal flag and the paramount power was to be restored to Bahadur Shah as the symbol of India's political unity. The consciousness of a foreign rule and a collective desire to uproot it is seen to emerge for the first time in Indian history. It was remarkable that, after prostration so complete, India should make an attempt so wide and so united; it was an entirely new phenomenon in Indian history. It was not just a confederacy of Indian princes which was fighting to overthrow a political adversary; the masses of the people in general were also openly aiding it. It was not a national movement but a national conspiracy and, as such, it was not the precursor of the national movement that was to come 25 years later. At the time of its occurrence, it portended the existence of a common will, a common objective and a united power of resistance which greatly disturbed the confidence and equanimity of the British rulers.

The failure of the Patriotic War of 1857 resulted in the ruthless repression of the Muslim community. The last of the Mughals, Bahadur Shah Zafar, also a poet of repute, wrote a pathetic verse on the misfortunes of the Muslim community after the fall of Delhi. He made particular mention of the fact that the Muslims were the special object of the wrath of the British rulers. The poem runs:

Gai yak-bayak jo hawa palat,
Nahin dil ko apne qarar hai;
Karun gham sitam ka main kya bayan,
Mera sina gham se fighar hai;
Ye riyaya-i-Hind tabah hui;
Kaho kya na inpe jafa hui.
Jise dekha hakim-i-waqt ne
Kaha yeh to qabil-i-dar hai.
Kahin aisa bhi hai sitam suna,

Ke di phansi lakhon ko be-gunah;
Wale kalma-goyon ki taraf se
Abhi dil men unke ghubar hai.[1]

[A dreadful change of atmosphere has overcome us,
And I know not one single moment's peace;
How may I tell my misery in words,
My heart is torn in two with agony;
The people of Hind are all doomed,
What depths of sufferings have they not known;
Whomsoever the masters of the day behold,
They say, 'Fit for the gallows is he too';
Had ever such tyranny been borne by men,
That lakhs are hanged, for no crime at all?
Still their hearts are full with venom and hate,
For those who utter the *Kalma* in prayer!]

On the pathetic condition of the Indian Muslims, W.W. Hunter wrote in 1868:

> After the mutiny, the British turned upon the Musalmans as their real enemies so that failure of the revolt was much more disastrous to them than to the Hindus. They lost altogether all their remaining prestige of traditional superiority over the Hindus. They forfeited for the time being the confidence of their foreign rulers. In every district, the descendant of some line of Muslim prince is sullenly eating his heart out in roofless palace and weed-choked tanks. The Musalmans are excluded from the Army and the law. The judiciary was either Anglicised or Hinduised; while Permanent Settlement led to the wholesale eviction of the Moslem land-lords.[2]

After the suppression of the revolt the British rulers lost no time in evolving a policy of divide and rule. In 1858 a commission was appointed to consider where the existing system had proved defective. Many high officers put forward their views before the commission. Lord Elphinstone, Governor of Bombay, in a minute dated 14 May 1858, wrote: '*Divide et impera* was the old Roman motto, and it should be ours. I might perhaps hesitate to express my conviction so decidedly if I were not able to show that my views upon this subject are entirely in accordance with those of the Duke of Wellington.'[3]

A glimpse into the official British records will show how this policy of *divide et impera* was taking shape. Wood, in a letter to Elign, says: 'We have maintained our power by playing off one part against the other, and we must continue to do so. . . Do what you can, therefore, to prevent all having a common feeling.'[4] Then again:

> I have been always very anxious to avoid any fraternizing and combining amongst the troops. It obviously is a cardinal point in India to keep races and classes so far away from each other as to obviate, as far as possible, all danger of this kind. Do the ordinary work of the North-Western Provinces with North-Western troops, Punjab ditto, and then have your Punjab troops ready to beat the Eastern with, and your Eastern troops to beat the Sikhs with, if occasion should arise.

In yet another letter Wood sagely remarks: 'We cannot afford in India to neglect any means of strengthening our position. Depend upon it, the natural antagonism of races is no inconsiderable element of our strength. If all India was to unite against us, how long could we maintain ourselves?'[5]

Discussing the relations of Turkey with India and the sympathies of Indian Muslims with the Ottoman Caliph, Lytton warned Salisbury that 'there is no getting over the fact that the British empire of India is a Mohammadan Power, and that it entirely depends on the policy of Her Majesty's Government whether the sentiment of our Mohammadan subjects is to be an immense security or an immense danger to us.'[6]

The launching of political agitation by Surendranath Banerjea through all-India tours, and the founding of the Indian Association in 1877-8, and the formation of the Indian National Congress in 1885 created a flutter in the official dovecots. Lord Reay, while forwarding a memorial from the Anjuman-i-Islam to Dufferin, remarks that 'the Mohammadans are undoubtedly handicapped in their competition with the Hindus; and I am anxious to see what can be done for them, though any increase of number of applicants for Government offices is not pleasant to contemplate.'[7] Sir Rivers Thompson, Lieutenant Governor of Bengal, welcomed the change in the government's policy of extending 'a helping hand to Muhammadans in securing appointments.'[8] Sir W.H. Gregory most heartily approved the resolution of the government on muslim education. He wrote to Dufferin:

> I am confident that it will bear good fruits; indeed, it seems to have done so already by the complete abstention of the Muhammadans from Brahmin and Baboo agitation. It will be a great matter to sweeten our relations with this portion of the Indian population, the bravest and at one time the most dangerous. But they all with one voice declared that they got their whipping in 1857, and they take it like men. They now look to us, and to us alone, not to be subject to Hindu domination.[9]

A year later, Gregory again wrote to the Governor-General: 'They [Muslims] see clearly they had best stick to us, as they would get scant favour from a Baboo or Brahmin ascendancy.'[10] Then, next year, he congratulated Dufferin in these words: 'It is a comfort to you to find how staunch you have made the Muhammadans to our Raj by your judicious treatment of them. You can well afford to smile at Baboo malignity.'[11] Colvin, Lieutenant Governor of the N.W. Province, assured Dufferin that the Muslims of that province would be bitterly hostile to Congress demands which they regarded as a claim for Hindu supremacy. He regarded the idea of a national movement in India as an absurd one, to which the Muslims would not subscribe.[12]

Sir John Strachey confessed that 'the truth plainly is that the existence of these hostile creeds side by side is one of the strongest points in our political position in India'.[13]

George Francis Hamilton, the Secretary of State for India, wrote to Curzon, the Viceroy:

> I think the real danger to our rule in India, not now but say 50 years hence, is the gradual adoption and extension of Western ideas of agitation and organization, and, if we could break the educated Hindu party into two sections holding widely different views, we would by such a division, strengthen our position against the subtle and continuous attack which the spread of education must make upon our system of Government.[14]

Lord Dufferin himself confided to Cross that 'The Muhammadans, whose goodwill I gained directly I arrived in this country, have also been very friendly and I am receiving addresses from the Muhammadan population of almost every town in India.'[15] And Cross had already informed him in the same strain, that 'this division of religious feeling is greatly to our advantage and I look for some good as the result of your Committee of Inquiry'.[16]

When the expansion of the legislative councils took place in 1892, the question of selecting members arose. Lord Lansdowne in his speech in the Imperial Legislative Council explained that there was no intention of setting up bodies possessing the attributes of parliamentary assemblies of the European type; what was desired was 'to obtain for these councils the services of members who will be in the truest sense representatives, but who will represent types and classes rather than areas and numbers'.[17]

Thus the principle of separate representation for religious communities and groups was introduced and India was treated as a conglomeration of varying interests, classes and cultures with no organic political unity — actual or potential.

The British conquest of India dealt a severe blow to its cultural unity and shattered its economic structure, social system and political organization. With the disruption of the social basis of culture, the culture itself was shaken to its foundations. New forces and factors were introduced into Indian life which added to the difficulties and rendered the task of rebuilding Indian society complicated.

It must be remembered that in the period before the British conquest, Indian society consisted of upper and lower classes. The upper class was composed of men of learning and of religion, pandits and maulavis, saints and Sufis, men of affairs and owners of landed property, military and civil servants of the state and zamindars; men of wealth, bankers, merchants, masters of guilds etc. The lower class was composed of artisans, craftsmen, peasants, workmen, etc. Devotion to learning and knowledge, service of the state and possession of property endowed men with a privileged status in society, but privilege carried with it the responsibility of political and cultural leadership. The builders of medieval civilization came from the ranks of these groups. The British conquest of India led to their ruination.

The introduction of western education created a revolution. The men of old learning lost their vital and organic relation with society. The new intelligentsia which arose in their place imbibed ideals which created a gulf between them and the mass of their countrymen. This uprooted class was long out of sympathy with the traditions of Indian life and looked upon the apish imitation of the west as the be-all and end-all of life.

The hereditary functionless property-owners, bereft of all spirit of adventure, became staunch supporters of the new political order, because it guaranteed them a life of ease, a life without ambition for power or fame. The men of wealth were ruined by the passing of business into the hands of the British merchants and by the deliberate policy of the British Government of strangling the trade and industry of the Indians, so that India might become a vast colony for the supply of raw materials to Great Britain, and in order that all competition between India and England might be eliminated.

But the worst effect of the conquest was to destroy the organic unity of the people. The several communities which inhabited the country had evolved a common way of life; they had become interdependent. While each group or caste followed its own pursuits, it was part of the society as a whole. By differentiation of functions, the groups avoided competition and conflict, and attained integrity of social structure. Religion did not hinder this cohesion. The British conquest broke up this structure. With the transfer of power and the concentration of authority and patronage in British hands, the mutual dependence of the communities lost its purpose and the groups began to drift apart. As every conqueror's success depends upon the weakness and disunity of the conquered, so the continuity of his power depends upon the perpetuation of this weakness and disunity. 'Divide and rule' is an ancient and well-tried maxim of statecraft. Thus the inner tendencies which had facilitated the overthrow of Indian society received a fresh impetus from the establishment of British rule, and the Indian people became a disorganized mass of humanity.

The British policy from the beginning of their rule in India was directed by a desire to maintain their power and supremacy. The chief instrument of this policy was to sharpen the lines of cleavage between group and group and community and community, by means of showing favours sometimes to the one and sometimes to the other, playing upon their greed for jobs, and arousing mutual jealousies between them. In their anxiety to obtain immediate relief from poverty and unemployment, the groups and communities played into the hands of the rulers.

The British conquest of India began in conflicts with the Muslim princes and governors. The Muslims were, therefore, regarded by them as their rivals for power and the principal object of their hostility. Everything was done to repress them, to destroy their influence and wealth. All doors to power and riches were shut to them. In the previous regime they had enjoyed grants of lands, for rendering service to the state in the army and in the land revenue department. Their learned men were employed in the judiciary and received royal patronage. Under the British, these sources of income and of advancement were much reduced. The Hindus were treated with special favour. Large tracts of land passed into their hands; government posts, such as were open to members of the subject race, were filled mainly by them; and they became apt and willing instruments of their masters. The Muslims sulked, and remained aloof and suspicious.

But the British never lost a chance of making use of them for their own purposes, when it was expedient. When Syed Ahmad of Bareilly began, about 1820, to preach holy war against the Sikhs, every facility was given to him and his followers to collect funds and raise men in British India to conduct the war against Maharaja Ranjit Singh, who was an avowed friend and ally of the British. But as soon as the Sikh power had been destroyed and Punjab had been annexed, the followers of Syed Ahmad were persecuted, hunted down, imprisoned, exiled, or executed.[18]

This trouble was not over when the Patriotic War of 1857 broke out, and the Muslims were held responsible for it. To the old suspicions new causes of wrath were added. Repression blazed with intense fury. But the more they were persecuted, the more disloyal and perverse they seemed to become, till at last widespread movements in Bengal, Bihar and the upper provinces opened the eyes of some of the British administrators, and the murder of Lord Mayo, the Governor-General, in 1873, shocked them into considering new ways of dealing with the problem.

The policy of repression had failed: the policy of reconciliation had to be given a trial.[19]

Indications of a change in the affections of the masters roused the jealousy of the Hindus. Their newspapers protested. They wrote long articles about the unwisdom of trying to reconcile the irreconcilables. But the die was cast. Besides, the mild, submissive and loyal Bengali Hindu was beginning to forget that he owed his rise to the favours of his rulers. He was beginning to protest against the iniquities of the white indigo planters, to claim the right of trying white criminals and offenders, to agitate for high posts and high emoluments.

In the Deccan, the smouldering embers of discontent were fanned into a flame by the activities of the Maharashtrian Brahmins of Pune. Conspiracies were discovered in 1862, insurrections were apprehended, and political dacoities actually took place. In the Punjab, Kukas (a Sikh sect), who were pre-eminently protectors of the cow, rose in rebellion under the leadership of their guru, Sant Ram Singh, but were put down with much severity in 1872. Guru Ram Singh along with a large number of followers were sentenced to life transportation.[20]

To counteract the rising tide of opposition, the government adopted a number of measures, whose underlying principle was the balancing of groups against one another. The old aristocratic class of taluqdars, zamindars and jagirdars was rallied by throwing open and restricting to them the membership of the newly constituted Legislative Council, and by conferring honorary magistracies upon them. Another measure was the reconstitution of the army. The pre-1857 army of the Bengal command had a preponderance of Brahmins and Rajputs, and the Madras and Bombay commands consisted of regiments of Tamils, Telugus and Marathas. After the Revolt, mixed regiments were broken up and class regiments were recruited. Brahmins and Rajputs began to disappear from the ranks; the number of Hindustanis, Tamils, Telugus and Marathas was reduced; Pathans, Gurkhas, Sikhs and Punjabi Muslims took their place.

But, of course, the trump political card to counter the growing influence of the Hindu intelligentsia was the reversal of the policy concerning the Muslims.

The Hindu educated class was now showing signs of intransigence. After the Ilbert Bill controversy they had founded political associations in different parts of the country. Hindu reform movements, such as the Arya Samaj, the Brahmo Samaj and the Theosophical Society were strengthening the sentiments of racial pride and fostering the desire for self-assertion. The passionate claim of the European to predominance was being answered by the passionate claim of the Indian to equality. The Indian National Congress had sprung into existence. Disaster seemed to loom large on the horizon for the British in India. In order to avert it, every endeavour had to be made to prevent the Muslims from co-operating with the Hindus.

W.W. Hunter (afterwards Sir William) sounded in *The Indian Musalmans*, published in 1870, the first note of warning. James O'Kinealy, the officer in charge of Wahabi prosecutions, wrote a series of articles drawing the attention of the government to the problem. He wrote, 'I attribute, the great hold which Wahabi doctrines have on the mass of the Muhammadan peasantry to our neglect of their education'. E.C. Bayley, Secretary to the Government of India in the Home Department, analysing the causes of Muslim discontent pointed to the need of reconciling them. Ultimately, 'from the highest official to the lowest (and no one has penetrated into the wrongs of the Musalmans more deeply than the present Viceroy) [Lord Mayo], there is now a firm conviction that we have failed in our duty to the Muhammadan subjects of the Queen'.

In a memorandum which the Governor-General Lord Mayo drew up, he laid down the following points in regard to the education of the Musalmans:

> (1) That a Muhammadan is not a gentleman until he has acquired a certain amount of Arabic and Urdu learning,
>
> (2) That he will not come to a Hindu School to be taught by a Hindu teacher,
>
> (3) That we must, therefore, give way somewhat to their national prejudices and allow to Arabic, Persian and Urdu a more prominent place in many of our schools and examination tests.
>
> In avowedly English schools established in Muhammadan districts the appointment of qualified Muhammadan English teachers might with advantage be encouraged . . . assistance might justly be given to Muhammadans by grants-in-aid to create schools of their own.

Lord Mayo hoped, 'a resolution of this kind would be justified by the circumstances of the case, and would have an excellent effect on the feelings of the Muhammadan population at this moment'.[21]

In the Fort William College, Calcutta, Indian languages received special encouragement. The language of the courts then was Persian, but Persian was confined to a small circle, and the language most commonly known in Northern India was Urdu. It was the language of polite speech among Hindus and Muslims and it was used both in prose and poetry, while Braj Bhasha was the medium of poetry. Gilchrist, the principal of the college in the opening years of the 19th century, sent for scholars of Urdu to compile textbooks. Thus a number of prose books were compiled in Urdu.

Then it struck the British that that was not enough. In the words of F.E. Keay:

> Urdu, however, had a vocabulary borrowed largely from the Persian and Arabic languages, which were specially connected with Muhammadanism. A literary language for Hindi speaking people which could commend itself more to Hindus was very desirable and the result was obtained by taking Urdu and expelling from it words of Persian or Arabic origin, and substituting for them words of Sanskrit or Hindi origin.[22]

Thus a new literary language was brought into existence which had not been used till 1800. By this clever device the seeds of the Urdu-Hindi controversy were sown. According to Sir G.A. Grierson, an authority on Indian languages:

> Unfortunately the most powerful English influence has during this period been on the side of Sanskritists. This Saskritized Hindi has been largely used by missionaries and translation of the Bible has been made into it. The few native writers who have stood up for the use of Hindi undefiled have had small success in the face of so potent an example of misguided effort.

The Hindi so inaugurated had little success till the war of 1857. Then the British hatred of Muslims and their culture attained extremes of ferocity. Persian had ceased to be the language of the courts in 1837. Urdu was still regarded as the *lingua franca* of India and the Delhi College which was established in 1829 to impart western education through the medium of Indian languages rendered a great service through translations of English scientific and philosophic works into Urdu. But the college was closed in 1857.

Now many British administrators took up the cause of Hindi which had made little progress so far. Articles were written in newspapers advocating its cause, grammars of the Hindi language were compiled, textbooks for schools were prepared, and demands that Hindi should be recognized as a court language were advanced. The Hindus swallowed the bait, although such an eminent writer as Bharatendu Harischandra recognized, as late as 1871, that 'the speech of the Agarwallas of both their men and women, is *Khari Boli* or Urdu'.

Sir George Campbell, Lieutenant-Governor of Bengal, Bihar and Orissa, announced in 1872 his resolve to stop the use of Urdu in the courts of Bihar and its teaching in the schools of the province. In 1882, the Hindus pressed the cause of Hindi before the Education Commission, but Hunter, the chairman, who was pro-Muslim, disregarded their request. In 1900, the Government of the United Provinces admitted the claim of the Hindus and sanctioned the use of Hindi language and letters in the courts. The 'unexpected' results followed. The gulf between Hindi and Urdu was widened.

Since 1900, modern Hindi has made great strides and developed a considerable literature, but this progress has been achieved at the expense of growing hostility to the language among the Muslims. Contrast with this the advance which medieval Hindi made during Mughal times, an advance more glorious and which was effected with the willing co-operation of the Muslims who enthusiastically adopted its cause and rendered invaluable services to it. Malik Mohammad Jaisi, Abdur Rahim Khan Khana, Tulsidas, Surdas, Meera and Keshavdas were the product of this period.

Over and above there were three other factors which disturbed the relations between Hindus and Muslims and fostered separatism among them. One is the revivalist movement. Hindus and Musalmans have both succumbed to it, in the fond belief that they could make the stream of time flow backwards and recapture the spirit, the customs and institutions of an age that is past. The Hindus were the first to come under the sway of revivalism. Western oriental scholars made them aware of a remote past which was pleasingly different from the present and the recent past, the stress of political influences raised in them the desire to improve their lot and they began to entertain the belief that they could do so in isolation from other Indian communities.

Thus it happened that from the first the movements of social, moral and religious reform, instead of following the footsteps of medieval pioneers like Kabir and Nanak, Raidas and Tukaram, began to seek inspiration from the ancient past. Raja Rammohun Roy, the first of these reformers, was a man of great learning, a scholar of Sanskrit and of Persian and Arabic, but he wanted the help of the British in cleaning the Augean stables of Hindu society. So he turned to the ideals enshrined in the *Vedas* and *Upanishads.* Dayanand Saraswati, the founder of the Arya Samaj, preached with the whole strength of his soul the gospel of 'back to the Vedas'. The Theosophical Society under the lead of Colonel Olcott, Madam Blavatsky and Mrs Besant, used Western scientific ideas to justify Hindu customs and institutions and traced them to the *Puranas* and other sacred texts.

On the other side, Hindu revivalism and Christian antagonism led to similar results among the Muslims. Wahabism of the second quarter of the 19th century was an endeavour to cut through the complexities of *Fiqah* and *Hadith* to the original word of the Quran. Sir Syed Ahmad Khan ridiculed the scholastic subtleties of the interpreters of the Quran and appealed for its rational and naturalistic understanding. Other reformers drew attention to the simplicity and austerity of the first followers and successors of the Prophet and denounced the softness and corruption of the later Muslims.

The efforts to revive the purity of their early religious life could not be confined within any narrow and arbitrary limits. Naturally, revivalism in religion led to a hankering for the revival of the entire way of life — social, economic, political and cultural, as it was lived in those ages when man seemed so pious, so righteous, so god-fearing.

The great national upheaval which commenced in India in 1905 produced leaders like Bal Gangadhar Tilak, Lajpat Rai and Aurobindo Ghosh. Tilak drew his inspiration from the history of Maratha achievements. He revived the Ganapati festival and Shivaji worship. Lajpat Rai was an eloquent propagator of the Arya Samaj doctrines, and Aurobindo Ghosh put the teachings of Shri Krishna in the hands of the revolutionary youth of Bengal.

Many young Muslims were also swept into the national movement. Among them was Mohammad Iqbal. In the beginning, Iqbal was a pure nationalist burning with zeal for the improvement of the whole Indian nation. He poured the volcanic fervour of a patriotic heart into the strangely fascinating moulds of Urdu poetry. His poems, *Naya Shivala, Hindustan Hamara, Rama,* moved equally the Hindus and the Muslims. His songs flew from house to house and village to village till they were on the tongues of vast multitudes in Northern India.

But then came a change. The first flush of national enthusiasm passed, and the phase of reflective thought supervened. And the currents of this thought came from two sources. Along one stream flowed the ideas that had their affiliations in the world of Islam. The philosophies of the great thinkers like ibn-Sina (Avicenna), ibn-Rushd (Averroes) and Ghazali, and the stirring ideas of Jamal Uddin Afghani and Sheikh Muhammad Abduh and the leaders of the Turkish revolution who urged the Muslims all over the world to shake off the domination of the West and revive the glories of the times when the conquering flood of Islam had overrun Asia and Europe. From India, on the other hand, came another kind of impulse. The nationalism of the partition of Bengal era laid emphasis upon the iniquity of breaking the unity of the educated class in Bengal, in other words the Hindu intelligentsia, and was, therefore, coloured with strong sentiments of Hindu resurgence. In this atmosphere, what happened may best be described in the words of Bipin Chandra Pal:

> If the Muslim leaders tried to wipe out the memories of the Sikhs and the Marathas, the Hindu nationalist leaders sought to revive them. It was no doubt a supreme psychological need of nationalist propaganda, and as far as these memories were revived to create the self confidence of a people

suffering from a state of hopeless and listless inertia they did only good and no harm . . . It gradually awoke, at least in a section of the nationalists, the foolish and suicidal ambition of once more reestablishing either a single Hindu state or a confederacy of Hindu states in India. Some people, thus, secretly interpreted Swaraj as Hindu Raj.[23]

Attracted by the first and repelled by the second, Iqbal placed all the resources of an imaginative and philosophic mind at the service of revivalism. For over a quarter of a century the spell of his magic verse and ardent discourse moved powerfully the thought of his community. The revivalism of the renaissance in Bengal had its natural reaction in promoting the revivalism of Islam. The growing estrangement of the communities received a powerful stimulus.

In the case of Iqbal, towards the end of his life, when the lengthening shadow of death began to fall upon him and the revivalist passion abated, the smouldering embers of the nationalism of his youth sparkled into life again. In his last moments, he appealed pathetically to his Hindu countrymen to obliterate the distinctions of 'self' and 'other', if they desired to end the slavery of the country, for in love alone is hidden the secret of freedom:

Banayen kya samajhkar
Shakhe-ghul pe ashiyan apna,
Vatan men ab kya rahna
Jo ho be-abru rahna![24]

[With what hope may we build our nest
On the flowered branch of the tree!
Oh, how can one live in the Motherland
If one has to live with dishonour!]

In the latter half of the 18th century, big landowners were created by the British after the English pattern, chiefly because it was far easier to deal with a few individuals than with a vast peasantry. The objective was to collect as much revenue and as speedily as possible. If a landowner failed at the stipulated time, he was immediately pushed out and another took his place. It was also considered necessary to create a class whose interests were identified with those of the British. The fear of revolt filled the minds of British officials in India and they referred to this repeatedly in their papers. Governor-General Lord William Bentinck said in 1829:

If security was wanting against extensive popular tumult or revolution, I should say that the Permanent Settlement, though a failure in many other respects, has this great advantage at least, of having created a vast body of rich landed proprietors deeply interested in the continuance of British Dominion and having complete command over the mass of the people.[25]

British rule thus consolidated itself by creating new classes and vested interests who were tied up with that rule and whose privileges depended on its continuance. There were the landowners and the princes, and there was a large number of subordinate members of the services in various departments of government, from the *patwari*, the village headman, upwards. The two essential branches of government were the revenue system and the police. At the head of both of these, in each district, was the Collector or District Magistrate, who was the linchpin of the administration. He functioned as an autocrat in his district, combining in himself executive, judicial, revenue and police functions. If there were any small Indian States adjoining the area under his control, he was also the British agent for them.[26]

The 19th century produced a galaxy of brilliant Hindus in Bengal, and yet there is hardly a single Muslim Bengali leader of any note who stands out there during this period. So far as the masses were concerned, there was hardly any appreciable difference between the Hindus and Muslims; they were indistinguishable in habits, ways of living, language, and their common poverty and misery. Indeed, nowhere in India were the religious and other differences between Hindus and Muslims of all classes so little marked as in Bengal.

All these early consequences of the British connection, and the various economic, social, intellectual and political movements that they gave rise to in Bengal, are noticeable elsewhere in India also, but in lesser and varying degrees. The break-up of the old feudal order and economy were less complete and more gradual elsewhere. In fact, that order rose in rebellion, and even when crushed, survived to some extent. The Muslims in upper India were culturally and economically far advanced compared to their co-religionists of Bengal, but even they kept aloof from Western education. The Hindus took this education more easily and were more influenced by Western ideas. The subordinate government services and the professions had far more Hindus than Muslims. Only in the Punjab was this difference less marked.

2. Syed Ahmad Khan and the Muslim Renaissance

Lord Ronaldshay has, in his *Heart of Aryavarta*, thus described this period:

> By the middle of the nineteenth century, a period of intellectual anarchy had set in which swept the rising generation before it like a craft which has escaped its moorings. Westernism became the fashion of the day and

> Westernism demanded of its votaries that they should cry down the civilisation of their own country. The more ardent their admiration for everything Western, the more vehement became their denunciation of everything Eastern. The ancient learning was despised, ancient customs and traditions were cast aside, ancient religion was decried as an outmoded superstition. The ancient foundation upon which the complex structure of Hindu society had been built was undermined and the new generation of iconoclasts found little enough with which to underpin the edifice which they were so recklessly depriving of its own foundation.[27]

Such conditions must naturally have very strongly distressed Swami Dayanand and generated a repugnance for Western civilization and a wholehearted desire to fall back on the great past of his own country. He felt it his mission to re-civilize India along lines that would combine the good in both East and West, but under the inspiration and guidance of the Vedic Dharma. He preached against idol-worship and hereditary caste. His Arya Samaj was, in fact, a Hindu protestant movement. The doctrines that he preached were nearer to Islam in its conception of fundamentals than the current popular forms of Hinduism against which his movement was a revolt.

While the Arya Samaj was thus making headway and bringing about a transformation in the religious and social outlook of the Hindus of Northern India, the Brahmo Samaj founded by Raja Rammohun Roy was working in Bengal. Its lines of work were, however, in some respects, different from those of the Arya Samaj. Its efforts were not only in the direction of social reform but that of a higher religious and moral synthesis.[28]

On the Muslim side arose an important reformer, Syed Ahmad Khan (1817-98). In Syed Ahmad's time, the Muslims of India took no interest in modern education and considered it a sin to learn English or Western science and philosophy. Being a man of great initiative and perseverance, although he never had the advantage of European education, he propounded successfully the view that Muslims in India would never be able to rise unless they adopted the current technique of educating youth as developed and understood in Europe and specially in England. He, therefore, founded the Anglo-Muhammadan College which later became the Aligarh Muslim University, a house of secular learning for Muslim youth. The 'Aligarh Movement' produced a progressive modernized Muslim 'gentleman' of India who combined in him the courtesy of old-world Islam, with a background of modern knowledge.

Like Dayanand, Syed Ahmad Khan was not English-educated, but unlike him, he had acquired a strong fascination for Western civilization and a yearning for securing for his community Western representative institutions. He could not dream of re-establishing Muslim political domination in India and, therefore, his first desire was to teach his community to bow to the inevitable and to reconcile them to the ways and methods of their rulers. He could read the signs of the time and could foresee the coming domination of Western civilization over his country. The one and only way in which he thought he could save his community from isolation and decay was to draw it into its vortex. Therefore, from the first to the last, he continued to concentrate on popularizing and organizing Western education in his community.

His efforts were successful because, in the meantime, a change had come over the government in its attitude towards the Muslims. The resurgence of the Hindu community had excited its fears and it had already begun to look about to discover a counterpoise to break its rising influence. Thus, though the motives were different, the schemes of the government and Syed Ahmad were converging towards the same centre. He went to England and there he studied at the Universities of Cambridge and Oxford. On his return, after preparing the ground for a few years, he founded the Muslim Anglo-Oriental College at Aligarh in 1874, the same year in which Swami Dayanand founded his Arya Samaj in Bombay. The M.A.O. College was started under government auspices; its grounds had been secured by the Lieutenant-Governor of the U.P.; its foundation was laid by the viceroy himself and the retiring viceroy made the first donation of ten thousand rupees.[29]

Syed Ahmad Khan and his associates had witnessed the futility of the attempts to drive out the British from India. To them 'independence' was not practical politics. The only practical objective was the betterment of the community under British dispensation. This required the removing of feelings of mutual suspicion and hatred between the Muslims and the British; convincing the British that the Muslims were not the inveterate enemies of their rule, provided it did not interfere with their religious beliefs and practices; and convincing them also that Islam did not enjoin hostility towards the Christian people who exercised power over them. For this purpose, a re-interpretation of religion was necessary.

It was also necessary for three other reasons. *Firstly*, the Christian missionaries had been merciless critics of Islam and had held up the religion to contumely and scorn. Their propaganda through books and pamphlets and public preaching and debates were reinforced through school and educational institutions and was proving effective. *Secondly*, the moral and social laxity and religious indifference of sections of the community, while giving to its rivals abundant grounds for attack, made it hard for its protagonists to defend it. To vindicate Islam, a fresh interpretation on modern lines was imperative to restore self-respect. *Thirdly*, the spread of Western ideas and expansion of Western education threatened to subvert the very basis of the Islamic faith. The challenge of modern science had to be met. Syed Ahmad Khan was not fully equipped with the philosophical and theological scholarship needed for the battle, but he possessed tremendous courage and a burning zeal. He took upon himself the triple task of religious reinterpretation, social reform, and education. But he did not lose sight of the fact that they were also the necessary and preliminary conditions for the rehabilitation of the community, economically and politically.

He was convinced that the only way of achieving satisfactory results in his polemics with the Christian missionaries and writers was to employ the weapons of debate of the West against them. If they attacked Islam in the name of reason and science, he should reply to them in the same coin. So, he sought to prove that the teachings of the Quran were wholly in accord with reason and nature. The principles on which he relied were:

(1) The teachings of the Quran are divinely inspired and eternal; therefore, faultless and binding in both word and meaning. No deviation from them is permissible.
(2) The *Hadith* comprise the sayings of the Prophet reported by narrators *(rawi)*, whose character and credibility as witnesses needed investigation. Hence they were subject to criticism and acceptable only after scrutiny.
(3) The authority of the *Hadith* was obligatory only in matters of religion, but was permissive in worldly affairs.
(4) The will of man is free.

On social, cultural and political matters, Syed Ahmad Khan's point of view was equally independent. The most controversial among the problems were those related to slavery, polygamy, *jihad*, interest and treatment of captives of war. His exposition made out that the Islamic view of these problems was both rational and in conformity with natural laws. He pointed out that Islam had laid down such liberal conditions for the treatment of slaves as to alter the very character of slavery; polygamy was allowed but only in rare circumstances; holy war was not justified against non-Muslims except when Islam was attacked; not every type of interest, but only the usury of pre-Islamic times was prohibited; men captured in war were not to be executed, nor women made slaves. Regarding the pious Caliphate, his view was that it ended with Imam Hasan on the expiry of thirty years after the death of the Prophet. It followed that the Sultan of Turkey had no justification to claim the title of Caliph, and that loyalty to the British rulers was obligatory.[30]

The most significant implication of his theology, so far as Indian society was concerned, was the repudiation of view held by some narrow-minded theologians that the Hindus were infidels *(kafirs)*. The enunciation of the principle that the laws of Islam were identical with the laws of nature and that all human beings were bound to obey them, led to the logical conclusion that the differences between those who avowed faith in the Quran and those who did not, was merely verbal and not real. Again, in so far as man was free to choose between good and evil, a Muslim was as much liable to go wrong as a non-Muslim and, in fact, both would have to answer for their deeds before the tribunal of God without the intercession of prophets and redeemers. Thus, Syed Ahmad Khan's liberalism opened wide the gates for social accommodation and co-ordination between Muslims, Hindus and Christians.

It is not surprising that, in his writings and speeches, Syed Ahmad Khan laid stress upon the unity of Hindus and the Muslims. In the speech which he delivered at Patna on 27 January 1883, he said:

> Now both of us, Hindus and Muslims, live on the air of India, drink the holy waters of the Ganga and Jamuna. We both feed upon the products of the Indian soil. We are together in life and death; living in India both of us have changed our blood, the colour of our bodies has become the same, our features have become similar; the Musalmans have adopted numerous Hindu customs; the Hindus have adopted many Muslim traits of conduct; we became so fused that we developed the new language of Urdu, which was neither our language nor that of the Hindus. Therefore if we accept that part of our lives which belongs to God, then undoubtedly, in consideration of the fact that we both belong to the same country, . . . both of us depend on our unity, mutual sympathy, and love, while our mutual disagreement, obstinacy and opposition and ill-feeling are sure to destroy us.

Further, he compared Hindus and Muslims to the two eyes of a beautiful bride whose face would be disfigured if either one or the other was injured.[31]

Addressing the Hindus of the Punjab, he asked complainingly why he was not regarded as a Hindu, and said, 'You have used the term Hindu for yourselves. This is not correct. For, in my opinion the word Hindu does not denote a particular religion, but on the contrary, everyone who lives in India has the right to call himself Hindu. I am, therefore, sorry that although I live in India, you do not consider me a Hindu.'[32]

In one of his last articles, he wrote: 'In our opinion just as the difference of religion which exists between the Mussalmans and the Hindus ought not to prevent social dealings, mutual affection, love and sympathy between them so also differences on political questions ought not to prevent social dealings, mutual affection and love and sympathy.'[33] He added, 'Undoubtedly, just by ignoring difference of religion we desire that there should be established between the Hindus and the Mussalmans friendship, affection, sympathy and brotherhood among them.'[34]

Syed Ahmad Khan was a believer in Hindu-Muslim political co-operation. It is a travesty of truth to regard him as the author of the theory that the Hindu and the Muslim were two separate nations. In fact, he was a supporter of Hindu-Muslim unity. For him there was no religious barrier in the way of this unity, no objection on the grounds of conscience. His differences with the Congress were based on considerations of political expediency alone.

Before the birth of the Indian National Congress, Syed Ahmad Khan had been a strong advocate of the association of all Indians in the councils of the government through their chosen representatives and also in the administration of district and local boards through their elected members. He had opposed the idea of special favours for the Muslims and had instead advised them to rely upon self-help. In his pamphlet, *Causes of the Indian Mutiny* (1863), he had stated that

> the original cause of the outbreak was the non-admission of a native as a member into the Legislative Council. I believe that this rebellion owes its origin to one great cause to which all others are but secondary branches, so to speak, of the parent stem. I do not found my belief on any speculative grounds or any favourite theory of my own. For centuries many able and thoughtful men have concurred in the views I am about to express.
>
> Most men, I believe, agree in thinking that it is indeed highly conducive to the welfare and prosperity of Government, essential to its stability, that the people should have a voice in its councils. It is from the voice of the people only that Government can learn whether its projects are likely to be well received. The voice of the people can alone check errors in the bud and warn us of the dangers before they burst upon, and destroy us.
>
> There is no reason, however, why the natives of the country should be excluded from the Legislative Councils, and here it is that you come upon the one great root of all this evil. Here is the origin of all the troubles that have befallen Hindustan . . . I do not wish to enter here into the question as to how the ignorant and uneducated nations of Hindustan could be allowed to share in the deliberations of the Legislative Council; or as to how they should be selected to form an assembly like the English Parliament. They are knotty points. All I wish to prove here is that such a step is not only advisable, but absolutely necessary and that the disturbances are due to the neglect of such a measure.[35]

In 1866, when he founded the British India Association, he exhorted Indians to try and secure proper representation of their interests in the Legislative Council. He told them that it would be folly and cowardice on their part if, out of fear of the government or the district officials, they refrained from demanding their proper representation. He was in favour of co-operation with the Hindus for securing better conditions. In fact, he went so far as to advise the Muslims that 'if the giving up of cow-slaughter will establish amity and friendliness among Hindus and Musalmans, then please do not sacrifice cows which is a thousand times better.'[36]

On the question of a common Indian nationality, he expressed very clear views. In his Patna speech on 27 January 1883, he said: 'Please remember that the Hindus and Muslims are religious terms. In fact, all the inhabitants of India whether Hindu, Muslim or Christian by virtue of the fact of their residence, constitute one nation. The time is past when merely on the ground of religion the inhabitants of one country could be regarded as members of two nations.'[37]

In his speech at Gurdaspur on 27 January 1884, he affirmed his faith in the unity of the two communities. He addressed the audience thus:

> We [Hindus and Muslims] should try to become one heart and soul and act in unison; if united we can support each other. If not, the effect of one against the other would tend to the destruction and downfall of both . . . .
>
> Hindu and Mahomedan brethren, do you people know any country other than Hindustan? Do you not inhabit the same land? Are you not burnt and buried on the same soil? Do you not tread the same ground and live upon the same soil? Remember that the words Hindu and Mahomedan are only meant for religious distinction — otherwise all persons, whether Hindu or Mahomedan, even the Christians who reside in this country, are all in this particular respect belonging to one and the same nation. Then all these different sects can only be described as one nation; they must each and all unite for the good of the country which is common to all.[38]

Syed Ahmad Khan had inaugurated a revolution in Muslim thought. He wanted to provide institutional foundations for his religious ideas and, therefore, he prepared a scheme for Muslim education which would satisfy their religious, cultural and material needs. So far as intellectual culture was concerned, Syed Ahmad Khan was not satisfied either with the traditional system of Muslim *madrasas*, or the modern teaching given in the colleges and universities established by government. About the *madrasas* he wrote: 'The Muslims have started in these days a number of institutions of old learning at Jaunpore, Aligarh, Kanpur, Saharanpur, Deoband, Delhi and Lahore, but I say, in all sincerity, that they are utterly useless and wholly futile.'[39]

The curriculum of the *madrasas* consisted of theology, language, logic, natural sciences, mathematics, astronomy and medicine. Syed Ahmad Khan's opinion was: 'Now the worthlessness of the Islamic sciences stands exposed and it has been abundantly clear that they do not comprise any useful knowledge, and this is the reason for their degradation and misery.'[40]

He enunciated the aims of education thus: (1) the strengthening of faith which required knowledge of religious truths, and the reconciliation of reason and tradition; (2) the training of character through establishing residential institutions and promoting healthy activities; and (3) the teaching of modern sciences up to the highest stage and evoking a rational outlook among students.

Under this scheme, the Aligarh Muhammadan Anglo-Oriental School was opened in 1874; it was raised to the status of a College in 1878. This venture served both a notice and a challenge to the Hindus and the British rulers that the Muslims in India were no more apathetic to the new education and its advantages.

The foundation of the Muhammadan Anglo-Oriental College marks a turning point in the life of Syed Ahmad Khan. He became so deeply concerned in its welfare and progress that all other interests were subordinated to it. Higher English education became for him the panacea for all the social and political ills of India. He deprecated political agitation for gaining political objectives. As the success of the College depended on the goodwill and co-operation of the community on the one hand, and the favour and support of the government on the other, he felt that the only way to secure both was by eschewing everything that offended the community or the government.

For Syed Ahmad Khan, economics and politics were thus inter-related and inter-dependent. He found that the Muslims as a community had economically sunk to a very low level; it was imperative that they should co-operate with the government and rebuild their economy with its help. Both economic advancement and political status depended on governmental favour. Herein lay the secret of Syed Ahmad Khan's anxiety to co-operate with the British rulers.

The tendency to isolate the Muslims from the main stream of Indian life, to lay stress upon particularistic Muslim interests and to deepen communal consciousness, were accentuated. The emphasis upon Muslim rights as distinct from the rights of the other communities was increased, either by ignoring the obligations of the Muslims towards their neighbours or by opposing their neighbours' claims even when they aimed at the general good.

Sir Syed's concept of loyalty to the government was based on his sense of the superiority of the British race and British institutions. His reverence for them has been characterized as bordering on 'almost cringing'.[41] The result was that he vehemently opposed any kind of dissent from the policies of government and advised his co-religionists to abstain from participating in any political movement. For him, politics was synonymous with criticism and disagreement, but loyalty, approval and support of government did not amount to politics.

Another fateful consequence of Sir Syed's unbounded admiration for the British was that he surrendered his own judgment to the opinions of his British mentors, such as Auckland Colvin, the Lieutenant-Governor of the United Provinces (now Uttar Pradesh), and Theodore Beck, the first Principal of the MAO College (1883-98). Under their inspiration he abandoned his earlier attitude on the Indian problem and made a speech in the Viceroy's Council (1883) condemning representative institutions on the ground that the Muslims would suffer under them, closely following the arguments of Beck. His antagonism to the Indian National Congress in 1887 emanated from the same source.[42]

3. Deoband and Indian Nationalism

Syed Ahmad Khan's views were challenged by two sections of Muslims: the bearers of traditional learning and the nationalist Muslims. While Syed Ahmad Khan became interested in the politics of the Muslims after the revolt of 1857, the *ulama* had been seized of them much earlier. The passing away of the Mughal Empire and the rise of British dominion was a terrible shock to them. Of the two pillars on which Islam seemed to rest, viz., faith and power, the latter had been lost. The question was whether the edifice of faith could endure without the support of the state. Syed Ahmad's answer was 'No'. But the answer of the *ulama* was that they could resuscitate Muslim political power. The *ulama* followers of Shah Waliyyul-lah undertook a dual task. Firstly, to purify the moral wellsprings of life, to lift the deadweight of legalistic dogma, and to bring the Muslims back to the pure teaching of the Quran and the shining example of the Prophet. In the second place, they tried to find a solution for the practical problems which the British conquest had created.

Shah Waliyyul-lah was born in 1703 and died in Delhi in 1762. The Mughal Empire had disintegrated; puppet kings, dissolute and degenerate, abject creatures of the growing British power, were the nominal rulers of the country. The religion of Islam was in danger of losing ground before the rising tide of Western influence, and in particular, the weakness of indigenous systems of law and legal procedure was compared with the English common law which had begun to assume prominence.

It was at this juncture that Waliyyul-lah arose to purify the faith of Islam, to make a working accord between Sufism and orthodoxy and to give a shining example of learning, piety, and philosophical profundity.

He was descendant of the great Omar-al-Faruq, the second Caliph of Islam, and had Central Asian Turkish blood in his veins. His father Abdur-Rahim, a mystic and theologian, was one of the compilers of the *Fatawa-e-Alamgiri,* and was the founder of the Rahimiyya Madrasa at Delhi. Waliyyul-lah had committed the Quran to memory by the age of 7; he completed his education at 15, and took charge of the Rahimiyya Madrasa at 17, on the death of his father. Between 1730 and 1732, he went on pilgrimage and stayed for some time in Hijaz. During the tumultuous span of his life, he saw seven kings of Delhi rise and fall. Shah Waliyyul-lah was the author of over a hundred tracts, monographs, and books. Some of his books are still studied at al-Azahar University in Cairo.

Waliyyul-lah was an original thinker, like al-Ghazali. He asserted the principle of independent interpretation of Islam. He opposed the slavery of mere imitation. A religious thinker of eminence, he was modern in his outlook and constantly urged that Muslim society should be purified and reconstructed.[43]

Shah Abdul Azia, son of Shah Waliyyul-lah, succeded his father. He issued a *fatwa* (decree) on the fall of Delhi in 1803 declaring that India was the land of war *(Dar-ul-Harb).* That decree made it incumbent on the Muslims either to declare a holy war *(jihad)* against the English conquerors or to migrate from India to Muslim lands.

In 1857, followers of Waliyyul-lah joined the revolt against the British. After the collapse of the Partiotic War the path of holy war was unthinkable.

A group of *ulama,* who had actively participated in the revolt and had organized a mass movement against British rule with its centre at Shamli in Muzaffarpur District of Uttar Pradesh, evaded the wrath of the government and established a school at Deoband in the Saharanpur District to train religious leaders for the community. Prominent among the founders were Muhammada Qasim Nanautavi (1837-80) and Rashid Ahmad Gangohi (1828-1905).

The school at Deoband was opened in 1867 with the following objectives:

(i) To exalt the word of God unaffected by any temptation, patronage, pressure and favour;
(ii) To extend contact with the Muslims in order to organize them for leading their lives according to the original Islamic principles;
(iii) To regard any co-operation with the government or the nobility as injurious to the interests of the school;
(iv) to follow firmly and strictly the teachings of Shah Waliyyul-lah;

(*v*) to avoid aristocratic and despotic ways and to work through co-operation and mutual consultation to set an example of democratic and republican methods of administration.

In education, the school at Deoband followed the curriculum prescribed by the *Dars-i-Nizami,* which concentrated on the traditional sciences. The school was wholly independent in finance and administration and its graduates had no openings in the departments of the government. It was a poor man's school and its teachers and pupils lived hard lives in most economical conditions. They wanted to keep their faith bright and did not care for worldly success. English education, Western culture and Western domination over Eastern land were hateful to them, and they longed to free Asian countries in order to bring about the moral and religious regeneration of the Muslim community.

Though the school was immediately concerned with the problem of education and character, the question of 'society and state' were as important for them as those of 'belief and practice' of the individual. The happenings in India and the world of Islam naturally demanded their attention. The Indigo Riots of 1859-60, the Deccan Riots of 1876, the famines and the deteriorating conditions of peasants and village artisans directly affected them. The political activity which started in Bengal and spread all over India and especially the agitation provoked by the Ilbert Bill in 1883, had aroused widespread anti-British feelings.

At the same time, events overseas were spreading dismay among the Muslims all over the world. The awakening of Muslims in Egypt, Turkey, West Asia, North Africa, Iran, had its repercussion in India. Jamal-al-Din Afghani's visit had stirred up the young Muslim scholars. His call to free Asia from the yoke of Western culture and political supremacy found an echo in many hearts.

The Deoband School was in agreement with Jamal-al-Din Afghani's views. Therefore, when in 1885 the Indian National Congress was founded to unite the people of India for political purposes, the school responded positively. Rashid Ahmad Gangohi, who was the head of the Deoband School, defined the attitude of the school. He held that, in accordance with the decree of Shah Abdul Azia, India was *Dar-ul-Harb* and, therefore, it was incumbent upon Muslims to drive the British out of the country.

On the question of co-operation in this task with the Hindus, Rashid Ahmad Gangohi expressed the opinion that for the fulfilment of national aims in temporal affairs, it was permissible, according to the Shariat, for Muslims to enter into agreement with Hindus. Hence he advised the community to co-operate with the Indian National Congress in its activities though he himself did not join it because he believed in the complete independence of India, unlike the Congress of those days. The declared opinion of the learned head of the Deoband School was unambiguous that the concept of nationality based upon the unity of all religious groups did not contravene the Islamic principle.

This decision created a gulf between Deoband and Aligarh. The pro-British attitude of Syed Ahmad Khan on the revolt of Arabi Pasha in 1881, Jamal-al-Din Afghani's condemnation of Syed Ahmad Khan's religious and political views, and lastly the support which Syed Ahmad Khan gave to the western powers in the Greco-Turkish war of 1897, against the Turks, widened the gulf between the principal centres of Muslim opinion in India. In spite of the attempts of Muhsin-ul-Mulk, it was not possible to bring the two together so that the Deobandi *ulama*, even in times of great communal dissensions, continued to uphold the cause of national solidarity and Indian independence.[44]

From amongst the Deoband *ulama* there arose another figure of entirely different character. Ubaydul-lah Sindhi, the spiritual descendant of Shah Waliyyul-lah, who was born in 1872 and died in 1944. Originally a Sikh, he ran away from home and went to Sindh, accepted Islam and returned for theological studies to Deoband at the age of 45. He travelled widely for 15 years in Afghanistan, Russia, Turkey and Hijaz. He was an ardent follower of Shah Waliyyul-lah and was both a political leader and an Islamic thinker. Because of his Sikh extraction, he understood clearly the affinities between the doctrine of *wahdat al-wujud* (unity of existence) and the Vedantic principle of pantheism. He always worked for a better understanding between Hindus and Muslims in India and had a great respect for the best in Hinduism. The principles for which he stood may be summarized as follows:

(1) There is no such thing as an Indian race. India is the home of many people and races. They must all live peacefully together.
(2) When certain people live in a compact geographical area, speak one language and create one culture, they are called one nation.
(3) As India is multi-racial and multi-lingual, each race and community has a right to develop its own language and culture. After such development, all these independent units must combine to form one political unit. This unit, the state of India, will be multi-racial. Such a unified state must possess the following characteristics:

(a) It should be a democracy with adult franchise which should encou age indigenous industries. The economic position of the workers should be improved. The working community should have equal rights with other sections. Agriculture should be aided. Old social forms must be changed and new forms evolved.

(b) All religions have the same end; the religions to be found in India have a unity of purpose. One example of this is the Islamic principle of *wahdat al-wujud* which is similar to vedanta. All religions in India should seek unity of purpose and factional tendencies should be avoided.

According to A.A.A. Fyzee, 'Ubaydul-lah Sindhi was one of the foremost Islamic thinkers and political leaders of the 20th century'. Shah Waliyyul-lah and Ubaydul-lah Sindhi represent the vanguard among the *ulamas* of their time. Their work has been an inspiration to the modernist school in India.[45]

The Deoband School welcomed the formation of the Indian National Congress and when, in 1888, Sir Syed Ahmad Khan, under the influence of his British mentors, counselled the Muslims to refrain from joining the Congress, the Deoband *ulama* condemned Sir Syed's attitude and issued a religious *fatwa* against Sir Syed's organization, the Patriotic Association, as well as the Muhammadan Anglo-Oriental Association whose secretary and moving spirit was Principal Beck of Aligarh College. The attempts of Sir Syed to obtain the co-operation of the *ulama* in his plans were rejected by the authorities of Deoband as the two differed widely in their political attitude.

Till the end of the 19th century, Deoband lay low for government kept it under careful watch. It was eking out an existence in extremely hard conditions — lack of funds was the greatest worry, for those in a position to help were afraid of the frowns of the powers that be, yet the school stuck courageously to its ideals and did not falter in its chosen path.

The sacrifices which the leaders of the Deoband School and the Jamiat made in the cause of freedom form a glorious chapter in the history of the freedom movement. Their intense devotion to the cause was manifest in their daily lives; there was no sacrifice which they did not or were not prepared to offer, financial or otherwise. They chose to spend their lives, from boyhood to death, eking out existence on a miserable pittance, stinting on creature comforts and, on many occasions, being obliged to put up with semi-starvation. They spent years in exile — voluntary or otherwise, or in British prisons — abused, maltreated, denied ordinary conveniences of life, and put on the poorest prison rations.

Among the earlier entrants to the school was Mahmud-al Hasan who spent practically all his life in the school, first as a pupil and then as a teacher and principal of the institution. He was born in 1851 at Bareilly and was in Meerut with his father when the Patriotic War of 1857 broke out. At home he heard the stories of the heroic exploits of the patriots as well as the gruesome tales of British atrocities. He witnessed the widespread ruin of the upper-class Muslims of northern India and the iron entered into his soul.

Mahmud-al-Hasan joined the Deoband School at the age of 15 and after completing the course of studies became a teacher there in 1875-6. He had studied under such accomplished scholars and affectionate teachers as Muhammad Qasim Nanautavi and Rashid Ahmad Gangohi. He imbibed from them learning, deep piety and love of freedom.

In 1887-8 he rose to the position of the head of the school. Early in life he had made up his mind about his mission which he pursued till his last day. His object was the liberation of India. In 1905 he began to promote his plans actively, and started his work on two fronts — within the country and abroad. The two were to rise simultaneously in armed revolt and drive the British out of India.

Within India, the mission had its headquarters at Deoband and branches in Delhi, Dinapur, Amrot, Karanji Kheda and Chakwal. Outside India, Yaghistan, a small independent principality on the north-western frontier, was chosen as the centre of activity. The followers of Syed Ahmad Shahhid and Maulavis Inayat Ali and Sharafat Ali who still continued to carry on *jihad* against the British supported the nucleus of the armed forces. Haji Turang Zai was appointed their leader. The neighbouring tribes and men and volunteers from India were expected to join them. It was hoped that the Amir of Afghanistan would lend his support.

The armed rising was not planned as a purely Muslim affair. From Punjab the Sikhs and from Bengal members of the revolutionary party were invited to co-operate. A house was taken on rent to accommodate them near Mahmud-al-Hasan's residence in Deoband. These preparations were carried out in secret. Ubaydul-lah Sindhi worked at Deoband and organized the Jamiat-ul-Ansar. Later he was sent to Delhi where the school, Nazarat-ul-Masrif, was established with Hakim Ajmal Khan and Vaqaral Mulk of Aligarh as patrons.

The year 1911 was critical in the history of the Indian Muslims. The partition of Bengal was revised, the capital of India was transferred from Calcutta to Delhi. The Balkan War was started with a revolt by the Christian provinces against the Ottoman Empire. This was immediately followed by the First World War in which Turkey fought in alliance with Germany against Britain and her allies. The frontier Muslim province of Sinkiang in China declared war against Britain.

Mahmud-al-Hasan was greatly excited by these developments and he thought that the time had come for armed action against the British. A plan was prepared and letters inscribed on silk were circulated to all the participants in the plan. Ubaydul-lah was sent to Afghanistan and he planned to proceed to the frontier himself. Unfortunately for the scheme, Amir Habib Ullah could not be persuaded to give his support. On the contrary, he kept the Government of India informed of the activities of the Indian revolutionaries and later of the Indo-German mission which came to Kabul to seek his intervention on the side of the Central powers. Raja Mahendra Pratap and Barkat Ullah were members of the mission who remained in Kabul after the departure of the Germans, to continue their efforts for the liberation of India.

At this juncture, Mahmud-al-Hasan came to know that the Government of India had decided to arrest him. With the help of Dr M.A. Ansari of Delhi, he hastily left India for Mecca in 1916. On arrival in Mecca he met Ghalib Pasha who was then the Turkish governor of Hejaz and induced him to give him a letter promising full sympathy and support to the Indian revolt against the British. This letter was smuggled into India and copies of it were distributed.

When, some time later, Anwar Pasha, the Defence Minister of Turkey, and Jamal Pasha, the commander of the southern forces, arrived in Mecca, he asked them to make arrangements for his journey to the Indian frontier, as well as to Constantinople. But, as misfortune would have it, Sharif Husain of Mecca, instigated by the British, rose in revolt against the Ottoman Empire. Mahmud-al-Hasan with Husain Ahmad Madni and two other companions were handed over to the British who exiled them to Malta, where they were kept prisoners.[46]

On the termination of the war, Madni and his companions were taken to Bombay and released in January 1920. After disembarking, he immediately proceeded to the office of the Khilafat Committee and threw himself heart and soul into the movement, in spite of his ailments and advanced age. He visited Aligarh and appealed to the staff and students of the university to boycott the government-aided institution and join the new national university, Jamia Millia Islamia, which he helped to establish.

He presided over the conference of the Jamiat-ul-Ulama at Delhi and, in winding it up on 21 November 1921, gave expression to his views on Indian politics. He called upon the religious leaders of the Muslims to continue their fight for the restoration of Muslim authority over their holy lands and for the liberation of India from the imperialist yoke. He advised them to maintain and strengthen the ties of unity and social cohesion between the communities in these words:

> You should know if the contrary conditions [disunity] prevailed they will make the freedom of India unattainable for all time. The iron claws of the bureaucratic government will grip closer every day and whatever dim imprints of Islamic influence have remained will be wiped off the page of existence, like a letter which is crossed out. Therefore, if the two communities of India and including the martial race of the Sikhs — all the three, will live in friendship and peace, then I cannot understand how a fourth community — however strong it may be, can defeat the common ideals of the Indian by its violence and despotic rule.[47]

Five hundred scholars *(ulama)* assembled at the conference signed the decree calling upon the Muslims to non-cooperate with the government and withdraw from all civil and military services.

Mahmud-al-Hasan died shortly after the conference. His mantle fell upon the worthy shoulders of his favourite pupil, Husain Ahmad Madni, who had been his companion in Malta, and who shared his ideas on Islamic revival and Indian independence.

Husain Ahmad Madni (1879-1957) had been the favourite pupil of Mahmud-al-Hasan at Deoband. But before he could complete the course at the school his father decided to migrate to Mecca in 1889-90. The whole family consequently left for Mecca. Husain Ahmad spent the next sixteen years of his life mainly in Hejaz, with occasional visits to India. When in 1916 Mahmud-al-Hasan arrived in Mecca, Husain Ahmad, who had till then taken no interest in politics, became an enthusiastic supporter of the mission for India's liberation. The faithful disciple became the confidant and counsellor of his master and accompanied him in his enforced exile and incarceration in Malta. On release, he became a zealous worker in the Khilafat and Congress movements.

Husain Ahmad had entered the field of politics at the instance of his revered teacher and leader Mahmud-al-Hasan. But his politics was not emotional. His was an intellectual approach to the problems of society and state. This is amply proved by his writings on India's politics and economics and on international affairs. On religious matters his knowledge was both in depth and breadth extraordinary. He had gathered a vast amount of information on the political and economic history of India and on the international relations of the Western powers with Islamic countries. There is no doubt that his residence in Mecca, the hub of the Muslim world, for over a decade and half and his incarceration in Malta for nearly five years, brought him into contact with many men from Muslim countries as well as Europeans — Germans, Austrians, Italians and others, from whom he learnt a great deal about international affairs.

As a Muslim scholar he was convinced that the Quran — the word of God, and *Hadith* — the record of the Prophet's sayings and deeds, offered complete guidance in the two realms of human living. It followed that religion was an all-pervasive, all-comprehensive rule of life and, therefore, not only matters of belief, worship and morals ought to be under its direction, but also matters relating to social, economic, political and cultural life. There can be no discord between eternal and temporal affairs.

A true Muslim, then, is one who seeks to obey the divine will in thought, word and deed, and refuses to obey any authority which commands to the contrary. A necessary consequence of this principle is that a Muslim cannot mortgage his freedom to any earthly ruler, and in no circumstances to an alien whose law and government aim at the ruin of Islamic ideals and ways of living. It was the religious duty of every Muslim, therefore, to strive to the utmost of his capacity to overthrow the British dominion over India. Numerous passages may be quoted in which Muslims are exhorted to rise against the foreign rulers and, in co-operation with the other Indian communities, to end their slavery.

This appeal was accompanied by an elaborate justification for revolt. In the first volume of his autobiography, out of 336 pages over 200 are devoted to an examination of the destructive consequences of British imperialism in India. Among these he mentioned:

(1) the humiliation of the people by racial and national discrimination and exclusion from higher services;
(2) the economic ruin of the country through land revenue administration, and disruption of industry and trade;
(3) the misconceived judicial system which encourages litigation and corruption and makes justice too dilatory and too expensive;
(4) the elimination of Indians from the processes of law-making; and
(5) the moral deterioration of the people as an effect of foreign domination.

In the second volume of the work, considerable space is devoted to an account of the breaches of solemn agreements and of other treacheries of Western powers in their dealings with the Muslim countries, especially the Ottoman Empire. It was pointed out that, among these powers, the record of the British is the blackest.

From these facts the conclusion is inevitable; the British are the most inveterate enemies of Islam, and the Muslims owe it to themselves and their future existence that they should destroy the British Empire which is a menace to all the people of Asia and Africa.[46]

But the redemption of the Muslims of the world, according to Madni, depended upon the liberation of India. It was to secure this that a movement was started based on the teachings of Shah Waliyyul-lah in the early 19th century which continued in the form of the revolt of 1857.

But the ruthless repression following the revolt slowed its tempo, and a fresh turn had to be given to the struggle. This was done by the Indian National Congress, which realized at the very start the supreme need of communal unity.

Husain Ahmad recognized that the Congress was the chief instrument for seizing power, and in spite of provocations and differences, he never wavered in his decision to support the organization, especially after the Congress declaration that India's goal was complete independence. He held that the people of India, irrespective of religious differences, ought to form a united nation in order to secure independence and pursue policies of common welfare. In a speech he stated that the modern nations were constituted on the principle of territoriality and not race or religion.

Iqbal regarded the statement as an attack upon his theory that the only basis of nationality *(qaum)* was religion, and that nationality founded upon race, language, territory, was accursed. In his view, territorial nationality was an unislamic concept. He published an article which argued that neither Arabic philosophy nor Islamic literature supported Madni's contention. He made uncomplimentary remarks on his learning, and ridiculed him in verse.

Hussain Ahmad was pressed to write a rejoinder, because Iqbal's views were likely to do a great deal of damage to the nationalist cause. This is contained in a monograph entitled 'United Nationality and Islam' *(Mutahadda Qauimyat aur Islam)*.[49] It discusses with great scholarship two aspects of the problem (1) the meaning and definition of the term *qaum* and its distinction from *millat*; and (2) the views of the Quran, *Hadith* and Islamic history on the problem.

Ahmad refers to the Arabic lexicons of early, middle and recent times to prove that the word *qaum*, apart from other meanings, denotes any group of men and women bound together in the pursuit of a common purpose, not necessarily religious.

The usage of the Quran confirms this meaning, for it speaks of the common nationality of the prophets of God and their unbelieving people, e.g., Muhammad and the Quraish. The Quran also contemplates a community consisting of groups following different religions, e.g. the followers of Ad and Faraun.

The example of the Prophet himself, however, is the most convincing argument in favour of this interpretation. For in the fourteenth year of his prophethood Muhammad united the Jewish tribes of Medina with his Muslim followers by a solemn covenant to fight against the pagan Arabs who were preparing to attack Medina. The terms of the agreement were that each party would be free to follow its own religion, but in all other matters the Muslims and the Jews would be regarded as one community.

The term *millat* has a different connotation. It applies only to the community of faith *(iman)* and canonical law *(Sharia)*. It applies to every religious community, whatever the common religion.

Accordingly it follows that Islam not only does not raise any obstruction to the formation of a united nationality with non-Muslims, it positively encourages it. Other considerations lend strong support to this consummation. The Hindus and Muslims are mostly decendants from the same race. Their residence in the same country for centuries together has moulded their common attitudes and ways of living. They speak common languages and share common historical traditions. They built together a common culture — literature, fine arts and music, while retaining their individual faith and personal law. They co-operate in numerous walks of life in villages and towns, in economic affairs, in schools and colleges, in district boards, municipalities, and provincial legislatures. In short, this common nationality may be defined in the following words:

> By united nationality I mean the same type of united nationality which was founded by the Prophet, for whom be praise and on whom be peace, among the people of Medina. That is, I desire that the inhabitants of India — whatever their religion, ought in their capacity as Indians and residents of one country to become one nation. . . . No one should obstruct the other in any religious matter. On the other hand, all the people inhabiting India ought to be free in the profession of their religious beliefs, ideals and worship. They should be free in following their religious customs, ritual and precepts, and in so far as their religion permitted in the propagation of their religion in a peaceful manner.[50]

4. Muslim Attitudes towards the Congress

Western education brought with it a yearning for participation in the democratization of the country and for the development of Western political institutions. This yearning continued to grow till it began to take the shape of an all-India demand and all-India organization. The government was aware of this yearning and was extremely uncomfortable about it. The government lacked sufficient means in those days to gauge its real depth and intensity and it wanted to get at the truth. In 1885, the psychological moment arrived, when actual attempts began to be made for the attainment of self-rule.

The idea began to take the form of an All India Social Organization to be organized under the presidentship of the viceroy. The viceroy, when approached, thought otherwise. He thought that an All India Organization of the Western educated class would be a better barometer of real

Indian feeling if left free from all official links and control. Therefore, he advised the organization of an independent association which might serve in India the purpose which Her Majesty's opposition served in the British Parliament. As a consequence, in 1885, at Bombay, a great gathering met which adopted the name and laid the foundation of the Indian National Congress.

It was only 72 delegates that met and they represented only 27 districts of India out of 250; but it was in the idea they represented and the feeling they embodied that the real importance of the movement lay. The soul of India was yearning to find some avenue of self-expression and self-assertion and the Indian National Congress afforded her such an opportunity. At the time itself, the movement was taken as a portent, and the people and the Government were both struck by the phenomenon. The tone of the correspondent of the *Times* gives an idea of the feelings with which this new organization was received at the time:

> This last week, the Bombay leaders have again given proof of their organising powers. They have brought together a National Congress composed of delegates from every political society of any importance throughout the country. The whole of India was represented from Bombay to Calcutta, Madras to Lahore. For the first time, perhaps, since the world began the Indians as a nation met together. Its congeries of races, its diversity of castes, all seemed to find common ground in their political aspirations.

It was indeed for the first time in Indian history that India was acting as a political unit, not through her kings but through her people. The formative stage had ended with the kings. Political unity had now become an accomplished fact. Henceforward the responsibility for her life and growth would rest wholly on her people. It was this aspect of the movement, the claim of the people of India to come into their own, that excited the fears and roused the indignation of her foreign rulers. And it was this which constituted an irresistible appeal for her own people, and drew them towards it as no other secular movement had drawn them together. The real nature of the movement and the challenge that was potential in it was apparent and unmistakable.[51]

The *Times* correspondent tried to play upon the pride of the Muslims and deflect their latent hostility from the British to their Hindu countrymen:

> Only one great race was conspicuous by its absence; the Mohammedans of India were not there, they remained steadfast in their habitual separation. They certainly do not yield to either Hindu or Parsi in their capacity for development. But they persistently refuse to act in common with the rest of the Indian subjects of the Queen Empress. The reason is not hard to find.

They cannot forget that less than four centuries ago, they were the dominant race while their present rivals in progress only counted as so many tax-paying units which contributed, each his mite, to swell the glory of the Islam.

K.T. Telang, the Secretary of the Reception Committee, replied in a letter to the newspaper:

The first point is in reference to your remark that the Mohammedans of India were conspicuous by their absence at the Congress. Although it must be admitted that the Mohammedan community was not adequately represented at our meeting, your remark is not an altogether accurate one. Two leading Mohammedan gentlemen did attend the Congress, viz., R.N. Sayani and A.N. Dharamsi. Both of these gentlemen are graduates of the University and attorneys of standing at the High Court of Bombay. R.N. Sayani held the office of Sheriff of Bombay last year, was a Member of the Khoja Law Commission appointed by Government some years ago and had for many years past been a member of the Municipal Corporation and Town Council of Bombay. Dharamsi is also a member of the Municipal Corporation of Bombay. Further, Badruddin Tyabji, a member of the Legislative Council at Bombay and Kamruddin Tyabji would have attended the Congress had they not been absent from Bombay at the time the Congress was sitting. Badruddin is the Chairman of the Managing Committee, Bombay Presidency Association, which, in concert with the Poona Sarvajanik Sabha convened the Congress.[52]

In the second Congress 55, and in the third 76 Muslims attended as delegates. Badruddin Tyabji was President of the third session held at Madras which made the famous safeguard clauses, regarding the protection of minorities, a part of the Congress Constitution. Syed Ahmad Khan abstained from commenting on the Congress for three years, but on the occasion of the fourth session, he openly declared himself against the Congress movement. A Mohammedan Educational Conference was held at Lucknow during Christmas week in 1887. There, at a special meeting of delegates, Syed Ahmad Khan spoke against Muslims joining the Congress. In August 1888, the so-called Patriotic Association was formed in opposition to the Congress.

The reasons which influenced Sir Syed Ahmad Khan to withhold support to the Congress have thus been described by one of his friends, Nawab Mushtaq Husain:

Syed Ahmad Khan closely watched the movement for three years. But when he found that it was not moderate or reasonable in its aspirations, nor sufficiently careful about interests of the minorities, and very far from respectful or fair in its tone as regards its relations with the Government of the country or the ruling race, he did not hesitate to warn his excitable co-religionists that participated in the agitation such as the Congress advocated, by precept and example, was against their best interest.[53]

Syed Ahmad Khan kept his judgment in suspense for three long years during which government itself was undecided about its attitude towards the movement and finally declared himself against it at the same time as the attitude of the government became openly antagonistic. His opposition supplied a new plank to the government, which henceforward began to justify its control of Indian affairs on the ground of its being the real champion of Indian minorities.

Syed Ahmad Khan argued that independence was no more than a wild dream, for British rule was too powerful to be shaken easily. Therefore, it was bad tactics to annoy the Government by exposing its mistakes and spreading disaffection. Theodore Beck, who was at once the confidant and adviser of Syed Ahmad Khan, made this clear in a letter to Badruddin Tyabji on 7 May 1888:

> Our chief objection to the National Congress is one more fundamental than any objection to any specific proposal. We believe that its methods — holding public meetings, showing the ills of the people and circulating pamphlets like the one printed at the end of the Congress report, etc., — will sooner or later cause a mutiny among the inhabitants of these provinces and the Punjab. If this be joined with a Frontier War, it will be a disastrous affair.

And he added:

> In the first place, the whole Mohammedan community of Upper India is distressingly poor. If they are led to believe, as they are already inclined to do, that this is due to the British Government, they will be ready to rise. They feel passionately the loss of their glory. The old Imperial buildings of Delhi and Agra are a living sign of their degradation. The older people of Delhi remember the last Emperor of the House of Timour. Add to this their religious fanaticism, which is not dead. The cry of Jehad is heard now and again. And add, moreover, that the people are really excitable and love a fight, as we saw at Delhi and Etawah — and we have the gravest reasons that if this kind of agitation spreads, the whole of Upper India may one day be aflame. Personally I should dislike this for two causes: first, because I have no desire to have my throat cut, and secondly, because the cause I have given my life to, would be hopelessly ruined, and the Mohammedans would fall perhaps never to rise again. We, therefore, do not like agitation of any sort.[54]

In another letter, he explains his views, which were also the views of Syed Ahmad Khan, regarding the future of India. He writes:

> The one thing of importance in India is the stability of the Government; for then we have every reason to expect the gradual progress of education and prosperity. I want to see the people enjoying a share in the Government of the country, but not by means of a representative system, which I believe is unadapted to India, but by means of occupying high positions in the bureaucracy.[55]

A second Muslim group which supported the Congress, consisted of educated Muslims, most of whom belonged to the Bombay and Madras Presidencies. Their outlook was nationalist in the modern sense of the term. They supported the political advancement of India along democratic lines, and they were deeply devoted to the cause of Hindu-Muslim unity. For them, there was no conflict between their faith in Islam and their love for India.

Badruddin Tyabji (1844-1906) was, in the early days of the Congress, one of the foremost nationalist leaders. He belonged to an Arab family, which came to India and settled down in Bombay. In early life, he was educated in a Muslim *madrasa*, and then in the Elphinstone Institute at Bombay. He began to take a lively interest in politics when, in 1878, Lord Lytton promulgated the Vernacular Press Act and suggested to the Secretary of State for India, Lord Salisbury, that Indians should be excluded from the Covenanted Services. Badruddin reacted vehemently against this. The Ilbert Bill controversy of 1883 brought him to the fight for the Indian cause. He was then rapidly climbing upwards in his profession as a barrister. He had been already appointed an additional member of the Legislative Council of Bombay, where by his eloquence and advocacy he gained great popularity among the people. On 31 January 1885, the Bombay Presidency Association was established, and he gave expression to his political opinions in the following words:

> It is, I think, with the nations as with individuals that with the growth of political life new aspirations arise, and those aspirations require an organisation to give them due expression and the organisation in its turn watches, regulates, develops, and directs national aspirations. . . . We have awakened to a sense of our political rights, and the distinctions of race, colour and creed, which have so long and unfavourably divided us, have at last disappeared under the softening and enlightening influence of education.[56]

Along with Kashinath Trimbak Telang and Pherozeshah Mehta, Badruddin Tyabji was the recognized leader of all public movements in Bombay. As Sir H.P. Mody points out, 'the brilliant triumvirate were carrying on a ceaseless campaign for reforms in every branch of the administration. From various platforms and through diverse organizations they laboured to promote the public good in every sphere of public life.'[57]

When the Indian National Congress met in Bombay in December 1885, Tyabji not only supported the Congress but took pains to repudiate the charge of the London *Times* that the Muslims of Bombay had kept aloof. In a speech at the Bombay Presidency Association, he said, 'I assure you of my perfect sympathy with the movement, and the sympathies of my co-religionists at large. The English *Times*, in writing about the movement, mis-stated that the Muhammedan community refrained from having anything to do with it. This I deny'.[58] Although it is a fact that, for some reasons, Tyabji was unable to attend the session, Rahmatullah Sayani and Abdullah Dharamsi, two equally influential Muslim leaders of Bombay, were present. And Tyabji reaffirmed his views thus: 'The Muhammedans have their Anjuman-e-Islam to represent to Government the wants of the community, and to urge them to adopt measures for its general improvement, but I deny that they are not one with their countrymen of other creeds and persuasions in the movement for the political improvement of their country.'[59]

Feelers were thrown out by the Governor of Bombay, Lord Reay, to dissuade the Muslims from supporting the Congress. Lord Dufferin, who had already had a very satisfactory interview with Syed Ahmad Khan, personally tried to influence Badruddin Tyabji also. The viceroy met Tyabji, presented to him a group photograph of himself and his family, and professed great admiration and friendship for the Muslims, whom, as British Ambassador in Turkey, he had come to love. But the effort of the viceroy had no effect. Badruddin confessed, 'I am much afraid of donees bringing presents'.[60] Syed Amir Ali also tried to win him over. As secretary of the Muhammedan Association of Calcutta, he invited him to join the proposed Muhammedan Political Conference. Tyabji declined the invitation saying:

> You are no doubt aware that I have always been of opinion that in regard to political questions at large, the Muhammedans should make a common cause with their fellow countrymen of other creeds and persuasions, and I cannot help deprecating any disunion on such questions between ourselves and the Hindus and Parsees. On this ground I have highly regretted the abstention of the Mussalmans of Calcutta from the National Congress held both in Bombay and Calcutta. If, therefore, the proposed Muhammedan Conference is started simply as a rival to the National Congress, I should entirely oppose it, as it seems to me that the proper course is to join the Congress and take part in its deliberations, from our peculiar circumstances.[61]

In a subsequent letter, too, Badruddin Tyabji reiterated his political views in these words: 'My own views are that in regard to general political questions affecting India as a whole, it is the duty of all educated and public-spirited citizens to work together, irrespective of their caste, colour or creed.'[62]

In 1887, the Indian National Congress held its session at Madras and elected Badruddin Tyabji as President and he paid no attention either to the displeasure of the government or the frowns of Syed Ahmad Khan and Syed Ameer Ali. In his presidential address, he laid stress on the desirability of all communities of India joining together 'in their efforts to obtain those great general reforms, those great rights which are for the common benefit of us all, and which I feel assured have only to be earnestly and unanimously pressed upon'. He refuted the charge that the Congress was merely a crowd of people. He challenged any person who made that assertion, stating, 'come with me into this hall and look around you, and tell me where you could wish to see a better representation of the aristocracy, not of birth and of wealth, but of intellect, education, and position, than you see gathered within the walls of this hall'.[63]

For several years after 1887, Tyabji was a decisive factor in the deliberations of the Congress. On the one hand, he attempted to convince the Muslims of India that, in matters of religion, they were free to act as they pleased and that the Congress would not interfere. But so far as national activities were concerned, the Indian Muslims should consider themselves as Indians and for all national advance — better government, better treatment of Indians, less taxes, better educational arrangements for all the communities — they should struggle together as one people to achieve their end. At the same time, he tried to dispel the fears of the Muslim community regarding the grant of representative institutions which would result in the preponderance of the Hindus, which might endanger the interests of Muslims by making laws and regulations affecting Muslim sacrifices on the occasions of Id and Muharram and Muslim ceremonies. He wrote to Muslim leaders of the north that it was the duty of all educated and public-spirited citizens to work together, irrespective of caste, colour or creed, and called upon all enlightened Muslims to do what they could individually and jointly to ameliorate the conditions of the people. As long as he lived, he remained a devout Muslim, but at the same time a devoted, loyal and fearless leader of the Indian National Congress.

Syed Ahmad Khan sought to collect the opponents of the Congress in the United India Patriotic Association which was founded in 1888. But it did not last long. In 1893, a number of communal disturbances occurred in many places including Bombay. Principal Beck took advantage of the situation to found the Muhammadan Defence Association of which he and Syed Mahmud became the secretaries. In his inaugural address, he pointed out the defects of the Patriotic Association, the desirability of establishing a purely Muslim body, and the need of a political organization to fight the Congress, which, according to him, aimed at the transfer of power into the hands of Hindu groups and the Hindu revivalists, who threatened the very existence of the Muslims. He explained: 'With the press pouring out a stream of political articles, our young educated Mahomedans will be drawn into the current to support or oppose the measures proposed. I think it would be a mistake to leave them without guidance.'[64]

Addressing the London Muslim Association in 1895, Beck impressed upon them the impossibility of Hindu-Muslim unity, and, therefore, of a democratic system of Government, because such a system would make the Muslims slaves of the Hindu majority for all time. He warned them not to repeat the mistake of 1857, and not to join the seditious Indian National Congress led by Dadabhai Naoroji and Bengali politicians. For, if they did so, they would lose their posts, their independence and their status.

It is regrettable that Syed Ahmad Khan adopted the views of Beck and continued till his death to oppose every Congress resolution. His activities during the last fifteen years of his life, under the influence of Beck, were so unexpected that even his close friends were surprised. Some of them ceased to co-operate with him. Samiullah Khan and his friends resigned from the trusteeship of the college, partly on account of Beck's increasing influence over the college affairs. Shibli Numani also retired from the college, because he completely differed with the political views of Syed Ahmad Khan. Other trustees were so worried that they intended to appeal to the community through a series of articles in the press to intervene and save the institution, but Sir Syed's death led them to desist. His last days were unhappy — a domestic calamity, the breakdown of his son's mind, the troubles in the college due to defalcation of funds, and public events, e.g., Sir Antony Macdonell's orders permitting the employment of Hindi in courts were shocks which shattered his health.

Unfortunately, the Muslim community abdicated the control of Aligarh into the hands of the British principals, who became virtually the leaders of the community in all political matters, and who for the next quarter century remained their philosophers, friends and guides. The famous Urdu poet Akbar Allahabadi commenting on the hold of British principals on the leaders of Aligarh movement wrote a satirical couplet:

Ye tifl-i-nadan, ghari-i-ke ghaflat,
Hawai-e-zillat men tan rahe hain,
Samajh nahin hai, Aqil nahin hai,
Banaye jate hain ban rahe hain!

Like immature and irresponsible children
Feeling proud in the humiliation
They possess neither understanding
Nor intelligence
And are willingly being made fools of!

Mr (afterwards Sir) Theodore Morrison who succeeded Mr Beck successfully kept the Muslims out of all political agitation. During his regime efforts were made to develop Aligarh into a Pan-Islamic centre. Agents were sent to outside countries like Persia to induce their wealthy youth to proceed to Aligarh and receive education there.

Mr Archbold, the next principal, played an important role in Muslim politics during his period of office from 1905 to 1910. When he arrived in Aligarh, India was seething with agitation against the partition of Bengal. In order to meet the situation, the government was considering measures for rallying the moderate and loyal Muslim elements. One of the measures contemplated was expansion of the Indian councils. Mr Archbold became the medium between the Government of India and the Muslim leaders. He met the private secretary to the viceroy at Simla and settled with him that a deputation of Muslims should wait upon the viceroy and present an address asking for separate representation for Muslims in the new constitution. The history of the deputation led by H.H. the Agha Khan is so well known that it need not be repeated here. It resulted in the granting of special representation to the landholders of each province, for commerce, and a separate representation for Muslims.

Lady Minto in her biography of her husband records the feeling of the official class in India regarding the proposal for separate representation. She says, 'on the very evening of his address to the Muslim League, Minto received a letter from an official: "I must send Your Excellency a line to say that a very very big thing has happened today. A work of statesmanship that will affect India and Indian history for many a long year. It is nothing less than the pulling back of 62 millions of people [Muslims] from joining the ranks of the seditious opposition [Congress]."'[65]

The seed had germinated and it attained luxuriant growth. In 1906, the Muslim League was founded which declared its three objects:

(1) To promote among Muslims feelings of loyalty towards the British Government and to remove possible misunderstandings against the Government.
(2) To watch the political interests and rights of the Musalmans and to bring to the notice of the Government their needs.

(3) Without injuring the objects of the League to discourage the growth of ideas hostile to other communities.

For a number of years Muslim politics continued to be guided in this manner, but at last the shock of events in India and abroad broke the spell. In 1911, the partition of Bengal, which had been heralded with so much trumpet-blowing to please the Muslims, was rescinded. In 1912, the Balkan War roused the Indian Musalmans who sent a mission under Dr Ansari in aid of Turkey. In 1914, the Great War broke out and the Turks joined the enemies of England. The Indian Muslims were deeply affected by these events and by the general awakening which was taking place.

5. Muslims and the Bengal Partition

Curzon's masterstroke, the partition of Bengal, was really a measure whose object was to break the growing solidarity of the political community which led India in opposition to the government. Ibbetson applied the doctrine to Bengal. He minuted:

> The influence of Eastern Bengal in the politics of the province is great, out of all proportion to the real political importance, in so much that the Bengali altogether overshadows the Behari, who is in every thing save the use (or abuse) of language immeasurably his superior. It is an object of great political and administrative importance to diminish this influence by separating one of its great centres from the others.[66]

Curzon completely agreed with these views, 'these Eastern districts of Bengal are the hotbed of the purely Bengali movement, unfriendly if not seditious in character'.[67] Thus, taking advantage of the necessity for reorganizing the oversized province of Bengal, Curzon contemplated the execution of his imperious design of destroying the influence of the intelligentsia over Bengal and of Bengal over the whole of India.

When the scheme for the partition of Bengal was published in December 1903 there was a hue and cry against it. The press denounced it. *Ananda Bazar Patrika* (Calcutta), *Charu Mihir* (Mymensingh), *Sanjivani* (Calcutta), *Basumati* (Calcutta), *Dacca Prakash* (Dacca), *Jyoti* (Calcutta), *Bengali* (Calcutta), *Dacca Gazette* (Dacca), and a host of other papers wrote angry condemnatory articles.[68] A number of associations presented memorials to government pointing out the grievous consequences of the scheme. The Bengal National Chamber of Commerce protested strongly and in its well-reasoned memorial covered the entire range of objections against the scheme. The Central National Muhammedan Association of Calcutta conveyed its disapproval of the scheme. It said in its memorial, 'Judged by the standards of civilization, languages, habits, past traditions, nature of revenue settlements, and a hundred other matters more or less important, the people of Dacca, Mymensingh, Tippera, Noakhali, and Chittagong have infinitely more in common with Bengal.'

Curzon in a despatch to Brodrick, the Secretary of State, wrote:

> Calcutta is the centre from which the Congress party is manipulated throughout the whole of Bengal and indeed the whole of India. Its best wire-pullers and its most frothy orators all reside here. The perfection of their machinery is truly remarkable. They dominate public opinion in Calcutta, they affect the High Court. They frighten the Local Government and they are not sometimes without serious influence upon the Government of India. The whole of their activity is directed to creating an agency so powerful that they may one day be able to force a weak government to give them what they desire.[69]

On the eve of his Dacca speech he wrote to the Secretary of State:

> The Bengalis who like to think themselves a nation, and who dream of a future when the British will have been turned out and a Bengali Babu will be installed in Government House, Calcutta, of course bitterly resent any disruption that will be likely to interfere with the realization of this dream. If we are weak enough to yield to their clamour now we shall not be able to dismember or reduce Bengal again, and you will be cementing and solidifying in the eastern flank of India a force already formidable and certain to be a source of increasing trouble in future.[70]

Lieutenant Governor Bampfylde Fuller had let loose unbridled coercion in East Bengal, humiliating and insulting respected leaders, ruthlessly punishing teachers and students — even flogging them, besides imposing fines and rusticating many. Loud demands for his removal had arisen. Gokhale in England addressed meetings of protest, and asserted, 'there is no hope of peace till he is relieved of his duties'.[71]

Minto was alarmed, 'I was not at all pleased with what I have gathered of Fuller's doings', he wrote to Morley.[72]

Morley agreed. He replied, 'I cannot but read in Fuller's utterances a most stupid misconception of the prudent policy. Partition was a disagreeable pill and Fuller had gilded the pill with wormwood.'[73]

A war of pamphlets and propaganda was let loose. The notorious Red Pamphlet, inspired by Fuller, preached the boycott of Hindu shops, products of Hindu industry, and the opening of Muslim schools.

'The Hindus have robbed us of wealth, honour and the glory of Islam. They spread the Swadeshi net to take our lives. O Mohammedan, give not your wealth into the house of Hindus. Lowest of all is he who cries Bande Mataram with the Hindus.'[74]

In an atmosphere made tense by propaganda and counter-propaganda it is not surprising that clashes occurred. Rioting had begun in the Mymensingh district in April and May 1906 causing panic among the Hindus.[75]

Communal riots on a bigger scale recurred in 1907 at Comilla in Tipperah district and in Jamalpur Taluk of Mymensingh district. At Comilla the occasion was the visit of the Nawab of Dacca who had undertaken a tour in the first week of March 1907 to strengthen the morale of his co-religionists. The provocation was provided by someone throwing brickbats at the nawab's procession. A melee ensued in which a Muslim was shot and killed. The indifference of the police led to killings, looting and arson, which continued for nearly a week.[76]

In Jamalpur Taluk disturbances began on 21 April and continued till 10 May. Markets were plundered, houses and offices of zamindars and other well-to-do persons were burnt, Durga temples were desecrated, women abducted, and much loss of life took place. In the trials which followed, the Calcutta High Court made caustic remarks about the partisanship of the Sessions Judge who had tried the Hindu accused.

In early 1906 the Muslims formed a committee which collected numerous signatures to the request to meet the viceroy to present an address. They prepared an address whose contents had been discussed between Muhsinul Mulk, S.H. Bilgrami and Archbold.[77] The text of the address was finalized by 16 September and an advance copy was despatched to the viceroy soon after. He was already acquainted with the general trend of the contents and had written to Morley on 18 September about the line he would take in his reply. Morley had given him the signal to go ahead.

The address was presented to Minto on 1 October at Viceregal Lodge in Simla. It contained a number of demands among which were:

(1) Adequate representation in all services — civil and military and in the High Courts; appointment to higher posts without competitive examinations.
(2) Guarantee of a number of seats in the councils of the municipal and district boards and the syndicates and senates of the universities.
(3) Election of Muslims to the Provincial Councils through separate Muslim electorates, and in numbers not in proportion to their population, but in accordance with their political importance.
(4) Election of Muslims to the Imperial Legislative Council through a separate electorate, in sufficient number so that the Muslims may not be an ineffective minority.
(5) Aid in founding a Muslim University which would be a centre of Muslim religious and intellectual life.

In his reply Minto addressed the delegates as 'the descendants of a conquering and ruling race', and 'welcomed the representative character of the deputation, as expressing the views and aspirations of the enlightened Muslim Community of India'.[78] He reminded them that the British rulers of India had been helping the Muslims in the spread of education in order to enable them to enter government service. He lauded the services of Sir Syed and the Aligarh College for their brilliant record in giving training to the Muslims in loyalty, commonsense and sound reasoning. Concerning the demand included in the address he gave a general assurance:

> I am as firmly convinced as I believe you to be that any electoral representation in India would be doomed to mischievous failure which aimed at granting a personal enfranchisement regardless of the beliefs and traditions of the communities composing the population of the continent.[79]

Thus the principle of special electorates for communities was officially accepted. Further, the assurance was given that the political rights and interests of the Muslims as a community would be safeguarded in any reorganization of the administration.

The delegation was mainly representative of the landed aristocracy of the community in northern India. Of the 35 delegates, eleven belonged to the N.W. Province, eight to the Punjab and eight to Bengal (Bihar included), Bombay provided four, three other provinces one each and the Nizam's State one. Excepting Ebrahimbhoy Adamji Peerbhoy, there was no other delegate from the large and prosperous commercial class.

Again the delegates were not chosen by any public organization or association of Muslims. They were members of the delegation only in their personal capacity. A group of equally eminent persons could have been hand-picked to make different demands.

Shibli's assessment of the Simla affair brings out the artificial character of the deputation and its claims:

> The object of the Simla Deputation was, and it was frankly expressed, to get a share for the Muslims in the political rights obtained by the Hindus . . . Day and night its constant refrain was that the Muslims were oppressed by the Hindus and so they must be given safeguards. We do not understand the importance of the Simla deputation. It was the biggest show staged on the communal platform.

Shibli refused to dignify the Simla transaction as a piece of politics, for, according to him, 'politics arouses a nation into action and inspires men for suffering and the highest sacrifice. But have our politics evoked these qualities in a single individual?' he asked.[80]

On the question of education, Shibli held a position midway between the school at Deoband and the school of Syed Ahmad Khan. He was in favour of reforming the traditional Islamic system of education by cutting down its verbal and formal studies and including the English language and the European sciences. He founded the *Nadwat-ul-Ulama* and *Darul Ulūm* in Lucknow in 1894-6, where he tried to give effect to his educational ideas. At first, he met with the determined opposition of the traditional *ulama*, but ultimately succeeded in convincing them of the desirability of changing the old courses and introducing the teaching of English.

In political matters, he held that Islam was a liberal religion, which promoted progress and civilization. It upheld the dignity of man, asserted human equality, championed the rights of women and favoured a democratic form of government. It taught tolerance and prohibited war, except in the defence of faith. It forbade the propagation of religion by force. Islam did not believe in the polarisation of life between temporal and eternal and rejected asceticism and monasticism.

Shibli was a democrat, an anti-imperialist, and a pan-Islamist. Naturally, he deplored Syed Ahmad Khan's attitude of loyalty to the British and opposition to the Congress. He thought the Aligarh School was too much under the influence of the English staff of the college. Syed Sulaiman Nadvi, the pupil and biographer of Shibli says:

> The English professors had created the conviction in Sir Syed's mind that opposition to the Congress and friendship for the British were in the true interests of the college and the Musalmans. He had been so charmed by their magic that his own opinions had been submerged and now whatever he saw he saw with the eyes of Mr Beck and the English staff, and whatever he heard he heard with their ears.[81]

Shibli admired the Congress for its high idealism and for its solicitude for the welfare and advancement of the Indian people. So far as the Muslims were concerned, he realized that, as a minority, they had a dual status. They possessed a distinctive religion and culture, their part in the history of India had been glorious, they belonged by faith to a universal society. At the same time, the Muslims were citizens of India and they owed loyalty to their motherland. They shared with the other communities the deprivations which British rule imposed, and the aspirations for the future which all Indians entertained. He knew that it was not possible to revive medieval Muslim rule, but he was convinced that the Muslims could, jointly with the Hindus, create a state in which both could live honourably and happily, and without any reproach from their conscience or any violation of their creed.

That the rulers did not entertain a high opinion of pro-British Muslim leaders is abundantly manifest from the opinion which Morley and Minto expressed in their correspondence in regard to them. For instance, Minto wrote about the Aga Khan that he knew more about second-class music halls of Europe than about Indian affairs.

According to Morley, Ameer Ali was an egoistical windbag who was fishing for a knighthood. Yet the Aga Khan wrote in a vainglorious mood to Dunlop Smith, the Private Secretary to Minto:

> I have asked all the members of the Muslim Deputation . . . to form a permanent committee, and I have given to my old friend Muhsinul Mulk who as you know is a most loyal and zealous Mohammedan, certain instructions regarding the method by which he is to proceed. . . . I have also asked him not to move in any matter before first finding out if the step to be taken has the full approval of Government privately.[82]

Muhsinul Mulk was equally exuberant in subservience. He told Dunlop Smith after the deputation that Minto's speech 'has put a new heart in us, and will always, with gratitude, be treasured by us and our posterity as a historical declaration of the policy of the Indian Government'.[83]

The government was anxious to counteract the rising mass movement which threatened the existence of irresponsible authority and demanded an end to exploitation. In the Muslims they found a counterpoise which could effectively serve their purposes.

Dunlop Smith wrote about the Indian nationalist movement to Lady Minto:

> There is hardly a country in Asia where there is not a strong national movement going. It has manifested itself in India in many unmistakable ways, but until lately, it was not at all religious in character . . . the national movement was at first non-religious. The leaders guided it on purely secular lines. But of late, there has been a somewhat rapid Hinduising of national ideas, especially, among the younger men, and the religious element has become infused into the political.[84]

The infusion served the purpose of the government well. It could exploit religious differences to its own advantage. It made use of them to provide plausible justification for communal representation. Dunlop Smith advised Minto to tell the objectors to separate electorates that the Indian Muslims 'are much more than a religious body. They form, in fact, an absolutely separate community, distinct by marriage, food and custom and claiming in many cases to belong to a different race'.[85]

The argument went home. The Muslim Leaguers began to believe it.

Religion became the handmaid of politics. The seed of separatism thus sown was nurtured by lack of understanding, unwisdom and the chauvinistic attitude of some sections of the Hindus. It was nourished by the British imperialist interests. The Muslim League had become conscious that they were a prize for which the Indian nationalists and the government were both competing and they started bargaining for their price.

The Congress which met in December 1909 strongly disapproved the creation of separate communal electorates, and objected to the excessive representation given to the Muslims. But Gokhale differed from this point of view. The Hindu Sabha of Lahore presented an address to Minto in April 1909 in which they protested against the special concessions to the Muslims on the ground of religion. The nationalist press echoed these sentiments.

On the other hand, the Muslim Leaguers rejoiced at their triumph, believing proudly that Morley had to bend before their powerful organization. The *Aligarh Institute Gazette* remarked on the resignation of Morley in November 1910 that the services of Morley to the Muslims of India, in spite of Muslim fears that he was a die-hard radical, were worthy of recognition and praise. He had given them important rights which, as Malaviya pointed out, were denied to the Hindus.

The Muslim electors were enrolled as such if they paid income-tax on an income of Rs 3,000 per annum, while Hindu electors were enrolled only if they had an income of three lakh rupees a year. A Muslim graduate of three years standing acquired the right to vote, but a Hindu graduate had to be of 30 years standing. Apart from all this, the Muslims were given direct elections and weightage.

After long delays and interminable discussions, the Secretary of State and the Government of India agreed upon a scheme of reform which embodied Minto's conception of 'constitutional autocracy'. It did not affect the supremacy of the imperial power in the slightest degree and hence maintained the autocratic character of government. In fact, one of the main purposes of the reforms was to create a counterpoise to the Congress which stood and worked for national unity. Both Morley and Minto were keen on rallying the 'loyal' elements, that is, the groups which wanted to perpetuate British rule in India, support the foreign government in maintaining its hold upon the country.

Earlier, in his correspondence with Morley on the subject of reforms, Minto had declared his intentions: 'We are here a small British garrison surrounded by millions composed of factors of an inflammability unknown to the western world, and we must be physically strong or go to the wall.'[86]

In order to avert this danger it was necessary to think 'of a possible counterpoise to Congress aims'.[87] The most effective counterpoise, apart from the Council of Princes, was to win over the Muslims to the support of the government, and 'to undermine the feeling of a growing nationality which was already doing much to unite Hindus and Mahomedans in a common cause'.[88]

Minto had laid the foundation of this policy when on 1 October 1906 he assured the Muslim Deputation that, because the system of election or nomination to the legislative councils prevailing hitherto had failed to give the Muslims adequate protection, he was in favour of accepting their claim to representation not only commensurate with their numerical strength, but with their political importance and the value of the contribution which they made to the empire. He recognized also their right to send their own representatives through separate electorates. He had asserted that 'any electoral representation in India would be doomed to mischievous failure which aimed at granting a personal enfranchisement regardless of the beliefs and traditions of the communities composing the population of the continent.'[89] Morley gave his assent to Minto's promises.

The Indian National Congress consisting of the Moderates met in December 1908 at Madras, just after Morley had introduced his bill in Parliament on 17 December 1908, and unreservedly welcomed the reforms. It resolved:

> The Congress desires to give expression to the deep and general satisfaction with which the Reform proposals formulated in Lord Morley's despatch have been received throughout the country; it places on record its sense of high statesmanship which has dictated the action of the Government in the matter and it tenders to Lord Morley and Lord Minto its most sincere and grateful thanks for their proposals.[90]

Rash Behari Ghose, the President, rhapsodized:

> [The clouds] are now breaking in blessings over your heads, slaking the parched and thirsty earth. English statesmanship which, as Lord Morley justly boasted, has never yet failed in any part of the world, has risen to its fullest height at this critical time, and has seized the golden moment, for it knows the season when to take occasion by the hand, not to suppress but to guide the new spirit which England has created in India.[91]

Unfortunately, the jubilation proved premature. Morley's surrender on the question of Muslim representation came to the Moderate Congressmen as a great shock. In 1909 the Congress deemed it its duty to place on record its strong sense of disapproval of the creation of separate electorates on the basis of religion; its regret at the excessive and unfairly preponderant share of representation given to the Muslims; the unjust, invidious and humiliating matter of elections, the franchise and the qualifications of the candidates; and deplored the general distrust shown towards the educated classes. It also drew attention to the defects in the constitution of the provincial councils.

Next year, at Allahabad, the criticism was reiterated, though in milder terms. The Congress President, Wedderburn, attempted to bring about conciliation between the Congress and the Muslim League, but without success.

In 1911 the Congress met at Calcutta with Bishan Narayan Dar in the chair. The announcement of the modification of the Bengal partition evoked the gratitude of the Congress. But the resolution about separate representation was repeated.

In the following year Congress demanded a revision of the Government of India Act of 1909, and deprecated the extension of the principle of separate communal electorates to the local bodies. A welcome feature of the Congress session of 1912 at Bankipore (Patna) was the large attendance of Muslims.

In 1913 the Congress placed on record its warm appreciation of the change in the objects of the Muslim League, and welcomed the proposal of the League to find a *modus operandi* for joint and concerted action on questions of national interest.

The succeeding year the Congress met after the outbreak of the first World War on 4 August 1914. It expressed its profound devotion to the throne, its unswerving allegiance to the British connection, and its resolve to stand by the empire, at all hazards and at all costs. It appealed to the government that, in view of the manifestation of loyalty by the people of India, the British Government should take such measures as might be necessary for the recognition of India as a component part of a federated empire, in the full and free enjoyment of the rights belonging to that state.

Bhupendra Nath Basu, the President of the Congress session for the year said:

> The world is swinging onward on the uplifting ropes of time. . . . The war of nations will knock off the vestiges of medieval domination of one man over many, of one race over another, it is not possible to roll back the tide of wider life which is flowing . . . into the still waters of the East. . . . India wants that her government should be consistent with her growing self-respect and intellectuality. . . . India wants that her Government should be an autonomous Government under the British Empire.[92]

Communal differences constituted the main obstacle in the way of constitutional advance. Efforts had been set afoot at the Karachi session of the Congress in 1913 to bring the Muslim League and the Congress to an agreement on the political goal of India. The Bombay session, 1915, marked a notable advance towards this objective.

Meanwhile, the Muslims were shedding their old leadership and their policy of dependence upon the rulers. In 1913 they came under the liberal and dynamic influence of Jinnah and Mohammad Ali, and abandoning their old creed, accepted the goal of self-government for India suited to its conditions. The League decided to enter into negotiations with the Congress to formulate a scheme for the future government of India. Other forces joined in these endeavours. The war had produced a new stir, which shook the West and the East.

Mrs Annie Besant who had till then devoted her energies to religion, entered the field of politics. She started the weekly *Commonweal* in January 1914 and a few months later the daily *New India*. With her characteristic zeal she threw herself into the Indian struggle for independence. At first she tried to unite the two factions of the Congress, but failed. Then in 1915 she published her plea for India's autonomy in her book, *India a Nation*, which was followed by a series of articles on the history of the freedom movement under the title *How India Wrought for Freedom*. She laid the foundations of the Home Rule League.

About the same time, Tilak, who had been released in 1914 from a prison in Mandalay, started a Home Rule League in Pune. Tilak, the responsivist co-operator, and Annie Besant, the radical politician, joined their forces to rouse the country out of the lethargy of the past decade.

In 1916, at Lucknow, the Moderates and the Extremists, as also the Home Rulers and the Muslim Leaguers came together, and unanimously adopted the agreement known as the Lucknow Pact. Its main proposals were:

(1) Special or separate electorates for the Muslims in the Provincial Councils in accordance with the following proportions: Punjab — 50 per cent, United Provinces — 30 per cent, Bengal — 40 per cent, Bihar — 25 per cent, Central Provinces — 15 per cent, Madras — 15 per cent, Bombay — 33⅓ per cent.

(2) The Imperial Legislative Council should consist of altogether 150 members, of whom 120 should be non-officials and one-third of the elected members Muslims.

(3) No bill, nor any clause of a bill, nor a resolution introduced by a non-official member affecting one or the other community shall be proceeded with if three-fourths of the members of the community in the Provincial or Imperial Council oppose the bill, clause or resolution.

(4) Defence, foreign and political affairs — war, peace and treaties — were considered outside the powers of the Imperial Legislative Council.

With one voice, the united Congress told the government that 'it is of opinion that the time has come when His Majesty the King-Emperor should be pleased to issue a proclamation announcing that it is the aim and intention of British policy to confer self-government on India at an early date'.[93]

Ramsay MacDonald recorded in his book: 'Some of the far-seeing members of the Mohammedan community are already beginning to feel that they have made a mistake. Several spoke to me with bitterness about the way that certain of their leaders had consented to play a game planned for them by Anglo-Indian officials'.[94]

The Muslim euphoria was short-lived. Developments both within India and outside administered unexpected shocks of great severity. In 1910, Morley resigned. The portfolio was transferred to Crewe. His deputy and spokesman in the House of Commons was Montagu. In India Minto's term was ending and a successor had to be found. Hardinge who was then the Permanent Under Secretary of State in the Ministry of Foreign Affairs was chosen for the viceroyalty.

The Liberal Party's policy towards the Muslim countries was not likely to give satisfaction to the Indian Muslims. Crewe refused to receive the London Muslim League Deputation to discuss the Turkish question. Hardinge was equally unfavourable towards Ottoman rule. On the constitution of the Aligarh Muslim University also differences arose between the government and the trustees of the MAO College.

Outside India the Muslim countries were exposed to mortal dangers. The westernmost bastion of Islam in North Africa, Morocco, had already passed under the French Empire. At the eastern end, Egypt had become a British protectorate. England and Russia had entered into a convention by which Iran was divided into spheres of influence. The British had already established special interests in the Persian Gulf. Italy seized Tripoli, a province of the Ottoman Empire, in 1911. The dismemberment of Turkey followed. An alliance of the Christian principalities of the Balkans was formed with Russian support in 1912, in order to attack Turkey which was in the throes of the Young Turk Revolution. In the war that followed (October 1912) Turkey suffered terrible defeats. The result was that the Ottoman Empire lost all its possessions in Europe, except a small foothold in Eastern Thrace (including Adrianople, Constantinople and the Straits).

The Balkan Wars were hardly over when the First World War started. As England, France and Russia, the Triple Entente, had upheld the claims of the Balkan states against Turkey, and Germany had shown sympathy for the Muslims, it was natural that the Turks should fight in the War on the side of their sympathisers, the German Empire.

The Indian Muslims, especially the *ulama,* were greatly exercised over the wars. For the first time it had happened that the *ulama* — the custodians of religion, 'who hold sway over the hearts of the entire community, from Peshwar to Burmah and Kashmir to Madras',[95] joined the middle class educated Muslims in opposition to the government.

The educated Muslims were upset by the change in the policy of the Indian Government. The era of upper class politics of loyalty was coming to an end. The Montagu-Chelmsford report noted that 'throughout the troubled years 1907-10, the Muslims, with a few unimportant exceptions, held severely aloof from the revolutionary movements and retained their traditional attitude of sturdy loyalty. . . . Since 1911 their attitude has been growing far less acquiescent'.[96]

6. The Lucknow Pact

These bitter experiences were destined to be followed by others still more bitter. In the autumn of 1912 the great Balkan War broke out which at one time threatened to drive the Turks out of Europe. The whole Muslim community was stirred to its depths. Shaukat Ali, for the first time, entered politics and began to organize his famous association known as Khuddaman-i-Kaba. Mohammad Ali began to write bitterly and vigorously in his *Comrade* that the bureaucracy tried to gag under the Press Act.

The Turkish Balkan War brought young Dr M.A. Ansari to the forefront of public life in India. He organized a Red Crescent Medical Mission to Constantinople. The position of Leader of the Medical Mission enabled him to establish close contact with leading Muslim organizations in India. The success of the medical mission received wide publicity. It brought acclaim and admiration from his co-religionists in India.

During the First World War, Sheikh-ul-Hind Mahudal Hasan, Husain Ahmad Madni, Abul Kalam Azad, Mohammad Ali, Shaukat Ali and scores of other Muslim leaders were arrested and detained. Ansari started a Detenue Relief Fund in May 1915. The Detenue Relief Committee elected Ansari as its chairman. The helpless families of political detenue heaved a sigh of relief at this much-needed timely help. The relief work made Ansari ever more popular.

When the feelings of the Muslims were at this pitch of bitterness and resentment, came the incident in Kanpur in 1913, when a large number of Muslims were shot down mercilessly by the minions of the British Raj while protesting against the destruction of the sacred precincts of a major mosque in the city. The Hindu community extended solid support to the Muslims over this episode. The educated section of Muslims seized on this incident and successfully roused the masses to an extent never previously achieved. In the electrified atmosphere of the country, the agitation spread like wild fire, and in a few short months the country was all ablaze. Before the year was out, Lord Hardinge had himself to go down to Kanpur and settle the affair.[97]

These happenings were bound to create a profound change in the angle of vision of the Muslim community. This expressed itself in its coming closer to the Congress and in its taking greater interest in movements inside the country. It was during this period that the Muslim League changed its goal and adopted the attainment of self-government for India as its main objective. The clause relating to loyalty to the British Government was dropped after a heated discussion in the year 1912. In 1914, the World War broke out. While *Al-Hilal* had from its very inception been pointing out to the Muslims the suicidal nature of their policy of aloofness from the Congress, and had been asking them to take their share in the Indian political movement, even the *Comrade*, which had so far been an exponent of the Aligarh school of thought, changed its policy in 1914 and began to draw the Indian Muslims towards the National Congress. The government, under the excuse of protecting India against German invasion and machinations, passed the Defence of India Act in 1915, and in the same year interned all prominent Muslim leaders under its provisions.

In reply to questions put by Mazharul Haq in the Imperial Council, it was actually stated from the side of the government that Abul Kalam Azad was suspected of sympathy with the Indian revolutionary movement and had persuaded Muslims to join it. As a reaction against the government's repressive policy, the Muslim League continued to drift towards the Congress. In 1915 this movement reached its climax and in its session at Bombay the League authorized Mazharul Haq, a sturdy and prominent Congressman, whom it had advisedly chosen its president, to arrive at a permanent settlement with the Indian National Congress.

The year 1916 is an epoch-making year in the history of Indian nationalism. It was the year in which the Muslim community, after wandering away from the national ideal for over a generation, returned to the national fold. Its wanderings had been full of varied experiences of which disappointments and sufferings had formed the major part, but through these it had gained in experience, strength, and organization. It was also in this year that the advanced wing of Indian nationalism, which had been exiled from the Congress since 1907 on account of its irrepressible and irreconcilable anti-British bias and tendencies towards direct action, rejoined the Congress.

Lokamanya Tilak had come back after serving his six years of incarceration and the nationalist forces had already begun to cluster round him. Mrs Besant also, who had at her back the powerful Theosophical organization and commanded great resources in men and money, decided all unexpectedly to throw herself wholeheartedly into the political struggle. Her first achievement had been to bring about a reconciliation between the Moderate and Extremist parties by evolving a compromise formula for the Congress creed. Thus the Muslims, the Extremists, the Moderates, all met together at the Lucknow Congress. By this time, the Home Rule Movement was in full swing. The Muslims had joined the movement wholeheartedly, and so powerful was its sweep that, within a few months, a situation was created which pushed the government into a corner and compelled it to arrest Mrs Besant. This incident convulsed the country like a tempest and the whole nation concentrated as one body for securing her release.

At this time Gandhi also appeared as a silent spectator on the Indian scene. The Lucknow Congress held in 1916 united the Extremist and the Liberal factions of the Congress on a common platform. The Lucknow Congress session enabled the Hindu and Muslim leaders to forge a bond of unity — the Lucknow Pact. The Muslim League joined hands with the Congress and its sessions began to be held along with the Congress sessions in adjacent pandals.

Lokamanya Tilak, after a long lapse, attended the Congress session of 1916 at Lucknow. A large number of delegates of his Nationalist Party were also elected from the Bombay Presidency. They accompanied Tilak to Lucknow. Tilak was rejoining the Congress after the Surat split. He also got Gandhi elected to the subjects committee of the Lucknow Congress. The session was presided over by Ambica Charan Mazumdar.

Nevertheless, the Lucknow session did not proceed smoothly. The secretariat of the U.P. Government issued a warning to the Reception Committee against seditious speeches in the Congress session, and a copy of the letter was served upon Mazumdar, the president-elect of the Congress, through the Government of Bengal. The Reception Committee gave a fitting reply to this gratuitous insult while the president treated it with the contempt it deserved. But the Lieutenant Governor of U.P., Sir James Meston, averted all complications by attending the Congress session with Lady Meston and staff. The president extended a welcome to Sir James, to which he gave a suitable reply.[98]

The great achievement of the Congress session held at Lucknow in December 1916 was the completion of Congress-Muslim League scheme of reforms, the achievement of a Hindu-Muslim concordat. The preliminaries of this concordat were gone through at a Joint Conference of the League and the Congress Executive at Allahabad in April 1916, and in Calcutta in November 1916.

The Lucknow session of the Congress was altogether a unique one, for the fraternization of Hindus and Muslims as well as for the formulation of a scheme of self-government. No less important was the reunion of the two wings of the Congress, the Extremists and the Liberals, which had been separated since the Surat Congress held in December 1907. It was a unique spectacle to see Tilak and Khaparde sitting side by side with Rash Behari Ghosh, Motilal Nehru and Surendranath Banerjea. Besant was there with Arundale and Wadia. Amongst the Muslims were men like Maharaja Mahmudabad, Mazharul Haq, Mohammad Rasul, Ajmal Khan and M.A. Ansari. Jawaharlal Nehru, for the first time, attended this Congress session. Gandhi and Polak were also there. The Lucknow session passed the following resolutions:

(a) That having regard to the fact that the great communities of India are the inheritors of ancient civilizations and have shown great capacity for government and administration, and to the progress in education and public spirit made by them during a century of British Rule, and further having regard to the fact that the present system of Government does not satisfy the legitimate aspirations of the people and has become unsuited to existing conditions, and requirements, the Congress is of opinion that the time has come when his Majesty the King-Emperor should be pleased to issue a Proclamation announcing that it is the aim and intention of British policy to confer Self-Government on India at an early date.

(b) That in the reconstruction of the Empire, India shall be lifted towards Self-Government by granting the Reforms contained in the scheme prepared by the All-India Congress Committee in concert with the Reforms Committee appointed by the All-India Muslim League.

The Lucknow Pact was largely the result of the efforts of Lokamanya Tilak. In speaking on the resolution of self-government he said in regard to the Pact:

> It has been said by some that we Hindus have yielded too much to our Mohammadan brothers. I am sure I express the feelings of the Hindu community all over India when I say that we could not have yielded too much. I would not care if the rights of self-government are granted to the Mahammaden community only. When we have a fight against a third party, we stand on this platform united; united in race, united in religion, united as regards all different shades of political creed. That is the most important event of the day.[99]

It is unfortunate that Tilak's attitude on the question of social reform and communal harmony has been much maligned by interested parties who disapproved of his policies. Indeed, Tilak was a follower of Sanatan Dharma but he strongly objected to an alien government whose powers he wanted to limit and, in fact, scale down through alteration, imposing reforms in matters which affected society intimately. Such reforms antagonized the orthodox. It was not worthwhile to incur their displeasure for such dubious progress.

In fact, Tilak favoured improvement in the status of women — their participation in public affairs, education, and raising the minimum age of marriage. His views about caste distinctions and untouchability were such as to delight the heart of any social reformer. He considered absurd the contention that certain castes alone should have the privilege of performing the Vedic rites. And he looked upon untouchability as an outrage upon Hindu society. He declared at the Depressed Classes Conference in Bombay in March 1918:

> If a God were to tolerate untouchability. I would not recognize Him as God at all. Whatever may be the genesis of untouchability, the sinful nature of the notion is beyond dispute. Untouchability must go . . . mistakes committed by the Brahmin bureaucracy of old require to be rectified.[100]

When Paranjpe asked him to sign a manifesto condemning untouchability, Tilak wrote to him, 'I am for removing all caste distinctions regarding interdining and untouchability'.[101]

While the movement for communal harmony was thus in full swing and the Hindus and Muslims were acting with great co-operation and goodwill all over the country, an incident occurred which was as strange as it was out of tune. It fell like a bomb on the movement, and would altogether have broken its momentum, had it not been irrepressible at the time in its onward course. Hindu-Muslim riots broke out in Arrah on a scale so extensive and with a virulence so startling that up to that time nothing like them had been heard of in the history of Hindu-Muslim differences. The riots began on 22 September 1917, and within two days rioting had spread throughout a large tract of 40 square miles which passed into the hands of Hindu mobs.

The effect of an outbreak of this nature on the feelings of the two communities can well be imagined. The whole Muslim community was staggered at the unexpected nature and extent of the calamity, harrowing details of which continued to appear in the press for months. But with a serenity praiseworthy and unprecedented, it passed through the painful ordeal without permitting itself to be deflected from its political objective and effort. And the national movement continued as vigorously as before.

History was repeating itself. While the calamity was still fresh, came a stroke of British policy calculated to divide the Moderates and Extremists. Mr. Montagu, who had already made his famous announcement in August 1917, fore-shadowing constitutional reforms, came to India about this time to see things personally and to create opinion in favour of the proposed reforms. An effort was made to divide the Muslim League from the Congress in making their demands. But in spite of this, a joint memorandum was submitted by the leaders of both the organizations. As a result of Mr Montagu's policy of conciliation, Mrs Besant was released. Her release was hailed by the whole country as its first unmistakable victory, and the movement continued to grow and spread among the masses.[102]

In 1918 another serious Hindu-Muslims riot broke out in Katarpur, in the Saharanpur District of the United Provinces. The Chief fact to be noted in this connection is that in 1918 Hindus and Muslims had been absolutely united in political objective and effort for almost five years, and that therefore their social relations had much improved and their religious bitterness much lessened. Still the nation as a whole remained helpless to protect itself from external underhand machinations. The reason for this helplessness was that the upper and educated classes took no or little interest in the life of the common people, and the Congress, engrossed in political matters, could not take any effective action to protect itself from these flank attacks. As a consequence, political unity failed to bring with it social and religious peace. However, in spite of the most powerful influences from outside and great distractions from within, the wave of Hindu-Muslim unity and co-operation continued to rise higher and higher.[103]

7. *Al-Hilal* and *The Comrade*

Analyzing the trend of Muslim politics after the Balkan War, Nehru in his *Discovery of India* wrote:

> Many prominent Muslims joined the National Congress. British policy became definitely pro-Muslim, or rather in favour of those elements among the Muslims who were opposed to the national movement. But early in the twentieth century the tendency towards nationalism and political activity became more noticeable among the younger generation of Muslims. To divert this and provide a safe channel for it, the Muslim League was started in 1906 under the inspiration of the British Government and the leadership of one of its chief supporters, the Aga Khan.[104]

In the early years of the 20th century, there were two trends among the Muslim intelligentsia; one, chiefly among the younger element, towards nationalism, the other was a deviation from India's past and even, to some extent, her present, and displayed a greater interest in Islamic countries. This tendency was especially encouraged by Sultan Abdul Hamid of Turkey and had found some response in the upper strata of Indian Muslims, and yet Sir Syed had opposed this and written against Indians interesting themselves in Turkey and the sultanate. The Young Turk movement produced mixed reactions. It was looked upon with some suspicion by most Muslims in India to begin with, and there was general sympathy for the sultan who was considered a bulwark against the intrigues of European powers in Turkey. But there were others, among them Abul Kalam Azad, who eagerly welcomed the Young Turks and the promise of constitutional and social reform that they brought.

When Italy suddenly attacked Turkey in the Tripoli War of 1911, and subsequently during the Balkan Wars of 1912 and 1913, an astonishing wave of sympathy for Turkey swept through Indian Muslims. All Indians felt that sympathy and anxiety, but in the case of Muslims this was keener and something almost personal. The last remaining Muslim power was threatened with extinction; the sheet-anchor of their faith in the future was being destroyed. As mentioned earlier, Dr M.A. Ansari led a strong medical mission to Turkey and even the poor subscribed to support it. Money came in more rapidly for this than for any proposal for the uplift of the Indian Muslims themselves. The First World War was a time of trial for the Muslims because Turkey was on the other side. They felt helpless and could do nothing. When the war ended, their pent-up feelings were to break-out in the Khilafat movement.[105]

The year 1912 was notable also in the development of the Muslim mind in India because of the appearance of two new weeklies — *Al-Hilal* in Urdu and *The Comrade* in English. The *Al-Hilal* was started by Abul Kalam Azad, a brilliant young man of 24, who had received his early education in Al Azaar University of Cairo and, while yet in his teens, had become well-known for his Arabic and Persian scholarship and deep learning. To this he added a knowledge of the Islamic world outside India and of the reform movements that were coursing through it, as well as of European developments. Rationalist in outlook and yet profoundly versed in Islamic lore and history, he interpreted scripture from a rationalist point of view. Soaked in Islamic tradition and with many personal contacts with prominent Muslim leaders and reformers in Egypt, Turkey, Syria, Palestine, Iraq and Iran, he was powerfully affected by political developments in these countries. Because of his writings he was probably better known in Islamic countries than any other Indian Muslim. The wars in which Turkey became involved aroused his intense interest and sympathy. And yet his approach was different from that of the older Muslim leaders.

Abul Kalam had a wider and more rationalist outlook which kept him away from the feudal and narrowly religious and separatist approach of the older leaders, and inevitably made him an Indian nationalist. He had himself seen nationalism growing in Turkey and the other Islamic countries and he applied that knowledge to India and saw in the Indian national movement a similar development. Other Muslims in India were hardly aware of these movements elsewhere and, wrapped up in their own feudal atmosphere, had little appreciation of what was happening there. They thought in religious terms only and if they sympathized with Turkey it was chiefly because of the religious bond. In spite of this intense sympathy, they were not in tune with the nationalist and rather secular movements in Turkey.[106]

Abul Kalam Azad spoke a new language in his weekly *Al-Hilal*. It was not only a new language in thought and approach, even its texture was different, for Azad's style was terse and virile, though sometimes a little difficult because of its Persian background. He used new phrases for new ideas and was a definite influence in giving shape to the Urdu language, as it is today. The older conservative leaders among the Muslims did not react favourably to all this and criticized Azad's opinions and approach. Yet not even the most learned of them could easily meet Azad in debate and argument, even on the basis of scripture and old tradition, for Azad's knowledge of these happened to be greater than theirs. He was a strange mixture of medieval scholasticism, eighteenth century rationalism, and the modern outlook.[107]

There were a few among the older generation who approved of Azad's writings, among them being the learned Maulana Shibli Numani. The tradition of Aligarh College was, however, different and conservative, both politically and socially. Its trustees came from among the princes and big landlords, typical representatives of the feudal order. Under a succession of English principals, closely associated with government circles, it had fostered separatist tendencies and an anti-nationalist and anti-Congress outlook. Abul Kalam Azad attacked this stronghold of conservatism and anti-nationalism, not directly but by spreading ideas which undermined the Aligarh tradition. This very youthful writer and journalist created sensation in Muslim intellectual circles, and though the elders frowned upon him, his words created a ferment in the minds of the younger generation. That ferment had already started because of events in Turkey, Egypt and Iran, as well as the development of the Indian nationalist movement. Azad gave a definite trend to it by pointing out that there was no conflict between Islam, and sympathy for Islamic countries, and Indian nationalism. This helped in bringing the Muslim League nearer to the Congress. Azad had himself joined the League, whilst yet a boy, at its first session in 1906.

The *Al-Hilal* was not approved of by the representatives of the British Government. Securities were demanded from it under the Press Act and ultimately, in 1914, its press was confiscated. Thus ended the *Al-Hilal* after a brief existence of two years. Azad thereupon brought out another weekly, *Al-Balagh,* but this too closed in 1916 when Azad was interned by the British Government. For nearly four years he was kept in internment and when he came out at last, he took his place immediately among the leaders of the National Congress. Ever since then he remained continuously in the highest Congress executive body, looked upon, in spite of his youthful years, as one of the elders of the Congress, whose advice both in national and political matters as well as in regard to the communal and minority questions, was highly valued. Twice he became Congress President, and repeatedly he spent long terms in prison.

The other weekly that was started in 1912, *The Comrade,* influenced especially the younger English-educated generation of Muslims. It was edited by Maulana Mohammad Ali, who was an odd mixture of Islamic tradition and an Oxford education. He began as an adherent of the Aligarh tradition and was opposed to any aggressive politics. But he was far too able and dynamic a personality to remain confined in that static framework, and his language was always vigorous and striking. The Balkan Wars moved him and he wrote passionately in favour of Turkey and the Islamic tradition it represented.

The year 1912 witnessed a series of incidents both inside and outside India. News began to arrive in India that Turkey, Persia and Morocco were being torn apart by internal disruptions and commotions and by external diplomacy. By autumn came news of the unforgettable massacres on the oasis of Tripoli and of Italy's lawless usurpation of that rich and fertile province. Russia, about this time, with the connivance of the British, hanged the Siqatul-Islam, who was the highest religious dignitary in Persia and commanded much reverence in the Muslim world; Meshed was bombarded, and Mecca itself was threatened with aerial bombing.

While the Muslims were smarting under these blows, another incident occurred nearer home which convulsed the whole community. All of a sudden, in January 1912, the partition of Bengal was annulled, and thus were lost to certain elements all the hopes which the bureaucracy had engendered and encouraged and for which they had fought with their brethren with such bitter results. Nawab Salimullah Khan of Dacca died within a few months of a broken heart. The general situation among Indian Muslims may well be described in the words of Maulana Mohammad Ali:

The benighted and uneducated Musalmans wanted the Bengal partition to remain unaltered. But really I never believed in that partition. Only I ask you to realize the fact that this Government had to call upon the Musalmans to fight as its auxiliaries against the Hindus in Bengal. Undoubtedly, I say, the partition of Bengal, although it, e.g., was most unjust and carried out in the most vindictive spirit by Lord Curzon, did benefit the Muslims to a certain extent. Yet, when the Government found that things were getting too hot for it, it dropped the Musalmans like a hot potato. Never was a more ignoble betrayal perpetrated in the whole history of Indian politics.

Nothing could have more clearly convinced them that their dependence upon a foreign Government, for support as against sister-communities, laid them perpetually open to such betrayals. They now realized that they could place no reliance on such support, whether at home or abroad, and it set them thinking that perhaps at a much smaller sacrifice of their interests they could purchase lasting peace and even secure the friendship of their neighbours and fellow countrymen.[108]

Progressively, Maulana Mohammad Ali grew more anti-British, and the entry of Turkey into the First World War completed the process. His famous, and enormously long article, in *The Comrade*, 'The Choice of the Turks' roused widespread interest. Soon after, government arrested him and his elder brother Shaukat Ali, and interned them for the duration of the war and a year after at Chhindwara. They were released at the end of 1919 and both immediately joined the National Congress. The Ali brothers played a very prominent part in the Khilafat agitation and in the Non-cooperation Movement in the early twenties and suffered imprisonment for it. Mohammad Ali presided over an annual session of the Indian National Congress and was for many years a member of its working committee.

The change that took place in Mohammad Ali [wrote Jawaharlal Nehru in his *Discovery of India*] was symbolic of the changing mentality of the Indian Muslims. Even the Muslim League, founded to isolate the Muslims from nationalist currents and completely controlled by reactionary and semi-feudal elements, was forced to recognise the pressure from the younger generation. It was drifting, though somewhat unwillingly, with the tide of nationalism and coming nearer to the Congress. In 1913 it changed the creed of loyalty to Government to a demand for self-government for India. Maulana Abul Kalam Azad advocated this change in his forceful writings in the *Al-Hilal*.[109]

8. Simultaneous Congress and League Sessions

The practice of holding the sessions of the Congress and the Muslim League in the same city and on the same dates on adjacent sites was started in 1915 at Bombay and was continued at the Lucknow and Calcutta sessions in 1916 and 1917. The practice was also followed in Delhi in 1918. Hakim Ajmal Khan was elected Chairman of the Reception Committee of the Congress and Dr M.A. Ansari was elected Chairman of the Reception Committee of the Muslim League session.

Dr Ansari, in his address as Chairman of the Reception Committee of the Delhi session of the Muslim League held in December 1918 dwelt at length on many problems facing the Indian Muslims as well as the Muslims all over the world. He felt that the session was being held at the most critical period in the history of the world. The Great War, in which the nations of the East and the West were engaged had come to an end. But, although the war was over, the anxieties of the Muslims had only begun. Momentous issues hung in the balance and the entire course of human history was to be determined, at least for a very long time to come, by the decisions of the Peace Conference. It was an anxious moment for the Muslims. Never in their varied history of over 1,300 years had they been faced with such a situation. Ansari traced the consistent hostility of the Western powers towards the Islamic states:

> We all know how Islam has suffered in its temporal power since the latter half of the nineteenth century. Each succeeding generation has witnessed the gradual disruption of the House of Islam. Lofty political doctrines have been invented to screen aggressive designs. The humanitarian principles have been advanced to justify the acts of robbery done to Islamic kingdoms. The white man's burden too has been paraded before an innocent and all-believing world. But bereft of all the verbiage of innocent looking doctrines and high sounding principles, this tragedy can be traced to the common dislike of the Muslim of the avarice and greed of the chancellories of Europe.[110]

Tracing the history of the question of Khilafat, Ansari said:

> It is an acknowledged fact of history that in 918 A.H. the last Khalifa of the house of Abbas, Mohammad Abbasi of Egypt, transferred, with the consent and concurrence of the Musalman people, the office and dignity of the Khilafat and the spiritual sovereignty of Islam along with the symbols of this exalted office, the sword, the standard and the cloak of the Prophet, to Sultan Saleem, the Great. The Sultan, accompanied by Mohammad Abbasi, took these holy relics to Istanbul. It is from this day that the Sultans of the House of Osman have received the honoured appellations of *'Khalifat-ul-Muslimeen'*, *'Sultan-ul-Islam'* and *'Khadim-in-Haramain-ish-Sharifain'* and the Musalmans of the world have recognised them as their spiritual Imams and the successors of the messengers of God. Not only the Holy Houses of Mecca and Medina but throughout the wide expanse where the religion of Islam is practised, prayers for their success and glory are offered every Friday and on the occasions of the two Idds.[111]

Commenting on the contemporary position, Ansari explained that, Shareef Barakaat of Mecca, on getting a *firman* from Sultan Saleem, acknowledged him as Khalifa and ordered the name of the Turkish Sultan to be introduced in the prayers. No Shareef has, since then, questioned the authority of the rulers of Turkey and even Shareef Hussain recognized the Sultan as the lawful Khalifa and submitted to his spiritual overlordship.

During the course of the war, actuated by personal ambitions and selfish interests, Shareef Hussain raised the standard of revolt against the unquestioned Khalifa of Islam whom he himself had recognized as such. By this action of his, he not only disregarded a rule of political morality, but, according to Muslim belief and religious teaching, broke an explicit and clear commandment of God and His Prophet. It has been distinctly ordered in the Holy Quran that, 'If one party becomes disloyal to the other [which is in power], fight against the one that has become disloyal until it returns to the bidding of God.

Ansari, elaborating the current situation said:

> It is the firm conviction and deliberate judgement of the Muslim world that, from the time of Sultan Saleem down to the present day, the House of Osman has discharged its duties in respect of the Holy Places, to its entire satisfaction. Therefore, His Imperial Majesty Sultan Waheeduddin Muhammad VI, is the one and the only Musalman who is and can be the rightful Commander of the Faithful and the Khalifat-ur-Rasool, capable of protecting the two Harams along with the Holy Places of Islam and of successfully combating against the intrigues and secret machinations of non-Muslim Governments.[112]

That the opinion of the Musalmans alone is the determining factor in this matter was officially acknowledged by Lord Robert Cecil, on behalf of His Majesty's Government, in the House of Commons, on 29 November 1917:

> Mr King asked the Secretary of State for Foreign Affairs whether, since the outbreak of war, Russia had any communications with this country relating to the proposals that the Sultan of Turkey should no longer be recognised as Khalifa; if so, what attitude was assumed on behalf of this country; and whether he will now declare that the Khilafat is a question for Islam alone to decide?
>
> *Lord R. Cecil:* 'The answer to the first part of the Hon'ble Member's question is in the affirmative, but His Majesty's Government have never departed from the attitude that the question of the Khilafat is one for Moslem opinion alone to decide.'

Mr King: 'We demand that this decision of the Government be put into practice and be not relegated to the domain of pious hopes and broken promises.'

Describing the sanctity of Mecca and Medina, Ansari narrated their religious significance:

In the Jazirat-ul-Arab is situated the Holy City of Mecca which contains the Baitullah, the first house of God, built by Abraham and reconstructed by the last of the prophets, towards which the Muslims of all countries turn their faces five times a day. It is the birthplace of the Prophet and it was to Mecca that he addressed the words:

> 'O land of Mecca, I love thee better than any other portion of God's earth and if my people had not driven me out I would never have forsaken thee.'

Surrounded by Mina, Arafat and numerous other places, a visit to which is an essential part of the Hajj, every inch of Mecca and the land around it is sacred territory, where never since the days of the Abraham, has a bird been shot or a tree felled. For, has not Allah Himself said:

> 'Do they not behold that we have made Mecca a safe sanctuary.'

Yasrib, where the Prophet found safety and a home after his migration from the city of his birth, became renowned as the Madinat-un-Nabi or 'the city of Prophet'. God named it Taiba [holy] as the Prophet once said:

> 'God has named it the holy city.'[113]

Medina was raised to the high dignity of a haram (sanctuary) by the Prophet who said:

> 'Abraham made Mecca a haram and I declare Medina to be one.'[114]

It is of this city that the Prophet declared:

> 'He who comes with the intention of seeing me will be near me on the Day of Judgment; I shall be his witness and intercede on his behalf on the Day of Judgment who adopts Medina as his home and bears its hardships with patience; while he who dies within the holy precincts of Mecca Medina will be immune from punishment on the day of Judgment.'[115]

A major portion of the Divine Book was revealed in Medina and from here were issued the orders and instructions which gave final shape and form to the constitution and organization of the Islamic theocracy. Medina again was the centre from which radiated the resplendent rays of the Light of

Islam and it was here that the mortal remains of the Prophet were entrusted to the earth.

Bait-ul-Maqdis, 'city of the Holy House', is also held sacred by the Muslims. This was the city towards which, not only all the prophets of Beni Israel turned their faces in prayers, but it was also the *Qibla* of the Prophet of Islam and his followers for full 14 years. After the Kaaba, the Masjid-il-Aqsa of Jerusalem is the first house of God of Islam. It has been referred to in the Qur'an in connection with the Mi'raj where it is said:

> Glory be to Him who took his servant a journey by night from *Masjid-il-Haram* to *Masjid-il-Aqsa* whose precincts we have blessed.

Referring to the case of Palestine, Ansari pleaded:

> Palestine cannot be handed over to the Zionists, whose sole claim to that land is that centuries before the birth of Christ the ancestors of the wandering sons of Israel had once lived in it. The achievements of Salahuddin Ayyubi and the blood of millions of *mujahideen* did not flow, in the days of the Crusades, to lose it to a people who cannot put forward any recognizable claim to it. The Muslim rulers of Palestine have, as acknowledged by Christians and Jews themselves, always kept the door open to all. It has given no amount of pain and much resentment has been created, among the Muslims of India, to see that the attitude of their own Government in connection with this matter, has been diametrically opposed to their wishes and sentiments.[116]

During the debate on Palestine, Mr King asked the Secretary of State for Foreign Affairs (on 19 November 1917) whether the desire of the government to see established a Jewish Zionist nationality in Palestine has been communicated to the Allied Powers, especially to France, Russia, Italy, and the other Allied States, and whether it was one of the Allied war aims or only a British war aim, to set a Zion community in the Holy Land.

Mr Balfour: 'No official communication has been made to the Allies on the subject, but His Majesty's Government believes that the declaration referred to would meet with their approval. His Majesty's Government hopes that the establishment in Palestine of a national home of the Jewish people will result from the present war.'[117]

This decision on the part of the cabinet was served out to India by Reuter and the official censor with the following addition:

> [His Majesty's Government] will use their best endeavours to facilitate the achievement of this object, it being understood that nothing will be done to prejudice the civil and religious rights of the non-Jewish communities in Palestine or the rights and political status of the Jews in any other country.

Najaf-i-Ashraf contains the sacred remains of Ali, the Lion of Allah and Khalifa of Islam. He is regarded as the fountain-head of the different schools of spiritualism by the sufis.

In Karbala-i-Maulla is buried the great martyr of Islam, Hussain-ibn-i-Ali, who gave his life to uphold right against wrong.

Baghdad with its mausoleum of Shaikh Abdul Qadir Jilani is the centre of the Qadiria school of sufis which claims millions of votaries among Muslims all the world over. The remains of Maroof-i-Kakhi, Ibn-i-Jauzi, Imam Ghazzali and that greatest of Muslim jurists, Imam Abu Hanifa, endear the city of Baghdad to the heart of every Muslim.

The Government of India published, on behalf of His Majesty's Government and on behalf of the Governments of France and Russia, a declaration on the 2 November 1914, which says:

> In view of the outbreak of war between Great Britain and Turkey, which to the regret of Great Britain has been brought about by the ill-advised, unprovoked and deliberate action of the Ottoman Government, His Excellency the Viceroy is authorised by His Majesty's Government to make the following public announcement in regard to the Holy shrines of Mesopotamia and the port of Jedda, in order that there may be no misunderstanding on the part of His Majesty's most loyal Muslim subjects as to the attitude of His Majesty's Government in this war in which no question of a religious character is involved. These holy places and Jedda will be immune from attack or molestation by the British naval and military forces so long as there is no interference with pilgrims from India to the Holy Places and shrines in question. At the request of His Majesty's Government, the Governments of France and Russia have given them similar assurances.

Commenting on the above Ansari said:

> I have already reviewed the painful history of the fate of Muslim people before you. As men and as Mussalmans we cannot be indifferent to the fate of 40 millions of our co-religionists in the world. We are deeply interested in their future and demand that not only integrity and independence of the present Muslim States be maintained intact but the wrong done to the Arabs of North Africa and the Tartars and Turks of Central Asia be redressed and all these people be given a free chance of determining their own form of Government.

Referring to the efforts of Gandhi, Ansari declared:

> I feel it my bounden duty to offer on your behalf and mine, our grateful thanks to that acknowledged intrepid leader of India Mr M.K. Gandhi, who is never afraid to speak out the truth and who has, by his noble actions, endeared himself, as much to the Musalmans as to the Hindus. In his famous letter of the 29th April, 1918, addressed to His Excellency the

> Viceroy, he has laid down the correct definition of Indian nationalism and explained the attitude that should be adopted by Indian politicians towards Muslim sentiments.

Dr Ansari described the policy of suppression of the Muslim press and the methods adopted by the bureaucracy to strangle it and destroy the organs of Muslim public opinion, one by one, so much so that in the whole of India not a single free Muslim newspaper existed. 'Our voice has been silenced and we have been prevented from carrying our views to the public, the Government and the British democracy.' Where the omnivorous Press Act could not catch its prey, the Defence of India Act was brought in to assist it in devouring, one after another, the *Zamindar*, the *Muslim Gazette*, the *Comrade*, the *Humdard*, the *Tarjuman*, the *Sadakat*, *Al-Hilal*, *Al-Balagh*, the *New Era*, the *Jamhoor*, and many others.

A.K. Fazlul Haq presiding over the Muslim League session at Delhi observed:

> To me the future of Islam in India seems to be wrapped in gloom and anxiety. Every instance of a collapse of Muslim powers of the world is bound to have an adverse influence on the political importance of our community in India.[118]

> . . . we are loyal subjects of the rulers, and are prepared to prove our loyalty in actual practice by making sacrifices. But this temporal loyalty is subject to the limitation imposed by our undoubted loyalty to our faith. We wish to warn our rulers that in making sacrifices one after another, the dividing line may soon be reached; and we need hardly emphasize that in case there is a conflict between Divine Laws and the mandates of our rulers, every true Musalman will allow the Divine Commandments to prevail over human laws, even at the risk of laying down his life.[119]

The speeches of Ajmal Khan, as Chairman of the Reception Committee of the Delhi session of the Indian National Congress held in 1918, Dr M.A. Ansari and A.K. Fazlul Haq set the tone of the ensuing Khilafat Movement. Among the Congress leaders, Gandhi read the Muslim sentiments and helped in establishing his unquestioned supremacy in the Khilafat and the Non-cooperation Movement.

Prominent Muslim divines attended the Muslim League session including Abdul Bari, Azad Subhani, Ibrahim Sialkoti, Sanaullah Amritsari, Ahmed Saeed, Kifyatullah and Abdul Latif which gave a new turn to the Muslim politics. Another significant incident of the session was the withdrawal of M.A. Jinnah and Mahmudabad from the Muslim League because they were opposed to the Resolution on Khilafat.[120]

The stage was now set for a political upheaval which during the short period it lasted, changed the face of the country. Gandhi launched a mass struggle against the government with the triple purposes of winning swaraj, rectification of the Punjab wrongs and rehabilitation of the Khilafat. For the first time after 1857, the stage was ready for launching a nation-wide programme in which millions of Hindus and Muslims were eager to participate.

Notes and References

1. Sunderlal, *History of the Hindu-Muslim Problem; Kanpur Riot Enquiry Committee Report*, 1931, p. 130.
2. W.W. Hunter, *The Indian Musalmans*, 1870; Sunderlal, *History of the Hindu-Muslim Problem*.
3. Elphinstone Papers, 14 May 1858. Wood Papers: Wood to Elgin, 3 March 1862.
4. Wood Papers: Wood to Elgin, 10 May 1862.
5. Ibid., 19 May 1862.
6. Lytton Papers: Lytton to Salisbury, 31 May 1885.
7. Dufferin Papers: Reay to Dufferin, 31 May 1885.
8. Ibid., Sir Rivers Thompson to Dufferin, 14 January 1886.
9. Ibid., Sir W.H. Gregory to Dufferin, 21 February 1886.
10. Ibid., Sir W.H. Gregory to Dufferin, 27 March 1887.
11. Ibid., Sir W.H. Gregory to Dufferin, 16 May 1888.
12. Ibid., Sir Aukland Colvin to Dufferin, 24 May 1888.
13. Quoted by P. Moon., *Strangers in India*, p. 99.
14. Hamilton to Curzon, 2 September 1897.
15. Cross Papers: Dufferin to Cross, 26 March 1888.
16. Ibid., Cross to Dufferin, 14 January 1887.
17. Lansdowne, Speech in the Imperial Legislative Council, 16 March 1893.
18. B.N. Pande, *The Hindu-Muslim Problem*, 1939, p. 48.
19. Ibid., p. 49.
20. Ibid., pp. 49-50.
21. Ibid., pp. 51-3.
22. Ibid., pp. 68-9.
23. Ibid., pp. 76-7.
24. Ibid., p. 78.
25. Jawaharlal Nehru, *The Discovery of India*, pp. 358-9.
26. Ibid., pp. 358-9.
27. Lord Ronaldshay, *Heart of Aryavarta;* Sunderlal, *History of the Hindu-Muslim Problem*, K.R.E.C.R., pp. 131-2.
28. Farquhar, *Modern Religious Movements in India*, p. 56.
29. Sunderlal, op. cit., pp. 134-5.
30. Sir Akhiri Mazamin, *Syed Ahmad Khan* (A.H. 1314-5; A.D. 1897-8), printed by M. Fazulddin, Bazar Kashmiri, Lahore, 1898, pp. 50 ff.
31. *Majmua Lecturehai Sir Syed* (Urdu), Munshi Sirajuddin edition, Balaji Press, 1892, pp. 117-21.
32. Ibid.
33. Ibid.
34. Ibid., pp. 56-7.

35. *Eminent Mussalmans*, G.A. Natesan & Co., Madras, pp. 8-9
36. *Akhari Mazamin*, p. 70.
37. *Majmua Lecturehai Sir Syed* (Urdu), pp. 117-21.
38. *Eminent Mussalmans*, G.A. Natesan & Co., Madras.
39. *Tahdhibul Akhlaq* (Lahore, Fazulddin edition), Vol. II, p. 457.
40. Ibid., Vol. I, pp. 429-31.
41. K.K. Aziz, *The Making of Pakistan*, p. 20.
42. M. Noman, *Muslim India*, p. 52.
43. A.A.A. Fyzee, *Modern Approach to Islam*, pp. 68-70.
44. Tarachand, *History of the Freedom Movement in India*, Vol. II, pp. 382-5.
45. M.A. Sarwar, *Mawlana Ubaydul-lah Sindhi: His Life, Teachings and Political Views*, Sindh Sagar Academy, Lahore, 1943.
46. The account is based upon Husain Ahmad Madni's autobiography (*Nawsh-i-Hayat* 1953). In his earlier book, *Safarnama-i-Shaikh-ul-Hind*, written in 1922, these facts were either omitted or denied, because the conditions did not then permit their revelation.
47. Ibid., p. 33.
48. Husain Ahmad Madni, *Nawsh-i-Hayat* (Urdu), 2 volumes; Tarachand, *History of Freedom Movement in India*, Vol. III, p. 259.
49. Husain Ahmad Madni, *Mutahadda Qaumiyat aur Islam* (Urdu), published by the Nazim Majlisis Qasim al Maarif, Deoband, p. 260.
50. Ibid., p. 260.
51. Sunderlal, *A History of the Hindu-Muslim Problem*, 1951, pp. 138-40.
52. Ibid., pp. 142-3.
53. Ibid.
54. Vide Badruddin Tyabji's correspondence in the National Archives of India, New Delhi; also Husain B. Tyabji, *Badruddin Tyabji, A Biography*, Thacker & Co., Bombay, 1952, p. 208.
55. Ibid., p. 209.
56. Husain B. Tyabji, op. cit., p. 160.
57. Ibid., p. 213.
58. Ibid., p. 167.
59. Ibid., p. 168.
60. Letter dated 3 December 1887; ibid., p. 178.
61. Letter dated 3 December 1887; ibid., pp. 178.
62. Letter dated 13 January 1888; ibid., p. 191.
63. Presidential Address, Madras Session, 1887.
64. *The Aligarh Institute Gazette*, 30 January 1894.
65. Mary, Countess of Minto, *India — Minto and Morley*, p. 47.
66. Ibbetson's Minute, dated 23 April 1903.
67. Curzon's note, dated 6 March 1903.
68. Report on the Native Newspapers, Bengal, July-December 1903.
69. Curzon Papers: Curzon to Brodrick, 2 February 1905.
70. Ibid., Curzon to Brodrick, 17 February 1904.
71. G.K. Gokhale, *Speeches and Writings*, Vol. II, 19 May 1906, p. 336.
72. Minto Papers: Minto to Morley, 29 March 1906.
73. Ibid., Morley to Minto, 25 April 1906.

74. For translation of the pamphlet, see Home Department Political A, Progs. July 1907, No. 189-92.
75. Home Department, Public A, Progs. July 1906, No. 124; also H. Risley to Arthur Godley, Under Secretary of State, 12 July 1906.
76. Home Department, Pub. A, Progs. May 1907, Nos. 159-71.
77. Muhsinul Mulk's Letter to Archbold, 18 August 1906, refers to Archbold's draft and his own reaction. M.A. Das, *India Under Morley and Minto*, pp. 167-8.
78. Tarachand, *History of the Freedom Movement in India*, Vol. III, p. 395.
79. Ibid., Vol. III, p. 396.
80. Shibli Numani, *Muslim Gazette of Lucknow*, 9 October 1907.
81. Syed Sulaiman Nadvi, *Hayat-i-Shibli*, Darul Musannafin, Azamgarh, 1943, p. 296.
82. Martin Gilbert, *Servant of India*, bearing correspondence and Diaries of Sir James Dunlop Smith, p. 57.
83. Ibid., p. 6.
84. Ibid., p. 135. Letter from Dunlop Smith to Lady Minto, 11 March 1908.
85. Ibid., p. 189.
86. Minto Papers: Minto to Morley, 28 May 1906.
87. Ibid.
88. Minto's Memorandum, 21 March 1907.
89. Minto's reply to the Muslim Deputation, Lady Minto, *India — Minto and Morley*, pp. 46-7.
90. *Report of the Indian National Congress*, 1908, Resolution II.; G.A. Natesan, *The Indian National Congress*, 2nd Edition, Part II, p. 127.
91. Ibid., Part I, p. 900.
92. *Congress Presidential Addresses* (2nd edition, Second Series, 1934), pp. 167-71, Natesan (1934).
93. *The Indian National Congress* (Natesan), 2nd Edition, 1917, Part II, p. 180.
94. R. MacDonald, op., cit., p. 179.
95. Muhsinul Mulk's speech, quoted in Ram Gopal, *Indian Muslims*, p. 115.
96. *Report on Indian Constitutional Reforms*, p. 14.
97. Sunderlal, *History of the Hindu-Muslim Problem*.
98. Pattabhi Sitaramayya, *The History of the Indian National Congress*, Vol. I, p. 129.
99. B.G. Tilak, Indian National Congress, Lucknow Session, December 1916, *Writings and Speeches*, pp. 223-4.
100. S. Bapat (ed.), *Tilak Reminiscences*, Vol. II, pp. 204-5; and *The Maharatta*, 20 March 1918.
101. Tilak's reply to Paranjpe, 12 December 1919, in *All About Tilak*, p. 323.
102. Sunderlal, *History of the Hindu-Muslim Problem*, p. 166.
103. Ibid., p. 167.
104. Jawaharlal Nehru, *Discovery of India*, p. 411.
105. Ibid., pp. 412-3.
106. Ibid., p. 413.
107. Ibid., p. 414.
108. Maulana Mohammad Ali, Presidential Address at the Coconada Congress, 1923.

109. Jawaharlal Nehru, *The Discovery of India*, p. 416, first edition, 1946, Calcutta.
110. Report of the Muslim League Session, 1918, Address of the Chairman, Reception Committee.
111. Ibid.
112. Ibid.
113. *Saheeh Muslim.*
114. Ibid.
115. *Mishat Belihaqi.*
116. Report of the Muslim League Session, 1918.
117. Parliamentary Debates, Commons, Vol. XCIX, p. 838.
118. Fazlul Haq's Presidential Address, cited in Khalid Bin Sayeed, *Pakistan, the Formative Phase*, 1960, p. 46.
119. Syed Sharifuddin Pirzada (ed.), *Foundations of Pakistan*, Vol. I, New Delhi, 1982, pp. 497-8.
120. Tarachand, *History of the Freedom Movement in India*, Vol. III, pp. 416-7.
121. Ibid., Vol. III, pp. 282-3.
122. Santimoy Roy, *Freedom Movement and Indian Muslims*, Peoples Publishing House, pp. 94-8. By permission of the author.

APPENDIX 4.1

The Ahrars

In 1857 the leading family of the *ulama* of Ludhiana threw in their lot with the revolutionaries. At Bahadur Shah's command they marched to Delhi, fighting their way through British forces. Abdul Qadir, the head of the family, and his sons showed indomitable courage during the siege. When Delhi fell they retired to the jungles of Patiala and evaded all attempts of the government to arrest them. On the proclamation of general amnesty they decided to return to Ludhiana. Abdul Qadir died on the way, but his family was warmly welcomed by the people.

The sons resumed their ancestral profession of religious teaching. In 1885, when the Indian National Congress met, they welcomed its formation. When two years later Sir Syed Ahmad Khan announced his opposition and advised the Muslims to abstain from participating in the Congress, Shah Muhammad, son of Abdul Qadir, issued a *fatwa* condemning Sir Syed's attitude, declaring co-operation with the Hindus for political purposes lawful and desirable. The *fatwa* was signed by nearly one thousand maulavis from all parts of India. It was printed under the title of *Nusrat-al-Ahrar* (Victory of the Good) and distributed in the meeting of the Congress at Allahabad in December 1888.

Ludhiana became a well-known centre of the liberal nationalist movement. In 1896, a weekly paper was issued which was succeeded by an English daily, the *Observer*. Its independent views attracted the wrath of the government and it had to cease publication in 1919.

The *ulama* of Ludhiana were greatly agitated and when Gandhi offered to start the movement of non-cooperation for the rectification of the Khilafat wrong and the restitution of the Holy Lands, Habibur Rahman, the grandson of Shah Muhammad, a young man of 27, joined the Congress. He never looked back till his death. He was a man of amazing courage and endurance. His devotion to principles was such as martyrs might envy. He never deviated from his beliefs and he stood by them firm as a rock.

On the advice of Abul Kalam Azad, he founded the *Majlis-e-Ahrar* (The Society of Freeman). Among its aims and objectives were:

(1) The complete independence of India;
(2) In independent India, freedom of religion, culture, civilization and education for all.

The sacrifices which the Ahrars made, and the sufferings which they cheerfully bore in the cause of Indian independence constitute a shining chapter of Indian history.[121]

APPENDIX 4.2

Muslim Martyrs in Jallianwala Bagh, Amritsar 13 April 1919[122]

Abdul Karim: born 1901 at Amritsar, Punjab, son of Pir Baksh, washerman, killed at the Jallianwala Bagh.

Abdul Karim: born 1902 at Amritsar, Punjab, son of Lal Mohammad, student, killed at the Jallianwala Bagh.

Abdul Khaliq: born 1859 at Amritsar, Punjab, son of Rahim Khan, worker in carpet factory, killed at the Jallianwala Bagh.

Abdul Majid: born at Peshawar, North-West Frontier Provinces (now in Pakistan), son of Rahim Baksh, killed at the Jallianwala Bagh.

Abdulla: resident of Amritsar, Punjab, son of Pir Baksh, washerman, killed at the Jallianwala Bagh.

Abdulla: born 1899 at Amritsar, Punjab, son of Lal Mohammad, killed at the Jallianwala Bagh.

Ahmad Din: born at Amritsar, Punjab, son of Karim Baksh, killed at the Jallianwala Bagh.

Ahmad Khan: born 1903 at Amritsar, Punjab, son of Dare Khan, killed at the Jallianwala Bagh.

Ahmad Ullah: born 1884 at Amritsar, Punjab, son of Karim Baksh, seriously wounded at the Jallianwala Bagh, died on 25 May 1919.

Ahmed Din: born 1886 at Gujranwala, Punjab (now in Pakistan), milk vendor, killed at the Jallianwala Bagh.

Allah Baksh: born 1864 at Lahore, Punjab (now in Pakistan), blacksmith, killed at the Jallianwala Bagh.

Allah Ditta: born 1874 at Amritsar, Punjab, son of Megha, killed at the Jallianwala Bagh.

Barkat: born 1899 at Amritsar, Punjab, son of Bhilla Sheikh, killed at the Jallianwala Bagh.

Barkat Ali: born 1881 at Amritsar, Punjab, son of Ilahi Bux, carpenter, killed at the Jallianwala Bagh.

Bheru alias *Nizam Din:* born 1901 in Hoshiarpur district, Punjab, son of Labhi Gujjar, labourer, killed at the Jallianwala Bagh.

Charagh Din: born 1901, district Lahore, Punjab (now in Pakistan), son of Mohammed Bux, labourer, killed at the Jallianwala Bagh.

Fateh Muhammad: born 1895 at Amritsar, Punjab, son of Ata Mohammad, dyer, killed at the Jallianwala Bagh.

Fazal: born 1904 at Gujranwala, Punjab (now in Pakistan), son of Maula Bux, labourer, killed at the Jallianwala Bagh.

Feroz Din: born 1900 at Amritsar, Punjab, son of Sher Mohammed, goldsmith, killed at the Jallianwala Bagh.

Ghulam Molhammad: born in 1901 at Amritsar, Punjab, son of Rahim Baksh, washerman, killed at the Jallianwala Bagh.

Gulam Mohiuddin: born 1874, resident of Amritsar, Punjab, son of Mohammad Jan Butt Kashmiri, killed at the Jallianwala Bagh.

Ghulam Rasul: born in 1895 at Amritsar, Punjab, son of Ghani Shah Kashmiri, killed at the Jallianwala Bagh.

Ghulam Rasul: resident of Amritsar, Punjab, son of Samad Shah of Srinagar, Kashmir, killed at the Jallianwala Bagh.

Hamid: born in 1895, resident of Amritsar, Punjab, son of Ahmad Din Kashmiri, killed at the Jallianwala Bagh.

Hassan Mohammed: born in 1910 at Gujranwala, Punjab (now in Pakistan), son of Fazal Din Arain, student, killed at the Jallianwala Bagh.

Hassi: resident of Amritsar, Punjab, son of Sikandar, goldsmith, killed at the Jallianwala Bagh.

Ibrahim: born 1879, resident of Amritsar, Punjab, son of Imam Din, contractor, killed at the Jallianwala Bagh.

Ilm Din: born 1899 at village Chak Mokand, district Amritsar, Punjab, private employee, killed at the Jallianwala Bagh.

Imam Din: born 1879, resident of Amritsar, Punjab, son of Murad Baksh, blacksmith, killed at the Jallianwala Bagh.

Ismail: born 1887, resident of Amritsar, Punjab, son of Miran Baksh, goldsmith, killed at the Jallianwala Bagh.

Ismail: born 1905 at Gujranwala, Punjab (now in Pakistan), son of Nizam Din, killed at the Jallianwala Bagh.

Karim Baksh: born in 1879, resident of Amritsar, Punjab, watchman, killed at the Jallianwala Bagh.

Khair Din: born in 1894, resident of Amritsar, Punjab, son of Mangtu, oil merchant, killed at the Jallianwala Bagh.

Khuda Baksh: born in 1883, resident of Amritsar, Punjab, son of Wasan Saha Fakir, killed at the Jallianwala Bagh.

Mahbub Shah: born 1889, at Amritsar, Punjab, son of Mir Ahmed Shah Sayed, killed at the Jallianwala Bagh.

Mera Baksh: born in 1889, resident of Amritsar, Punjab, son of Nikka Kashmiri, potter, killed at the Jallianwala Bagh.

Mohammed Din: born 1894, resident of Amritsar, Punjab, son of Karim Baksh, goldsmith, killed at the Jallianwala Bagh.

Mohammed Din: born 1897, resident of Delhi, son of Khuda Baksh, took part in the public demonstration at Delhi against the Rowlatt Act on 30 March 1919, received bullet wound in firing by an army unit and died the same day.

Mohammed Ismail: born 1912 at Amritsar, Punjab, son of Karam Din alias Kalu Kashmiri, student, killed at the Jallianwala Bagh.

Mohammed Ramzan: born 1895, resident of Amritsar, Punjab, son of Rahim Bux Kashmiri, confectioner, killed at the Jallianwala Bagh.

Mohammed Sadiq: born 1894, resident of Amritsar, Punjab, son of Murad Buksh Sheikh, canal department employee, killed at the Jallianwala Bagh.

Mohammed Shafi: born 1889 at V. Dangerke, Zafarwal, district Sialkot, Punjab (now in Pakistan), son of Jan Mohammed, shopkeeper, killed at the Jallianwala Bagh.

Mohammed Shafi: born 1901 at Amritsar, son of Rahim Bux, killed at the Jallianwala Bagh.

Mohammed Shafi: born 1902 at Amritsar, Punjab, son of Abdul Rahim, died in firing by the police near the railway bridge, Amritsar, on 10 April 1919.

Mohammed Sharif: resident of Amritsar, Punjab, son of Mohammed Ramzan, mason, killed at the Jallianwala Bagh.

Mohammad Bux: born 1884, resident of Amritsar, Punjab, mason, killed at the Jallianwala Bagh.

Musa: born 1894, resident of Amritsar, Punjab, son of Jamal Din Kashmiri, killed at the Jallianwala Bagh.

Noor Mohammed: born 1894, resident of Amritsar, Punjab, son of Jhanda, oil merchant, killed at the Jallianwala Bagh.

Ramzan: born 1894, resident of Amritsar, Punjab, turner in a factory, killed at the Jallianwala Bagh.

Rehmat: born 1898 at Amritsar, Punjab, son of Nawab Din Sheikh, killed at the Jallianwala Bagh.

Rukan-Uddin: born 1901 at V. Thanda, district Amritsar, Punjab, son of Illahi Bux, farmer, killed at the Jallianwala Bagh.

Shamas Uddin: born 1895 at Amritsar, Punjab, son of Sikandar, goldsmith, killed at the Jallianwala Bagh.

Sharar Din: born 1900 at Amritsar, Punjab, son of Jamal Din, student, killed at the Jallianwala Bagh.

Shahjan: born at Peshawar, North-West Frontier Province (now in Pakistan), died in firing by the police at the railway bridge, Amritsar on 10 April 1919.

Sher Khan: born at Peshawar, North-West Frontier Province (now in Pakistan), died in firing by the police at the railway bridge, Amritsar on 10 April 1919.

Sherbaz: born at Peshawar, North-West Frontier Province (now in Pakistan), died in firing by the police at the railway bridge, Amritsar, on 10 April 1919.

Taj Din, Hafiz, alias *Mullan:* born 1894 at Amritsar, Punjab, son of Ali Mohammed, tailor, killed at the Jallianwala Bagh.

Umar Behi: born 1864 at V. Dulla, district Amritsar, Punjab, widow of Shri Iman Din, killed at the Jallianwala Bagh.

Umar Bux: born 1859, resident of Amritsar, Punjab, son of Ida Sheikh, killed at the Jallianwala Bagh.

Umar Din: born 1889 at Amritsar, Punjab, son of Mohammed Din, private employee, killed at the Jallianwala Bagh.

Chapter V

National Revolutionary Movements in India (1900-1918)

Santimay Ray

THE INDIAN REVOLUTIONARY MOVEMENT is a part of the broader national movement which had its formal beginning in the foundation of Indian National Congress on 28 December 1885 in the city of Bombay.

Any serious undertaking of scientific narration of historical events requires a word of explanation on the key concept around which the threads of historical events may be woven and causal relations between the different ebbs and tides may be measured. Here, in this case, the term 'national revolutionary' needs to be clearly defined.

In the Indian context, 'national movement' clearly implies a movement directly and indirectly against colonial rule. 'National revolutionary', in this particular context, represents the ideals, methods and activities of certain organizations and groups of people inspired by the avowed object of creating terror, uncertainty and extreme uneasiness amongst the ruling class, so as to make their life insecure and unbearable, and of instilling courage and hope in the minds of the dismayed and demoralized people; their cherished objective was the attainment of independence.[1] In British administrative records they were termed 'terrorists' and occasionally 'anarchists'. In course of time, the revolutionaries themselves accepted this terminology, on the basis of their short-term aims, as evidenced by their party literature.

In this brief survey of the movement, an attempt will be made to highlight the correlation between the streams of the broad national movement, spearheaded by the Indian National Congress from its inception to the end of the First World War in 1918, when the national revolutionaries, may broadly be said to have integrated themselves into the mainstream of anti-imperialist national movement led by the Indian National Congress under Gandhiji's leadership.[2]

1. Background

What then was the situation at the turn of the 19th century which led to the emergence of militant nationalism of the type branded by the British rulers as revolutionary terrorism?

The first important development was the emergence of a middle class, educated on western lines, sensitive to the appalling misery of the Indian people, but unable to express openly their growing indignation and taking positive action to improve their lot.

The chronic visitations of famines, especially the one in 1877, which cost some five to six million human lives, and the growth of unemployment to massive levels amongst the educated middle class, and amongst landless peasants, made them sullen and apprehensive about their future.[3] Amongst school teachers, the problem of under-employment became particularly acute. According to Vereney Lovett, a well-known British columnist, the number of school teachers was very large because many educated persons opted for this profession, in spite of the incredibly low salaries offered, since no better alternatives were available.[4]

This desperate situation was compounded when every attempt at individual or national advancement was undermined by the obstruction and hostility of an all-powerful, tyrannical alien rule. The press was gagged in 1876, the Drama Performance Act (1878) denied them the right to stage any exposure of the tyrannical system; the Arms Act (1878) deprived them of all means to protection against predators — animal and human; the failure to pass the Ilbert Bill (1884) as originally drafted, in the face of determined European opposition, caused frustration and helplessness.

The second important factor which shaped the ideas, quickened the intellect and fired the emotions of the revolutionaries was the positive intellectual influence of the Bengal Renaissance initiated by Rammohun on the one hand, and the resurgence of the neo-humanism of Ramkrishna Paramahansa, Vivekananda and Bankim, on the other. Derozian revolutionary ideas, invoked the spirit of rationalism, while the literature of the British and French enlightenment left a powerful intellectual legacy. These factors led to the rise of a group of fearless rationalist journalists and writers like Devendra Nath Tagore, Rajendralal Mitra, Ramgopal Ghosh, Peary Chand Mitra, Harish Mukherjee, Sisir Ghosh and Suren Banerjea, among others. They fertilized the soil to a very large extent and created the climate for the defiance that characterized the flaming rise of *agnijuga*.

Swami Vivekananda

Amongst the savants who shaped the ideas of the revolutionary terrorists, especially in Bengal, Swami Vivekananda's name is the outstanding one.[5] Without going into an examination of the vast mass of writings and speeches of Vivekananda, a few significant aspects of his speeches may be illustrated here.[6]

At Kumbha Konam in 1897 he declared:

> What our country now *wants are muscles of iron and nerves of steel, gigantic wills which nothing can resist,* which can penetrate into mysteries and the secrets of the universe and will accomplish their purpose in any fashion even if it meant going down to the bottom of the ocean and meeting death face to face. This is what we want and this can only be created, established and strengthened by understanding and realising the ideal of the Advaita, that ideal of oneness of all.

The second element in Swami Vivekananda's nationalism was his tireless efforts to propagate, in his unique way, *love for one's own people — that is, the starving millions of India.* He asks:

> Has it gone into your blood, coursing through your veins, becoming consonant with your heart beats? Has it made you almost mad? Are you seized with the one idea of the misery of ruin and have you forgotten all about your name, fame, your wives, your children, your property, even your own bodies? Have you done that? That is first step to become a patriot, the very first step.[7]

The service of man, he preached, was the highest form of religion. He raised the most pertinent question: 'If you cannot worship your brother, man, the manifested God, how can you worship a god who is unmanifested?'[8]

This firm belief in the divinity and essential quality of man led him to deliver this inspiring message:

> Forget not that thou art born as a sacrifice to the Mother's Altar; . . . forget not that the lower classes, the ignorant, the poor, the illiterate, the cobbler, the sweeper are the flesh and blood, the brothers. Thou brave one, be bold, take courage, be proud that thou art an Indian and proudly proclaim I am an Indian, every Indian is my brother, the poor and destitute Indian, the Brahmin Indian, the Pariah Indian is my brother.[9]

'Slaves can have no politics,' he asserted, *'It is preferable to play football than to study the Gita.'* Here his emphasis was quite clear. He had no time to build up a self-contained social philosophy. His career was short but resplendent with a glorious searchlight which enabled the first and second generation of the leaders of the national revolutionary movement to develop on a firm ideological foundation suited to the given historical situation. As Dr Biman Behari Mazumdar aptly writes:

> Swami Vivekananda is one of the greatest makers of modern India. . . . It is not a mere coincidence that his works along with Gita were found by the police in the possession of many of the revolutionaries in the early nineteenth century.
>
> He wanted to organise throughout Indian groups of youngmen, strong, physically and morally, who would willingly sacrifice comforts in the service of the suffering humanity, ready to undergo hardships for any noble cause and prepare the country for higher civilization and spiritual greatness. His stirring appeal to the nation's youth reverberated throughout the land.[10]

Bankim Chandra

Next to Swami Vivekananda, Bankim Chandra was regarded as a 'prophet of modern India' who was able to *foresee the need of creating a band of selfless sannyasis for achieving the liberation of the country.* His *Ananda Math* provided the model which inspired Nivedita and Aurobindo to prepare the blueprint for the revolutionary workers set out in their famous booklet, *Bhawani Mandir.* In it they openly urged their readers to self-sacrifice: 'Worshipers of the Mother are they from their birth in Her incarnation of the Sword, lovers of death are they — not lovers of life — and of storm and stress.'[11] Bankim's *Dharmatattva* and *Anushilan* also exerted great influence in shaping the mental outlook and physical organization of the underground revolutionary parties, like Anushilan (1902):

> It called for cultivation of the physical and moral qualities of man to perfection. . . . The concept of Anushilan stood for a structure of values that impelled one to seek happiness in harmonising bodily vigour, devotion and knowledge.[12]

It made a man duty-bound to serve his own self, his relatives, his country and the world. Patriotism, however, was the loftiest ideal that a believer in Anushilan would strive to realize. It was incumbent upon him to effect a synthesis between the scientific thought of the West and the passionate devotion to duty as prescribed by Shri Krishna in the Bhagavad Gita.[13]

Patriotic Poems, Songs and Plays

Along with moral and intellectual stirrings, the emotional fabric of revolutionary nationalism was prepared by the flow of patriotic songs and poems. These flowed from Michael Madhuśudan and Rangalal Bandopadhyay who in 1858, almost coincidentally with the Mutiny, exhorted the people to realize that death was preferable to serfdom and asked: 'Is there any fool who would [like to] put the shackles of slavery around his own feet? Hellish it is to remain a bondman for millenia; a moment's independence tantamounts to heavenly bliss.' Hemchandra Bandopadhyay exhorted the people to develop a martial spirit combined with matching physical fitness and mental vigour.

In 1874, Jyotirindra Nath Tagore, in a drama entitled *Puru Bikram* gave expression to the same feeling as that which inspired Rangalal. He wrote in verse:

> Fie to him who entertains fear for his life
> in emancipating the motherland from bondage!
> Let such a man suffer the eternal perdition of
> slavery. What is the use of life saved at
> the cost of independence? Fie to him who
> desires to tolerate such a miserable existence.[14]

It goes without saying that such writings and songs had a tremendous impact on the young minds of Bengal and the rumblings were heard of the mighty explosion during the first two decades of the 20th century.

Here it would be appropriate to quote what Mr Farquhar wrote on religious nationalism in 1912 and revised in 1915 for inclusion as an annexure in James Campbell Ker's *Political Trouble in India (1907-17).* It gives one an insight into the gradual transformation of the Indian mind:

> (a) In this new era we have the assertion of the full independence of the Indian mind. The educated Indian now regards himself as a full grown man, the equal in every respect of the cultured European, not to be set aside as an Asiatic or as a member of a dark race. . . . This adult self confidence was immeasurably strengthened by the victory of Japan over Russia (1905) and the temporary reverse of the British Army in the Boer War. The exultation which every Indian felt over these victories lifted the national spirit to its height and gave a new note of strength to the surging national consciousness.[15]
>
> (b) The new nationalism is much more serious and open eyed than the thin old politician. It is burdened, tortured, driven forward by the conviction that the whole national life needs to be reinspired, reborn.
>
> (c) . . . . Finally, whether in anarchists or in men of peace the new nationalism is willing to serve and suffer.

Amongst the causes of the sudden rise of the 'storm of furious hate', Mr C.R. Cleveland in his introductory observations in *Political Troubles in India,* lists the fact of foreign rule itself and the hatred and contempt Europeans displayed towards Indians:

> . . . . This behaviour of a small minority of our fellow countrymen which at all times has produced very serious results, necessarily stirred fiercest

passions, when national feeling and Indian self respect rose to floodtide. . . .[16]

Lord Curzon's contribution to this process was among the greatest:

Perhaps no man was ever so well prepared for the Viceroyalty as Lord Curzon was . . . yet it was his tragic destiny to be more furiously detested by the educated Indian [whom he called a nation of liars] than any other Englishman. The cause lay in his self confident and arrogant spirit and manner but contemporaneous with the rise of Indian mind to independence and national dignity and with the emergence of Asia from her secular slavery to Europe. They stung India to fury and worked wild ruin.[17]

The main antagonism between Hindu and Western Culture and the exaggerated praise of India and condemnation of the west had greatly heightened the ego of the new educated middle class. *But it was the partition of Bengal (1905)*[18] *that gave the anarchist party their opportunity to rouse the people, immediately when a new type of journalism had appeared in Calcutta.* The principal writers were Aurobindo Ghosh, who had been educated in England and had then spent some years in the service of the Gaekwad of Baroda, his brother Barindra, Bipin Chandra Pal and Bhupendra Nath Datta, brother of Swami Vivekananda. While Bal Gangadhar Tilak and his followers continued the campaign in Maharashtra, Lala Lajpat Rai and the followers of Dayananda Saraswati did all they could to rouse the Punjab.[19]

It had its echo too in the very heart of the British Empire, in London, where Shyamaji Krishnaverma launched a campaign through a new penny journal, *The Indian Sociologist*.[20]

One can only describe briefly the grim inadequacy of material and cultural components in the life of Indian youth, especially in Bengal, Maharashtra and the Punjab at the turn of the 19th century, which made them strongly react to 'the loss of identity' in their craving for a meaningful life in a background of racism, then rampant. Dr Sumit Sarkar puts this very appropriately when he sums up the situation:

Rigidly excluded from military service, constantly accused of effeminacy by the rulers, it was natural for young Bengalees to seek psychological compensation in a cult of physical strength and somewhat exaggerated faith in the efficacy of purely military methods and the mounting number of cases of intimidation and assault by Anglo-Indians must have helped to make the 'akharas' seem even more indispensable. With physical culture came to be combined in the course of 'Anushilan', the development of all human faculties in the service of the country and of a rejuvenated Hindu faith. Vivekananda's teachings in the 1890s, gave a tremendous stimulus to national pride, tacitly identified with Hindu resurgence and inculcated a spirit of social service. There was also the impact of events abroad — the Boer war, which set Rajnarayan Basu's nephew Janendranath thinking in terms of secret societies — and the meteoric rise of Japan, the influence in the early years of the new century of Okakura and Nivedita; as well as of course the reaction to Curzon's arrogant ways.[21]

The Roots

To trace the ancestry of revolutionary secret societies, one may be tempted to go as far back as sannyasis and fakirs at the early stage of British Rule, to be followed by the Waahabis during the 19th century. At a time when Vasudeo Balwant Phadke (1845-83) of Maharashtra, along with Ismail Khan, a Rohilla leader, took up the thread from the Waahabis and made an unsuccessful bid to rise against the British Raj, the great *ulema* leader, Jamaluddin Al-Afghani, made an extensive tour, contacting various brands of nationalist Muslims, like Shibli Nomani, Rashid Ahmed Gangoi, young Mahmud Hassain, a firebrand fighter and teacher in Deoband school, in order to bring them to the path of armed resistance against the infidel *firingis*.

But the classical *agnijuga* had yet to begin. To trace the history of the revolutionary movement in Bengal, in India, no less, one can go back to the endeavours of Nabagopal Mitra to set up a National Theatre, a National Paper and a National Press as well as *akharas* in Sankar Ghosh Lane.[22] Poet Tagore has left a well-known account of the secret conclave or game as played by the young Tagores in the 1870s, with Jyotirindranath as leader and Rajnarayan Basu as the principal motivator and chief architect. Surendranath's lecture on Mazzini also inspired many students and youth to imitate the Carbonari of the Italian national liberation movement.[23] Shibnath Shastri also caught the infection of revolutionary ideas. In 1876 he inspired a batch of young men, including Bipin Chandra Pal, to take a vow of 'Dedication to the Cult of Fire'.

While Bengal was in ferment, the nascent political community in India was suddenly thrilled by the meteoric rise of that remarkable figure, Vasudeo Balwant Phadke, in Maharashtra. The sufferings of the people during the famine in the Deccan (1876-7) made him sad and angry. He toured all over Maharashtra and roused the people from apathy. He, however, failed to educate the Ramoshi tribes. With the help of Ismail Khan, the Rohila leader, he organized an armed band prepared to die for the cause of freedom.

Early in May 1879 Vasudeo proclaimed a manifesto denouncing the British policy of ruthless exploitation of India and demanding redressal. 'The proclamation sent a thrill of excitement throughout India.' The Government ordered the army to suppress the uprising.[24] Avoiding pitched battle, Vasudeo reorganized his forces and started guerilla warfare. But he was ultimately betrayed and was captured in a Buddhist monastery and was sentenced to transportation for life. On 17 February 1883, in Aden Jail, he succumbed to the rigours of life in jail. Thus passed away one of the bravest freedom fighters of India since the mutiny. He left a diary which is the only first-hand source of information on this episode. As V. Joshi points out:

> The single handed fight of Vasudeo against the British Raj was bound to be a failure. But it left a legacy and the seeds he sowed, grew into a mighty banyan tree with its roots spread over India, in about quarter of a century. His daring spirit was later taken up by the Chaphekar brothers in Maharashtra and the revolutionaries in Bengal.[25]

Vasudeo was the link between the revolutionary ideas of Rajnarayan Bose, Surendranath Banerjea and Nabagopal Mitra and the revolutionary actions of Chaphekar and the Savarkar brothers in the early part of the 20th century.

The period following the death of Vasudeo Balwant Phadke, particularly the decade from 1897 to 1907, were the formative years of the classical *agniyuga*.

Revolutionary Writings

The first feature of this revolutionary movement was the remarkable growth of revolutionary journalism, particularly in Bombay, Bengal, the Punjab and the United Provinces. Representatives of this development were the *Kesari* edited by Bal Gangadhar Tilak (1897), *Poona Vaibhav* (1896), *Kal,* a weekly Marathi paper published from Pune by Shivram Paranjape (1898). Paranjape was warned by the authorities to desist from seditious writing in 1900, 1904, 1905 and 1907. In 1908 he was prosecuted and thrown into prison. Bal Gangadhar Tilak was jailed soon after for writing in *Kesari* in support of Khudiram's revolutionary venture.

All over the country, newspapers began to breathe fire and brimstone and received the kind of attention of the authorities that they 'deserved'. Among those to suffer were the *Poona Vaibhav* (1897), *Maḍavritta* (1897), *Kesari, Kal, Vihari, Bande Mataram* (1906), *Jugantar, Sandhya, Navasakti, Karam Yogin, Pratoda* (Bombay), *Sahayak* (Lahore), *Peshawal* (Lahore), *Hoonkar, Swaraj, Desha-Sevak, Amrita Bazar Patrika, Karmajogin* and *Swarajya* from Allahabad. The *Indian Sociologist* issued from London brought a sea of change in the mental outlook of the educated youth and urged them on to defiant revolutionary actions.

There was also a whole crop of defiant, inflammatory literature which was proscribed and confiscated as soon as the authorities could sign orders for the purpose. The *Laghu Abhịnay, Bharat Gatha* (Marathi poems of Ganesh Damodar Savarkar),[26] *Swadhinatar Itihash*, lives of Mazzini and Garibaldi, *Desher Katha* by Sakharam Ganesh Deuskar, deserve special mention.[27]

The act of clandestine distribution may be considered rightly as revolutionary actions, no less soul-stirring and effective than the consummation of revolutionary murders or daring robbery of later years. It had a resounding impact upon both the rulers and the ruled.

Revolutionary Societies (Samitis)

The third feature of the revolutionary movement was the growth of *samitis* which first sprang up in Maharashtra, particularly with the Chaphekar Group (in Pune) which later developed into the Mitramela. Then came Abhinava Bharati which subsequently developed into Naba Abhinav Bharati in Central India (in the Gwalior region). In Bengal, the Atmaunnati Samiti was established around 1900. Among the young men who founded it were Satish Mukherjee and Nibaran Bhattacharya, both of whom were students and later professors in Government Colleges. Like its sister organization, Anushilan, it adopted the cultivation of the potential faculties of man — the development of the self — as its main objective. It had its beginning in Central Calcutta (Bowbazar Byeam Samiti) and slowly spread over to the rural areas of the western Bengal. Chandannagar, then a French principality, became one of its main working centres. Amongst its early leaders, Bipin Behari Ganguly, Provash De and Indra Nath Nundy took an active part in various militant activities, occasionally initiated jointly with the Anushilan Samiti led by Pramthanath Mitra, Sister Nivedita, and later by Aurobindo Ghosh.[28]

Second in age after Atmaunnati, although not in importance, was the Anushilan Samiti (1902).[29] It was founded by Pramathanath Mitra with the ostensible purpose of developing the physical fitness and courage among young Bengalis. In those days there were frequent clashes between Indians and Anglo-Indians, Europeans and often European soldiers. Most of these clashes were provoked by the latter who insisted on getting privileged positions in parks, streets, public conveyance and other places. There was neither any remedy for the aggrieved Indians in court, nor did the police give them any protection. On the contrary, government agencies acted almost systematically in favour of the Anglo-Indians and Europeans. This convinced many that young Indians must be given proper physical training so that they might give a good account of themselves in such clashes. Societies for physical culture began to sprout in and around Calcutta as early as 1897. Anushilan was started virtually as a federation or co-ordinator of some of these *samitis*. But as A.C. Guha points out, 'It would be wrong to say that Anushilan Samiti was just a physical culture society and nothing more. It had also an intellectual side, as regular classes were held. It had even a political purpose though very incipient and undefined as yet.'[30]

Anushilan was followed by a host of other sister *samitis* like Suhrid and Sadhana in Mymensingh; Brati in Faridpur; Swadesh Bandhab Samiti in Bakharganj; Bharatmata Samiti in Punjab; Lotus and Dagger in London. But the Dacca Anushilan Samiti (where Pulin Das was the virtual leader), the Yugantar group of the Anushilan Samiti in Calcutta which flourished around 1906 and the Ghadar and Islamic (Fraternity) Brotherhood of later years were the major components of the national revolutionary movement in India till 1918.

2. Militant Action

Maharashtra (1897)

While the climate of revolutionary defiance evidenced in the flamboyant writings of groups of revolutionary thinkers can be traced in Maharashtra, particularly in the Pune region, to Tilak's writings and his speeches at the Ganapati and Shivaji festivals, it was further heightened in the militant protest of the Chaphekar brothers against the inhuman manner in which the Epidemic Disease Act of 1897 was implemented. According to the *Desh Mitra* (11 March 1897), 'one area in Budhwar Peth and part of Shukrawar were surrounded by 200 cavalry and 100 infantry'. The *Dnyansagar* (15 March 1897) described how 'men and women and children are marched off to the camps with guards at the back and the front, bare-headed, bare-footed as if they were a pack of lawless banditti'. It was no wonder that it could be said in such circumstances that 'men prefer death by drowning to removal to the plague hospital'.

The *Sudhakar*, on 19 April, and again on 3 May 1897, bewailed: 'Shame! There is not a country on earth whose whole people are so effeminate as ours.'

'It was now plain,' as Kalicharan Ghosh writes, 'that the moment had arrived in the revolutionary history of India when peace loving Indians began to talk freely about self defence, resistance and reprisal against the agents of the government for their misdeeds.'[31]

Rand and Ayerst were murdered by Damodar Hari Chaphekar, assisted by his brother Balkrishna, on 3 July 1897. On 9 August 1897 Damodar was arrested. He was sentenced to death and gallantly met it with a copy of the Bhagavad Gita tied up in his hand at Yeravda Central Jail on 18 April 1898 — 'a day that was remembered with gratitude by the whole nation'. Balkrishna was later arrested in Hyderabad, tried and also sentenced to death, which he met without regrets on 12 May 1899. Some time later, Wasudeo, Damodar's younger brother, and Ranade were also arrested. Wasudeo had vowed to avenge brother's death and had assassinated the two approvers in his brother's case, Ramchandra and Ganesh, and had allowed himself to be arrested on 10 February 1889. Wasudeo and Ranade were tried and sentenced to death. They were executed on 8 and 10 May 1899 respectively. They were calm and self composed in the face of death. Kalicharan Ghosh describes the revolutionary atmosphere:

> The spirit of sacrifice for a cause that was displayed by Chaphekar brothers can be traced back to the great mother who could offer three sons at the altar of the Motherland in the course of few months. Sister Nivedita came to know about the momentous event and thought of paying her respects in person to the mother then leading a life of devotion and retirement at Poona. The revered lady was engaged in her daily Puja. Nivedita was astounded to find the Mother completely self composed, no complaints; no regret. . . . The spirit of self respect and march towards self realisation of the Indian nation as well as its way and Nivedita came to realise that it has proceeded far ahead of the stage of which she had any idea.[32]

Revolutionary activities in Western India did not stop after the execution of Wasudeo and Balkrishna. The flame spread to other parts of Western and Central India — Nasik, Baroda and Gwalior.

Even Indians in London were soon roused. Shyamji Krishnavarma, a native of Kathiawar, a member of Mitramela-Abhinava Bharati Revolutionary Group, left Bombay in 1897 and went over to London. He started a monthly journal, *The Indian Sociologist*, an organ of freedom and of political, social and religious reform. It not only supported the programme of the Indian National Congress of its day, but also went one step further and gave a call for 'resistance to aggression' and established the Home Rule Society on 18 February 1905. Krishnavarma established a hostel for Indian students living in London called India House and instituted a fellowship for deserving Indian students from among whom he could pick his cadre for his revolutionary organization to undertake agitation and propaganda and, in later years, overt acts of resistance to British rule. It is no wonder that from amongst this conclave came great revolutionary patriots like Vinayak Damodar Savarkar and Madan Dhingra, Madame Cama, the 'Mother of Indian Revolutionaries', and Lala Hardayal.

Vinayak Savarkar, before leaving India, had been drawn into a movement initiated in 1905 by a sannyasi, Agamya Guru Paramahansa, who, according to an intelligence report,[33] toured throughout India and spoke fearlessly against British oppression and called for action to conquer fear. Vinayak joined the Abhinav Bharat Society founded by his elder brother Ganesh Damodar. At the time of his departure from India,

Savarkar and his brother were also the leaders of an association known as Mitramela, started around 1899. They organized Ganapati and Shivaji festivals and the physical training in Nasik and other areas.

In the meantime, Krishnavarma finding the situation uncongenial in London, shifted to Paris and, in collaboration with S.S. Rana, started a new centre.

Bengal (1907-14)

In view of the severe repression in Bengal after the partition in 1905, the Anushilan Party in Calcutta and later in Dacca and the Chandannagar Group of revolutionaries led by Srish Ghosh and Motilal Ray, along with the London Indian Sociologist group of Krishnavarma openly began to advocate Nihilist methods of revolutionary activity — a tooth for a tooth, an eye for an eye — to create a sense of terror amongst the officials of the Raj.

The anti-partition movement that started in Bengal, and got the sanction of the Banaras Congress in 1905 and the Calcutta Congress in 1906, produced a deep and sweeping emotional upheaval. In a sense, it was the first national mass upsurge which generated patriotic consciousness amongst the people in urban as well as rural areas. This political environment was further surcharged with great emotion when Rabindranath's swadeshi songs gave expression to the people's anguish and anger. The consequent resistance, suffering, sacrifices, and disappointment prepared the ground for some revolutionary action on the lines of that of the Chaphekar brothers. The Congress in those days was dominated by the Moderates. But the extremist leaders like Bal Gangadhar Tilak in Maharashtra, Lala Lajpat Rai in Punjab, and Bipin Chandra Pal in Bengal (Lal-Bal-Pal), were propagating day in and day out the need for a direct confrontation with the British Raj, as the only course left open to the oppressed people.

As in Maharashtra, the Bengal scene had also become surcharged. The arrogant Curzon had deliberately thrown down the gauntlet; the Lieutenant Governor, Sir Bamphylde Fuller's 'circular' had provoked the anti-circular movement amongst the students, particularly in East Bengal; the growth of the National Volunteer movement in 1906 had created a new atmosphere of vitality, strength and confidence. But the most significant development was the advent of Aurobindo on the political scene in 1906. Aurobindo, after organizing the Lotus and Dagger Society in London, returned to India and accepted the post of the Vice-Principal in Baroda College under the direct patronage of the Gaekwad of Baroda, Sayaji Rao, around 1898. Here he came in contact with one Thakur Saheb, a Rajput chief, who made him a practical revolutionary. It cannot be established whether Thakur Saheb was in any way connected with Abhinav Bharati or Vinayak Savarkar, but Aurobindo started writing inflammable articles in *Indu Prakash, New Lamp for the Old,* thus ushering in a new age in revolutionary journalism.[34]

In 1902 he brought Jatin Banerjee and his younger brother, Barin Ghosh, to Baroda and was instrumental in having Jatin appointed as a security guard to the Gaekwad. The same year, Aurobindo sent Jatin to Calcutta with a letter to Sarala Debi, then the main organizer of the Physical Culture Movement in Bengal. She introduced Jatin to P. Mitra, the President of Anushilan Samiti.[35]

In 1906, the All Bengal Political Workers Conference was held at Barisal (in spite of its being declared illegal) under the presidentship of Abdul Rasul. With a fierce lathi charge, a procession was dispersed. Quite a few eminent political figures of Barisal, including Chittaranjan Guha Thakurta (son of the eminent Manoranjan Guha Thakurta) suffered grievous injury. Surendranath Banerjea was arrested. This was closely followed by an unforgettable incident: Bipin Chandra Pal was tried before Kingsford, the Chief Presidency Magistrate, on a charge of contempt of court in September 1907 for refusing to give evidence. There was a tremendous rush in the court room.

A young student, Sushil Sen, aged 16, struck an English sergeant in reply to his bellicose, unseemly gestures. Sushil was tried and awarded 15 lashes on 26 August 1907, in front of the Town Hall in the presence of 20,000 Calcutta citizens. That very night, in Muraripukur Asram, the highest committee of the Calcutta Anushilan (Jugantar group) resolved to put Kingsford, who supervised the lashings, to death. According to Dr Jadu Gopal Mukherjee, the 'bench' consisted of revolutionaries like Aurobindo, Charu Dutta and Subodh Malik.[36]

Khudiram Bose, belonging to the Midnapore group led by Satyen Bose, and Prafulla Chaki, from the Rangpur group, were deputed to kill Kingsford, who had been transferred to Muzaffarpur. An attempt on his life had previously been made by the Chandannagar group by sending him a book bomb. But fortunately for Kingsford, the book was opened only after the scheduled lapse of time, while he was in Muzaffarpur. The renewed attempt by Khudiram and Prafulla to strike with bombs also ended unsuccessfully. Kingsford escaped unhurt. Mrs and Miss Kennedy were killed in error.

Even previous to this decision, the Jugantar group of the Calcutta Anushilan had embarked upon a programme of 'terror', dacoity and the publication of inflammable literature. In 1905, *Bhowani Mandir* was published (vide appendix). It was followed by *Mukti Kon Pathe* and *Bartaman Rananiti* in 1907. These made a tremendous impact on the minds of the youth.

Attempts were made to wreck the special train of Lieutenant Governor, Andrew Frazer, at Chandannagar on 2 December 1907 and Narayangarh (Midnapur) on 6 December 1907. This was followed by an attempt on 11 April 1908 to assassinate M. Tardival, the Mayor of Chandannagar, with a bomb. The report on the attempt to derail the special train of the lieutenant governor on 6 December had come to the notice of the Paris police and, in a secret memorandum, they had informed the British Government thus:

> That there was in Paris a Russian anarchist named Safranshi, an ex-officer of Engineers, who was in touch with some Hindu (Hindusthani) students in that city supposed to be Bengalis; and that they are supplying arms and ammunition to the anarchists of Calcutta and Chandannagar.[37]

On 23 December 1907, Allen, formerly District Magistrate of Dacca, was shot at and killed by Sisir Guha at Goalnundo station in Faridpur District. This was the work of the Dacca Anushilan Samiti.

Alipore Bomb Case

During the Alipore Bomb Trial, following the discovery of large quantities of explosives, arms and literature in Muraripukur Garden, after the Muzaffarpur bombings, there were 34 arrests of leaders and workers, including Aurobindo Ghosh, Barindra Kumar Ghosh, Upen Bandopadhyay, Debabrata Bose, Hemchandra Das, Abinash Bhattacharya, Hrishikesh Kanjilal, Ullashkar Dutta, Sailendra Nath Bose, Satyendra Nath Bose, Kanailal Datt, Sushil Sen, Nalini Kanta Gupta, Sudhir Sarkar, Abinash Chakraborty etc. of the Yugantar Group of the Calcutta Anushilan Party (henceforth referred to only as the Yugantar Party). Barindra Kumar, Upendranath and Ullashkar made confessional statements with a view to acquainting the country with the objectives, ideals and the nature of the activities pursued by the party.

Narendranath Goswami, a scion of the Uttarpara zamindar family turned approver in this historic trial, which lasted for more than a year. But on 1 September 1908, Kanailal Datta and Satyen Bose dramatically put an end to Narendranath's life. They had smuggled revolvers into the Alipore Central Jail from their party comrade Srish Ghosh of Chandannagar.[38] There was wild jubilation amongst the youth of Bengal and Maharashtra. The *Indu Prakash* made the following observation on the incident on 5 September 1908:

> The Bengal anarchists may be considered to be the most romantic lot in the whole anarchist world and in point of bravery, rascality and cunning they simply cast into the shade Russian and Spanish desperados — quick in action, quick in revenge, smart in overpowering powerful European Warders, and smart in getting rid of an approver.

> The anarchist law is terrible indeed and their creed in this respect was better let go half dozen spleen-cracking Europeans than allow a traitor to escape.[39]

The undying valour and superb philosophic detachment with which Kanailal Datta and Satyendra Nath Bose met death by hanging for assassinating the approver and traitor, Naren Goswami, deeply stirred the youth of the country. It even earned the applause of the French Socialist newspaper *L'Humanite*.[40] K.C. Ghosh described the reaction:

> The unprecedented and most unexpected manifestation of universal public grief and resentment at a time when British administration was held more in awe than respect, showed the direction in which the wind had started blowing. If it had gone to prove anything it was that the suppressed urge for political emancipation had discovered an avenue through which it erupted in an unwonted manner.[41]

Kanai admitted his guilt. In respect of Satyen a majority of three against two declared him to be not guilty. On 21 October 1908 the High Court pronounced its judgment awarding capital punishment to both the accused. On 10 November 1908, in the Alipore Central Jail, at about 7 in the morning, Kanai was executed. This was followed by unforgettable scenes of national mourning throughout Bengal. Satyendra Nath's execution was delayed for a few days, till the legal battle was completed. He was executed on 21 November 1908, and his body was cremated within jail grounds.

Earlier, the more outstanding and demonstratively striking incidents, were the self-immolation of Prafulla Chaki, the compatriot of Khudiram who preferred to die by his own hand rather than to surrender to the police at Mokama Ghat, Bihar, on 1 May 1908; and the hanging of Khudiram, a boy of 18, on 11 August 1908, who bemoaned the fact that he missed his target, Kingsford, and instead killed Mrs and Miss Kennedy. His execution roused profound indignation throughout the country.

All these incidents had far-reaching consequences. During the course of the Alipore conspiracy trial, some of the accused like Barindra Kumar Ghosh and Upen Bandopadhyay made startling disclosures about the objectives, method of organization and the nature of the activities undertaken to develop and expand the base of the revolutionary movement in Bengal. The High Court, on appeal, commuted the death sentence passed upon Barindra and Ullashkar Datta to transportation for life. Hemchandra Das and Upendra Nath Banerjee, Bibhuti Sarkar, Hrishikesh Kanjilal and Indu Bhushan Ray, received ten years' transportation. Sudhir Sarkar, Paresh Maulik and Abinash Bhattacharya received seven years' imprisonment. Aurobindo Ghose, along with 17 others, was acquitted. Some, like Sushil Sen, Nikhileswar Maulik and Abinash Chakravarty were to play an important role in the stormy years to come.[42] To quote K.C. Ghosh again:

> The echo of these incidents, particularly the Muzaffarpur explosion, reverberated throughout India and reached the shores of England before it died down. The Nationalist press while condemning the act commended the spirit of selfless sacrifice of the two young lads one of whom took away his life with his own hands and another who lost it on the gallows.

The British-owned papers all over India, as was not unexpected, went into hysterics and demanded the heads of the known and unknown leaders and men of the revolutionary movement.[43]

Some of the nationalist papers advised caution and urged the government to find out the real cause of such unrest and violent manifestations of temper of a class of people who had developed a passion for liberty, irrespective of the sufferings they might have to undergo in attaining it. 'The remedies suggested by the Anglo-Indian Press are sure to fail . . . as these have failed in Russia and elsewhere', wrote *Kesari* on 5 May 1908. The *Indu Prakash* observed on 5 May 1908: 'The English have been greatly frightened at the change which this engine of destruction has wrought in the politics of the country.'

Similarly, the *Panjabee* (6 May 1908); *Kal* (8 May 1908); *Hind Swarajya* (9 May 1908); *Maharatta* (10 May 1908); *Bhala* (11 May 1908); *Hind Punch* (13 May 1908); *Swarajya* (16 May 1908); *Sudhakar* (16 May 1908); *Vihari* (18 May 1908); *Yugantar* (5 May 1908) and *Aftab* (2 August 1908) reacted very sharply, reflecting the intensity and expanse of this movement.[44] Official reports too clearly discerned the gathering storm:

> The arrests of the Manicktala Garden Conspirators caused intense excitement among the extremists throughout India. The papers and in particular the Jugantar became more violent than ever and when their publication eventually was put a stop to, they continued to appear in the form of secretly printed leaflets openly and boldly inciting to murder and every conceivable form of violence.[45]

With the arrest of the Yugantar leaders on 2 May 1908, there was jubilation in police circles. The new Yugantar leadership consisted of Abinash Chakravarty of Pabna, Jatindra Nath Mukhopadhya (Bagha Jatin) of Nadia, in close collaboration with Dr Jadugopal Mukhopadhay, Motilal Ray of Chandannagar, Hemendra Kishore Acharjya of Mymensingh, Satish Mukherjee and Manoranjan Gupta of Barisal, Jatin Ray of Bogra, Purna Das of Madaripur, and Satkari Banerjee and Hari Kumar Chakravarty of 24 Parganas. They initiated a programme of revolutionary action throughout Bengal with increased vigour, tenacity and consistency to raise morale and self-confidence.

In East Bengal, in November 1908, the Anushilan Party, founded originally by its President Pramatha Mitra, entrusted its effective leadership to Pulin Behari Das and 'became the most powerful revolutionary organisation in India especially after the Alipore Conspiracy Case'.[46]

The intelligence report by Daly and special report by Magistrate Salked stressed the need for more effective vigilance to curb the power and ever-expanding influence of the Anushilan party. After his release from detention in 1908, he flung himself into a programme of revolutionary violence and in the process raised a band of revolutionaries on the model of the Santandal of Bankim's *Ananda Math.* He was flanked by a brilliant galaxy of revolutionary leaders, with Trailakya Chakravarty, the model of a revolutionary, in the vanguard, followed by Pratul Ganguly, Rabi Sen, Naren Sen, Makhan Sen, Kedareswar Guha, Ramesh Acharya and others.[47]

The two parties, Jugantar and Anushilan, though they formally both went under the name of Anushilan, maintained separate identities for all practical purposes. Atmaunnati led by Bipin Ganguly, Provash De and Indranath Nandy, was more closely integrated to the Jugantar group from its very inception, although always willing to cooperate with Anushilan. The Chandannagar group led by Motilal Ray, Manindra Naik, Kanailal Datta and Srish Ghosh, however, kept close contact with Jugantar (of Calcutta Anushilan as well as Dacca Anushilan led by Pulin Das and later on by Naren Sen). It was through the Chandannagar group that the Anushilan Samiti expanded their base in U.P. (Banaras). Rash Behari Bose, who got his first initiation from Srish Ghosh in Chandannagar, was mainly instrumental in carrying the burden of expanding the movement to U.P. He was destined to play a most dynamic role in Northern India — especially in U.P. and Punjab — in the years to come.[48]

Revolutionary actions, in the form of killings of officials and robberies, had started in Bengal from 1906. There were two references to minor robberies in Rangpur and Dacca in August and September. It may be recalled that on the question of collecting funds by recourse to armed robbery, there was a controversy amongst the early leaders of the Jugantar Group. Sister Nivedita, Aurobindo Ghosh and Barin Ghosh were opposed to it.

According to the Daly intelligence report, the names of the following were on record as leading financial supporters according to the confession of an informant who was deep in the revolutionary movement — Subodh Chandra Mallick; Nirode Chandra Mallick, wealthy Calcutta citizen residing in Wellington Square; Rajendra Nath Mukherjee, alias

Mistri Babu of Uttarpara in the Hughly District; Charu Chandra Datta, a judge of the Bombay Civil Service; P. Mitra, Bar-at-Law; and Monoranjan Guha, mineowner of Giridih in the Hazaribagh District, '. . . all of them belonged to supporting fringe of Manicktala Garden Party', according to Daly.

16 September 1908

After Aurobindo's withdrawal to Pondicherry, Jatin Mukherjee took over. The first revolutionary robbery took place in Bighati in the district of Hooghly under his leadership. Only Rs 536 could be collected. Three persons were sentenced to 5-6 years' imprisonment for this. Raids in Nadia on 29 November and Morchal in Hooghly on 2 December 1908 followed.

In the elimination programme, the Jugantar group had a better record of success than their bid to collect funds by dacoity. While their early attempts on the life of Bamphylde Fuller, Andrew Fraser, Kingsford and Hume (15 May 1908) proved ineffective, the attempt on the life of Allen, District Collector of Dacca by the Anushilan Sisir Guha on 23 December 1907 was remarkably successful from all points of view and raised the morale to a high point.[49]

After 2 May 1908, there was spate of bomb attacks. There were six in Kankinara, Shyamnagar, Belgharia, Agarpara, Sodepur and Kharda, undertaken more as demonstrations, but the police could take advantage of them. In East Bengal, the most important political incident was the political dacoity at Barrah in Dacca District on 2 June 1908. The victim was a moneylender. Rs 25,837 were seized — quite a considerable sum in comparison with earlier hauls. But more important was the battle royal against the combined fire power of villagers and police in mid-river at Dhaleswari, in broad daylight, which continued for nearly twelve hours. It created a sensation and quite a considerable stir amongst the youth and encouraged them to open more and more centres of the Anushilan Samiti. The police failed to collect any clue and failed to work out a viable criminal case, since there was no leakage and no betrayal.

This was followed by a series of dacoities by the Anushilan Samiti at Bajitpur (Mymensingh) on 15 August, Bighati (Hooghly) on 16 September, and Naria (Faridpur) on 30 October 1908.

The successive waves of political murders and dacoities and the climate of growing defiance that was manifested in every aspect of life, provoked the government to come down with a heavy hand on revolutionaries and the radicals alike under cover of a Draconian law. Prominent leaders were arrested on 16 December 1908 and sent to different distant jails under Regulation III of 1818. Among them were Pulin Behari

Das, Bhupesh Chandra Nag, Aswini Kumar Datta, Krishna Kumar Mitra, Satish Chandra Chatterjee, Subodh Chandra Basu Mallick, Monoranjan Guha Thakurtha, Shyam Sundar Chakraborty and Sachindra Nath Basu. On 14 January 1909, the government by virtue of a special power vested in it by the 14th Amendment Act of 1908 declared the following organizations unlawful:

1. Dacca Anushilan Samiti
2. Swadesh Bandhab Samiti of Bakharganj
3. Brati Samiti of Faridpur
4. Suhrid Samiti of Mymensingh
5. Sadhana Samiti of Mymensingh

According to K.C. Ghosh, a large number of actions were organized not solely to collect funds but also to prepare young minds for acts of daring, to inure them to suffering and privation and to cultivate an attitude of detachment to family and concern for life and limb.[50]

There were dacoities in Morchal (Hooghly) in March 1909. Netra (24 Parganas) on 25 April 1909, Nangla (Khulna) on 16 August 1909, Rajendrapur (Dacca) on 11 October 1909, Haludbari on 28 October 1909, and Mahisla (Jessore) on 5 July 1910. On 1 January 1909, the Anushilan revolutionaries committed a daring theft of three rifles at Comilla from the store of the Nawab of Dacca. On 10 February 1909 Ashu Biswas, Public Prosecutor in the Alipore Bomb Case, and Shamsul Alam, a police officer, were murdered by Charu Bose and Biren Datta, who belonged to the Jugantar group. They were both tried and hanged.

Following the Alipore Bomb Case (2 May 1908), the government initiated the Midnapore Conspiracy Case in September 1908, the Nangla Conspiracy (Khulna) Case on 18 July 1910, the Khulna Gang Case on 21 October 1910, the Munshiganj Conspiracy Case on 12 November 1910, the Dacca Conspiracy Case on 8 August 1910, and the Howrah Gang Case on 1 December 1910. Eminent figures like Pulin Das, Pratul Ganguly, Trailakya Chakraborty, Ramesh Acharya, Kedareswar Sen, Madan Bhowmick, Amrita Hazra or Sasanka Hazra of Anushilan Samiti, Narendra Bhattacharya (M.N. Roy) and Jatindra Nath Mukhopadhyay were involved in these cases.[51] Some of them were outstanding absconders hauled up later in the Barisal Conspiracy Cases (1913) and sentenced to long terms of imprisonment. Surendra Mohan Ghosh of Mymensingh was arrested with arms and convicted to a year's imprisonment in 1911. After his release in 1912 he was sent to Calcutta to take charge from Naresh Choudhury. It was from this time that Surendra Mohan was drawn closer to Jatin Mukherjee till his death in 1915.[51a]

Punjab (1907-1914)

In Punjab revolutionary nationalism was sparked off by Lala Lajpat Rai in 1906, when he went with Bal Gangadhar Tilak to Bengal to attend the Shivaji Utsav organized by Bipin Chandra Pal in collaboration with the Calcutta Anushilan. Punjab already had the background of the Kuka uprising of 1868 which continued till 1871. When Ram Singh was taken prisoner and sent to Rangoon for detention at the turn of the century, there was a great stir over the Land Alienation Act (1907) and the Colonisation Bill. The weekly journal *The Panjabee,* took up the cause of the aggrieved settlers. The paper faced prosecution and its editor was sentenced to two and a half years' imprisonment. This drew country-wide protest even in distant places like Madras and Calcutta. Lala Lajpat Rai took up the cause along with Sardar Ajit Singh, Kishan Singh, Aga Hyder, Sufi Amba Prasad and Syed Hyder Reza.

The genesis of revolutionary secret societies in Punjab came from a different background. In February 1907, was organized the Indian Patriots' Association, mainly for the betterment of the condition of the peasants. Another association was formed by Sufi Amba Prasad under the name of Bharat Mata Samiti. Thousands of people joined the movement and very soon it had infiltrated the armed forces. The demand was not limited to the removal of agrarian grievances but was avowedly for swaraj. Ajit Singh openly preached the removal of British rule. He frankly told the peasants that unless Swaraj were won, no real redress of grievances could be expected. He exhorted the people not to be afraid of the armed might of the government. 30 crores of Indians could easily defy the arms of the government. He even told them that it would be better and nobler to die for freedom of the country than to die of hunger and the plague.[51b]

Lala Lajpat Rai could not be indifferent to these developments and when he joined this movement, he became its natural leader. He was among the first to denounce the 'mendicant policy' of the Indian National Congress and to urge recourse to militant action.[51c] Although his connection with the revolutionary movement is still debated, the *Civil and Military Gazette* of Lahore (May 1907) described him as 'a rebel busily involved in the affairs of his insurrectionary enterprise with a hundred thousand desperados at his command'.[52] The *Englishman* openly charged him with having tampered with the loyalty of the Indian army, although on a suit filed by Lalaji he got damages of Rs 15,000 under a judgement of the Calcutta High Court.[53]

Lajpat Rai openly and vigorously supported Sardar Ajit Singh and Syed Hyder Reza and the cause they really represented, issuing a statement in which he asserted that the demand for swaraj was one 'which it will be madness to ignore or treat with contempt'. The whole of

Punjab was erupting like a volcano. Discontentment was spreading fast even in the army. It was reported that the 10th Jat Regiment was in a defiant mood. As Commander-in-Chief, Lord Kitchener was perturbed, he sent an urgent message to London suggesting the modification of some agrarian measures and the immediate arrest of Lajpat Rai and Ajit Singh. Their arrest in 1907 led to some decrease in the intensity of the agitation. But the struggle was continued by such revolutionary leaders as Sufi Amba Prasad, Pindi Das, Kishan Singh (uncle of Bhagat Singh), Lal Chand Falak and Bhai Paramanand. They too were prosecuted and convicted for inciting disaffection. Lajpat Rai and Ajit Singh were sent to Mandalay jail in Burma along with seven Bengal leaders. The Lieutenant Governor of Punjab, Sir Denzil Ibbetson, reported to London that 'Everywhere they could sense a new wind blowing through men's minds.' According to him, in the east and west of the province, new ideas were confined to the educated classes and amongst lawyers, clerks and students, but 'as the centre of the province is approached, however, the feeling in the towns grows strong and there is sign of activity and unrest'.

In Rawalpindi, Sialkot, Lyallpur, Amritsar, Ferozepur and Lahore 'an anti-British propaganda is being openly and sedulously preached'. In Bannu the army barrack was affected.[54] From 1908, a period of lull followed till the advent of Hardayal on the scene. Earlier, Sarala Devi had come and settled in Punjab. She was the first to become an organizer of revolutionary secret societies, to draw future revolutionaries in her husband's coterie. Later, Niralamba Swami (Jatin Bandopadhyay) made an extensive tour in that region to pick up prospective revolutionaries in order to form a society on the model of Bhowani Mandir. In all probability, Sufi Amba Prasad was introduced to Sarala Devi and they started to maintain contact with the Calcutta Anushilan centre in respect of their publicity media. *Jugantar, Mukti Kon Pathe, Bartaman Rananiti,* and other proscribed literature was available to them. This material created a great stir in the minds of the youth between 1907 and 1910.

Earlier, after his release from jail, Ajit Singh joined Sufi Amba Prasad and established a secret society in Lahore which very soon spread to urban and rural areas. The revolutionary leaders conducted a whirlwind campaign amongst the people throughout 1909.[55]

The government took a serious view of the situation since Punjab was the recruiting ground for the army and large scale arrests of leading workers soon followed throughout the province. Amba Prasad, Ajit Singh and Hrishi Kesh Mukhopadhyay, who came from Bengal to assist Amba Prasad, fled to Iran. Lal Chand Falak was arrested with bombs and seditious literature. He was sentenced to 15 years' imprisonment.[56]

Bhai Paramanand was also prosecuted on the charge of possessing incriminating material. A copy of the bomb manual used by the Alipore conspirators and other documents were seized from him. It may be recalled that Ajit Singh, Sufi Amba Prasad and others, had previous contacts with Jatin Banerji (Swami Niralamba) and Sarala Devi of Calcutta and later of Punjab.[57]

The next attempt to rebuild the organization was the work of a brilliant young student of Delhi named Hardayal who made his mark as a distinguished revolutionary of international fame.

Hardayal went to England on a state scholarship where he came in contact with Shyamji Krishnavarma and got initiated into the revolutionary party. As a protest against the tyranny of British rule in India, Hardayal refused a Fellowship and left England for Lahore. After his return in 1909 he started teaching students of post-graduate classes. Here, under the name Dinanath, he initiated two students, J.M. Chatterjee, and Abodh Behari, a school teacher of Delhi, into revolutionary activities. Before he left for England again in 1910, he introduced them to Rash Behari Bose, a clerk in the Forest Department, who was living in Dehra Dun.

In 1908, Rash Behari had been arrested in the Alipore Bomb Case but had secured acquittal. After nearly two years of hard work, he succeeded in co-ordinating the activities of different revolutionary groups and parties. One such centre was Chandannagar where Manindra Naik and Srish Ghosh were working hard to prepare a special type of bomb known later as the Rajabazar model on which Amrita (alias Sasanka) Hazra of Anushilan (Dacca) experimented. Very soon the Delhi centre was strengthened by the entry of Abodh Behari and Bal Mukund. Rash Behari then brought one Basant Biswas from Krishnanagar, a gift of Amarendra Chattopadhyay (Yugantar leader of Uttarpara), Srish Ghosh, and Manindra Naik of the Chandannagar centre.

Mention should also be made in this context of the part played by Sundarlal in spreading disaffection consistently and with incredible audacity through the paper, *Karmayogi* (Allahabad Edition) from July 1909 onwards. Sundarlal was also the chief promoter of the *Swarajya* of Allahabad, who managed to evade legal responsibility, according to an intelligence report. The four editors, including Shantinarayan, were convicted along with Ram Hari and Laddaram Sanyasi to 10 years' imprisonment in 1910. *Swarajya, Karmayogi* and *Hindi Pratap,* with which Sundarlal was deeply involved, defying all threats, became instruments of revolutionary actions in Northern India. 'This young man, born about 1885 in Muzaffarnagar, was responsible for stirring a great deal of trouble in the United Provinces.'[57a]

Earlier, Sundarlal had accompanied Lala Lajpat Rai in 1905 and B.G. Tilak in 1909 on tours in his role as an organizer of revolutionary cells in Kanpur, Lucknow and Allahabad. His speeches, according to the police record 'proved him to be a reckless youth of considerable ability; on account of his disloyal character he was expelled from Muir College boarding house'.[58] After 1910, he adopted a new name and called himself Someswarnand Swami and came in contact with Amir Chand and Hanumant Sahay of the Delhi Anushilan Centre. Soon after this, he went underground for the time being and probably filled the gap between 1908-13 in U.P. He worked with Rash Behari, when the latter started the *Karmayogi*, the paper then admittedly controlled by Aurobindo Ghosh, and edited by Amarendranath Chatterjee, who was well known to Rash Behari Bose. It has been established that Basanta Kumar Biswas, the person who threw a bomb at Viceroy Hardinge in Delhi on 23 December 1912, was recruited by Chatterjee before he was introduced to Rash Behari for more practical work. A.C. Guha describes his activities:

> Besides spreading sedition by means of his papers, Sundarlal was evidently, therefore, closely connected for the time being with this very dangerous gang of active revolutionaries. He spent most of his time in Allahabad, and so was not in the centre of the movement of Banaras, but his influence in preparing the ground in that part of India was very great . . .[59]

Attempts on British Dignitaries

In 1912 Rash Behari planned a big demonstrative action. On 12 December 1912 a grand Imperial Durbar was held at Delhi in honour of the visit of King George V. Two important announcements were made at the Durbar, one transferring the capital of India from Calcutta to Delhi, and another annulling the partition of Bengal. To inaugurate the new capital, Lord Hardinge, the then Viceroy of India, made a state entry into the imperial city on 23 December 1912. As the procession reached Chandni Chowk, a thickly populated part of the city, a powerful bomb was hurled at the *howda* on the elephants carrying the entourage of Lord Hardinge. The bomb exploded with a deafening blast but the Viceroy narrowly escaped death, although one of his A.D.C.s was killed.[60] The police could not trace the culprits.

Another operation was assigned to the Lahore Centre viz. to bombard Lawrence Gordon at Lahore. Gordon had earned notoriety while he was posted at Maulvi Bazar, Sylhet, by indiscriminate firing on followers of Swami Dayananda. He was now on transfer to Kasur, a district of Lahore. Prior to the Delhi episode, Basanta Biswas had been assigned the job of bombarding Gordon at the club which he was likely to visit.

The attempt, however, miscarried (17 December 1913). Tracing the leaflets distributed on this occasion, the police arrested Dinanath. He unfortunately turned approver in the famous *Delhi Conspiracy Case* (1913). Bal Mukund, Abodh Behari, Amirchand and Basanta Biswas were arrested, tried under section 121A and executed on the charge of waging war against the Emperor. A reward of ten thousand rupees was declared for information leading to the arrest of Rash Behari,[61] who started moving throughout northern India. The prospect of war between England and Germany opened up a new perspective. The period of self-assertion and conquest of fear which started in 1907 had ended. By 1914, war clouds had gathered on the international horizon. For the revolutionaries in India and abroad a new period with tremendous opportunities opened up.

Maharashtra — London — Paris — Tamil Nadu: 1907-14

Before giving an account of 1914 to 1918 period note must be taken of the position in other parts of India and particularly Maharashtra, and Tamil Nadu on the eve of the First World War.

The Chaphekar brothers were most valiant, but, as a reviewer of the revolutionary phase of our history observes, 'they had no definite political aims neither could they build up any political organization. They showed exceptional courage and made tremendous self-sacrifice indeed but it cannot be denied that, there was some childish element in their activities'.[62] The most active phase of revolutionary nationalism began in Maharashtra, in 1904, with the transformation of the Mitramela into the Abhinav Bharati Society — a name suggested by that of Young Italy Society of Mazzini. The object of the society was to put an end to the domination of the British and to achieve independence. After the execution of Damodar Hari Chaphekar, Vinayak took a vow to emulate his *guru*, and was formally initiated by a lame unlettered Maratha poet, Govind Trimbak Darekar, considered to be the most outstanding revolutionary poet of Maharashtra.

Along with his college-mate, Mahadev Bhat, Vinayak reorganized Mitramela around 1905. According to an Intelligence Report, biographies of revolutionaries like Mazzini were studied with great avidity as a means of attaining independence for India. At these study meetings the methods advocated were the education of the public through lectures and songs and collection of arms and ammunition in preparation for an uprising against the British Government.[63]

Vinayak got a scholarship from Shyamji Krishnavarma and set sail for England in June 1906. Henceforward he became one of the main activists in the London Centre of India House. He wrote a biography of Mazzini in Marathi and sent it to his brother Ganesh who had it published. The intelligence report on it runs thus:

> The suggested methods of preparation for war are the purchase and storage of weapons in neighbouring countries to be used when opportunity should occur; the opening of many very small but secret factories at some distance from one another for the manufacture of weapons clandestinely in the country; seeking independence and the purchase by secret societies of weapons in other countries to be secretly imported in merchant ships.[64]

The Maharashtra movement was in many ways linked with the movement in Bengal led by Aurobindo, Barin and Hem Das, but they preferred to have a number of independent societies for security reasons. Thus there sprang up separate units at Nasik, Bombay, Pune, Kolhapur, Aundh, Satara, Gwalior, Baroda, Amraoti, Yeotmal, Nagpur and many other places. Barin Ghosh states in his Memoirs that he convened an all-India meeting of the revolutionaries at the Surat Congress in December 1907.[65] This was corroborated by Dr V.M. Bhat who wrote: 'I told Karve that we had settled at Surat a joint programme with Bengal revolutionaries of simultaneous murders of English officials in at least 3 provinces and blowing up the bridges and railways and government offices.' But Karve in Maharashtra and the party of Barindra in Bengal precipitated matters by their rashness. In Paris, the Maharashtra revolutionary, Bapat, along with Mirza Abbas, met Hem Chandra Das and made a joint endeavour to manufacture bombs.[66]

A pamphlet entitled *Bande Mataram* issued from London, probably written by Vinayak Savarkar in 1909, made the following exhortation:

> Terrorise the officials, English and Indian, and the collapse of the whole machinery of oppression is not very far. The persistent execution of the policy that has been so gloriously inaugurated by Khudiram Bose, Kanai Lal Datta and other martyrs, will soon cripple the British Government in India. This campaign of separate assassination points out the conceivable method of paralysing the bureaucracy and of arousing the people. The initial state of the revolution is marked by the policy of assassination.[67]

The Bombay police found in the possession of Kashikar, a member of Abhinav Bharati, a composite photograph in which Khudiram Bose, Prafulla Chaki and the Chaphekar brothers were grouped as patriots. Secret collaboration between Maharashtra and Bengal is proved by the simultaneous outbreak of terrorism in both regions in April 1908. It was on 2 April 1908 that an attempt was made on the life of Anderson, Assistant Collector of Pune. Colonel Ferris was singled out at Kolhapur at about the same time as the revolutionaries in Bengal made efforts to eliminate Kingsford and others.

The revolutionary movement in Maharashtra was at its height in 1909. On 13 November, two bombs were thrown at the carriage of the Viceroy at Ahmedabad. On 21 December, A.M.T. Jackson, District Magistrate, was murdered in a theatre at Nasik by Anant Laxman Kanhere. Anant was captured in the hall itself. Subsequently, three persons, including Karve and Vinayak Narayan Deshpande, were sentenced to death and Shankar, Ramchandra Soman, Ganesh Balaji Vaidya and one, alias Daji Narayan Joshi, were transported for life.

On 28 February 1909, Ganesh Savarkar was arrested. His brother Vinayak, heart and soul of the London Centre, had made meticulous arrangements to receive a Browning pistol to add to the armoury of Abhinav Bharati. In the Nasik Conspiracy Case, while Vinayak Damodar Savarkar was transported for life, Keshav Sripat Chand Wadekar was transported for 15 years and 25 others were sentenced to various terms ranging from one to ten years.[68]

In 1910, Simooz, Collector of East Khandesh and Machnochie, Collector of Nasik, were threatened with murder. According to police reports a secret society styled as the Nava Bharat Society existed in the Gwalior State. Baroda was also a centre of considerable revolutionary activity. Of 167 revolutionary books and pamphlets proscribed in British India, at least 17 are known to have been printed at Baroda Press. One of these books was euphemistically called, *Vegetable Medicines* by Narsinghi Patil. It contained such remarks as 'to slay white officials is a merit not a sin'. The Nava Bharat Society tried to organize a band of strong, vigorous and fearless workers, ready to sacrifice their self-interest for promoting the larger interests of the nation.[69] When the Bombay police increased their vigilance, the centre of activity shifted to London and Paris.

Under Shyamji Krishnavarma, an avowed Arya Samajist, India House in London and Paris, after 1907, became the most dangerous revolutionary rendezvous for the British Raj. In 1909, Vinayak Savarkar rose to the position of acknowledged leader at India House. 'It became the fashion,' according to an intelligence report, 'to read at Sunday meetings passages from the book on the Indian Mutiny prepared by Savarkar.'[70] The practice gained in significance as preparations got under way to celebrate the Golden Jubilee of the First War of Independence, 1907. Fiery literature was written, published and distributed openly and clandestinely in India, especially in Bombay, Calcutta, Lahore and Madras.

The culmination was reached when Madan Dhingra, a Maharashtrian youth, shot and killed Colonel William Curzon Wylie, an A.D.C. to the Secretary of State for India. On 17 August 1909, Madan, with supreme self-confidence, went to the gallows. About the same time, Ganesh Savarkar, the elder brother of Vinayak, was convicted in Nasik on a charge of abetment to waging war against the King under section 121A of the I.P.C. He was sentenced to transportation on 9 June 1909. When Vinayak was informed about this, he thrice repeated his oath to wreak vengeance on the English. A statement of Dhingra's reasons for killing Curzon Wylie was found in his pocket when he was arrested. The first paragraph read: 'I attempted to shed English blood intentionally and with a purpose as an humble protest against the inhuman transportation and hangings of Indian Youth.'[71]

The murder of Jackson followed on 21 December 1909. Pistols sent by Vinayak were used.[72]

The arrest of Vinayak by the London police and his daring escape in Marseilles port from the ship carrying him back to India, and the subsequent last legal battle in an International Court made him at once a figure of political eminence. He was sent to Andamans Jail along with his brother Ganesh Savarkar to face inhuman torture, till the end of the decade.

Revolutionary Terrorism in Tamil Nadu

The contagion soon spread to the South, according to intelligence reports, from the fiery speeches of Bipin Chandra Pal in 1907 at Rajmahmundry, where he declared British rule as *maya*. The judgment of the Madras High Court in criminal appeals Nos. 491, 503 of 1908 show that Subramania, Siva and Chidambaran Pillai conspired together to excite disaffection towards the government. Two conspirators were arrested on 12 March 1908. This was followed by a serious riot in Tinnevelly. In March a critical article appeared on the arrest of Chidambaran Pillai the conclusion of which read: 'Hello : Feringi, Cruel tiger: you have devoured simultaneously three inoffensive Indians in a moment without cause. . . .'[73] For this article the printer and editor were tried and convicted. The cause was taken up vigorously by one M.P. Tirumal Acharya, who suddenly left Pondicherry for Europe and joined the India House Centre. In Madras his place was taken by Nilkanta Brahmachari who was going round Southern India in 1908 in company with Shankar Krishna Aiyar. Here Shankar introduced Nilkanta to his brother-in-law Vanchi Aiyar who was working in the Forest Department.

Early in December 1910, V.V.S. Aiyar, who had been the principal associate of Vinayak Savarkar at the India House and had subsequently gone to Paris and associated himself with Shyamji Krishnavarma, Madame Cama and others, arrived in Pondicherry and became the chief organizer of the revolutionary activities. Here he picked up Vanchi

Aiyar and trained him as a professional revolutionary and deputed him to assassinate Ashe, District Magistrate of Tinnevelly. On 17 June 1911, the action was consummated with rare perfection. Vanchi committed suicide as directed. Shankar Krishna Aiyar was arrested, tried and sentenced to death.

> Upon the body of the murderer was found a letter in Tamil language which asked every Indian to drive out the English and restore Swarajya and Sanatan Dharma. His model was Shivaji, Krishna, Gurugovind and Arjun. Three thousand Madrasis had taken a vow to kill George V, as soon as he landed in the country.[74]

Their ambition, however, was not to be fulfilled. There is unmistakable evidence of the complicity of the Bande Mataram group in Paris, directed by Madame Cama and its Mymensingh counterpart in the murder of Sub-Inspector Rajkumar Ray on 19 June 1911. An article published in the April issue of *Bande Mataram* of 1911, hinted at some action at the ceremony of the royal coronation.[75] It may have been a coincidence. Intelligence reports, however, considered that the movement in Tamil Nadu was more a by-product of Bengal or Paris, rather than a growth of indigenous character. Things quietened down there after 1912, but some of the leading conspirators like Champakaraman Pillai left the country and joined the Paris centre to collaborate in the wider international plot better known as the Indo-German plot led by Hardayal, Heramba Gupta, Dr Tarak Das, Dr Bhupendra Nath Datta, Professor Barkatulla and others at the approach of the First World War in 1914.[76]

Plans for an Army Revolt (1914-1918)

At the approach of the war, leaders of all the revolutionary parties — Anushilan (Dacca), Jugantar (which had already acquired an independent identity especially after the Howrah Conspiracy Case of 1910-11) and Atmaunnati — were contemplating preparations for the coming revolution, which they had been waiting for since Bernharde's article.[77] Jatin Mukherjee, the leader of the Jugantar-Atmaunnati combine, by and large unified the different federated district units under one central command. He had been aided since 1907 by Swami Prajananda Saraswati of the Barisal group, Hemendra Kishore Acharya of the Mymensingh group, Nani Gopal Sen Gupta of the Howrah group, Jatin Ray and Abinash Ray of the Bogra group, Bipin Behari Ganguly and Anukul Mukherjee of the Atmaunnati group, Bejoy Ray of the Jessore-Khulna Group, Srish Ghosh of the Chandannagar group, Satish Sen Gupta and Ashutosh Das of the Sreerampur group, Nibaran Ghatak of the Bankura group, Purna Das of the Madaripur group, etc.[78]

Thus organized, Jugantar seriously considered the German project of sending arms, money and technical assistance which had been decided upon at a meeting between the Indian representatives, Viren Chattopadhay, Dr Abinash Chandra Bhattacharya and Dr B.N. Datta and Von Oppenhiem, the German Foreign Minister.[79] A committee was formed to work out this plan. Albert Belin was appointed President, Oppenhiem and Dr Sukthankar Vice-Presidents, and Dhirendra Nath Sarkar was made its Secretary.[80]

The committee, named the Indian Independence Committee, took up its first programme of collecting together all the Indian revolutionaries working outside India. The German plot envisaged an attack on the Andaman Cellular Jail and liberating the revolutionary prisoners.[81] The second and most important task the committee decided to undertake was to send arms to India by the sea lines of the Pacific Ocean and Admiral Von Hintz was sent to Peking to arrange the deal. Both Jiten Lahiri of Yugantar and Kedareswar Guha of Anushilan returned to India, one by March 1915 and the other by November 1914.[82]

Intelligence records, however, speak of three schemes by the Germans to foster rebellion in India. The first depended on Muslim disaffection and was directed against British control of the North Western Provinces. The second was an attack on Burma by repatriated Gadar personnel, trained by German military officers. The third was the Batavian scheme for supplying arms to the Jugantar Party to foster rebellion, presumably in Bengal and North East India.[83]

One interesting point should not be missed here. The Ghadar constituted a common element in all the plans for an uprising in three sectors — Far East, Middle East and Northern India, in collaboration with the Islamic Brotherhood of Deoband, at least in the first two places. As such, the plan of raising an army revolt has to be reviewed first. In some areas, where the Turco-German Scheme was organized and put into action, the Berlin Committee played a considerable role in this ineffective undertaking.[84]

Army Revolt of 18 February 1915

1. *Call to Return to India:* The arrest and virtual deportation of Lala Hardayal from America and the formation of the Berlin Committee created an unprecedented stir amongst Indians staying abroad, especially amongst the Sikh community in America and Canada. A number of pamphlets containing an appeal in the name of Tilak, Barkatulla, Madame Cama, Ajit Singh, Savarkar, Aurobindo Ghosh, Krishnavarma, Hardayal, along with the names of many eminent Indian leaders staying abroad were distributed in USA and Canada. 'Let us rise in revolt,' it says, 'O Sikh, Hindu, Muslim brothers come, join us, let us return to our

motherland. This is our last chance; let us join under common flag of revolt.'[85] They openly called upon the large number of Indian passengers on the *S.S. Korea,* which carried the first batch of revolutionaries returning to India, to 'stir up rebellion in every corner of the country. Rob the wealthy. . . .'[86]

The ship left from San Francisco and halted at Yokohama and Manila. At Manila, Hafiz Abdullah, Nawab Khan and Jagat Ram addressed them. They were told that 'England was engaged in a war threatening her very existence; don't let this opportunity slip by . . . be ready to kill or be killed on arrival in India.'[87]

2. *Komagata Maru Incident, 1914:* Then came the famous *Komagata Maru* incident of 29 September 1914. More than 350 discontented Sikhs under the leadership of Baba Gurdit Singh, started from Vancouver on 23 July 1914, on the *S.S. Komagata Maru,* a Japanese ship. After passing through tremendous ordeals, the ship was allowed to enter the Hooghly river and stopped near Budge-Budge, 14 miles away from Calcutta. A party of British and Indian officers headed by Sir Fredrick Halliday, Commissioner of Police, Calcutta, came on board and peremptorily ordered the passengers to disembark at once and proceed to the train waiting at Budge Budge Railway Station to take them to Punjab. From the very beginning the passengers were very suspicious about the intentions of the authorities. They resisted desparately, and there was a near massacre of the unarmed Sikhs, in the course of which, according to official reports, 20 died while 211 were arrested out of the total 376 passengers. The actual number of deaths must, however, have been double the official figures according to local witnesses interviewed later.[88] Baba Gurdit Singh escaped alongwith 28 others, but not before he had entrusted the Granth Sahib, riddled with bullets and his young son, Balwant Singh, to the care of one of his faithful lieutenants.[89]

The *Komagata Maru* incident created great commotion in Punjab and also in Bengal. An exaggerated account of the resistance as well as the inhuman treatment meted out to the returnees travelled fast creating widespread resentment. Hundreds of Indian emigrants, mostly Sikhs, began attempting to return to India in various ships — *Tosa Maru, Korea, Mesha Maru, Siberia, Mexico Maru* and the *Canada Maru,* each carrying thousands of Indians. All these vessels touched at various ports in the Far East and the homeward emigrants everywhere tried to procure arms. Indian revolutionary leaders everywhere were urging them to rebellion and armed uprising. In all, seven to eight thousand returned. If arms and ammunition could not be supplied to them from abroad, the emigrants were urged to attack police stations and snatch away the arms of the police. They were also advised to encourage mutiny among

Indian soldiers. A fair number of the returnees managed to escape police arrest and somehow reached Calcutta where they contacted the Sikh community. With their help they came in touch with the Kidderpur group of the Jugantar Party. Some of the *Komagata Maru* emigrants were given temporary shelter in different colleges, hotels and boarding houses, where members of the Jugantar Party were residing. They had been given these addresses by Dr Tarak Das and other Indian revolutionaries abroad.[90] The Punjab authorities became alarmed over the sudden spate of revolutionary activities in the form of robberies on the Ferozepur-Ludhiana line, Hissar and Ambala.[91]

3. *Seduction of Army:* But more serious was the attempt of the returning emigrants to win over the Indian Army. From the police records it appears that the Ghadarities, in their anxiety to participate in an attempt to subvert the existing regime, initiated from any quarter, be it the Jugantar, Anushilan or the Islamic Revolutionary Brotherhood of Deobandis, exercised no discrimination.[92] In the middle of 1914, Satyen Sen and Pingle returned from abroad and met both the Jugantar and Anushilan leaders, especially Jatin Mukherjee and Rash Behari Bose. The two leaders had met previously and discussed the general strategy and tactical line to be followed in preparing for an all-India uprising. But the two leaders failed to formulate a common strategy with regard to the organizational pattern, as well as timing of the uprising. While the Anushilan claimed that it was by far the most centralized party with a base in Northern India, the Jugantar claimed that, after 1911, it had developed into an unified party in Bengal, with contacts with the 10th Jat Regiment in Fort William, Calcutta, and also that it had organized the prospective German assistance in the form of a supply of a huge quantity of arms, ammunition, money and a military training scheme. They expected to receive the assistance at the end of June as per negotiations with the Berlin Committee. According to Rash Behari Bose, the prospect of receiving German arms was highly uncertain, while Jatin Mukherjee felt the projected army revolt was too risky an enterprise, with no chance of success.[93]

Moreover, the two groups found it impossible to merge and give up their separate identities. They, however, agreed to co-operate if either of the parties could launch a rising against the British Raj in India in the coming months. It was probably more a clash of personalities than of ideals and objectives which hindered the process of building up a united centralized leadership at this historic juncture in the Indian revolution. The course of events proved this to be true.

To trace the course of attempts to win over the army, we will first have to look back over earlier endeavours of national revolutionaries in this direction which culminated in the event of 21 February 1915.

4. *The Search for Foreign Assistance:* The national revolutionaries of Jugantar and Anushilan (Dacca) were not unmindful of the tremendous potentiality of the foreign centres, both for publicity and for collecting resources. In this direction again, Maharashtra had been slightly ahead of other regions. The part played by Shyamji Krishnavarma, Vinayak Savarkar, S.S. Rana, Bhikaiji Rustamji Cama, Champakaraman Pillai has already been traced earlier. From Bengal, both the Jugantar and the Anushilan claimed to have sent their emissaries and cadres abroad since 1907.[94] Dhangopal Mukherjee, brother of Dr Jadugopal Mukherjee, Satyen Sen, Dr Bhupendra Nath Datta, Surendranath Kar, attached to Prem Mahavidyalay of Raja Mahendra Pratap, Bejoy and Dhiren Sarkar, brothers of Professor Benoy Sarkar, Jiten Lahiri and Pandurang Khankoje went to Europe and the USA. Around this time, Professor Barkatulla went to Japan on his way to America. But the most outstanding national revolutionary, who made singular contribution abroad during the first decade of the 20th century, was Lala Hardayal. In 1910, he left for the USA, after organizing a unit in Delhi. In 1911, Hardayal reached San Francisco where he found the soil fertile for starting revolutionary work amongst the emigrant Sikh peasantry. Even prior to that, Bhupendra Nath Datta had probably chosen New York as a place of voluntary exile, partly because of the help to be expected from the society founded there by his brother Vivekananda, and partly because it was already a centre of anti-British intrigue. In the autumn of 1906, a society had been formed under the name of Pan-Aryan Association at 1 West, 34th Street by Samuel Lucas Joshi, a Maharashtrian Christian and Md Barkatullah, a Muslim from Bhopal. In November 1907, the name of the society was changed to 'the Society for the Government of India' which was considered less likely to give offence to the class of wealthy and influential Americans whom it wished to interest. After the visit of Madame Cama, the effort received some encouragement. Her speeches in New York and elsewhere, exposing the oppressive character of British rule did 'not seem to have achieved conspicuous success' according to an intelligence report.[95]

At the end of 1908, George Freeman, a very prominent figure in the circle of disaffected Indian students in New York, was found to be taking keen interest in the publication of the *Free Hindustan* and was for some time regarded by the Indians in New York as the real leader of the anti-British movement. From the intelligence record it appears that George Freeman was actively committed to writing, activizing and guiding the Indian agitators, both Hindus and Muslims, as early as 1908. An incomplete letter was found in possession of one Fazlul Hassan and Hasrat Mohani of Aligarh wherein he instructed them to adopt Russian revolutionary methods with Fuller, which obviously meant Sir

Bamphylde Fuller, the first Lieutenant Governor of Eastern Bengal. In August of the same year, a letter from Barkatullah published in the *New York Sun* stated that Englishmen were getting nervous because the Hindus and Muslims were drawing together and the success of nationalism appeared to be nearer. In another letter written in Persian which appeared in the Urdu *Maulla* of Aligarh, he strongly advocated the necessity for unity between Hindus and Muslims and defined the chief duties of the Muslims as 'patriotism and friendship' with all Muslims outside India. The entry of Dr Tarak Nath Das into this arena added a new dimension to the anti-British movement. His close contacts with the Sikh community, especially those connected with the army, drew the attention of British intelligence. Several instances of bonfires of certificates and the return of medals by Sardar Ghalib Singh, a member of the committee of the Sikh temple and a former sepoy in the 14th Sikh Regiment, and Sardar Bag Singh of the 10th Bengal Lancers Regiment, Secretary of the Khalsa Diwan, clearly indicate the attempts of the national revolutionaries to win over the armed forces in India and outside.[96] The paper *Swadesh Sewak*, mainly addressed to the Sikhs in the Indian Army in their own Gurumukhi language, was despatched to India frequently in 1911.[97] A letter from a retired Hindu soldier appeared in Madame Cama's *Bande Mataram* in March 1913, stating that 'our revolutionary movement must culminate in open war against our tyrants. This war can only be successful if we be backed up by the mass of the people and the regular army.'[98]

The arrival in the USA of Lala Hardayal in 1911 was of great importance to the anti-British movement there. A distinguished Professor of Indian Philosophy in the University of California, he was very soon joined by Bhai Paramanand and Ramchandra (Peshawari). They toured the cities and towns of the USA and Canada which had Indian concentrations. At first they founded the Hindustani Association of Pacific Coast for Independence. A paper, *Ghadar*, was started as its mouthpiece on 1 November 1913 from San Francisco with Ramchandra as its editor. The entire setup was given the name, Yugantar Ashram. Very soon a new revolutionary party emerged out of this extraordinary revolutionary endeavour, the Ghadar Party, which was destined to play a most dynamic role in the revolutionary movement in India in the years to come.

The tremendous energies of Hardayal found an appropriate outlet in the activities of the Ghadar Party of which he became the Secretary and Baba Sohan Singh the President. From the very beginning, Hardayal had two priorities, viz. propaganda amongst the masses in India and the seduction of armed forces. The very first issue of *Hindustan Ghadar* declared on 1 November 1913:

> Today there begins in foreign lands, but in our country's tongue, a war against the British Raj. What is your name? Mutiny.
>
> Where will it burst out? India. When the time will come? When rifle and blood will take the place of pen and ink.[99]

Hardayal and his comrades anticipated the coming of the war between England and Germany, and also that the US Government would be involved in it. He was arrested by the American administration on 23 March 1914, just four months before the commencement of the war. He, however, jumped bail and left for Geneva alongwith Professor Barkatulla. Barkatulla was the living link between the Islamic Brotherhood (Fraternity), representing Muslim disaffection and the Ghadar current of the most advanced secular revolutionary movement in India and abroad. Very soon, both these currents spread to the Far East, Middle East, especially in Manila, Tokyo, Shanghai, Bangkok, Batavia, and Teheran, Constantinople, Baghdad and the Heja in the Middle East.

Meanwhile, a National Party was formed in Germany with Champakaraman Pillai as Secretary, in collaboration with Biren Chattopadhyay, S.S. Rana, Chandra Kumar Chakravarty, Abinash Bhattacharya, Heramba Gupta and Raja Mahendra Pratap. At the approach of the war, it was transformed into the Berlin Committee or Independence Committee. It started negotiations with the German Foreign Office who were deeply interested in the implementation of a scheme, widely known as the 'German Plot', to subvert British rule, by sending arms, money and technical military assistance to the revolutionaries.[100]

Volumes have come out regarding the actual negotiations between the German Foreign Office and the different functionaries of the revolutionary movement, representing the Jugantar, Ghadar and Anushilan parties. Lord Hardinge's Diary, and the Memoirs of Col O. Dwyer, do not provide a clear picture. Dr Bhupendra Nath Datta and Dr Abinash Bhattacharya have left for us their own version in their books *Aprakashita Rajanaitik Itihash* and *Bahir Bharate Biplab Prachesta*. Several papers on the Lahore Conspiracy Case and Sikh Conspiracy Case have left certain evidence which give us a one-sided picture. Out of the bewildering mass of literature one can very briefly sketch the main contours of the German Plot and the part played by the different revolutionary parties in India and abroad.

Wartime Venture

The history of the revolutionary movement during the war years, July 1914 to November 1918, may conveniently be dividend into four sections:

(1) The attempt to raise an army revolt which ended in failure in February 1915.
(2) The unsuccessful implementation of the German scheme in the Far East which ended by the end of December 1915.
(3) The unsuccessful implementation of the Turco-German Scheme in the Middle East which ended by the middle of 1916.
(4) The rearguard action by the fast dwindling, desperate revolutionary forces of the major parties like Anushilan, Jugantar and Ghadar between 1916 and 1917 to 'leave a moral and adorn a tale'.

Previous Efforts to Win Over the Army

From 1909 onwards, Europe was under the shadow of an impending war between Britain and Germany. Jatin Mukherjee, the great revolutionary leader, brought different political factions of Bengal, including the Adi (original) Anushilan or Calcutta Anushilan (Jugantar Group) and others under a single leadership. After the departure of Aurobindo Ghosh, he restablished contact with the army. A Sikh soldier was contacted through one Naren Chattopadhyay of Shibpur.[101] According to Dr Jadu Gopal Mukherji, Benoy Bhusan Datta, Bhimrao and Vir Savarkar's brother, Dr Savarkar opened a contact centre in Maharashtra. Dr Mukherjee also states that Sri Ashutosh Ghosh, a teacher of Khidirpur School, maintained regular contact with the Punjab centre. Arrangements had also been made to contact the army stationed at Fort William, Calcutta.[102] This is corroborated by Soviet sources:

> Early in 1910 the official Anglo-Indian press featured the sensational news of the arrest of 10 soldiers of the 10 Jat Regiment which was stationed in a suburb of Calcutta, the then capital of British India. The news agitated the public, all the more, because, the administration offered no explanation for its action and tried to belittle its importance. The regimental commander was forced to take 'a lengthy holiday'. The entire regiment was disarmed and despatched by sea to a remote spot in Sind Province. . . . It was rumoured that as the soldiers were being arrested an armed clash ensued, resulting in the death of several persons. It was also rumoured that the arrested soldiers had been put in solitary confinement in Alipur Prison.[103]

The above data was collected from the report of the Russian Consulate General, stationed at Calcutta, to St Petersburg on 6 February 1910, available in Soviet archives. According to A.V. Raikov, however, this information about the arrest of 10 sepoys was wrong. Consul Arseneyev named as many as 35, or even 42, sepoys on trial in a letter dated 11 March 1911. The report goes thus:

During the Christmas holiday in 1909 a ball was to be held at the residence of the Bengal Governor to which the Viceroy, C-in-C and all the high ranking officials of Calcutta were to be invited. The 10th Jat Regiment was to do sentry duty during the ball. The undercover patriotic organisation which had established contact with the soldiers decided to take advantage of this convenient ball to blow up the ball room and thus destroy the colonial Government.[104]

On the Eve of the First World War

On the eve of the First World War, when war between England and Germany was certainty, Rash Behari Bose made separate and collective efforts in Northern India to set up contacts with army personnel in different barracks.[105] He even tried to co-ordinate their operational strategy with Jatin Mukherjee.

Outside India, the famous Berlin Committee was formed and supported by the German Government. Under the leadership of Dr Tarak Nath Das, Raja Mahendra Pratap, Maulana Barkatulla, Obelidulla Sindhi, Lala Hardayal, Dr Bhupen Dutta, Biren Dasgupta, Abinash Bhattacharya, Madame Cama, Viren Chattopadhyay, C.R. Pillai and others, arrangements for importing arms and ammunition from abroad were made. In this connection the Rowlatt Commission observed: 'It was supported by efforts to evolve a system to affiliate all those behind the movement into an efficient working unit, the principal aim of which would be to cause mutiny among native troops in British India and in different centres engaged in War.'

Here was the confluence of the four main streams of Indian revolutionary currents — Ghadar, Pan-Islamic Revolutionary Brotherhood, Anushilan, and Yugantar.

One of the prominent Indian revolutionaries was given the responsibility to direct a campaign to win the allegiance of Indian prisoners of war captured by the Germans. But later on Anushilan and Jugantar co-ordinated this plan of action and made an areawise division. As a matter of fact links were then established between the revolutionaries and the 10th Jat Regiment stationed at Fort William in Calcutta. Maharaj Trailakya Chakroborty has made a few observations in this regard in *Trish Bachar Jele : Trailakya Maharaj on seduction Plan:*

> Meanwhile endeavours were going on inside the country to procure arms and ammunition, tamper with the allegiance of the Native Soldiers and to win them over. . . . Only in Bengal 1200 revolutionaries were arrested and confined in jail custody. But still attempts to organise the revolt went on unabated, leaders and workers of Anushilan Samiti such as Rash Behari Bose, Sachindra Nath Sanyal, Girija Dutta, Anukul Chakraborty, Amrita Sarkar, Pandit Paramananda, Prithvi Singh Azad, Joal Singh, Mohan

> Singh, Pandit Jagatram, Bishnu Ganesh Pingley, Binayak Rao Kapley and others moved from Lahore to Dacca and thence to Central Province to win over the support of the Army. For the said objective Rash Behari Bose, Sachindra Nath Sanyal and Damodar Swarup were sent to Ahmedabad, Zila Singh to Benaras, Biswanath Pandey and Mangal Pandey to Ramgarh and Jabbalpur, Kartar Singh and Prithvi Singh to Lahore, Ambala, Ferojpur and Rawalpindi, Bishnu Ganesh Pingley to Meerut, Pandit Jagatram to Peshawar, and Pandit Paramananda to Jhansi and Kanpur. Sardar Madan Singh and Hazra Singh established contact with Sikh Regiment No. 26 and Sardar Harnam Singh succeeded in doing so with the military cantonment at Mianwali.[106]

At the end of January 1915, Rash Behari deputed Hridaram to assess the political situation in Jullundar, establish contact with the Dogra Regiment stationed there and win them over. Hira Singh Charar was sent to Jacobabad, Piara Singh to Kohat and Sant Gulab Singh and Harnam Singh to Banu on similar missions.

All these envoys brought back encouraging reports. The 35th Regiment of Banu fully assured their support, as soon as it was transferred to Rawalpindi. Mohan Singh of Baring and Gurumukh Singh Lall, brought similar reports from Naushera, Peshawar, Haji Mardan, Jhelum and Rawalpindi. Soldiers at Kapurthala, Meerut, Agra, Allahabad, Banaras, Ferozabad and Lucknow expressed a similar willingness to take part in the rebellion at the appointed time. Sant Wasakha Singh was sent to Delhi to establish contact with the Indian soldiers there. Sucha Singh and Kartar Singh Saraba went to Meerut on a similar mission where Pingley was already working. They were successful in establishing links with Inder Singh and some other men of the 12th Cavalry. Main Mir and Ferozepur Cantonments were the main centres of activity of the Punjabi Ghadrites. Dafadar Lacharan Singh and Sowars Lal Singh and Natha Singh promised to side with the revolutionaries. Nidhan Singh and Kartar Singh Saraba who had frequently visited Ferozepur ultimately prevailed upon the soldiers of the 6th Pathan Regiment to hand over to them the keys of the arms depot. The Indian soldiers were generally discontented owing to the proportionately heavier casualties they were suffering on the European front as compared to British soldiers. Militarily too the British position in India at that time was shaky.

On receiving these encouraging reports, Rash Behari Bose took over the task of general direction and co-ordination with other revolutionary groups of Bengal led by Jatin Mukherjee. He expected that, as soon as the sepoy uprising turned into a popular insurrection, Afghanistan and the tribal people of the north-west frontier would be persuaded to accord diplomatic recognition to the revolutionary government. He pinned his hopes mainly on the defection of some men from the 23rd

Cavalry posted at the Main Mir Cantonment in the suburbs of Lahore, of the 26th Punjabi Regiment posted at Ferozepur, and the 28th Pioneers and 12th Cavalry posted at Meerut.[107]

Repeated reverses suffered by the British during the first phase of the First World War had a very adverse effect on the morale of the Indian Army. The message of freedom had also by then created an unprecedented stir in their minds. 'To fight for national independence appealed to them more than to die for alien Government.' Association with Rash Behari helped the native soldiers to regain their good sense and they realized that the attainment of independence was fully in their hands. At the time, barely twelve thousand British troops were stationed in India. The rebels among the Indian troops therefore decided to launch a sudden attack on the British troops, defeat and imprison them and thereafter proclaim a National Government. At that time, soldiers were permitted to retain their arms inside the Fort. Rash Behari Bose, who was an absconder, carrying a reward of several thousand rupees for his apprehension, was in a fort discussing plans and programmes of the future revolution with the army personnel.[108] He had secured entry by introducing himself as a kinsman of a soldier. This was possible because the sentry at the gate also happened to be his trusted follower. When these matters came to light, the sepoys were prohibited from keeping the guns with them. After daily parade, all the guns were deposited in the magazine and outsiders were no longer allowed to enter the fort. This was fully corroborated by the report of the Sedition Committee.[109] Contact was established with 26 cantonments, including those at Ferozepur, Rawalpindi, Meerut, Jabbalpur, Banaras and Allahabad. 'Rash Behari also tried to organise the collection of gangs of villagers to take part in the rebellion. Bombs were prepared, arms were got together, flags were made ready, a declaration of war was drawn up. Instruments were collected for destroying railways and telegraph wires.'

Ghadar Efforts in America

In America the Ghadar Party made serious efforts to collect money and to procure arms and ammunition in order to take part in the armed revolutionary struggle in India. To help the revolutionary movement in India, seeds of insubordination and patriotism in the Indian Army and the idea of revolt in the public at large were deftly sown. The 'Liberty' pamphlets issued by revolutionaries like Bhai Bal Mukand found their way into army units stationed at Dehra Dun, Kasauli, Ambala Cantonments and other military stations in Punjab and U.P. Flaming articles were written. One such was *Bande Mataram* issued from Geneva under the caption 'What shall we do?' 'Our revolutionary movement must cultivate open war against our tyrants. This war can only be successful if we are backed by the masses and the regular army.'

Baba Sohan Singh Josh was the President of the Ghadar organization. It had a good number of contacts in the army. The Punjabis are noted for their valour, and, as soon as the members of the Ghadar Party landed at Budge-Budge in Calcutta from the *Komagata Maru*, as mentioned earlier, they were engaged in a pitched battle with British forces. Prior to this, in a conference of the party held in Stockholm (in 1914) it was resolved that the organization should be affiliated with political parties in India and that contact would also be established with Indian soldiers abroad.[109A] Many Sikhs were able to fight and so reached Punjab. Hundreds of them took upon themselves the task of working within the army.

Pan-Islamic Brotherhood

The Pan-Islamic Brotherhood, a revolutionary party, was another group associated with these efforts. Most of the Muslim youths who passed out from Deoband School and had gone abroad for higher studies joined this organization and consolidated it. They also took upon themselves the sacred task of driving out the Britishers and freeing India from the foreign yoke. Obeidullah Sindhi was their leader and Anwar Pasha of Turkey, the Egyptian revolutionary, set up centres throughout the Middle East, North West Frontier Province, Sindh, Punjab, Kashmir, Iraq, Iran, Hedzaj in Arabia and elsewhere. They distributed leaflets and handbills among the soldiers and also abroad in various cantonments in Basra, Malaya, Singapore, Java and Shanghai.[110]

Efforts were made to knit all those behind the movement into an efficient working unit, the principal aim of which would be to cause mutiny amongst the native troops in British India and different war theatres. It was decided by common agreement that the Flag of Independence would be unfurled on 21 February 1915. But one Kripal Singh betrayed the plot and the British Government cracked down upon the revolutionaries. Large-scale arrests followed and Pandit Jagatram was interned in Peshawar. Pingley, while carrying a package of bombs and pistols, was arrested in Meerut Cantonment from the lines of the 12th Cavalry Regiment. Sardar Harnam Singh, the Sikh havildar of the 9th Infantry Division, Sardar Narayan Singh and Sardar Sohan Lal, both carrying pistols, were arrested at Maimo in Burma. The government also disbanned native army divisions at many places. Indian sepoys at Ambala and Ferozepur, who came in close contact with the revolutionaries, were court-martialled and executed. Around this time also nearly 200 mutinous soldiers in Basra were blown up from the mouth of the cannon.[110a]

Both in the Rowlatt Commission Report and David Petrie's report on Indian revolutionary activities in the Far East describe the plan for the uprising: 'The revolutionaries were to go through China, Japan, Borneo and Siam into Burma. In the west it was planned to seize the Suez canal to go through Persia and Afghanistan and thence to the West Coast of India.'

Middle East

The scheme which depended on Muslim disaffection was directed against the North West Frontier. The other schemes relied upon the Ghadar Party of San Francisco and the Bengali revolutionaries.[111] In Germany, the revolutionaries propagated the concept of one nationality and freedom amongst the Indian prisoners of war through the Berlin Committee. (The Rajputs and Sikhs greeted the revolutionaries with the cry *'Bande Mataram'.)* Dr Tarak Nath Das, one of the founder members of Ghadar, was entrusted with this task. Thanks to the constant campaign, Hindus and Muslims closed their ranks and participated jointly in their respective festivities.[112]

In 1915, a few Indian revolutionaries, including Heramba Gupta, Obeidullah Sindhi, Maulana Barkatullah and others went to Constantinople as representatives of the Berlin Committee. Their main task was to distribute propaganda leaflets among the Indian soldiers stationed in Mesopotamia. The rebellion in Basra was probably their handiwork. It failed owing to the treachery of one Muhammed Shariff, the Mayor of Hedzaj. Some of the participants were arrested, while on the way to Persia, and were sentenced to death. The case instituted in this connection is known as 'the Silk Conspiracy Case'. At least 30 revolutionaries, all of them Muslim students from Punjab and the North West Frontier Province were condemned to death. The rest were sentenced to long terms of imprisonment.[113]

Far East

The 5th Native Light Infantry, an Indian Muslim Unit stationed at Singapore, rose in rebellion on 15 February 1915, and declared Indian independence. The mutinous Indian soldiers put the British army personnel under arrest, captured Singapore and held it under their control for two weeks. Ultimately, the rebellion was put down, only with the help of allied Japanese warships.

Ismail Manjur and Sohanlal Pathak were the chief leaders of this revolt. Capital punishment was inflicted upon the participants. Rasullullah Imtiaz and Ruqunuddin were executed on 8 March and Havildar Naik Sulaiman, Naik Munshi Khan, Naik Jaffar Ali Khan and Abdur Reza Khan were executed on 13 March 1915. At the same time Bhagat Singh, Atar Singh, Tankar Singh, Rula Singh, Hazar Singh,

Tamer Singh and Bir Singh were blown up by cannon fire. Besides, 65 other army mutineers were also killed.

Simultaneously, there was a revolt in Malaya. Here the mutineers belonged to the State Guard Unit of Malaya. Subedar Dande Khan, Jamadar Chisti Khan, Havildar Rahmat Ali Khan, Sepoy Hakimali and Havildar Abdul Gani of these rebels were court martialled on 23 March 1916 and sentenced to death.

After the suppression of the rebellion in the Far East, two conspiracy cases were instituted. Sohanlal, the main accused to the Mandalay and the Burma Conspiracy Case, was charged with fomenting mutiny in military barracks and was hanged in the Mandalay Jail in January 1916. Before his execution, the governor visited him in jail and proposed that if he repented and prayed for mercy, the capital punishment inflicted on him might be commuted. In reply to this Sohanlal is reported to have said that if anybody is to beg for pardon, the British must do it, for they have no right at all to stay here in our country.[114]

About 200 soldiers of the mutinous 130th Beluch Regiment were handed out various prison terms and Mustafa Hussain, sentenced to death, was later hanged.[115]

The names of Lala Hardayal, Rash Behari Bose, Barkatulla and others were divulged in the course of this conspiracy case.[116] An approver deposed that 'Red', 'Blue' and 'Green' were the symbolic terms used respectively for the Hindus, the Sikhs and the Muslims. Sohanlal, Kriparaj Harnam Singh, Kala Singh and Basudev Singh, all accused in this case, were sentenced to death by hanging and Chaitram, Kapur Singh, Harjeet Singh, Badan Singh, Gujar Singh, Ramraksham and others were sentenced to transportation for life.[117]

After the failure of the rebellion in Northern India, the mutinous soldiers in various cantonments were put to death and the rest were put on trial in the famous Lahore Conspiracy Case on the charge of waging war against the King. Ninety of the accused in this case were given capital punishment in three successive batches and eight hundred were sentenced to transportation for life. It is learnt from the deposition of the approver of the case that, 'the revolutionaries had been to various cantonments in Meerut, Agra, Kanpur, Allahabad, Ferozepur and Ambala, etc. where they tampered with the allegiance of the native soldiers'. Sri Ganesh Vishnu Pingley, Sardar Jagat Singh, Sardar Suren Singh and Sardar Harnam Singh were among those who were sentenced to death.[118] Balwant Singh, Harnam Singh, Kedar Singh, Khusal Singh, Nanda Singh, Prithibi Singh, Rula Singh, Dewan Singh, Mohan Singh, Wasan Singh, Bhai Paramanand, Pandit Paramananda, Hirderam, Ram Saran, Pandit Jatrit Rao, Gurnam Singh, Joala Singh, Sher Singh, Pandit

Jagat Ram, Nidhan Singh, Keshar Singh, Bisakha Singh, Roob Singh, Bhel Singh, Udam Singh, Piyara Singh, Kripal Singh, Indra Singh, Lal Singh, Kala Singh, Natha Singh, Sahib Singh and Sajjan Singh were among those who were sentenced to transportation for life.[119]

Altogether nine conspiracy trials took place at Lahore. In one of these cases 61 were prosecuted, in another the number of accused was 45, and in a third, 12 were involved. As a result of all these cases, 28 persons were hanged, 29 were acquitted and the rest were sentenced to transportation and imprisonment.[120]

The most important of the charges as framed by the Magistrate in the Banaras Conspiracy Case of 1916 was to cause disaffection and resentment in various military barracks and to incite troops to rebellion by distributing seditious booklets. One of the accused of this case was the revolutionary leader, Sri Sachindra Nath Sanyal, a distinguished colleague of Rash Behari. He was sentenced to transportation for life alongwith Sri Damodar Swarup Ganeshlal, Nalini Mukherjee, Kalipada, Jitendra Nath Sanyal amongst others.[121] Rash Behari, after a brief hesitation, ultimately accepted the decision of the party to move to Japan in the guise of P.N. Tagore in May 1914.

Thus the heroic endeavours to bring about a rebellion which would culminate in national revolution with the help of the army fell through. What were the reasons for this failure? First, despite glowing evidence of communal unity and uncommon bravery, there was a serious lack of political consciousness. All plans and programmes were centred on, and dependent upon the victory or defeat of Germany and that was why the main source of revolutionary inspiration was cut off on the fall of Germany. Secondly, as the leaders of the rebellion could not project to the people a clear idea about their future state and society, the revolution could not take root in the solid base of mass consciousness. It could not gain a mass basis as the Italian or the Irish revolutions did. In 1888 the Decembrists in Russia too were also able to present a picture of the state structure they proposed to establish.[122] Thirdly, there were reasonable grounds to doubt the patriotism of many of those who provided the revolution with programmes and leadership from abroad. Squabbles over money, jealousy, and self-centered narrow-mindedness, among others, served as a stumbling block to the progress of the national revolution.[123]

But those who responded to the call of the leaders and sacrificed their lives were undoubtedly nobler than their leaders, though their names find no place in the roll of honour in history. There is an urgent need for research on these unsung heroes.

The Jugantar-Atmaunnati Bid for an Uprising (1914-15)

On the approach of the World War there had been complete unanimity that there must be an uprising led by the revolutionaries. But, as mentioned earlier, Jugantar and Anushilan failed to come to an understanding over the major tactical line. Jugantar waited for German arms for the final showdown from Bengal. Arms and money were the main problems they had to face. Manpower was not so much of a problem for them since they expected nearly 5000 revolutionary cadres to participate from almost all the districts of Bengal except Darjeeling.[124] Although the promised German help was not expected to reach before June 1915, Jugantar workers were not idle.

Rodda Arms Theft Case (26 August 1914)

As early as 26 August 1914, the Atmaunnati group, led by Bipin Behari Ganguly and Anukul Mukherjee, in collaboration with the group led by Hem Ghosh, allied with the Federated Jugantar and Naren Ghosh Choudhury of Barisal, one of foremost action leaders of Jugantar. They managed with remarkable skill to remove 50 Mauser pistols and a huge quantity of ammunition from stock meant for delivery to Messrs Rodda & Co., premier gun merchants of Calcutta. One Srish Mitra, an employee of Rodda & Co. and a 'trusted follower' of Anukul Mukherjee, along with Haridas Datta, accomplished the task with singular efficiency:

> This theft of 50 mauser pistols and 46,000 rounds of ammunition was an event of major importance in the development of revolutionary crime in Bengal. These pistols and ammunition had been distributed amongst nine different groups including Anushilanites and in the later years mauser pistols were freely used in revolutionary action.[125]

On the night of the theft itself, the pistols were despatched from Bhujanga Roy Choudhury's house to different centres. Ultimately, practically all of them came under the control of Atul Ghosh and Naren Bhattacharya, who had to organize the difficult task of its disposal and retention in safe custody.

This event caused a sensation among the people and also a sense of panic among government officials. Kalidas Bose and Bhujanga Roy Choudhury of the Atmaunnati group took grave risks and showed resourcefulness and boldness in handling this matter. It was their responsibility to arrange for the safe custody of arms. But most interesting is the involvement of G.D. Birla and Prabhu Dayal Himmatsingha. The former was released but the latter was interned. Hari Das Datta was convicted and important leaders of Atmaunnati were detained under the Defence of India Act and later under Regulation III of 1818. Bipin Behari Ganguly was convicted to a long term of imprisonment in another case. The young Srish Mitra went underground never to be seen again. 'His supreme sacrifice in effacing himself completely, marked him as a man of high idealism and great moral virtue,' writes A.C. Guha.[126] Srish Paul is also frequently mentioned as one of the leading figures in this group in the contemporary literature prepared by the Rodda Celebration Committee in Calcutta. He is mentioned in police record as their informer, planted within the party. But this needs verification and deeper examination in view of his later career and involvement in the revolutionary movement of the 30s.[126a]

In early 1915, Jatindra Nath Mukherjee, along with Narendra Nath Bhattacharya, Atul Ghosh, Amarendra Nath Chattopadhyay and Naren Ghosh Choudhury, made elaborate plans to collect a lakh of rupees in order to complete organizational arrangements to receive German arms, as per the information received from the Berlin Committee. Through a series of taxi robberies in Garden Reach (12 February 1915), Bird Co. in Beliaghata Gaddi, Sethbagan and Corporation Street the target was nearly fulfilled. The police failed to track down those responsible for any of these operations, none of which took more than ten minutes. The revolutionaries also secretly circulated pamphlets entitled, Jugantar, announcing that the money had been taken as loans to be paid back by the 'National Government'.[127]

These robberies provoked determined police investigation under Denham, Deputy Commissioner, and Charles Tegart.[128] Nearly all the Jugantar leaders had to go underground to avoid arrest. To deter investigations quite a few police officers were murdered, e.g. Suresh Mukherjee, Nirode Halder and Madhusudan Banerjee, who were killed by Chittapriya Roy Choudhury on 28 February 1915, and Radha Charan Pramanick and Benoyendra Ray.[128a]

In the meantime, Jiten Lahiri of Sreerampur had returned from Germany in March 1915 with the information that the *S.S. Maverick* would start for India with a huge load of arms in April. Jatin Mukherji and his colleagues made organizational arrangements to receive the expected arms and money. According to Arun Chandra Guha, one of the leading figures of Jugantar, in pursuance of the original plan, arms were expected to be landed at two or three places, e.g. at Raimangal in the Sundarban and on the Orissa coast. One such consignment was also expected to be delivered at Goa.

A two-pronged attack on the government with the German arms was planned, for which a guerilla force was necessary to help armed uprisings in different areas. This would have to be backed by a mutiny among the Indian armed forces. An estimate was made and it was found that during the war the British force in India was numerically almost negligible. Immediately on receipt of the arms, these were to be sent to different neighbouring districts. Party units were to be properly organized in all such places. It was decided that Chhota Nagpur on the one side and the Sylhet Hills on the other would form the flanks. Technical arrangements for blowing up the railway bridges were made. Bands of youths were taught gun-handling, as well as signalling. A medical unit with proper training was also organized. Emissaries were sent abroad and to different parts of India. Naren Bhattacharya (Mr Martin) and Bholanath Chattopadhyay were sent to Batavia to meet Theodore Hallferich, German Consul, and to discuss and settle the entire deal. Jiten Lahiri also went for the second time.

Unfortunately the plan was leaked by Czech revolutionary refugee residing in the USA, according to the Czech President Massaryck.[129] The British Government took every precaution to prevent the *Maverick-Larsena* from co-ordinating this exchange on the high seas. Fresh attempts using other ships also were prevented by the Dutch authorities in Batavia and the British authorities in Shanghai. Bhupati Mazumdar who went to the Far East along with Phani Chakravarty, were arrested in Singapore. They successfully withstood the ordeals of intensely severe interrogation by the army authorities and were kept in detention. Phani Chakravarty was convicted to a long term of imprisonment. Bholanath Chatterjee, who earlier went to Burma and Siam, came back safely but was betrayed in Goa. It was arranged that one shipload of arms would be unloaded at a place called Gokarn on the Konkan coast near Goa. They were arrested on 27 December 1915 after their return from the near east. On 27 January 1916, Bholanath committed suicide in the Yeravada prison at Pune. He was considered to be one of the most reliable and brilliant members of Jugantar, according to Dr Jadugopal Mukherji and Arun Chandra Guha. 'Hope of getting arms via the West Coast disappeared with Bholanath's arrest.'[129a] Naren Bhattacharya left Batavia for Tokyo via Shanghai when he found that the game was lost. He, however, made several futile attempts, with the help of Dr Sun Yat Sen to arrange the receipt of arms from the German ambassador in Shanghai.[130] He left for Mexico and assumed the name of M.N. Roy and was destined to play an important role in the freedom movement as a communist leader after his re-emergence.[131]

The last scene of this act is yet to be described. Ever since the murder of Nirode Halder and Suresh Mukherjee, two important police officers of Calcutta, the police were hot on the trail of Jatin Mukherjee and his aides. In the meantime, according to the plan of insurrection, the south-western theatre, covering an extensive area of the Chhota Nagpur Hills from Chakradharpur to Mayurbhanj and Balasore on the south needed to be properly organized. Satish Chakravarty was given charge of blowing up the Rupnarayan Bridge. Already two offices of trading companies under the name Sramajibi Samabay and Harry & Sons had been established to receive funds from the German sources in Batavia and other places. The police, however, got a clue of this plan, probably from one Kumud Nath Mukherjee, an infiltrator into the party in Bangkok.[132] The suggestion to set up a centre at Balasore made by Nalini Kar as early as 1910 was supervised by Naren Bhattacharya. A branch office of Harry & Sons under the name of Universal Emporium was started there as a petty cycle shop manned by cadres of Hari Kumar Chakravarty of the Changripota group. Jatin Mukherjee went there after a few days, along with Manoranjan Sen Gupta, Chittapriya Roy Chowdhuri, Niren Das Gupta and Jyotish Pal. They lived in a village called Kaptipada, 30 miles away from the Balasore town. The police unearthed a few slips of paper after a thorough search of Harry & Sons (Universal Emporium) at Balasore. They also got a clue of Kaptipada village. The police party was incidentally headed by important officials like G.C. Denham of the Central Intelligence and others from Calcutta along with Sergeant Rutherford and R.G. Kilby, District Magistrate of Balasore. In the meantime, Jatin and his companions left the village and decided to wage a last battle inside the dense forest nearby. After two days of weary walking they at last took up position near the crossing of Burha Balong river. Jatin was repeatedly implored by Chittapriya and Manoranjan to escape alone, while they held the police party till their death. But that was not to be.[133] Jatin was determined to have a show down, which probably as a leader he should have avoided. If he had survived he could have certainly played a most dynamic role in the years to come, just as Rash Behari did. M.N. Roy (Naren Bhattacharya) said of Jatin Mukherjee in his Memoirs:

> I admired Jatinda because he personified — perhaps without himself knowing it — the best of mankind. This was indeed a great heritage left for the future — to live, fight and die first, so that the ideal of establishing a social order in which the best in man could be manifest.[134]

The story of the martyrdom of this brave band is well known. Chittapriya became the first martyr while Jatin expired the next day in hospital. Manoranjan, Niren and Jyotish were tried. While Jyotish was awarded a life sentence, the other two were sent to the gallows. Thus ended a glorious but tragic episode in the history of the freedom struggle in India.

Last Phase of Rearguard Action

The successful escape of Rash Behari to Japan in May 1915 and the heroic death of Jatindra Nath on 10 September 1915, marked the beginning of the end of the final chapter of the abortive armed uprising in Bengal, North West or Northern India and the Far East.

But the revolutionaries did not give up the fight so soon. The subsequent period witnessed a grim battle for survival as well as a determined attempt to fight back, which in military terminology may be called rearguard action. The objective of an armed seizure of power having failed at least for the time being, they concentrated on organizing safe hiding places, robberies and political killings with the arms collected during the previous two years. Amongst nearly 260 revolutionary crimes committed during the last phase, some of the notable actions in which both Anushilan and Jugantar joined are mentioned below. They very often co-operated with each other.

The leaders of Jugantar after the tragic but glorious death of Jatin Mukherjee formed a small council composed of Dr Jadugopal Mukherjee, Amarendra Chattopadhyay, Nalini Kar, Satish Chakraborty and Atul Ghosh. Earlier, Bipin Ganguly had been arrested and convicted. Narendra Nath Bhattacharya left for Shanghai to make a last effort to despatch a considerable quantity of small arms from China through the North Eastern region bordering China. Purna Das was convicted. Amongst the action squads who were moving from place to place, the names of Manoranjan Gupta, Surendra Mohan Ghosh, Swami Prajnananda, Aswini Ganguly, Naren Ghosh Choudhury, Nagendra Shekhar Chakraborty, Kali Bagchi, Benoyendra Ray and Sanjib Ray appeared in the intelligence report.[135]

Among the many daring acts of the Jugantar revolutionaries the one at Masjidbari Street on the night of 21 October 1915 ranks very high. Girin Banerjee was spotted in a police den and shot by an unknown revolutionary. The Shibpur dacoity followed soon after on 27 October under the leadership of Naren Ghosh Choudhury. It was enacted on the Barrah Pragpur (April 1915) model, utilizing the superior fire-power from the Mauser pistols acquired from the Rodda theft, which broke the armed cordon put up by the police and the villagers. Three people, including one police constable, died in the fray.

Nagendra Shekhar Chakraborty and Benoyendra Nath Ray ultimately successfully retreated towards Calcutta, although their escape was fraught with grave risks. Both were, however, apprehended after two years, in 1917, and kept in prison till the amnesty of 1919. Naren Ghosh Choudhury, the real hero of hundred battles, was arrested and tried along with six others, including Nikhil Guha Ray, and convicted to a long term of imprisonment in the Andaman Cellular Jail.[136]

Anushilan, however, suffered a severe setback after the failure of the uprising and army revolt on 21 February 1915. But they regrouped their force and a comparatively younger leadership emerged. They had already suffered considerably when in the two Barisal and other conspiracy cases, some of the ablest leaders like Trailakya Chakraborty, Pratul Ganguly, Ramesh Acharya, Naren Sen, Khagendranath Choudhury, Ramesh Choudhury and Madan Bhowmick were awarded heavy sentences.

The void left by the arrest of the leaders was quickly filled up by a new batch. Anukul Chakraborty, Amrita Lal Sarkar, Nagendranath Dutta and Krishna Lal Saha, alias Kanai Ray, found no difficulty in receiving shelter at Chandannagar and other dens.

In the districts also, by the year 1916 the Anushilan Samiti had been reorganized with new vigour. Among the district organizers were Prakash Chowdhury (Chittagong), Prabodh Chandra Sen (Comilla), Amritalal Chakraborty (Dacca), Jamini Sarkhel (Madaripur), Probodh Chandra Dasgupta (Mymensingh), Ramani Chakraborty (Behrampur), Satish Pakrashi (Barisal), Sitanath Das (Khulna-Jessore), Dakshina Ranjan Sarkar (Purnea), Rebati Kanta Nag (Bhagalpur), Nibaran Chandra Pal (Faridpur), Nalini Bandhu Gupta (Howrah) and Jogendra Das Bhattacharya (Calcutta). All of them were absconders and were not expected to hold fast to their headquarters.[137]

The period which followed was one of rearguard actions by a desperate revolutionary community hunted by a repressive machine. 'In 1916 Amrita Lal Sarkar, Nalini Kanta Ghosh, Krishna Lal Saha constituted the leadership of the Anushilan Samiti. Later, however, Krishna Lal Saha lost his character and betrayed [on June 1918]. That gave of course a staggering blow to the party.'[138]

The two most outstanding actions of Jugantar and Anushilan were the determined attempts on the life of Basanta Kumar Chatterjee, a Deputy Superintendent of Police, in his residence at Musalman Para Lane (25 November 1915) and the murder of Madhusudan Bhattacharya, the I.B. Officer, responsible for the arrest and conviction of Naren Ghosh Choudhury, the leader of many actions committed by the Jugantar Party.

The attack was sudden and well planned. Chatterjee had a providential escape while his bodyguard was killed and three policemen were injured. Satish Pakrashi and Kalimohan Maitra, who took part in the attack, were injured but managed to escape. Nagendra Nath Sengupta was, however, arrested on the spot. But thanks to a remarkable legal battle waged by Norton and others, he secured his acquittal.

These outrages caused the government concern. In November, the police succeeded in arresting quite a number of leaders, including Narendra Mohan Sengupta at the Green Park of Calcutta.

But the most sensational revolutionary outburst of Anushilan was achieved on 30 June 1916, when in the third attempt on the life of Basanta Chatterjee, a most hated police officer, was fatally shot by Atindra Mohan Ray of Comilla and Suresh Chandra Chakraborty. Four persons, Probodh Biswas, Mohini Bhattacharya, Sisir Ghosh and Prafulla Dasgupta actively assisted in the plot. This murder showed once again the remarkable courage and discipline that characterized many of the actions of the Anushilan Samiti.[139]

After these murders, the government became furious and started wholesale arrests of young men. On 23 June 1916, two CID constables were shot dead at Bairagitola in Dacca. Atindra Mohan Ray was once again the main architect, along with Krishna Shah. On 1 July 1916, at the initiative of Charles Tegart, the then DIG, IB, CID, the government of Bengal had launched severe repressive measures, ordering a complete round-up of all the suspects. The entire family of Sett brothers, Naren and Phani, the Setts of Beadon Street, became victims of the extra-ordinary wrath, which evoked public criticism. Pulin Mukherjee of the Anushilan broke down under torture in Dalanda House. In Lower Circular Road, Kyd Street and Elysium Row, the police had established horrifying torture chambers.

The Anushilan, Jugantar and the entire revolutionary movement entered a phase of sharp decline by the close of 1916. The period that followed was not, however, barren and colourless. It was rather one of uncommon courage, matchless patriotism and a surprising display of self-sacrifice on the part of both young workers as well as of veterans. 'The months of July, August and September passed in this way. By that time about 1,500 workers were arrested all over Bengal. It was a period of diaspora for both the Jugantar and Anushilan parties.'[140] Regulation III of 1818 was in full force. Leaders of both Anushilan and Jugantar often had to live together and use common shelters.

On the Jugantar side, Surendra Mohan Ghosh, Amar Ghosh and many other important workers were arrested between July and December 1916. Arun Chandra Guha of Sankar Math, who was one of main planners of shelters, was arrested and put to a severe test in Dalanda House. But seven of its top-ranking leaders were absconders, namely Dr Jadugopal Mukherjee, Amar Chatterjee, Atul Ghosh, Satish Chakraborty, Nalini Kar, Manmath Biswas, and Panchu Gopal Banerjee, each carrying on his head a reward of Rs 5,000. Bhupendra Kumar Datta, a close associate of Jatin Mukherjee, remained almost the sole mobile worker who could maintain links and collect money. For some time he had the assistance of two other colleagues, Charu Ghosh and Kuntal Chakraborty. After a few months, he was also arrested. Kuntal and Charu remained free up to the beginning of 1918. Another important worker, Jiban Lal Chattopadhyay, was arrested around the end of 1916.[141]

In December 1917, on the eve of the visit to India of Montagu, Secretary of State for India, in the British Cabinet, a leaflet was circulated by the Jugantar group, then headed by Kuntal, calling on the people

> to spread terror to make this unholy government impossible. . . . Remember those who had died or had gone mad. Remember, watch and work we ask you once more, brothers, in the name of God and country and all young or old, rich or poor, Hindus and Mahomadans, Budhists and Christians, join this war of Indian Independence and pour forth your blood and treasure. Hark, the Mother calls and show the way, *NANYA PANTHA VIDYATE ANYANYA* [The only way and no other].
>
> (By order of the Executive Indian Revolutionary Committee.)[142]

Kuntal was the last of the important workers of Jugantar who was yet free. However, he died of T.B. due to malnutrition.

The government established machinery to break the nerve of the revolutionaries who were found to be extremely busy after Basanta Chatterji's murder. The Samiti suffered a further setback after the arrests of their remaining top-ranking leaders like Nalini Kanta Ghosh and Ashutosh Kahali at Allahabad station. 'The police failed to elicit any information from these two ardent revolutionary leaders even after putting them to torture of the most infernal kind.' Even the intelligence report admits the failure. On 9 October 1916, Narendra Nath Banerji was arrested at 39 Pathuria Ghata Street of Calcutta (the secret headquarters of Anushilan at that time). Jogesh Chattopadhyay, Sisir Kumar Datta and Jogendra Das Bhattacharya were also taken into custody by the police from the same house.[143]

In Dalanda Torture Chamber

Jogesh was put to the severest trial by a sadist police officer named Manoj Pal. L.H. Colson, one of the interrogators, recorded: 'This appears to be a very dangerous youngster (aged 21 only). I also told him that many leaders of his party had made full statement and he could neither save himself nor the Samiti, to which he made no reply.'[143a]

A full and graphic account of the inhuman tortures perpetrated on Chatterjee, Sisir Datta Gupta, Jogendra Das Bhattacharya, Atindra Mohan Ray, Amrita Lal Chakraborty, and Amrita Lal Sarkar, who were arrested around the middle of 1916, was provided by Jogesh Chandra in later years.[143b]

The dramatic escape of Jogesh Chandra Chatterjee and Nalini Kanta Ghosh from Dalanda Hall was considered to be among the most courageous exploits of Anushilan, comparable to the grand escapes of Purnananda Dasgupta and Dinesh Majumdar from the Presidency Jail and Midnapur Jail respectively in the late Nineteen thirties. These escapes gave a brief boost to the declining morale of the revolutionary movement in Bengal.

Wandering Revolutionary Community : 1917-18

Revolutionary campaigning through leaflets and occasional gun battles with the police became the main features of the activities of the wandering revolutionary absconders of the Jugantar and Anushilan. In the district of Mainpuri in Eastern Uttar Pradesh, revolutionary terrorist units sprouted as late as 1917 under the leadership of Gandelal Dixit, Roshan Singh and Ramprosad Bismail, who joined later.

Top leaders of Jugantar centering on Dr Jadugopal, Amarendra Chattopadhyay, Satish Chakraborty and Nalini Kar, left for the North Eastern Frontier, Bhutan and beyond, facing the Tibetan border, anticipating a cargo of arms to be sent by M.N. Roy through Dr Sun Yat Sen. They were expecting an uprising amongst the Abor tribe. Here Dr Jadugopal and others led the lives of a hotel keeper, village doctor, etc. and faced varied occupational hazards in Dhubri (Assam). They were undertaken along with a few of their most versatile comrades like Nagendra Shekhar Chakraborty, Kulendra Raha Ray, Satish Thakur (Chakraborty), who acted as their most loyal bodyguards, servants and cooks.[144]

Earlier, in Chandannagar, both the Anushilan and Jugantar leaders enjoyed the hospitality of Motilal Roy. Much earlier they lived in a shelter in Salkia (Howrah) and once had to confront a police party with a hot exchange of fire. Leaving Chandannagar, Satish Chakraborty and Panchu Gopal, avoiding the train journey, undertook a long trek for several weeks, reaching ultimately a village near the Bhutan border which was almost outside the pale of civilization. They lived through this ordeal upto 1922 in the hope of a tribal uprising.[145]

Gauhati Kalta Bazar Battle, 1918

Pressed hard by the Calcutta police in Chandannagar, the joint leadership decided to shift to a relatively insignificant shelter in Gauhati in Assam under the command of Nalini Ghosh, whose great escape from Dalanda House, made him the idol of Bengali youth. The party shifted to Gauhati in the beginning of 1917, taking the veteran Jugantar leader Amarendra Chattopadhyay along with them. But on 8 January 1918, Krishna Lal Saha one of the top leaders of Anushilan was arrested in Calcutta. 'He broke down under torture and gave out the clue of the Gauhati as well as many hideouts.'[146]

On the night of the police raid all the Anushilan members and Amarendra Chattopadhyay were sleeping at the Atgaon shelter while Satish Chakraborty had gone out in the daytime. The raid was led by Mr Fairweather, I.G. of Police, Bengal, with a large contingent. The entire operation is reminiscent of the Balasore battle of 9 September 1915.

Manindra Ray was on guard. Nalini woke up and on realizing their predicament wakened the others. In the meantime, the police were vehemently knocking at the closed door, shouting 'Open please'. Nalini retorted, 'It is open, enter and be killed.' Giving no time to Fairweather, the gallant band of revolutionaries like their counterparts in Balasore, began to shower bullets and forced them to retreat since they were confused and puzzled at the unexpected attack. They started running to and fro. Nalini ordered that they should reserve at least one bullet each for themselves. Just then the veteran revolutionary, Amarendra Chattopadhyay, intervened and requested Nalini to reconsider the decision of self-immolation and try to escape through the gap in the cordon that had been created. So they successfully marched through the disorganized policemen with loaded revolvers in hand. Their boldness produced a miraculous effect and all seven escaped unhurt. The next morning, their first job was to arrange the safe shifting of veteran Amarendra Chattopadhyay. Amarendra went to Punjab and took the garb of a Sikh monk. He travelled through the country and finally settled in Madras in the garb of a sannyasi, establishing an ashram.

Thereafter, seven brave souls — Nalini Ghosh, Nalini Bagchi, Narendra Banerjee, Manindra, Prabash Lahiri, Taraprasanna and Satish Pakrashi took up positions on the top of a hillock (Naba Graha hill) near the Kamakhya temple.

On 9 January they were surrounded by an armed contingent. The leader, Nalini, decided to carry on the fight alone and to keep the police engaged till his death. He ordered that, in the meantime his comrades must escape. His comrades seemed unwilling to leave him, but with a thundering voice, he ordered them to obey him saying, 'It was crime to waste seven valuable lives, when by sacrifice of one life only, six other lives could be saved.'[147]

In this unequal battle, Satish Pakrashi, Nalini Bagchi and Probodh Das Gupta were able to escape unhurt. All the others were injured, caught and tried. They were awarded detention ranging from 2 to 7 years, 20 white policemen received severe injuries.[147a]

The Gauhati episode was not just a 'skirmish' as one writer tries to belittle it. It excelled even the Balasore incident. Both in Balasore and Gauhati there is no dearth of the grandeur of human nobility, courage and revolutionary will power, but in Gauhati the leader of the group could keep himself sufficiently self-composed at the most crucial point, to make a realistic revolutionary decision and fought his way through the police cordon.

The last episode of these series was the Kalta Bazar incident. Nalini Bagchi and Prabodh Biswas, after their successful escapade, came to Calcutta. Here Nalini contracted a severe attack of small pox. He was very soon cured by the care of Satish Pakrashi and left for Dacca to reorganize the dilapidated party. In Kalta Bazar area, Dacca, they were, however, betrayed. The police cordoned the house in which the revolutionaries were sheltered. But they decided to fight unto death. Tarini died in the encounter after receiving bullet wounds, while Nalini was caught seriously wounded. As the Additional S.P. pressurized Nalini for disclosing his identity, he gave the reply with laconic unconcern, 'Don't disturb me, let me die in peace.'[148] This episode went round as a household story to be told to every youth of the next decade and influenced many cadres to lay down their lives with remarkable stoicism and valour.

In 1918, the curtain at last fell upon the drama that was being enacted since the commencement of the war in August 1914.

Where Do They Stand?

We are now at the end of the story. The question now is how far and to what extent did the national revolutionaries succeed in achieving their objective.

Their long-term objective, since the commencement of the revolutionary current in 1897, was to achieve the independence of India from the yoke of British rule. In each period they also had some immediate objective.

During the first phase, i.e. 1897 to 1907, the revolutionaries succeeded in developing organizations nearly all over India and even outside. Indian organizations had distinct religious overtones. Political actions in the form of murders, as in the case of Maharashtra, were mainly characterized by the crudity of religious and racist emotion in form, though the content was anti-imperialist. Popular participation therefore was seemingly passive and inert. During the second phase (1907 to 1914), the specificity of its revolutionary ideal, both social and political, may be discerned distinctly in the process of character-building as visualized by Swami Vivekananda and followed by other mythological and historical figures like Sree Krishna, Goddess Kali, Chatrapati Shivaji and Pratapaditya (in a lesser degree in the case of Bengal). Side by side, the western model also began to attract Indian revolutionaries, mainly in the persons of Mazzini, Garibaldi of Italian liberation, and to a certain extent

Russian nihilists like Vera Fignor. In short, the Italian and Russian models of revolutionary action were closely and avidly followed. The perspective of this period was to quicken the process of revolutionary struggle for independence as against the moderate Congressmen's plea for self-government under the tutelage of British Raj. In fact, it was a strident call for independence, for revolt against the policy of 'mendicancy' of a section of Congressmen led by Gokhale, Mehta and Lord Sinha. Dacoity for collecting funds became the subject of intense debate amongst the leaders of Anushilan. Sister Nivedita was definitely opposed to it, as also Pramathanath Mitra, the President of Anushilan. But political assassination was willy nilly accepted and sympathized with once it was committed and the extreme price paid for it. Commenting on political murders, W.S. Blunt writes in his Diaries:

> People talk about political assassination as defeating its own end, but that is nonsense. It is just the shock needed to convince selfish rulers that selfishness has its limits of impudence. It is like the other fiction that England never yields to threats. My experience is that when England has her face well slapped she apologises, not before.[149]

The method of terrorist actions became the subject matter of heated debate amongst the Liberals and the Congress-minded public figures like Lala Lajpat Rai, Surendranath Banerjea, not to speak of Gokhale. But one must try to appreciate the specific historical situation in which it was born. A study of the autobiographies of few of the erstwhile revolutionaries like Barindra Kumar Ghosh, Upendra Nath Bandopadhyay, Hemchandra Kanungo, Dr Jadugopal Mukhopadhyay, and Sachin Sanyal, have revealed the fact that they were drawn to the path of violence on account of the repressive measures of the British Raj, against which they found no other remedy. The arrest of Sushil Sen, a young boy of 16, followed by 15 lashes as a measure of punishment; the brutal lathi charges on Chittaranjan Guha Thakurtha at the Barisal Conference (1906); the arrest of Aswini Datta, Lala Lajpat Rai (1908) and the barbarous sentences on Bal Gangadhar Tilak (1909), and on Ganesh Savarkar, have been cited as the immediate causes for the shift of public sympathy in favour of terrorism.[150]

The statement of Madan Dhingra, who shot at Curzon Wyllie in London provides a true insight into the mentality of a national revolutionary during this formative decade when the conquest of fear of death and assertion of revolutionary personality as the process of new political perception were the main phenomena. Dhingra stated:

> I admit, the other day, I attempted to shed English blood as an humble revenge for inhuman hangings and deportations of patriotic Indian

> youths. . . . I believe that a nation held in bondage with the help of foreign bayonets is in a perpetual state of war. Since open battle is rendered impossible to a disarmed race, I attacked by surprise since guns were denied to me, I drew forth my pistol and fired. . . . I feel that a wrong done to my country is an insult to God. . . . The war of independence will continue between India and England so long as the English and Hindu [Hindusthani] races last.[151]

During the preparatory period (1907-14), despite the expansion and, to a certain extent, the consolidation of revolutionary parties, the number of actions in the form of dacoities and murders of suspected people and their own cadres were quite impressive in point of numbers but not in quality. Except the murder of Naren Goswami within the Alipur Central Jail, the Jackson murder in Maharashtra, of Curzon Wyllie in London, of Ashe in Tinnevelly and the attempt on the life of Hardinge in 1912 (23 December), most of the outrages failed to create a positive sentiment of enlightened nationalism, as happened in Italy and Ireland. Later reports on the commission of frequent dacoities, as revealed by intelligence reports and corroborated by the authors themselves in jails, created political and organizational problems at a time when it was imperative to remain inconspicuous in view of the preparations for a much bigger action like the commencement of insurrection in 1915. More or less, both Anushilan and Jugantar, failed to rise to the great occasion for which they were preparing themselves, though on parallel lines, in 1915.

Revolutionary insurrection is a serious undertaking. There should have been other effective devices to raise funds than by committing dacoities of the Pragpur, Khidirpur, and Bighati type, inviting more undesirable organizational and political hazards, leading to the damage of the infrastructure necessary for a large-scale insurrection. Both the parallel schemes associated with the names of Rash Behari Bose and Jatin Mukherjee proved to be quite inadequate in terms of political and organizational preparation, especially for a country like India, then ruled by the most astute imperial despotism on earth, after the Romans.

But what is significant here is not the degree of failure, but the moral and political legacy left for future generations of national revolutionaries in particular, and freedom fighters in general, and their contribution to the growth of political consciousness amongst the militant youth, drawn from all classes, communities and regions who flung themselves headlong into the mass struggles of 1920s, 30s and 40s.

It is true that initially upto 1910, the linkage with the Muslim community was weak owing to the peculiar historical situation that prevailed in some parts of Maharashtra and Bengal. Anushilan (of Dacca) had been affected by an anti-Muslim bias as a reaction to the 'loyalist' stance of some Muslim leaders. But that barrier was slowly removed when the movement expanded its base in northern India under Rash Behari. With the entry of Ghadar, there was a qualitative shift in the political complexion of the national revolutionary movement from that of 1913. Revolutionary literature from Paris, Zurich, San Francisco, Constantinople and Shanghai, prepared by the Jugantar, Ghadar, Islamic Fraternity combination went a great way towards the creation of a militant, secular national outlook. A vague conception of the Republic was thrown in a seal prepared by Kuntal Chakraborty, the leader of Jugantar as late as 1918.[152] Confusion and ambiguity on the ideological plane was due to the peculiar historical situation generated by the uneven social, economic and cultural heritage and backlogs accumulated within India as a whole through the ages and more intensely under colonial rule.

The charge that the national revolutionaries were anti-Muslim is, in a small degree, true for a very short period, may be up to 1910. Even Vinayak Damodar Savarkar, who in the closing years of his life became the pillar of Hindu communalism, glorified both Hindu and Muslim heroes of the rebellion of 1857 in his book, *The First War of Independence*.

It is true that, during the formative years, national revolutionaries, especially in Maharashtra and Bengal, had to use Hindu mythological traditions, precepts, concepts and models as means of political mobilization against tyrannical alien rule. Moreover,

> they found among the members of that [Hindu] community worst vices and evils being practised in the name of religion. They were steeped up to the neck in the most nonsensical superstitions, irrational prejudices and taboos erecting insurmountable barriers between man and man, a spineless dependence on fate, fear of their own shadows and of evil spirits lurking at every corner making them incapable of taking a single step off the beaten track, incapability of looking beyond narrow selfish personal or caste or parochial interests. They had become totally callous to the sufferings not only of other fellow countrymen but also of the members of their own community. It is with such human material that the pioneers of radical militant nationalism had to begin their work. Under these circumstances, in the initial stages of national awakening, those pioneers, sought to impart new consciousness among the people with the help of religion itself. But with a big difference. They sought to purge the Hindu religion and society of all the degenerate practices, beliefs and superstitions which in their opinion were responsible for the downfall of the society and the country.[153]

It is important, before we conclude, to draw attention to the part played by women, known and unknown, during the third phase of the movement (1914-8). They took a full share in the most dangerous assignments of keeping arms, organizing shelters for absconding leaders, playing the role of camouflaged housewives, nurses, hotel managers, mistresses of police officers, etc.

The names of Sarala Devi, Sister Nivedita, Madame Cama, are well known. But few people know the names of Sarojini Devi, the elder sister of Swami Prajnananda; Binode Bala, widowed elder sister of Jatin Mukherjee; Manorama Mazumdar, wife of Nagen Mazumdar (Mymensingh); Dukuribala Devi of Birbhum, tortured and convicted; Nanibala Devi, the first woman state prisoner, brought from Punjab and tried in a torture chamber in Kyd Street; Shindhu Bala Ghosh, wife of Deben Ghosh, tortured and jailed for harbouring absconders;[154] Ambika Devi of Palong, mother of Jogen Ray of Tilliha Manickganj. These women showed exemplary courage in keeping (Kalicharan) Trailakya Maharaj and others underground.[155] A Muslim lady, sister of Abdul Waheb, who was the proverbial *didi* of Shahid Khudiram[156] moved heaven and earth to get the death sentence on Khudiram commuted, in complete disregard to the possible consequences for her because of her open display of her concern and regard for the young revolutionary.

These and hundreds of others should be remembered along with many unknown martyrs, Hindus, Muslims and Sikhs, in far off lands.

The history of the revolutionaries is not just an account of heroic deeds, but, at the same time, it cannot cynically reflect only its negative features in the name of so-called realism. After all, the success or failure of a movement should be viewed from a long-term historical viewpoint in which the evolution of enduring structures of universal human value should take precedence over short-term considerations relevant only to a specific historical period.

In our time, Che Guevera may be considered a highly romantic revolutionary, but his last words sum up the essence of the true revolutionary spirit:

> In our country if the individual knows that the glorious period in which it has befallen him to live is one of sacrifice — he has learned its meaning. The true revolutionary is moved by strong feelings of love. It is impossible to conceive of an authentic revolutionary who lacks this quality. Herein lie what are perhaps the great dramatic challenges to a leader, he must combine an impassioned spirit with coolness of mind and he must make painful decisions unfalteringly.[157]

Notes and References

1. Bhupendra Rakshit Ray, *Bharater Shashstra Biplaber Itihas*, Calcutta, p. 14. Satyendra Nath Majumdar, *In Search of Revolutionary Ideology*, New Delhi, p. 18.

2. Jadugopal Mukhopadhyay, *Biplabi Jibaner Smriti* (first edition), Calcutta; Arun Chandra Guha, *The Spark of Indian Revolution*, Calcutta, p. 386; Intelligence report on Congress alliance with terrorists (Home Pol. F. No. 4/21/1932).
3. Lester Reginald Hutchinson, *Empire of the Nabobs*, p. 189.
4. Verene Lovett, *History of Indian National Movement*, p. 232; Rowlatt Commission Report (GOI), pp. 26-7.
5. The writer interviewed more than a hundred former revolutionaries and read 12 biographies where they have mentioned Vivekananda as one of the primary sources of their inspiration and of the sustenance of revolutionary ideals.
6. Vivekananda, *Collected Works*, Calcutta, p. 190.
7. Ibid., pp. 225-6.
8. Biman Bihari Majumdar, *Militant Nationalism in India*, Calcutta, 1966, p. 44.
9. Ibid., p. 480.
10. Ibid., p. 46. Kalicharan Ghosh, *Roll of Honour*, Calcutta, 1965, p. 31.
11. Bhupendra Nath Datta, *Aprakasita Rajnaitik Itihash*, Vol. I, p. 212. Jugantar Party; James Campbell Kerr, *Political Troubles in India 1907-17*, Calcutta, p. 64.
12. Bankim Chandra Chattopadhyay, *Dharmatattva, Anushilan*, pp. 1-11, 26-8.
13. Pradyot Kumar Ghosh, 'Ideology of a Revolutionary Secret Society — Anushilan Samiti, 1902-1918' in *India Past and Present*, Vol. I, No. 1, Surindra Nath Ray Commemoration Volume, IHR Bombay.
14. Kalicharan Ghosh, op. cit., pp. 26-7.
15. J.C. Kerr, op. cit., pp. 6, 8; Reginald Reynold, *White Shahib in India*, p. 34.
16. J.C. Kerr, op. cit. (henceforth J.C.K.), p. 8.
17. J.C.K., p. 5.
18. Ibid., pp. 8-9.
19. Ibid., p. 10.
20. Ibid., p. 12.
21. Sumit Sarkar, *Swadeshi Movement*, New Delhi, 1973, pp. 470-1.
22. Ibid., p. 468.
23. *Daly Report* (Intelligence), A Strictly Confidential Report: Note on the growth of 'Revolutionary movement in India 1900-12', edited by Sankar Ghosh, Calcutta, 1981, p. 276.
24. Arun Chandra Guha, op. cit., pp. 55, 164.
25. V. Joshi, *Vasudeo Balwant Phadke*, p. 46 ff; K. Maitra, 'Phadke, Father of the Movement', in *Conflux*, September 1971, Vol. III.
26. J.C.K., vide Appendix.
27. Ibid., p. 25.
28. Ibid., p. 28; Dr Jadugopal Mukhopadhyay, op. cit., p. 185.
29. Jadugopal Mukhopadhyay, op. cit.; Budhadev Bhattacharjee, *Freedom Struggle & Anushilan Samiti*, Vol. I, Calcutta, p. 34.
30. A.C. Guha, op. cit., p. 84.
31. Kalicharan Ghosh, op. cit., p. 41.
32. Ibid., p. 53.
33. Rowlatt Committee or Sedition Committee Report (henceforth RCR), p. 36.
34. J.C.K., p. 28.

35. *Daly Report,* pp. 12, 13.
36. Ibid., p. 134.
37. Ibid., p. 134.
38. Motilal Roy, *Amar Dekha Biplab O Biplabi,* p. 32.
39. K.C. Ghosh, op. cit., p. 183.
40. Bhupendra Nath Dutta, op. cit., p. 60.
41. K.C. Ghosh, op. cit., p. 187.
42. B.N. Datta, op. cit., p. 60.
43. K.C. Ghosh, op. cit., p. 187.
44. K.C. Ghosh, *Philosophy of Bomb,* p. 177.
45. *Daly Report,* pp. 4-5.
46. *Salkeld Report on Anushilan Samiti,* p. 90.
47. *Freedom Movement & Anushilan Samiti,* p. 135.
48. Motilal Roy, p. 46; R.C.R., p. 127; Trailakya Chakraborty, op. cit., p. 110.
49. Ibid.
50. K.C. Ghosh, p. 192.
51. J.C.K., p. 151; *Daly Report,* pp. 192, 210.
51a. Interview with Surendra Mohan Ghosh.
51b. A.C. Guha, op. cit., p. 329, J.C.K., p. 329.
51c. J.C.K., p. 23; B.B. Majumdar, *Militant Nationalism in India,* p. 22.
52. *Pol-File Home Freedom Movement,* No. 935; B.B. Majumdar, op. cit., p. 122.
53. *Lajpat Rai — Autobiography,* Delhi, pp. 82, 965; *Englishmen,* 10 September 1907; *Young India,* 182.
54. *Home Political File-113,* August 1907; *Minto Papers; New Age,* 30 July 1972.
55. R.C.R., p. 142.
56. B.N. Datta, p. 65.
57. A.C. Guha, p. 262.
57a. Ibid., p. 141.
58. Ibid., pp. 342-3.
59. Ibid., p. 343.
60. Ibid.; Hardinge Diary; B.B. Majumdar, op. cit., p. 88.
61. Ibid., p. 88.
62. Ibid., p. 89.
63. *History of Freedom Movement Source Materials File 11-394.*
64. Ibid., pp. 11-401.
65. Ibid., pp. 11-345.
66. Ibid., pp. 11-401.
67. Ibid., pp. 11-481.
68. B.B. Majumdar, op. cit., p. 95.
69. Ibid., p. 99.
70. R.C.R., p. 109.
71. Ibid., p. 71.
72. Ibid., p. 72.
73. Ibid., p. 165.
74. Ibid., p. 166.
75. A.C. Guha, op. cit., p. 150.
76. Jadugopal, op. cit., p. 421.
77. R.C.R., p. 134.

78. A.C. Guha, op. cit., pp. 157-8.
79. P.K. Ghosh, *Freedom Struggle and the Anushilan Samiti*, Vol. I, pp. 101-2.
80. J.C.K., pp. 197-9. D. Petrie, *Report on the activities abroad, Home Pol. A + B.*
81. Ibid., pp. 209-10.
82. Ibid., p. 210.
83. Ibid., p. 214.
84. Lahore Conspiracy, Trial Papers, 1st/2nd: Lala Hardayal Dharmavira, p. 213.
85. Ibid., J.C.K.
86. A.C. Guha, op. cit.; Jadu Gopal Mukherji, op. cit.
87. J.C.K., p. 218.
88. R.C.R.; Hardayal, p. 219.
89. Lahore Conspiracy Trial Papers, N.A. Freedom Movement files.
90. Interview with Dr Balwant Singh, son of Baba Gurdit Singh.
91. A.C. Guha, op. cit., p. 350.
92. R.C.R., p. 136.
93. R.C.R., p. 110; Dr Jadugopal Mukherji, op. cit.
94. Bhupendra Kumar Datta, *Biplaber Padachinha*, Calcutta, p. 87.
95. J.C.K., pp. 197-8.
96. Ibid., pp. 209-10.
97. Ibid., p. 218.
98. Ibid., p. 214.
99. A.C. Guha, op. cit., p. 368; Jadu Gopal, op. cit., p. 425; B.N. Datta, op. cit., p. 178.
100. Lahore Conspiracy Trial Papers, *Home Pol. File No. 364.*
101. Dr Jadugopal Mukherji, op. cit.
102. K. Singh and S. Singh, Ghadar Benares Conspiracy Trial Papers, Home File No. 364; Sachin Sanyal, *Bandijiban*, Vol. I, p. 158.
103. A.V. Raikov, Soviet Academi in *New Age*, 30 July 1972 quoting Soviet archival sources.
104. Ibid.
105. Trailakya Maharaj, op. cit., p. 138; R.C.R., p. 172.
106. Sachin Sanyal, op. cit., Vol. I, p. 160; Bala Shastri Haridas, *Armed Struggle*, p. 228.
107. Sachin Sanyal, op. cit., Vol. I, p. 87; R.C.R., p. 172.
108. Ibid.
109. Ibid.
109a. *Freedom Struggle and Anushilan Samiti*, Vol. I, Chapter IV.
110. K. Singh and S. Singh, op. cit; R.C.R., Appendix on Muslim., disaffection.
110a. Interview with Abdur Rezzaque Khan and Amir Hyder Khan.
111. R.C.R.; David Petrie, *Report on the activities of the revolutionaries in Far East.*
112. Ibid., pp. 97-8; B.N. Datta, op. cit., Vol. II, p. 85.
113. Ibid., p. 112; Abinash Bhattacharya, op. cit., p. 74; A.R. Khan, interviewed.
114. A.H. Khan, interviewed, April 1944; R.C.R.; R.W. Mosbergan, *The Sepoy Rebellion — A History of Singapur Mutiny of 1914*, unpublished thesis, University of Malaya, 1954.
115. R.C.R.; *David Petrie Report;* A.R. Khan and A.H. Khan, Interview.

116. Trailakya Maharaj, op. cit.; R.C.R., p. 170, *David Petrie Report.*
117. Trailakya Maharaj, op. cit.
118. Ibid.
119. R.C.R.; Sachin Sanyal, op. cit., Vol. I, p. 90.
120. R.C.R., p. 143.
121. B.N. Datta, op. cit.; Lahore Conspiracy Trial Papers, *Home Pol. A+B,* March 1916.
122. Ibid.
123. Ibid.; B.N. Datta; Microfilm record — NAI; M.N. Roy, *Memoirs.*
124. Interview with B.N. Datta, 7 October 1967; A.C. Guha, op. cit.
125. R.C.R., p. 65; Nalini Kishore Guha, op. cit., pp. 109-11; A.C. Guha, op. cit., p. 365.
126. A.C. Guha, op. cit., p. 367; R.C.R., p. 66.
126a. *Home Pol. Police record,* Vol. V, pp. 3-13.
127. Vide Appendix — R.C.R., p. 69.
128. A.C. Guha, op. cit., p. 375.
128a. Motilal Roy, *Amar Dekha Biplab-O-Biplabi,* pp. 135-7.
129. A.C. Guha, op. cit., p. 362; Arun K. Bose, 'On German Scheme to supply arms', Seminar paper on the occasion of Golden Jubilee of Chattagram youth uprising.
129a. A.C. Guha, op. cit., p. 400.
130. Ibid., p. 387; M.N. Roy, op. cit., pp. 4-5; J.C.K.
131. Ibid., p. 400.
132. A.C. Guha, op. cit., p. 401; J.C.K.
133. Dr Jadugopal; J.C.K.; A.C. Guha, op. cit.; B. Bhattacharya (ed.), *Freedom Struggle and Anushilan Samiti,* p. 126.
134. M.N. Roy, op. cit., p. 56.
135. Dr Jadugopal; R.C.R.; A.C. Guha, op. cit.
136. Ibid., p. 128. Statement of Nagendra Sekhar Chakravarti.
137. *Freedom Struggle and Anushilan Samiti,* p. 126.
138. Ibid., p. 126.
139. Ibid., p. 127.
140. A.C. Guha, op. cit.
141. Ibid., p. 418; vide Appendix R.C.R.; Anushilan, op. cit., p. 128.
142. R.C.R.; A.C. Guha, op. cit., p. 421.
143. *Freedom Struggle and Anushilan Samiti,* p. 128.
143a. Note by L.H. Colson, 23 October 1916, Home Pol. Progs, January 1917, Nos. 364-72.
143b. Jogesh Chandra Chattopadhyay, op. cit., p. 63.
144. Dr Jadugopal, op. cit., p. 428; A.C. Guha, op. cit., p. 421; *Interview with Nagendra Sekhar Chakravarty*: Benoyendra Ray; M.N. Roy, *Memoirs,* p. 24.
145. Satish Pakrashi, op. cit., pp. 100-4; Diary of Political Events of 1919; Home Pol. A. Progs — January 1919, No. 3; Dr Jadugopal, op. cit., p. 448; A.C. Guha, op. cit., p. 423.
146. Anushilan Samiti, op. cit., p. 133.
147. Ibid., p. 138.
147a. Satish Pakrashi, op. cit., pp. 100-4.

148. Diary of Political Events 1928; Home Pol. A. Progs — January 1919, No. 3; A.C. Guha, op. cit., p. 423; Anushilan Samiti, p. 133; Interview with Provesh Lahiry.
149. W.S. Blunt, *Diaries*, Part II, p. 288. Quoted in B.B. Mazumdar, op. cit.
150. R.C. Majumdar, *History of Freedom Movement*, Vol. 2, p. 450.
151. Dhananjay Kir, *Savarkar and his times*, p. 558.
152. R.C.R.; p. 110.
153. Satyendranarayan Majumdar, *In search of Revolutionary ideology and a revolutionary programme.*
154. Dr Jadugopal; A.C. Guha, op. cit.
155. Trailakya Chakraborty; *Writer's Personal Experience.*
156. B.N. Datta, op. cit., Vol. I.
157. Che-Guevera, *Reminiscence of a revolutionary*, p. 3.

Chapter VI

Worker, Peasant and Tribal Movements (1885-1919)

Sunil Kumar Sen

THE SECOND HALF of the 19th century witnessed an important development in the Indian economic situation: the emergence of the working class as a group conscious of their rights. Industrial development was sluggish, and industrial workers were not numerous in relation to total population. But they were concentrated in the industrial centres and developed into a potential force in political movements in this country. There was a great deal of migration of peasants and artisans from the villages to the industrial centres, railway workshops and mining towns. It seems that railway building helped labour mobility. By 1882, 10,144 miles of railway line had been laid. In Bengal the main streams of immigration flowed from Bihar, Orissa, Central Provinces and the United Provinces to the metropolitan industrial area, from Nepal into Darjeeling and Jalpaiguri, from Chhota Nagpur to Jalpaiguri tea gardens. In the steel mill in Jamshedpur the workers came not only from neighbouring villages in Manbhum and Singbhum but also from Orissa, Punjab, the United Provinces and North-West Provinces and even from Bombay and Madras. The workers in the Bombay cotton mills were drawn mainly from Ratnagiri, Satara, Kolaba (now Raigad) and Pune; from 1911 onwards the mill-owners recruited workers from the United Provinces whose proportion rose from 3.5 per cent in 1911 to 9.42 per cent of the total millhands in 1921.[1] It does not seem that the joint family, caste and village system stood in the way of labour mobility. As time passed, peasants and agricultural labourers became increasingly absorbed in the system of capitalist production.

As table 6.1 shows, the cotton textiles industry employed the largest number of workers; the industry apparently continued to expand despite the imposition of the cotton excise duty in 1896 (which was not repealed until 1926). Female workers constituted a large proportion of the labour force. Most of the workers were peasants and artisans, and for a long time remained scarcely differentiated from the agricultural population; the official reports allude to high labour turnover and absenteeism in organized industries. The lingering habits of the old peasant life partly explain the workers' lack of capacity for organization. Nevertheless the industrial proletariat was emerging, albeit slowly, in iron and steel and engineering industries. By 1905 railway workshops employed 79,000 workers; the employees in Tata Iron and Steel Company rose from 4,000 in 1907-8 to 25,221 in 1920-1; a few thousand workers were employed in the ordnance factories and private engineering works.[2]

TABLE 6.1

Distribution of Labour Force, 1911

(in thousands)

	Persons	*Males*	*Females*
Food stuffs	2,077	749	1,328
Beverages	20	12	8
Tobacco and tobacco products	30	21	9
Cotton textiles	3,340	2,014	1,326
Jute textiles	228	187	41
Wool textiles	170	104	66
Silk textiles	123	72	51
Miscellaneous textiles	713	451	262
Wood and wooden products	1,449	1,075	374
Paper and paper products	4	3	1
Printing and publishing	43	42	1
Leather and leather products	1,101	907	194
Chemical and chemical products	37	25	12
Non-metallic mineral products	1,129	726	403
Metals and metal products	660	584	76
Transport equipment	10	10	—
Miscellaneous manufacturing	573	536	37
	11,707	7,518	4,189

Source: J. Krishnamurty, The Occupational Structure, *Cambridge Economic History of India*, Vol. 2, 1983.

1. Working Conditions

That the condition of the workers remained appalling until the 1930s has not been denied by any reasonable observer. Indeed, the workers lived, as Nehru wrote years ago, 'at an incredibly low level of existence — in filthy disease-ridden hovels, with no window or chimney, no light or water supply, no sanitary arrangements'.[3] In his report on Indian Coal,

Dunstan vividly described the condition of miners in the British-owned collieries in 1898:

> The working hours are from 6 a.m. to 6 p.m., and perhaps later, when extra work is required. . . . The miners live in small villages, aggregations of huts of mud walls with thatched or tiled roof. The hut consists of one room, sometimes two, of from 6 feet by 6 feet. . . . Women and children work underground, and are principally employed in carrying the small coal and dust. The women often take their babies, two and three months old, down the mine. The light which the collier carries with him is exceedingly primitive. . . . The ventilation of the underground workings receives very little attention, and in most collieries none at all. The ignorant native has not yet realised that his health and longevity are in question.[4]

Morris had made a detailed study on the conditions of the working class in Bombay. The average worker in a cotton mill had a 13-hour day; this sometimes increased to 14 hours during the summer months. By 1904 mills were working longer hours with the help of electricity. In 1905 the average number of working hours went up to 15, with a half-hour midday break; the 15-hour day continued till 1911 when the Factory Act provided that no worker could be employed for more than 12 hours; the weekly holiday provision was tightened. The mills relied heavily on the jobbers who had the power of engaging and dismissing workers. In the absence of leave rules the workers had to bribe the jobbers when they went on leave and returned to the mills. The mill-owners' claim that the powers of the jobber had been restricted and transferred to the managers and departmental heads cannot be substantiated; the jobbers' control over the workers was hardly broken until the coming of independence. The regular workers were paid once a month; mill-owners often withheld a minimum of a month's pay, which was apparently a weapon against strike; over the years fines were imposed on the workers for breakages, late attendance, underproduction etc.; in the 1880s fines amounted to the loss of from half to a full day's pay. Morris tells us that the powers of the employers were restricted in the 1930s thanks to state intervention.[5]

In Jamshedpur the compulsion of creating a permanent labour force led the management to offer some amenities to the workers. In 1912 an 8-hour day was introduced, although a weekly or fortnightly holiday was not provided for. The permanent employees got a month's leave on full pay in a year while the daily-rated staff could get a fortnight's leave. In 1924 housing was provided for only 33 per cent of the employees, with the result that several families had to live in quarters meant for one family. The women workers did not enjoy maternity benefits. There was no provision for gratuity or profit-sharing. After the war there was an extraordinary rise in accidents in this sector; in 1920, out of a total of 926 accidents in India, the steel works accounted for 651 accidents.[6]

The workers in the Bengal jute mills averaged a 10-hour day till 1872; from 1873 onwards they worked for 12 hours a day. In 1895 the multiple shift system was introduced with the help of electricity, and the working hours were increased to 15 hours. Most of the workers lived in *bustees;* in 1897 only 13.5 per cent of the mill workers lived in company-built coolie lines. As labour supply rose, the *bustee* owners, mostly local landlords, invariably increased their rent. As the Deshpande report shows, the conditions of labour in the jute mills remained deplorable over the years; even in 1939, only 39 per cent of the labour force was housed by the mill-owners. The *sirdars* behaved like nawabs, and there was a great deal of corruption and bribery with regard to employment, promotion and granting of leave.[7]

Few capitalists conceded that higher wages or shorter hours might increase productivity. They showed a tendency to pay the lowest wages for the longest hours so that they could maximize profits. There was no minimum wages legislation. But the employers had to retain a certain number of core workers who were often paid higher wages. The white-collar employees constituted a privileged category, although clerks remained poor by middle-class standards. As the Royal Commission has pointed out, wages were lowest in Madras and Cawnpore (Kanpur), and highest in Bombay.[8] The wages in the jute mills in Bengal were appreciably lower than in Bombay cotton mills; there had been no important change in the basic wage structure until 1939.[9] In his meticulous study on the condition of Indian workers Professor Kuczynski has made a survey of the movement of wages from 1880 onwards. It appears from his findings that money wages showed a tendency to rise upto the

TABLE 6.2

Money Wage and Real Wage Index

(1900 = 100)

Year	*Money Wage*	*Cost of living*	*Real Wage*
1880-89	87	69	127
1890-99	94	83	112
1900-09	107	97	111
1910-19	135	143	98
1920-29	211	207	103

Source: J. Kuczynski, 'Condition of Workers, 1880-1950', in V.B. Singh (ed.), *Economic History of India, 1857-1956*, 1965.

First World War, while real wages fell. As he puts it: 'The inflation served Capital as a means of grossly deceiving the worker.' Real wages rose in the post-war years in India as in most capitalist countries. Kuczynski, however, adds a note of caution. The nominal wages of the worker were reduced by wage deductions as punishment, bribes to the jobbers, and the heavy burden of indebtedness.[10]

It does not seem that factory legislation helped to improve the conditions of factory employment. The first Indian Factory Act, passed in 1881, due largely to the pressure campaign mounted by Lancashire, prohibited the employment of children under seven and limited the hours of work for children. It is noteworthy that the number of children employed in large-scale industries was never large, and their proportion was considerably reduced in subsequent years. The Factories Act, 1911, limited the hours of work for all employees and made recommendations for better ventilation, supply of water and fencing of machinery. As Morris writes, factory legislation prohibiting night work for women proved to be a major factor in reducing the proportion of female workers, particularly in cotton mills and coal mines. It was in the 1930s that the powers of the mill-owners were restricted: the position of workers in the Bombay mills improved when the Payment of Wages Act, 1937, and Industrial Disputes Act, 1938, were enforced. What needs to be noted is that state intervention came in the wake of workers' movements that flared up in the major industrial centres. To the subject of workers' movements we now turn.

2. Workers' Movements

Although the trade union, the fundamental institution of working-class self-defence, came late in the day, strikes became frequent in the industrial centres from the last decade of the 19th century. The *Indian Textile Journal* reported in 1892 that there was 'a strike mania'. As recent research shows, numerous strikes occurred in railways, cotton mills and jute mills between 1892 and 1908. Broadly speaking, nationalist leaders hardly took any notice of the social discontent reflected in these strikes. A few nationalist intellectuals tried to mobilize labour during the Swadeshi Movement, but they did not include the leadership of the Bengal Congress. Tilak, who sought to build a popular movement, caused the first political strike in this country to flare up when he was sentenced to six years imprisonment. Nehru, then a student in Cambridge, recalls his admiration for Tilak, the father of Extremism:

> News of Tilak's activities and his conviction, of Aurobindo Ghose and the way the masses of Bengal were taking the Swadeshi and boycott pledge stirred all of us Indians in England. Almost without an exception we were Tilakites or Extremists, as the new party was called in India.[11]

In 1883-4 about 38,000 workers were employed in the British-owned jute mills which were scattered in north 24 Parganas, Hoogly and Howrah districts; the Hindustani workers from the U.P. and Bihar had started replacing the Bengali workers. Sasipada Banerjee, a radical Brahmo, founded the Workingmen's Club and published a journal, the *Bharat Sramjibi*, the first labour journal in this country in 1874, and organized night schools in Baranagar, a centre of the jute industry. In an appeal to the labourers the *Bharat Sramjibi* wrote in 1897: 'All men are equal. . . Then why do you wallow in misery?. . .The rich are only a handful, you are the majority, and the country is yours.'[12] Sasipada hardly dealt with the housing conditions, long working hours and low wages of the labourers; the labouring poor remained unorganized. But unrest was growing among the workers; and the Indian Jute Mills' Association requested the government in April, 1895 to send additional police forces for 'controlling riotous combinations of mill hands'. In October 1895 there was a strike in the Budge Budge Jute Mills that continued for eight days; as the *Amrita Bazar Patrika* reported, about 7,000 labourers fell out with the *sirdars*, raided the bungalows of European officers, assaulted two police constables and a *darwan* of the mills; the 'Europeans fired on the mob', and two workers were 'seriously wounded'. There was another strike in this mill in the summer of 1896.[13] It is noteworthy that the increase in the working hours as a result of the introduction of the electric light had created considerable discontent among the workers. While the workers launched sporadic strikes, the immigrant Muslim workers demanded paid holidays on festivals like Id and Muharram, and communal riots broke out in some mills in 1896-7. What was reflected in these riots was, as Chakravarty puts it, 'community consciousness' that was 'an imported social outlook' of the immigrant Muslims who were acquainted with cow-killing riots in the U.P. and Bihar.[14] With the influx of immigrant workers in the jute mills, the growth of 'community consciousness' among the workers became a new reality in the 1890s. What is not clear is whether this factor inhibited the growth of class consciousness among the workers in the 1920s when trade unions were being formed.

The labour movement made a notable advance in Bengal during 1905-8, and formed part of the national upsurge. The press employees, jute mill workers, railway employees organized strikes, which led to the formation of the Printers' Union and Indian Mill Hands Union. In September 1905, the workers of Burn and Co. struck work. On 16 October 1905, the day of national upsurge, twelve jute press factories, one sugar factory, one shellac factory, one gun factory and about seventy local mills were closed. There were strikes in Jamalpur, Kharagpur and Samastipur workshops, where hundreds of workers were concentrated. On 19 August 1906, the Indian Mill Hands Union was formed at Budge Budge which had witnessed militant strikes in 1895 and again in 1906. The leader of this Union was Aswinicoomar Banerjee, a barrister, a nationalist associated with the Anushilan Samiti, who recalled in his old age that he had organized 'more than 50,000 mill-hands' and become a terror to the mill-owners. Closely associated with him was Prabhat Kusum Roy Chaudhari, also a barrister, who did not lose interest in the labour movement until his death in 1921. Another labour leader was Premtosh Bose, owner of a small press in north Calcutta, an extremist nationalist who was prominent in the strikes of press employees and railway workers. Apurbakumar Ghosh, a Christian barrister, emerged as a leader of the East Indian Railway strike of 1906. A less known labour leader was Suren Halder, also a barrister and a nationalist, who was associated with the press employees' movement and became the first president of the Jamshedpur Labour Union in 1920. On 14 September 1907, a Bengali journal drew attention to the potentiality of the still weak labour movement:

> The thousands of mill and factory hands also have several unions. . . . If these unions could manifest their anger at the imprisonment of Bepinbabu [Pal] through some effective action, that would inspire the entire country. . . . Our country's chains will never be broken until our workers learn self-sacrifice in these matters. . . .[15]

Curiously enough, nationalist interest in the labour movement in Bengal 'suddenly slumped' in the middle of 1908. A few sporadic strikes occurred in 1908-9, but the nationalists were not much involved in them. In sharp contrast to Bombay, workers in Bengal were not mobilized in protest strikes when nationalist leaders were thrown in jail. The labour movement became moribund; when it revived in the 1920s, men of a new generation emerged as its leaders.

In Bombay the situation was different, partly because many of the workers in the cotton mills were Maharashtrians. In Bengal Sasipada had founded the Workingmen's Club which hardly focused on the economic demands of the workers; in Bombay N.M. Lokhande, a middle class philanthropist, held labour meetings and founded the Bombay Mill-Hands Association in 1890 which put forward the demands for reducing working hours, a weekly holiday, a midday recess and compensation for injuries suffered during work at the mills. Karnik has described Lokhande, who edited *Dinbandhu*, as 'the first labour leader' who tried to formulate the demands of labourers. The government appointed the Factory Labour Commission with Lokhande as one of its members. The Factory Act, 1891, sought to limit the working hours of children and women. During 1892-3 workers in several cotton mills struck work as the mill-owners tried to reduce their wages. There was considerable labour unrest in 1897 when the dreaded plague broke out in Bombay. As hundreds of workers left for their villages, the mill-owners thought it wise to introduce the daily-wage system in order to contain labour unrest. As soon as the epidemic subsided, they reverted to the system of monthly wages. The workers fought back with spontaneous strikes.[16]

The labour movement in Bombay reached its highwater mark in 1908. On the one hand, Tilak's trial and conviction created indignation among all sections of Indians and the political situation had become tense. On the other, the mill-owners increased the working hours as electric light was introduced in the mills. In an excellent piece on the 1908 strike Gordon has related the labour upsurge to the concentration of workers in Bombay and their acute discontent. About 100,000 workers were concentrated in the cotton mills; there were 11,000 workers in the railway workshops, 16,000 dockers, and 15,000 tramway workers. The level of wages remained low, although food prices had gone up. Many workers were perpetually in debt. Working hours in the mills had been raised to 15 hours in 1905. The labour force had become multilingual; but the majority of the workers were Marathi-speaking. As Gordon writes: '. . . the Maratha majority made it easier for the national democratic elements of Maharashtra to establish contacts with the workers of Bombay'.[17] The Tilakites did appeal to the 'religious sentiments' of the workers, to draw them into the national movement, but 'the operatives were beginning to combine. . . . Mohammedans and Hindus would now mix together in decided contrast to the conditions prevailing a few years ago.'[18]

Many writers have pointed to the high wind of discontent that blew across Maharashtra during the trial of Tilak, the tallest leader in the country. Chirol has noted that Tilak's followers showed 'a genuine desire to mitigate the evils and hardships to which their humbler fellow-creatures were exposed'; they told the workers that Tilak was arrested 'because he was their friend and had sought to obtain better pay for them'.[19] On 17 July 1908, a procession of 20,000 workers moved in the industrial area urging the workers to launch a strike. On 19 July thousands of workers struck work. On 22 July, the concluding day of Tilak's trial, the dockers joined the strike. The mill-owners did not realize that these were only pre-storm signals. On 23 July, the political strike began as the news of Tilak's conviction spread in the city. D.C. Home and Chicherov have vividly described the sweep and intensity of the six-day political strike. On the first day about 20,000 workers struck work at noon; there was also a hartal in the city. On 24 July, fighting between the workers and the police broke out in the streets; all the mills remained closed. The *Times of India* reported on 25 July:

> . . . Since day-break mill-hands were seen collecting at different places. . . . The crowd then numbering more than twelve thousand began to put stones at E.D. Sassoon Mills. . . . The Officers used their revolvers in self-defence, but yet the crowd was undaunted and hence military help was called for. They defied the troops and refusing to disperse began to stone the military and the police . . . Mr Setalvad, Magistrate, . . . gave orders to fire, as a result of which several men fell to the ground.

The strike spread to Colaba; in Mahim, the police opened fire on the workers, killing three persons. On 26 July, Vithaldas Thakersay, a cotton merchant and mill-owner, called a meeting of the Bombay Native Piece Goods Merchants Association which requested the members 'to open their shops'. On 27 July, the 'poorer sections of the business community' as well as the coolies joined the demonstrations; a Gujarati handbill which carried Tilak's portrait and the slogan *'Tilak Maharaj-ki-jai'* was distributed among the people. On 28 July, the clerks 'were prevented' from going to work, and trams were stoned; domestic servants showered stones on the police from the roofs of many buildings. The strike was called off after six days — one day for every year of the savage sentence imposed on Tilak.[20]

Chicherov emphasizes the fact that the Tilakites were 'objectively instrumental' in arousing 'the class consciousness' of the Indian working class. As the exponents of 'petty bourgeois yet revolutionary democracy', they often appealed to the religious sentiments of the workers.[21] It is noteworthy that a large proportion of the workers came from Tilak's home district, Ratnagiri. In his speeches at labour meetings Tilak hardly advocated 'class struggle' and seemed to rely on the jobbers who were instructed to form 'committees of mill-hands'.[22] As a pragmatic politician Tilak knew that the jobbers had enormous influence over the workers and hence their initial support would be of much help to draw the unorganized workers in the nationalist movement. The fact has to be admitted that the jobbers continued to play an important role in the labour movement until the emergence of the Communists in 1926; the cotton textile workers hardly built viable unions until 1928.

The labour movement was moribund on the eve of the First World War. In fact, the whole national movement was at an impasse. As Nehru puts it:

> Towards the end of 1912 India was politically very dull. Tilak was in gaol, the Extremists . . . were lying low without any effective leadership. Bengal was quiet after the unsettling of the partition of the province, and the Moderates had been effectively 'rallied' to the Minto-Morley scheme of Councils.[23]

But the horizon began to light up when the labour movement revived from 1918 onwards. The immediate post-war years witnessed a wave of strikes in most industrial centres. In a graphic passage the Royal Commission on Labour described the new wave:

> The two or three years following the close of the war saw the formation of a large number of organizations, owing their origin mainly to the grave economic difficulties of industrial labour. . . . The world-wide uprising of labour consciousness extended to India and for the first time the mass of industrial workers awoke to their disabilities, particularly in the matter of wages and hours and to the possibility of combination.[24]

During the war Indian industries made fabulous profits; the shareholders of the companies received large dividends, but there was a steep decline in the real wages of the workers owing to the abnormal rise in prices of food and essential commodities. In most of the strikes in this period, the demand for higher wages figured prominently.

But the political situation was fast changing. In the winter of 1916 unity between the Moderates and Extremists was achieved; the famous Congress-League Pact, ratified at Lucknow, has been described by Coupland as 'the most striking expression of Indian nationalism so far achieved within the bounds of British India'.[25] The Home Rule movement had begun; in Madras some of the leaders of the Home Rule League became involved in the labour movement. As we shall see, Tilak began to take considerable interest in labour movement in Bombay after his return from England. In Ahmedabad, Gandhi personally led a strike of cotton textile workers. In the summer of 1919, the Rowlatt satyagraha was launched; on 6 April, the first all-India *hartal* was observed. Nationalism was sweeping the country. It would be fatuous to ignore its impact on the working class, although the strikes, mostly spontaneous, reflected the economic discontent of the labouring men.

It was in this period that the labour movement spread in South India; and the Madras Labour Union was formed on 27 April 1918. In a note prepared by the Home Department labour unrest in Madras figured prominently; the strike wave had spread among the workers in the Carnatic and Buckingham Mills, and tramway workers and rickshaw pullers in Madras City; there had grown 'considerable industrial organizations' in the cotton mills of Tinnevelly and Coimbatore, sugar factories at Samalkota, railway workshops at Negapatam and the timber mills on the west coast. Although high prices of foodgrains, cloth and kerosene oil had 'material bearing on the labour unrest', there was 'clear connection between the activities of the labour branch of the Home Rule agitation and the strikes', which were mainly directed against enterprises financed by European capital. It was pointed out that no attempt had been made 'to approach the agricultural labourer whose condition in many parts of the Presidency is more degraded . . . than that of the industrial labourer'.[26]

It seems that the attitude of the Home Rule agitators to Indian labour was influenced by the British Labour Party which had become a force in England. The Madras Government related labour unrest to the activities of the Home Rule League, stressing the role of the contemporary newspapers controlled by the League. The *Indian Patriot* published an appeal in early February 1918 by Diwan Bahadur P. Kesava Pillai under the heading 'A Labour Organization : an urgent and immediate need'. In March, labour meetings were held in Madras, which were addressed by Kalyansundaram Mudaliar, a Tamil Pandit of the Wesleyan Mission College, who gave up his profession to become a Home Rule journalist and edited *Desabhaktam*. *New India* published a special article entitled 'Capital and Labour in India', which enjoined the Home Rule League 'to encourage and direct the awakening of labour'. Annie Besant showed her personal interest in the labour movement in an article published in *New India* on 21 May, in which she focused on the failure of the government to enforce the Factory Act and on the manner in which the mill-hands were 'cruelly overworked' for the benefit of the mill-owners. In June, B.P. Wadia, a close associate of Mrs Besant, formed a Rickshawallas Union in Madras following a temporary strike; Wadia established control over the *Indian Patriot* by advancing a sum of Rs 9,000 from the Home Rule League Funds. Mrs Besant took much interest in the Madras Rickshawallas Union and sought to form low-price co-operative stores. In July, Besant and Arundale addressed a labour meeting held in the central hall of the Theosophical Society. Although the labour movement was quiescent in October, the Home Rule 'politicians' continued to hold 'weekly meetings' of groups of labourers in Madras. They seemed to be specially active in founding an all-India Labour Organization; Besant addressed a meeting on 18 October in the Young Men's Indian Association hall emphasizing the need to organize labour and 'to make the European capitalists respect Indian opinion'. On 29 October, *New India* announced the formation of the Central Labour Board in Madras whose main objects would be 'to create harmonious relations between employers and employed', and to endeavour to get increased wages and promote legislation for fixing a minimum wage.[27] Apparently, the Home Rulers anticipated the formation of the All-India Trade Union Congress.

Meanwhile B.P. Wadia had formed the Madras Labour Union in April 1918 with Besant's approval. Wadia writes that 'a few ill-treated labourers' came to him seeking his help, and he decided to form a labour union after he had collected facts on ill-treatment by European officers and inadequate wages of the workers. The executive committee of the Madras Labour Union was formed at a mass meeting of the mill-hands. Ever since its formation the Labour Union had to face the opposition of Binnys as well as of the Madras government. With the increase in food prices, labour unrest in the Buckingham and Carnatic mills became intense in 1918; Binnys ignored the demands of the Union for increased wages, extension of the lunch hour, and better treatment of Indian workers by the European supervisors. Although Wadia was not in favour of a strike, the workers took matters into their hands in October; the management declared a lock-out on 29 October. Trouble broke out again in November when the workers allegedly assaulted the European manager and members of the staff. The management declared a second lock-out on 27 November, and later confiscated a quarter of the gratuity fund credits held by the workers. The Union demanded wages for the period of closure, restoration of the gratuity fund and cancellation of the orders of dismissal. Since the management rejected these terms, the lock-out continued. In an article published in the *Pioneer* Wadia pointed out that the primary object of the British company was 'to disband our labour union'. At this point Wadia appealed to Gandhi to come to Madras. Although Gandhi could not come, he sent his trusted friend Andrews to Madras. Thanks to the intervention of Andrews, the strike was settled on 16 December; the management undertook 'to restore the confiscated portion of the gratuity fund'. Andrews also intervened in the strike at the Burma Oil Company's engineering works, which was quickly settled.[28] It is noteworthy that labour unrest in the Buckingham and Carnatic mills flared up in 1920 and the confrontation between the Labour Union and Binnys continued unabated.[29]

A labour union was formed in Ahmedabad in the wake of a strike, which was led by Gandhi. By 1916 Ahmedabad had 51 cotton mills employing 41,000 workers. In this industrial town, Miss Anasuya Sarabhai, sister of Ambalal Sarabhai, a leading mill-owner, had started night schools for the workers just before the start of the war. The Home Rule movement spread to Ahmedabad in the autumn of 1916, in which Maganbhai Patel and Jivanlal Desai played a leading role; in March 1918 Besant herself came to Ahmedabad and addressed public meetings. As in Madras, discontent grew among the workers, mostly Gujaratis, with the rise in prices of food, cloth and kerosene; tension was exacerbated when the mill-owners replaced 'plague bonus' which came to about 70 per cent of wages by a mere 20 per cent increase in wages. The demand of the weavers for an increase of 50 per cent (later reduced to 35 per cent on Gandhi's advice) was rejected by the mill-owners.[30] At this point Gandhi became involved in the strike. As Gandhi, writes:

> . . . there came a letter from Shrimati Anasuyabai about the condition of

> labour in Ahmedabad. Wages were low, and the labourers had for long been agitating for an increment. . . . Anasuyabai had to battle against her own brother, Sjt. Ambalal Sarabhai, who led the fray on behalf of the mill-owners. My relations with them were friendly. . . . I had consultations with them and requested them to refer the matter to arbitration, but they refused to recognize the principle of arbitration. I had therefore to advise the labourers to go on strike.[31]

The strike continued for 21 days. Gandhi held daily meetings of the strikers; the workers paraded the streets in peaceful procession. The jobbers were in the forefront of the strike. The workers showed, as Gandhi tells us, 'great courage and self-restraint' during the first two weeks, but later showed 'signs of flagging'. Gandhi began a fast; after three days a settlement was reached.[32] The mill-owners agreed to grant 35 per cent increase in wages and appoint an arbitrator. In 1920 Gandhi formed the *Majur Mahajan* which stood for peaceful relations, class co-operation, arbitration, and social service. Gandhi personally guided the work of the *Majur Mahajan,* which was never affiliated to the All-India Trade Union Congress. One may say that the Ahmedabad workers remained isolated from the mainstream of the working class movement that continued to grow from 1919 onwards. But the fact remains that the workers were politicized and massively participated in the Rowlatt satyagraha in 1919. On 10 April, as the news of Gandhi's arrest spread, there was a spontaneous strike in most of the mills; two European weaving masters who allegedly said 'Damn Gandhi' were chased and stoned; a crowd of 2,000 to 3,000 people gathered in the streets and clashed with armed police; at least 28 persons were killed and 123 wounded in police firing. On 13 April Gandhi arrived in Ahmedabad, condemned violence and asked the people to stop the demonstrations. Of those tried by the special tribunal set up by the government, about half were mill-workers.[33]

On 9 January 1919 about 250,000 cotton textile workers, concentrated in Parel, Chinchpokli and Byculla struck work, pointing, as never before, to the potential power of the working class. Masselos and Kumar have emphasized the spontaneous character of the strike that could be related to the abnormal rise in prices of food and consumer goods. The cotton mills obtained colossal profit during the war; the average dividend paid by the leading cotton mills in Bombay was 120 per cent in 1919-20; in some cases it reached 200, 250 and 365 per cent.[34] The mill-owners granted a small increase in the workers' wages in 1918, which proved inadequate. The cost of food had gone up by 93 per cent; there was an influenza epidemic and a rise in cholera deaths. The demand of the workers for an increase of 25 per cent in their wages was rejected by the mill-owners, and the workers embarked on a strike.[35]

The official reports indicate that the Home Rule League was involved in this strike, as it supported earlier strikes of postmen and railway workers. Kanji Dwarkadas, a leading figure in Besant's League, prided in the fact that the league participated in the 1919 strike.[36] The Home Rule Leagues of Tilak and Besant, though functioning separately in Bombay, generally supported the demands of the workers; they carried on relief work in mill areas during the influenza epidemic. When the strike began, the *Bombay Chronicle* advised middle class young men to join and work in trade unions.[37] We do not know the position of Tilak who had gone to England, where he became acquainted with the labour movement; but a few Home Rule advocates, notably Sathaye (a Tilakite), Jamnadas Dwarkadas and Umar Sobhani, addressed working class meetings. The *Pioneer* reported on 13 January 1919 that they had advised the workers to return to the mills so that negotiations with the management could be undertaken. The workers rejected their advice and chose to continue the strike. Masselos rightly stresses that the Home Rule Leagues were sympathetic to labour upto a point; the 1919 strike was 'organized on an *ad hoc* basis by the strikers themselves through leaders thrown up from their ranks'.[38] Dwarkadas writes that the Home Rule League requested Gandhi, who led the Ahmedabad strike in 1918, to help them; it is not clear why Gandhi refused to lead the Bombay strike in which the Marathi-speaking workers were ranged against Gujarati and Parsi mill-owners.[39]

In his detailed study of this great strike, Kumar emphasizes the solidarity of the workers who lived together in the chawls, their militancy in the face of police repression, their determination not to surrender to the mill-owners even when the *Kamgar Sabha* advised them to resume work. As the strike continued unabated, the dockers and railway workers of the Parel workshops went on strike. The strikers consistently refused to withdraw the strike on only 'verbal assurance'. At last, the mill-owners who had stubbornly opposed any wage increase announced a 20 per cent increase in wages.[40]

What needs to be noted is that the great strike of 1919 was a part of the strike-wave that continued in 1920 and prepared the ground for the formation of the All-India Trade Union Congress. As Das has shown, strikes broke out in most industrial centres, revealing an upsurge among the working-class:

> November 4 to December 2, 1919, woollen mills, Cawnpore, 17,000 men out; December 7, 1919 to 9 January 1920, railway workers, Jamalpore, 16,000 men out; January 9-18, 1920, jute mills, Calcutta, 35,000 men out; January 2 to February 3, general strike, Bombay, 200,000 men out; January 30-31, mill workers, Rangoon, 20,000 men out; January 31, British India Navigation Company, Bombay, 10,000 men out; January 26 to February 16,

mill workers, Sholapur, 16,000 men out; February 24 to March 29, Tata Iron and Steel workers, 40,000 men out; March 9, mill workers, Bombay, 60,000 men out; March 20-26, mill workers, Madras, 17,000 men out; May 1920, mill workers, Ahmedabad, 25,000 men out.[41]

On his return from England, Tilak began to show considerable interest in labour, addressing labour meetings and advising labourers to form trade unions, while advocating peaceful agitation. When N.M. Joshi was nominated by the government to represent India at the Washington Conference of the ILO, Tilak explained in a workers' meeting that 'he declined to go as an assistant to the man selected by the government'.[42] Although Tilak did not go to Washington, he was, as Dange writes, 'the moving spirit of the AITUC formation in its first phase before his death'.[43] Lala Lajpat Rai presided over the inaugural session of the All India Trade Union Congress, which was attended by prominent nationalists and independent trade unionists, notably Motilal Nehru, Vithalbhai Patel, Annie Besant, C.F. Andrews, K.F. Nariman, B.P. Wadia, J. Baptista, Dewan Chaman Lall, N.M. Joshi. Gandhi did not give his blessings to the formation of a central organization of Indian labour.[44] In 1930 there were 125 unions with a total membership of 250,000. Vast sectors of the economy remained still unorganized. It seems that the leading functionaries were drawn mostly from the educated middle class and white-collar employees.[45] The official reports allude to the dominant role of 'the outsiders'. The fact is that their assistance was indispensable in the initial period. Social consciousness had to be shaped from above, and hence the role of the radical intelligentsia was of crucial importance. But the question may be asked whether any attempts were made for the creation of leaders and organizers from the working class. There is an element of truth in R.P. Dutt's contention that 'the outsiders' often came 'without understanding the aims and needs of the labour movement, and brought with them the conception of middle class politics'.[46] Nevertheless, a central trade union organization had come to India, and with it the era of trade union movement.

3. Plantation Labour

We will deal, briefly and in passing, with plantation labour which remained virtually unorganized until the coming of independence. It is well-known that the Indian tea industry owed its development to British capital; tea companies headed the list of sterling companies registered between 1874 and 1904 (out of 63 sterling companies, 30 were tea companies). The first garden in Cachar was opened in 1855; the industry spread in the Tarai in Darjeeling district in 1862 and in the Dooars in

Jalpaiguri district in 1874. There was a crash in 1866 when many companies collapsed; from 1870 onwards the industry once again made steady progress. The capital sunk in the industry rose from £ 25 million in 1902 to £ 28 million in 1922; the area under tea cultivation increased from 520,000 acres to 707,733 acres in this period.[47]

Many writers have drawn a lurid picture of labour recruitment and conditions of plantation labour. The planters relied on the *arkatis* who recruited poor peasants mainly in Chhota Nagpur and brought them to the tea gardens under inhuman conditions; between 1863 and 1866, of 84,915 recruits for Assam, 30,000 died. As the Royal Commission on labour noted: 'Factories ask for individuals, plantations want families.' Very often entire families were enticed to and settled on the plantations; under the Workmen's Breach of Contract Act, 1859 the absconding labourers were hunted down and punished. Even so, the remarkable increase in the labour force seems to indicate that poor tribal peasants who had been dispossessed of land chose to build a new life in the tea gardens. The number of tea garden labourers in Assam leaped from 34,433 in 1867-8 to 417,262 in 1905-6; by 1911 there were 191 gardens in the Dooars employing 75,315 labourers. It is noteworthy that female labourers formed a large proportion of the labour force; they invariably received lower wages than men.[48]

Fortunately, a few radical intellectuals, most notably Dwarkanath Ganguly, a Brahmo who fought for female education, became interested and began to visit Assam tea-gardens, collecting facts on the coolies, and wrote a series of articles in *Bengalee* and *Sanjibani* which created a stir in the country. We quote some excerpts from Dwarkanath's articles:

> We have already seen that overwork is one of the principal causes of high mortality in tea gardens, and that neglect on the part of women who are not allowed to stay at home . . . is the chief cause of excessive infant mortality. . . . We know of several instances where coolies . . . have committed suicide. . . . The next mode of punishment is the lock-up. It is a dreadful place. . . . Having been systematically maltreated, some 110 coolies, men and women, came in a body from the Rajberia Tea gardens, and made complaints before the Assistant Commissioner. . . . Gordon has found some of the serious charges to be correct . . . .[49]

In 1888 the Indian Association, of which Dwarkanath was a prominent leader, submitted a memorandum to Ripon on the horrid conditions of the Assam coolies; Bipin Pal, a young Brahmo who later emerged as an Extremist leader, moved a resolution in the Bengal Provincial Political Conference, demanding the appointment of 'an independent commission to enquire into the conditions of the coolies'. The resolution was passed, although Surendranath, who seldom adopted a radical stance, pointed out that the planters as well as the coolies 'should make a common effort towards amending a law which was shown to have been such a source of hardships'.[50] At last, recruitment of labour through contractors and *arkatis* was made illegal under the Assam Labour and Emigration Act, 1915.

Over the years the labourers remained unorganized. But the simmering discontent of the labouring poor led to sporadic 'riots' and strikes. As Fuller wrote on his experiences during 1902-6: '. . . there was bound to be some revolt . . . they sometimes ended in the burning of the manager's bungalow'. Between 1905-6 and 1920-1 there were 141 cases of rioting; planters and/or their assistants were assaulted in the gardens. There was a wave of looting of rural *hats* (market places) in 1918 as prices of food and cloth rose steeply; strikes broke out in a few tea gardens. In the wake of the non-cooperation movement, politics came into the tea gardens, and there was the remarkable Chargola exodus in the summer of 1921 when thousands of striking labourers left the gardens and walked miles to reach the railway station, shouting 'Gandhi Maharajki Jai'.[51] This was followed by the great Assam-Bengal railway strike which lasted for about two and a half months, revealing, as never before, the solidarity of the railway workers and the tea garden labourers.[52] Even so, plantation labourers were not organized in trade unions.

4. Agrarian Conditions

Although capitalist industry developed in a few regions, India remained an agricultural country; the factories were like islands in a vast agricultural sea. While the population increased from 315 million in 1911 to 385 million in 1931, the proportion of those employed in industry decreased; the percentage of industrial workers in the total population was 5.5 in 1911, 4.9 in 1921, and 4.3 in 1931. Agriculture continued to employ the largest number of hands. In all the regions the landlords and rural middle class dominated the agrarian social structure.

All the evidence that has accumulated in recent years makes it clear that Indian agriculture was stagnant. What needs to be asked is whether the stagnation in agriculture could be related to the agrarian structure. The nationalist writers, most notably Romesh Dutt, consistently focused attention on the high incidence of land tax, neglect of irrigation, famines, and showed a tendency to exaggerate the benefits of a permanent settlement of land revenue.[53] What is clearly missing in their interpretation is an analysis of the structural changes in the agrarian system. When we view the country as a whole, some crucial changes become evident. Land transfer continued unabated; land was passing from the hands of peasants into the control of non-agriculturists. By the mid-19th century land had become a favourite form of investment for traders and the urban middle classes; since the pace of industrialization was slow, the urban middle classes seemed to be anxious to acquire landed property. The growth of a class of non-productive rent-receivers was accompanied by the dispossession of impoverished peasants with miniature holdings. There started the 'de-peasantizing' process to which official reports drew pointed attention. The Strachey Commission, 1880, for instance, referred to the erosion of 'cultivators' rights' with the result that owner cultivators were swelling the ranks of 'rack-rented tenants-at-will who, owning no permanent connection with the land, have no incentive to thrift or improvement . . .'[54] In Bengal the peasants who had reclaimed wastes and jungles were reduced to share-croppers known as *adhiars, bargadars, bhagchasis;* they paid 50 per cent of the gross produce while bearing most of the expenses of cultivation; significantly, the scheduled castes and tribes constituted 40.8 per cent of the share croppers in West Bengal in 1915. The Settlement Officer of Midnapore wrote in 1917:

> . . . far from bhag rent showing any tendency to disappear in favour of money rent it seems to be on the increase. When a tenant of the latter class is sold up for arrears of rent, it is a common practice for the purchaser to resettle the land with the defaulter on bhag rent.[55]

In the U.P. *zamindars* and *taluqdars* employed *shikami* tenants on their *sir* land who had no occupancy right; there was another class of tenants, called *bataidars,* who paid produce rent and had no security of tenure. In Bihar rent-paying tenants that included *bataidars* were mostly employed on zamindar's *khas* and *bakasht* lands; the Collector of Champaran reported in 1896-7: the creditor 'can either cultivate the land himself or as is more usual he lets it out to the former ryot at an exorbitant produce rent'. In Punjab the Land Alienation Act, 1900, which was designed to restrict the sale of land by agricultural tribes to non-members, hardly checked mortgages of land; land tranfer continued and the peasant was often resettled on the land as a *bataidar.* In ryotwari areas in Madras a large proportion of the land was cultivated by tenants on *varam* or crop-sharing basis; the tenants paid as rent 40 to 60 or even 80 per cent of the produce and remained sunk in poverty.[56]

Professor Morris argues that land transfers merely meant the legal titles to the lands being transferred to non-agriculturists, since the old peasants continued to cultivate the lands.[57] What actually happened was that the old peasant was resettled on the land as a share cropper or under-ryot who had no security of tenure and was separated from the means of production. Much land was also sold during land transfer, and in such cases the expropriated peasants were reduced to agricultural labourers who lived on wages in cash or kind. In 1882 the census returned a total number of 7.5 million agricultural labourers; the number rose to 21 million in 1921. In 1888 the Dufferin Enquiry Committee noted the miserable conditions of rural labourers in Punjab, Agra and Oudh. Professor Mukherjee drew attention to the growth of agricultural labourers in Bengal from the 1880s:

> The number of transfers of occupancy holdings effected by registered deeds have risen from 43,000 in 1884 to 2½ million in 1913. . . . This implies the displacement from the soil of a highly desirable class of cultivators who . . . must swell the ranks of the landless proletariat.[58]

By 1901 the agricultural labourers had become a large group in Bengal, Bihar and Orissa; they formed 17.5 per cent of the agricultural population.[59] In western India labourers fluctuated between 22 and 23 per cent of the male agricultural work force between 1881 and 1921.[60]

It seems that tenancy legislation only resulted in safe guarding the interests of the rural elite represented by the middle classes and landlords. The Bengal Tenancy Act, 1885 allowed the *zamindar* to increase the rent if it was below the prevailing rate in the village or if there was a rise in prices. In this Act there was no provision for treating the *bargadars* as tenants. In the U.P the Rent Act of 1886 hardly checked the eviction of tenants; eviction was a device of the *taluqdars* to make it difficult for old tenants to become occupancy tenants. Further, landlords received *nazarana* from new tenants. The Deputy Commissioner of Pratapgarh reported in 1920: 'Fathers have sold their daughters for *nazarana* money to husbands of advanced years.'[61] An official note of 1892 vividly described how tenancy legislation failed to protect the tenants in Bihar:

> . . . The Rent Act of 1859 was passed a third of a century ago, you go to any village in Bihar and ask an average raiyat about the commonest provisions of the law, and he will be found to display a remarkable amount of ignorance. . . . Notwithstanding successive rent laws, the zamindar in Bihar is malik or lord in every sense of the word. He ejects raiyats at pleasure, and in many cases enhances rent at will . . . raiyat is too poor to come to court to get redress for eviction, and even if he has the means, he has no documentary evidence wherewith to substantiate his title.[62]

5. Tribal Peasants

The second half of the 19th century witnessed the long series of tribal peasants' movements which could be related to the introduction of the new land system and the 'environmental revolution' caused by deforestation. On the one hand, the tribal peasants were dispossessed of their land which passed into the hands of non-tribal landlords. On the other, the government encroached on their traditional rights in the forests which supplied them food, fuel, honey, fodder and housing material. In the Bengal districts the Santals who cleared the jungles were reduced to *bargadars* when the work of reclamation was done; the land was often leased to non-tribals who could pay high cash rent. In the Santal Parganas increase in rents continued unabated, particularly in those areas where the *Zamindars* appointed Europeans to farm their estates; Santal tenants were induced to sign *Kabuliyat* (contracts) agreeing to pay rent at an enhanced rent; they lost their traditional rights on the *mahua* trees. With the introduction of the Rent Act, 1859 in the Santal Parganas in 1865, the Santal peasants were very often shifted from one village to another so that they could not acquire occupancy rights. What caused considerable bitterness was the persistent attempt of the government to undermine the *manjhi* system, the basis of communal life. As O'Malley writes, the *manjhi,* the Santal headman, was 'essential to Santal life, every public sacrifice, ceremony and festival requiring his presence'. The government seemed to encourage the wholesale dispossession of the *manjhis* who were denied occupancy rights on their land and had to pay increased rents.[63] In Chhota Nagpur the tribal *jagirdars* or tribal chiefs were replaced by non-tribal landlords; in Palamau Rajput *jagirdars* became the dominant force; in Ranchi district the old Munda and Oraon chiefs were replaced by Hindu farmers. Raising of rents by the landlords continued unabated; *begari* (free labour) for a number of days on the *khas* land of the landlord had become pervasive; in some areas the landlords had succeeded in levying 50 to 60 days' *begari* in one year on the peasants. There was large-scale land alienation among the tribal peasants whose land passed into the hands of non-tribal landlords and moneylenders.[64] As the Settlement Report of 1920 showed, the landlords evaded the Chhota Nagpur Tenancy Act, 1908 and the Oraons and Mundas swelled the ranks of non-occupancy tenants and agricultural labourers.[65]

Deforestation came in the wake of railway building and multiplication of urban centres. There was an enormous demand for timber, and the timber merchants and contractors became familiar figures in the forest areas. In Pratapgarh in the U.P., for instance, there was wholesale destruction of *mahua* groves; the fruit of *mahua* was a source of food for the tribal peasants who also used its seed for fuel-oil. As the jungles were cleared, the peasants were faced with the scarcity of firewood and fodder; cattle starvation became a regular occurrence, particularly during the lean period before the rains. With the dwindling wastelands the pressure to use dung as fuel increased among the peasants who, alas, were hardly much impressed with government advice to preserve dung for manure.[66] In all the regions the clearing of wastes and jungles went hand in hand with railway building and urbanization. In the Sundarbans in Bengal, 493,907 acres or 771 square miles of jungle had been cleared between 1830 and 1872. In 1880 Captain Gray, the Settlement Officer, drew attention to the wholesale destruction of forests as a result of the trade between Chhota Nagpur and East India Railway in respect of sleepers; in Ranchi district the area under forest decreased from 2,281 square miles in 1902 to 1,956 square miles in 1927.[67]

McLane emphatically asserts that the early Congress showed little interest in landless labourers or tenants; few politicians had 'face-to-face relations' with the peasants.[68] But the fact is that the Congress adopted resolutions focusing on the tribal peasant's problems and the 'oppression of forest subordinates' in 1891, 1892, 1893, 1895. Moving the resolution on forest laws in the Congress session in 1891, Peter Pillai pointed out that 'the communal rights' of the tribal peasants had been effaced with the result that 'criminal prosecutions' took place for 'petty infringement' of forest laws and cattle mortality increased 'for want of pasture'. Another speaker, coming from a hill district, noted: 'fuel, wood, grass, stones, earth, leaves, bark, roots — all had been taken away from them not by God but by avaricious men.' Pleading for an amendment of forest laws the Congress resolution adopted in 1895 stated: '. . . the action of the Forest Departments under the rules framed by the different Provincial Governments, prejudicially affects the inhabitants of the rural parts of the country. . . .'[69] It seems that the interest shown by the early Congress in the tribal peasants survived, and the Congressmen working at the grass roots became involved in forest satyagraha in Madras in 1920-1 and again in Central Provinces in 1930-2.[70] In the wake of forest satyagraha the tribal peasants were drawn into the mainstream of the nationalist movement.

Meanwhile Chhota Nagpur had become a volcano whose rumblings the ruling class dreaded. One finds some continuity in tribal peasant's struggles in this area. The Hos, Oraons and Mundas joined hands in the Kol insurrection that started in the winter of 1831. By January 1832, the Kols in Chhota Nagpur and the five parganas of Tamor, Bunda, Barendra, Rai and Silli had 'taken up arms', as Cuthbert reported, against the new non-tribal landlords to whom the Maharaja of Chhota Nagpur had leased lands cultivated by the tribal peasants. There were clashes between the armed forces and tribal peasants; in a memorable resistance Bhundu Bhagat and his followers fought with bows and arrows until they perished to the last man. The Kol insurrection was followed by the Sardari agitation in the 1880s which was directed against *beth begari* and rent enhancement. It seems that the Sardars started with peaceful agitation, sending petitions to the government and even contacting Calcutta lawyers for drafting a memorial to the British Parliament. By 1887 the agitation developed into a no-rent movement when the tribal peasants declared that they would pay rent only to the *sarkar*.

Although the agitation petered out, the Sardars remained restive and played a leading role in the famous *ulgulan* led by Birsa Munda.[71]

It appears from Suresh Singh's excellent account that the Munda revolt, which had considerable popular support, had millenarian overtones. Birsa, a young handsome Munda peasant who received education in a missionary school, became popular in his village as a healer, miracle-worker and preacher; his declared object was to establish Munda raj in which land was to be held rent-free. The Birsaite *ulgulan* was 'spontaneous' sudden in its eruption, elemental in its character like a volcanic outburst'. When Birsa was arrested in the summer of 1895, there was great tension and an immense crowd, about 7,000 peasants, collected at Chalkad waiting for the return of the master. Released from jail after two years, Birsa found that the Sardars had revived 'their revolutionary propaganda'; in fact, the Sardars broached the proposal of armed resistance, and their determination influenced Birsa who had initially advocated peaceful means of struggle.

The official reports refer to numerous meetings held in the villages, transmission of news to distant villages, and the formation of a fighting force. On 24 December 1899 arrows were shot at a few missions. The *ulgulan* started in early 1900. On 6 January two constables were killed at Etkedih; when Gaya Munda returned home with his followers after this incident 'their women turned out to greet them and wash their feet with water while the men sang hunting songs'. On 7 January about 300 Munda peasants attacked the Khunti police station, killed one of the constables and set fire to the houses of a few banias. On 9 January a memorable fight took place on Sail Rakab hill, a little away from Dombari. About 200 Mundas, including women, were killed, while the majority managed to take shelter in the jungles. The revolt quickly collapsed. Hunted by the police, Birsa lived in the forests for two years evading arrest, was betrayed by the Mundas, and died of cholera in Ranchi jail.[72] The Chhota Nagpur Tenancy Act, 1908 hardly improved the condition of the Mundas; although *beth begari* was abolished, land alienation and moneylender's oppression continued as before.[73]

The Birsaites lived as a district sect that became a dwindling community as time passed. Although there was no recrudescence of Munda revolt, the Oraons launched the Tana Bhagat movement which had a family resemblance with the Birsaite movement. It also started in a religious form and developed into an agrarian movement. Unlike the *ulgulan*, it remained peaceful and merged in the non-cooperation movement. In 1914 Jatra Oraon, who was then 20 years of age, proclaimed that God had asked the Oraons to give up the worship of *bhuts* (spirits), abstain from taking meat and liquor and stop working as coolies or labourers; through *bhakti* they could attain a better and higher position in society. What started as a reformist movement grew into a popular movement as the Tana Bhagats, led by Sibu and Maya, refused to pay rent or chaukidari tax; they brought out processions blowing conches and distributing leaflets. The objective of the movement was explained in one of the leaflets circulated among the peasants:

> It is no longer the Raj of the zamindars. The land belongs to pious men. None should pay rent or chaukidari tax. The Banias must not attend bazars. They rob the men. Marwaris sell cloth at high rate and cheat religious men. Marwaris, may your cloth be burnt to ashes.[74]

The movement spread to Ranchi, Palamau and Hazaribagh. On 20 April 1919 the D.I.G. of police wrote to the government: 'It is very important that Tana Bhagat movement should be stamped out . . .'[75] There was hardly any resistance by Oraon peasants when their leaders, Sibu and Maya, were arrested. But the movement could not be crushed. Under the leadership of Turia Bhagat, crowds of Oraon peasants moved in the villages, holding meetings and refusing to pay rent or chaukidari tax. The Deputy Commissioner of Ranchi wrote to the Commissioner on 9 March 1921: 'The Tana Bhagat movement continues to give trouble and there is ample evidence that the efforts of agitators to associate it with Non-cooperation has given the movement a new life.'[76] The Tana Bhagats were drawn into the nationalist movement, and some of their leaders attended the Gaya session of the Congress in 1922.[77] Apparently they had become wedded to the Gandhian ideals of satyagarha and ahimsa.

The tribal peasants' struggles which flared up in other parts of the country were ruthlessly suppressed. Broadly speaking, these struggles reflected ethnic solidarity as well as acute discontent. In Manipur there was an uprising of the Thadoe Kukis in 1917-9 which was led and organized by the Thadoe chiefs when the British tried to recruit them in the labour force to be employed in France. The uprising, based on the support of 40,000 rebels, continued for two years; the British army destroyed 85 Thadoe villages, while the Kukis burnt 34 villages and killed 28 persons of the Assam Rifles. By the middle of 1919, all the leading chiefs were arrested, and the uprising petered out. As Bhadra tells us, the uprising was secular and free from millenarian overtones.[78] In the Godavari forests in Madras disturbances broke out in 1840, 1858 and 1862, culminating in the Rampa rebellion of 1879 which affected 5,000 square miles. It seems that the tribal peasants resented the oppression of the *mansabdars* as well as the loss of their traditional rights in the forests; the Koyas and the Reddies, for instance, clung to *podu* or shifting cultivation while 'making clearings in the heart of the forest by felling and burning the trees'. There was growing discontent against the new *Abkari* regulation preventing the drawing of toddy for domestic purposes; when the *mansabdar* imposed an additional tax called *madalupannu*, the tribal peasants broke into rebellion, blaming the government for 'all this injustice'. They virtually carried on a guerilla war which the British suppressed in the winter of 1880 by deploying six regiments of Madras infantry and a squadron of cavalry. The deposition of the *mansabdar* and the collaboration of the *muttadars* who were given extra allowances 'did much to allay the excitement', although disturbances continued in the Vizagapatam district till the winter of 1881.[79] In 1910 there was a rebellion in Bastar led by a former *diwan*, which was mainly directed against the curtailment of rights enjoyed by the tribal peasants in the forests; the rebels attacked police stations and forest outposts and tried to besiege Jagdalpur town.[80] It is noteworthy that the Koyas organized an uprising in the Vizag agency in Andhra in 1922, which was led by Seerama Raju, a sannyasi, who came from West Godavari, lived among the Koyas and became a charismatic leader; the uprising, which hardly received the blessings of the Congress, was suppressed in 1924.[81]

6. Peasant Mobilization

It was not until the Gandhi era that the Congress embarked on peasant mobilization. In a country where the peasants comprised 90 per cent of the population, the Congress could not ignore the agrarian problem, and regularly adopted resolutions on the extension of the Permanent Settlement in different provinces, reduction of the land tax and 'modified fixity of tenure' for the tenants.[82] In the early Congress, Tilak was the only leader who tried to organize a no-revenue movement in the Maharashtra Deccan in 1896-7 when famine broke out in the area, anticipating the Gandhian technique adopted in later years. The Poona Sarvajanik Sabha, captured by Tilak, sent members in the villages who held meetings and asked 'uneducated landholders to withhold payment of revenue due by them to the state'; even students in Pune colleges were asked 'to advise the peasants in their villages not to pay taxes'.[83] It was certainly not a 'no-rent campaign' as McLane writes. The fact is that the Congress consistently stuck to 'no-revenue' movements; only in eastern U.P did the Congress, prodded by Jawaharlal Nehru and Baba Ramchandra, approve a rent-strike in 1931.[84] Tilak advocated non-payment of revenue when the government adopted coercive measures in collecting revenue from the landholders; the number of notices served for non-payment of revenue in the Central Division, that included Pune, leaped from 35,284 in 1896-7 to 126,668 in 1897-8; the government singled out the leaders of the no-revenue movement by attachment of their movable property.[85]

In the agrarian disturbances which broke out in Punjab in 1906-7, the nationalists took the side of affluent peasants that benefitted from the extension of irrigation. The scene of the disturbances was the Chenab canal colony where vast tracts of desert land had been brought under cultivation with the help of canals. The rich peasants launched a movement when the Punjab government brought a bill in October 1906 stipulating that the ryots would have to fulfil the conditions concerning sanitation, tree planting and construction of houses, and that fines would be collected as before in case of breach of the conditions. It seems that the government wanted to tighten its control in the thriving canal colony from which it received over seven lakhs of rupees annually as net profit from water charges and land revenue. Lajpat Rai was drawn into this movement along with Ajit Singh, the revolutionary leader, who called upon the peasants to launch a no-revenue movement; as the movement gathered momentum the peasants raised the cry of non-payment of the new water rate. Lajpat was deported in May 1907. There were disturbances in Amritsar, Lahore and Rawalpindi. Discretion is the better part of valour. Minto decided to veto the Bill which affected 'a warlike and loyal section of the Indian community'. Ten days after the veto, Popham Young, the Settlement Commissioner, was greeted with garlands when he visited the canal colony.[86] Apparently, the rich peasants had won the battle. Irrigation made further advance; the Triple Canal Project was completed by 1920. With the extension of irrigation, commercial agriculture made considerable advance. Surely the peasants received an impetus from high prices during the First World War, and began to use new implements from 1921 onwards. The basis was laid for a change in production conditions.[87]

What we witness in Malabar is a new type of peasant unrest, much more complex than the tribal peasants' movements to which we have referred. In the agrarian society in Malabar the *jenmis,* propped up by the British, were the dominant section; land was concentrated in the hands of the *jenmis,* while the *verumpattamdars* who paid produce rent as well as the agricultural labourers remained at the bottom of the social pyramid. There was another rising category, the *Kanamdar,* to whom the *jenmi* leased his land. The large proportion of the Moplahs came from the non-occupancy tenants who held land from the Hindu *jenmis* or from the intermediaries. It was in this background that a series of Moplah revolts flared up in the 19th century; the Moplahs often attacked the *jenmis,* burning or looting their houses. Between 1855 and 1896 several Moplah outbreaks were reported in the official documents; there was severe repression and the Moplahs became increasingly anti-British. As they bitterly said, 'there is no room for Mussalmans in the country'. Over the years the government did little to cope with the tenancy probem. In 1916 the Malabar Tenants' Association was formed, and it seems that the *kanamdars,* representing the landed gentry, tried to mobilize the rent-paying tenants; meetings were held in Ernad and Walluvanad in which the Moplah tenants participated. Then came the Khilafat agitation and the Moplah rebellion swept south Malabar like a tidal wave in the summer of 1921. It will be beyond the scope of this paper to deal with the nature of the Moplah rebellion, which has been researched intensely.[88]

It was Gandhi who embarked on peasant mobilization. One may say that it was the Mahatma's *tour de force.* At last the Congress became linked with the peasant masses. The techniques of struggle evolved by Gandhi — meetings, processions, signature campaigns, satyagraha — helped to generate among the peasant a spirit of defiance against the British. It is significant that in Champaran the movement was directed against the British planters, while in Kaira (Kheda) Gandhi launched a no-revenue movement. The rent-paying tenants, drawn mostly from scheduled castes and tribes, were not mobilized against the landlords. It seems that the overriding consideration was to maintain unity among all categories of the rural people so that there could develop a broad platform of the national movement.

When Gandhi came to Champaran in the summer of 1917, the Congress was, as he writes, 'practically unknown in those parts. Even those who had heard the name of the Congress shrank from joining it or even mentioning it'.[89] The campaign started in April 1917. Gandhi moved from one village to another collecting evidence of the ryots. There was spontaneous response from the peasants. As Rajendra Prasad who had joined Gandhi in the Champaran campaign tells us: 'The statements of tenants continued to be recorded the whole day. There was such a continuous stream of these tenants that there was not a minute's break between 6.30 a.m. and 6.30 p.m.' On 16 July about 10,000 peasants collected for 'darshan' of the Mahatma at the meeting place of the Enquiry Committee set up by the government. Gandhi sought to keep the movement 'within its non-political limit', hoping that 'disinterested service of the people in any sphere ultimately helps the country politically'.[90] Under the Champaran Agrarian Act, 1917, *tinkathia,* which had continued for over a century, was made illegal; *sharabeshi* was reduced by 20 or 26 per cent. Gandhi agreed to a compromise as he felt that 'peasants and planters had still to live together'.[91] The positive effect of this campaign has been noted by Gandhi: 'The ryots who had all along remained crushed now somewhat came into their own . . .'[92]

In the spring of 1918 Gandhi launched the satyagraha of Patidar ryots in Kaira (Kheda) in Gujarat. Since there was a failure of kharif crops due to excessive rains, the ryots demanded suspension of land revenue. The government rejected the demand on the ground that the harvest was more than 25 per cent of the normal yield. On 22 March 1918 Gandhi launched the satyagraha which continued in full swing till June; village meetings were held; 2,337 ryots signed the pledge not to pay land revenue. A section of the educated middle class represented by Vallabhbhai Patel, Indulal Yagnik and Mahadev Desai stood by Gandhi; subscriptions were raised from the Gujarati merchants. As the government tried to suppress the movement by attaching the ryots' property and imposing fines on the defaulters, the peasants began to waver.[93] As Gandhi tells us, some of the ryots paid up their dues while 'some were prepared to fight to the bitter end'. Gandhi became anxious to find 'some graceful way of terminating the struggle'.[94] The satyagraha was suspended when it was agreed that rich Patidars would pay up their dues and poor peasants would be granted suspension.

Willingdon wrote to Chelmsford that Gandhi and Patel suspended satyagraha when they saw 'the game was up'.[95] The fact is that Gandhi's main object was to help the poor peasants who were assured of suspension of revenue. Gandhi was not happy on the outcome of the satyagraha: '. . . the end was far from making me feel happy. . .' But the satyagraha helped to politicize the peasants. As Gandhi writes, Besant's Home Rule agitation had touched the peasants, but 'the Kheda satyagraha marks the beginning of an awakening among the peasants of Gujarat, the beginning of their true political education'.[96] Indeed, the satyagraha radicalized the patidars who rallied behind the Congress during the Rowlatt satyagraha of 1919. Kheda was in the vortex of the disturbances: a train carrying British troops was derailed.[97]

Barrington Moore, who describes Indian peasants as 'docile', writes that the alliance between the Congress and the peasants was forged and maintained via non-violence; the bourgeoisie hardly found it difficult to become reconciled with peaceful peasant movements.[98] What Moore has not cared to examine is that the political education of the peasants who were mostly illiterate and lived in scattered villages had begun. Looking back one may say that a ground swell was discernible among the peasants. Once the path of peasant mobilization was taken, it was difficult to halt. The 1920s marked a distinct turning-point: the rural poor were drawn into the nationalist movement. As an official report described the new trend in Indian politics in 1921:

> In various parts of India the movement for tenants' unions or Kisan Sabhas has become increasingly prominent. In many cases these unions have confined themselves to collective bargaining with local landholders and overlords and to secure improved conditions of tenure. . . . This has been considerably increased by the policy of hostility to the government

preached by the Non-cooperation Party . . . there is a considerable increase in the class consciousness of the rustic.[99]

The Kisan Sabhas remained in a rudimentary stage. Nevertheless, they promoted the growth of agrarian movements. This was particularly evident in the U.P. where the Congress seemed to show a great deal of interest in the Kisans. Madan Mohan Malaviya organized the U.P. Kisan Sabha in 1918, which generally represented Rajput tenants and small landlords. In 1919 Nehru was drawn into the peasant movement directed against 'the barons of Oudh'. There were Kisan Sabhas in the villages manned by local Congressmen. The most prominent local leader was Baba Ramchandra, who, dressed like a *sannyasi*, remained sunk among the peasants in Pratapgarh, holding village meetings and reciting melodious verses from the *Ramayana*. About 60,000 peasants assembled to see Ramchandra Maharaj when he was arrested. In 1920-1 the non-cooperation movement and peasant mobilization went hand in hand.[100] Indeed, peasant mobilization made a remarkable advance in eastern U.P. where the *zamindars* and *taluqdars* dominated the agrarian social structure and stubbornly opposed tenancy legislation.[101]

Notes and References

1. M.D. Morris, *The Emergence of an Industrial Labour force in India, 1854-1946*, 1965, pp. 70-1.
2. S.K. Sen, *Economic Policy and Development of India, 1848-1939*, 1972, pp. 7, 47, 66. In 1913, 35,000 persons were employed in the engineering firms.
3. J. Nehru, *The Discovery of India*, 1960, p. 359.
4. W.R. Dunstan, 'Report on the Coal Supply of India, 1898', *Commerce Department, Coal and Iron*, July, 1908.
5. Morris, op. cit., pp. 104-5, 110-11, 128, 152. Morris writes that the payment of Wages Act, 1937 restricted the employer's authority to fine workers and withhold wages.
6. See the present writer's *The House of Tata, 1839-1939*, 1975, pp. 97-8.
7. S.R. Deshpande, *Report on An Enquiry into conditions of labour in the Jute Mill Industry, 1946*; R. Das Gupta, 'Factory Labour in Eastern India', *Indian Economic and Social History Review*, No. 3, 1976.
8. *Royal Commission on Labour*, 1931, Vol. 5, pp. 208-10.
9. Deshpande, op. cit.
10. J. Kuczynski, 'Condition of Workers, 1880-1950', in V.B. Singh, ed., *Economic History of India, 1857-1956*, 1965.
11. J. Nehru, *An Autobiography*, 1936, p. 21. Nehru was extremely critical of the Moderates.
12. K. Chatterjee, *Brahmo Reform Movement, 1858-83*, 1983, p. 99.
13. Sukomal Sen, *Working class of India : History of Emergence and Movement, 1830-1970*, pp. 21, 197.
14. D. Chakravarty, *Communal Riots and Labour : Bengal Jute Mill-hands*, Calcutta, 1976.

15. S. Sarkar, *The Swadeshi Movement in Bengal, 1903-8*, 1973, pp. 201-27; also P. Saha, *Working class Movement in Bengal*, 1978, pp. 17-25.
16. V.B. Karnik, *Strikes in India*, 1967, pp. 14-6.
17. L.A. Gordon, 'Social and Economic Conditions of Bombay Workers', in I.M. Reisner and N.M. Goldberg, eds., *Tilak and the Struggle for Indian Freedom*, 1966, pp. 475, 479, 495, 504.
18. Gordon, op. cit., p. 542.
19. V. Chirol, *Indian Unrest*, 1910, p. 53.
20. D.C. Home, Bombay Workers' First Political Strike, *New Age*, June, 1953.
21. A.I. Chicherov, *Tilak's Trial and the Bombay Political Strike of 1908*; Reisner and Goldberg, op. cit., pp. 602-9.
22. Sukomal Sen, op. cit., p. 114.
23. J. Nehru, *Autobiography*, p. 27.
24. *Report of the Royal Commission*, 1931.
25. R. Coupland, *The Indian Problem, 1833-1935*, p. 47.
26. Home Department Proceedings, March 1919, Labour Unrest in Madras.
27. Fortnightly Reports of Madras Government, February 1918 to October 1918.
28. Ibid., December 1918 to January 1919.
29. E.D. Murphy, 'The Madras Labour Union, 1918-22', *Economic and Social History Review*, July-September 1977.
30. K. Gillion, 'Gujarat in 1919', in R. Kumar, ed., *Essays on Gandhian Politics*, 1971, pp. 134-6.
31. M. Gandhi, *The Story of My Experiments With Truth*, 1929, pp. 411-3.
32. Ibid., pp. 419-22.
33. Gillion, op. cit., pp. 138-9.
34. S.K. Sen, op. cit., p. 62.
35. J. Masselos, 'Bombay City Politics in 1919', in R. Kumar, op. cit., pp. 166-7.
36. K. Dwarkadas, *Forty-Five Years*, 1969, pp. 3, 18.
37. *Bombay Chronicle*, 6 January 1919. They were asked to become secretaries of labour unions.
38. Masselos, op. cit., p. 170. Masselos seems to underestimate the part played by the Hóme Rulers.
39. Dwarkadas, op. cit., p. 21.
40. R. Kumar, 'The Bombay Textile Strike, 1919', *Economic and Social History Review*, March 1971.
41. R. Das, *Labour Movement in India*, 1923, pp. 36-7; also Sukomal Sen, op. cit., pp. 131-7.
42. Sukomal Sen, op. cit., p. 162.
43. *AITUC — Fifty Years, Documents*, Vol. I.
44. Ibid.
45. R. Roy, *Urban Roots of Indian Nationalism*, 1979, pp. 92-5. The white-collar employees formed the largest unions.
46. R.P. Dutt, *India Today*, 1947, pp. 333-4. Dutt writes that the AITUC in its early years was 'mainly a top organisation'.
47. S.K. Sen, op. cit., p. 52.
48. A. Guha, *Planter Raj to Swaraj*, 1977, p. 37; S. Bhowmik, *Class Formation in the Plantation System*, 1981, p. 53.

49. K. Chatterjee, op. cit., pp. 127-34.
50. Chatterjee, op. cit., p. 134.
51. Guha, op. cit., pp. 106-8, 129.
52. Guha, op. cit., p. 130; P. Saha, op. cit., pp. 47-56.
53. For an account of nationalist thinking on the agrarian problem see B. Chandra, *The Rise and Growth of Economic Nationalism in India*, 1966, Chapters 9, 10. Chandra argues that R.C. Dutt, while pleading for the extension of permanent settlement of revenue did not want the extension of Bengal *zamindari* system. Curiously, Chandra hardly notes Dutt's views on the positive effects of the *zamindari* system which was described as 'a boon to Bengal', 'a protection to agriculture'.
54. *Report of Indian Famine Commission*, 1880, p. 118. Richard Strachey was the Chairman of this commission.
55. *Settlement Report*, Midnapore, 1911-7.
56. See the present writer's book, *Agrarian Relations In India, 1793-1947*, 1979, pp. 28-31.
57. M.D. Morris, 'Economic Change and Agriculture', *Indian Economic and Social History Review*, June, 1966. Dharma Kumar, writing on Madras, seems to hold the same view: '. . . there seems to have been no largescale dispossession of the peasantry by moneylenders and traders'. D. Kumar, *Land and Caste in South India*, p. 179.
58. R. Mukherjee, *Land Problems of India*, p. 157.
59. B. Chaudhuri, Agrarian Relations in N.K. Sinha, ed., *History of Bengal*, 1757-1905, pp. 320-2. The percentage of agricultural labour in Bengal rose from 17 in 1921 to 33.2 in 1931.
60. H. Fukazawa, 'Agrarian Relations, Western India', *Cambridge Economic History of India*, Vol. 2, p. 204. The number of agricultural labourers 'did not grow rapidly or steadily in western India'.
61. S. Gopal, *Jawaharlal Nehru : A Biography, 1889-1947*, 1976, p. 43. In Pratapgarh 936 notices of eviction were served on the tenants in 1906-7; this figure rose to 2,593 in 1919-20. For tenancy system in U.P. see W.C. Neale, *Economic Change in Rural India*, 1962.
62. Revenue Proceedings, Bengal, December, 1892, cited in G. Mishra, *Agrarian Problems of Permanent Settlement : A Case Study of Champaran*, 1978, pp. 130-1.
63. Bengal Judicial Proceedings, May, 1872, cited in B. Chaudhuri, 'Peasant Movements in Bengal', 1850-1900, *Nineteenth Century Studies*, 1973. The English view of property rights proved to be incompatible with 'the Sonthal view of the rights of the village'.
64. N. Kumar, *Bihar District Gazetteers : Ranchi*, 1970, pp. 66-8.
65. K. Suresh Singh, 'Tribal Land Organisation in Chotanagpur', in *Trends of Socio-economic Change in India, 1871-1961*, Simla, 1969. In 1918 there were about 60 thousand Kamias in Palamau who were mostly serfs.
66. E. Whitcome, *Agrarian Conditions in Northern India*, 1971, pp. 94-6.
67. N. Kumar, op. cit., pp. 166.
68. J.R. McLane, *Indian Nationalism And The Early Congress*, 1977, p. 267.
69. AICC papers, 1885-1919; also Annie Besant, *How India Wrought For Freedom*, 1915, pp. 132, 153, 170.

70. For an account of forest satyagraha in Madras see C. Baker and D. Washbrook, *South India : Political Institutions and Political Change, 1880-1940*, 1975, and for CP see D.E.U. Baker, *Changing Political Leadership : The Central Provinces and Berar, 1919-39*, 1979.
71. Kumar, op. cit., pp. 68-9.
72. S. Singh, *The Dust Storm And The Hanging Mist*, 1966; K.K. Datta, *History of the Freedom Movement in Bihar*, Vol. I; Ranajit Guha has concentrated on The Santal Rebellion and the Munda Revolt in *Elementary Aspects of Peasant Insurgency in Colonial India*, 1983.
73. Singh, op. cit.
74. Note of H.W.P. Scroope, 19 March 1919, Political Department, Bihar, File No. 860 of 1919. Also Oraon Unrest, Home (Political), September, 1915, No. 58.
75. Note of C.C. Ryland, DIG, 20 April 1919, Political Department, Bihar.
76. Confidential diary of the Superintendent of Police, Ranchi, 15 March 1919; also K.K. Datta, *Freedom Movement in Bihar*, Vol. I, 1957, p. 333.
77. Kumar, op. cit., p. 74. The Tana Bhagats, wearing Gandhi caps, went to jail during the non-cooperation movement in 1920-2.
78. G. Bhadra, 'The Kuri Uprising, 1917-9', *Man in India*, March, 1975.
79. F.R. Hemingway, *Gadavari District Gazetteer*, 1907; S. Sarkar, *Popular Movements and Middle Class Leadership*, 1983, pp. 13-4.
80. Sarkar, op. cit., p. 16.
81. V. Raghavaiah, 'Tribal Revolts' in A.R. Desai, ed., *Peasant Struggles in India*, 1979.
82. AICC papers, 1885-1919. The Congress opposed the measures adopted by the Government in 1893-4 to give greater security to the tenants on the ground that these were 'reactionary attacks on the Permanent Settlement'. The 1899 session presided over by R.C. Dutt adopted a resolution on tenancy legislation, this session also adopted a resolution protesting against the Labour Laws of Assam. The Congress session of 1901 proposed the establishment of Agricultural Banks and deplored recurrence of famines throughout India.
83. Gordon Johnson, *Provincial Politics and Indian Nationalism : Bombay and the Indian National Congress, 1880-1915*, 1975, p. 96. Tilak was arrested in 1897 and sentenced to eighteen months' imprisonment.
84. S. Gopal, op. cit., pp. 165-6. As the rent-strike was launched, Jawaharlal said: 'It is war, war now and ever till the end of our lives.'
85. McLane, op. cit., p. 263.
86. N.G. Barrier, The Punjab Disturbances of 1907, *The Punjab : Past and Present*, October, 1974.
87. S. Sen, *Agrarian Relations*, pp. 79-82.
88. D.N. Dhanagare, *Peasant Movements in India, 1920-1950*, 1983, pp. 59-60, 77, 81-2; Conrad Wood, 'The Moplah Rebellions, 1802-1922', *Economic and Social History Review*, January-March, 1976; R.E. Miller, *Mapila Muslims of Kerala*, 1976; S.F. Dale, *The Mappilas of Malabar, 1498-1922*, 1980.
89. Gandhi, op. cit., pp. 369-70.
90. Ibid., pp. 382-3.
91. J. Brown, *Gandhi's Rise to Power*, 1972, p. 72.

92. Gandhi, op. cit., p. 396. Also S. Henningham, *Peasant Movements in Colonial India,* 1982. He refers to the continuing peasant-planter conflict during 1919-23.
93. Brown, op. cit., p. 110.
94. Gandhi, op. cit., p. 440.
95. Brown, op. cit., p. 111. Throughout her study Brown emphasizes Gandhi's political manipulation and tries to denigrate him.
96. Gandhi, op. cit., p. 443.
97. Gillion, 'Gujarat in 1919', in R. Kumar, op. cit., p. 142. The Patidars played no mean role in peasant mobilization in Bardoli, a taluk in Gujarat; the Patidar Yuvak Mandal, founded in 1908, spread nationalist ideas among the common people; the Spinners' Association maintained contact with the *Harijans,* see A. Bhatt, 'Caste and Political Mobilization in a Gujarat District', in R. Kothari, ed., *Caste in Indian Politics,* 1970.
98. B. Moore, *Social Origins of Dictatorship and Democracy,* 1967, see ch. 6. K. Gough has tried to refute Moore's statement that Indian peasants were 'docile' and drawn attention to numerous peasant revolts in different parts of India. See 'Indian Peasant Uprisings', *Economic and Political Weekly,* August 1974.
99. R. Williams, *India in 1920-1,* 1922.
100. M.H. Siddiqi, *Agrarian Unrest in North India, 1918-22,* 1978. Siddiqi presents a documented account of peasant mobilization in eastern U.P.; also S. Choudhury, *Peasant's and Workers' Movements in India, 1905-27,* 1976, pp. 36-7.
101. For an intensive study of peasant mobilization in eastern U.P. in the 1930s see G. Pandey, *The Ascendancy of the Congress in U.P., 1926-34,* 1978.

Chapter VII

Healing the Breach and the Home Rule Movement

S. Vijayalakshmi

1. The Urge for Unity

THE SPLIT IN THE CONGRESS at Surat in December 1907 was the first of many vicissitudes that were to beset the Congress organization during the hundred years of its history. The imperialists were happy over the break-up of the Congress. The enemies of Indian freedom were jubilant and hoped that the rift was unbridgable. The years 1907-10 were crucial years for both the Congressmen and the national movement.

The Surat split was an unfortunate episode occurring under most painful circumstances. It ranged Congressmen in two rival camps as Moderates and Extremists or Nationalists. The conflict between the two wings was not over office or position. It concerned ideology: its content, and the methodology to be followed to attain the goal; and also the goal itself.

The discontent and revolt within the Congress at Surat might have temporarily rendered the movement weak, but soon the Congress was to emerge as a powerful force challenging the imperialist grip. Both wings of the movement learnt valuable lessons from this episode. It proved beyond doubt that what was disrupted or broken could also be mended or united. The split was healthy; it activized Congressmen to expand the Congress base and marked the beginning of a new phase in the history of the Congress.

The Anglo-Indian Press, jubilant over internal strife in the Congress, were soon to witness, to their grave disappointment, the quick recovery, the prompt action and the businesslike procedures in the Congress ranks. These were far better proof of their fitness to rule the country than the capacity for peaceful and orderly meetings. The courage to meet the emergency, and grapple with it, and to secure the continuity of the Congress were indications of the statesmanlike qualities and judgment that Congressmen were capable of, even in critical moments.

During the 1904-8, the consensus among Congressmen was broken. They were divided into Moderates and Extremists or Nationalists. There were many wordy conflicts over the drafting and content of the resolutions to be adopted at annual sessions. There was public divergence of opinion about both the content and interpretation of the resolutions. The leadership came in for severe attack. As a result, the Congress became more active than ever before. Commenting on this Bal Gangadhar Tilak observed:[1]

> We have been accustomed to be united for the last 22 years but unfortunately within this particular year, five or six months ago . . . differences of opinion gave rise to a controversy among the members of the Congress, and that controversy culminated in a split in the Congress camp. The Congress is for national purposes and for all the people of India; people of all shades of opinion.

The split made Congressmen of all shades of opinion unhappy, but they got over the feeling soon enough. Congressmen in different corners of India manifested tremendous zeal to preserve the unity of the organization. Bengal appeared to have displayed an extraordinary sense of unity in the face of the all-India split.

The split had occurred between the 'reconcilables' at a time when the Congress had become the focus of all organizations engaged in public service. As the main vehicle of nationalism, the Congress had begun to acquire increasing significance in political life and a capacity to exert independent influence on Indian politics. Commenting on the split, *The Madras Standard* wrote:[2]

> How foolishly and criminally have the irreconcilables acted; That there should be diversity of opinion in the Congress camp was not only inevitable but desirable. It showed that the Congress was not a moribund mass, but full of vitality and brimful of energy, an augury of a long life of splendour and sure sign of ultimate triumph. If the two parties had kept together, each would have imparted to the other something of the qualities each excelled. The extremists could have communicated to the moderates something of their fire, their electric energy, their passion, their self-help and their love of self-sacrifice for the sake of our Motherland.

A series of provincial Congress conferences at Pabna, Dhulia and Pune, that were held soon after Surat, simply ignored the split in the all-India body. In Pabna (Bengal) the Congressmen of both the Extremist and Moderate wings exhibited warmth and friendliness.[3] A conference at Satara, in the heart of Maharashtra, adopted a resolution urging the reunion of the Congress.

Congressmen at large were afraid that a rift would inflict lasting injury on the organization and that, unless a compromise was effected, unhealthy repercussions might follow. Advice to this effect poured in from different directions to both the camps of Congressmen to reunite and remain united, and to act with restraint, ignore differences and manifest a spirit of compromise.

There was an intense desire on the part of the Extremist Congressmen to reunite in the interests of the Congress. *Mahratta,* Tilak's paper observed: 'In fact the split of the Congress and desire for reunion were simultaneous.'[4] The parties themselves had begun to manifest something more than a pious desire for compromise.[5] The Extremist Congressmen were not unaware of the kind of organization that the Congress ought to be. Tilak, their unquestioned leader, was quite clear on the type of political organization required to win Indian independence. He said:[6]

> If the National movement was to embrace every caste, class and religion which it must, then its leaders had to make compromises with each other; they [leaders] had to realise that the Congress existed for specific political purposes.

Tilak was never in favour of a split, and when it came, he was most anxious to heal the breach as soon as possible. This is evident from his writings and activities in the first six months of 1908. The Poona District Conference and the Dhulia Provincial Conference in Maharashtra and the Pabna Conference in Bengal were all organized jointly by the Nationalists and Moderates. The *Kesari* fully supported such conferences for Congress unity. Constant efforts were being made by Tilak to deem the next session of the Congress as a continuation Congress session. Tilak regarded the Congress as the principal political organization of the country in which every shade of political opinion should find room. He was firmly of the opinion that its proceedings and decisions should be completely democratic. The difference in approaches 'was not such an insurmountable difficulty in reaching the compromise, [nor was] the schism an irreparable one,'[7] he said. All his writings in *Kesari* during these months bear testimony to the fact that Tilak wanted to adhere to the Congress very closely.

The desire among Congressmen for unity was intense. Efforts in that direction were also not wanting. All attempts to effect a compromise and to enable Tilak and his followers to return to the Congress, however, proved, for the time being, futile. The Moderates had gone ahead with drafting a constitution for the Congress. Before any moves for unity could be pursued, the government unleashed a series of repressive measures. The country witnessed a reign of terror under Lord Minto's regime in the following years. Tilak was prosecuted for seditious writing. He was sentenced in September 1908 to transportation for six years in Mandalay Jail thus making impossible any united Congress till his release.

For the eight years after Tilak's deportation there were no prospects of the Congress being united, though regular district, state and national sessions of the Congress continued to be held. Acrimony and bitterness of temper that the split had generated amongst erstwhile colleagues continued to persist during these years in varying degrees.

The immediate effect of the Surat split was that the Indian National Congress came under the exclusive control of the Moderates. The Extremists or the Nationalists, as they preferred to call themselves, seceded from the parent body and remained separate for nearly a decade. Almost every Congress session that was held since Surat adopted a resolution calling for the reunification of the Congress.

The spirit of the nationalist movement passed to the hands of the Extremist Congressmen and their followers everywhere in the country and they were soon to emerge as the major challenge to the British.

The split might well have ruined the Congress for ever. The resourcefulness and the earnest desire on the part of the Moderate Congressmen to continue Congress work helped a great deal in preserving this mighty organization. Whatever might have been their shortcomings, the Moderates' historic role in shaping the Indian National Congress in its early and formative years cannot be denied. They slowly built an all-India organization which grew to be a mighty challenge to the alien rulers of the country in the early decades of the 20th century. It would be unfair to minimize the stupendous work done by the early Congressmen considering the limitations under which they functioned. Dr Rash Behari Ghosh observed in this connection:[8]

> Some kindly thoughts for those who too, in their days strove to do their duty, however imperfectly, through good report and through evil report, with it may be somewhat chastened fervour, but a fervour as genuine as that which stirs and aspires younger hearts.

As the split occurred at Surat and the 23rd session of the Congress was abruptly suspended, the leading Moderate Congressmen called a convention the following day[9] and adopted a creed for the Congress that stated:[10]

(a) that the goal of our political aspirations is to attain self-Government similar to that enjoyed by the self-governing colonies of the Empire.

(b) that the advance towards the goal is to be strictly constitutional, by bringing about a steady reform in the existing system of Government by the promotion of national unity and improving the condition of the mass of the people.

(c) that all meetings held for the promotion of these objects should be conducted in an orderly manner.

Of the 1,663 delegates who attended the session at Surat, over 900[11] subscribing to the creed mentioned above attended the convention held on 28 December[12] in the Congress pavilion.

On a motion of Pherozeshah Mehta seconded by Surendranath Banerjea, with Dr Rash Behari Ghosh in the chair, G.K. Gokhale proposed a committee of 100 names to draw up a constitution for the Congress.[13] Pherozeshah Mehta, Gokhale and Wacha were nominated secretaries. The President R.B. Ghosh dissolved the convention thereafter.

The constitution for the Congress was drawn up by the convention committee at Allahabad in April 1908. A set of rules was also framed. That constitution and those rules have been followed by subsequent Congresses. It became necessary thereafter for delegates to be elected by a few recognized and affiliated bodies and, further, that each delegate had to subscribe to a stated creed by signing the formula embodying the creed of the Congress or the declaration of the aims and objects of the Congress.[14]

During 1908-14 the Congress passed through a period of depression. These years were marked by lacklustre AICC sessions. The two wings of the national movement remained aloof. The years were to witness distressing events in India; they saw great stress and storm. Taking advantage of the rift in the Congress, the British Government in India pushed through unpopular measures. Already a spirit of distrust was gathering in the minds of the Indian people and a wave of awakening was seen in India from 1905 when Lord Curzon partitioned Bengal. The country entered the phase of militant nationalism. Revolutionary youths in Bengal and elsewhere lent support to and strengthened the new political trend, which was revolutionary in character. It came to be recognized as the New Party. Its leaders were Lala Lajpat Rai, Bal Gangadhar Tilak and Bipin Chandra Pal (Lal-Bal-Pal). People became restless and discarded display of loyalty to and faith in the British as something obnoxious. Tilak had stressed earlier the need for radical change in the Congress programme. He preached everywhere the tenets of the New Party. B.C. Pal lectured widely to revolutionize the thinking of the youth. The reality of the situation coupled with the bitter feelings of the people towards their alien rulers rendered the whole atmosphere tense.

The administration were alarmed at this situation which came to be described as the 'Indian unrest'. Relations between the rulers and ruled were very strained as the unrest enveloped the nation in a massive way. Soon even the most optimistic of Moderates was to be unnerved in the face of the severe persecution and the deportation, jail sentences under 'lawless laws', and the repressive measures unleashed by the imperialist government. The Boycott and Swadeshi Movements initiated after the partition of Bengal, had come to acquire a massive dimension. It became a mass movement. In fact, the partition receded into the background. The Boycott and Swadeshi Movements were transformed into a massive movement for self-government or swaraj. The swadeshi spirit pervaded all aspects of the nation's life. A confidential report of the government observed:[15]

> The Collector of Customs hears that more or less determined efforts were being made to enforce boycott. It is said that Bengali priests at that time refused to conduct marriage unless the marrige parties take the Swadeshi vow and wear country-made clothes. The support of the priests might, it was feared, give the boycott movement a new stimulus.

2. Rising Unrest, Intensified Repression

The year 1908 was to witness great unrest in many parts of the country — North Western Frontier, Bengal, East Bengal, Assam, Deccan, Western India, Madras Presidency and the United Provinces. The country passed through an unprecedented period of storm and stress. The Bengal revolutionaries established secret societies, as the repressive policy of the government was severe, and introduced the cult of bomb. Young men all over India, inspired by Bengali youths, performed many daring acts, despite government's repression and persecution. Youths in Maharashtra, Punjab and in the Madras Presidency took to a revolutionary programe and systematically promoted it through secret societies, on the Bengal model. These societies were in regular contact with Bengal.[16] The existence of a secret society in Maharashtra pledged to winning freedom, proved by official evidence, led to the execution of three Brahmins. B.C. Pal's tour of Madras in 1907 revolutionized Tamil and Andhra youth. Many youngsters were inducted into the revolutionary circle. B.C. Pal's collected speeches in Madras ran into several editions.[17] The Swadeshi and Boycott Movements had spread in a most aggressive form in the distant provinces and remote villages. The whole nation, down to schoolboys, had begun to act with enthusiasm. Demonstrations, marches by masses of people and public meetings became the regular means adopted to propagate the concepts of boycott and swadeshi. Incoherent economic ideas came to be welded into common economic nationalism. Poet Bharati's poetry reflected the spirit of swadeshi and the new awakening in the land. Propagation of swadeshi reached its pinnacle when V.O. Chidambaram in Tuticorin in the South inaugurated the Swadeshi Steam Navigation Company with the moral support of B.G. Tilak, with a view to crippling the British Navigation Co.[18] Lala Lajpat Rai, B.C. Pal, B.G. Tilak, Chidambaram Pillai and Hari Sarvothama Rao became the idols of the youth.

In Madras Presidency, swadeshi coins were manufactured and circulated as the token of the peoples faith in swadeshi and with the circulation of the coin, intensive swadeshi propaganda was planned.

Newspapers like *Yugantar, Bande Mataram, Sandhya, Kesari, New India* and *Swadeshamitran* became powerful instruments of political education and were prosecuted for sedition. The youth of the country became impatient everywhere and took to terrorist activities. Political terrorism was on the increase due to severe repressive measures unleashed by the government.

The government came down heavily on Extremist Congressmen and the revolutionary youth. Even moderate politicians and their papers, and editors like G. Subramania Iyer, were not spared.

Tilak was arrested on 23 June 1908 for his series of articles in *Kesari* on the repressive policies of the government. Tilak had commented on the Muzaffarpur bomb outrage in Bengal, in which two English-women were killed 'as the political thermometer showing how greatly the people were becoming desperate and exasperated'.[20] In an article on 9 June Tilak had refused to believe 'that the bombs of Bengalis were subversive of society'. He explained that 'there was an excess of patriotism at the root of the bomb in Bengal'.[21] As mentioned earlier, Tilak was sentenced to six years imprisonment and was deported to Mandalay in September.[22]

It was indeed a most barbarous sentence. Its severity shocked men like Gokhale. Tilak's conviction was resented at many places. Western India was in a state of ferment. There was an unprecedented mass upsurge in the country. The Marathi press was vehement in its criticism, and its tone bold and outspoken.

In December 1908 nine prominent Bengali leaders were deported.[23] On the same day Hari Sarvothama Rao and others were arrested in Andhra. Rao was a great patriot who sacrificed everything for the national cause. A student of the Madras Christian College,[24] he preached swadeshi and boycott of foreign goods.

1908 was a year of repression in every part of the country. The *Swarajya* paper, with which Hari Sarvothama Rao was connected, was proscribed. The District Court sentenced Rao to simple imprisonment for six months, but the government preferred an appeal to the High

Court which sentenced him to three years' rigorous imprisonment. The policy of repression continued in 1909 too.[25]

Just two weeks before Tilak was sentenced, in Tuticorin in Tinnevelly District of Madras Presidency, V.O. Chidambaram was sentenced to rigorous imprisonment for 'life' (usually 14 years)[26] which was later reduced to six years.[27] Along with him his illustrious colleague, Subramania Siva, a fiery patriot, was sentenced to ten years' imprisonment for spreading the message of boycott, swadeshi, national education and swaraj. The immediate occasion for their arrest was the organization of felicitation meetings in celebration of Bipin Chandra Pal's release from prison.

In delivering judgment on V.O. Chidambaram, Justice Pinhey observed that 'the conviction of the man was not merely to punish him, but also to deter the others from committing the same crime'.[28]

The government of Lord Minto promulgated a series of measures to suppress the revolutionary activities and seditious writings and propaganda by the newspapers. Bhupendra Nath Dutta, the editor of *Yugantar* was given a long sentence. Aurobindo Ghosh was kept in prison for a year awaiting his trial. *Swadeshamitran* and *India* of Madras were proceeded against and Editor G. Subramania Iyer was prosecuted.[29]

Lord Minto succeeded in suppressing the Extremists and apparently restored calm in the country. Already in 1907, the Seditious Meetings Act had been passed. To it the government added in 1908 the following far more severe measures:[30]

(a) The Explosive Substance Act, 1908
(b) The Newspaper Incitement Act, 1908
(c) The Criminal Law Amendment Act, 1908

These were soon to be followed by the Indian Press Act, 1910, and several ordinances and circulars suspending the rights of free speech and free criticism.

The societies that were propagating swadeshi and boycott in Bengal, Maharashtra, Madras and other places were raided by the CID. Police raids, house searches, confiscation of property, espionage, became the order of the day. Press prosecutions and proscription of newspapers and journals was witnessed every day and everywhere.[31]

The severity of the repression drove revolutionary activity underground, while superficial calm was restored. That the terrorist movement continued unabated during Minto's regime was demonstrated by the murder of Jackson, Collector of Nasik, by a youth; an attempt on the life of Minto in 1909; and the assassination of Collector Ashe, ICS, of Tinnevelly District in the South in June 1911.

So severe was the repression that even Lord Morley was horrified, and on 14 July 1908 he is said to have protested and written to Minto:

> I must confess to you, that I am watching with the deepest concern and dismay the thundering sentences that are being passed for sedition; we must keep order, but excess of severity is not the path to order; on the contrary it is the path to the bomb.[32]

Such was the situation when the Indian National Congress held its session in Madras in December 1908, in an atmosphere of uneasy calm, while a thick cloud of sorrow and anger seemed to float over the country. The session was presided over by Dr Rash Behari Ghosh, the President-elect of the memorable Surat Session, the previous year. During the period of 1908-14, the Nationalists or Extremist Congressmen were either in prison or outside India. The Moderates or the old party were at the helm of affairs. With their firm faith in the efficacy of constitutional methods, they desired that conflict with the government should be averted at any cost. They eschewed violence. Their old methods of prayer, petitions, representations, and deputations for gaining political concessions continued. They avoided sharp attacks and adopted a friendly, accommodating and conciliatory attitude towards the government. Their expectation was that, if the Congress and the country acted within a particular framework, a liberal measure of political reform would follow, and that if it did not, there would be repression. But later events were to prove that they neither got a liberal measure of reforms nor could they save the country from repression. The British, true to their instinct of 'divide and rule', and faced with the task of quelling the stirring forces of the Indian unrest since the Bengal partition, had already worked out their line of action. The Morley-Minto regime had begun to befriend and rally the Moderates to their side and play up the loyal elements against the Nationalists or Extremists and their leaders against whom they unleashed a wave of repressive measures.

The British were alarmed at the growing strength of nationalism. The revolutionary activities of the youth and Extremist Congressmen caused them much concern. They had also begun to pamper Muslim communalism in order to counteract or contain the patriotic forces among Muslims, and of the country as a whole, whether represented by Tilak or by Gokhale. Both policies moved simultaneously. Added to this, they gave wide publicity to their famous despatch on the reform proposals.

Minto split the Congress by holding out a promise of constitutional reform to Moderates. He wrecked the unity of the country and the Indian people by framing special rules for the Muslims under the same reform. He was the originator of the 'two nation theory'. Minto gave not only a sympathetic reply to the famous memorandum presented by a group of Muslim leaders in 1906, he assured them that in any scheme of associating the people of India with its government, he would undertake to see that Muslim interests did not suffer.[33]

The Madras Congress Session came to be known as the constitutional Congress. It was deemed the reassembling of the twenty-third session adjourned *sine die* at Surat, the previous year. 626 delegates from different parts of the country attended this resurrected Congress session.[34] The ex-presidents of the Congress were present. The session was wholly Moderate in complexion. The Nationalists (Extremists) were absent. The non-attendance of the Extremists was largely due to the repression unleashed against them. Many besides Tilak were languishing in jails. Some like Lala Lajpat Rai and B.C. Pal were abroad.

The announcement of reforms gave hope and satisfaction to the Moderate Congress leaders as they were in session in Madras. The reform bill was introduced in the House of Lords on 17 December 1908. The Congress, under the leadership of Dr Rash Behari Ghosh, G.K. Gokhale, Pherozeshah Mehta, Surendranath Banerjea and others, were hopeful of a new era opening and praised the reform bill and its author Lord Morley. The Congress welcomed Morley's reform scheme but expressed the fear that it might be frustrated by the rules framed by men on the spot — the bureaucracy.

The president of the Congress session condemned the successive repressive laws and deportations under a 'lawless law'. Several resolutions were adopted after full-fledged debates. The most important among them was the one on the forthcoming reform scheme. It expressed deep appreciation of and satisfaction with the proposals. The Congress leadership ardently believed that the proposed expansion of the legislative councils constituted a large, liberal instalment of reform that would usher in representative government and that Indians would henceforth have an effective voice in directing the policy of the government and a substantial say in the management of their affairs.[35]

The grievances of the Indians in South Africa, the partition of Bengal, and the severe repressive measures promulgated by the government came in for criticism by the delegates. The speakers condemned the policy of deportation without trial and observed that 'such a policy could never succeed except to help the government to convert the prison house into martyrdom'.[36]

3. Reforms

The Morley-Minto reforms were neither calculated to satisfy the legitimate political aspiration of India, nor expected to end the activities of the extreme sections of the national movement by conceding their demands. The reforms did not transfer even a particle of responsibility to Indian hands in spite of the enlargement of the councils as well as admission of Indians to the executive councils of the viceroy and governors of Bombay and Madras Presidencies. The real intention of the government was to strengthen its hands in dealing with revolutionary activities and political terrorism, and in that they succeeded. In the face of the danger confronting them, the government was driven to adopt drastic measures to prevent the spread of unrest and to strike at the root of the political crimes.

While the much-expected reforms could not concede real rights to people, it laid emphasis on communal and group interest as the foundation of the future political arrangement in India. The separate representation for Muslims amounted to a denial of Indian nationalism. Minto succeeded in diverting important section of the Muslim community from the Congress, thus weakening the national movement.

A confidential account of Minto's Administration mischievously recorded that it appeared that Congress had admittedly lost its claim to be designated a national institution. From the beginning, the Nationalists despised the reform proposals and expressed their misgivings even before they were announced. The revolutionary section pronounced the reform scheme as an 'ingenious fraud', a *Delhi ka laddu'*, and termed the Moderates 'old fossils', and continued to meet the executive lawlessness of the government with increased resistance.[37] The revolutionaries intensified their propaganda and other activities.

Towards the end of 1909 Gokhale himself was driven to the conclusion that disunity and dissensions within the Congress would threaten the very existence of the Congress.

The Congress constitution of 1908 framed by the Allahabad convention was conceived by its founding fathers in a state of excitement and anger against Extremist Congressmen. Ever since the Surat episode, Gokhale had become a sad man. He realized that the Indian National Congress had to put up a facade of unity and strength if it was to gain any tangible concessions from the British. He wanted that the next Congress session which was scheduled to be held in Madras should realize this and urged his friends to make the session an eventful one. But it was not to be. It was a wholly 'Moderate Congress'.

As a result of the absence of the Extremists, the Indian National Congress lost its influence with the people, especially after the announcement of the reform scheme. The small number of delegates at the Lahore Session was no surprise, and with Lala Lajpat Rai keeping aloof, even Punjab was very poorly represented by only 76 delegates.[38]

Bengal had insisted that both wings should be invited. In the absence of such a move, they boycotted the session. The Madras delegates excused themselves on the plea of the severe Punjab winter. The total number of delegates at the Lahore Congress of 1909 was only 243. Attendance from all other provinces was equally unsatisfactory. Writing to William Wedderburn on the situation of the country and the Congress, Gokhale observed:[39]

> The Lahore Congress was the poorest gathering on record. Bengal had all but seceded. The bulk of the Punjab was not only indifferent but actively hostile. The attendance from other provinces too was unsatisfactory. There were two main causes of this. One was opposition to the Congress constitution framed at Allahabad, on the part of many, who in their views and convictions are no more with us than with the Extremists, but who think that the constitution stands in the way of a reunion on the Congress platform of all parties in the country. The other was the feeling that has no doubt been rapidly spreading in the Hindu community, since last year that the Congress had done no good to it: that while it borne the brunt of the struggle all these years, the Muhammedans have walked away with the greater part of the spoils, and that it was necessary for Hindus now, first and foremost, to look after their own interest, as distinguished from those of the Muhammedans.

The mood of the country and the disappointment in the Congress ranks were well reflected in the Lahore Session. Pherozeshah Mehta declined, at the last minute, the invitation to preside over the session. The choice fell on Pandit Madan Mohan Malaviya. The Congress leaders realized that the great expectations raised by the reform scheme had, after all, come to nothing. Lord Morley said that the policy of the Government of India should be to rally the Moderates. To their dismay the Congressmen found that the new regulations under the reform scheme were disappointing and the legitimate aspirations of the Indians remained unfulfilled. The Congress expected at least the withdrawal of the partition measure. The other promised political privileges under reform did not come. Congressmen were annoyed that, despite protest, caste distinctions were given undue importance. It may be remembered that the President of the Madras Congress Session in 1908, Dr Rash Behari Ghosh, had extolled reforms and said they heralded a bright era for India. But in the very next session at Lahore, Dr Ghosh issued a manifesto pointing out its shortcomings.

The prevailing trend appeared to be that, before the session at Lahore, no efforts should be spared to reunite the two wings of the Congress and win back the esteem of the people. The President, Madan Mohan Malaviya, stressed the desirability of putting the rules of the Congress into better shape to conciliate all wings. The consensus was that the

Allahabad Constitution required amendment in the light of the present situation, since it created some hurdles in the way of the re-entry of the Extremists.

The Lahore Congress reflected the growing tension between the Congress and the government. The reforms had lost their attraction for the Moderates. The prospect of reconsideration of the constitutional issues in the light of Congress suggestions appeared remote and was not to take place for another decade. Senior Congressmen ardently believed that the Congress must be united and that Hindu-Muslim unity was the need of the hour. They spared no efforts in this direction.

Gokhale wrote to Wedderburn, inviting him to preside over the Allahabad Session, since his presence, Gokhale believed, would enable the old Congress elements of the country to revive their old faith and strength.[40]

The Allahabad Session of 1910, with William Wedderburn as President, is significant for its attempted move in the direction of unity between the Congress and the Muslim League and efforts to reconcile the two wings of the Congress. It had become obvious that the Congress could not present an image of strength unless the two wings united to restore to the organization its former status, strength and representative character as the spokesman of all patriotic forces in the country, and to resume work among the masses. It is appropriate to reproduce here extracts from a letter written to *The Madras Standard* by its Allahabad Correspondent which reveals the state of public life at this period and the attitude of the politically oriented section to the Indian National Congress:[41]

> The break-up of public life that has followed the rigorous working of the new repressive Acts has led to complete demoralisation in portions of Bengal and the Central Provinces. Active public life has not only become impossible in them but also is positively dreaded because of the increase of police activities to which it leads. In one word, the Congress is the only avenue left in all India for the ventilation of just grievances, and this point is receiving greater and greater attention at the present moment

G.K. Gokhale and William Wedderburn, the President-elect of the Allahabad Congress made sincere efforts to achieve a rapprochement between the Muslims and the other communities and as well as between the Moderates and extremist Congressmen. Wedderburn sounded the watchwords of *'Hope'*, *'Conciliation'* and *'United Effort'*. He emphasized the identity of interest of all sections in India and appealed to the Extremists not to lose faith in constitutional agitation.[42] The session proposed some well-thought-out amendments of reforms announced by the government. The Congress saw in the existing system of separate electorates a strong divisive influence and demanded its abandonment before the next election. Very lengthy debates took place on the question of the council regulation and the Muslim leaders themselves admitted the disintegrating tendencies of the methods of election chosen by the government and they saw the imperialist game behind this move. The grievances of South African Indians and the partition of Bengal dominated the delegates' session.[43]

What came as a rude shock to the liberty-loving people of India and the Congress was the passing of the Indian Press Act of 1910 and the extension of the Seditious Meetings Act. The delegates criticized these invasions of the freedom of the people. This Act came in the wake of the introduction of the Morley-Minto Reforms. Speaking on the occasion of the inauguration of the reforms, Minto had said that he would 'no longer tolerate the revolutionary Press and that he was determined to restrain it'.[44]

In their anxiety to curtail terrorism and anarchist outrages, the government enacted one stringent measure after another to curb the liberties of the people. These became fetters affecting the rights and liberties of innocent citizens.

4. Moves towards Unity

The year 1911, after Lord Minto's retirement, saw one of the greatest changes in the annals of Indian history. The country witnessed in this year the pomp and splendour in connection with the visit to India of King & Emperor George V for his Coronation Durbar. The king's visit was marked by an announcement at the Delhi Durbar annulling the partition of Bengal. This pacified Bengal which had passed through seven years of sorrow and tribulation. The capital of India was shifted from Calcutta to Delhi to commemorate the king's visit. In an unusually pleasing atmosphere, the annual Congress Session met at Calcutta in 1911 under the presidentship of Pandit Bishen Narayan Dar. The nullification of the partition of Bengal dominated the Session. Bhupendra Nath Basu, Chairman of the Reception Committee observed:[45]

> From the Congress platform year after year, there went forth unqualified condemnation of the measure, and resolutions were passed praying the Government for its annulment or modification, a modification of the kind which has now been promised to us. That great wrong has now been remedied, that grievance has been redressed, and it is our duty, we men from other parts of India, not only to congratulate Bengal, but all of us.

The President criticized the bureaucracy for its policy of repression to curb the new spirit and the progressive forces that were gathering strength all over the country. He condemned the coercive measures and the Anglo-Indian opposition to Congress attempts at Hindu-Muslim unity. He disapproved and repudiated in strong terms the proposed communal representation in politics.[46]

The six Congress sessions since Surat had been marked by an atmosphere of chilliness and the absence of enthusiasm. They had been monotonous and the low key was marked by the decreasing number of delegates, which reached the lowest ever figure of 207 at Bankipur (Bihar) in 1912. Earlier, the attendance at the Convention Congress (1908) at Allahabad had also not been flattering. On the whole, the annual Congress meets had become humdrum affairs; routine, heavy and lacklustre affairs. The table below gives the number of delegates attending the Congress at Surat in 1907 and over the ten following years:

Surat	— 1907	— 1663
Madras	— 1908	— 626
Lahore	— 1909	— 243
Allahabad	— 1910	— 636
Calcutta	— 1911	— 446
Bankipur	— 1912	— 207
Karachi	— 1913	— 550
Madras	— 1914	— 866
Bombay	— 1915	— 2259
Lucknow	— 1916	— 2350
Calcutta	— 1917	— 4792

The Bankipur Session in 1912 was also a listless one. Nevertheless, with R. N. Mudholkar, the stalwart from Maharashtra presiding, and the great Muslim nationalist of Bihar, Mazhar-ul-Haque, as the Chairman of the Reception Committee, it was significant in one respect like the one that was to follow in Karachi the next year (1913). The significant feature was the large number of Muslim delegates that had deliberately attended the session. Their presence greatly enhanced the prestige and importance of the Indian National Congress as a national political organization. Mazhar-ul-Haque in a thought-provoking speech observed:[47] 'Already a great and powerful body of liberal Mussalmans had arisen, whose aims and ideas were the aims and ideas of the Indian National Congress. . . . And this was the party which was bound to lead in future, the Muslims of India.' It was at the Bankipur Session that Ibrahim Rahimtoola persuaded the Muslim League to accept the Congress ideal.

R.N. Mudholkar, presiding over the session, made a spirited speech expressing trust in the sympathetic attitude of the new Viceroy, Hardinge and hoping that this would lead to a relaxation in the Government's repression policies.

The Hindu-Muslim problem had assumed serious dimensions following the introduction of communal electorates under the 1909 reforms. These, as already mentioned, were created by the bureaucracy to keep the Muslims from joining the Congress. Various Congress sessions had, with utmost earnestness and sincerity, and with great tact, dealt with this question. Bankipur represented a distinct landmark in this respect. The President observed:[48]

> A highly objectionable feature of the present regulations in the matter of communal representation is the constitution of separate Mohammedan electorates. Gentlemen, in my opinion nothing is more calculated to retard the concord and harmony between Mohammedans and Hindus, to obstruct the intellectual and political advancement of the Mohammedans themselves, and the growth of a sturdy catholic public spirit and life among them than these water-tight compartments of separate electorates. The undesirability of these separate electorates is acknowledged by several of the leaders of the Mohammedan community, by some of those very persons who were elected to represent its interest in the Viceregal and Provincial Councils.

The most crucial resolution at Bankipur was the one concerning the hardships experienced by the Indians in South Africa. On the basis of a motion of G.K. Gokhale, who had been to South Africa to inquire into the grievances of the Indians there, the Congress adopted a resolution

> drawing attention to the position of Indians in South Africa and other British Colonies and urging that the system of indentured labour was undesirable and should be abolished, and called on the Government to prohibit further recruitment of Indian labour under contract of indenture whether for service at home or abroad.

In a moving speech, Gokhale described the insults and hardships which Indians in South Africa were subjected to and described the non-violent struggle organized and carried on by M.K. Gandhi and his companions. This form of struggle captured the imagination of all who heard about it. It was the precursor of the far greater passive resistance movement for Indian freedom which the country was destined to witness in the coming years. That struggle was to be waged under the auspices of the Congress with Mahatma Gandhi as its leader.

The Government of India, under the new Viceroy, Lord Hardinge, indicated a slight change in their attitude towards Indian aspirations by their Despatch on 25 August 1911 which announced provincial autonomy as the definite aim of the administration. The Congress session attached profound significance to this announcement. It put new hope into the hearts of the Congress leaders.

The 28th session of the Congress held at Karachi in 1913 was again somewhat routine in nature. Many of the senior leaders could not attend. Nevertheless, the session was memorable for the significant progress achieved in the direction of Hindu-Muslim unity. In the history of efforts at rapprochement, Karachi is an important milestone. It was presided over by Nawab Syed Muhammed Bahadur from Madras, a descendant of Tipu Sultan. His presidentship marked the beginning of a new relationship of amity and comradeship between the two communities. The President discussed at length the question of rapprochement between the two communities. The All India Muslim League, which since its foundation had kept aloof from the Congress and had in some measure shown hostility towards it, passed a resolution in this session accepting 'the Congress ideal of Self-Government' as their goal.[49] M.A. Jinnah actively participated in the deliberations. Nawab Syed Muhammed Bahadur noted this development with pleasure and the view expressed by leaders on both sides that they should meet periodically 'to find a *modus operandi* for joint and concerted action on all questions of national good'. He appealed for the unity of all communities in India and added: 'The tide of national unity . . . will surely sweep away in its majestic onward course the unnatural and artificial barriers of race, colour and religion'.[50]

> The Congress has from its very inception set before itself the ideal of a united Indian Nationality and has been consistently advocating the cause of the Indian people as a whole without being influenced by party or sectarian considerations incompatible with that high ideal. The changes that the country has undergone during the last one generation, that is since this organisation came into existence, are immense and the Congress, I think, may well take credit for bringing about not a few of them.

An important resolution was the one moved by Bhupendra Nath Basu welcoming the resolution of the Muslim League. 'The India of the future,' he said, 'will be a stronger, nobler, greater, . . . a brighter India than was revealed to Akbar in the wildest of his visions.' The 28th Congress was the forerunner of the Lucknow Pact and was symbolic of the Muslims' loyalty to the Congress that was to be displayed during the Non-cooperation days.

The major preoccupation of the Congress Session at Karachi was the question of the status of the Indians in South Africa. Gokhale devoted his attention to finding a permanent solution to the problem. During the discussion on the issue in the Subjects Committee, M.K. Gandhi's name and the heroic struggle carried on by him and his co-workers were frequently mentioned.[51] It was at that time that the epithet 'Mahatma' came to be associated with Gandhi's name. The Indian people were called upon by the Congress leaders to contribute funds to help the cause of Indians in South Africa.

Gokhale, despite his illness, pleaded the cause of the Indians in South Africa who had offered passive resistance in Natal. The struggle had come to a pause before the Congress met at Karachi. Gandhiji had been released in order to carry on negotiations with General Smuts at Pretoria. Lord Hardinge had expressed his sympathies with the Indian cause. In a classic statement at Madras, he expressed deep anguish and genuine sympathy for the Indian cause in South Africa:[52]

> They have violated, as they intended to violate, those laws, with full knowledge of the penalties involved, and ready with all courage and patience to endure those penalties. In all this they have the sympathy of India — deep and burning — and not only of India, but of all those who like myself, without being Indian themselves, have feelings of sympathy for the people of this country.

The 29th Congress held at Madras in 1914 was in many ways a distinct advance on previous Congresses. The number of delegates was the largest since Surat, but of the 866 delegates, 784 were from the Province of Madras itself. The increase in the number of delegates was due to the impact of war conditions, and more directly to a series of articles on the Congress published in *New India* edited by Mrs Annie Besant.

It was a common complaint that the Congress was only a 'grievance manufacturing machine' and the succession of articles in *New India* helped it overcome much of lifelessness and lethargy into which it had sunk since Surat.

There were certain persons at the Madras Congress who were obsessed with the war. The bureaucracy had warned that no matters that might embarrass the government should be raised there. In fact, their object was to see that the Congress did not meet. It was this that led the Muslim League to abandon the idea of holding its annual session in 1914. But the articles in *New India,* mostly by eminent men, focussed national feeling, a vigorous propaganda was kept up in the press of Bengal and Madras, emphasizing the need to continue the series of annual sessions of the Congress unbroken, and the importance of examining Indian questions in the light of the prevailing situation and the outbreak of the World War.

S. Subramania Iyer, the Chairman of the Reception Committee, justified the holding of the Congress session and stated that 'if they had not met in the Congress they would have lost a golden opportunity of giving expression in their united capacity as Congressmen, to their unswerving devotion and attachment to the King Emperor'.[53]

The Congress met under the Presidentship of Mr Bhupendra Nath Basu. It is important to note that, in his presidential declaration,[54] he stated that what was wanted was neither separation from nor subordination to Britain, but a 'Joint Partnership' on equal terms. The idea of 'Joint Partnership' was a distinctive advance from the imperial to the federal ideal and was due to the wider vista opened out by the War. For the first time a resolution of the Congress session did not speak of 'loyalty to British rule', as in the past, but of 'allegiance to the British connection', a change most significant and far-reaching. Among the earliest resolutions passed at the session was one expressing 'profound devotion to the Throne' and 'unswerving allegiance to the British connection', and a 'firm resolve to stand by the Empire at all hazards and at all costs'.[55]

5. Annie Besant and 'Home Rule'

The chief resolution of the Session was the one on Self-Government moved by Surendranath Banerjea and supported by Mrs Annie Besant. The resolution demanded self-government in clear terms:

> In view of the profound and avowed loyalty that the people of India have manifested in the present crisis, the resolution called upon the Government to remove all invidious distinctions between the Indian and other subjects of the King Emperor's British Empire.[55a]

Further the resolution called upon the government

> to give effect to the Despatch of 25th August 1911, proclaiming Provincial Autonomy as the Government's aim and redeem its pledge.

Surendranath appealed to Congressmen to formulate a scheme for the purpose. Mrs Besant supported the resolution and exhorted the younger men to practise the art of government in the local bodies. The resolution was a distinct and momentous advance, and in this lay the importance of the Madras Congress of 1914. The absence of Pherozeshah Mehta, Gokhale and Pandit Madan Mohan Malaviya in the Session left a sad gap in the ranks of leaders usually adorning the dais. Gokhale was then laid-up with a heart ailment to which he succumbed two months later, in February 1915. But the absence of these stalwarts at what was certainly an important session of the Congress was amply compensated for by the presence of Mrs Besant. Not many realized then the significance of her participation. Within a few months, she was destined to capture the imagination of India by holding aloft the banner of Home Rule and sounding its battle cry. Those present at the session long remembered the enthusiastic greetings with which she was welcomed. None in that Congress spoke as forcefully as she did. The President of the Session, Bhupendra Nath Basu, made a fitting reference to Mrs Besant amidst loud applause while welcoming her to the Congress. He conveyed thanks to the venerable old lady who had joined the cause which she had made hers and 'had brought to it so much of her wisdom, energy and ardour'. She was henceforth to be a potent factor in the fortunes of the Congress, and her personality was very closely bound up with the subsequent politics of the country. It is impossible to proceed further without a digression to describe Mrs Besant's talents, capacity and character. As Pattabhi Sitaramayya wrote in his pioneering history:

> She brought new ideas, new talents, new resources and altogether a new method of organisation and new outlook into the field of the Congress. She was already a great world character and had millions of followers in the East and in the West.[55b]

She was a dominating figure. A great orator of her times, Mrs Besant belonged to a restless and eager generation. A gifted organizer, she was to involve Congressmen deeply in the Home Rule Movement. With her immense following and with her inexhaustible energy, she gave new direction and new life to Indian politics.

The 29th Congress may thus be considered significant in that Mrs Besant demonstrated India's worthiness for freedom and asked the Congress to formulate a definite scheme of Self-Government to present to England after the War. This was the task that Mrs Besant herself took up after she appealed to the country to secure India's place in the readjustment that was to follow the termination of the War. She exercised all her influence on the Congress Committee to deliberate, discuss and formulate the scheme of Self-Government. Of the many schemes which were prepared by the Congress Committees for discussion by the All-India Congress Committee, the one sent by Madras was the best planned and the most perfect. The Madras Congress Committee discussed the subject most thoroughly and no one had a greater share in the moulding of the scheme than Mrs Besant.

Through a resolution, the Congress recorded its warm appreciation of and admiration for the heroic endeavours of Gandhiji and his followers and their unparalleled sacrifice in their struggle for the maintenance of the self-respect of India and the redressal of Indian grievances.

The War was to give rise to new conditions and unleash new forces and their impact on India was profound as immense possibilities unfolded themselves. India had to organize herself to articulate her views, before the psychological moment had passed.

After the Madras Session, there were rapid developments. Mrs Besant had already entered the Indian political arena and was to set the pace for agitational activities through the Home Rule League. The Madras Session was the prologue of the new and epilogue of the old era.

6. Impact of First World War

The declaration of War by England on Germany in August 1914 had its impact on the Indian political scene. It opened a new chapter in the history of the Congress. One significant change that occurred was the co-operation and fellowship among the different units of the British Empire. The racial arrogance and colour prejudices of the rulers received a setback. India was automatically drawn into the war on the side of the Allies. The war widened the horizons of both India and England and their angles of vision appeared to have changed. It made the Indian people conscious of their position and as well as their responsibility as a distinct national unit.

What was India to do? In the complex world situation no nation could remain isolated. The other major British colonies were ethnically and culturally bound to England by many ties — especially a tie of racial concatenation. But Indians were an alien people administered by a bureaucracy they distrusted. The bureaucracy always saw sedition in every movement of Indian youth. In the name of quelling the revolutionary forces of 'Indian unrest' which had been active since the partition days, the Minto regime had unleashed severe measures of repression. Action under a virtually defunct regulation of 1818 and the arrests and deportations without trial of political leaders were the darker aspect of the picture which no patriotic Indian was prepared to forget or ignore, in spite of the War.

But still, India acted with dignity and magnanimity. Gandhiji who arrived in London from South Africa a few weeks before the War broke out, observed, 'India would do her duty'. In a letter to the Secretary of State for India, Gandhiji offered to take up active service during the War. He wrote:

> It was thought desirable by many of us that during the crisis that has overtaken the Empire and whilst many Englishmen, leaving their ordinary vocation, in life, are responding to the Imperial call, those Indians who are residing in the United Kingdom and who can also do so should place themselves unconditionally at the disposal of the authorities.

'Gandhiji became the self-appointed recruiting sergeant for the army.'

On the eve of the outbreak of War, a deputation of Congressmen consisting of B.N. Basu, M.A. Jinnah, Lajpat Rai, N.M. Samarth,

B.N. Sarma and S. Sinha, alongwith other prominent Indians, addressed a letter to the Secretary of State for India for submission to the King. 'We have not the slightest doubt,' the letter stated,

> that, as on previous occasions when the British forces were engaged in defending the interests of the Empire, soon the princes and peoples of India will readily and willingly co-operate to the best of their ability and afford opportunities of securing that end by placing the resources of their country at His Majesty's disposal.

The Indian National Congress meeting at Madras in December 1914, under the Presidentship of Bhupendra Nath Basu, expressed similar sentiments. One of the first resolutions passed expressed, 'its profound devotion to the Throne', 'its unswerving allegiance to the British Connection and its firm resolve to stand by the Empire at all hazards and at all costs'.[56] India contributed splendidly to the War efforts. The Indian Government with the loyal consent of the people despatched expeditiously forces to the War front. India's part was big.[57] India contributed £ 100 million sterling to the expenses of the War.[57] Lord Hardinge trusted the Indian people. In despatching the Indian Expeditionary Forces to the front, he put the warriors of India alongside the best of Europe. The Indian troops fought on the fields of France and Flanders, the deserts of Mesopotamia, in Africa and on the shores of Gallipoli and other theatres of War. The blood of Indian soldiers mingled with that of Englishmen in the comradeship of death. Nearly a million Indian soldiers fought in the War and, according to one computation, 36,696 Indians died in the various theatres of War.[58]

> The Indian Muhammadan troops fought against the Turks valiantly without reservation, though the Muslims were against the War. Several Indian Princes made large contribution of men (troops) and more, for the War. They themselves served personally in War theatres of France and Flanders. Besides ambulances, hospital ships were subscribed. The first hospital ship was from Madras. Supply of food stuff, mill goods from Indian Cotton Mills, large quantity of timber for laying Railway lines and ship building followed. India provided ammunition and other War requirements. The reaction in England was marvellous. The English were surprised at the splendid manner in which the Indians rallied to their cause by fighting in defence of the Empire.[59]

The Times, a journal that always harboured rancour and animosity towards Indian aspirations, changed its tone and talked of the ushering in of a new era. It observed, 'On our part when we have settled account with the enemy, India must be allowed a more ample place in the Councils of the Empire.'

B.G. Tilak, preoccupied as he was with his activities, negotiations, and conferences with Congress leaders regarding his re-entry into the Indian National Congress, lost no time in declaring Indian loyalty to the British Throne and the desire to support the Government in the great hour of crisis, when England had been compelled by the actions of Germany to take up arms. He wrote in the *Mahratta*:[60]

> At such crisis, I firmly hold that the duty of every Indian, be he great or small, rich or poor, is to support and assist His Majesty's Government, to the best of his ability. No time in my opinion should be lost in convening of public meetings of all parties, classes and sections in Poona, as they have been elsewhere to give an emphatic expression to the same. It requires hardly any precedent to support such a course.

Tilak further added:

> The present crisis in my opinion is a blessing in disguise, in as much as it had universally evoked an united feeling and sentiments of loyalty to the Throne.

The World War brought about tremendous changes in the country. The political principles for which Great Britain and her allies fought Germany evoked unprecedented enthusiasm and a yearning for political liberty in the Indian mind.

The Indian Nationalists were emboldened by the Irish rebellion. The Muslims were concerned about the Caliph and the Turks. The Extremists gathered strength under the leadership of Tilak and the Indian National Congress began to swing towards the Extremist line. Thus nationalist politics took a radical turn.

India's emergence on the international arena attracted the notice of the rest of the Empire. Keen observers of the Indian situation called for a change in the 'angle of vision', in their perspective, of the Indian problem. The Indian contribution to the war effort in terms of men, money and other resources was tremendous. The Government was urged to take cognisance of the situation and placate Indian feelings in a suitable manner.

The War created a new awakening and self-consciousness among the Indians. It imparted a sense of self-confidence among the Indian people and demonstrated the importance of India for the British Empire. It thus materially advanced India's claim to Self-Government.

In the face of the world crisis, the need for unity was being felt in the country. There had already been a move to effect Hindu-Muslim unity and rapprochement between the All India Muslim League and the

Indian National Congress was on the agenda. Simultaneously, efforts for unity within the Congress were intensified.

The year 1914 is significant in the history of the Congress, dividing the period of stress and strain and ushering in the era of changes that were to follow. It may be termed the end of an era. As 1914 dawned, political life and public activities were at their lowest ebb. Indian political life smacked a stagnant pool; there was very little activity from the Congress platform between annual sessions.

Efforts towards reunion of the two wings of the Congress snowballed with Tilak's release. Mrs Besant had joined the Congress and had begun to activize the Congress Committees that were defunct. With Madras as her base, she devoted herself to rejuvenating the Indian National Congress. Her first and foremost mission was to unify the Moderates and the Extremists.

Tilak was released from Mandalay in June 1914. After his return he too began to work for Congress unity and his re-entry into Congress. Realizing that a united Congress was the need of the hour, Tilak involved himself in a series of parleys in October and November that year. It was all set that the Nationalists would attend the Congress Session at Madras in December 1914 and there was hardly any time to lose. Mrs Besant took the initiative for negotiations. She realized the impact the War was to make on the Indian political situation and wished for a unified and strong Congress to utilize that situation to demand Home Rule for India. She also desired that the Hindus and Mussalmans make a reappraisal of their respective positions and work together instead of through separate organizations.

Mrs Besant and the General Secretary of the AICC, N. Subba Rao of Madras, went to Bombay at Gokhale's suggestion. They met Gokhale and also held discussions with Tilak and Moderate leaders like Sir Pherozeshah Mehta. A series of parleys took place. Tilak expressed his ardent desire for unity in the interest of India's political progress. It was not the creed of the Congress that disturbed Tilak. He did not relish the method and approach of the then leadership and the inactivity of the Congress. But the inveterate opposition of Sir Pherozeshah Mehta irritated him. The compromise effort stalled. The electoral procedure that the convention and the Congress constitution prescribed for the election of delegates to the AICC session, especially Article X of the Congress constitution, created a practical difficulty for a Nationalist re-entry.

The most encouraging factor at that time was that the release of B.G. Tilak heralded a revival of the political life in Western India, especially in Maharashtra. Nationalist activities soon gathered momentum. Tilak and his followers dedicatedly addressed themselves to the task of organizing the Home Rule League. His acceptance of the ideal of Home Rule was an indication of a major step towards compromise between the two wings of the national movement on the issue of self-government for India. He wrote a series of articles on the Home Rule idea in *Kesari* on the eve of the Bombay Congress and suggested that the World War, in which India was helping Britain's War effort, was an appropriate time for India to demand Home Rule.

Tilak was impatient. He could not bear to wait till his readmission was formalized. He inaugurated his branch of the Home Rule League on 28 April 1916 and confined his area of operation to Maharashtra and Karnataka, leaving the rest of India to Mrs Besant's charge. Both roused the Congressmen to activity. The demand for Home Rule began to be pronounced more keenly from Congress platforms.

The year 1915 was destined to be the beginning of a new era in the history of the Congress, or perhaps the prelude to that new era. As the War prolonged, India's importance to the British Empire was becoming obvious. Her contribution to the War effort had become a topic of discussion and her share of the burden was far greater than that of any other unit of the British Empire. Inspired as they were by freshly enthused self-confidence, the Indians realized how indispensable their help and support was for the British Empire.

In this period the Congress lost two of its ablest leaders, G.K. Gokhale and Sir Pherozeshah Mehta. February 1915 saw the demise of the former. It was a great blow to the Congress organization. Thirty years of strenuous political life and absolute dedication to the country's cause had made him the idol of the nation. At a time when his mature wisdom and understanding of political question were most needed, he was snatched away by the cruel hand of death. The entire nation mourned his death and felt desolate. Within few months of this calamity, another of India's stalwarts and a giant among men, P.M. Mehta, expired in November 1915. The death of these two outstanding leaders, who had played no small part in nurturing and developing the national movement, left a great void in the Congress. This period was also marked by the death of another stalwart, Sir Henry Cotton, who had been actively associated with the nationalist movement since its formative years.

The prolonging of the war naturally increased the hardships of the common people. The Defence of India Act was in operation. The government had assumed special powers under it to control all aspects of life. Political repression added to the sufferings of the people.

Public activity had become well-nigh impossible in India in 1914-15. Political workers were prosecuted on the slightest pretext. There were growing symptoms of discontent in the country. Prosecutions were to follow in intensified form in the post-war years. Maulana Mohammed Ali and Shaukat Ali, known as the 'Ali Brothers', were interned. The country once again witnessed a period of discontent. The Lahore Conspiracy Case (1909-15) dragged on. Ominous clouds loomed large. The situation was such as to inspire hardly any hope. The only silver lining was Mrs Besant's efforts to activize the Congress. She left for Bombay on the eve of the 30th session to enlist the support of the Congress leaders for her Home Rule League.

7. Bombay Congress, 1915

It was against this background that the Congress assembled in Bombay in December 1915 for its 30th annual Session. In many respects, the Bombay Session was remarkable. The agenda was quite heavy. The problem of reunion of the Congress was before the session. The propriety of starting the Home Rule League was another issue. The Muslim League was to meet simultaneously, alongside the Congress Session, to evolve a joint plan of action with the Congress for drafting a reform scheme. All this made the 30th Session of the National Congress at Bombay momentous in the annals of Indian political life. The country looked to it with high expectations and 2,259 delegates converged from all parts of India to attend it. The assembled visitors were estimated at 15,000. The Session was important for the unity it marked between Hindus and Muslims and the Moderates and Extremists. As the Congress met, with Sir Satyendra Prasanna in the chair, so far as the bulk of delegates was concerned, it was a Home Rule Congress, throbbing with life and energy. The President, however, disappointed these delegates: the emphasis on Self-Government was not pronounced in his speech, which was out of tune with the prevailing trend.

The delegates looked forward to Mrs Besant starting the Home Rule League. The younger generation of politicians craved for sustained political activity. On the eve of the Bombay Session, Mrs Besant had convened a conference of her adherents to discuss the Home Rule programme. Senior leaders like S. Banerjea and Pandit Madan Mohan Malaviya discouraged the proposal. The objects and constitution of the proposed Home Rule League had already been published in Mrs Besant's *New India*.

But the leadership of the Congress at the Bombay Session decided that Congress must itself take up the question of Self-Government for India and popularize it by educative and propagandist work. It was felt that the Congress which had laboured hard for thirty years through storm and stress and had withstood many an onslaught, should continue with that work and not delegate it to a newborn association, however strong, better mobilized and loyal, even subordinated, to the Congress. Still, it was widely felt by a segment of Congressmen that, however excellent the annual sessions of the Congress had been, it had failed in these years to engage in healthy and vigorous political activity. The absence of sustained and continued political activities from the Congress platform between the annual meets was much regretted by the young and rising generation of political workers.

Mrs Besant, as a member of the AICC, was prepared to abide by the ruling of the High Command. She would give up her venture if the Congress so desired, though she had come fully prepared to start the Home Rule League. She made it clear that the Home Rule Movement was not antagonistic to the Congress but was intended to break the static and routine functioning of the Congress and to impart dynamism to it.

Mrs Besant appealed to the Congress to concentrate all its energy and efforts on this one question of Home Rule instead of dissipating them over various resolutions moved again and again in nearly identical form. She was instrumental in making the Congress adopt, in the Bombay Session, a resolution approving in principle the necessity for the establishment of the Home Rule League in India. The National Congress openly accepted Self-Government as an immediate problem and the need to use its resources and organization to attain that end. The Congress leaders solemnly agreed to undertake all efforts necessary to undertake all that the Home Rule League had proposed to do. The spirit of compromise being one of her strongest traits, Mrs Besant suspended her proposal, though her followers insisted that she should go ahead with it. The Congress at Bombay had become, in the words of Dadabhai Naoroji, 'the Home Rule Congress' through its famous resolution on Self-Government.[61] This resolution on Self-Government was the main political resolution of the session. It categorically stated that 'the time had arrived to introduce further and substantial measures of reform towards the attainment of Self-Government.' The word 'Self-Government' was a specific, not a vague term, unlike those used hitherto. The resolution demanded among other things:

(a) The introduction of Provincial Autonomy including financial independence.
(b) Expansion and reform of the Legislative Councils so as to make them truly and adequately representative of all sections of the people and to give them an effective control over the acts of the Executive Government.
(c) The reconstitution of the various existing Executive Councils and the establishment of similar Executive Councils in Provinces where they do not exist;

(d) The reform or the abolition of the Council of the Secretary of State for India.
(e) Establishment of Legislative Councils in Provinces where they do not now exist;
(f) The readjustment of the relations between the Secretary of State for India and the Government of India; and
(g) A liberal measure of local Self-Government.

The Resolution also authorized the All India Congress Committee to frame a scheme of reform and a programme of continuous work — educative and propagandist — on the basis of the principles embodied in this resolution. The Congress Committee was further authorized to confer with a similar Committee that might be appointed by the All India Muslim League for the same purpose and to take necessary steps and submit its report on or before 1 September 1916 to the General Secretaries of the AICC who should circulate it to the different Provincial Congress Committees as early as possible.

Mrs Besant, who seconded the resolution, described it as the most momentous that had ever been adopted by the Indian National Congress in the thirty years of its history.

The Bombay Session made another departure by demanding, through a resolution, complete fiscal independence for India, with special reference to import and export and excise duties to be conceded to the Government of India.

8. Hindu-Muslim Unity

The Bombay Congress was also significant as it marked the beginning of great fraternization between Hindus and Muslims. Subsequent events revealed that the unity between the two political parties could be real. When Mazhar-ul-Haque arrived in Bombay, the leaders of the Indian National Congress were present to receive him. Likewise, the leaders of the Muslim League assembled in large numbers to receive Sir S.P. Sinha, the President-elect of the Congress Session. The Muslim volunteers joined those of the Congress to escort the president in procession. Some of the prominent leaders of the Congress attended the session of the Muslim League that was being held simultaneously at Bombay. The leaders of the Muslim League reciprocated by participating in the Congress Session. The League leaders were received with warmth at the Congress pavilion. It was a manifestation of warmth, cordiality and perfect understanding between the two major communities in the interests of India's future. That it was a spectacle of Hindu and Muslim unity is confirmed by the following:[62]

> The fact that the All India Muslim League was to meet — for the first time in the history of the body — at the same place at which the Congress was to meet and the opportunity that the event afforded for cordiality between Hindus and Mohammedans and for cordial co-operation between that body and the Indian National Congress for the promotion of their common political aspirations, attracted to Bombay a large number of members of both the bodies from the different Provinces. For the first time also in the history of the Congress, the representatives of the All India Muslim League attended the Congress Pandal in front of the Congress delegates and were received by the vast assemblage with hearty applause and enthusiastic manifestations of cordiality as they entered the Pandal and took their seats in the prominent place reserved for them.

What was striking was the realization on the part of Muslims that they must throw in their lot with the nationalist forces like the Congress in order to challenge the imperial power. The Muslim League appointed a committee to formulate a scheme for self-government in consultation with other political bodies. This committee was to confer with a similar Committee appointed by the Indian National Congress on the basis of its political resolution.

The intra-Congress division was discussed and a mutually satisfactory solution was found. The Nationalists (or Extremists) had already made up their mind to return to the Congress fold; on the platform of self-government both had already mingled and begun to press for self-government.

Since the surat split, the Nationalists had courageously faced the repression unleashed by the bureaucracy against the Extremists and the revolutionary movements. It was not as though there had been no desire or efforts for unity during the eight years that had elapsed since the Surat episode. The Moderates in Bengal (even leaders like Bhupendra Nath Basu), Punjab and other regions had strained every nerve to achieve unity. Acrimony and bad temper apart, there had been moments of friendly gesture on the part of both the sections.

In the Bombay Session it had become clear that a united Congress was a reality. The creed of the Congress was intact and the acceptance of it was an essentiality for participation in the Congress activities. But Article XX of the Congress Constitution was suitably modified to satisfy the Extremists. The union was cemented.[63] It was expected that in 1914 itself the Madras Congress Session would see a united Congress; but the credit was to go to the Congress at Bombay in December 1915. Even in Bombay, it was too late for Extremist delegates to enter and participate in the session; but they participated fully at Lucknow in December 1916.

Writing in *New India* (31 December 1915) Mrs Besant observed:

> A matter of great rejoicing is the closing of the breach between the two wings of the National party and the declaration that it is not necessary that a delegate should be a member of a Congress Committee in order that he should be elected — thus forbidding any unfair order such as the one by the Bombay Provincial Congress in order to shut out people they disliked. We shall have a united Congress at Lucknow — the first since the Surat split; the wound has been healed and what Madras began Bombay has completed. Let us now all work together for the common motherland and be rivals only in devotion to her.

The Bombay Congress laid the foundation for the new era. The air of monotony and the state of depression that enveloped the Congress was over. The resolution presented under the title 'Self-Government', was a momentous one. The decision to frame a scheme of reform and a programme of sustained activity, educational and propagandist, was another major stride in the direction of progress. The conference with the Muslim League Committee was the most hopeful of all. The first of September was the date fixed as the deadline for Mrs Besant to start the Home Rule League, if, by then, the Congress had not already taken up the tasks outlined in the Home Rule resolution.

The AICC continued its work on the basis of the Bombay resolution and a reform scheme was drawn up. Conferences were held with the Muslim League and, after prolonged discussion between the two bodies, the famous Congress-League Scheme was adopted. It envisaged quite a substantial measure of self-government. Never before was witnessed a spirit of compromise to match that which pervaded the conference. The proposal was to be placed before the Lucknow Session of the Indian National Congress in December 1916 as the main political resolution.

In 1916, when the agitation for Home Rule was raging in the country, at the initiative of C. Sankaran Nair, the Member for Education in the Viceroy's Council, nineteen members of the Imperial Legislative Council submitted a memorandum with proposals for post-war reforms in India. These had been drafted in the light of the discussions all over the country. It was despatched to the Secretary of State for India. The memorandum rightly summed up what India wanted: 'What is required is not merely good Government or efficient administration but Government that is responsible to the people, because it is responsible to them.'

The bureaucracy was highly critical of the Memorandum of the Nineteen; they accused it of 'hasty draftsmanship and faulty logic'. This act of the Central Legislators angered the authorities. Referring to the recommendation of the Memorandum of the Nineteen, the British Government characterized them as catastrophic and embodying revolutionary proposals, constituting danger to India *(Wednesday Review,* 18 October

1916). The bureaucracy believed that the move was German-inspired and ordered severe repressive measures.

The Government sent out a secret circular laying down the policy line to be pursued for curbing popular agitation for self-government. The utterances and attitude of the authorities well reflected their mood and irritation. Sir Michael O'Dwyer, Lieutenant Governor of the Punjab, and Lord Pentland, Governor of Madras Presidency, did not mince matters. They warned the Indian people against high expectations in matters of political reform.

The suppression of the Home Rule Movement, the internment of Mrs Besant and two of her colleagues, and the externment of B. G. Tilak and B. C. Pal from the regions of Punjab and Delhi are indications of how the government had prepared themselves to put down the agitation.

The Lucknow Congress of 1916 was not only a memorable event but also a historic one in many respects. Ambica Charan Mazumdar was President. During the boycott days, the British bureaucracy had called him a 'notorious misleader of students and youths'. The Nationalist Congressmen desired that Mrs Besant should preside over the session but she was to be the choice for the very next year, for the 32nd session to be held at Calcutta in December 1917. The practice of holding simultaneous sessions of the Congress and the League in the same city which had been inaugurated the previous year in Bombay (1915) was continued in Lucknow.

An unusual reaction was anticipated from the authorities. Suddenly the bureaucracy in UP issued a warning to the Reception Committee of the Lucknow Congress against speeches of a seditious nature in the AICC Session. A copy of the letter was also served on the president. Both the President and the Reception Committee treated the warning with the contempt it deserved. Mrs Besant was already under the orders of externment from Berar and Bombay.

The Session at Lucknow commenced its sitting on 26 December 1916. It turned out to be an epoch-making one. Events in 1916 which have been narrated earlier had made the Congress a truly national and united body. The Lucknow Session attracted a splendid gathering and marked a record attendance of delegates. There were 2,298 delegates and ultimately it was claimed that there were as many as 2,500. About 4,000 visitors, including 500 women, were present. It is significant to observe here that most of the delegates were below 35. This clear indication of the new era was discernible in the session. It was the Congress of the young in age and the young in spirit; it was the Congress for Swaraj. After a decade of disunity, the two wings stood shoulder to shoulder to voice India's determination to be great and free. Hindus and Muslims realized for the first time that their ideals were 'indivisible and identical'. Speaking in the Congress camp, B.G. Tilak said:[64]

> I am glad to say that I have lived these ten years to see that we are going to put our voices and shoulders together to push the theme of Self-Government. Not only have we lived to see the differences of Hindus and Muslims closed as well. So we have now united in every way in the United Provinces and we have found that *luck in Lucknow.*

The utterances of the Muslim leaders were equally forceful and joyous. Mazhar-ul-Haque of the Muslim League said:

> All my political life I have been of this opinion that our Motherland cannot advance without the unity of the Hindus and the Muslims and that has been achieved today in the town of Lucknow.

The Congress President, Ambica Charan Mazumdar, observed:

> If the United Congress was buried nine years ago in the debris of the old French garden at Surat, it was reborn that day in the Kaiserbagh at Lucknow. Both the wings of the Indian Nationalist Party had come together and had realised their true position and responsibility. So long as there were honesty of motive and singleness of purpose the widest divergence of opinion need not frighten them.

Tilak and Mrs Besant contributed in no small measure to making the Lucknow Congress a success. It was truly a National conference of Moderates, Extremists and the Home Rulers. G.S. Arundale, the Organizing Secretary of the All India Home Rule League of Mrs Besant, appealed to every member of the Muslim League to get himself elected as delegate to the Congress session and ensure that the Lucknow Congress was committed to Home Rule. Both in the open session and in the Subjects Committee, the Home Rulers were in a majority. Tilak organized 'Congress Special' trains to enable the delegates from Maharashtra to attend the session. This became the practice for subsequent sessions. After quite a long break there was a record gathering of Congress leaders in the session, including Pal, Tilak, Malaviya, Mrs Besant, Sarojini Naidu and S. Banerjea.

The World War had changed the Indian political scene and the outlook of Indians. The old thinking was yielding place to new. The Moderates too appeared to have broadened their outlook. The presidential address was a stirring appeal to Congressmen to take advantage of the new situation and the new spirit prevailing in the country. While referring to this new spirit the president categorically stated that 'the system of Government that Britain had given to India had become obsolete'. He observed that:[65]

> the Indians were no longer willing to wait for the British to grant them Self-Government. The new spirit that had arisen in the country was the manifestation of democratic force transforming the old world into a new order of things. It was no longer the question of fitness for reforms. India must govern herself.

This was well manifested in the resolution of Self-Government adopted by this historic Congress session. It was based on the reforms scheme evolved jointly by the Congress and Muslim League, as called for by the Bombay Session.

Many other resolutions were moved in the session and some were of extraordinary interest. The Press Act Resolution was moved by B.G. Horniman, the stalwart English friend of India and gifted editor of the *Bombay Chronicle*. The Patna University Bill Resolution was moved by Principal Paranjpe and the one on National Education was moved by Mr G.S. Arundale. Lucknow was also the first Congress to protest against the lawless use of the Defence of India Act. Mrs Sarojini Naidu was one of the speakers on the Arms Act Resolution, raising her voice she pleaded

> that in view of the brave deeds of India's martyred sons in the War and India's splendid response to Britain's need in her great hour of crisis, the right to bear arms be restored to the Indians.

The most significant resolution at Lucknow was the one on Self-Government. Speakers on the subject were listened to with rapt attention. The best speakers and the foremost leaders of all schools and communities expounded the great subject and articulated the feelings of India. One whole day was dedicated to it. The resolution was unique in its contents and approach. It observed:[66]

(a) the great communities of India are the inheritors of ancient civilisations and have shown great capacity for Government and administration and to the progress in education and public spirit made by them during a century of British rule, and further having regard to the fact that the present system of Government does not satisfy the legitimate aspirations of the people and has become unsuited to the existing conditions and requirements, this Congress is of opinion that the time has come for His Majesty, the King-Emperor to issue a proclamation, announcing that it is the aim and intention of British policy to confer Self-Government on India at an early date.

(b) The resolution further demanded that 'a definite step should be taken towards Self-Government by granting the reforms contained in the scheme prepared by the All India Congress Committee in concert with the Reforms Committee appointed by the All India Muslim League'.

(c) That in the reconstruction of the Empire India shall be lifted from the position of a dependency to that of an equal partner in the Empire with the self-governing Dominions.

The statement that 'the time had arrived for the attainment of the freedom' was no longer a mere statement. A detailed and definite scheme of reforms was now being demanded by elected representatives of the Hindu and Muslim communities with the support of the entire country. The Moderates and Extremists buried deep their differences and old distinctions of moderation and extremism, stood united on the common platform of the Indian National Congress and, with Parsis and Muslims, offered the strength of their support to the Congress-League Scheme of reforms. Speaking about the scheme, Tilak obsrved:[67]

> I do not care to call it by any name. I do not mind the name but I believe you have hardly realised the importance and character of that Scheme or Reform. Let me tell you that it is far more liberal than the Irish Home Rule Bill and then you can understand what possibilities it carries. It may not be complete Self-Government. It may not be Swaraj in the wider sense of the word but it is far better than Swadeshi and Boycott. It is in fact a synthesis of all the Congress resolutions passed during the last thirty years, a synthesis which will help us all to proceed in a definite and responsible manner. We cannot now afford to spend our energy on all the resolutions on the public services, the Arms Act and others. All is comprehended and included in this one resolution.

The resolution was moved by Babu Surendranath Banerjea with his usual eloquence. Referring to the warning of Lord Chelmsford that 'revolutionary tendencies should be guarded against', the mover said:

> We are the friends of reforms because it is the surest safeguard against revolution. All history proclaims the truth that reforms indefinitely postponed or tardily carried out, are inadequate in their scope and comprehension, prepare the ground for revolutionary propaganda. God grant that this blunder may not be committed in India.

Mrs Besant seconded the resolution and made a moving speech.

The leaders of the Congress who spoke on this historic resolution in the Lucknow Session of the Indian National Congress included, besides the President, A.C. Mazumdar, Tilak, Surendranath Banerjea, B.C. Pal, Dr Besant, Joseph Baptista, Pandit M.M. Malaviya, Mazhar-ul-Haque, C.P. Ramaswamy Iyer, Sir Dinshaw Petit, Sarojini Naidu, Tej Bahadur Sapru and many more stalwarts of Indian political life.

The reforms proposal thus evolved and adopted at Lucknow demanded self-government as an inalienable right and no longer as a reward for proven loyalty; nor was it demanded on the grounds that the country was now mature enough for it.

Indian self-government was thus no longer urged as a long-term goal, a far-off vision. Delegates from all parts of India had flocked to Lucknow to acclaim it. The Congress had been revitalized by the enthusiasm generated by the simple but forceful cry of Home Rule.

9. The Home Rule Movement

Immediately after the Lucknow Congress, home rule activities were intensified by both Tilak and Mrs Besant who undertook tours of different regions. They drew large crowds even in small towns. The government could not but sense the new strength behind the resolution on self-government. The Indian National Congress and the Muslim League had entered into a pact (Lucknow Pact) in December 1916 and this spelled imminent danger to the government which saw in it a threat to the untrammeled power enjoyed by the bureaucracy. Indian political aspirations were taking definite shape.

The government had begun to make free use of its powers of internment under the Defence of India Rules. There was an organized drive against revolutionary activities based on extensive use of powers of internment without trial and a free use of the infamous Regulation of 1818. There was also increased political repression all round.

The year 1916 was important in many respects in the history of the Congress. It saw the reunification of the Congress and the establishment of the Home Rule League. The Congress grew in strength and influence. The Congress and the Muslim League united on the platform of self-government to fight the common foe — British Imperialism. One big hurdle in the way of Indian political advancement had been communal differences. In 1916 the two great communities — the Hindus and the Muslims — had freely made friendly adjustments among themselves — which augured well for the forthcoming political struggle.

The events leading to the Lucknow Pact need to be examined. The call for an inter-community understanding came from the annual Congress sessions at Bankipur (1912) and Karachi (1913). Since 1911 a perceptible change was seen in the western-educated Muslim's attitude to India's internal situation. These educated, middle-class Muslims with progressive ideas were alienated from the British. The rich elements representing the landed aristocracy alone were loyal to the government on which they depended for their status and security. There were several reasons for the shift in the attitude of Muslims with modern education. The British had not cared to consult the Muslims concerning the annulment of the partition of Bengal announced at the Coronation Durbar in 1911. This irritated educated Muslims.

A more significant and a far more important factor was the policy of the British towards the Muslim states in the Middle East. In this period

European states like France, Italy, the Balkan states and Russia were pursuing a policy of aggression against and encroachment upon the Islamic states, more or less in alliance with Britain. Many Muslim states lost their independence during the Balkan War of 1912-13. The Triple Entente of Britain, France and Russia had supported the Balkan states' attack on Turkey. Turkey's defeat and the plight of the Muslim countries and their exposure to aggression by the European powers shocked Indian Muslims. Germany was sympathetic to the Muslim cause. The Turks were keen to fight on the side of the Germans when the World War broke out immediately after the Balkan War.

10. A New Muslim Leadership

Educated middle-class Muslims deeply hurt by the march of events, felt that Britain was responsible for the collapse of the Islamic states. They were greatly alarmed at the calamity facing the Muslim brotherhood and they realized as never before that it would be folly to depend on the imperialists to look after Muslim interests in India. In this situation, the Muslim League could no longer pursue their old line of loyalty to the British.

The old leadership of landlords and aristocracy withdrew and the Muslim League came under the influence of a more dynamic and educated middle-class leadership under M.A. Jinnah and others. Nationalist Muslim leaders like Maulana Abul Kalam Azad and Mohammad Ali through their papers *Al Hilal* and *Comrade* roused the Muslim population in India. This development, while alienating the Indian Muslims from the British, drew them closer to the National Congress. Under the new leadership, the Muslims, though belatedly, realized that their political interests were identical with those of the Hindus. Separate electorates and weightage were no doubt gifts of imperialism, but it became obvious to educated Muslims that Minto and Morley's interest in them was not genuine. Whatever they had done was only with the purpose of driving a wedge between the Hindus and the Muslims to serve their policy of divide and rule and weaken the national movement. From then on Muslim politics flowed strongly towards accommodation with the Indian National Congress and were designed to hasten constitutional and political change at the all-India level. A definite advance in that direction was made by the All India Muslim League at its session in 1912 when it formally adopted self-government within the British Empire as its ideal.

As mentioned earlier, this was immediately responded to by a resolution passed at the Karachi Congress of 1913, warmly welcoming the advance made by the Muslim League and offering it the friendship and co-operation of the Congress in all matters affecting the national welfare. The change in the attitude on the part of the Indian Muslims and the negotiations that continued between the Congress and the League led to the holding of simultaneous conferences of the two bodies in Bombay in 1915. (The All India Muslim League did not hold its annual session in 1914.) At Bombay, the Congress and the Muslim League resolved to formulate a scheme of reforms calculated to secure for the people of India, a substantial step forward in the direction of self government.

On the basis of a resolution moved by M.A. Jinnah in the League Conference in Bombay (1915), a committee was appointed to formulate a scheme of reform and to confer with the committee of the National Congress that was being formed for the same purpose.

For the next few years there was great fraternalization between the Congress and the Muslim League. Simultaneously sessions of the two bodies were held again at Lucknow in December 1916. A scheme of reform proposals framed by a Joint Committee of the Congress and the League was considered at a joint meeting of Congress and League representatives at Calcutta in October 1916. As a result of their delibera-tion, a plan was evolved and finalized. At the Lucknow session the plan was accepted and agreed to by both bodies. This agreement be-tween the Congress and the Muslim League came to be known as the Lucknow Pact.[68]

Under the Lucknow accord, the Congress and the League had agreed to work more or less as a single body. The League accepted the Congress ideal of self-government as its goal. This enabled the two political bodies to come together against the common foe — the British.

The Lucknow Pact may be remembered in history for both its strong and weak points. Since its inception, the Indian National Congress had been keen to achieve unity between the Hindus and the Muslims for India's political advance. The Lucknow Pact, in this context, is signifi-cant for the rapprochement achieved. It was the natural culmination of the great era of fraternalization between the Congress and the League since 1912. The myth that the two communities were irreconcilable and could not be united, was exploded.

The Lucknow Pact was the achievement of the leaders of the two major communities who had a similar ideological background, intellec-tual calibre, outlook and approach to India's political problems. Leaders like Jinnah, Ansari, the Raja of Mahmudabad conferred with Ambica Charan Mazumdar, S. Banerjea, Motilal Nehru and Tilak on the home rule, self-government, constitutional amendments and other issues of common political interest. The Lucknow Pact was the basis for the resolution on self-government adopted at the Lucknow Session of the Indian National Congress in December 1916. From 1918, the Congress and the Muslim League, under Gandhiji's guidance and that of the Khilafat Committee, were to be engaged in a combined fight against the British.

The pact, however, had certain weaknesses. The Indian National Congress's acceptance of separate electorates and weightage amounted to the Congress sacrificing its secular principles and accepting a communal ideology. This was a blemish on the reputation of the Congress. The National leadership, though fully realizing the havoc that the system of communal electorates was bound to cause, failed to plead for its replacement by a joint electorate. This was a setback to the secular principle for which the Indian National Congress stood.

The rapprochement between the Hindus and the Muslims was only short-lived. Soon, mutual distrust and misunderstanding raised their heads and the two communities began to drift apart, to pursue their separate lines of politics, ultimately strengthening the 'two-nation' concept. It was not long before it became clear that the Lucknow Pact was a 'blunder of first magnitude', having adverse repercussions on the future politics of India. What was done in good faith to unify the Indian communities in a common fight against imperialism unfortunately amounted to recognition of the communal principle.

Between the Lucknow and Calcutta sessions of the Congress lies a historic and stirring record of events. The Calcutta Congress was initially expected to be the most fiery and the most determined of all held. The middle of the year saw the internment of Mrs Besant. In June she was served with the order and the three months of her exile witnessed unparalleled demonstrations of anger and protest by the Indian people. One after another, the Provincial Congress Committees were returning Mrs Besant to the presidential chair. Her release in time for the Congress appeared unlikely. It was decided that if her presence was not possible, Sir S. Subramania Iyer would substitute for her.

Following Mrs Besant's internment, a campaign of passive resistance was planned to secure the release of the Home Rule internees. In the meantime, the All India Congress Committee and the Muslim League, at a joint meeting held on 28 and 29 July, discussed the question of passive resistance for political ends. The provincial Congress committees were asked to express their opinion on the issue. In response to Sir William Wedderburn's suggestion, the meeting appointed a deputation comprising M.A. Jinnah, V.S.S. Sastry, C.P. Ramaswamy Iyer, Tej Bahadur Sapru and Wazir Hassan to go to England in September 1917, to explain the general political situation in India and to create a favourable atmosphere for strengthening the cause and scheme of reforms adopted.[69]

In the meantime came the Secretary of State, Edwin Montagu's declaration announcing the British policy for 'the increasing association of Indians with Self-Governing Institutions in India'. The country was pacified and public feeling subsided on the release of Mrs Besant on 17 September 1917.

11. The Montagu Mission

Montagu visited India on a political mission. He met representatives of various political parties, leaders of public opinion and other interests clamouring to be heard. Numerous memoranda and petitions were presented to him. Deputation after deputation waited on him, the two most influential being the Congress-League Joint Deputation and that of the Home Rule Leagues.

The Joint Deputation presented a memorial demanding Home Rule. It was read to the Secretary of State by Surendranath Banerjea. The Home Rule Leagues were represented by Tilak and Mrs Besant. Both presentations were on 26 November 1917. They stated in clear terms that nothing less than the Congress-League scheme would satisfy Indians.

In Madras the All India Home Rule League presented Montagu with a monster petition with a million verified signatures, gathered in the presidency and conveyed to him in cartloads.

Ten long years had passed since the Congress had last met at Calcutta in December 1906, to raise the banner of swaraj. In December 1917, the Congress met for its 32nd session in the same city. The Calcutta Congress voiced India's resolve in an unflinching tone. Mrs Besant, the president of the year, delivered her address, a masterly study of the Indian situation. She referred in her speech to a new and rising spirit in India. Analysing the factors and special forces responsible for the rise of the new spirit, Mrs Besant listed the following:[69a]

(1) The awakening of Asia
(2) Discussions abroad on alien rule and imperial reconstruction
(3) Loss of belief in the superiority of the white races
(4) The awakening of the merchants
(5) The awakening of the women to claim their ancient position
(6) The awakening of the masses.

After declaring that freedom was India's birthright which she had earned the right to enjoy through her services and sacrifices, Mrs Besant concluded:[70]

> To see India free, to see her hold up her head among the Nations, to see her sons and daughters respected everywhere, to see her worthy of her mighty Past, engaged in building a yet mightier Future — is not this worth working for, worth suffering for, worth living and worth dying for?

The number of delegates which was about 2,500 at Lucknow had doubled to 4,967 which showed the remarkable leap in the public spirit and patriotism of the people. Besides delegates and 10,000 visitors, thousands outside the Congress pavilion also declared their will, their longing and their determination to be free. Montagu was still in the country studying the situation. The country had spoken in a thousand ways demanding self-government.

The Calcutta Congress of 1917 marks the beginning of a new phase in the battle for freedom.

Since the Surat split, the national movement had continued on its placid and humdrum course. Political activity was at its lowest ebb when the First World War broke out in 1914. The deterioration in relations between the Moderates and Extremists since 1908 had rendered the Congress movement weak. The annual sessions of the Congress after Surat were orderly and harmonious but they were also dull and monotonous. Under the leadership of the Moderate leaders the Congress continued to affirm its faith in British justice and, through resolutions which had become stale by repetition over the last twenty years or more. The political methods of the Moderates were powerless to bring the people any relief against the despotic rule that trampled upon all their rights. There was complacency among the British. Tilak's incarceration, had silenced the voices of the other Extremists. Maharashtra had become comparatively quiet. Western India came to be dominated by the activities of the Moderate Congressmen of Bombay. Leaders like Lala Lajpat Rai and B.C. Pal were out of the country. Bengal and Punjab suffered repression during the boycott and swadeshi agitation. In Punjab, the Nationalists' activities had become virtually impossible due to war time emergency proclaimed there in 1914-17. The southern region, especially the Tamil and Telugu areas, which had earlier been greatly influenced by the revolutionary doctrines preached by B.C. Pal, fell back into Moderate politics. With the annulment of the partition, Bengal had receded into the background and political activities, except those of the secret societies, had come to a standstill. The other parts of India had not been drawn into the vortex of the national movement in a big way during the Swadeshi and Boycott Movement. There was on the whole very little political activity in the country. The split in the Congress and the repressive measures of the Minto Government had weakened the national movement.

The provincial, district and taluk Congresses and the network of Congress Committees set up by the leadership following the Surat split had ceased to be active by 1914. There was no sustained activity throughout the year from the Congress platform. Annual Congress sessions had become mere rituals and the number of delegates had declined sharply, falling to 207 at the AICC Session at Bankipur in 1912.

This state of affairs led those deeply committed to the national cause to make a deeper study of political problems than had been done in the past. This was the rising generation of leadership consisting of persons who had been students during the Swadeshi days.

The Extremists had left a legacy of struggle and agitation. When they withdrew from the parent body in 1907, they captured the imagination of the youth by their activity and sacrifice. These were the people who forced the British Government to introduce the Minto-Morley Reforms. While the Moderates, though honest and patriotic, were not prepared to make sacrifices, the Extremists by their suffering and sacrifices in the cause of the national movement inspired a whole generation of youth and students to plunge into active struggle to achieve the cherished goal. The examples of leaders like Tilak, Lajpat Rai, B.C. Pal, V.O. Chidambaram, Subramania Siva and Hari Sarvothama Rao inspired the younger generation who had joined the Congress since 1905.

This emerging generation of nationalist leaders had become impatient and saw the necessity for nationwide agitation in India to resist the British. In the face of Congress inactivity and lethargy coupled with inability to organize an effective resistance movement against the imperialists, these young men did not lose heart but looked eagerly for a leadership to spearhead an anti-British agitation. The Morley-Minto Reforms had been a great disappointment, having failed to satisfy the legitimate aspirations of the Indians. The political atmosphere in the country was thus favourable for the Home Rule agitation. Tilak was released from Mandalay after six years of detention (June 1914). He confided to a friend after his release that 'his days were numbered'. Nevertheless he resumed his activities with his old zeal and thoroughness. Tilak and his followers realized the importance of being part of the Congress and began to work towards that end.

12. Annie Besant at the Helm

At a time when the Congress was torn asunder over methods and goal and the Indian national movement was devoid of dynamism and leadership, Mrs Besant entered the Indian political scene. Madras became her base. She undertook the task of revitalizing the Indian National Congress. She aimed to woo the Indian youth and students and promoted activities to wean them away from violence and passive resistance. Since the Congress was inactive between annual sessions, the need for a body like the Home Rule League to carry on a continuous and powerful agitation for home rule was felt. The emerging generation of the western-educated Nationalist Congressmen looked forward to Mrs Besant's leadership for spearheading the agitation against the British.

Dr Annie Besant (1847-1933), Irish by birth,[71] a gifted journalist, an able organizer and the greatest orator of her generation, used her eloquence for propagating several noble causes. She devoted herself to social reform. She stood for free thought, radicalism and socialism. She worked with Charles Bradlaugh in his National Secular Society. Later she joined the Fabians and worked with the Socialist leaders like Lansbury, Sydney Webb, George Bernard Shaw, Ramsay Macdonald and several other Socialists of England of that time. It was observed in 1889 that there was 'scarcely any modern reform for which she had not worked, written, spoken and suffered'.

Theosophy brought Mrs Besant to India. As Madame Blavatsky's prime disciple, Mrs Besant soon attained prominence in that body. In 1893 she arrived in India, to work for Theosophy with Banaras as her headquarters. In 1907 she was elevated to the post of the President of the Theosophical Society, following Colonel Olcott's death. This position she held till her death in 1933 and Adyar (Madras) became her headquarters. Hindu metaphysics fascinated her. She translated several sacred texts, including the *Bhagavad Gita,* into English and lectured all over the country on Hinduism, on New Education, the status of women, and the social liberation of the poor and the oppressed. In 1914 she joined the Congress to espouse India's demand for Self-Government. She ardently believed that the Indian National Congress was the only political organization capable of leading India to her cherished goal. She planned to lead the agitation for Indian Home Rule, on the model of the agitation led by her in the 19th century in the company of the British Radicals and Fabians for the abolition of slavery, repeal of the Corn Law and for Irish Home Rule. She readily offered to use her journalistic skill, her eloquence and organizing ability for the cause.

Mrs Besant founded, in January 1914, a weekly newspaper *Commonweal* as her political organ. In July 1914 she purchased the *Madras Standard* and renamed it *New India.* She took pains to activize the Congress everywhere. She urged that 'instead of asking for Reforms or Home Rule, we make the reforms for ourselves'.[72] *New India* became her chosen organ for propaganda for India's freedom. She was a delegate to the Congress Session held at Madras in 1914. Through a series of articles on the Indian National Congress in *New India* on the eve of the 29th session of the Congress at Madras, Mrs Besant created a new atmosphere and stirred the thinking of nationalist-minded men. This was reflected in the Congress Session of 1914 held in Madras under the shadow of the World War.

Mrs Besant planned to reunite the two wings of the Congress before the session opened. She believed that India would get an opportunity to act promptly with the outbreak of the World War. The situation created by the war and India's splendid contribution to the war effort, her generous help in men and material, had altered India's international status. A shift in the British attitude to India was visible. When the future of the Empire was considered, Mrs Besant pointed out, as it would be after the war, India's silence might be understood as India's contentment and she might be left out of account altogether. Mrs Besant, therefore, thought this was the opportune movement to put forward the Indian claim for self-government. For India to make this demand forcefully, unity in the Congress was essential. Mrs Besant realised the importance of the unified Congress and the need for the Extremist Congressmen to return to the parent body. She wrote in *New India*[73]: 'If we are to win Home Rule, union is absolutely necessary; the Right and the Left wings of the National Party are to be united by the Congress.'

Many eminent public men in India, journalists and Moderate Congress leaders like G. Subramania Iyer, C.P. Ramaswamy Iyer and several other leaders of the south and north appealed to Mrs Besant to play the role of the unifier. Even those Congressmen identified with the Moderates during 1907 were in general ready to go to any extent to pull the Congress out of its old rut. But Mrs Besant's efforts to achieve unity in the Congress of December 1914 did not succeed and negotiations dragged on till the following year. Her proposed amendment of the Congress Constitution, modifying it in order to enable the re-entry of the Extremist Congressmen on the eve of the Madras Session of the Indian National Congress could not be carried.

The failure of Mrs Besant's mission had far-reaching consequences. It resulted in the formation of a new political organization, viz. the All India Home Rule League, which campaigned for self-government, which was spontaneously and eagerly welcomed all over the country. It was to become a common political platform for both Moderate and Extremist Congressmen over the next two years and more.

Mrs Besant went to Bombay on the eve of the 30th session of the Congress to seek the permission and support of the senior Congress leaders and of the All India Congress Committee to launch her new political organization for the purpose of educative and propagandist work throughout the year for self-government or home rule for India. She secured the blessings of India's 'Grand Old Man', Dadabhai Naoroji. She held consultations with Gandhiji. In a conference of her adherents drawn from both the Congress and the Muslim League, held on 27 December 1915, Mrs Besant put forward her scheme for a Home Rule Organization. Opinion was divided on the issue of the immediate formation of the Home Rule League. A resolution was adopted approving the establishment of a League to carry on educative propaganda on the principles of and the necessity for self-government in India.

The resolution, when referred to the Congress Committee (Subjects Committee) was carried but the AICC decided that, instead of a newly founded organization, the Congress itself should take up the work of educative propaganda for home rule throughout the year. The older Congressmen were not in favour of a separate body and advised Mrs Besant to suspend her Home Rule campaign since the Congress itself had decided to undertake the educative propaganda work throughout the year. Mrs Besant was given a deadline up to 31 August 1916. By then, if the Congress had failed to act, the Home Rule League might be launched. Despite Mrs Besant's assurance that the Home Rule League was intended to strengthen and not to weaken the Congress, she met with failure. In this context, it is of interest to quote the following extracts from Mrs Besant's letter to *New India*, written from Bombay in December:[74]

> I expect as this resolution has been carried, the Home Rule League will not be sanctioned this evening. The opportunity of joint action on a common platform between Hindus and Muslims will thus be destroyed. I am, of course, bound by my promise not to start the organisation if the Indian leaders disapprove it, deep as will be the disappointment felt all over the country by the rank and file, who have come to the Congress with the object of joining it.
>
> As regards the suspension of the formation of the Home Rule League, the position is really quite clear. I had said from the beginning that it was intended to strengthen, not to weaken the Congress. I had further said, that I would not organise the League if the Indian leaders were against it. The enthusiasm raised by the brief three months' work brought a huge number of delegates to the Congress; the resolution which was carried took up the proposed work of the Home Rule League. I had to choose, on the 29th between obeying this mandate as a member of All India Congress Committee or starting a new Organisation to do exactly the same thing, creating a split for the mere sake of leading a new Body when the old one had taken up the work. All the well-known Congress leaders were against the formation of a new Body under the changed conditions, and my own judgment agreed with theirs . . . .
>
> The formation was therefore adjourned. If the All India Congress Committee does not carry out the mandate of the Congress, and if the Congress Organisation goes to sleep, then we can go on with our adjourned meeting. But we have no right to insult the trusted men elected by the Congress Circles by assuming that they will disobey the Congress.

The object of the Home Rule Movement was to achieve self-government for India. 'Home Rule is the cry of a Nation for Self-Rule or

Self-Government,' observed Mrs Besant. The purpose of the Home Rule League was defined as the securing of Home Rule for India through constitutional methods, maintaining the connection with Great Britain by becoming a free nation within the British Empire, and supporting and strengthening the Indian National Congress. Further clarifying the concept of Home Rule, Mrs Besant wrote in *New India*:[75]

> India to be governed by her own men, freely elected by herself, to make and break ministers at her will; carry arms; to have her own army, her own navy; to levy her own taxes; to make her own budget; to educate her own people to irrigate her own land . . . to be sovereign Nation within her borders, owning the paramount power of the Imperial Crown and sending her sons to the Imperial Council.

Mrs Besant preferred to call her objective Home Rule for two reasons. For any popular cry, she emphasized, a short and precise title was better than a longer one. Her preference for the Home Rule to Self-Government was also for the reason that the latter would mean independence and a break with the British.[76] To indicate that by independence she did not mean a break between India and Great Britain, it was necessary to add 'within the Empire' wrote Mrs Besant. 'Home Rule hence stood for the Self-Government within the Empire on colonial lines.' 'This freedom without separation,' Mrs Besant explicitly stated, 'was Home Rule.'

Mrs Besant, explaining why India should demand Home Rule, wrote:[77]

> India demands Home Rule for two reasons, one essential and vital, the other less important but weighty: First, because Freedom is the birthright of every Nation: secondly, because her most important interests are now made subservient to the interests of the British Empire without her consent, and her resources are not utilised for her greatest needs. It is enough only to mention the money spent on her Army, not for local defence but for Imperial purposes, as compared with that spent on primary Education.

Mrs Besant had already set the pace for starting the Home Rule League in Madras and much had been done throughout 1915. The country responded splendidly to the home rule slogan.

Owing to her commitment to the Congress in Bombay, Mrs Besant had to wait. But Tilak had made no such commitment. On 28 April 1916, he inaugurated in Pune the Home Rule for India League prior to that of Mrs Besant. He invited her to address a mammoth gathering in Pune. Tilak and Joseph Baptista were the leaders of the League. Tilak's colleagues and followers were distinguished men who included Khaparde, Dr B.S. Moonje, M.S. Aney, R.P. Karandikar, S.K. Altekar, C.M. Desai,

N.C. Kelkar, V.R. Patwardhan and C.V. Vaidya and several other outstanding men from Maharashtra, and C.P. and Berar. Both Tilak and Mrs Besant (who was free to announce the birth of the Home Rule League, as conceived earlier, on 1 September 1916, i.e. five months later than Tilak) initiated sustained political activities in the country. Tilak confined his area of operation to Maharashtra and Karnataka, leaving the rest of India to Mrs Besant's charge. Within a year, on account of the sustained work of Tilak himself and Baptista, the Home Rule League had begun to gather much support. It was received with unprecedented enthusiasm. Tilak gave a democractic constitution to his League. The area under his charge was divided into regions like Central Maharashtra, Bombay City, the Karnataka, Berar and the Central Provinces. In each of these regions, Tilak got a Home Rule Branch inaugurated. All these branch offices worked very effectively.

Many professional men joined the Home Rule League and placed their resources and time at its disposal. Great was the zeal and fervour exhibited by these men. The ever-growing membership of the League was a true indication of the fact that the home rule demand was getting stronger.[78] Branch offices became virtual recruiting centres. The home rule message reached far and wide. Tilak's papers, *Kesari* and *Maharatta,* played a crucial role in educating the people on the home rule ideal. The League did a marvellous job. The propaganda went on vigorously and support for the home rule cause spread, involving increasingly large numbers of Indians.

The authorities grew nervous at the vigorous home rule propaganda launched by Tilak. Of the many causes that helped the spread of the home rule ideal and the scattering of the seeds of the freedom movement, none was more effective than the attitude of the bureaucracy. The bureaucracy, with a view to striking a blow, accused Tilak of indulging in seditious activities. They rejected his application for a passport to proceed to England to fight his libel suit against Valentine Chirol. They also tried to gag him and stall home rule activities. In July 1916, the authorities demanded Rs 40,000 from Tilak as security for his 'good behaviour' on the ground that his speeches were of a highly seditious nature. The supporters of the Home Rule League were warned against lending any support to the movement. Tilak appealed to the High Court of Bombay and obtained a ruling 'that Home Rule League was not seditious'. The policy of repression only enabled the Home Rule League to grow in strength and influence. This had a great impact on Tilak's membership drive on account of the wide publicity the League had acquired. Commenting on the vindictive attitude of the bureaucracy to Tilak, Mrs Besant wrote in *New India:*[79]

> The impertinence of the Magistrate in hoping that Mr Tilak would take the warning, and in telling him that he was fortunate in not being prosecuted for sedition may pass. Mr Tilak had already suffered seven and half years of prison for his love of India and his health will never recover from the sufferings which have added twenty years to his age. His body has been weakened but his mind is as vigorous as ever and his spirit as unbroken. The cruel gagging will only strengthen his determination to free India from the yoke of a bureaucracy, which makes it impossible for such a man speak to his own people.
>
> First comes the refusal of a passport, Secondly, the binding over in exorbitant securities.
>
> Mr Tilak is bound over, so as to silence him, for any political speech of his would obviously be held to forfeit the Rs 40,000. I am excluded from the Presidency. So I can only conclude that Lord Willingdon chooses to consider my speeches at Poona as seditious . . . .
>
> What will the Bombay Government do next? We have had three actions: (1) My own exclusion, without cause shown, and therefore presumably unjustifiable (2) The refusal of a passport to Mr Tilak thus, whether intended or not, preventing him from carrying on his case against Sir Valentine Chirol (3) The binding over of Mr Tilak. What will be the fourth step? When a Government enters on the downward path of repression, it is difficult for it to stop. What is H. E. the Viceroy doing, that he allows the Government of Bombay thus to stir up the fire of anger in Maharashtra?
>
> Of one thing I am sure; that every act which strikes at the champions of Home Rule makes it dearer to the hearts of the people and the last word lies with them. We have to face a period of difficulty and danger but the agony of the Cross preceded the Resurrection of India — A Nation.

In June 1916, Mrs Besant's friends in the Theosophical Society organized in England an Auxiliary Home Rule League. In fact the Auxiliary Home Rule League preceded the Leagues in Madras and Bombay. It worked most effectively in Britain.

13. The All India Home Rule League

Mrs Besant had agreed to defer the inauguration of the Home Rule League to September. As a member of the AICC she was bound by her promise to the Congress High Command, unlike B.G. Tilak who was yet to be readmitted into the Congress. Mrs Besant was agreeable even to drop the proposal altogether if the Congress really took up home rule work. It was a great achievement, getting the Congress to commit itself definitely to the home rule ideal. The Congress had also decided to carry on educative and propagandist work on a continuing basis, but the AICC was busy in the preparation of the reform scheme in consultation with the Committee of the Muslim League.

The first of September arrived and Mrs Besant was true to her promise. She did everything possible in the meantime to implement the Congress resolution. But the Congress was too heavy to move and years of slumber and lethargy had rendered it somewhat immobile. On 1 September, therefore, Mrs Besant launched her All India Home Rule League. The League was formally inaugurated on 3 September in Madras in the YMIA hall at a largely attended, enthusiastic public gathering. It had a branch in Bombay where Jamnadas Dwarkadas and P.K. Telang were the leading members. The *New India* became the main vehicle to disseminate the home rule ideas. Mrs. Besant's immense resources were wholeheartedly dedicated to the sacred cause.

Mrs Besant and Tilak, through the home rule agitation, revived healthy political activity in the entire country. Agitation had begun to grip the thinking of Congressmen. Within months, every principal town in the southern provinces had set up a unit of the League and not a day passed without fresh accession to the number of Home Rule League Branches.

Mrs Besant envisaged a less rigid and more informal set-up then that of B.G. Tilak's League. Initiated with a seven-member executive, excluding Mrs Besant, these seven were to represent the thirty-two founder branches. The office bearers of the League were colleagues and followers of Mrs Besant. The All India Home Rule League commenced its work with Mrs Besant as its President, C.P. Ramaswami Iyer as its General Secretary, and B.P. Wadia and G.S. Arundale as its Treasurer and Organising Secretary respectively. A very simple procedure marked the opening of branches. Any three individuals could open a branch. It was not long before it came to be felt that for a town to be without a branch of the Home Rule League was a disgrace. It became a status symbol.

The All India Home Rule League was to take up the work in the entire country to the exclusion of the region which was covered by B.G. Tilak's League, but the strong base of the League was in the south where the Theosophical Society had penetrated deeply. The Theosophical Society had fertile soil in the south, since no other reform movement had ever flourished there. Of the 200 and odd branches of the League claimed by the documents, 132 were in the Madras Presidency alone. Mrs Besant depended initially on her Theosophical Society followers for the spread of the home rule message. *New India* devoted a page for home rule news. G.S. Arundale, who edited the news, bulletined its affairs. His exquisite sense of humour and fervent enthusiasm made his writings popular. Through his work among the students he inspired the new generation of leaders of the freedom movement. The propaganda was pursued vigorously through the press and the platform and the home rule cause spread far and wide, enlisting larger and larger number of members.

Following Mrs Besant's clash with the bureaucracy in the Madras Presidency in 1917 over her political writings in *New India*, the League's membership increased from 7,000 in March 1917 to 27,000 in December that year.[80]

The Home Rule League mapped out an elaborate programme of action to involve every section of the Indian community in the movement. Mrs Besant involved the students in a variety of intellectual, educative, sports and public activities through the organization of Boy Scouts and other bodies. A Young Men's Indian Association soon came to be established. A network of debating societies, mock parliaments, libraries and reading rooms sprang up all over.

The Home Rule page in the *New India* advised the branches on the modality of the activities to be undertaken. Several branches opened libraries and reading rooms and organized lectures and group discussions. In major cities like Karachi, Bombay, Calcutta, Madras, Madurai, Trichy, Masulipatnam and Vijayawada, group discussions spearheaded by Congressmen, became a regular feature. The subjects ranged from Indian Finance and Local Self-Government to Literature. The discussions ultimately led up to the need for home rule, an issue that moved all sections of Indian society. Its vibrations were felt in every sphere of life.

Mrs Besant established the 'Madras Parliament', a debating Society observing parliamentary forms and methods. The cream of Indian society joined this body: 'since we aim at Home Rule it would be well to train ourselves in Parliamentary methods'. Several of the aspiring nationalist politicians and future Congress leaders were involved in the activities of this body.

In the Madras Presidency, the existence of a network of Theosophical lodges facilitated the intensive home rule propaganda. The membership drive had phenomenal success. By September 1917, Madras could claim 132 branches. Theosophists were also the office bearers of the Home Rule League. There was a close and intimate link between Home Rule League and the Theosophical Society.

Bengal was initially slow to act. Political activity had been dormant there since the annulment of the partition in 1911. However, Bengal soon fell in line and inaugurated a provincial branch. Besides the South, Mrs Besant's strongholds included Bombay city, Gujarat, Sind, Uttar Pradesh and Bihar, where her Theosophical Society was also quite strong.

In her intensive campaign for home rule, Mrs Besant was ably aided by her two papers, *Commonweal* and *New India*, which rendered tremendous service. *New India* was particularly her chosen instrument to propagate the ideology of home rule while condemning the repressive policy of the bureaucracy and exposing its misdeeds. From 1915, *New India* began to assume an aggressive tone and inaugurated the campaign for home rule in a crusading spirit. Its influence came to be felt in all provinces.

As for the main political programme to back the demand for home rule, Mrs Besant planned her activities on the basis of the agitation for Irish home rule spearheaded by the English radicals and Fabians. It was to be through monster meetings, press pamphleteering, and having the demand relayed through local branches to different parts of the country. In the event of government trying to smother and suppress the movement, the law courts would be moved which would help the movement to acquire greater publicity.

The most far-reaching part of the home rule campaign was Mrs Besant's personal activities. In addition to her daily journalistic chores, she addressed meetings in Madras, travelled to all centres of political activity in the country, lectured to monster gatherings, interviewed all the leading Indian personalities on the subject of home rule. It was a phenomenal performance for a woman of 70. She roused unprecedented enthusiasm, encouraged prompt and vigorous action and the response astonished the whole nation.

Inspired by Mrs Besant, leaders from all over the country joined the Home Rule Movement. Among them were Sankarlal Banker, Jamnadas Dwarkadas and Kanji Dwarakadas of Bombay; Indulal Yagnik of Gujarat; Motilal Nehru with his son Jawaharlal from the United Provinces; Jitendralal Banerjee and later C.R. Das from Bengal; S. Subramania Iyer, A. Rangaswamy Iyengar, C.P. Ramaswamy Iyer, V.S. Srinivasa Sastry and many more from the south. M.A. Jinnah, Tej Bahadur Sapru, Madan Mohan Malaviya and others also joined the Movement.

In Madras, Justice Sadasiva Iyer was induced to join the Madras 'Parliament' and also to lend his name to the elaborate scheme of National Education, intended as a counterblast to the Order (G.O. No. 559) of the Government prohibiting the participation of students in political movements in the Madras and Bombay Presidencies, and in Central Provinces.

The *mantra* of home rule as Gandhiji called it, reached every section of Indians by 1917. Many government servants who were Theosophists began devoting time to propagating the home rule cause.

A Deputy Collector in Bellary who was a Theosophist was alleged to have persuaded a number of people from the villages under his charge to become Theosophists and Home Rulers. In April 1915 he resigned his official position in order to devote himself entirely to political work.[81]

The Bihar Government was worried about the effects of some of Mrs Besant's pamphlets and books on the student community. A Home Rule Series pamphlet was found in the hands of students of Patna College. The Government of Bihar could not take any action as the publication was from Madras, and it was also hesitant since proscribing the book or forbidding the students to read it would only lend publicity to the cause of home rule.[82]

Many elder politicians now began to feel 'out of the picture'. They found it difficult to cope with the work of the League and its new ideas. One had to address gatherings of not fifty or a hundred, but of five thousands. 'The polite and well-bred middle-aged Congress politicians found it a strain not only on their voice but on their temper and nerves too.' Mrs Besant knew no rest. She and Tilak attracted huge crowds even in small towns. Their popularity was immense. The whole country rang with the demand for home rule. Large numbers of Moderate Congressmen, craving for activity under the Congress banner responded eagerly to the home rule agitation and swelled its ranks.

In her whirlwind campaign for home rule, Mrs Besant's paper, *New India*, was the main means of spreading ideas of freedom to every corner of India. In a series of articles of self-government in March and April 1915, Mrs Besant indicated her intention to lead a political campaign in favour of *swaraj* or home rule. Her articles in *New India* talked of the drain of India's wealth: 'the drain had left Indian children starving on one meal a day'. She attributed India's poverty to British rule. In her opinion, the British administration in India was the costliest on earth and the Indian legislative councils were becoming farces. *New India* observed:[83]

> India has outgrown the need for officialdom. We have demanded so long for reforms from the Congress platform and have not got them. The children of the soil go forth with the brand of inferiority on their brows. Subjection had stunted their growth and dwarfed their stature. Foreign rule had demoralised them. The bureaucracy is based on distrust. It must go; India's claim is for freedom. It was never conceded by any country as a boon. It is a right to be fought for and won. Agitation must be constitutional, but it must be manly, resolute, unceasing and based on impregnable facts. Let India shake off the hallucination that her freedom would be given as a bounty by any Nation. It is her right to be wrung from unwilling hands.

The British Government in India was alarmed at the phenomenal growth in the number of Home Rule branches and the intensity of the movement launched by Mrs Besant. They contemplated severe action as in the case of Tilak, since *New India* was Mrs Besant's chosen instrument in spearheading a raging campaign against the British. The paper became the first target of the bureaucratic attack.

By the end of 1915, *New India* circulation was 10,500 copies. Mrs Besant's articles in the paper were viewed with great concern by the government who were convinced that she was out to undermine their authority through constant vilification. In July 1915 Mrs Besant was warned by Lord Pentland, the Governor of Madras. He addressed her a friendly remonstrance on the subject of the general tendency and tenor of articles appearing in *New India*.[84] Unmindful of the remonstrance, she continued her vigorous campaign for home rule in her paper.

The government initially planned to deport Mrs Besant. In October 1915 the Madras Government addressed a letter to the Government of India,[85] proposing that drastic steps be taken to check Mrs Besant's activities and suppress her agitation which they apprehended 'was fraught with danger to the public peace and security'. The Government of India did not agree to this but suggested[86] that, in the event of Mrs Besant infringing the law either through her written or spoken word, the government should not refrain from the application of provisions of the law to deal with her. The Government of Madras was thus advised to resort to action if the situation required it, either by demanding a security deposit from her paper or any other action which they deemed expedient.[87]

From then on, the authorities resorted to severe repressive measures against the Home Rule Movement and to muzzle Mrs Besant's journalistic campaign. They invoked both the Defence of India Act and sections of the Indian Press Act of 1910 to gag her.

The Indian Press Act of 1910 empowered District Magistrates to require the keeper of a printing press and publisher of a newspaper to deposit security from Rs 500 to Rs 5,000 which was liable to be forfeited in the event of the newspaper publishing seditious or objectionable matter and in case the tone of the paper came to the adverse notice of the authorities to the extent of disturbing public peace, as they saw it. This provision had been used to kill several newspapers,[88] since the outbreak of the War. Under the Act, the owners of the press and the editors and publishers of the newspapers were at the mercy of the local government which was the authority to decide whether a particular piece of writing or news item was objectionable. Appeals against such order were, however, possible.

At the time of the registration of *New India* as a newspaper in 1914 it was exempted from the liability to deposit security. Special reasons had to be stated for such exemption. In the absence of any such reasons in this case, the authorities took a view that Mrs Besant did not deserve this concession. In view of the continued aggressive tone of *New India* and the sharpness of the articles appearing in it, the Government of Madras moved the Chief Presidency Magistrate's court on 15 May 1916 to cancel the order which exempted Mrs Besant from the obligation to deposit security in connection with the New India Power Press.

This provoked Mrs Besant to launch an even more forceful anti-Government campaign than hitherto. Her powerful tirade against the Indian Press Act, in general, and its application to her own press, in particular, was pursued with great vigour. In view of this, the government thought it expedient to proceed further against the paper. In May 1916, a security deposit of Rs 2,000 was demanded from *New India*. That was the first blow, but every time Mrs Besant and her paper were suppressed, they were able to rise again with redoubled might and glory. The agitation spread over the entire country. Security demands only helped to enhance the circulation of the paper and its influence rendered more forceful the demand for home rule in the face of increasingly severe repressive measures.

A major cause of anxiety for the government was that Mrs Besant's followers were effectively emulating her methods in the propagation of home rule ideas all over the country. Home rule literature — pamphlets and books — were written in or translated into vernacular languages. This was the first indication that the movement was well on the way to reaching the masses.[89]

In July 1916 came an order from the Bombay Government which under Rule No. 3 of the Defence of India Act prohibited Mrs Besant's entry into the Bombay Presidency. Soon, on the heels of the agitation against the Bombay order, came another. In November 1916, the Government of Central Provinces and Berar also excluded Mrs Besant from their territory.[90]

What greatly alarmed the authorities was the impact of the irrepressible *New India* in other provinces. The Punjab Government had drawn the attention of the Government of India to the influence of *New India* on the press of that province. In Sir Michael O'Dwyer's opinion, 'the significance of the *New India* propaganda lay in the fact that it was following the traditional lines of sedition and aims at creating a feeling of dissatisfaction towards the Government established by law'.

Mrs Besant's hold on the student community and youth and her influence with teachers was tremendous. Besides writing and speaking with a view to directly influencing young minds, Mrs Besant had instituted home rule classes. Through the formation of troops of Boys Scout and volunteers, she directed youth to do social work, help the poor and band themselves together to keep order in public meetings, which the government hardly did. The sedulous diffusion of the home rule ideas, the government was worried, had the effect of 'thoroughly unsettling' the minds of youngsters and poisoned their thinking against the government in India.[91] Mrs Besant was a strong advocate of National Education. 'Education in India is hopelessly backward and reactionary,' Mrs Besant wrote, 'it deadens all patriotic impulses and is a continued menace to the vitality of the country'. Such writings in *New India*, the Government believed, sowed seeds of discontent in the minds the students, Mrs Besant's public meetings were largely attended by the student community. The CID police reporters were, on more than one occasion, manhandled by the students for spying. Mrs Besant called the CID the 'Crush India Department'. The home rule ideal and propaganda in favour of it penetrated so deep into the student community that its reaction was visibly felt. The students of the Madanapalle College (in Andhra Pradesh), for example, once wrote up on the blackboard: WE DO NOT ASK FOR HOME RULE, WE DEMAND IT.

The authorities attributed the prevailing serious unrest in the country to home rule ideas and Mrs Besant's influence on the students and youth. They linked the several expressions of discontent and acts of indiscipline over the preceding fifteen months in the Madras Presidency and in other provinces to the propaganda and the writings of Mrs Besant.

To checkmate this trend, the Governments of Madras, Bombay and Central Provinces issued a prohibitory order on 1 May 1917 to direct that 'no undergraduate of any college and no student of any school should be permitted to take part in public, political discussion, to attend political meetings, to join a political association or to take part in any movement.'[92]

Mrs Besant described this order as 'the most repressive edict so far issued in India'. She cautioned the government against turning the province into another Bengal:

> . . . they [Government] were heedless and in fact were converging towards that undesirable state of affairs; when young men are driven out of the area of constitutional politics which is their right to study and discuss, [they] will run into dangerous channels of anarchical crime.

The authorities believed that here was a sinister influence over the students; that they were being used to discredit the existing educational machinery as 'out of sympathy with Indian aspirations'.

What made the government panic was Mrs Besant's use of the machinery of the Theosophical Society for her political work. 'Theosophical lodges were understood in many places to have become the potential centres of local agitation for Home Rule,' observed a Government communique.[93]

In August 1916 the government ordered the forfeiture of the security of Rs 2,000 deposited earlier by *New India* and all copies of the paper, wherever found, were seized. The government served an order on Mrs Besant demanding a fresh security of Rs 10,000 for continuance of *New India*. The order also required a fresh press declaration for publishing the journal. Three days later, on 29 August, as the keeper of the Vasantha Press where her weekly *Commonweal* was printed, Mrs Besant was asked to furnish under Section 3(2) of the Indian Press Act 1910, a security deposit of Rs 5,000 with the District Magistrate, Chingleput, within five days from the service of the notice.[94]

Mrs Besant was enraged. By another executive order, the Government had interned hundreds of young people in Bengal to weaken the Home Rule campaign there. Repression bestrode the land and popular feeling ran high. *New India* became even more forthright in its criticism.

Mrs Besant decided to move the High Court of Madras under Section 17 of the Indian Press Act and presented an application to have the forfeiture set aside. The High Court rejected Mrs Besant's petition.

While Mrs Besant lost the case, the wide publicity acquired by the security issue strengthened the home rule agitation and it intensified, not only in Madras but in other parts of India, especially in Bombay and Bengal.

The *New India* Security Case drew the attention of the entire nation. There was a nationwide protest against the Madras Government's demand. National leaders like Pandit Madan Mohan Malaviya, M.A. Jinnah, Tej Bahadur Sapru and C.Y. Chintamani raised their voice of protest. Mammoth public meetings were held in the Madras Presidency, in Bombay, Bengal and the United Provinces. Congress committees in Tirupur, Tanjore, Erode and Cuddalore, Ahmadnagar, Bombay, Allahabad and other towns in India voiced their protest. The Home Rule Movement thus acquired a new dimension. Several associations and societies like the Bombay Presidency Association, the Servants of India Society and the Hyderabad Citizens' Association expressed their solidarity with the Home Rulers in support of *New India*. The Malabar Congress Committee and merchant bodies gathered funds for the defence of *New India*. At no time earlier had such a unanimous cry been raised all over the country, demanding the repeal of the obnoxious Indian Press Act of 1910.

The press itself vehemently voiced its deep concern at this attack on the freedom of the press. 'Liberty of the Press in India is a myth,' the *Amrita Bazar Patrika* declared.

The official position was that Mrs Besant's charges were groundless and that she had made wild charges against a settled government and that her political writings and speeches amounted to calumny and went far beyond the limits of honest and legitimate criticism.[95]

In her attempts to influence students, Mrs Besant's most active associate was G.S. Arundale who had long been connected with her educational work in India. B.P. Wadia, the sub-editor of *New India* shared responsibility for the tone and policy of both *New India* and *Commonweal* and government took action against both of them.

14. Government Reaction to Home Rule Demand

Government repression and efforts to block her activities through repeated attacks on her paper, *New India*, did not deter Mrs Besant one bit. *New India* continued publication. She also resorted to other channels to rouse the people. After a strong home rule speech she delivered at Cuddalore in May 1917, the Governor of Madras, Lord Pentland, sent for Mrs Besant and offered her two alternatives: either to leave the country or get interned.[96] As Mrs Besant refused to leave India, she was interned along with G. S. Arundale and B.P. Wadia (June 1917).

But the Home Rule Movement could not have reached the heights it did without the suffering which is the characteristic of all great movements in history. The internment had to be undergone. It marked a peak in pre-independence Indian politics. Mrs Besant and her two colleagues were ordered to be confined to Ooty in the Nilgiri District.[97]

The deep resentment at Mrs Besant's internment was manifested in many ways. What disturbed the British was the Moderate Congressmen's involvement with the Home Rulers and their participation in the agitation.[98] It was an unparalleled demonstration of anger and protest. The country made clear that it would not brook the blow struck at the strongest propagandist of home rule who had done more than any other individual person to make it an immediate issue.

India witnessed unprecedented scenes for three months following Mrs Besant's internment. There was a nation-wide protest and agitation for Mrs Besant's release. The Home Rule League gained in strength and influence. Several new branches sprang up in various parts of India. Protest meetings were held everywhere. Members of the Theosophical Society were active everywhere. Hari Sarvothama Rao agitated widely for Mrs Besant's release; he recruited propagandists for the spread of home rule ideas. Senior Congressmen, who had earlier kept aloof, also joined the Home Rule League willingly. They fanned the agitation everywhere and openly identified themselves with it.

The protests soon snowballed into action. Men like Madan Mohan Malaviya, C.Y. Chintamani, Motilal Nehru, Tej Bahadur Sapru, Jehangir Petit hastened to join the issue against the policy of repression by announcing their membership of the Home Rule League. The non-official members of the legislative councils contemplated resignation. Mrs Besant said: 'Unless I suffer, people could not believe that I am not the hidden instrument of Imperialism and that I am not the mere agent of the British Government.'

The representatives of the Indian National Congress and Muslim League met at a joint Conference in Bombay on 28 and 29 July 1917 to consider the situation consequent on Mrs Besant's internment and to discuss the issue of passive resistance. The meeting resolved to request the provincial Congress Committees and the Council of Muslim League to examine the proposal of passive resistance suggested by Gandhi and convey their views to the AICC.[99]

In the thick of the protest meetings and agitation for Mrs Besant's release, came Sir S. Subramania Aiyer's famous letter to President Wilson of USA.[100] Aiyer, a senior Congressman and co-founder of the Indian National Congress in 1885 was a retired judge of the Madras High Court and the Honorary President of the All India Home Rule League. He apprised the US President of the situation in India following Mrs Besant's internment and the oppressive policy pursued by British Government in India. The Madras Government and the Government of India took serious objection to this letter, calling it disgraceful. However, in view of Aiyer's old age, took no action against him. Sir S. S. Aiyer resigned his knighthood to register his protest against Mrs Besant's internment.

With the Home Rule League at the height of its popularity, the Government of India resorted to every means to thwart it. The Non-Brahman Movement was encouraged and induced to oppose the home rule agitation. Communal riots were engineered in parts of Andhra and Tamil regions, to represent to the visiting Secretary of State Edwin Montagu, that the demand for home rule came only from a small section of the people and that the non-Brahmins, who constituted the majority of the people, were opposed to it. Communal riots were staged to establish the old theory that, in a land where acute caste and communal divisions existed, a democratic system and representative institutions could not function.

In recognition of her sacrifice and in appreciation of her contribution to the cause of Indian Nationalism, Mrs Besant was elected to preside over the thirty-second session of the Indian National Congress at Calcutta. It was felt that the best reply to the Government of India in the matter of the internment would be to elect the subject of their displeasure to the greatest honour which the nation could confer on those who served its cause.

This marked the end of three crowded years of strenuous struggle. Never before in India had a single movement in the short span of three years accomplished so much to transform and energize the national movement, to change its course and character as the Home Rule Movement had done.

The Home Rule League was to be an auxiliary body to undertake, on behalf of the Congress, educative propaganda on the principles of and necessity for self government in India. The Indian National Congress and the Home Rule League had an identical objective: Home Rule for India.

This movement was to be a turning point in the history of the National Congress. The Congress came to be transformed into an active agitating body on account of the Home Rule League. The Congress organization was drawn into the nation-wide agitation for Home Rule, especially during the year 1916-1917. Congressmen were roused to action, thereby activizing their committees. The country-wide agitation, raging throughout the year, was a novel experience for the Congress. 'If political work were to be successful, it was necessary to keep the flame of agitation burning continually from day to day,' observed Mrs Besant. The formation of Home Rule League was welcomed by the progressive sections with their new line of leadership in the Indian National Congress as they opted in favour of agitation against the British. But conservative sections feared that the League might overlap and weaken the Congress and also reduce its political importance. Mrs Besant, however, dispelled this impression. Writing in *New India* she said that the 'Home Rule League would "supplement" and not "supplant the Congress" '. She further made it clear that 'the League was to be a kind of an executive arm of the Congress to rouse them to activities instead of being a rival to the National Congress'. The League was designed everywhere to help the Congress in its work by carrying on an intensive political campaign.

The home rule activities acted like magic in reviving the Congress which had become dull and heavy and showed signs of exhaustion. Both Mrs Besant and B.G. Tilak and their Leagues had addressed themselves to purging the Congress of its lethargy and promoting healthy political activity from the Congress platform throughout the year.

The Home Rule Leagues chalked out their programme and agitation objectively, hastening the evolution of self-government as the Congress goal. The impact of Mrs Besant's and Tilak's active propaganda for self government was visibly felt in the Congress party right from the beginning of the former's efforts. The Congress, by applying itself to home rule activities, began to breathe new life. Mrs Besant's lofty idealism, organizing calibre, promptness, capacity for resolute action, devotion to the Congress cause, eloquence and journalistic talents stirred the lethargic Congressmen to activity.

At a time when disappointment and frustration were rampant in the country, the Home Rule Leagues breathed activity into the Congress, dull, drab and nearly defunct till then. Mrs Besant was weary of the dullness and tediousness that marked the Congress and the activities of the Home Rule League generated a new enthusiasm in the country.

The tremendous response in the ranks of Congressmen to the activities of the Home Rule League was reflected in the attendance at the 1915 annual session of the Congress at Bombay. This Session was termed the Home Rule Congress, though the League could not be launched at that time. The home rule campaign that was carried on in the months preceding the Lucknow Session in 1916 and the Congress-League understanding, coupled with Mrs Besant's persistent agitation, was largely instrumental in drawing the Congress and the Muslim League together. At a time when the Congress lacked machinery, the Home Rule League imparted vigour to its central organization.

Many Congressmen were effective Home Rulers, of whom A. Rangaswamy Iyengar, Pattabhi Sitaramayya, and younger Congress leaders like Jawaharlal Nehru, S. Satyamurti, Choudhuri Khaliquazzaman and others were soon to dominate the Indian political scene.

The home rule resolution adopted in the Bombay Congress Session was largely due to the influence and pressure exerted by Mrs Besant for the establishment of her League. Again, in the same session, Mrs Besant was instrumental in securing the adoption of the political resolution demanding substantial measures of reform leading to self-government in India. Though short-lived, the Home Rule Movement raged like whirlwind and transformed the Congress and prepared it for a sustained movement for freedom under the leadership of Gandhiji.

15. The Impact of the Home Rule Movement

Any endeavour to study or estimate the impact of the Home Rule Movement and its organization on the National liberation struggle will necessitate an objective analysis of its ideology, goals and limitations.

The movement developed into a fairly widespread one with substantial mass participation and following within a short span of time. Despite its immense popularity and mass following, however, the Home Rule Movement had certain limitations.

The Home Rule League, with its weak mass base, and short-lived character was more like a trend than a regular party. Its organization and structure were far from adequate for building up a sustained movement. Its branches had tenuous links with their headquarters and soon began to disintegrate and decline in strength as Mrs Besant's influence and popularity waned. Attempts to revive them were all failures.

The serious shortcoming of the ideology of the Home Rule Movement was its acceptance of the link with imperialism. At a time when the Home Rule League was growing and had frontally clashed with imperialism, Mrs Besant defined the 'Home Rule' as 'Self Rule' or 'Self-Government within the Empire'.

This was a serious flaw imposing certain limitations on the Home Rule Movement. In the face of these limitations the League could not develop into a sustained anti-imperialist body which could lead the next phase of the liberation struggle. On this account, the League failed to pursue its efforts in continuation of the agitation after Mrs Besant's release. The absence of an anti-imperialist stance rendered it weak. The Home Rule League was thus on the wane when the avalanche of the Non-Cooperation Movement was launched under the leadership of Gandhiji.

In the special session of the National Congress held in September 1918, the younger and progressive Congressmen rejected Mrs Besant's leadership since she had suddenly altered her strategy and opposed any resistance movement.

In changing the character and direction of the national movement, the Home Rule League's role is significant. The old Moderates and the Extremists were brought closer together. The demand for self-government was clearly articulated. The British Government's assurance of an advance towards self-government was largely a response to the home rule agitation.

The home rule agitation was a prelude to mass politics. Though the Leagues of both Tilak and Mrs Besant were not mass-based organizations, the activities of the movement touched the broad Indian masses, and particularly after the internment of Mrs Besant, there were widespread protest gatherings, mass meetings and processions involving large numbers of people.

Predominantly moderate in politics, the Madras Presidency underwent change with the emergence of Mrs Besant on the national scene. It was drawn into active participation in agitational political activities.

The Brahmins dominated the Home Rule League in Maharashtra, Karnataka and Madras. In Maharashtra, besides the Brahmins, the participation of the Marathas and other non-Brahmins was equally substantial. But in the Madras Presidency, the Brahmins held a predominant position in the All India Home Rule League of Mrs Besant to the exclusion of other communities. The Brahmin response was phenomenal.

The increased participation of the upper caste Hindus and the

Brahmins in the National Congress in the first decade of this century in the south naturally led to their effective association with the Home Rule Movement as it was a suitable outlet for them. Mrs Besant's deep involvement in Hinduism and metaphysics, her discourses on Hindu philosophy, her translation into English of the Hindu scriptures probably drew Brahmin adherents to the Home Rule League in large numbers. The immediate reaction to the Home Rule Movement in Madras was the Non-Brahmin Movement as the League's narrow social base had provoked the non-Brahmins. The British too tried to weaken the Home Rule Movement in the south by prompting the non-Brahmins to oppose it by encouraging the formation of the Justice Party. The Justicite contention was that the transfer of power to Indian hands would mean predominantly Brahmin Rule. They therefore tried to stall the freedom movement. Their opposition, though lost in the avalanche of the Non-Cooperation Movement, was to lead to the ascendance of regional forces and somewhat deflect this region from the national mainstream.

Mrs Besant had established a network of local committees for propagating home rule. This was a new development and a departure from the pattern of the Swadeshi-Boycott Movement which was confined to certain areas in British India. The League branches, however imperfect and loosely knit, 'underlined the importance of an All India Organization at the local level for conduct of nation-wide agitation and provided the necessary guidance for the future leadership in Indian politics'. Gandhiji was to benefit from this experience. The Home Rule Movement encompassed regions and areas hitherto untouched by political movements and agitation.

In the short period of its existence the Home Rule League confronted the British frontally. It received repeated blows from the imperialist government, but it carried on undeterred. The Home Rule Leagues of India contributed effectively to the sustained political propaganda, thus preparing the nation to meet the enormous challenge from imperialism in the coming years.

The Indian political cauldron had begun to boil. The expectations of the Indians had been roused and hopes had been held out that, after the War, Indian demands would be looked at from 'a new angle of vision'.

Britain's response to the Indian home rule demand for self-government, came in the shape of an announcement by Edwin Montagu, the Secretary of State for India, in the British House of Commons on 20 August 1917:

> The policy of His Majesty's Government with which the Government of India are in complete accord, is that of the increasing association of Indians

> in every branch of administration and the gradual development of Self-Governing institutions with a view to the progressive realisation of responsible Government in India as an integral part of the British Empire.

Owing to public resentment and indignation, coupled with the situation created by the nation-wide protests and mass upsurge, the government ordered, in September 1917, the release of Mrs Besant, G.S. Arundale and B.P. Wadia. In view of Montagu's political mission to India the government wished to restore normalcy and her release was regarded as a triumph for Indian nationalism. The reception accorded to her by the masses was a true index of the popularity of the slogan of home rule.

Following the Calcutta Congress of 1917, there were important developments. The Montford Report was published on 12 July 1918 and a fierce controversy raged in the country over it. Indian political opinion was sharply divided over the reform proposals.

The cleavage between the moderate and the liberal-minded politicians and the left-wing nationalists was real. The Moderates hailed the proposals as a 'definite stage in the progressive realisation of responsible Government'. The left-wing Congressmen condemned the proposals as falling short of legitimate Indian political aspirations. They failed in their efforts to bring the Moderate Congressmen to the special session of the Congress at Bombay (1918) to consider the Reform Proposals. The Moderates not only chose to stay away from the special session, but, according to Dinshaw Wacha, were constrained to hold an All India Conference of the Moderate Party to endorse the reform proposals and to stall the danger of the new reform scheme being wrecked by the Extremists. The split this time saw the Congress in the hands of the nationalist and progressive sections, while the Moderates walked out to constitute a separate political group.

The issue was further complicated by the publication of the recommendations of the Rowlatt Commission. Its Report, reviewing the revolutionary and conspiratorial activities of the seditionists of Bengal and elsewhere, saw a German connivance in all these activities and recommended imprisonment without open trial and arbitrary internment of the revolutionary suspects.

The Indian people were told in so many words that the Self Government of India would not be a factor in the reconstruction of the Empire after war; those who worked for freedom would be put down. Undeterred by the government's warning and not tempted by bureaucratic favours, wihout 'falling a prey to any system of political jobbery', the Indian people resolved to rise as one man under Gandhiji's leadership to struggle for swaraj or self-government. From Dadabhai Naoroji, Tilak,

Mrs Besant, the mantle of leadership passed to Gandhiji, prophet of the new philosophy of non-violent non-cooperation.

Notes and References

1. B.G. Tilak's speech: Extracts from Police Abstracts Bombay History of the Freedom Movement vide C.I.D. Reports, Vol. I, File No. IV-1909 (Madras Archives).
2. *The Madras Standard,* 29 Dec. 1907.
3. Home Political A. Proceedings, 26 Feb. 1908. Also see *Hindu,* 13 & 17 Feb. 1908.
4. *Mahratta,* 2 Feb. 1908 — vide C.I.D. Reports 1909. Vol. I, File No. 4 (Tamil Nadu Archives).
5. Ibid.
6. *Mahratta,* 26 April 1908.
7. Tilak's main speech in the Dhulia (Maharashtra) conference, 27 April through to 1 May 1908, *Mahratta.*
8. Presidential speech by Dr Rash Behari Ghosh in the Congress Session at Madras, Dec. 1908.
9. *Proceedings of the Surat Convention,* 28 Dec. 1907.
10. C.I.D. Report, Vol. I, 1909, File No. 4.
11. Ibid.
12. *Proceedings of the Surat Convention,* 28 Dec. 1907.
13. See the printed Proceedings of the Surat Convention, 28 Dec. 1907 (Madras Archives).
14. See the Congress Constitution adopted at the Allahabad Convention, 18 April 1909. *C.I.D. Reports, Vol. I, 1909. File No. 4 (INA) and the Proceedings of the Convention of Allahabad 1908* 18, 19 April.
15. Letter from Chief Secretary Gait, ICS, Bengal, to Home Secretary 4 Dec. 1907, vide *Home Political Jan. 1908 No. 499 Confdl. on partition agitation and Boycott.*
16. *C.I.D. Report* Vol. I, Part II, 1909.
17. *C.I.D. Report* Ibid.
18. G.O. No. 1542. Judicial dt. 3-10-1911. Also *C.I.D. Report 1909, File No. V, Vol. II* (Confdl).
19. *Home Political B.* dt. 21-1-1909, No. 33.
20. Confidential Report of the Native Newspaper — *Kesari,* 26 May 1908.
21. Articles in *Kesari* 9 June 1908. Native Newspaper Report Jan.-June 1908.
22. *See Home Political A — Oct. 1908* No. bi-103.
23. *Home Political A — Proceedings Nov. 1909-10,* 31.
24. *Home Political A — March 1910, 79-87.*
25. *C.I.D. Report Vol. I Part II (Bundle No. 63)* 1909.
26. *Home Political A — March 1910, 79-87.*
27. *G.O. No. 1542 — Judicial, dt. 3-10-1911.*
28. *G.O. No. 1542 — Judicial. dt. 3-10-1911* containing C.I.D. Compiled Report and the Judgment. *Home Political A. April 1908 Nos. 9-87.*
29. *Home Political A — Dec. 1908 Nos. 6-14.*

30. *C.I.D. Report*, op. cit.
31. *C.I.D. Report*, op. cit.
32. Morley to Minto 15 April 1908.
33. *Home Political A. Proceedings No. 118 dt. Oct. 1913.*
34. *Proceedings of the Congress 1908, Madras.*
35. Presidential speech delivered by Dr Rash Behari Ghosh in the Madras Session of December 1908.
36. Ibid.
37. *Home Political A. Proceedings No. 34*, Feb. 1910 (Confdl).
38. *Native Newspaper Report 1910* (Vol. Jan. to April).
39. G.K. Gokhale to W. Wedderburn, 30 June 1910, *(Gokhale papers)* NMM, New Delhi.
40. G.K. Gokhale to W. Wedderburn, *(Gokhale Papers)* NMM.
41. *Native Newspaper Vol. Jan.-June 1910.*
42. Presidential speech : William Wedderburn. *Proceedings of the Indian National Congress at Allahabad 1910.*
43. Ibid.
44. Lord Minto's opening speech in the Central Assembly in Jan. 1910.
45. *Proceedings of the Indian National Congress at Calcutta 1911.* Speech by the Chairman Reception Committee.
46. President Pandit Bishan Narain Dar's speech.
47. See the *Proceedings of the Indian National Congress* Session at Bankipur. Chairman Reception Committee Speech.
48. *Proceedings of the twenty-seventh Congress at Bankipur 1912.* Presidential Speech by R.N. Mudholkar in *Encyclopaedia of the INC* pp. 318-19. Vol. VI, 1911-1916, by A.M. Zaidi and S.G. Zaidi.
49. *Resolution No. IV Indian National Congress Session at Karachi.*
50. The Presidential Address to Karachi Session 1913.
51. See the *Proceedings of the 28th Session of the Indian National Congress at Karachi, 1913.*
52. Viceroy Hardinge's speech at Madras, *The Encyclopaedia of the Indian National Congress* Vol. VI, 1911-1916, by A.M. Zaidi and S.G. Zaidi p. 419.
53. Welcome Speech by S. Subramania Iyer as Chairman Reception Committee of Madras Session of Indian National Congress, December 1908. See printed Proceedings (Tamil Nadu Archives).
54. Presidential Speech by Bhupendranath Basu, Madras Session : Indian National Congress, Dec. 1908 from the printed proceedings of the twenty-third Session of the Congress (Tamil Nadu Archives).
55. Resolution 4.
55a. Resolution No. XII. See *Proceedings of the 29th Session of the Indian National Congress; Madras, 1914.*
55b. *The History of the Indian National Congress*, P. Sitaramayya, p. 202.
56. Resolution No. V, Madras Session of Indian National Congress, December 1914.
57. *C.I.D. Report—File No. 6*, 1916-19.
58. C.S. Srinivasachari *History of India.*
59. Dr Annie Besant's speech. See *Besant Papers Vol. III*, Sir James Willcocks 'With Indians in France'.

60. T.V. Parvate *Bal Gangadhar Tilak.*
61. Resolution No. XIX—Thirtieth Session of the Indian National Congress from *Congress Encyclopaedia Vol. VI.*
62. *The Encyclopaedia of Indian National Congress Vol. VI* 1911-1916 by A.M. & S.G. Zaidi, *Proceedings of the Thirtieth Session of the Indian National Congress,* Bombay, December 1915.
63. See the *Proceedings of the Thirtieth Session of the Indian National Congress,* Bombay—Dec. 1915.
64. Tilak's speech in Lucknow Session (from *Proceedings of the Indian National Congress Session, Lucknow* — Dec. 1916).
65. Presidential Address of A.C. Mazumdar at Lucknow Session — 1916.
66. *A.I.C.C. Files 1885-1947* — Resolution of Lucknow Session — December 1916 (Nehru Memorial Museum).
67. At the A.I.C.C. Session — Lucknow — Tilak's speech.
68. See *Annexure I* — For Provisions of the Lucknow Pact.
69. Letter from W. Wedderburn to the General Secretaries, A.I.C.C., A.I.C.C. Files 1885-1947 N.M.M.L. collections.
69a. Dr. Annie Besant's Presidential Address to Calcutta Congress Session — December 1917.
70. Ibid.
71. *Biography of Dr Annie Besant.*
72. Series of articles in *New India* 1914.
73. *New India* — 6 Jan. 1916 p.10
74. *New India* — 31 December 1915 p. 11.
75. *New India,* 6 January 1916.
76. *G.O. No. 836 — Public Confidential 23.6.1917 also Besant Papers Vol. I.*
77. The future of Indian Politics by Mrs Annie Besant paper. 181.
78. From 1400 in early Nov. 1916 to 32,000 in early 1918 See report in *Maharatta* in the *Native Newspaper Jan.-July 1918 Report Volume July-Dec. 1916. Jan.-June 1917.*
79. *New India* 14 August 1916. Besant Papers Volume IV Paper 4445 (Madras Archives).
80. Cuttings from *New India* in Besant Papers Vol. III.
81. *G.O. 836 Public Confidential dt. 23.6.1917.*
82. *Home Political, Deposit — Sept. 1917* — File No. 50.
83. New India — Articles — 1915-16 appended in *Besant Papers* Vol. II.
84. *G.O. No. 836 — Public Confidential dt. 23.6.1917 also G.O. No. 3112. Public Confidential dt. 11 December 1915 Op. cit. Home Rule File No. 4.*
85. Butterworth's letter No. 44961 dt. 8 October 1915, Vol. II — *Besant Papers.*
86. Wheeler's (Home Secretary), Government of India letter No. 833 dt. 28 Feb. 1916, *Besant Papers* Vol. II.
87. *G.O.No. 582, Public Dept. (Confdl.) dt. 8 July 1918* a Memorandum on Newspapers.
88. *Besant Papers* Vol. I Paper 37 — 44.
89. *G.O. No. 744 — Public Confidential* dt. 7.6.1917.
90. Order No. 40 dt. 7.7.1916 of Bombay Government from *Besant Papers* Vol. II.
91. *G.O. No. 836 — Public Confidential dt. 23.6.1917.*

92. *G.O. No. 559 Home-Education* 1.5.1917 in Home Rule File No. 7(k).
93. 836, *Public Department, Government of Madras* — 23.6.1917 and also Besant Paper Vol. III.
94. *Besant Paper* — Vol. IV
95. Editorial: *Wednesday Review*: 31 May 1916.
96. G.O. No. 836 — *Public Confidential* dt. 23.6.1917. *also* pages 20, 102, 103 — *Besant Papers* Vol. II.
97. G.O. No. 836 — *Public Confidential* dt. 23.6.1917 *also* Home Political A. August 1917 No. 80-106.
98. *Fortnightly Report* — 17.7.1917
99. *Home Political, Deposit 48, September 1917;* also *Home Political, 4 Confdl. December 1917,* No. 628-38.
100. *Home Political D. February 1918* — File No. 36 *Text of the Letter — Annexure III.*

APPENDIX 7.1

G.O. No. 836 Public Confidential dt. 23 June 1917

The Governor of Madras in exercise of the powers conferred in him by rule 3 of the Defence of India Rules 1915, served the order for internment on Mrs Besant and her two colleagues on 17 June 1917, prohibiting them from attending or taking part in any speech and from publishing or processing the publication of any writing or speech compared by them placing their correspondence under censorship. Further the order directed that after the expiry of seven or fourteen days from the date of service of the order, they shall cease to reside in the city of Madras or in the district of Chingleput and shall take up their residence within any one of the following six areas:

1. The Nilgiri District
2. The Coimbatore District
3. The Bellary District
4. The Palani Hills
5. The Shevaroy Hills
6. The Municipal Town of Vizagapatnam

APPENDIX 7.2

S. Subramania Iyer's Letter to President Wilson*

On 24 June 1917, S. Subramania Iyer, Honorary President of the Home Rule League addressed a letter to Woodrow Wilson, President of the United States of America. The letter made the authorities in India and Britain very angry and wild allegations regarding receipt of money by Annie Besant, Lala Lajpat Rai and others from Germany were levelled against them. Excerpts from this letter are reproduced below:

Madras, India, 24th June

To His Excellency, President Wilson.

Honoured Sir:

I address this letter to you as Honorary President of the Home Rule League in India, an organisation voicing the aspirations of a United India as expressed through the Indian National Congress and the All India Muslim League. These are the only two bodies in India today which truly represent the political ideals of that Nation of more than three hundred million people, because [they are] the only bodies created by the people themselves.

Over five thousand delegates of these two popular assemblies met at their annual convention in Lucknow last December and they unanimously and co-jointly agreed upon identical Resolutions, asking His Majesty, the King of Great Britain, to issue a proclamation announcing that it is the aim and intention of British policy to confer Self-Government on India at an early date, to grant democratising reforms and to lift India from the position of a Dependency to that of an equal partner in the Empire with the Self-Governing Dominions.

While these Resolutions, Honored Sir, voiced India's aspirations, they also expressed her loyalty to the Crown. But, though many months have elapsed, Great Britain has not yet made any official promise to grant our country's plea. Perhaps this, because the Government is too fully occupied with the heavy responsibility of the War.

But it is the very relationship of the Indian Nationalist Movement to the War that urges the necessity for an immediate promise of Home Rule — Autonomy — for India, as it would result in an offer from India of at least five million men in three months for service at the front, and of five million more in another three months.

India can do this because she has a population of three hundred and fifteen millions — three times that of the United States, and almost

*Extracted from *Home Political D.*, Feb. 1918, File No. 36.

equal to the combined population of all the Allies. The people of India will do this, because then they would be free men and not slaves.

At present we are a subject Nation, held in chains, forbidden by our alien rulers to express publicly our desire for the ideals presented in your famous War Message: " . . . the liberation of peoples, the right of nations great and small, and the privilege of men everywhere to choose their ways of life and of obedience. The world must be made safe for democracy. Its place must be planted upon the tested foundations of political liberty."

Even as conditions are, India has more than proved her loyalty to the Allies. She has contributed freely and generously of both blood and treasure in France, in Gallipoli, in Mesopotamia, and elsewhere, Mr Austen Chamberlain, British Secretary of State for India said: "There are Indian troops in France to this day; their gallantry, endurance, patience and perseverance were shown under conditions new and strange to them." Field Marshall Lord French said: "I have been much impressed by the initiative and resources displayed by the Indian troops." The London Times said concerning the fall of Baghdad, "It should always be remembered that a very large portion of the force which General Maude had guided to victory are Indian regiments. The cavalry which hung on the flanks and demoralised the Turkish army and chased to the confines of Baghdad, must have been almost exclusively Indian cavalry. The infantry which bore months of privation and proved in the end masters of the Turks, included Indian units, which had already fought heroically in France, Gallipoli and Egypt."

If Indian soldiers have achieved such splendid results for the Allies while slaves, how much greater would be their power if inspired by the sentiments which can arise only in the souls of free men — men who are fighting not only for their own liberties but for the liberties of mankind. The truth is that they are now sacrificing their life to maintain the supremacy of an alien Nation which uses that supremacy to dominate and rule them against their will.

Under these conditions, it is not surprising that the official Government in India utterly failed to get a response to its recent appeal to Indian volunteers for military service. Only five hundred men came forward out of a possible thirty million.

It is our earnest hope that you may so completely convert England to your ideals of world liberation that together you will make it possible for India's millions to lend assistance in this War.

Permit me to add that you and the other leaders have been kept in ignorance of the full measure of misrule and oppression in India. Officials of an alien nation speaking a foreign tongue force their will upon us; they grant themselves exorbitant salaries and large allowances; they refuse us education; they sap us of our wealth; they impose crushing taxes without our consent; they cast thousands of our people into prisons for uttering patriotic sentiments — prisons so filthy that often the inmates die from loathsome disease.

A recent instance of misrule is the imprisonment of Mrs Besant, that noble Irish woman who has done so much for India. As set forth in the accompanying statement signed by eminent legislators, editors, educators and pleaders, she had done nothing except carry on a law-abiding and constitutional propaganda of reforms; the climax being her internment, without charges and without trial shortly after printing and circulating your War message.

I believe His Majesty, the King, and the English Parliament are unaware of these conditions, and that, if they can be informed, they will order Mrs Besant's immediate release.

A mass of documentary evidence, entirely reliable, corroborative and explanatory of the statements in this letter is in the hands of Mr and Mrs Henry Hotchner, who would esteem it a privilege to place it at your disposal. I have entrusted this letter to them because it would never have been permitted to reach you by mail. They are loyal Americans, editors, authors and lecturers on educational and humanitarian subjects, who have been deeply interested in the welfare of India. They have sojourned here off and on during the last ten years and so have been eyewitnesses to many of the conditions herein described. They have graciously consented to leave their home in India in order to convey this letter to you personally in Washington.

Honoured Sir, the aching heart of India cries out to you, whom we believe to be an instrument of God in the reconstruction of the world.

I have the honour to be, Sir,
your most obedient servant:
S. SUBRAMANIA

Knight Commander Indian Empire;
Doctor of Laws;
Honorary President of
the Home Rule League in India;
Co-Founder of the
National Congress of India in 1885;
Retired Judge and frequently
Acting Chief Justice of the
High Court of Madras.

Chapter VIII

Congress during 1917-1919 The Environment in Motion

Tarasankar Banerjee

1. The Position of the Congress

THE CONGRESS DURING 1917-19 stood at the threshold of a mighty change both in terms of the magnitude of the conflict with the Raj and the dynamics of the movement. The position of the Congress in national political life also underwent a significant, qualitative transformation. The rise of a new star on the political horizon of India — the rise of Gandhiji — brought about a refreshing promise in the national struggle, which was destined to give an altogether new direction to the efforts of the people to achieve their cherished goal — freedom. In a sense, the period between 1917 and 1919 was a great divide in the history of the Congress before independence. It was a sort of hyphen that connected two momentous epochs, each with distinct characteristics and shades of ideas.

As it stood in 1917, the Congress presented a united appearance once again, organically speaking. The Moderates and the Extremists had no doubt, closed their ranks in 1916, but the scars of the Surat split in 1907 were yet to be completely healed. Events during this period proved that the attitude towards the nationalist path among the erstwhile Moderates and Extremists still continued to be different, notwithstanding the outward unity. Nationalists of all shades, however, had already suffered a traumatic experience at the hands of the imperialist rulers. The Congress was now standing on firm foundations, particularly after the victory it had achieved in 1911, when the nefarious partition of Bengal by Curzon was annulled. The Congress had come to stay, effectively belying the fond hopes of Curzon that he would ultimately witness its 'peaceful demise'. The Congress in 1916 had, undoubtedly, become a great, viable nationalist body, upholding the cause of the people of India as a whole and not merely that of any particular sect or group. Both the rulers and the politicians came to recognize that it was a great spokesman for the Indian people and their political demands. The Raj could not ignore it as it had done in the 19th century; it had to heed it in the interests of the empire itself. On the other hand, Indian politicians had also clearly realized that the Congress had already become an effective political platform and they aspired to control it in spite of the existence of 'in' and 'out' groups, so to say. This had become evident during 1898-1911 and was climaxed by the Surat split in 1907. Prior to the emergence of Gandhi, the struggle for leadership was never due to purely personality conflicts; it stemmed, by and large, from differences in principle regarding the nature of the movement against the Raj. This difference in approach imparted a particular character to the Congress over the years. It may be noted that in 1917 the final shape of things for the future struggle against the rulers was yet to be determined, even though the Congress had become the pivot of the Indian national movement.

The history of the evolution of the Congress and its achievements cannot be judged in isolation. Two other factors have to be taken into account for a proper assessment of the developments during 1917-19. These are the relationship of the Congress with the Muslim League that was founded in 1907, and international developments. It is true that the Congress is always regarded as the prime nationalist body in Indian political life. But the establishment of the Muslim League in 1907 injected a new factor into Indian politics which had its repercussions on the Congress policies and approach as well. Towards the fag end of 1906 Nawab Salimullah of Dacca confidently declared: 'India was on the eve of a new era and Mohammadans were awakening from the coma into which they had fallen. The new political movement had been forced on them.'[1] The story of the rise of the Muslim League has been recounted elsewhere; but it is necessary here to state the aims and objectives of the League for a reapprisal of the position of the Congress vis-a-vis the League in 1916. The League objectives were

(a) to promote amongst the Mussalmans of India, feelings of loyalty towards the British Government, and to remove any misconception that may arise as to the intentions of Government with regard to any of its measures;
(b) to protect and advance the political and other rights of the Mussalmans of India and respectfully represent their needs and aspirations to the Government;
(c) to prevent the rise among the Mussalmans of India of any feeling of hostility towards other communities, without prejudice to the other aforesaid objects of the League.[2]

The bold declaration of Zaka Ullah, Secretary of the Muslim League in 1907 gave a foretaste of the future tendency. He said, 'We are not opposed to the social unity of the Hindus and the Mussalmans . . . . But the other type of unity [political] involves the working out of common political purposes. This sort of unity with the Congress cannot be possible because we and the Congressmen do not have common political objectives.'[3] Till 1907 the Congress was virtually the unrivalled political institution in the country. Now the position was changed. While the Raj found a new ally, the Congress stood face to face with a determined political adversary. The Indian Muslims as a political body could not be taken for granted. There is no denying the fact that the League, since its birth, 'possessed alarming portents against the Congress in particular and the national aspirations in general'.[4] A period of competition and collaboration between the Congress and the League began, in which bouts of hostility and friendliness alternated. Since the first decade of the present century, the Congress was thus faced with a new political situation and it had either to contend with or adjust to the Muslim League in the interest of the larger national struggle.

If the decade following the partition of Bengal witnessed strained feelings and political opposition between the Muslim League and the Congress over the anti-British, anti-partition agitation led primarily by Hindus, a wind of change began to blow with the commencement of World War I. It is ironical that the outbreak of the war was indirectly a boon to the Indian national movement in general and the Congress-League relationship in particular. Since its foundation, the League had kept aloof from the Congress and maintained a posture of hostility towards it. But the stress of political events in and outside India gradually alienated the League from the British and drew them closer to the Congress. It has been rightly remarked that the 'annulment of the partition of Bengal in 1911 gave a rude shock to the Muslim faith in the British Government'.[5] The Indian Muslims were further disillusioned when, on the eve of the Great War, the Muslim countries in Africa and Asia received a new deal from the European powers during 1912-13. This was 'interpreted as a definite move for the extinction of the power of Islam'.[6] Political as well as emotional factors thus compelled the League to gradually veer around to the Congress for support. A welcome wind of change, much to the satisfaction of the Congress, started blowing in 1913 when both the Congress and the League discussed at length, at their own sessions, the question of a rapprochement. The Karachi Congress in 1913, presided over by Nawab Syed Mohammad of Madras, adopted the following resolution:

> That this Congress places on record its warm appreciation of the adoption by the All India Muslim League of the ideal of self-government for India within the British Empire and expresses its complete accord with the belief that the League has so emphatically declared in its last session that the political future of the country depends on the harmonious working and

> cooperation of its various communities in it, which has been a cherished ideal of the Congress.

It has to be noted that M.A. Jinnah played an important role in the Karachi Congress deliberations. On the other side of the curtain, under the presidentship of Muhammad Shafi, the All India Muslim League adopted a resolution in its annual session in 1913, defining its object as 'the attainment under the aegis of the British Crown, of a system of self-government suitable to India'. The League resolved to achieve this object by promoting national unity and co-operation with other communities.

The Karachi Congress is rightly regarded as 'the forerunner of the Lucknow Pact and also of the wonderful loyalty the Muslims showed to the Congress in the days of Non-cooperation movement'.[7] While the League was changing its character from diehard conservatism and hostility to co-operative progress, the Congress was also closing its ranks under the shock of the war. The climax was reached in the famous Lucknow Pact in 1916 when there was a complete rapprochement between the Congress and the League. The year 1916 was significant in more than one way. The erstwhile moderate and extremist wings united after a decade of differences. In the Congress Presidential Address at Lucknow it was emotionally remarked: 'If the United Congress was buried in the debris of the old French Garden at Surat, it is reborn today in the Kaiser Bag of Lucknow, the garden of the gorgeous King Wajed Ali Shah.' The united Congress showed political wisdom in taking the warm, co-operating hand of the Muslim League which also had its session at the same place. The Lucknow session was climaxed by the signing of the Congress-League scheme, the draft of which was prepared by a Joint Committee earlier. This scheme was the high-water mark of the joint efforts of the two political bodies for furthering their common goal. An unusual fraternity and co-operative spirit opened a new vista in the history of the Indian national struggle.

The welcome change in the political atmosphere in the country due to the rapprochement between the Congress and the League put the Congress in a better position to devote its energies to the fight against the Raj. It undoubtedly put the lever once again into the hands of the Congress during 1917-19 to act more effectively. It also prepared the backdrop for Gandhi's wholehearted attempt to achieve Hindu-Muslim amity. In his speech at the Mohammedan Association at Surat on 3 January 1916 Gandhi referred to the picture of South Africa where different communities worked shoulder to shoulder against White repression. He said, 'We shall accomplish the tasks that face us in India only when my Hindu, Muslim and Parsi brethren feel that they are all one.'[8] Thus, in more than one way the year 1916 was a turning point in the history of the Congress.

International events indirectly acted as a catalytic agent in India's struggle against the Raj and helped the Congress to ride the saddle and lead the country in the company of the Muslim League. World War I and the Russian Revolution of 1917 cast a deep shadow on Indian politics which entered a new phase and acquired a new dimension. As R.P. Dutt observed: 'It was the shock of the first world war with its lasting blow to the whole structure of imperialism, and the opening of the world revolutionary wave that followed in 1917 and after, which released the first mass movement of revolt in India.'[9] In two different ways these two events were corrosive in their impact on the British Empire in India. If the Great War had suddenly increased India's importance to the British, necessitating a change in the attitude of the imperial rulers, the Russian Revolution brought up the issue of national self-determination that was going to affect the relationship between India and Great Britain. The declaration of war against Germany automatically dragged India in without her explicit consent. Indian newspapers like *Amrita Bazar Patrika* recorded that 'the whole of India was at once thrown into a state of excitement'.[10] *The Statesman* recorded on 7 August 1914:

> Our very existence as a nation is at stake. If we are found wanting, it will not be the England hitherto known to us that will emerge from the trial. This reflection is enough to make every Englishman and, as we believe, every Indian resolve that, come what may, in the final result we shall not fail and that the people who ended the domination of Napoleon will prevail against the public enemy of modern Europe.[11]

The Congress had to cope with this unusual situation. They were hitherto mainly concerned with the internal problems which revolved round the question of political reform, adjustment with the Muslim League, and preservation of communal harmony. The Congress was not actually ready for an external exigency of such magnitude as faced them after the start of the war. The suddenness of the war demanded an immediate response and in the process it hastened the political evolution of the Congress vis-a-vis the Raj as well as the Muslim League.

By and large, the Congress did not subscribe to the view that England's disadvantage was India's advantage. The popular feeling found expression in Subramania Bharati's letter to *The Hindu* on 3 September 1914. He wrote: 'We shall always adopt peaceful and legal methods to achieve our object. In peacetime we shall be uncompromising critics of England's mistakes. But when trouble comes, we shall unhesitatingly stand by her and if necessary defend her against her enemies.'[12] Similarly, notwithstanding his motto to 'oppose and oppose the Government',

Motilal Ghose also thought that 'this was an occasion when Indians ought to co-operate with the Government'.[13] The Madras Congress of 1914 under the presidentship of Bhupendranath Basu gave expression to similar feelings. In one of its resolutions this Congress expressed its profound devotion to the Throne and 'its unswerving allegiance to the British connection, and its firm resolve to stand by the Empire at all hazards and at all costs. . .' R.C. Majumdar was not ready to accept the utterances and resolutions of the Congress at their face value. He wrote:

> On the other hand, there was, at least outwardly, an effusion of loyal sentiments which found expression in public sympathy with Britain and offers of active support to her in her fight against Germany. The whole of India seemed to be full of enthusiasm for the cause of the Allies, and eager to assist and co-operate. All this might have been partly genuine as far as the ruling chiefs were concerned, but it would be a grievous mistake to take the words of the common people or their leaders at their face value. Some of the British writers and statesmen committed this mistake, and wondered why the Government of India did not turn to the best account this universal enthusiasm of the people and desire to serve, by canalizing it into voluntary organizations and subsidiary service. They held that it was due to the failure of the government to do so that the bulk of Indian opinion gradually relapsed into comparative apathy. But the hard-boiled bureaucrats, who ruled India, knew better. A modern historian would undoubtedly endorse their view that there was no real and genuine war-enthusiasm or even loyalty among the people of India. Indeed there can be hardly any doubt that the pious platitudes uttered by Indian leaders indicating the support of, and sympathy with, the British during the First World War, did not represent the real feelings of India.[14]

Majumdar has perhaps come to this conclusion by way of easy generalization of the opinion expressed by some leaders like Tilak. If newspapers are any index of popular feelings, the only conclusion will be that during 1914-15 there was a genuine feeling of sympathy for and an urge for support to the Allied powers. The disillusionment of the Congress came towards the end of 1915 when they realized that, in spite of apparent softening in the attitude of the Raj, the rulers were not keen about favourably responding to the aspirations of nationalist India. The initial response of the British Government was extremely friendly as 'it was the need of the hour for the Government to try to woo the Congress'.[15] The war had kindled many political hopes which were not linked with India's support to the war effort. The *Bengali* in a leading article on 6 January 1915 rightly pointed out:

> This war has created a new self-consciousness and self-confidence in our people. It has revealed the need of our help and support for the Empire to which we belong. . . It is folly and suicidal conceit to ignore these new

conditions and to talk and act as if nothing had happened to affect the Indian mind since the war commenced.[16]

Actually, the Congress realized that it was a time for mutual understanding between England and India. The leaders did not want to support the British conditionally, though there was a firm natural expectation that the Raj would sympathetically appreciate the nationalist aspirations of India. In other words the Congress wanted to make it clear that Indian demands were the natural outcome of India's growing political needs, war or no war. In his Presidential Address at the Bombay Session of the Congress in 1915, Sir S.P. Sinha declared, 'There is not, I trust, a single person in our camp who expects reforms as the price or reward of our loyalty. That loyalty would indeed be a poor thing if it proceeded from a lively sense of favours to come.' This did not mean that the Congress should go on tolerating the British attitude of 'promise, pause, prepare, postpone, and end by letting things alone' with regard to reforms. There was a growing realization in the Congress that there was a necessity to press for demands. There was no denying the fact that the war had put the Congress in a better bargaining position by 1916, when the rapprochement within ensured a favourable climate for political struggle. According to Sitaramayya, 'here was then in 1916, a Nation whose cause went unheeded, and whose leader remained yet to be found',[17] as Tilak, hitherto the uncrowned leader of nationalist India, was failing in health, which stood in the way of his undertaking strenuous propaganda tours throughout India. A new leader with revitalizing power was the need of the day, when the country was on the verge of political take-off. Such a leader was soon to rise in the personality of M.K. Gandhi.

2. Emergence of Gandhi

Gandhi's emergence on the Indian political scene was spectacular as well as interesting. A panoramic glance at his career will show that his rise was neither sudden nor accidental, as it has been sometimes supposed by some scholars.[18] Objective conditions in India had directly contributed to the success of Gandhiji as a political leader. On his part he was shrewd enough to gauge the pulse of the people, and at the right moment he projected himself armed with his conviction in some basic principles, so different from the prevalent Indian political practices, and a new technique of struggle he had already developed in South Africa.

To understand the emergence of Gandhiji in Indian politics is not easy. There are two main trends to note in this phenomenon. Some scholars like Judith Brown view his rise primarily in the context of Indian power politics. Some look at him with unquestioned reverence and consider him basically as humanist *par excellence*, elevating him to the level of a saint. But it is true that the political Gandhi cannot be divorced from the other Gandhi who held some firm ideas which appeared to be obscurantist to many. Interestingly, this amalgam of opposites gave Gandhiji a unique strength and enabled him to gain a grip over the masses.

For students of history there are several basic difficulties in making an objective assessment of Gandhiji and his phenomenal rise. First of all, there had been some confusion among contemporaries as well as later critics as they confronted an enigmatical and, to some extent, mystic personality in whom saintliness was intertwined with shrewd political vision and a firm conviction in his own principles and methods.

> Here was a man who announced that he wished to live the life of a Hindu ascetic, yet plunged into politics and parleyed with viceroys. Here was an Indian who castigated his compatriots as unfit for Home Rule because of their moral and social failing, yet presented them with a novel technique of revolution with which to undermine the might of the British raj. Here was a nationalist who preached love of the imperial opponent. In the face of this phenomenon both rulers and ruled were at a loss. They had only a dim idea of Gandhi's ultimate goal, and consequently were often unable to understand or anticipate the steps he took towards that goal.[19]

Secondly, the attitude to their subject of authors writing on Gandhi sometimes created difficulty, since they were constantly aware that, for the people of India, Gandhi was something more than a political leader and could not be evaluated only as such. Thirdly, if Gandhiji's actions have often been ill-documented, his intentions have suffered still more from conjectures based on inadequate evidence. There are lots of 'private papers of Gandhiji; but there may be a debate over the question whether these were *really* private, that is, whether Gandhiji's innermost thoughts had come out in them. A recent British scholar has rightly commented: 'Gandhi was one of the most public of public men. He lived in full view of friends and followers . . . and kept a mound of papers and correspondence, knowing that these would probably be made public.'[20] In other words, these so-called 'private' papers are actually the conscious projections of Gandhiji, the astute politician. Nevertheless, their bona fides cannot be denied for purposes of historical analysis. Lastly, one great obstacle to a proper study of Gandhi is that he did not systematically and clearly delineate his ideology in English or any Indian language. We only get some glimpses of his ideas in a rather pedestrian form in his *Hind Swaraj* — the true testament of Gandhian ideology. These difficulties, however, do not prevent scholars from attempting a study of the rise of Gandhi in Indian politics during 1917-9.

Gandhiji returned to India — 'the land of deliverance' — in 1915, never to go back again to South Africa where he had had his early experience of public life. His political potential was, by then, an established fact. The fact that the British in South Africa heaved a sigh of relief when Gandhi announced his decision in the latter part of 1914 to return to India bears eloquent testimony to his qualities as a great leader. The Secretary of State for the Colonies wrote in March 1914 that 'the best possible outcome will be if Gandhi will return to his native land.'[21] Writing in August 1914 General Smuts said, 'The Saint has left our shores, I sincerely hope for ever.'

When he arrived in his motherland, Gandhiji was little known to the public. But Gokhale, whom Gandhiji considered as his political guru, had a clear idea of his potential and described him as 'wonderful personality'. As early as 1912, Gokhale commented. 'He [Gandhi] is without doubt made of the stuff of which heroes and martyrs are made. Nay, more. He has in him the marvellous spiritual power to turn ordinary men around him into heroes and martyrs.'[22] However, when Gokhale read Gandhiji's *Hind Swaraj* (English translation) in 1912 he found it so 'crude' and 'hastily conceived' that he prophesied 'Gandhi himself would destroy the book after spending a year in India.'[23]

The prophecy did not come true. After spending more than a year in India, Gandhiji declared that 'the views expressed in *Hind Swaraj* are [still] held by me'.[24] Some years later he again wrote, 'Except for withdrawing the word prostitute used in connection with the British Parliament which annoyed an English lady, I wish to make no change at all.'[25] Much later, in 1938, Gandhiji once again asserted: 'I might change the language here and there, if I had to rewrite the booklet. But after the stormy thirty years through which I have since passed, I have seen nothing to make me alter the views expounded in it.'[26]

Gokhale was deeply impressed by Gandhi's humanism; but being a refined, intellectual politician thought that he would be 'a liability in Indian public life'[27] because of his ideals and methods of work. Gokhale had taken a promise from Gandhiji that, for a whole year after his arrival in India, he would not take the initiative in any direct political work, but watch the trend of events silently. Gandhiji scrupulously kept his promise and established an ashram on the banks of the Sabarmati at Ahmedabad in 1915, where he planned to train his followers in his own methods and ideals to which he had given shape in South Africa. It was necessary for him to make experiments in Indian conditions before he could apply them to the general political situation. Gokhale did not live long after Gandhiji's return to India, but his fears indicated that 'a leader of disturbing quality was returning to India in 1915'.[28]

It is also interesting to find that the British authorities in India also became alert. The Governor of Bombay, Lord Willingdon, who had expressed to Gokhale his keen desire to meet Gandhi, told him, when the latter called on him, 'I ask one thing of you. I would like you to come and see me whenever you propose to take any steps concerning Government.'[29] Gandhiji replied: 'I can very easily give the promise, inasmuch as it is my rule, as a satyagrahi, to understand the viewpoint of the party I propose to deal with, and to try to agree with him as far as may be possible. I strictly observed the rule in South Africa and I mean to do the same here.'[30] All these only tend to prove that here was a leader who had to be taken note of, although he was so different from other Indian leaders of the time.

Most political leaders in the making are usually trained by seasoned seniors in the trade. But Gandhiji was virtually a self-made politician. His politics at the initial stage, though it looked somewhat obscurantist in its approach, was

> rough and ready because there was none to help him, and he was pushed into action by the pressures of the situation in which he found himself. The techniques he evolved were those of a pragmatist; in particular he was limited by the people he had to organise, the audience at which he aimed, and the nature of the issues at stake.[31]

These were the basic reasons why Gandhiji's political philosophy as reflected in *Hind Swaraj* and his techniques of political agitation became so different from those practised by the elite in India at that time. Gandhiji wrote *Hind Swaraj* in Gujarati in 1908, when he was forty years old. This was the original testament of Gandhian ideas. Divided into twenty chapters it was written in dialogue form, 'in perfect Gandhian style — terse, simple and logical'. It dealt with practical questions in an original way. Western influence, particularly that of Tolstoy, on the framing of ideas in this work is quite evident. Gandhiji himself said, 'I have but endeavoured humbly to follow Tolstoy, Ruskin, Thoreau, Emerson and other writers, besides the masters of Indian philosophy. Tolstoy has been one of my teachers for a number of years.'[32] Gandhiji had sent an English translation of the work to Tolstoy who wrote back: 'I have read your book with great interest, for I consider the question there dealt with — passive resistance — to be of very great importance, not only for India, but for the whole humanity.'[33] On the face of it, *Hind Swaraj* appears to be an angry work. But on a careful examination one can find that it was based on some of Gandhiji's firm convictions which might not be agreeable to Westernized minds. Certainly he was reacting to the situation in which he found himself in South Africa and what he heard about the developments in India following the partition of Bengal.

Actually, he wrote *Hind Swaraj* 'in answer to the Indian school of violence and its prototype in South Africa.'[34] In a letter to a friend in India, Gandhiji summarized *Hind Swaraj*; and some of those points may be cited as follows:

1. There is no impassable barrier between East and West.
2. There is no such thing as Western or European civilization, but there is a modern civilization which is purely material.
3. The people of Europe, before they were touched by modern civilization, had much in common with the people of the East.
4. It is not the British people who are ruling India, but it is modern civilization, through its railways, telegraph, telephone and almost every invention which has been claimed to be a triumph of civilization.
5. Bombay, Calcutta, and the other chief cities of India are the real plague-spots.
6. If British rule were replaced tomorrow by Indian rule based on modern methods, India would be no better, except that she would be able to retain some of the money that is drained away to England.
7. East and West can really meet when the West has thrown overboard modern civilization, almost in its entirety.
8. India's salvation consists in unlearning what she has learnt during the past fifty years or so.
9. India should wear no machine made clothing whether it comes out of European mills or Indian mills.[35]

After summarizing the points, Gandhiji wrote:

> It is the true spirit of passive resistance that has brought me to the above almost definite conclusions. As a passive resister, I am unconcerned whether such a gigantic reformation, shall I call it, can be brought about among people who find their satisfaction from the present mad rush. If I realize the truth of it, I should rejoice in following it, and therefore, I could not wait until the whole body of people had commenced.[36]

In a word, Gandhiji denounced Western civilization in its entirety. He even dubbed Western medicine as 'black magic'. His repugnance for Western institutions also was so strong that he denounced the British system of parliamentary government. In *Hind Swaraj* he declared that 'the mother of Parliaments is a sterile woman and prostitute'. Later, however, Gandhiji modified his opposition to the parliamentary system when he found that by and large educated Indians favoured that system; but his primary goal, swaraj, remained. Gandhiji wrote in 1921:

'I am individually working for the self-rule pictured therein *[Hind Swaraj]*. But today my corporate activity is undoubtedly devoted to the attainment of parliamentary *swaraj* in accordance with the wishes of the people of India.'[37] His condemnation of Western civilization as such remained unaltered. 'We consider our civilization to be far superior to yours', he told Englishmen, 'We consider your schools and law courts to be useless. We want our own ancient schools and courts to be restored. The common language of India is not English but Hindi. . . . We can hold communication with you only in our national language.'[38] Gandhiji's diagnosis was that the pristine condition of India could be restored by only one effort, and he unhesitatingly advised: 'drive out Western civilization. All else will follow.'

If *swaraj* was Gandhiji's goal, and driving out the West was the panacea of all ills, *satyagraha* was the method or the means to attain it and to him both the end as well as the means must be morally justifiable. The positive teaching of *Hind Swaraj* was 'the gospel of love in place of that hate. It replaces violence with self-sacrifice. It pits soul force against brute force.'[39] Some scholars have noticed strains of the Vaishnava tradition of *ahimsa* in the ideology of *satyagraha*. The aim of satyagraha is the conversion of the opponent to one's own view by self-suffering, and not by violence. How it triumphs over the opponent has been clearly described by P. Sitaramayya:

> It involves self-chosen suffering and humiliation for the resisters. If it is effective, it is so by working on the conscience of those against whom it is being used, sapping their confidence in the exclusive rightness of their case, making their physical strength impotent, and weakening their resolution by insinuating a sense of guilt for the sufferings they have a part in causing.[40]

Attempts are sometimes erroneously made to equate the ideology of 'passive resistance' with the philosophy of satyagraha. But as Gandhiji himself said:

> Satyagraha differs from Passive Resistance as the North Pole from the South. The latter has been conceived as a weapon of the weak and does not exclude the use of physical force or violence for the purpose of gaining one's end; whereas the former has been conceived as a weapon of the strongest, and excludes the use of violence in any shape or form.[41]

If passive resistance is actually at a lower level of evolution of Gandhian ideas, satyagraha represented a much higher level of thought which is a curious blend of philosophical, ethical and mystic elements. Satyagraha in its operative form denotes non-violence. It rejects violence absolutely as a matter of principle and not as a matter of expediency. The satyagrahi must have infinite trust in human nature and in its inherent goodness. However, it was not at all easy to be a 'real satyagrahi'. It required a lot of training and control over both body and mind and Gandhiji emphasized on this when he started the Satyagraha Ashram at Sabarmati. This concept was a different one no doubt, but Gandhiji refuted criticisms of leaders like Motilal Nehru and C.R. Das who held the view that his theory was 'impractical and visionary'. He contended: 'I am not a visionary. I claim to be a practical idealist. The religion of nonviolence is not meant for *rishis* and saints. It is meant for the common people as well. Non-violence is the law of our species as violence is the law of the brute.'[42] In its practical application satyagraha has several offshoots or ramifications:

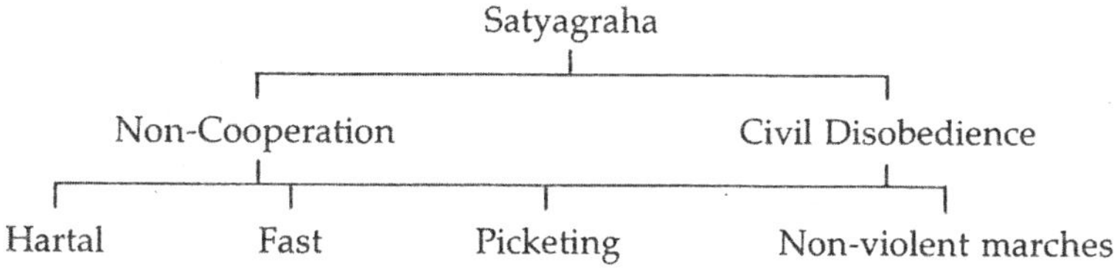

In all the offshoots, the basic theory of ahimsa was to rule and they were all elevated to a higher plane of moral discipline.

Notwithstanding several contradictions in *Hind Swaraj* and its revivalist nature, Gandhiji held on to these ideas. Indeed it would be difficult for most Western educated Indians of this century to subscribe to the ideas expressed in the work. Whatever might have been the criticism against Gandhian ideals and methods, the fact remained that the doctrine preached by Gandhiji changed the whole nature of Indian politics. As a modern Indian writer observed, 'Formerly mental brilliance, a glib command of English, a comfortable bank account, noble birth, and the stamp of Oxford or Cambridge were the assets that made a leader in India. Today the tables are turned.'[43] Here was something that was so different from the existing pattern which drew its life blood from Western ideas and institutions. His philosophy and techniques electrified the masses in general who were hitherto mute spectators of the changing political drama since the inception of the Congress. Here was the clue to his phenomenal rise in Indian politics during 1917-19. For the first time the tender mental chord of the common man was touched and it began to respond in a great way. Gandhiji believed that no one had the right to represent the masses unless he identified with them. Later, he said that the masses were 'as yet untouched by politics. . . . Their politics are confined to bread and salt. . . . We must share their sorrows, understand their difficulties and anticipate their wants. . . . Then and not till then shall we truly represent the masses and they will respond to every call.'[44]

Gandhiji had one great asset when he came back from South Africa and waited in the wings to enter the Indian political stage — it was his intimate and rich experience of working with the masses for realizing a common goal. This was his strong point *vis-à-vis* the English-educated elitist leaders of the time in India. It can be safely said that the masses began to play a role in Indian politics after Gandhiji appeared on the Indian political scene. Even Communist writers acknowledged this contribution of Gandhiji. R.P. Dutt commented: 'The achievement of Gandhi consisted in that he, almost alone of all the leaders, sensed and reached out to the masses. . . . This positive achievement of Gandhi is bigger than all the idiosyncrasies and weakness which may be brought against him, and constitutes his real contribution to Indian Nationalism.'[45] M.N. Roy also complimented Gandhiji for his method of non-violent mass struggle against the established regime.[46] It was but natural that Gandhiji was easily enthroned in the hearts of the people who became the main source of strength when he rose high in Indian politics. Very soon he converted nationalism into a practical and intelligible creed for the masses and brought it down from the English-educated political platform to the soil of the country.

Gandhiji considered his struggle against the British rule as a 'spiritual crusade'. The Indian freedom movement was projected by him as a 'religious crusade' and his method of satyagraha was actually an attempt to spiritualize politics. It may be conceded that Indian elitist politicians of the time could not subscribe to this religious politics of Gandhiji, but the common man accepted this creed and gradually leaned towards the Gandhian path which clearly manifested itself in the non-cooperation movement. Gandhiji firmly believed that politics bereft of religion was 'absolute dirt'. He said, 'Those who say that religion has nothing to do with politics do not know what religion means.'[47] There is no denying the fact that by spiritualizing politics Gandhiji could convert the Congress from 'a middle class debating club to a mass organization'. The process of this conversion was not without tough opposition and it could take place only when the Congress politics of the time proved to be hollow by 1917-19.

It has been rightly remarked that 'South Africa had transformed Gandhiji from a shy and youthful pleader with no experience of public life into a mature idealist and leader. By 1915 he had become a skilled political mobilizer and had evolved a political technique of super flexibility which was to be his hall mark when he returned to India.'[48] Congress was the apex of institutional politics in which Gandhiji found himself to be a misfit at the outset. He was wise enough to understand and follow the advice of Gokhale to remain silent for a year and watch the trend. This vow of silence resulted in his isolation from institutional politics for a little more than a year. From 1915 to 1917 he remained in what may be called 'peripheral politics' with Sabarmati Ashram as the new nationalist training base.

Gandhiji preferred to remain in the background and refused to be drawn into any particular political network, although he attended the Congress session in 1915 and was nominated a member of the Subjects Committee. In April 1916 he attended the Belgaum Conference, when he supported the reunification of the two wings of the Congress; but he declared that 'he himself was an outsider who did not belong to any party, and was merely present because he thought it was his duty as a servant of his country.'[49] He attended the reunited Congress in 1916 but scrupulously kept aloof from being aligned with any power group. Thus he remained away from the main currents of politics and, instead, devoted all his attention and energy to a slow as well as steady preparation for launching his own weapon — satyagraha — when there was no other alternative to his countrymen but to look to him for a new leadership.

Gandhiji had a wonderful sense of timing in applying his techniques and was only prepared to plunge into the main vortex of Indian politics on his own terms. There is no clear written evidence, but it may be conjectured that he realized his shortcomings *vis-à-vis* the trend of Congress politics of the time. Perhaps, he was no match for the elitist politics of the Moderate as well as Extremist groups which had one thing common — the dominance of the English educated middle class. His own convictions also stood in the way of accepting either of them. He had to wait till the prevalent brand of politics reached a dead-end in the face of imperialist repression at the end of the World War. He would either have his own way, without compromise, or else he would remain aloof. This dogged conviction ultimately paved the way for the emergence of Gandhi as generalissimo of the Congress in 1919.

For the first thirty years of its history the Congress by and large acted on the Western idea of nationalist movements. Till 1905, when the Congress was under the control of the Moderates, constitutional agitation was the technique in obtaining concessions from the Raj. The Moderates had a firm faith in the sense of justice of Englishmen and advocated the concepts of liberty, patriotism and nationalism. Violence of any kind was scrupulously eschewed. During this phase, the Congress believed in gradualism and conceded that democratic institutions in India could be best ensured by a laborious process of training in the art of parliamentary self-government. The shock of the partition of Bengal disillusioned even the staunchest of the Moderates. R.P. Dutt rightly commented that 'frustration was consequently the fate of the Moderate school'.[50] Even Gokhale, the veteran leader of the Moderates, bitterly complained that 'the bureaucracy was growing frankly selfish and openly hostile to national aspirations. It was not so in the past.'[51]

For some time the old school was in disarray but Curzon's wishful thinking that 'the Congress is tottering to its fall' did not prove true. The new school, otherwise known as the Extremist school, under the leadership of B.G. Tilak, had a spectacular rise when Moderate politics reached a dead end. Drawing inspiration from revivalism and religious nationalism the new school criticized the bankruptcy of the policy of compromise and conciliation of the old guard and was in favour of a more positive programme. The belief in gradualism and the unbounded faith in British parliamentary institutions came under heavy fire. The Extremists advocated militant methods in politics and preached a policy of direct action in place of 'the political mendicancy' of the earlier phase. During the period of 'the revolt of the Congress' between 1905 and 1915 the watchwords of the new school thus became, Swadeshi, Swaraj, Boycott and National Education. Tilak and his followers believed that however much British rule might be improved or liberalized, it could never be as beneficial to Indians as an indigenous Indian rule — self rule. The revocation of the partition of Bengal in 1911 was a great triumph for the Extremist school. But it must be noted that the main debate and dispute between the Extremists and Moderates was on the question of the political method that should be applied in the struggle against the Raj and not in the form of government that was to be established.

Self rule or Home Rule advocated by Annie Besant and Tilak became the new expression when the Congress reunited in 1916. It was undoubtedly an advance in terms of ideas, though it signified the continuance of constitutionalism in one form or the other among the intelligentsia. The Lucknow Congress which Gandhiji attended just as a non-aligned leader, passed a resolution demanding self-government at an early date; and since the reunification, it became more difficult for the British to play off one group against the other.

Congress policy till 1916-7 did not break away from the elitist politics which was confined primarily to the middle class intelligentsia; the Congress movement did not reach the common masses till Gandhiji appeared on the scene. The hollowness as well as the limitations of elitism in politics became patent at the end of 1918 when the hell of repression by the British was let loose in India, the exigencies of the War situation no longer existing. In spite of pressure tactics through strikes and boycott, all shades of nationalists had supported British war efforts in India and now their disillusionment was complete. In the face of British repression the elitist leaders could not prescribe any new technique to fight the Raj. They could neither support revolutionary terrorism as a means to attain nationalist objectives, nor could they give any new direction to the Congress movement which had a promise of success. It became clear to the countrymen that the elitist leaders were successful only as long as the British gave them a long rope and tolerated their activities. No promising alternative was forthcoming from the established leaders of the Congress when government repression assumed menacing proportions in 1919. It now fell to Gandhiji, who was waiting in the wings, so to say, with his technique of satyagraha, to fight against the British Raj. This was something new and people became hopeful, and nationalist India looked towards Gandhiji for new leadership. By that time Gandhiji was ready to launch the new method, the efficacy of which had been proved in the Champaran, Kheda and Ahmedabad movements during 1917-8. The limited experimentation by Gandhiji in these three local disputes — peasants against landlords in Champaran, farmers against revenue officials in Kheda, and mill-workers against the Indian millowners in Ahmedabad — could not minimize the importance of the new technique, even when those issues were considered outside the normal range of political activity.

But it would be wrong to suppose that 'Gandhi's entry into Indian politics occurred almost fortuitously in 1917 and 1918'.[52] The situation in India had been slowly ripening since the last quarter of the 19th century, while the change in the character of the British rule became gradually manifest. Recent researches have shown how 'the extension of Government activity from the late 19th century onwards had disrupted local patterns of power and interest, made the Raj more obstrusive and disliked', and 'provided new issues and avenues for the ambitious to fight over'.[53] The 'strains of devolution' told very heavily on the middle-class intelligentsia in the first quarter of the 20th century, making them restive and aggrieved.[54] The changing conditions in India indirectly helped Gandhiji who had an uncanny sense of choosing the right moment to take the initiative and was never unduly in a hurry to thrust himself upon the political scene. Gandhiji triumphantly emerged when there was no other viable alternative left to the people in general and Congress in particular.

The Special Calcutta Congress of 1920 was the turning point in the history of the Congress, when it formally gave a stamp of approval to the ideas and methods of Gandhiji. Sitaramayya recorded: 'It left every one of the older Congressmen — seniors, leaders and patriarchs — aghast, asking themselves and each other, "Who is this man that speaketh with a tone of authority and whence doth he come?" Seasoned men like Pal and Malaviya and Jinnah and Khaparde, stalwarts like Das and Lalaji were simply overpowered'.[55]

3. The Environment in Motion

By 1917 the Congress found its new leader in the personality of Gandhiji and the masses got an effective weapon in satyagraha. When these two brought a new promise to the nationalists, the events during 1917-19 set the whole environment in motion for realization of the nationalist objectives *vis-à-vis* the Raj. The emergence of Gandhiji in Indian politics, 'to a certain extent, slowed down the advance of Western thought. In spite of all the attraction for Western thought, among many Indians there was yet a deep-rooted and instinctive hostility towards it.'[56] The disillusionment of the middle class, the frustration of the nationalists in general, and the 'instinctive hostility' of the masses all burst forth into the political struggle during 1917-19, when the policy of repression of the British became manifest in several events. By then new important trends in Indian politics had appeared which have already been discussed in the preceding analysis. *Swaraj* became the Congress ideal and *satyagraha* was the new technique of conflict, while the spirit of non-violence lent a new colour to the Congress movement.

The British response to the Indian situation during the war was apparently sympathetic. While the war was going on, the British thought it wise to respond rather positively, and their policy was 'repression coupled with concessions'. On the one hand they went all out to suppress revolutionary terrorism and to maintain order and tranquility in India at any cost through measures like the Defence of India Act; on the other, they announced concessions to satisfy the Congress aspirations. Montagu's famous Declaration of 20 August 1917 was a step in that direction. The Declaration ran thus: 'The policy of His Majesty's Government . . . is that of the increasing association of Indians in every branch of the administration and the gradual development of self-governing institutions with a view to the progressive realisation of Responsible Government in India as integral part of the British Empire.' Montagu came to India, toured the country extensively, and, in collaboration with Viceroy Chelmsford, submitted a report which was published on 8 July 1918. On the basis of the recommendations of the report the Government of India Act was later passed (December 1919) by the British Parliament. Attention may be drawn to the time sequence of these developments to analyze the British attitude. When the Montagu Declaration was made, the Allied powers were unsure of their victory and continued Indian support was essential. When the report was submitted, victory over Germany was clearly within sight. When the Act was passed, Indian support had become meaningless. Similarly, the Indian reaction also changed from jubilation to utter disappointment, from friendliness to hostility, and from thaw to ice again.

During the initial years of the war, the Congress leaders of both hues were preaching loyalty and support to the British. Gandhiji went a step further and advised his countrymen to 'think imperially'. Disappointment loomed large when the Montagu-Chelmsford Report was published. The British Committee of the Indian National Congress also recorded its mixed reaction in its report for 1917-18 *(See Appendix 8.1).* There was widespread indignation at the way the British had manipulated the reform proposals to suit imperialist purposes. True, responsible government within the framework of the British Empire was a far cry, not to speak of the type of system which persons like Motilal Ghosh wanted. When Montagu invited schemes of government from responsible Indians, Motilal suggested in a series of articles in the *Amrita Bazar Patrika* that India should be given the type of self-rule granted to the Philippines by the USA.[57] Montagu who had an interview with Motilal, thought that the idea was too premature to be considered. In *An Indian Diary*, under the date 4 December 1917, he wrote:

> We had a long interview with Moti Lal Ghose, the charming old editor of the Amrita Bazar Patrika . . . He reminded me that five years ago he had told me that our Indian Empire was slipping away from us . . . Moti Lal Ghose has abandoned the Congress-League Scheme, and goes for complete responsible government in the Provinces, with Congress-League Scheme for the Government of India. He is in a great hurry and I begged him to be a little more patient — ten years was a long stretch in the life of a man, but very little in the life of a country.

There were by and large three lines of thinking in the Congress itself: (1) total acceptance advocated by the moderate leaders; (2) total rejection urged by the diehards among the Extremists led by C.R. Das; (3) a middle path of 'responsive co-operation' with the reform scheme. It is interesting to find that Gandhiji was still on the borders of institutional politics, isolated from the elitist politicians at large. These early events, however, brought Gandhiji from peripheral politics to the main political stage. He did not clearly align himself with any of the shades of opinion, although he was ready to co-operative with the British in translating the reform scheme into practice. The Delhi Congress in December 1918, unanimously passed the following resolutions putting forward the claims of Indians:

> No. 2. That this Congress reaffirms the principles of reform contained in the resolutions relating to Self-Government adopted in the Indian National Congress and the All India Muslim League held at Lucknow in December, 1916, and at Calcutta in December, 1917, and declares that nothing less than Self-Government within the Empire can satisfy the Indian people and by enabling it to take its rightful place as a free and self-governing Nation

in the British Commonwealth, strengthen the connection between Great Britain and India.

No. 3. That this Congress declares that the people of India are fit for responsible government, and repudiates the assumption to the contrary contained in the Report on Indian Constitutional Reforms.[58]

From the middle of the year 1919 the Congress was seriously engaged in an exercise over the Reform Bill which was before the British Parliament for consideration and acceptance. The Act of 1919 based on the Montford Report finally belied the expectations of the Congress leaders and a battle royal ensued on the crucial point — co-operation with the British Government in working out the reforms. Within the Congress also a sharp tussle ensued over the question of acceptance or rejection. In the Congress Session at Amritsar a heated debate took place over the resolutions moved by C.R. Das and seconded by B.G. Tilak. Three amendments were moved against the resolutions proposed by Das. While the amendments of Mrs Besant and Bipin Chandra Pal were put to vote and lost, the amendment proposed by Gandhiji was given serious consideration. While Das was in favour of rejecting the reforms, Gandhiji took the opposite view. It was on this occasion that Gandhiji took a leading part in the discussion for the first time. He had entered the main stage only to take an initiative in his own way to put the whole environment in motion. Gandhiji explained his attitude in regard to reforms in the issue of *Young India* of 31 December 1919. He wrote: 'The Reforms Act . . . is an earnest intention of the British people to do justice to India and it ought to remove suspicion on that score. . . . Our duty therefore is not to subject the Reforms to carping criticism but to settle down quietly to work so as to make them a success.' After an acrimonious debate, a compromise was reached and the following resolution was passed by an overwhelming majority in the Congress of 1919:

(a) That this Congress reiterates its declaration of last year that India is fit for full Responsible Government and repudiates all assumptions and assertions to the contrary wherever made.

(b) That this Congress adheres to the resolutions passed and is of opinion that the Reforms Act is inadequate, unsatisfactory and disappointing.

(c) That this Congress further urges that Parliament should take early steps to establish full Responsible Government in India in accordance with the principle of Self-Determination.

(d) Pending such introduction this Congress trusts that so far as may be possible the people will so work the reforms as to secure an early establishment of full Responsible Government and this Congress offers its thanks to the Right Hon'ble E.S. Montagu for his labours in connection with the Reforms.[59]

Another issue that made the British intention quite clear in the closing stage of the war and led to the hardening of the Congress attitude was the question of application of the 'principle of self-determination' to India. The principle was an offshoot of the war situation affecting the national boundaries of various countries. It should be conceded that 'the issue of national self-determination was brought to the forefront by the Russian Revolution'[60] in 1917. Though President Wilson, Lloyd George and other statesmen advocated this lofty principle, it was not to be applied in the case of India. The Congress was sore over this attitude and adopted a categorical resolution in the Delhi Congress, 1918:

> In view of the pronouncement of President Wilson, Mr Lloyd George, and other British Statesmen, that to ensure the future peace of the world, the principle of Self-Determination should be applied to all progressive nations, Be it resolved —
>
> That this Congress claims the recognition of India by the British Parliament and by the Peace Conference as one of the progressive Nations to whom the principle of Self-Determination should be applied.

The Congress resolved further

> That in the reconstruction of Imperial polity, whether in matters affecting the inner relations of the nations constituting it, in questions of foreign policy or in the League of Nations, India shall be accorded the same position as the Self-Governing Dominations.[61]

In spite of professions of appreciation of Indian support, the imperialist interest was much more weighty, and the British government turned an absolutely deaf ear to the Indian demands. The principle of self-determination ran counter to the idea of imperialism, and nationalist India continued to smart in the stranglehold of British imperialism.

A great contributing factor to the Congress success during the period 1917-19 was the disillusionment of the Indian Muslims with the British as a result of which they came closer to the Congress and co-operated with that body for common benefits. Earlier in this volume, this process of gradual disillusionment, leading to Congress-League co-operation being established under the Lucknow Pact in 1916 has been described. The disenchantment of the Indian Muslims was nearly complete by 1917, although they were still divided among themselves, and the League was not the sole representative body. The intrusion of English education and the psychology of loyalty towards the British had created interest groups among the Muslims who could not speak in one voice before 1917.

It is well known that there was a great divergence of opinion over the Lucknow Pact which meant, for many of the Muslims, co-operating with the Hindus. They still had some faith in the British when the Montagu Declaration was made. The communal riots in Bihar in September-October 1917, commonly known as the Bakri-Id riots stood in the way of complete collaboration between the Congress and the League. As a result of the disturbed Hindu-Muslim relations, many conservative Muslims began to doubt whether 'a joint political programme at the top could at all safeguard the minority privileges',[62] while antagonism between the two communities was continuing at the lowest level. Secondly, the conservative section of the Muslims could not heartily accept the idea of separating religion from politics. Thirdly, they were not very enthusiastic about the representative systems at a time when the fate of the Caliphate looked uncertain and when the Hindus in general were unconcerned about the dangers faced by the Caliph. There was a turn in the tide as soon as the Montagu-Chelmsford Report was published. A certain amount of Muslim unrest followed this all over India. Lord Sydenham drew the attention of the government in the British Parliament in November 1918 to the fact that 'the Report is regarded by Mohamedans generally as having dealt too lightly with their interests'.[63]

The politically conscious section among the Muslims, not to speak of the conservatives, became more anti-British than before when the war was brought to a close. Turkey's defeat and the consequent humiliation of the Caliphate had been too much for the Muslims to swallow without resentment. 'Loyalty towards their spiritual head and consideration for his temporal interests weighed more heavily on the Muslim mind than their regard for the British rulers.'[64] As a result, they now came closer to the Congress in an effort to redress their grievances.

Meanwhile, a new wave of Pan-Islamism swept over Asia and Africa which had a great influence on the Muslims in India. 'Pan-Islam was an ideal with many facets and many modes of expression; but at its core lay the Muslim belief in the brotherhood of all believers and the organization of society for the practice of faith, under a Khalifah or successor of the Prophet.'[65] Thus the Caliph was the symbol of Islam, of Muslim hopes and identity. Pan-Islamism gathered momentum towards the close of the war.

To assuage the restive Indian Muslims, British Prime Minister Lloyd George declared on 5 January 1918 that the Allies were 'not fighting to deprive Turkey of the rich and renowned lands of Asia Minor'. This was endorsed by President Wilson. But all the hopes of the Muslims were dashed when the terms of the Armistice were known. Under the Armistice, the Asiatic portion of the Turkish Empire came under the control of England and France. The Caliph was deprived of all real authority even in the remaining portion of his territories. Indian Muslims became seriously aggrieved and considered the treatment of Turkey 'a great betrayal' on the part of the British. A storm of indignation gathered on the horizon.

While all these developments were taking place, Gandhiji had appeared on the Indian political stage. It is interesting to find that Gandhiji was particularly concerned for Indian Muslims. In South Africa Gandhiji was quite close to the Indian Muslims settled there and knew their sentiments when he championed their cause as a pleader. He maintained that sympathetic contact with the Muslims when he returned to India. Gandhiji later said, 'With that object I came to India. My first duty was, when I came to India, to find out such Muslim brethren who would give their lives for truth and for unity between Hindus and Mussalmans.'[66]

While Gandhiji was willing to espouse the Muslim cause, they had confidence in him. Perhaps, he was more acceptable to the Muslims than any other leader of the Congress. It was therefore only to be expected that Gandhiji would be closely associated with the agitation that was brewing in India over the Khilafat question. He missed no opportunity of pressing the Government of India for a solution of the problem. In his letter to the viceroy immediately after the War Conference at Delhi, Gandhiji laid emphasis on the question and urged the viceroy to take steps in the right direction.

When the All India Khilafat Conference met at Delhi on 23 November 1919, Gandhiji was elected its President and he readily accepted. He thought that something must be done to avoid any turn towards violence. In April 1919 he had written a demi-official letter to the viceroy drawing his attention to such an eventuality. He wrote:

> I would like, too, to place before you my reading of the situation. The ferment among the Mohamedans is too great to be checked for ever. It may burst like a torrent at any moment and behind the present disturbances are to be traced the results of extreme Moslem dissatisfaction. It is not confined to classes but it is most decidedly permeates the masses. I venture to submit that it will be a most disastrous thing if the questions affecting Islam are not settled by the League of Nations in accordance with enlightened Mohamedan opinion, and I suggest that the Brothers Ali may be invited to give their opinion. You cannot do better than having the Brothers in London to give the Home Government the benefit of their advice. They are among the honestest of the Mohamedans. They are independent and able. It is their opinion and that of such Mohamedans which will count in the end with the vast masses of the Mohamedan population. I have not hesitated to tell the Mohamedans whom I meet that rather than harbour discontent, ill will and finally hatred, and depend upon

> methods of violence, it behoves them to depend on the peaceful and loyal way of Satyagraha. My reliance upon Satyagraha is so great that I do not despair of securing its acceptance by all the classes and communities in India on the one hand, and Government on the other. For to me it is the rule of life, to which we subscribe, more or less, consciously or unconsciously often even against our will.[67]

In the Amritsar Congress of 1919 leading Khilafatists had assembled along with the Congressmen and the Khilafat question was thoroughly discussed. It was also decided that the Khilafat work should be organized under the guidance of Gandhiji. The Congress adopted a resolution on the Khilafat question in no uncertain terms as Gandhiji could carry the general body with him in favour of the Khilafatists. The resolution proposed by Bipin Chandra Pal was seconded by Pandit Rambhaj Dutt Choudhury of Punjab:

> This Congress respectfully protests against the hostile attitude of some of the British Ministers towards the Turkish and 'Khilafat' question as disclosed by their utterances and most earnestly appeals to and urges upon His Majesty's Government to settle the Turkish question in accordance with the just and legitimate sentiments of Indian Musalmans and the solemn pledges of the Prime Minister, without which there will be no real content among the people of India.[68]

The Khilafat issue was of great importance in setting the environment in motion, because it was one of the two 'wrongs' which Gandhiji wanted to 'undo' when he launched the Non-Cooperation Movement. The Khilafat issue was basically a religious issue which had nothing to do with the country's political issues directly. Critics of Gandhiji often questioned the wisdom of fighting political issues in 1920-21 with the prop of religion. R.C. Majumdar wrote:

> The Hindu leaders failed to realize that the Khilafat agitation was really inspired by the Pan-Islamic movement, and the policy of Hindu-Muslim entente was merely an ingenious device on the part of the Muslim leaders to secure help against British imperialism, then regarded as the greatest enemy of Islam. There was no reason to suppose, as subsequent events clearly proved, that the Muslim leaders were inspired by a genuine desire to make up their differences with the Hindus in order to form an Indian nation.[69]

Majumdar was perhaps a little too sceptical, but it is not true that all the leaders of the two communities contributed to the idea of the Hindu-Muslim entente *a priori*. Majumdar's analysis reflected only a point of view. Gandhiji, on the other hand, propagated the Khilafat issue, because he thought that it provided an opportunity to unite the

Hindus and the Muslims that might not come in a hundred years' time. Whether this was the genuine feeling of Gandhiji or whether he used this as a convenient lever is extremely difficult to decide. But in the absence of clear evidence we cannot conclude that Gandhiji upheld the Khilafat cause only for reasons of political expediency.

It is, however, very difficult to reconcile genuine concern on Gandhiji's part with the fact that, before the sudden withdrawal of the Non-Cooperation Movement, he did not feel it necessary to consult his Khilafatist associates whose cause he wanted to advance. Angry Muslim reactions and communal bitterness had been the outcome of the unilateral action of Gandhiji. Politics is a game of wits and Gandhiji could support his actions by suitably adjusting his arguments. The plain truth was that in 1919 the Khilafatists required Congress support without which they were ineffective against the British; and the best means to secure that support was to have Gandhiji associated with their agitation. The surest channel to get Congress support was through Gandhiji, whose magnetic personality did really work miracles. Gandhiji, on the other hand, required unhesitating support in 1919 when he was at the centre of the political stage but yet to gain an unquestioned grip over the Congress by turning the tables against the established elitist leaders of that organization. He made absolutely sure of that valuable support when he wholeheartedly espoused the cause of the Khilafatists. 'His Muslim allies might be in a minority in their community, but they were strategically placed to arouse far deeper and wider support than the older politicians of either community had been able to muster.' Whatever was the motive of either the Khilafatists or Gandhiji, the Khilafat issue was of pregnant importance in the history of the Congress during 1917-19.

The occasion for vigorous action by the Congress for the realization of nationalist aspirations was provided by the Rowlatt Act in 1919. This issue, and the agitation following the enactment, also gave a chance to Gandhiji to prove his mettle and to pass from peripheral local politics to committed participation in mainstream national politics. While Gandhiji came out of the shell of measured isolation, the Congress got a new fillip to march forward in a determined way.

When the war was drawing to a close, revolutionary terrorism continued to be a cause for anxiety to the British authorities. The Defence of India Act had enabled them to cope with the situation while the war was on. But with the end of the war in sight, the Raj was confronted with the problem of how to tackle revolutionary activities, since the Defence of India Rules would automatically lapse at the conclusion of the war. A Committee headed by Justice Rowlatt was appointed to devise effective ways and means to tackle revolutionary activities. On the basis of the

Rowlatt Committee Report, two bills were initiated and one was enacted by the Legislative Council in March 1919 as the Indian Criminal Law (Amendment) Act. The other enactment came to be known as The Anarchical and Revolutionary Crimes Act. This was popularly called the Rowlatt Act, and it vested in the government wide dictatorial powers to detain without warrant, set up special courts for summary trial of the revolutionaries in camera without jury, and legalized admission of evidences not permissible under ordinary criminal procedure.

Ever since the publication of the Rowlatt Report in July 1918, nationalist India had been greatly agitated and politicians of all shades of opinion considered it as a blow to Indians in general. The Delhi Congress in 1918 resolved:

> That this Congress views with alarm the recommendations of the Rowlatt Committee which, if given effect to, will interfere with the fundamental rights of the Indian people, impede the healthy growth of public opinion and would also prejudicially affect the successful working of constitutional reforms.[70]

All over India the press became very vocal against the Report and the proposed bills. *The Hindu* commented in one of its issues in January 1919:

> It is a well grounded apprehension that the two sedition bills . . . will prove destructive to the personal liberties of the people, will impair the sense of personal freedom and sap the elements which go to make up national solidarity and resentment among the best and most reflective minds in the Indian community.[71]

When the Imperial Legislative Council referred the Rowlatt bills to a Select Committee on 10 February 1919, *The Hindu* once again wrote: 'No Indian question has evoked such unanimous and indignant protest throughout the country as the pernicious piece of legislation embodied in the Rowlatt bills.'[72] Gandhiji sent a telegram on 24 February 1919 to the Private Secretary to the Viceroy, J.L. Maffey, in which he categorically stated:

> In my opinion bad in themselves Bills [Rowlatt] are but symptoms of deep seated disease among the ruling class, coming as they do on eve [of] Reforms. Bills augur ill for their success. Those who have been associated with me in public work and other friends met me today and after greatest deliberation have decided to offer Satyagraha and commit Civil Disobedience of such laws as Committee to be formed from ourselves may decide.[73]

This was a storm signal to which the Private Secretary replied to Gandhiji on 13 March 1919:

> You succeeded in South Africa because you had a cause worthy of your countrymen's enthusiasm and lives. Can you say the same today? You have a magnetic personality, and proportionate responsibility rests upon you. People will follow you not because they think they are right, but because they think Mr Gandhi is right. . . . Government may conceivably be wrong, but you have to consider whether you are not more wrong.
>
> It is ridiculously easy, for a leader with your record to throw dust in people's eyes, and even to upset the smooth tenor of a country's affairs, but in times such as these a heavy responsibility rests on those who rock the boat when all hands are wanted to keep her steady. As a 'bureaucrat' I should of course be sorry to see a 'struggle' such as you indicate as possible, but those of us who know you, even 'bureaucrats', will be equally sorry to see you come down from the lofty plane where you have always claimed our admiration.[74]

It was a beautiful exposition of the way the government looked at Gandhiji and also an indication of the government's mind, as well, *vis-à-vis* the proposed struggle of Gandhiji who was equally determined and made a last appeal in his telegram dated 11 March 1919 to the Private Secretary to the Viceroy:

> Even at this eleventh hour I respectfully ask His Excellency and his Government to pause and consider before passing Rowlatt Bills. Whether justified or not there is no mistaking the strength of public opinion on the measures. I am sure Government do not intend intensifying existing bitterness. Government will risk nothing by delay, but by expressly bowing to public opinion will smooth down feeling and enhance prestige.[75]

The last-minute appeal fell on deaf ears, and the bills were passed. Once the bills became law, verbal protest was useless and Indian politicians in general were at first somewhat bewildered, not knowing exactly what to do to meet the situation. It was at this stage Gandhiji stepped to the forefront to take the reins of leadership in his hands and give a new direction to the nationalist movement.

Gandhiji spent a few months working out his next step. He knew what he was talking about and what he intended to do. About the Rowlatt Bills which became Acts, his own analysis was clear and he expressed it in his 'Letter to the Editor' of *The Times of India*, Bombay, on 1 March 1919:

> Now look at the setting of the Bills. Their introduction is accompanied by certain assurances given by the Viceroy regarding the Civil Service and the British commercial interests. Many of us are filled with the greatest misgivings about the Viceregal utterance. I frankly confess I do not understand its full scope and intention. If it means that the Civil Service and the British

> commercial interests are to be held superior to those of India and its political and commercial requirements, no Indian can accept the doctrine. It can but end in a fratricidal struggle within the empire. Reforms may or may not come. The need of the Government is a proper and just understanding upon this vital issue. No tinkering with it will produce real satisfaction. Let the great Civil Service Corporation understand that it can remain in India only as its trustee and servant, not in name, but in deed, and let the British commercial houses understand that they can remain in India only to supplement her requirements . . .
>
> It will now be easy to see why I consider the Bills to be an unmistakable symptom of a deep seated disease in the governing body. It needs therefore, to be drastically treated. Subterranean violence will be the remedy applied by impetuous hot headed youths who will have grown impatient of the spirit underlying the Bills and the circumstances attending their introduction. The Bills must intensify the hatred and ill will against the state of which the deeds of violence are undoubtedly an evidence. The Indian covenanters, by their determination to undergo every form of suffering make an irresistible appeal to the Government, towards which they bear no ill will. . . . We must ascertain whether the disease is sufficiently great to justify the strong remedy and whether all milder ones have been tried. They have convinced themselves that the disease is serious enough, and that the milder measures have utterly failed. The rest lies in the lap of gods.[76]

Gandhiji thus strongly felt that the national wrong could only be righted through satyagraha. He called a small conference attended by about twenty persons, including Vallabhbhai Patel and Sarojini Naidu. There the Satyagraha Pledge was drafted and signed by all present on 24 February 1919. A separate body, the Satyagraha Sabha, was also established with Gandhiji as its President and Bombay as the headquarters. The pledge was published in *The Times of India,* Bombay, of 1 March 1919. Bulletins were issued, public meetings were held and more people signed the pledge. The whole country was expectantly preparing for the 'Rowlatt Satyagraha'.

Gandhiji then gave a call for hartal on 30 March 1919 but the date was later shifted to 6 April. As timely information regarding the new date could not reach Delhi, the hartal was observed there on 30 March. It was a tremendous success. Unfortunately, a confrontation with the police followed resulting in casualties. The hartal then spread all over India accompanied by violence and repression. Particularly in the Punjab, the situation became pretty bad, as the province was already seething with intense discontent as a result of the strong-arm tactics of the lieutenant governor. Within a week after the Delhi hartal, the whole of the Punjab was aflame, and to put down the disturbances severe repression was let loose. Gandhiji was arrested but later released on condition that he would not leave the Bombay Presidency where he had been sent by the police. There was no doubt that the 'Satyagraha Day' was observed with great enthusiasm and spontaneity. *The Hindu* in one of its issues in April 1919 reported: 'The absolute spontaneity of the movement, its vast scale, the tremendous enthusiasm which it aroused . . . all these unmistakably show the intensity of feeling in the country.'[77]

But faced with police repression the patience of the masses broke and widespread disturbances took place in various parts of India. The climax was reached at Jallianwala Bagh where a large number of unarmed and innocent people fell to the bullets of the army under the command of Brigadier General Dyer on 13 April. This was followed by the imposition of martial law in the Punjab and brutal repression by the government. The records of the Home (Political) Department of Government of India are virtually littered with documents telling tales of this repression. There were indignant reactions as well as appeals from all over India. Worried and pained by the government's repressive policy, *The Hindu* of 17 April appealed to the viceroy 'to put aside the sword for the sceptre of justice and truth'. It was, however, clear that Gandhiji's instructions to the Rowlatt Satyagrahis on 7 April 1919 did not produce the desired results when repressive measures were applied by the Government. Gandhiji instructed:

> We are now in a position to expect to be arrested any moment. It is, therefore, necessary to bear in mind that, if anyone is arrested, he should without causing any difficulty allow himself to be arrested and, if summoned to appear before a court, he should do so. No defence should be offered and no pleaders engaged in the matter. . . . There should be no demonstration of grief or otherwise made by the remaining satyagrahis by reason of the arrest and imprisonment of their comrade. . . . When once imprisoned, it is our duty to conform to all prison regulations, as prison reform is no part of our campaign at the present moment. A satyagrahi may not resort to surreptitious practices, of which ordinary prisoners are often found to be guilty. All a satyagrahi does can only and must be done openly.[78]

It is clear that the people were not trained well enough to carry out the instructions implicitly, and they were not yet ready for the technique Gandhiji applied in the form of the Rowlatt Satyagraha. It was also true that even in that critical hour all the nationalist leaders did not speak in one voice. Ten prominent members of the Imperial Legislative Council headed by Sir Dinshaw Wacha, Surendranath Banerjea, Muhammad Shafi and Srinivasa Sastri had issued a 'manifesto' in March 1919 opposing the idea of the passive resistance movement. The manifesto declared:

> While strongly condemning the Rowlatt Bills as drastic and unnecessary, and while we think we must oppose them to the end, we disapprove of the passive resistance movement started as a protest against them and dissociate ourselves from it in the best interests of the country, especially in view of the Reforms Proposals, which are about to be laid before Parliament in the form of a bill.[79]

Gandhiji was definitely not ready for the enormous magnitude of violence that erupted in the country. There were angry reactions, demands for enquiries, condemnations of the brutal repressions by the government, but the stone-hearted rulers stuck to their guns. However, Gandhiji's mind worked in a mysterious way. He was mortally wounded by the violence. He declared that he had committed 'a blunder of Himalayan dimensions' which had enabled ill-disposed persons, not true passive resisters at all, to perpetrate disorders. He first suspended the satyagraha movement on 18 April, and called it off on 21 July because of the violence. In his letter to the Private Secretary to the Viceroy dated 14 April 1919 he revealed his own thinking in regard to the movement. He wrote:

> I wanted to reach a decided stage before writing to you again and I have alas reached more than a decided stage, and in the place I have made my abode I find utter lawlessness bordering almost on Bolshevism. Englishmen and women have found it necessary to leave their bunglows and to confine themselves to a few well-guarded houses. It is a matter of the deepest humiliation and regret for me. I see that I over-calculated the measure of permeation of Satyagraha amongst the people. I underrated the power of hatred and illwill. . . . My Satyagraha, therefore, will, at the present moment, be directed against my own countrymen.[80]

At the same time, he pointed out in his letter that

> the Rowlatt Legislation has passed the stage of controversy on merits. In my opinion everything happening in India today points to the desirability of the withdrawal of that legislation and the Government will only enhance its prestige by definitely announcing its withdrawal out of regard for Indian opinion so definitely expressed.

The satyagraha ended but Gandhiji miscalculated the government intentions. They were in no mood to retreat on this point; rather they wanted to go further, which was evident from a curious circular containing some resolutions passed at a meeting of the principals of colleges and headmasters of high schools in Lahore on 21 April 1919, which was presided over by Rev Dr Ewing, a former Vice-Chancellor of the Panjab University. One of the resolutions was:

> That all college students be directed to read these [copies of the abstract of 'the Rowlatt Act prepared by the Hon Mr Fagan] and invited to ask questions about anything in the Act. They are all liable to be called upon for *viva-voce* examination on the main features of the Act.[81]

Even when the Rowlatt satyagraha was withdrawn, the Congress did not give up the issue. The Amritsar Congress offered 'respectful condolence to the relatives of those persons whether English or Indian who were killed.' The Congress also resolved that 'the site known as Jallianwala Bagh in Amritsar be acquired for the Nation.' The Congress left no doubt about its mood when it adopted the following resolution in the Amritsar Session, 1919:

> This Congress is of opinion that it is impossible to have real peace in India until the legislation popularly known as the Rowlatt Act which was passed in the face of the unanimous opposition in the country is repealed . . .

The struggle remained unresolved in 1919 and it was to take a new shape in 1920 when Gandhiji made a decisive change of front and started the historic Non-Cooperation Movement. The year 1919 thus signified a sort of 'passing of the frontier' in the history of the Congress. The period which followed with Gandhiji as the supreme leader of the Congress, came to be known as 'the Gandhian era'. The period under examination (1917-9) was marked by a traumatic experience and uncertainty not only without, but also within the Congress. Nevertheless, the Congress emerged from the fleeting fortunes and failures of the time as a more mature and bolder organization.

Notes and References

1. *Pioneer*, 2 January 1907; Quoted in M.N. Das, *Indian National Congress versus the British*, p. 294.
2. Quoted in R.C. Majumdar, *History of the Freedom Movement in India*, Vol. II, p. 282.
3. See Lal Bahadur, *Muslim League*, p. 43.
4. M.N. Das, op. cit., p. 295.
5. R.C. Majumdar, op. cit., p. 332.
6. Ibid.
7. C.F. Andrews, G.K. Mookerjee, *The Rise and Growth of Congress in India*, p. 145.
8. *Collected Works of Mahatma Gandhi*, Vol. XIII.
9. R.P. Dutt, *India Today and Tomorrow*, p. 130.
10. Paramananda Dutt, *Memoirs of Motilal Ghosh*, p. 210.
11. See *The Statesman: An Anthology, 1875-1975*, p. 320.
12. See *A Hundred Years of The Hindu*, p. 227.
13. Paramananda Dutt, op. cit., p. 220.
14. R.C. Majumdar, op. cit., p. 349-50.

15. M.N. Das, op. cit., p. 327.
16. Andrews and Mookerjee, op. cit., p. 150.
17. B.P. Sitaramayya, *The History of the Indian National Congress*, p. 212.
18. M.N. Das was of opinion that 'Gandhi's rise to power and prominence was sudden and spectacular'. op. cit., p. 404.
19. Judith Brown, *Gandhi's Rise to Power: Indian Politics 1915-22* (Introduction).
20. Ibid.
21. Quoted in ibid, p. 3.
22. Gokhale's Speech in Bombay, 14 December 1912. *Collected Works of Mahatma Gandhi*, Vol. XI.
23. See Sankar Ghose, *Political Ideas and Movements In India*, p. 87. Also see D.G. Tendulkar, *Mahatma*, Vol. I, p. 109.
24. Tendulkar, op. cit., p. 109.
25. Ibid.
26. Louis Fischer, *The Life of Gandhi*, p. 12.
27. *Collected Works*, op. cit., Vol. XII, p. 360.
28. Judith Brown, op. cit., p. 2.
29. Gandhi, *An Autobiography*, p. 276.
30. Ibid.
31. Brown, op. cit., p. 3.
32. Tendulkar, op. cit., p. 109.
33. Ibid.
34. Ibid, p. 106.
35. Ibid, pp. 107-8.
36. Ibid, p. 108.
37. *Young India*, 26 January 1921.
38. *Hind Swaraj*, pp. 94-5.
39. Ibid, p. 95.
40. *Gandhi and Gandhism*, p. 111.
41. Ibid, p. 101.
42. Quoted in R.C. Majumdar, op. cit., Vol. III, p. 10.
43. K. Sridharani, *My India, My West*, p. 224.
44. *Young India*, 11 September 1924.
45. R.P. Dutt, *Modern India*, p. 72.
46. See M.N. Roy, *Memoirs*
47. Quoted in Ghose, op. cit., p. 77.
48. Brown, op. cit., p. 8.
49. Ibid., p. 48.
50. R.P. Dutt, *India Today and Tomorrow*, p. 123.
51. Quoted in ibid.
52. Brown, op. cit., p. 52.
53. D.A. Low, (ed.), *Congress and the Raj: Facets of the Indian Struggle 1917-47*, p. 7. Also see D.A. Washbrook, *South India: Political Institutions and Political Change, 1880-1940*, and C.A. Bayly, *The Local Roots of Indian Politics, Allahabad 1880-1920*. These works clearly prove Low's contention.
54. See R.J. Moore, *The Crisis of Indian Unity, 1917-40* for an analysis how these strains developed.
55. Sitaramayya, op. cit., p. 348.

56. Ghose, op. cit., p. 82.
57. Dutt, op. cit., p. 297.
58. See A.I.C.C. File No. 9 of 1918.
59. A.I.C.C. File No. 1 of 1919.
60. R.P. Dutt, op. cit., p. 133.
61. A.I.C.C. File No. 9 of 1918.
62. M.N. Das, op. cit., p. 374.
63. Quoted in ibid, p. 395.
64. Ibid, p. 317.
65. Brown, op. cit., p. 136.
66. Quoted in ibid., p. 47.
67. Govt. of India. Home (Pol.) A. Progs. Nos. 455-72 of May 1919.
68. A.I.C.C. File No. 1 of 1919.
69. Majumdar, op. cit., Vol. III, p. 63.
70. A.I.C.C. File No. 9 of 1918.
71. *A Hundred Years of the Hindu*, p. 250.
72. Ibid, p. 251.
73. Govt. of India: Home (Pol.) A. Progs. No. 250 of March 1919.
74. Ibid.
75. Ibid.
76. Ibid.
77. *A Hundred Years of The Hindu*, p. 252.
78. B.N. Pandey, (ed.) *The Indian Nationalist Movement, 1885-1947: Select Documents*, p. 52.
79. Govt. of India: Home (Pol.) A. Progs. No. 250 of March 1919.
80. Ibid, Nos. 455-72 of May 1919.
81. See 'Oppression in the Punjab and C.F. Andrews' in *Andrews' Papers* published by the Deenabandhu Andrews Centenary Committee.

APPENDIX 8.1

Report of The British Committee of the Indian National Congress 1917-1918

Since the last Annual Report of the Committee, the cause of Indian self-government has made great progress both in India and in this country. While we congratulate ourselves on this advance, we have also sadly to deplore the loss of our esteemed Chairman, Sir William Wedderburn, Bart. The very last occasion upon which Sir William appeared in public was to take the chair at a Memorial Meeting on the passing away of Dadabhai Naoroji, one of the founders of the Committee. Sir William had been for some time in weak health, and his visit to London left him exhausted. He returned home so enfeebled that he never recovered strength and vitality, and he passed away peacefully on January 25, 1918, at the age of 79, to the great grief of his many friends in this country and in India. During his long life, he served India faithfully and lovingly. From the day of his return to this country, after long service in India, that country was ever in his mind and heart, and he was ever ready to plead her cause, in the House of Commons, on the platform, and in the Press. One of the last acts of his long life was to draft a magazine article on the need for a large measure of constitutional reform for India.

Sir William had rejoiced when, on August 20, 1917, the Home Government's momentous declaration of British policy in India was made. He rejoiced still more when Mr Montagu announced his intended visit to India in order to prepare a draft scheme of reform in consultation with the viceroy, the heads of the public services, and the principal exponents of public opinion in India. So eager was he to help to the utmost of his power that he offered to accompany the Secretary of State, in order to assist him in his mission. Had Sir William lived long enough, and with his unique experience of official methods in India and public life in this country, there is no doubt that he would have cordially welcomed the spirit of the Report that has now been presented for discussion and criticism by the Secretary of State and the Viceroy, as being the precursor of a better form of Government in India and far more cordial relations between India and this country. Especially would he have welcomed this new State document as recognising the validity and strength of India's claim to responsible self-government, and seeking to provide the machinery for its attainment in due course, with the goodwill and co-operation of government and people alike, along the lines laid down in the pronouncement of August 20, 1917 — a pronouncement gladly accepted by this Committee, and one that was partly the result of its work.

Unfortunately, Sir William did not live to read the Report, and his loss at this critical period in India's history is irreparable, not alone to the Committee over which he presided from its inception, but to the whole Congress movement. His wise counsel, mature judgment, and unrivalled experience would have been invaluable to the Committee and to India to-day in considering the detailed features of the Report, but they are unavailable, and with him has passed away the last of the great figures around which Congress influences in this country had gathered. A Memorial Meeting was held at the Cexton Hall, Westminster, on March 5, 1918, presided over by Sir J. Herbert Roberts, M.P., at which occasion was taken to pay a last tribute by many Members of Parliament, Peers and other notable persons.

The Committee, in common with the Congress itself, frankly accepted the declaration of British policy in India made by the Secretary of State, on behalf of the British Government, and felt it to be its duty to examine the proposals relating to constitutional reform in India contained in the Montagu-Chelmsford Report in the light of that pronouncement and its clear implications. Upon the publication of the Report, which expressly called for reasoned and constructive criticism of its proposals, the Committee, recognising the generous spirit in which its authors had applied themselves to the difficult task of framing a Scheme that would be generally acceptable, and with a full sense of its own responsibility in exercising its well recognised function of tendering independent and disinterested advice to the Congress, came to the conclusion that, in its broader features, but without binding itself in any way in matters of detail, it was the Committee's duty to offer support to the general principles of self-government proposed in the Report, subject to the right to submit such constructive criticism, in due course, as a closer study of the methods proposed to carry them out and a wider survey of the situation and its possibilities might require. The Committee accordingly telegraphed to the General Secretaries of the Congress, stating that it supported the proposals in principle, and enquiring the views of the Congress as regards the Report and the detailed proposals.

The Committee has watched with growing concern the trend of events within the Congress, resulting at length in the abstention of a number of old and respected Congressmen (some of whom have been for years among the Committee's most valued counsellors, and whose names are among the best known in this country as those of leaders of a great and inspiring national movement) from the recently held special session of the Congress at Bombay. The fact is fully recognized that there has been a cleavage in Indian opinion upon the proposals for self-government, but the Committee hopes that, with further light and information, misconceptions will be dispelled, and strongly recommends that all possible avenues should be thoroughly explored, with a view to securing unity of action and sacrifice at this momentous hour in the history of the Indian Motherland. This is surely a time when party divisions in India are a deadly peril to political progress, and disunion, weakness, or schism among the Indian reformers will certainly be used for the purpose of playing off one party against another and of delaying or frustrating constitutional reform by those whose interest lies in the preservation of the *status quo,* and who have always sought to prevent the fulfilment of pledges and opposed the transfer of power from the bureaucracy to the people.

There are several very important questions affecting the future government of India which are left open in the Report of the Secretary of State and the Viceroy. Committees have been appointed to deal with the subject of the franchise and to determine the subjects to be reserved, etc., and until these Committees have reported, the Cabinet will not be in a position to introduce a Bill. The measure of reform will be considered by the government that will represent the next Parliament. It will be the most democratic Parliament in British history, and any measure that will be passed by such a Parliament should be of a democratic character.

The Committee has rejoiced to note that, of the Indian members appointed to the two Committees that have proceeded to India to report on the questions of franchise and electorate and of reserved and transferred functions of government, four are prominent and respected Congress leaders whose sagacity, maturity of experience, and independence have stood the country in good stead on many an occasion, and that a fifth, though temporarily holding office, is a progressive and patriotic supporter of Indian reforms. The Committee feels that such appointments indicate a radical change in the attitude of the government towards Indian problems and the Indian nationalistic cause.

The Committee will support to the utmost of its power the demand for such modifications in the Reform proposals as are deemed to be essential to the due fulfilment of the pledges and promises contained in the pronouncement of August 20, 1917, and it will seek and use every opportunity to influence public opinion here to that end. But it would fail in its duty to India if it did not have regard to developments, Parliamentary and otherwise, in this country, and emphasise the paramount importance of the fullest possible agreement in attitude and spirit as to the essentials of the Reform Scheme on the part of all sections of Indian opinion. When the proposals reach Parliament, in the form of a Bill, then alone it will be possible to form a final judgment on them as a whole, much will depend upon the reasonableness and statesmanship of the Indian reformers. If mere hostility and acrimonious, not constructive, criticism prevail, if the tension between the two wings of the Nationalistic Party remains acute, this it is evident, must seriously endanger the passage of the Reforms, and the Committee would make the most urgent appeal for such a measure of support from India for the proposals as will enable the government in this country, in the face of many urgent claims and undoubted difficulties arising out of the inevitable consequences of the present situation, to carry this great constitutional reform in its main principles, with necessary amendments, through Parliament.

The Committee would take this opportunity of sharing in the rejoicing of India at the splendid part that she has been privileged to take in three continents, in the historic events and the remarkable victories that are rapidly leading to the final triumph of the Allied cause. India has reason to be proud of her great effort and the result of her immense sacrifices in men, money and material.

The Committee especially welcomes the action of the Imperial Government in inviting to this country, as guests of the British nation, a party of Indian editors, representative of different points of view, with the object of enabling them to see at close quarters something of the extraordinary effort of Britain and her Allies, by land and sea, to bring about an era of renewed confidence in the sanctity of treaties and the publicly pledged word of the nations.

Following the usual procedure, the Committee has availed itself of the presence in London of representative Indian gentlemen known to be in general sympathy with it, to obtain their advice and services. The Committee has specially welcomed the presence in London of the three distinguished Indians who have been appointed to the Secretary of State's Council — namely, Sahibzada Aftab Ahmad Khan, Sir Prabhashankar Pattani, and Mr Bhupendranath Basu. The first is known as an ardent educationist and a broad-minded and progressive member of the Mussulman community in India. The second, a distinguished administrator, has served as a member of the Bombay Government. The third has been for long an independent leader of the Indian National Movement, and was the President of the Congress and the chosen spokesman of his compatriots at the outbreak of the War. All three have been, it is believed, a source of strength to the Secretary of State, and have added greatly to Indian prestige by their quiet and patriotic labours.

For the second time, Sir Satyendra P. Sinha came to this country to attend the Imperial War Conference, and the Maharaja of Patiala was appointed as the representative of the Indian Princes. For the first time, an Indian representative, Sir Satyendra Sinha, was invited to attend the Imperial War Cabinet as a full member, and it is known that he rendered valuable services in that capacity to the Empire and to India alike — not merely as the sole representative of the Government of India, but as a distinguished and representative Indian, upon whom the King was pleased to confer the honour of appointment as one of His Majesty's Counsel. Both he and Mr Basu have earnestly warned the British public against the dangers of delay in the adoption of a large and far-reaching measure of reform, and their efforts have done much to strengthen the hands of friends of India against the powerful reactionary forces arrayed against the grant of political reforms.

When it became known that Mr Tilak and other members of Home Rule League deputations, who had received from the Government of India passports to proceed to this country to enlighten people here upon the situation in India, had been prevented from continuing their journey by the arbitrary action of the Home Government, the Committee submitted to the government a strong protest against this unworthy attempt to stifle an expression of Indian public opinion, especially as a known opponent of any large measure of constitutional reform was permitted to come to this country and to address the British people.

During the year, there has been registered in London a limited liability company, known as the Indo-British Association, presided over by Lord Sydenham, and whose principal members and shareholders include a number of retired Anglo-Indian officials and merchants. The Association is provided with large funds, it is said, principally by business houses that have been invited to subscribe by way of business insurance connected with their Indian commercial interests. As a body it has done everything possible, through the Press and by pamphlets and other literature, to discredit the Secretary of State, and to malign the leaders and the purpose of the Indian National Movement. At first, it tried to stampede public opinion here against all idea of political reform, by the circulation of a pamphlet containing (as Mr Charles Roberts, M.P., has shown) garbled and misleading extracts from selected addresses presented to Mr. Montagu and Lord Chelmsford, purporting to prove that large and influential bodies of people in India were strongly hostile to such reforms. Later, it endeavoured by a frontal attack to overthrow the Reform proposals put forward by the Secretary of State and Viceroy, on the ground that they were subversive of British rule in India, and calculated to play into the hands of those they term Indian 'Bolsheviks'. Being defeated in the House of Lords and not venturing to seek a hearing in the House of Commons on August 6 last, it has since sought to undermine and whittle away the Scheme by the suggestion of impossible and reactionary amendments. It is true that some of the members of the Association have publicly and emphatically dissociated themselves from these questionable methods. But it is clear that the Association is endeavouring to rally to its banner all that is most reactionary in English life, the retired bureaucrats that have failed to keep in touch with the rapid growth of Indian political sentiment, especially during the war and vested interests of every kind, based upon a determination to retain power and privilege, material and official, so long as possible. These, as before, will do their utmost to frustrate any Scheme of reforms, and will use every division, weakness, and error of judgment of the Indian reformers to injure the National Movement.

The Committee has carried on its general propaganda by meetings, lectures, the circulation of literature, etc., and, as far as circumstances have permitted, has placed the views of the Congress before the British public and official circles. It has also associated itself with such organizations as the British Auxiliary of the Home Rule for India League, Britain and India, and some societies of Indian gentlemen, in the holding of public meetings, and it has further co-operated with them in joint conferences, in which questions of policy and joint public action have been considered. The desirability of having branches of the Committee in some of the large towns is under consideration. Some of these towns, such as Glasgow, have fifteen members of Parliament; others have ten or eleven.

The Fraternal greetings of the Congress were presented to the Annual Conference of the Labour Party, in January, by Mr Polak, and the response of the large audience was very hearty and generous.

The death of Sir William Wedderburn has been a most severe loss to the Committee. He was its most prominent and influential member, devoting almost his entire time to its work. We have no one who can replace him. One by one, the men who have held important offices in India, such as Mr Hume and Sir Henry Cotton, have passed away, and none of those who have held such high official posts have joined the Committee to take their places. There are but few in this country who have knowledge of the Indian National Movement or sufficient sympathy with it to do the work which needs to be done. The Committee ought to be strengthened by the addition of members from India, and by the appointment of a chairman who will be able to devote a considerable time to the work. Since Sir William's death, Dr G.B. Clark, ex-M.P. (who was the Chairman of the Indian Reform Association, formed in 1882 to support Lord Ripon's policy) has been acting as Chairman, but age and other duties make it impossible for him to give the time necessary.

The closed accounts for 1917, duly audited, are presented along with those covering the period from January 1 to September 30, 1918. The increase in the ordinary expenditures of the Committee is due to the grant of increments long overdue and to special war-charges. In accordance with the resolution of the Congress, the journal 'India' has been regularly issued. In 1917, the Committee's funds were charged with a sum of £500 on account of the deficit incurred. For the current year, part of the deficit to date has been met by payment of £300, and it is estimated that a further sum of £475 will be required to cover the loss for 1918. While part of this result is due to a falling off in the number of paying subscribers in India, the main cause is the serious advance in the cost of production owing to the War. The cost of paper is now seven times its pre-war value, whilst that of printing and distribution is increased by about 120 per cent. The deficit on the publication of 'India' for the complete year 1919 is estimated at £1,050, if prices do not further increase. The General Secretaries of the Congress have been fully informed on these matters, which, it will be seen, are entirely beyond the control of the Committee and the Directors of the Company. The further work of the Committee will be determined by the amount of financial support it receives from India.

The Committee desires to place on record here its deep sense of appreciation of the valuable services rendered to the national cause by Mr H.E.A. Cotton, L.C.C., M.P., during the twelve years in which, as editor, he had the conduct of the journal 'India'. It is confident that, in his new sphere of activity in Parliament, Mr Cotton will continue to serve India to the best of his ability.

The value of a weekly paper as a form of propaganda is inestimable, and increasing, particularly in highly influential circles, and the Congress would do well to provide additional funds for its maintenance and improvement. Today and during the critical period ahead, when such far-reaching changes are contemplated, such a journal as 'India' is a vital necessity.

Signed on behalf of the Committee,

G.B. CLARK,
Acting Chairman.

OFFICES OF THE BRITISH COMMITTEE
OF THE INDIAN NATIONAL CONGRESS,
14, HENRIETTA STREET, CONVENT GARDEN, W.D.2.
October 22, 1918.

APPENDIX 8.2

The Pledge

Being conscientiously of opinion that the Bills known as the Indian Criminal Law (Amendment) Bill No. I of 1919, and the Criminal Law (Emergency Powers) Bill No. II of 1919, are unjust, subversive of the principle of liberty and justice, and destructive of the elementary rights of individuals on which the safety of the community as a whole and the State itself is based, we solemnly affirm that in the event of these Bills becoming law and until they are withdrawn, we shall refuse civilly to obey these laws and such other laws as a Committee to be hereafter appointed may think fit, and we further affirm that in this struggle we will faithfully follow truth and refrain from violence to life, person or property.

Chapter IX

The Evolution of the Congress Party and Organization

Ashim Kumar Datta

1. First Congress

THE 72 'REPRESENTATIVES'* who attended the First Congress held in Bombay on 28 and 29 December 1885, came in response to the letter that had been drawn up by Allan Octavian Hume some time in the middle of 1885. Some points from the letter that will be relevant to a discussion on the development of the Congress as an organization are set out below:

1. The 'Conference' of 'the Indian National Union' would 'discuss and decide upon the political operations to be undertaken during the ensuing year'.
2. Conferences will be held every year.
3. The delegates will be the 'leading politicians' of the country.
4. They will be 'well acquainted with the English language'.
5. Besides 'the Poona friends' [that is to say, leading personalities of the Sarvajanik Sabha], about 70 delegates were expected.

It will probably never be known who exactly had been considered by Hume to be worthy of being personally contacted by him for attending what was named in his above letter the conference of the 'Indian National Union', and in another contemporary document of his, 'the National Party', which acquired its permanent name, the 'Indian National Congress' in December 1885. Nor is any list extant of the individuals or organizations which were approached by him or by the Sarvajanik Sabha of Pune which had been selected by him to organize the proposed conference.

---

* Mano Mohun Ghosh, Narayan Ganesh Chandavarkar, and Sivalaya Ramaswami Mudaliar had been sent to England in the middle of 1885 as 'delegates' of the 'Indian National Union' to plead the case of India, and so the delegates to the First Congress were referred to as 'representatives'. From the Second Congress onwards, the word 'delegates' was used.

That Hume was being rather selective from the very beginning is beyond doubt. The letter was treated as a private and confidential document and it circulated amongst a very small number of people whom he called 'the inner circle' of his contemplated organization. When he was engaged in exploring the idea and toured different cities like Bombay, Pune, Madras and Calcutta between November of 1884 and April of the next year, he took some like-minded leaders into confidence. In the correspondence of the time, he stressed the need for 'linking in'. The estimate of Dr S.R. Mehrotra is that the controversy over the Ilbert Bill had given an opportunity to Hume to establish himself at the head of a network of contacts throughout India *(The Emergence of the Indian National Congress,* Chapter VII). Hume referred to this as 'our party' in some of his correspondence of 1883-4. In 1885, he gave it the name 'Indian National Union'. It is very likely that he drew up the circular letter after he had had discussions with the Viceroy Lord Dufferin in Simla in May 1885. During this private tour he made his own selection of persons with whom he chose to discuss his plans. For instance, during his stay in Calcutta in March 1885, though he met Ananda Mohan Bose and discussed with him other matters, the plan of holding a national convention at the end of the year was not disclosed to him, and he chose not to see Surendranath Banerjea. His confidants in Calcutta seem to have been W.C. Bonnerjee and Narendra Nath Sen, the two of the three persons from Bengal who attended the First Congress. There is no evidence of how and when the third 'representative', Girija Bhusan Mukherjee, a lawyer and a journalist, came to be invited. The Report of the First Congress says that some more representatives from Bengal had been expected — who they were and what organizations they belonged to are not known.

The three bodies on which Hume had put his reliance were the Sarvajanik Sabha of Pune, the Bombay Presidency Association of Bombay, and the Mahajana Sabha of Madras. The Sarvajanik Sabha was entrusted with the responsibility of organizing the conference, and had not cholera broken out in Pune in December, the conference would have been held in that city. The arrangements at Bombay, the substitute venue, were also made by the Sarvajanik Sabha, but with active co-operation from the Bombay Presidency Association.

It can be guessed that the Sarvajanik Sabha conducted the correspondence, be it with associations, or individuals, regarding the selection of 'representatives' especially because Hume himself did not come back to India till 2 December from the trip that he had undertaken to England in the summer of that year. There is indirect evidence that 'Select Committee', that is to say, committees to select delegates had been appointed in some places, because when the venue as also the dates of the meeting were changed, telegrams were sent to these committees informing them of the new arrangements.

In his 'Introductory Article' for the report of the Second Congress in Calcutta in 1886, Hume anonymously admitted: 'The Congress of 1885 had been got together with some difficulty by the exertions of a few leading reformers, and included less than one hundred of the more advanced thinkers belonging to the most prominent centres of political activity.'

In the official report of the First Session held in Bombay on 28 and 29 December 1885, details about the delegates and the bodies to which they belonged are probably incomplete. For instance, one Mr J. Ghoshal of Allahabad is mentioned in the proceedings as a speaker, but his name is not found in the list of delegates. This was no other than Janaki Nath Ghoshal who attended almost every session of the Congress during the next twenty-five years, as long as he was alive, and though not mentioned as a speaker for or against any resolution on any occasion, often features in the reports of the early sessions as the person reading out the rules of procedure and presenting the list of delegates elected to the Subjects Committee. His home was in Calcutta, he owned lands in Nadia District and so in the reports of other sessions, he is mentioned as a delegate elected by either the Bengal Landholders' Association or the British Indian Association of Calcutta, or both, and how he happened to be a 'representative from Allahabad' to the First Session is not known.

The places from which the delegates to the First Session came and their professions and standing in society, as far as can be gathered from the Report, are tabulated below:

AGRA: 2 (both pleaders, one also a municipal commissioner and editor of a paper).

AHMEDABAD: 3 (two *vakils*, one also a municipal commissioner, the third name is not mentioned).

ALLAHABAD: 1 (name was omitted in the list, but from the detailed proceedings one knows that it was J. Ghoshal, that is to say, Janaki Nath Ghoshal, a zamindar, has already been mentioned).

AMBALA: 1 (pleader and also a journalist).

ANANTAPORE: 1 (pleader and also a member of the Local Board).

BELLARY: 1 (merchant and also chairman of the municipality).

BENARES: 1 (retired Subordinate Judge).

BERHAMPORE (Ganjam): 1 (pleader and also municipal commissioner).

BOMBAY: 18 (three barristers; three *vakils*; four solicitors; two merchants; two editors of newspapers; profession not mentioned for two Members of Legislative Council, one member of the Bombay Presidency Association, and one otherwise undescribed person).

CALCUTTA: 3 (one barrister; one pleader and also editor of a journal; one editor of a newspaper).
CHINGLEPUT: 1 (pleader).
COIMBATORE: 1 (editor of a newspaper and member of Local Board).
CUDDAPPAH: 1 (pleader).
KARACHI: 2 (both pleaders).
KUMBHAKONAM: 1 (landholder).
LAHORE: 1 (Brahmo missionary).
LUCKNOW: 3 (one pleader, one professor, one proprietor of a newspaper).
MADURA: 1 (no mention of profession).
MADRAS: 8 (four *vakils*, one of whom was a member of the Legislative Council and another a Commissioner of the Municipality; two newspaper editors; one merchant and also a municipal commissioner; one medical doctor).
MASULIPATTAM: 1 *(vakil)*.
POONA: 8 (two pleaders; two newspaper men one of whom was also a professor; two professors, one, as mentioned before, also editor of a journal; three described as representatives of the Sarvajanik Sabha).
SALEM: 1 (occupation not mentioned).
SIMLA: 1 (retired member of the I.C.S., that is to say, Hume himself).
SURAT: 6 (four pleaders two being also municipal commissioners, one merchant; profession of one not mentioned).
TANJORE: 2 (one lawyer and also President of an Association, another landholder).
TINNEVELLY: 1 (landholder and school teacher).
VIRAMGAM: 1 (municipal commissioner).

Summarizing these statistics, Hume wrote anonymously in the official report:

> Not only were all parts of India thus represented, but also most classes; there were barristers, solicitors, pleaders, merchants, landowners, bankers, medical men, newspaper editors and proprietors; principals and professors of independent colleges, headmasters of schools, religious leaders and reformers.

The government servants who attended were eight in number, and amongst them were Mahadev Govind Ranade, then a Judge of the Small Causes Court and also a member of the Legislative Council, Professor Ramakrishna Gopal Bhandarkar, and D.S. White, at that time President of the Eurasian Association. Excepting one, they did not take part in the deliberations, the exception being Ranade.

The details given in the list of delegates state that one delegate from Bombay was a representative of the Bombay Presidency Association, two of Madras were representatives of the Mahajana Sabha, three of Pune were representatives of the Sarvajanik Sabha and three of Surat were of the Praja Hitawardhak Sabha.

In his presidential speech, W.C. Bonnerjee stated that 'the representatives of Lahore, Lucknow, Agra, Allahabad, Benares, each represent political associations collectively of very widespread influence' and that the editors or delegates of the *Indian Mirror*, the *Hindu*, the *Indian Spectator*, the *Tribune* were present. It appears to be impossible to say now how the particular 63 delegates who, in the list of delegates, are not specifically mentioned are representatives of any association, were chosen or invited. In Bonnerjee's view 'it might be said they were self-elected but that was not so'. From the short summary of his speech, one learns that

> the news that this Congress would be held had been known throughout the year in the different Provinces of India and they all knew that everywhere the news had been received with great satisfaction by the people at large and though no formal elections had been held, the representatives had been selected by all the different Associations and bodies, and he only wished that all thus selected had been able to attend, instead of their having now to lament the absence of many valued co-adjutors whose attendance had been unhappily barred by various unfortunate circumstances.

Dr S.R. Mehrotra who while preparing his book *The Emergence of the Indian National Congress* (1971) had scanned the important newspapers of 1885, found only two references to Hume's activities from November 1884 to mid-1885. One reference was to a private meeting that Hume had in January 1885 with select leaders from Bombay. The other news item indicated that the reporter had only a very vague idea of what was being planned. Surendranath Banerjea's autobiography, *A Nation in the Making* would also suggest that some of the very important people in the field of political activities also did not come to know of the proposed conference. It was at a very late stage that W.C. Bonnerjee invited him to attend the conference, and Surendranath Banerjea seems to have heard about the matter only then for the first time. Newspapers started mentioning the conference only after Hume had come back on 2 December; the first reference seems to have been on 5 December.

Hume's letter had indicated that such a conference was to be an annual event. Hume of course hoped for something more than a mere annual conference — his letter stated that 'indirectly, the Conference will form the germ of a Native Parliament'. One of the Resolutions of the First Congress was that the resolutions passed by this Congress be communicated to the Political Associations in each province and that these Associations be requested with the help of similar bodies and other agencies within their respective provinces, to adopt such measures as they consider calculated to advance the settlement of the various questions dealt with in these resolutions.

It was also decided that the Second Congress would meet in Calcutta around Christmas time the following year. The official report of the First Congress does not contain any information on matters like who could elect the delegates to the Second Congress, what procedure was required to be followed, how many delegates were permissible from one constituency or whether territories or institutions formed constituencies. Nor does the report disclose that Hume was going to function as the General Secretary of the organization — however amorphous it might have been at that time, by reason of the fact that it was going to hold a conference year after year, to 'discuss and decide upon the political operations to be undertaken during the ensuing year', it aspired to assume a role of almost continual activity. Bonnerjee, in his presidential speech attempted to define the aims and objects of the organization that was in the process of coming into being, though 'not exhaustively'. In his view, they were:

(a) The promotion of personal intimacy and friendships amongst all the more earnest workers in our country's cause in the parts of the Empire; (b) The eradication by direct friendly personal intercourse of all possible race, creed or provincial prejudices amongst all lovers of our country, and the fuller development and consolidation of those sentiments of national unity that had their origin in their beloved Lord Ripon's ever memorable reign [sic]; (c) The authoritative record, after this has been carefully elicited by the fullest discussion, of the matured opinions of educated classes in India on some of the more important and pressing of the social questions of the day; (d) The determination of the lines upon and methods by which during the next twelve months it is desirable for native politicians to labour in the public interests.

2. Second Congress

The report of the Second Session held in Calcutta in December 1886, contains greater details about the election of delegates and their status and occupation, but no information is available on the directives which might have had been issued by either the General Secretary of the Congress — Hume was functioning in that capacity (the confirmation in print is available in the Report of the Fourth Congress, Allahabad, 1888) when he was 're-elected' to the office — or the Reception Committee, in relation to who could elect delegates, and how, and up to what limit. That at least in one of the meetings held for electing delegates, the letter of Mr J. Ghoshal, Secretary of the Reception Committee, was publicly read out, we can gather from the reports of such meetings collected in Appendix II of the Report of the Second Session, and the 48 such meetings referred to there are going to be mentioned soon.

At least 69 associations, some of them like the Bombay Presidency Association of Bombay and the Indian Association of Calcutta having branches in other places, are mentioned in the Report of the Second Congress as having sent delegates. The actual number might have been greater, inasmuch as the Prajahit Vardhak Sabhas of Surat, Broach, Viramgam, and Nadiad might have been quite separate institutions, although they all shared the same name — the title would mean 'association for increasing the welfare of the people'. The same might have been the case with the three Sindh Sabhas (Sind Associations) featuring in the list of delegates, one located at Karachi, one at Hyderabad, and one at Sukkur. Two Mahajan Sabhas, one at Majdia and the other at Kissengunge both rather small places in the Nadia District of Bengal, similarly are likely to have been separate entities, and the word *mahajan* most probably meant wholesale merchants, whereas the same word in the name of the well-organized Mahajana Sabha of the Madras Presidency meant people. It is perhaps superfluous to mention that the associations represented a very wide spectrum in membership, status, influence and the like. Whereas bodies like the British Indian Association of Calcutta, Mahajana Sabha of Madras, Sarvajanik Sabha of Pune, Bombay Presidency Association of Bombay, Indian Association of Calcutta, were well-organized bodies, some of them of long standing, many others might have been very small and also recent in origin. The very name of the 'Habiganj People's Association of Silchar', which sent a delegate, indicates that it could not have been either a numerous or an influential body — Silchar itself was a small district town of some four or five thousand people at that time, and the people from the subdivision of Habiganj in the neighbouring district of Sylhet who resided in Silchar, though they included some of the leading citizens of the town, could not have been very many in number. Similarly, the 'Agricultural Society' of Tahirpur of Bengal which became a constituency, is very unlikely to have been professionally at all significant — Tahirpur was the seat of a fairly big zamindari and the association most probably was founded and run by the zamindar of the day. The names of the associations which sent delegates are given below.

Associations Which Sent Delegates to the Second Congress (Calcutta, 1886)

1. Arya Dnyan Vardhak Sabha, Bombay
2. Agricultural Society, Tahirpur (Bengal)
3. Arbelia J.V. Sabha (24-Parganas, Bengal)

4. Agra Association, Agra
5. Bombay Presidency Association, Bombay and other places
6. Ballia Institute, Ballia (NWP)
7. Bengal National League, Calcutta
8. British Indian Association, Calcutta
9. Burrabazar Political Association, Calcutta
10. Bengal National League, Calcutta
11. Bagirhat People's Association (Bengal)
12. Barisal People's Association (Bengal)
13. Baranagore Working Men's Club (24-Parganas, Bengal)
14. Baranagore Ratepayers' Association (24-Parganas, Bengal)
15. Central Indian Association, Mhow
16. Chinsural Wellwishing Club (Bengal)
17. Dacca People's Association
18. Furreedpore People's Association (Bengal)
19. Gooty Union (Madras)
20. Gooty People's Association (Madras)
21. Gujarat Sabha, Ahmedabad
22. Ghatal Association (Midnapore, Bengal)
23. Hindu Excelsior Reading Rooms, Madras
24. Hindu Samaj, Allahabad
25. Howrah People's Association (Bengal)
26. Habiganj People's Association, Silchar (Assam)
27. Indian Association, Calcutta and different places including Lahore
28. Indian Union, Calcutta
29. Jhinkargacha Ryots' Association (Jessore Dist., Bengal)
30. Jnan Pradayini Sabha, Joyrampur (Bengal)
31. Kalia Youngmen's Association (Bengal)
32. Khetripara Ryots' Association (Bengal)
33. Katdah Association (Bengal)
34. Khirpai Association (Midnapore Dist., Bengal)
35. Lokasabha, Nagpur
36. Mahajana Sabha, Madras
37. Meerut Association
38. Moorshedabad Association (Bengal)
39. Mahajan Sabha, Majdia; Kissengunge (Both in Nadia District, Bengal)
40. Malda Association (Bengal)
41. Mirzapur Institute, Mirzapur
42. Nowgung Ryots' Association (Bengal)
43. Natshal Gramya Samity (Midnapore District, Bengal)
44. Neelphamari Association (Bengal)
45. Nattore People's Association (Bengal)

46. National Society, Balasore (Orissa)
47. Orissa People's Association
48. Prajahit Vardhak Sabha, Surat, Broach, Viramgam, Nadiad
49. Paschim Mymensingh Association, also mentioned elsewhere as West Mymensingh Association
50. Purulya Gramya Samity (Midnapore District)
51. Purbasthali Hitakari Sabha (Bengal)
52. Patriotic Association, Rohora (24-Parganas, Bengal)
53. Rifah-am Association, Lucknow
54. Rajshaye Association (Bengal)
55. Russapagla Improvement Association (Calcutta)
56. Ryots' Association, Nowgong (Assam)
57. Sarvajanik Sabha, Poona
58. Sindh Sabha, Sukkur; Hyderabad; Karachi
59. Serampore Muffasil Association (Bengal)
60. Seebpore Ratepayers' Association (Bengal)
61. Seebpore Association (Bengal)
62. Senhati People's Association (Bengal)
63. Sherpur Landholders' Association (Bengal)
64. Sankrail Hitasadhini Sabha (Bengal)
65. Suburban Ratepayers' Association, Bhawanipur (Calcutta)
66. Triplicane Literary Society, Madras
67. Unjuman-i-Tehzib, Fyzabad (N.W.P. and Oudh)
68. Utterparah Union (Bengal)
69 Vaidik Samaj, Farukhabad (N.W.P. and Oudh)

Either the editor or the proprietor of each of 24 newspapers and periodicals from different corners of the land and which varied a great deal in circulation and importance, came as delegates to this Second Session of the Congress at Calcutta in 1886, and here is a list of those papers:

1. *Ahmedi*, Sakrail, Mymensingh
2. *Amrita Bazar Patrika*, Calcutta
3. *Andhra Prakasika*, Madras
4. *Behar Herald* and *Indian Chronicle*, Patna
5. *Bengalee*, Calcutta
6. *Bharatbasi*, Calcutta
7. *Christian Herald*, Calcutta
8. *Crescent*, Coimbatore
9. *Gujarati*, Surat
10. *Hindu*, Madras
11. *Hindu Patriot*, Calcutta
12. *Indian Mirror*, Calcutta

13. *Indian Nation,* Calcutta
14. *Indu Prakash,* Bombay
15. *Kerala Patrika,* Calicut
16. *Kohinoor,* Lahore
17. *Naseem Agra,* Agra
18. *Prayag Samachar,* Allahabad
19. *Reis and Rayyet,* Calcutta
20. *Sanjivani,* Calcutta
21. *Sar Sudhanidhi,* Calcutta
22. *Sind Sudhar,* Hyderabad
23. *Sind Times,* Karachi
24. *Sitara-i-Hind,* Moradabad

What is certainly more indicative of the extent to which the interest of the people had been roused is the collection of news items from newspapers about the elections of delegates held in November and December, given in Appendix II of the report of the Second Congress. 48 such items were included, and a list of the places where such meetings were held or from where the departure of the delegate(s) was mentioned, is given here.

Meetings mentioned in Appendix II of the Report of the Second Congress (Calcutta, 1886)

1. Allahabad — 19 December
2. Arbalia J.U. Sabha (24 Parganas) — 19 December. J.U. were probably abbreviations of Jatiya Unnati (Betterment of the Nation)
3. Arrah — 13 December
4. Balliah — 13 December
5. Bankipur (Patna) — 28 November
6. Bareilly, Bareilly Institute
7. Bellary — 13 November
8. Berhampore (Ganjam)
9. Bombay, Bombay Presidency Association
10. Mention of delegates of 'Arya Jnana Vardhak Sabha' Bombay. (*Jnana* = knowledge; *Vardhak* = that which increases; *Arya* = noble)
11. Burrabazar Political Association, Calcutta — 24 December
12. Calcutta; *Hindusthanis* elected a representative who is listed as a Representative of the Burrabazar Political Association in Appendix II
13. Russapagla (Calcutta) — 24 December
14. Calicut — 6 November
15. Chittagong — 16 December

16. Coimbatore; called by Sudasa Dharma Ratchani Sabha (the People's Association)
17. Conjeeveram
18. Cuddalore — 1 November
19. Dacca — 1 December
20. Dibrugarh; Council of Upper Assam Association appointed 2 delegates
21. Ghatal (Bengal) — 26 December
22. Gooty; called by Gooty People's Association
23. Gudivada — 31 October (affiliated to Madras Mahajana Sabha)
24. Halisahar (Bengal) — 25 December
25. Hosangabad — 21 December
26. Hospet (held under the auspices of the Ryots' Sabha) — 4 December
27. Jubbulpore — 21 December
28. Kisengunge (Nadia District) — 22 December
29. Lucknow; representative of Jalsa-i-Tahzib mentioned in a report of 10 December
30. Madras Mahajana Sabha — 27 November; central office delegates elected, and list of members nominated by branches (15 districts in all and two 'estates' of zamindars?) drawn up. (Some of the meetings are separately mentioned in the citations above.)
31. Mylapore (Madras) — 21 November
32. Mahishadal (Bengal), Branch of Indian Association
33. Mhow, Central Indian Association — 25 December
34. Midnapore, Branch of Indian Association — 12 December
35. Delegates of Nagpur mentioned
36. Natore (North Bengal) — 28 November
37. Nellore — 13 November
38. Patna, Branch of Indian Association — 19 December
39. Penukondah — 13 November
40. Rahara (near Calcutta), called by Rohora Patriotic Association — 16 December
41. Rajamundry — 7 November
42. Ranaghat (Bengal) — 28 November (affiliated to Indian Association)
43. Sholingur
44. Surat, called by Surat Sabha
45. Sylhet (Assam) — 16 December
46. Tanjore — 7 November
47. Vizianagram — 4 December
48. Wallahjanagar, North Arcot District.

A note at the bottom of Appendix II says:

> A vast number of brief telegraphs so and so appointed delegates at today's meeting will arrive Calcutta at such and such hour on such and such date were received. . . . Only in the Madras Presidency were full reports of all the meetings immediately published in the local Press; many of these Madras Reports have been reproduced above; the rest are similar.

These newspaper reports furnish three instances of the constituency offering to meet the cost of the delegates and their refusing the offer in each case. A proposal was made at the meeting of the public of Wallah-janagar (North Arcot District), to raise a fund for the expenses of the delegates, and he, 'a patriotic gentleman', declined the offer. He was a pleader by profession. The same thing happened at Sholingur — the delegate, a *vakil*, did not agree to accept any monetary help. A proposal to raise a fund at Bellary was abandoned when the delegates said that they would meet their own expenses. The Report of the Third Congress states that some constituencies subscribed the travelling expenses of delegates too poor to pay themselves.

The report of the Second Congress also set the pattern of how the names of the delegates were to be mentioned in the official reports henceforward. The list was to constitute *Appendix I*, and the particulars of each delegate were entered under seven columns in this Report in this order: Serial number; Presidency; Province; District or City; Name of the delegate; Place, or Association, which he represented; Remarks as to his profession or status. Particulars of 436 delegates will be found in the Report, but it is also mentioned that some delegates had not cared to fill in the proforma that was distributed for this purpose, or did not record all particulars. A note appended at the end of *Appendix I* informs the readers that,

> This list, it is feared, is not quite complete as to names even, since it is believed that some few gentlemen left without recording their names. It *certainly* is incomplete as to many whose names *are* recorded, owing to gentlemen failing to note their academical degrees, professions, and other particulars opposite their names before leaving. [Emphasis in the original.]

Another footnote there deserves to be quoted:

> Besides these delegates, several Visitors — the Honourable Mr Ranade, Rajah Lutchman Singh, the Honourable Mr Baijnath (Chief Justice, Indore) and others were present, and though taking no part in the Public Proceedings, assisted the Delegates at some of their committees, with informal advice.

The report of the Fifth Congress held in Bombay in 1889 states that the break up of the delegates who attended the Second Congress at Calcutta in 1886 by Presidencies or Provinces was as follows:

Madras Presidency	47
Bombay and Sind	48
Punjab	17
Northwestern Provinces and Oudh	74
Central Provinces and Berar	10
Bengal, Bihar, Orissa and Assam	240

Some more details tabulated by Hume, the anonymous author of the report of the Second Congress, are also quoted below.

Places from which Delegates came to the Second Congress in Calcutta, 1886:

1. *Madras Presidency:* Anantapur, Bellary, Berhampore, Bezwada, Calicut, Chingleput, Chittur, Cuddalore, Gooty, Gudivera, Kumbhakonam, Kurnool, Madras City, Masulipatam, Nayaveram, Nellore, Ongole, Penukondah, Raichur, Rajmundry, Wallajanagar.
2. *Konkan:* Bassein, Bombay.
3. *Deccan:* Belgaum, Poona, Sangli, Satara.
4. *Gujarat:* Ahmedabad, Baroda, Broach, Nadiad, Surat, Viramgam.
5. *Sind:* Hyderabad, Karachi, Kotri, Sukkur.
6. *Punjab:* Ambala, Amritsar, Dera Ismail Khan, Gurdaspur, Lahore.
7. *North Western Provinces:* Agra, Aligarh, Allahabad, Almora, Azamgarh, Ballia, Basti, Benares, Farrukhabad, Gazipur, Kankhal (Hardwar), Mainpuri, Meerut, Mirzapur, Moradabad, Tajpur (Bijnore).
8. *Oudh:* Barabanki, Fyzabad, Lucknow, Partabgarh, Unao.
9. *Central Provinces:* Hosangabad, Khandwa, Jubbalpore, Nagpur.
10. *Bihar:* '. . . representatives came from Patna, Bankipur, Behar, Shahabad, Doomraon, Chupra, Gya, Mozufferpore and Bhagalpore'.
11. *Lower Bengal:* (that is to say, Bengal more or less as it came to be constituted in 1912): 'The list of places represented in Lower Bengal is almost a list of all the districts.'
12. *Chota Nagpur:* Hazaribagh, Purulia, Ranchi.
13. *Orissa:* Balasore.
14. *Assam:* Sylhet, Cachar, Shillong, Nowgong and Dibrugarh.

Then, a calculation of the distances travelled was given in the report: 300 delegates made long journeys, 30 of them travelled 2,000 miles, average distance travelled being 903 miles.

It would be appropriate here to quote how Hume himself assessed the attendance at the Second Congress. This is what he wrote in the opening paragraphs of his essay, 'The Congress — An Introductory Article', prefacing the formal report of the proceedings:

> The leading characteristic of the Congress of 1886 was, that it was the whole country's Congress. The Congress of 1885 had been got together with some difficulty by the exertions of a few leading reformers, and included less than one hundred of the more advanced thinkers belonging to the most prominent centres of political activity. The Congress of 1886 may be said to have grown, almost spontaneously, out of the unanimous resolve of the educated and semi-educated classes, throughout the Empire, to take a decisive step towards the attainment of that political enfranchisement to which they have come, of late years, to attach so much importance.
>
> In all the more advanced provinces action commenced early in the autumn, and it soon became apparent that the second Congress was destined to be, in many essential respects, a decided advance on the first.
>
> The delegates or representatives who attended the first Congress, though representatives of the highest culture of the land, and fully qualified to speak as to the wants and wishes of the nation, yet appeared as volunteers in the good cause, uncommissioned, as a rule, by any constituencies, local or general, to appear on their behalf. Very early it seems to have occurred, simultaneously, to all those most interested in the renewed movement, that something more than this was requisite, and that the gentlemen who were to take part in the second Congress ought to receive some public authorisation from the bodies and committees (or leading members of the latter) whom they were to represent. Accordingly, as the time of the Congress drew near, the leading Associations at all the more important towns and cities proceeded to elect delegates, and great public meetings, embracing all classes of the community, who were interested in the matter, were also held, almost throughout the country, at which representatives were designated.
>
> It has not been possible to collect the records of all these elections, but a sufficient number of notices of these, gleaned from papers of different presidencies and provinces, have been placed on record in *Appendix-II*, to show how thoroughly and systematically this new feature in the arrangements have developed. . . . But the great advance lay, perhaps, in the total change in the character of the Congress. In the previous year people had to be pressed and entreated to come; to the late Congress *everybody* wanted to come of their own accord. The first Congress was erected by the labour of a few who had to nurse carefully the young plant; the second Congress burst into vigorous growth on its own account, with a luxuriance that demanded careful pruning. From some provinces double, or more than double, the members actually delegated would have been sent, but for inter-provincial communications as to the numbers other provinces contemplated sending, and remonstrances against one province swamping the others.

> For the first Congress there was no enthusiasm until after it was over and its results had been announced (though then indeed the entire country endorsed those results and warmly approved the new departure); but in regard to the second Congress, the greatest enthusiasm prevailed, especially throughout Bengal. . . .

Analysing the occupational background of the delegates, Hume made some generalizations of the following nature: No representatives of the 'old aristocracy' were there, for government had excluded them from all positions worthy of their rank; higher landed interests were well represented; the higher commercial class, bankers, merchants, were fairly represented, but the shopkeeping class sent no delegates — his comment was that petty moneylenders and shopkeepers are generally ignorant and entirely immersed in their own personal concerns. He also admitted, '*ryots* and cultivating classes' were 'insufficiently represented'. According to his analysis, five *ryots* came as representatives, six other gentlemen came as the elected representatives of different Ryots Associations, and also came 'representatives who are known champions of the *ryot*'. His own assessment was that the great bulk of the *ryots* 'have as yet but a very imperfect knowledge of political matters', and he added that 'to educate them in all such matters is one of our most pressing duties'. Hume added a second reason why he thought there were no delegates from among the *ryots* themselves — they were poor. In his opinion, with these exceptions, all classes were adequately represented. The legal profession 'mustered very strong'; some forty editors came; 'two dozen', principals, professors, and masters of schools attended; twenty merchants; the same number of bankers; sixteen medical men; small groups of millowners, manufacturers, tea and indigo planters; a couple of contractors; a single engineer; and three Christian missionary ministers, came as delegates. About seventy delegates were presidents, vice-presidents, or elected members of municipalities, some thirty held similar positions in local boards and subdivisional boards. There were fifteen Honorary Magistrates.

This short passage from his 'Introductory Article' deserves to be quoted in this context:

> We have said nothing yet of religious distinctions, because we consider that it is community of temporal interests and not of spiritual convictions that qualify men to represent each other in the vast majority of political questions. We hold that, their general interests in this country being identical, Hindus, Christians, Mahomedans and Parsees may, as fitly as members of their respective communities, represent each other in the discussion of public secular affairs. . . We deprecate the introduction of any religious sentiment, or any reference to gentlemen's religious beliefs into political movements of the nature of these Congress. . .

He then proceeded to discuss the charge that Muslims were inadequately represented.

3. Third Congress

As against 436 delegates to the Second Congress (Calcutta, 1886), 607 attended the Third Congress (Madras, 1887) although 760 had been elected. 90 of the 153 who failed to come sent messages of regret and the Report makes a guess that about 70 could not come because of the length and expense of the journey, as most of them belonged to the Punjab, North-West Provinces, Oudh, and Bihar. A comparative table is given in the Report about the attendance province-wise to make the point that long distances stood in the way of attending the Congress, and the table is reproduced here.

Delegates from	*Second Congress (1886) at Calcutta Number of Delegates*	*Third Congress (1887) at Madras Number of Delegates*
Madras	47	367
Bombay and Sind	47	99
Punjab	17	9
N.W.P. and Oudh	74	45
Central Provinces	8	13
Bengal, Bihar, Orissa and Assam	238	79
Total	431	612

(In the Report of the Fifth Congress, the count is 436, the Bombay-Sind figure being 48, the C.P.-Berar figure 10, and the Bengal figure being 240).

Not much information has survived about the elections held to choose delegates, and this is what one would find in the Report of the Third Congress:

> All through October, November, and December, elections were going on. So far as these went, they were regularly and properly conducted, and the fact of the elections having been held and the names of the parties delegated were duly and regularly notified to the Reception Committee at Madras. There was no attempt, so far, to divide the country into definite electoral divisions, or restrict the number of delegates that might be sent from any particular locality; the one suggestion that was made was, that no province (other than that in which the Congress was held) should, as a

whole, send more than two delegates per million of its total population. Any town, any of whose inhabitants felt interested in the question, held a public meeting, often consisting of only one or two hundred people, but, in some cases, mustering several thousands, and thereat, after speeches explaining the nature and the objects of the Congress, elected as delegates those men who were generally looked up to as leaders. Again, any association, (no matter whether it numbered only fifty or five thousand members), that desired to be represented, called a general meeting and thereat elected one or more of its leading members. But, except in Madras, where they were only too successful, no persistent efforts were made to make all towns and all associations do their duty in this matter, or to get the smaller towns and villages to hold preliminary meetings and select thereat several of their number to represent them at the election meetings in the bigger towns. This was done in several cases, but only just where the people, of their own accord, saw fit to do it. Again, except in Madras, where the political organization is more advanced than in any other province, no regular system was adopted to ensure the adequate representation of all creeds, classes, and interests; anyone who wanted to be represented could be represented, but no one troubled about those who did not themselves come forward, and if, after all, the representation was singularly exhaustive, it is due to the general interest in the Congress which pervades the community. In all these matters the idea has been to let the thing develop in its own fashion for a year or two before attempting to lay down any fixed rules.

The Report had this to say about the quality of representation to the Third Congress:

. . . But though the representation was unequal (Provincewise) and still far from perfect, yet, considering that this was only the second Congress for which any attempt at elections had been made, a glance at the list of delegates *(Appendix I)* will show that it was such as no men could, even three years ago, have believed that the people could have spontaneously created for themselves, not only without Government assistance but, in many places, in the face of the opposition of the local officials. Every province, every sub-province, and except in the Punjab, almost every large city was represented; while in Bombay and Madras every town, every district, and almost every association were represented. The representation, too, was more satisfactory than in 1886. There was this time no class or community that had no spokesmen. . . . There were quite a number of shopkeepers, (last year, conspicuous by their absence), and no less than ninety-five *ryots* or cultivators, against only five last year. Doubtless, Madras sent the bulk of these; for poor men cannot unaided travel huge distances, but twelve came from the Bombay Presidency, one from the Central Provinces, four from lower Bengal, and three from the North-Western Provinces. . . . The higher landed interests . . . were well represented from every Province. The legal profession again mustered very strong, and while in 1885 [misprint for 1886?] there were only about 40 merchants and bankers, in 1886 [misprint for 1887?] they numbered 144. The principals, professors, and masters of Indian schools and colleges were far more numerous than on the previous occasion, and it may be noted that as in 1885 [misprint for 1886?] so in 1886 [misprint for 1887?] 25 per cent of all the delegates were graduates. There were the usual quotes of newspaper editors, 43 in number, of medical men, millowners, manufacturers, ministers and missionaries — and what was very satisfactory, 19 artisans, 2, 3, 4, 6 from every great province (except the Punjab), one of whom, be it noted, a carpenter by trade, made a most sensible speech in Tamil, on the necessity of a regular system of technical education.

From the Third Congress (Madras, 1887), the particulars of delegates given in *Appendix I* of the Reports were put under the following 9 headings: (Serial) number; Presidency; Province; District; Name in full with honorary titles, scholastic degrees, etc.; Religious denomination and caste, if any; Occupation, address etc.; Place or places or associations, etc. which they represent; How and when elected.

Among the delegates were the editors or proprietors of some 50 newspapers and periodicals and the delegates represented more than 100 associations, the separate branches of a body not being counted, nor all the Ratepayers' Associations being shown separately. Lists of these are given below:

Newspapers Represented through Delegates at the Third Congress (Madras, 1887)

1. *Advocate,* Lucknow
2. *Ahmedabad Times* (Gujarati Weekly), Ahmedabad
3. *Akbhar-i-Am* (Urdu tri-weekly), Lahore
4. *Andraprakasika* (Telegu Weekly), Tiruvateswaram-pettah
5. *Baisack Tattva* (Bengali), Rajshahi
6. *Bharat Bandhu* (Anglo-Hindi Weekly), Aligarh
7. *Bharat Jivan* (Hindi), Benares
8. *Behar Herald* and *Indian Chronicle* (English Weekly), Patna
9. *Bengalee* (English Weekly), Calcutta
10. *Brahman* (Hindi monthly), Kanpur
11. *Christian Herald,* Calcutta
12. *Crescent,* Coimbatore
13. *Dharma Jivan* (Urdu Weekly), Lahore
14. *Dharwar Vrit* (Marathi and Kanarese Weekly), Dharwar
15. *Dnyan Chakshu* (Marathi Weekly), Poona
16. *Dnyan Prakash* (bi-weekly), Poona
17. *Eastern Star,* Egmore, Madras
18. *Hindu,* Madras
19. *Hindu Punch,* Poona

20. *Hindu Rangini* (Bengali Weekly), Maldah
21. *Hindustani* (Urdu Weekly), Lucknow
22. *Hindusthan* (daily), Allahabad
23. *Indian Mirror*, Calcutta
24. *Indu Prakash*, Bombay
25. *Jaridai Rozyar* (Hindustani Weekly), Royapettah
26. *Kalanidhi*, Coimbatore
27. *Kalpataru* (Marathi Weekly), Poona
28, *Kerala Patrika* (Calicut)
29. *Kundandai Mitram*, Kumbhakonam
30. *Lokananda Samaj Patrika*, Madras
31. *Madura Mail* (English Weekly), Madras
32. *Mirat-ul-Hina*, Lucknow and *Murasila*, Lucknow; written *'Miratul Hina and Murasila'* (either two or one)
33. *Mitra Vilasa* (Hindi Weekly), Lahore
34. *Naseem Agra* (Urdu Weekly), Agra
35. *Native Opinion*, Bombay
36. *People's Journal* (English Weekly), Lahore
37. *Prakasika* (Telegu fortnightly), Vizagapatam
38. *Prayag Samachar*, Allahabad
39. *Rajyavakta* (Gujarati bi-weekly), Ahmedabad
40. *Ramdoss* (Marathi and Kanarese weekly), Bijapur
41. *Silpa Krishi Patrika* (Bengali), Rajshahi
42. *Sitara-i-Hind*, Moradabad
43. *Sungbad Pravakar* (Bengali Daily), Calcutta
44. *Swadeshamitram* (Tamil bi-weekly), Madras
45. *Telegu Harp* (English Weekly), Vizagapatam
46. *Tribune* (Lahore)
47. An unnamed Oriya Weekly edited by Gouri Sankar Roy

Associations mentioned to have sent Delegates to the Third Congress (Madras, 1887).

1. Agricultural Association, Hospet
2. Agricultural College Society, Saidapet
3. Agricultural Society, Tahirpur (Bengal)
4. Akhila Jana Manoramya Sabha, Kovaripak, Kondapuram
5. Anjuman Mufid-i-Islam, Madras
6. Artisan Association, Kumbhakonam
7. Aryadesh Opkarini Sabha, N.W. Province
8. Arya K.N. Sabha, Jubbulpore
9. Arya Samaj, Agra
10. Arya Samaj, Jubbulpore
11. Arya Vardhak Sabha and Samaj, Bombay
12. Ballia Institute, Ballia

13. Bassein Prant Association
14. Behar Landholders' Association, Patna
15. Behar People's Association, Patna
16. Bengal Congress Committee
17. B(engal) N(ational) Chamber of Commerce, Calcutta
18. Bengal National League, Calcutta
19. Berhampore Association (Ganjam)
20. Bharatvarshya National Union, Aligarh
21. Bombay Anjuman, Bombay
22. Bombay Presidency Association, Bombay and branches in different places.
23. Bhratre Association Sabha, Dera Ismail Khan
24. British Indian Association, Calcutta
25. Central Indian Association, Indore
26. Committee of Arbitration Court, Bombay
27. Council Association, Satara
28. Desabhimana Sabha, Madras
29. Deshorpaini Sabha, Meerut
30. Devanagri Sabha, Meerut
31. East Bengal Association, Calcutta
32. Goraksha Sabha, Navsari
33. Gorakshini Sabha, Tahirpur
34. Gorakshare Sabha, Jubbulpore
35. Graduates' Association, Madras
36. Hazaribagh Association
37. Hindu Brethren's Association, Wallajanagar
38. Hindu Nidhi, Deccan
39. Hindu Sabha, Ambala
40. Hindu Samaj, Allahabad (could be a misprint for Madhya Hindu Samaj)
41. Hit Sabha, Jubbulpore
42. Indian Association, Calcutta, branches at different places including Lahore
43. Indian Union, Calcutta
44. Jain Association of India, Bombay
45. Jalsa-i-Tahzib, Lucknow
46. Jalsa Tazib, Basti
47. Kashi Sarvajanik Sabha, Benaras
48. Koza Hitakari Sabha, Nadia (Bengal)
49. Kumbhakonam Club
50. Kumbhakonam Mill
51. Literary Association, Cuddapah
52. Literary Society, Triplicane
53. Lokananda Samaj, Madras

54. Loka Sabha, Nagpur
55. Madhav Sabha, Madras
56. Madhya Hindu Samaj, Allahabad
57. Mahajana Sabha, Madras and branches in other places
58. Mahajan Sabha, Majdea (Bengal)
59. Mahajan Sabha, Khulna
60. Mahomedan Association, Bangalore
61. Maldah District Association
62. Merchants' Association, Negapatam
63. Metal Trading Company, Madras
64. Moorshedabad Association
65. Mutual Improvement Society, Madras
66. Mymensingh Association
67. Mymensingh Ryots' Association
68. Native Association, Chittore
69. Orissa Association, Cuttack
70. Patriotic Association, Srirangapatam
71. People's Association, Barisal
72. People's Association, Faridpur
73. People's Association, Gooty
74. People's Association, Howrah
75. People's Association, Khandwa
76. People's Association, Magurah
77. People's Association, Ranigunge
78. Poona Mercantile Association
79. Praja Hitavardhak Sabha, Surat
80. Rajshahy Association
81. Ranchi Association
82. Ratepayers' Association (different places)
83. Ratnagiri District Association
84. Reading Room, Trichinopaly
85. Reading Room and Victoria Jubilee Library, Tiruvalur
86. Reform Association, Cochin
87. Rifa-i-am, Ambala
88. Rifa-i-am Association, Lucknow
89. S.D.R. Sabha, Coimbatore
90. S.V. Sabha, Bellary
91. Sadhupati Association, Nadia (Bengal)
92. Sarva Jana Sabha, Igatpuri
93. Sarva Jana Sabha, Nasik
94. Sarva Jana Sabha, Ratnagiri
95. Sarva Jana Sabha, Tinnevelly
96. Sindh Sabha, Karachi
97. Social Progressive Association, Kangra

98. South India Merchant Company, Madras
99. Sukhdaik Sabha, Bannu
100. Tanjore People's Association
101. Tripura Hita Sadhini Sabha, Calcutta
102. U.K. Sabha, Tellicheri
103. Union Club, Madura
104. Vidya Dharma Vardhini Sabha, Allahabad
105. Vidya Vivardhani Sabha, Vizianagram
106. Viveka Vridhi Sabha, Muttiyalpet

4. Fourth Congress

The Report of the Fourth Congress (Allahabad, 1888) contains this information about the election of delegates:

> During the year, the greater part of the country was regularly divided into electoral divisions, and the minimum number of delegates to be elected by each was settled. These divisions, for the double purpose of the education of the people and the convenience of voters, were re-divided into sub-divisions, and divisional and sub-divisional committees were created in all these, composed either of the delegates to previous Congress with others whom they co-opted, or, as in Berar for instance, of men specially elected *ad hoc* by the people.

There is a footnote on the minimum number of delegates and this will be considered later. Another footnote there says: 'Electoral divisions are of two kinds, first Territorial, as in England, and second (to secure the representation of Minorities), Sectional, each including a special community, or an Association, *Sabha* or *Samaj*, representing such.'

Of the 1,248 delegates who attended the Fourth Congress (Allahabad, 1888), as given in the Report,

> 455 [were] in one branch or other of the legal profession, 42 in the medical profession, 5 engineers, 127 merchants and traders, 85 bankers, 73 editors and journalists, 297 landed proprietors, 102 landholders, 17 *ryots* or cultivators, 2 artisans, 7 shopkeepers, 31 clergymen, missionaries, priests and religious teachers, 59 educationalists, principals and professors of colleges, masters of schools, and public teachers, 6 printers, 18 contractors, etc.

The Report of the next year's Congress (Fifth, Bombay, 1889), supplies the information that of the 1,248 delegates, 95 were from Madras, 163 from Bombay and Sind, 80 from the Punjab, 73 from the Central Provinces and Berar, 254 from Bengal, Bihar, Orissa and Assam, and 583 from the North West Provinces and Oudh.

It is necessary to draw attention to two points in connection with the mention of delegates being ryots or artisans by occupation in the early

Reports of the Congress. The Report of the Second Congress (1886) states that five ryots attended and six gentlemen came as representatives of different ryots' associations. In the List of Delegates which is *Appendix I*, four persons altogether seem to have the word *ryot* associated with their names, either as being so themselves or representing a body of such men. Of the two delegates elected at the meeting of the Ryots Sabha of Hospet, one was a 'Rao Saheb, Member, District Board, Honorary Magistrate', and the other, 'Row Saheb, Landholder, 1st Grade Pleader'. The Report of the Third Congress mentions that ninety-five ryots and nineteen artisans came. The word *ryot* is appended to a few names only in the List of Delegates in that Report. Delegates 296 and 297 are stated to have been ryots themselves and elected representatives of ryots. Four delegates, serial numbers 311 to 314, are stated to have been elected at two meetings of ryots of two areas, and the occupation of one of them is mentioned as *'Mirasdar'*, and of the other three, 'Landed Proprietor'. Three delegates, numbers 562, 585, and 598, are mentioned as 'zamindars' and also as representatives of ryots. Of a fourth, number 554, the Assistant Secretary of the Indian Association, it is stated that in addition to being elected from two other constituencies, he was also elected at a meeting of 'cultivators'. A fifth such person, described as the 'Superintendent of Tezpur Mills', is stated to have been a member of the Ryots' Association of that town. It is stated in the Report that one of the nineteen artisans, 'a carpenter by trade, made a most sensible speech in Tamil, on the necessity of a regular system of technical education'. One delegate who delivered such a speech according to the report of the proceedings, had the title of 'Rao Saheb', was a municipal commissioner, and his recorded occupation was 'Iron Merchant', but he had been elected by an association of artisans.

Since it is difficult to agree with Hume as to who amongst the delegates were ryots or artisans on the basis of the data available in the printed Reports, one has to assume that more details were available to him when he made his analyses. It is not absolutely certain that every time he used the word *ryot* he meant a peasant. The Congress was urban-based. A general statement may be made that during the period 1885-1919, peasants and artisans did not play any role at any session of the Congress. Well-to-do members of the middle class who knew English well ran the organization, and among them again, lawyers played the dominant role.

The Report of the Third Congress (Madras, 1887) provides information on what the central leadership was doing at this time to make the Congress and its programme known to the common people. This line of thinking was also reflected in the draft constitution that was prepared at this session. Hume's circular letter of 1885 had mentioned that the delegates would be 'leading politicians well acquainted with the English language'. At the Second Congress (Calcutta, 1886) the character of the Congress at least in appearance was radically different from this idea. Not all of the 436 delegates could be described as 'leading politicians'. And there were a sprinkling among them who did not use English while addressing the house and some amongst such delegates might not have known the language at all. On the very opening day of the Second Congress, one of the speeches supporting the motion to elect Dadabhai Naoroji the president was in Urdu and the next speaker gave a summary of that speech in English. The Report mentions at least one more speech in Hindustani at that session. At least one speech was in Tamil at the Third Congress, and the President of the Fourth Congress gave a ruling that only those delegates who had difficulty in delivering speeches in English may use other language and that otherwise the proceedings would be conducted in English. 607 delegates attended the Third Congress (Madras, 1887), and 1,248 the Fourth Congress (Allahabad, 1888).

Hume's reference to the different classes of people assembled at the Second Congress and in particular, to ryots, shopkeepers and the like to which attention has already been drawn, shows that the central leadership was keen that common people, at least those who were literate, also attend the Congress. One great advantage that the Congress enjoyed throughout its battle for freedom was that even if it had not taken the trouble of publishing any pamphlets or similar literature, the nationalist newspapers, in English and in Indian languages, would have given — as they in fact did give — the fullest publicity to its activities, plans of future action, appeals for co-operation and the like. There is evidence that the Congress published during this period a number of tracts for the common people. The report of the Third Session (Madras, 1887), contains in its *Appendix III* English translations of two pamphlets that had been issued by the Congress soon after this session.

One was a catechism in Tamil written by M. Viraraghava Chariar, Editor of the *Hindu*, and a regular delegate to the Congress sessions. The final paragraph of this was as follows: 'Read [this catechism] to all your friends . . . read it to everyone in your village . . . make everyone in the neighbouring villages understand . . .Let your cry be *"Congress ke jai"* and God will help those who thus prove that they are anxious to help themselves.' It is interesting to note that way back in 1887, the translator chose to put the slogan 'Victory to Congress' in Hindustani: *'Congress ke jai'*. It might have been at the instance of Hume, the anonymous editor of the Report. He claimed in a speech of 1888 that this slogan had been heard at the Third Congress (Madras, 1887). As the name indicates, the pamphlet was in a question-answer format. It stressed the situation that though the British people through their Parliament and the party in power had the last say in deciding the fate of India, neither the common people in England nor their leaders had enough information on our country, and that the English officials in India did not send trustworthy reports. So a question was put: 'What then should we do to inform the English people of our wants and wishes and obtain justice at their hands?' The answer was that Indians should set up a representative council similar to Parliament, obtain the permission of Parliament to elect members of that council, that the Queen should make the resolutions of that council binding on the governor general and governors, that there should be one grand council for the whole country and five or six smaller councils for the more important provinces, and that Indians should go on sending telegrams, reports as also delegations to keep the people in England informed of the situation in India and to put forward their demands. It was added in another answer that members of the Legislative Councils in India were not chosen by Indians - the government chose 'foolish big men' for this purpose, and that, in any event, the Indian members had no right to ask questions in the councils. Then coming to the Indian National Congress itself, it was mentioned that 'for the last three years, many of the *zamindars*, merchants, landlords, and men of other professions living in different parts of India, have made it a point to meet once in a year in some Presidency town and discuss public questions of the most vital importance.' In yet another answer, information was furnished that the 'Proceedings of the Second Congress were published in a book and 5,000 copies of this were distributed by Mr Dadabhai Naoroji in England.' It was commented elsewhere that whereas delegates to the First Congress 'were not appointed by the people'. . . 'for the Second Congress, members of the people at public meetings and through public associations, elected their representatives', that 'all kinds of people were elected delegates to the Third Congress, great men like Sir T. Madhava Row and little men like artisans and petty tradesmen.' Answering the question, 'were there *zamindars*, were there *ryots*, were there Municipal Commissioners' (in the Third Congress), the author wrote, 'yes, there were all these . . . out of the 604, there were 61 *zamindars, jaigirdars,* and *taluqdars,* and there were 95 *ryots* and other small landholders. Then there were 144 merchants, traders and shopkeepers, 55 school masters, 206 members of legal profession, retired judges, barristers, advocates, pleaders, solicitors etc. 43 editors of newspapers, 19 artisans, 8 doctors, etc.' Among them were members of (legislative) councils, '31 were Honorary Magistrates, 10 were Fellows of one or other University, 103 had seats on municipal boards, and 56 on local fund boards'. A comment was added thereafter: 'It is difficult to imagine a more representative gathering.'

Other points worthy of note from the catechism are that, probably,

10,000 copies of the Report of the Third Congress would be sent to England; that 'We must have a permanent Congress Fund'; that 'a multitude of small donations' would be welcome; and that in every Province there was a 'Standing Committee'.

The other pamphlet was in Hindustani and the title in English translation was, 'A Conversation between Molvi Farid-ud-din, M.A., B.L., Vakil (Barrister) of the High Court, practising in the Zillah Court of Hakikatabad, and Rambaksh, one of the Mukaddams [Chief villager] of Kambakhtpur'. Hume was the author, and before publishing the brochure, he showed the manuscript to friends in India and in England.* Kambakhtpur would mean the village of people of little understanding, while Hakikatabad can be translated as the city where truth prevails or where rights are honoured. Farid-ud-din first explains what representative government is, and then stresses that for the proper functioning of such a government, it is necessary that the people should take an interest in public issues and also discuss them. He expressed the hope that, because the government in Britain was a constitutional one, if the people there understood the problems of India, then the right steps would be taken. Farid-ud-din then said that he would set up a political association in Hakikatabad and that it would be a branch of the larger association at the capital, and that small branches would be set up in every village where there were intelligent people; that people should pay small subscriptions. Talking about the activities of his proposed association, he said that pamphlets would be published, and that each district should send elected representatives to the annual session of the Indian National Congress. He added that delegates should be sent to England. A final piece of advice was: 'Trouble yourself little about what men call themselves, Hindu, Moslem or Christian. Look to what they are, and if good, remember that they may wear different liveries, they are all servants of one Lord.'

The back cover of the Reports of the Congress in this period contained in some cases lists of priced pamphlets available on sale. The Report of the Fourth Congress (Allahabad, 1888), says:

> Hundreds of thousands of tracts, pamphlets, speeches and leaflets were put into circulation in all the languages of India. Thousands of public and semi-public meetings and gatherings were held, not in one province, but in almost every district of the Empire. Hundreds of missionaries of the cause travelled from town to town and village to village expanding the good tidings of the Congress, and the fiercer the opposition raged and the more

---

*In a letter to Ripon, dated 13 January, 1889, Hume stated that 20,000 copies in Hindi and Urdu had been distributed. Briton Martin, *New India, 1885,* (1970), p. 325.

persistent the efforts of the adversaries of the movement, the more strenuous became the efforts of the supporters'.

Hume, however, had thought it necessary to add a word of caution about these publications in the last paragraph of the Introductory Article in the Report of the Fourth Congress. It is stated there that the

> Congress Party as a party . . . is responsible for the formal resolutions passed at its sittings and for nothing else. Day by day, as the movement spreads, men who accept its principles write and publish books, pamphlets and leaflets and make speeches in a dozen languages, here, there, and everywhere. For all these productions, the individual authors and creators are alone responsible. The Congress Party, as a whole, may not agree with what this or that speaker or writer puts forth, but it holds itself *responsible* only for the resolutions it passes. . . . [emphasis in the orginal].

J.C. Bagal in his *History of the Indian Association* quotes from its Report for 1885 where an account of what it had done in its first ten years from 1876 to 1885 was compiled, and it is said there that:

> The idea of holding meetings of the *ryots* and of teaching them rights and obligations also originated with the Indian Association. During the Rent Bill controversy, several meetings of the *ryots* were held under the auspices of the Association to discuss the Rent Bill. . . . At present the Association is actively engaged in forming village organisations; for, to invest our political demonstrations with the reality of power, they must be supported by the great body of the people. It is too often brought forward as a matter of reproach that our political agitation is confined to a few educated *Babus*. The Association is resolved to wipe off this reproach and a considerable success has already attended its efforts in the direction as is apparent from the numerously attended meetings . . . to protest against the *Chowkidari* Bill.

The Congress benefited from the activities of such organizations. Speaking about the Indian Association's role after 1886, its historian Bagal says: 'In Bengal, the Indian Association took upon itself the self-imposed task of popularising the ideals for which both the Association and the Congress stood.'

It was perhaps no problem to find volunteers for the Congress to organize such work, for what the Congress was saying was in the heart of every member of the Indian intelligentsia, with the solitary exception of the followers of Sir Syed Ahmed Khan. The Anglo-Indian community, using the word in its 19th century sense, meaning Britishers living in India, was another group opposing and ridiculing the Congress. Sir Auckland Colvin wrote pamphlets against the Congress and these were answered not only by Hume but also by Eardley Norton, a British barrister practising in Madras and a steadfast supporter of the Congress. Lord Dufferin, the viceroy also ridiculed the Congress, saying in a speech in 1888 that the educated class in India was 'a microscopic minority'. These particular pamphlets and speeches in English can be found in libraries but, alas, no details regarding the work of the 'missionaries' of the Congress of this period or of the pamphlets that were printed in the different languages, other than the English translations of the two referred to above, are documented or available.

In this background of adverse propaganda, Pherozeshah Mehta, in his presidential speech at the Sixth Congress (Calcutta, 1890) said with some amount of exultation:

> We have survived the charge of sedition and disloyalty. We have survived the charge of being a microscopic minority. We have also survived the charge of being guilty of the atrocious crime of being educated, and we have even managed to survive the grievous charge of being all *Babus* in disguise . . .

Nonetheless, it would not be correct to characterize the Congress of this period as an organization of any group other than the intelligentsia of the country. What Man Mohun Ghose said at the Sixth Congress (Calcutta, 1890) may be taken as the correct summing up for the period: 'It is asked whom does the National Congress represent? What right has it to speak on behalf of the masses of people who know nothing about the Congress? My answer is, the National Congress represents the thinking portion of the people of India.' So also the statement of Pherozeshah Mehta made some ten years later at the Eighteenth Congress (Ahmedabad, 1902) may be accepted as a correct assessment: 'the Congress is the work of the educated classes'.

Hume used to claim, as he did for instance in the Report of the Fourth Congress (Allahabad, 1888), that the Congress also represented the semi-educated classes. He did not however choose to define or describe the exact group he meant. That common people who could read their own language were supporters of the Congress aims is beyond doubt. It is they who read the thousands of pamphlets that we are told were printed in the different Indian languages by and for the Congress at this time. It is they who were behind the increase in the circulation of the newspapers printed in Indian languages. Their contribution to the debates of the Congress was nil though a few of them are found as delegates in the different sessions, but neither their support of the ideology of the Congress nor their admiration for the top leaders can be doubted.

Can we answer the question as to who had the right to send one or more delegates to a session of the Congress? The conclusion that comes to mind from a perusal of the reports of the Congress for the years up to 1908, when a formal constitution was adopted by a Convention which called the Congress of that year, seems to be that *(a)* any association that was contacted by the Reception Committee or a Standing Committee could send as many delegates as it wished to; *(b)* any association *suo motu* could write to the Reception Committee or even send a telegram at the last moment stating that it was deputing a delegate or delegates; *(c)* any *ad hoc* public meeting, however small the attendance, could also similarly inform the Reception Committee that it had elected the named delegate or delegates, and no one of the persons who, on the basis of such a meeting, claimed the status of being a delegate was refused that status by the Reception Committee, provided he brought with him a letter of authorization. There is evidence that such papers were checked. For instance, the Report of the Fourth Congress (Allahabad, 1888) has a footnote at the end of the List of Delegates, stating that some names were 'intentionally omitted of gentlemen who did register because on enquiry from the local Standing and Divisional Committees, it did not appear that these gentlemen had been duly elected'. Some very eminent people of Calcutta, however, attended the Sixth Congress held in that city in 1890 without producing any such formal papers, as mentioned at the foot of the List of Delegates to that session.

A more fundamental question is, how could such a system, under which any association or any public meeting could send an unlimited number of delegates to a session of the Congress, work at all for so many years? It can be safely stated that the answer is that the intelligentsia thought alike on the political, administrative, and economic issues that were being discussed in the sessions of the Congress or on other platforms or in the press, at the time, despite the fact that the country was vast, the distances great and differences of language, religion, caste and the like also existed. One group of people had called a conference in Bombay and another in Calcutta, in the last week of December, 1885, but both conferences passed resolutions on almost identical lines. Those who had not been informed of the First Congress and joined at a later session, became steadfast workers for the cause from the time they joined. Persons who chose to be elected delegates from some constituency or other were basically of the same point of view on all public issues. Hardly ever was it necessary in any session of the Congress to settle any issue by counting votes — the resolutions were always unanimous. A Congress session was thus a gathering together of like-minded people. Personal differences undoubtedly existed among them — the styles of functioning of the leaders too was anything but identical — but the basic unity on the fundamental aims and values was as strong among the leaders as among the general body of delegates. The twenty or so leaders who guided the affairs of the Congress in the first two decades enjoyed the confidence of the general body of delegates and supporters of the cause. Till the time of the open split at the twenty-third Congress at Surat in 1907, the Congress could very well carry on with its work with a very informal constitution.

How did the First Congress tackle the problem of agenda and rules of procedure for the conference? The official report says: 'During the whole day [of 26 December] and far into the night of 27th, informal discussions were carried on between the representatives and the order of the proceedings for the next three days was thus settled.' There is evidence that drafts of resolutions were prepared at a private meeting held at the residence of William Wordsworth, Principal of Elphinstone College, and at which meeting Wedderburn, Ranade and others were present.

Thanks to the offer of active co-operation from the Sarvajanik Sabha of Pune, Hume was able to mention in his letter of announcement that the same premises in that city that would be used as the venue for the conference would also be available for the residence of the delegates. His letter said: 'Much importance is attached to this since when all thus reside *together* for a week, far greater opportunities for friendly intercourse will be afforded than if the delegates were . . . scattered about in dozens of private lodging houses all over the town' (emphasis in the original). They were fortunate that when the venue had to be shifted to Bombay, suitable accommodation could be found for holding the formal sessions in the place where the delegates would also be lodged for the three or four days of the session. At the Second Congress in Calcutta, the delegates from other Provinces lived in a number of houses, all on Park Street, but the Bengal delegates were scattered. Hume referred to the importance of informal discussions among delegates in his 'Introductory Article' in the Report of the Second Congress and stated that 'from the first the idea in regard to these public sittings has always been that they should do little more than formally and publicly record the conclusions arrived at 'in committee'. (Hume had said in his letter that the conference would form the 'germ of a Native Parliament' and so it was perhaps natural that he thought in terms of the British Parliament's way of functioning.) He added: 'Before formal session began some leaders met and talked over certain draft resolutions. These were altered at "friendly conferences" and even further altered at the public sittings.'

The Report of the Second Session (Calcutta, 1886) indicates that the organizers took the initiative in circulating some suggestions as to topics to be discussed at the Congress. According to the Report:

> Another point that grew to be generally insisted on, was that the representatives ought to be made aware, beforehand, of the principal subjects

> likely to come under discussion at the Congress, and so be in a position to ascertain, in advance, the views of their constituencies. Accordingly, printed suggestions as to subjects for the consideration of the Congress were issued from several of the provinces and circulated to all the others. The first was issued from Calcutta (where the general feeling on the subject first took a tangible form), and is reproduced in *Appendix III* as sufficiently indicating the nature of these preliminary steps. Unfortunately, admirable as the idea was, the necessary machinery (now provided by the Standing Congress Committees, *Resolution XII of 1886*), did not exist for carrying it out in its entirety, and a considerable proportion of the delegates never saw, or even if they saw, never properly considered, in consultation with their constituents, these important papers of suggestions, which constituted the foundation stones of the subsequent congressional deliberations.

Appendix III of the Report of the Second Congress contains copies of two circular letters sent out from Calcutta, one, dated 5 November, on the reform of the Legislative Councils, and the other, dated 7 November , on the subject of Indians seeking election to the House of Commons from constituencies in Great Britain.

The Subjects Committee which became a permanent feature of the Congress had its origin at the Third Session (Madras, 1887). This is the history as given in the Report of that Session:

> Standing Congress Committees all over the country, were [requested by the Reception Committee] to set on foot the necessary elections in their several jurisdictions and to ascertain and communicate to them the subjects that their people desired to be brought forward at the coming Congress. A long list of subjects was thus collected and compiled, and then, through the several committees, and through the medium of the native newspapers, circulated about the middle of November, in the several Provinces. This list of proposed subjects, therefore, became known to all the delegates a month before they left, and all were thus in a far better position than in the previous year, to consider the questions that were to be discussed, maturely, with the assistance of the more intelligent of their constituents. But there were still two defects; the list was far too long, and though it gave the subjects (e.g. 'reduction of military expenditure'), it in no case formulated the Resolution that the proposer desired to have set forth in regard to them. Of course, the delegates were able to learn generally what their constituents' views were of the leading subjects, but in many cases they did not know exactly what they thought upon the details of these or exactly how far they desired the Congress to go in regard to them. Moreover, it was apparent to the great bulk of them, that a very large proportion of these subjects (for everything that anybody had formally proposed had been honestly included), were, for one reason or another, unsuited to, or still unripe for, discussion by the National Congress. So, after much private discussion amongst the delegates who had assembled, as many did, before the Congress met, on the day of the inaugural sitting, the whole Congress

> appointed a very strong 'Subjects Committee', comprising representative men from every province, to weed the list, and to draft Resolutions on such of the subjects as all were agreed in retaining. Their report formed the basis of the subsequent proceedings (though several of the Resolutions were greatly much modified and some subjects added during the course of the debates), and all this constituted a distinct advance on the procedure of former Congresses.

From now onwards, the timetable for a Congress session became like this: the inaugural session took place on the first morning, and agreed lists of members elected from each Province (or, later on, Circle) to the Subjects Committee were read out after the president's speech was delivered; the plenary session did not meet again till the next afternoon, and the afternoon and evening of the first day, and the morning of the second day were utilized for holding meetings of the Subjects Committee and getting drafts of resolutions prepared; almost everywhere, printed copies of draft resolutions were distributed to the delegates when they met at the formal meeting of the Congress in the afternoon of the second day.

The composition of the Subjects Committee at the Fourth Congress (Allahabad, 1888) was as given in the table below:

Circle	*Number of members*
Calcutta Circle (viz lower Bengal, Orissa, and Assam)	18
Bihar (viz Patna, Bhagalpur and Hazaribagh Division)	7
Benares and N.W. Provinces	16
Oudh	8
Punjab and Delhi	17
Sind	3
Gujarat	4
Bombay	4
Pune	6
Berar	3
Nagpur (viz the Central Provinces)	8
Madras	12
	106

The Report says that this number of 106 for the Subject Committee,

> was fixed after much previous consultation among the leaders of the several circles, partly with reference to the population, wealth, educational status and general importance of the circle, but more especially with regard to limiting the representatives to the smallest number that would adequately represent all different shades of opinion and views among the delegates of each circle.

The members of each circle elected their representatives and the lists of members chosen were read out. With reference to this session, the Report says that some months previously, the Reception Committee called upon all the Standing Congress Committees to report the subjects which

> the people of their respective circles desired to have brought before the Congress. All those subjects, proposed by more than half the Committees, were then re-circulated, with tentative resolutions framed in regard to each, to all the Standing, and by them, to Divisional Committees, so that in regard to all these subjects, which comprised the great majority of those actually brought before and discussed by the Congress, the delegates came fully prepared.

The Subject Committee in 1888 met after the inauguration, sat until late at night, and the next day, sat from morning till 1 p.m., the Congress reassembling at 2.

The Report of the Sixth Congress (Calcutta, 1890) contains interesting information about the way in which the Subjects Committee functioned. Reporters and spectators were excluded from the sittings of the committee; speeches were short, lasting two or three minutes only; there were rapid questions and answers; every member took an active part, matters were rapidly and satisfactorily disposed of.

This Report also explains what matters were put up before the Subjects Committee:

> Months before the Congress meets, the Committee of the circle in which it is to assemble, calls upon all the Standing Committees (of which there is one to each circle), to submit, after consultation with their divisional and sub-divisional Committees, a list of the subjects which they suggest for the consideration of the coming assembly. Their replies are compiled by the Committee first mentioned; subjects proposed by a majority of the Committees are accepted and are embodied in a circular to all the Standing or Circle Committees, notifying that these are the Subjects which will be submitted by the Reception Committee to the Subjects Committee when it is formed. Subjects proposed by less than half of the Committee are not included. Every delegate, therefore, nowadays, knows, or can know if he chooses, and ought to know, before he leaves his Province, what the subjects are which will primarily engage the attention of the Congress.

At the Subjects Committee, it is said, 'subjects in regard to which, after full discussion, considerable difference of opinion continues to exist, are *ipso facto* thrown out'. The logic behind this is stated thus: 'the main object of the Congress is to press upon the attention of the Government of India and the people and Government of England those reforms, and those reforms only, in regard to which the whole country has come to a substantial agreement; in regard to which the people of all provinces, of all races, castes, and creeds, are practically of one mind.' It was stated that 'this is the explanation of that marvellous unanimity often suspiciously commented upon by European critics, that characterizes, as a rule, Congress debates. The Congress itself, through its elected representatives, weeds out all subjects in regard to which a practical agreement, in all parts of the country and by all parties, has not been arrived at.' It is claimed that 'it is this, too, which ought to give weight to the formal recommendations of the Congress, since these are not proposals advocated by this or that body, this or that province, but only such as are concurred in by the educated and semi-educated classes throughout the Empire.'

The Subjects Committee was not restricted to what the Reception Committee placed before it and

> many other [subjects] are brought forward in the Subjects Committee, by one or more province, or even by individual members, and duly discussed; but these rarely secure a sufficient unanimity of assent to permit of their being then submitted to the Congress, though having thus been brought within the sphere of practical politics, and hence being during the year talked of all over the country, they not infrequently, are sent up next year, from a majority of the Committees, and so find a place in next year's Reception Committee's list.

A very important matter and which had the support of the top leaders, could be introduced at the Congress even without the stamp of authority of the Subjects Committee.

The practice of setting up something like a small township for the stay of the delegates, as also for their deliberations, at a session of the Congress, started with the Third Congress (Madras, 1887). With very rare exceptions, this became a regular feature with every Session. The 72 delegates to the First Congress (Bombay, 1885) could all be accommodated in Gokuldas Tejpal Sanskrit College, the institution selected for the purpose of holding the session. The arrangements at the Second Congress, for which 436 delegates registered, were not satisfactory in this respect. The inaugural meeting took place at the Town Hall, and, for the business session, the delegates had to assemble in the hall of the British Indian Association, and from there, for want of space, press reporters had to be excluded against the wishes of all. Madras, the venue of the Third Congress, did not happen to have a capacious hall for seating six to seven hundred delegates, and so a temporary hall 130 feet long by 92 feet wide, was put up, where as many as 3,000 people could gather, proper accommodation could be provided to the press, and acoustics were excellent. The delegates also lived in tents near the temporary hall. The Report of the Third Congress said that 'in all these matters too, the late Congress was a marked advance on its predecessors'.

The Fourth Congress (Allahabad, 1888) marked further advance in the matter of accommodation for delegates. Because of the opposition of the local government, the Reception Committee had difficulty in getting a public park for setting up a temporary hall for the session. But the resourceful organizers found a private property with extensive grounds and there long rows of tents were pitched for the delegates, 'dining and meeting halls for each block were created', and 'a splendid hall', 150 feet by 100 feet, capable of accommodating 5,000 persons, was erected for the sittings of the Congress. A *shamianah* (marquee), some 100 feet square was pitched to serve as a drawing room, another *shamianah* was pitched to serve as a reading room where copies of almost every newspaper, supplied free of charge, were kept. Some shops were set up, and every conceivable article that might be needed by a delegate was available for purchase, the only prohibited merchandise being spirituous liquor.

The third occasion when the delegates lived in a small township temporarily put up for them was the Seventh Congress held at Nagpur in 1891. Referring to the fact of the delegates all living together 'permitting the constant daily and hourly interchange of thought and opinion,. . . practically from dawn till midnight', the Report of the Session said,

> It is impossible to overrate the importance of this close intimate personal intercourse. It has been often said that these Congresses have made a nation of India's multitudinous peoples; and that they have done so has been, in a great measure, due to this intimate personal association of all delegates during the Congress weeks.

It may be remembered that the Report of the Third Congress (Madras, 1887) contained a statement that when the election of delegates was going on, there was some thinking that no province, other than that in which the Congress was held, should, as a whole, send more than two delegates per million of its total population. That, for the Fourth Congress (Allahabad, 1888), the country was divided into electoral divisions and the minimum number of delegates to be elected by each was settled, has also been mentioned. A footnote under the word *minimum* in this context in the Report of the Fourth Congress says:

> The education in political work, that a personal participation in these Congresses affords, is so valuable that it was considered inexpedient in

> 1888 to limit the number of delegates that each division might elect. But some 1,500 (of whom 1,248, at least, actually took their seats at the Congress) were elected in 1888, and there is little doubt that in 1889, if no limits be fixed, 3,000 will be elected. It is felt that these huge members are unsuited to a deliberative assembly, and hence it is in contemplation to limit the number to 1,000, which allowing for death, sickness and other unavoidable causes of absence, would reduce the number of actual sitting members, in future Congresses, to between 800 and 900.

This thinking, coupled with the fact that 1889 delegates came to the Congress held in Bombay in 1889, formed the background to a resolution passed there in these terms:

> Resolved that, in view of the large number of delegates this year assembled and the possibility, arising from past experience, of their number continuing to increase year by year, henceforth the number of delegates to be allowed from each Congress Circle be limited to five per million of the total population of the circle: the Standing Committees of each Circle allotting the number which their jurisdiction, as a whole is entitled to elect, amongst their several electoral divisions, as may seem most expedient.

995 delegates were elected to the next Congress, the Sixth, held in Calcutta in 1890, and of them, 702 actually attended. The attendance at the next three Congresses was below 1,000 every time — 812 at the Seventh Congress at Nagpur in 1891, 625 at the Eighth at Allahabad in 1892, and 867 at the Ninth that met at Lahore in 1893. This may be the reason why the limiting of the number of delegates with reference to the population of a province as directed by the above resolution was never required to be put into practice. Though 1,163 delegates came to the Tenth Congress that met in Madras in 1894, and as many as 1,584 delegates assembled at the Eleventh Session in Pune in 1895, the number was below 1,000 in the other sessions of the period — 784 at the Twelfth, Calcutta, 1896; 692 at the Thirteenth, Amraoti, 1897; 614 at the Fourteenth, Madras, 1898; 740 at the Fifteenth, Lucknow, 1899; 567 at the Sixteenth, Lahore, 1900; 896 at the Seventeenth, Calcutta, 1901; 471 at the Eighteenth, Ahmedabad, 1902; and 535 at the Nineteenth, Madras, 1903.

A possible explanation for the rise and fall in the number from about 1905 is that, when a burning political issue agitated the minds of the educated middle class, many of them felt interested to join a session as delegates. An additional explanation for the rather thin attendance for a few years after 1908 is that the construction that came into force that year took away the right of a public meeting to elect delegates. The privilege was restored in a modified way in 1915. The Congress of 1916 was expected to be important as some joint proposals with the Muslim

League for constitutional reform were going to be considered at this session. The period of the First World War saw the Home Rule Movement, the announcement by Montagu that 'progressive self-government' was the aim of the British Government, his visit to India and the different formulas for reforms, etc. In 1919, came the Rowlatt Act and the Jallianwala Bagh massacre. The Moderate leadership withdrew from the Congress and the organization reached the stage for the participation of the masses.

A table showing how many delegates were present at the different annual sessions of the Congress is given in the table.

Number of Delegates at the Annual Session of the Congress, 1885-1919

Year	*Number*	*Year*	*Number*
1885	72 (or 73)	1903	535
1886	431 (or 436)	1904	1,010
1887	607	1905	758
1888	1,248	1906	1,663
1889	1,889	1907	1,200/1300*
1890	702		
1891	812	1908	626
1892	625	1909	243
1893	867	1910	636
1894	1,163	1911	446
1895	1,584	1912	207
1896	784	1913	550
1897	692	1914	866
1898	614	1915	2,259
1899	740	1916	2,301
1900	567	1917	4,967
1901	896	1918	4,881
1902	471	1919	7,031

*No report; Tilak's estimate

5. Fifth and Sixth Congress

We may now examine the status and profession-wise break-up of the delegates to the Fifth and Sixth Congresses as given in the official Reports. The Report of the Fifth Congress states that of the delegates, 7 were 'Princes', 7 'Sardars and Chiefs', 7 'Rajahs', 10 'Nawabs', 8 Members of Council, past or present, 269 chairmen or members of municipal, district or local boards, 50 honorary magistrates, 250 or so graduates of universities. It is stated in parentheses that this list is not complete as many delegates failed to record all the details. Occupation-wise, the delegates were classified into these fifteen categories in the 'Introductory Article' of the Report:

Barristers and Advocates	23
Pleaders	582
Attorneys and Solicitors	23
Landholders ('a great many of them *ryots* cultivating, under the *ryotwari* system, their own lands, and so entitled to be classed as landowners')	541
Cultivators *'pur et simple'*	41
Bankers and money dealers	147
Mercha :ts, traders, brokers and shop-keepers	417
Medical profession	56
Engineers	8
Christian clergymen and missionaries	9
Non-Christian religious leaders and priests	19
Educationalists	104
Journalists	88
Printers and publishers	10
Working artisans	2

The 'Introductory Article' of the Report of the Sixth Congress (Calcutta, 1890) gave this break-up:

Zamindars, talookdars, landholders of various kinds, and cultivators	Some	250
Bankers	Some	30
Merchants and traders	Some	70
Barristers, advocates, solicitors, pleaders, *Mukhtears*	Nearly	300
Principals, professors, masters of colleges and schools		41
Journalists, newspaper proprietors		41
Medical men		31
Engineers		6
Millowners, contractors, indigo and tea planters		a few
Missionaries and religious teachers of various creeds		16

Status-wise, it was observed that there were 10 'Nawabs', 2 or 3 'Rajahs', several members of Viceroy's and other Legislative Councils, more than 200 Chairmen, Vice-Chairmen or members of District or Local Boards and Municipalities, nearly 100 Honorary Magistrates, 160 graduates, and many fellows of universities.

That women were present at the Fourth Congress (Allahabad, 1888) as visitors, we learn from an indirect reference in the Report for the session where it is stated that when an appeal was made to the delegates for contributing to the Congress fund, some women visitors gave their jewellery.

The first time any woman attended a Congress as a delegate was at the fifth one at Bombay in 1890 when ten were present. Of their election, the Report says that 'one [was] elected by men at a public meeting, the others by various ladies' associations — the Women's Christian Temperance Association, the Bengal Ladies' Association, and the Arya Mahila Samaj. It is stated that 'with one exception [they] have for years done a good work for India' — the exception must have been the traveller from America. From the information contained in the 'Introductory Article' and in the List of Delegates, one finds that they were:

1. Pandita Ramabai, 'teacher'.
2. Miss S. Manookjee Cursetjee, 'Lady Superintendent, Alexandra Girls' School'.
3. Swarna Kumari Devi (Mrs J. Ghoshal), 'sister of Bengal's most thoughtful poet', 'Editor of *Bharati*'. (It is stated that she was elected at a meeting of the Arya Mahila Samaj of Bombay).
4. Miss Jessie Royce Carleton, M.D., (from Ambala).
5. Mrs D.N. Ganguly (nee Kadambini Bose), 'graduate of Calcutta University', 'Lady Doctor', elected at a meeting of the Bengal Ladies' Association.
6. Miss Emma Brainerd Ryder, M.D., 'now travelling in India'.
7. Mrs Trimbuck (Shevantibai), 'directs schools'.
8. Mrs Kashibai Kanitkar, 'biographer of Anandibai Joshi, wife of editor of Marathi *Manoranjan*'.
9. Mrs Nikambe, 'teacher'.
10. Mrs G.N. Dass of '44 Mulunga Sain, Calcutta' (possibly a misprint for Mulunga Lane which is a street in Central Calcutta), also elected at a meeting of the Arya Mahila Samaj of Bombay.

A list of Congress publications available on sale from the office of the *Advocate* of Lucknow and printed at the back of the official Report of the Sixth Congress (Calcutta, 1890), mentions that a 'chromolitho' picture of the lady delegates to the session in 1889 was available for sale.

It appears from the 'Introductory Article' of the Report of the Sixth

Congress (Calcutta, 1890) that some of the ladies who attended the Fifth Congress were eager to address the house also. The first occasion when a woman delegate spoke at a Congress was in the next year, when at the Sixth Congress, Kadambini Ganguly proposed the customary vote of thanks to the President of the Session at the end. It is stated that the innovation was due to Man Mohun Ghose and Sir Ramesh Chandra Mitter, the Chairman of the Reception Committee. Kadambini had been in 1883 one of the first two women graduates of the University of Calcutta; she was the first woman student in Calcutta Medical College, and in addition to being licensed to practise medicine by the Government of Bengal, also obtained qualifications from Edinburgh, Glasgow and Dublin, and set up practice in Calcutta. Her husband Dwarka Nath Ganguli (1844-98) was a keen Congressman, and he might have had played a role in women being present as delegates in 1890. One of the passions in his life was the education and emancipation of women. At the age of 25, he started publishing a journal named *Abala-bandhav* ('Friend of Women') from a village, and his sobriquet became *Abala-bandhav;* one song of his became very popular and it proclaimed, 'unless the women of India wake up, India's slumber will continue'.

The four women delegates who attended the Sixth Congress are mentioned to have been elected delegates at a 'Ladies Meeting held at 81 Baranasi Ghose Street, Calcutta', on 24 December. They were:

> Mrs Hemanta Kumari Sukul, 'Brahmo', of no occupation;
> Mrs Sushila Mazumdar, 'Brahmo', 'Lady Superintendent of Girls Boarding School';
> Mrs Hemanta Kumari Chaudhurani, 'Brahmo', 'Editor, *Sugrihini,* a monthly journal';
> Mrs Kadamdini Gangooly, 'B.A., G.M.C.B.', 'Brahmo', 'Lady Doctor'.

Mrs Amelia Sophia West, 'Eurasian', attended the Seventh Congress (Nagpur, 1891) as a delegate, and it is stated that she had been elected at a public meeting held at Serampore (Bengal). The Report of the Thirteenth Congress (Amraoti, 1897) mentions that one woman attended as a delegate, many women came as spectators, and an exhibition was held of silk and lace embroidery work of women. Six women attended the Seventeenth Congress (Calcutta, 1901) as delegates — they were *abadhutis* (nuns) from Benares and were elected at a meeting of *sannyasis* (monks) held there. Some *abadhuts* (monks) also came as delegates from Benares. One Miss Florence Belgarnie from England is found speaking at the Nineteenth Congress (Madras, 1903), on a resolution supporting the candidature of Dadabhai Naoroji, W.C. Bonnerjee, Sir Henry Cotton, and Sir John Jardine for the House of Commons.

Generally speaking, women did not take any prominent role in Congress work during this period, 1885 to 1919, and it was rarely that women attended sessions as delegates. Some women played a significant part in the Swadeshi Movement in Bengal following its partition in 1905, but always behind the scenes. Sarojini Naidu came into prominence towards the end of the period, and there was Annie Besant, who led the Home Rule Movement during World War I and who presided over the Thirty-second Congress (Calcutta, 1917), being the first woman to be elected to that office.

The celebrated letter of Hume calling a conference in the name of the 'Indian National Union' indicates that in his thinking the body to be set up would be concerned with 'discussing' and 'deciding upon' political operations in addition to meeting in a conference from year to year. From almost the very beginning, one can discern that the Indian National Congress had two aspects. The more spectacular of the two was the annual 'congress' where delegates came in hundreds from all corners of the country and where, in the shape of a number of resolutions, the political demands of the time were formulated. The other was the work carried on to take its message to the educated, half-educated and even non-educated public, to create a political force behind its resolutions, to make the British public aware of the Congress stand, to maintain continuity in the work from session to session, in one word, running a permanent organization with a network spread all over the country and with an agency in England. In fact, in some of the earlier and even later Reports and Resolutions, two distinct expressions, 'Congress' and 'Indian National Congress Organization', are used to indicate the two different activities, namely, the annual gathering, and the work spread over the year. No doubt the two activities were inseparably linked and complemented one another but yet, in nature, they were different to some extent. Even if the aim at first had been to hold only a conference every year, a central secretariat of some sort would have been necessary, at least for the purpose of maintaining link with the Reception Committee of each year, to ensure that the annual 'Congress' was properly held, and to see that a report of the session was duly published.

The realization that there should be both a national network as also a central secretariat must have come as soon as the First Congress was over, if not earlier. One of the decisions of the First Congress was that 'the resolutions passed by this Congress be communicated to the Political Associations in each Province, and that these Associations be requested, with the help of similar bodies and other agencies within their respective provinces, to adopt such measures as they may consider calculated to advance the settlement of the various questions dealt with in these resolutions'. So a secretariat of some sort may be presumed to have started functioning with this initial activity as also the likely duty of despatching the report, when printed, to individuals and associations. Hume handled the work, though his role came to be mentioned somewhat later. The committee appointed at the Third Congress (Madras, 1887) to draw up a constitution for the Congress, stated in Rule III of their draft that 'there is at present a General Secretary holding office at the pleasure of the several Congress Committees [presumably meaning the 'Standing Committees' set up under a resolution of the Second Congress of 1886] but henceforth a General Secretary shall be elected at each Congress for the ensuing year'. At the Fourth Congress (Allahabad, 1888), a resolution was passed that Hume be 're-appointed' the General Secretary. Moving the resolution, W.C. Bonnerjee said that 'it is a privilege to have Mr Hume as our General Secretary'. Hume had started functioning in that capacity from the first session so to say. It was he who had drawn up the report and got it printed. In fact, he wrote the reports for the later sessions too, certainly up to 1891, and documentary proof of this is available in a 'confidential' letter that he sent out in 1892. The letter was printed and one copy is found attached to the copy of the Report of the Seventh Congress (Nagpur, 1891) in the National Library. The full text is given below:

CONFIDENTIAL *NOT FOR PUBLICATION*

To The Secretary of the Standing Congress Committee

March 16, 1892

Dear Sir,

Will you kindly inform your Committee that this year, the Congress Report will appear in India without any introductory article.

I prepared one as usual, which was approved by the Chairman of the Reception Committee and also by Messers W.C. Bonnerjee and Mano Mohun Ghose who have most carefully considered it. But Pandit Madan Mohan Malaviya in a most earnest letter, apparently on behalf of the Allahabad Committee, condemned it as seditious, as calculated to harm the cause irreparably, as certain to frighten most of our party, and so on.

Now, though we do not agree in all this, we feel that we could not publish this article, here, in the report, in the face of such a protest from the Committee where the next Congress is to be held and I, personally, compelled as I am to leave the country, do not choose to leave behind a cause of quarrel. It is impossible to *modify* this review. Every word and every section has been so carefully considered that it constitutes a single piece. It would be useless cutting out this or that; the only thing to be done is to rewrite it entirely, which, of course, is now impossible, even if we thought this desirable, which we do not. Therefore we have decided to issue the report in India without any introductory article, but to print this later in the

English Edition, and separately, as a pamphlet, in England and I will of course see that copies of this latter reach all of you.

There is this much to be said in favour of the Allahabad Committee's position. Mr Mano Mohun Ghose informs me that in the Bungabasi case, Sir Comer Petheram (though he has turned it down in the printed report) did lay down broadly that anything tending to bring the Government into discredit was seditious. This is directly opposed to the best English authorities; it is a monstrous doctrine, which if I have been correctly informed, I shall endeavour to bring before the bar of English public opinion. But if this be the Chief Justice of Calcutta's Law, then the whole review, showing how cruelly the Revenue and Forest systems work and insisting on all the shortcomings of the existing administration *is* seditious, and it is best not to publish it here, where in cases like that against the Bungabasi, the juries are packed and it is hopeless to expect justice.

I hope you will kindly explain privately to all Congress men in your circle the reason why the Indian Report will appear this year without the customary introductory article.

Yours truly,

A.O. Hume

P.S. I sail from Bombay on the morning of the 22nd.

Hume continued to be the General Secretary till 1903. The fact that he had gone back to England in 1892 for permanent stay and visited India only in the winter months apparently did not make him any the less qualified to hold the office. Much of the work of publicity and lobbying on behalf of the Congress used to be done in England in this period and Hume remained deeply involved in that work. However, from 1889, started the practice of appointing a Joint General Secretary, and the text of the resolution explains why this was felt necessary. The relevant resolution of 1889 says that 'from the date of Hume's departure for England the Hon. Pandit Ajodhyanath be appointed Joint General Secretary'. Hume was not going away for good this time. The same resolution authorized 'that Rs 5,000 be assigned for the payment by him (the Joint General Secretary) of such Assistant Secretaries as he may find it necessary to employ, clerical assistance, postage, telegraph and printing'. The resolution also added that 'W.C. Bonnerjee be appointed Standing Counsel for Bengal; Pherozeshah Mehta Standing Counsel for Bombay, and Ananda Charlu Standing Counsel for Madras'. It is likely that Hume was in the habit of consulting them on organizational matters connected with the respective Presidencies and it was felt expedient to record that their services would be available to the Joint General Secretary too. Pandit Ajodhyanath was appointed Joint General Secretary in

1890 and 1891 also, only unfortunately, he died soon after the Congress of 1891. The office of the General Secretary was a key office in the early days and the succession in the office may be brought down to 1919. P. Ananda Charlu was appointed the Joint General Secretary with Hume at the Congress of 1892. The Congress of 1893 and of 1894 made Hume the sole General Secretary, and in 1895, Dinshaw Edulji Wacha was added as the Joint General Secretary. This arrangement continued till 1903 when Gopal Krishna Gokhale was appointed Additional Joint Secretary. The three of them functioned together till 1908 when Wacha and Daji Abbaji Khare took over as Joint General Secretaries, Article XXIX of the Constitution adopted that year having provided that there would be two General Secretaries. This team worked till 1913. To complete the story — Nawab Syed Mohamed Bahadur and N. Subba Rau Pantulu were appointed Joint General Secretaries in 1913 and they continued till 1917. In the latter year, the Constitution was changed and there were to be three General Secretaries. The three elected that year were C.P. Ramswami Iyer, G.M. Bhurgi, and Kesava Pillai. In 1918, Vithalbhai Patel, Fazlul Haque, and Gokaran Nath Misra took over. At the Congress of 1919, M.A. Ansari was elected in the place vacated by Fazlul Haque.

The need for setting up a national network found expression in this resolution adopted at the Second Congress (Calcutta, 1886): 'Resolved that Standing Congress Committees be constituted at all important centres'. While proposing this, W.C. Bonnerjee said:

> My opinion is that permanent Committees of this Congress ought to be constituted in all the provinces of India. Each province will, no doubt, fix the number of its own committee and appoint its own committee man, but a committee, small or large, is absolutely requisite in every province. Without such Committees it is quite impossible to keep up a regular correspondence between all the different parts of the country, and so to arrive in due time at a general agreement as to the various questions on which action is to be taken at the Congress.

Narayan G. Chandavarkar supported him by saying, 'We are all agreed as to the necessity of that arrangement.' And the resolution was immediately passed unanimously.

The constitution that was drafted by the committee appointed at the Third Congress (Madras, 1887) was largely based on the practices current at the time, and Rule III therein laid down that 'the delegates from any jurisdiction attending a Congress shall form the Standing Committee for that jurisdiction for the ensuing year and they shall have power to add to their number and appoint their own executive'. Thanks to the fact that the records of the Indian Association had been preserved and that these were looked into by J.C. Bagal while writing its history, we know how one Standing Committee was formed. Bagal writes that the Indian Association bore the brunt of the work in securing the attendance of delegates from different parts of Bengal to the Second Congress, and sent a letter to the Bengal delegates stating that it would make arrangements for their hospitable reception. On the day preceding the inauguration of the Congress, the Association called a meeting of the Bengal delegates and draft resolutions were considered there. At the end of the session, another meeting of the Bengal delegates was called jointly by the British Indian Association, Indian Association, and Indian Union, and at this meeting, 'a Provincial Committee to give effect to the Resolutions of the National Congress was appointed', and this became the 'Bengal Standing Committee'.

Some organizational steps were taken in course of 1888 but unfortunately, all the details cannot be ascertained. The constitution drafted at Madras during the Third Congress there in 1887 provides some clues, for although the constitution was not adopted, the Standing Committees were requested by the resolution on the subject that 'they will during the coming year act in accordance with these rules so far as this may seem possible and desirable. . . .' That the country was divided into electoral divisions has been mentioned earlier. A footnote on the Standing Committees in the Report of the Congress of 1888 says: 'There is one such supreme managing body for each Circle, which controls the Divisional Committees, each of which has charge of one electoral division, and of the several sub-committees which manage the several included sub-divisions.' Apparently, Standing Committees were expected to bring their annual reports to the Congress in terms of the draft constitution of the previous year, for this is implied in one place in the Report of the Congress of 1888:. . . . one or two Standing Committees laid their annual reports for 1888 on the table; but the majority unfortunately had either prepared no formal reports or had not them printed. It was the first year of systematic organization, and so allowance must be made.'

The representation to the Subjects Committee in the Congress of 1888 was on the basis of Circles, and twelve circles are mentioned in this connection.

18 Circles are mentioned in the Report of the Fifth Congress (Bombay, 1889): Calcutta (including the Presidency, Burdwan and Chittagong Divisions, Assam, and Orissa); Dacca; Rajshahi; Bhagalpur; Chota Nagpur; Bihar; Benares; Allahabad; Oudh, Delhi; Lahore; Karachi; Gujarat; Bombay; Poona; Amraoti; Nagpur, and Madras.

The report of the Ninth Congress (1893, Lahore) mentioned as many as 29 Circles in connection with the election of the Subjects Committee, and these were: Calcutta (including Presidency and Burdwan Divisions, Orissa, Assam, Sylhet and Cachar); Dacca District; Faridpur District;

Circle	*Members*
Calcutta Circle, viz Lower Bengal, Orissa and Assam	18
Bihar Circle, viz Patna, Bhagalpur, and Hazaribagh Divisions	7
Benares and North West Provinces Circle	16
Oudh Circle	8
Punjab and Delhi Circle	17
Sind Circle	3
Gujarat Circle	4
Bombay Circle	4
Poona Circle	6
Berar Circle	3
Nagpur Circle, viz the Central Provinces	8
Madras Circle	12

Barisal District; Rangpur District; Pabna District; Jalpaiguri District; Rampur Boalia, (that is to say, Rajshahi District); Bhagalpur Division; Chota Nagpur Division; Bihar (Patna Division but not including Muzaffarpur District); Benares District; North West Provinces Circle (not including Benares); Oudh; Delhi; Punjab (not including Delhi); Sind; Ahmedabad (including Ahmedabad, Kutch, Kathiawar, Rajkot); Surat (Surat and Broach); Sholapur District; Belgaum District; Bhusawal District; Satara District; Deccan (not including Sholapur, Belgaum, Nagpur, but including Khandesh minus Bhusawal); Ichalkaranji (Southern Maratha country); Bombay (Bombay Island, Colaba, Thana, Ratnagiri); Berar; Nagpur (Central Provinces); Madras (entire Presidency).

A further organizational step was taken in the Fourteenth Congress (Madras, 1898) when these two resolutions were passed:

(a) Resolved that all Standing Congress Committees be requested to form Central Committees in their respective Provinces, for the appointment of agents and adoption of other measures, for furthering the objects of the Congress, such Central Committees submitting annually at the meeting of the Congress, a report of the work carried out in their Provinces during the year.

(b) Resolved that the Standing Committees at Madras, Bombay, Nagpur, Amraoti, Calcutta, Allahabad and Lahore be requested to take measures to give early effect to this Resolution.

Next year when 11 basic rules on the constitution were adopted, a new name, 'Provincial Congress Committee' replaced the earlier name 'Standing Committee'. The Constitution of 1908 contained some Provisions on Provincial and District Committees. The constitutional changes are referred to later. At the Twenty-first Congress (Benares, 1905), a Standing Committee of fifteen members was appointed 'to promote the objects of the Congress and to take such steps during the year as may be necessary to give effect to the Resolutions of the Congress'.

A permanent fund was created early in the career of the Congress and a reference to the trustees of the fund is found in a resolution of 1892. The practice of remitting a big sum to England every year, for publicity and lobbying work there, started in 1889. As a matter of strategy, the leaders of the Congress of the time believed that since the last word lay with the Cabinet, Parliament, and the electorate in Britain, the point of view of the Congress must be made known there if it were to become effective. And it was an axiom with them that if the case of India could be properly placed before the British electorate, remedy would follow forthwith. The logic was that the common people of Britain themselves believed in constitutional government and so they would not withhold this privilege from the Indians the moment they were convinced that Indians had become fit for participating in governing themselves and also that British officials in India often acted unlawfully or arbitrarily.

The Indian Association of Calcutta was the first to conceive the idea of sending someone to England as a spokesman for India. Lal Mohun Ghose was the delegate of the Association in 1879, and he was sent again next year that being an election year. He was chosen by the 'United Indian Committee' to visit England in the summer of 1883 to counter the propaganda of the Anglo-Indian Defence Association against Lord Ripon and his Ilbert Bill. This association had been set up in Calcutta by W.C. Bonnerjee a little earlier and was renamed 'Indian Union' in 1884. 'The Indian National Union', that is to say, Indian National Congress in embryo, sent three delegates to England — Mano Mohun Ghose, Narayan Ganesh Chandavarkar, and Sivalaya Ramaswami Mudaliar — in the middle of 1885. When the Congress came to be established within a few months, Dadabhai Naoroji, who used to live in England, volunteered to act as the agent of the Congress in England. A statement in the Tamil 'Catechism' of 1888 may be recalled as stating that Naoroji had arranged to distribute several thousand copies of the Report of the Congress of 1886 in England. W.C. Bonnerjee and Eardley Norton, a British barrister practising in Madras, visited England in 1886 and helped Naoroji in his work. One important result of their efforts was that they succeeded in enlisting the support of Charles Bradlaugh, M.P.

The 'British Committee of the Congress' was set up in London in July 1889, and when the Congress met in the following December, this was confirmed and a contribution was voted for its work. A delegation was also appointed for going to England. The relevant resolutions were as follows:

This Congress does hereby confirm the appointment of Sir W. Wedderburn, Bart., and Messrs. W.S. Caine, M.P., W.S. Bright Mclaren, M.P., J.E. Ellis, M.P., Dadabhai Naoroji, and George Yule as a Committee (with power to add to their number) to guide and direct the operations and control the expenditure of the National Congress Agency in England, and does further tender its sincere thanks to these gentlemen and to W. Digby C.I.E., the Secretary, for the service which they are rendering to India.

This Congress does formally appoint Mr George Yule, Mr A.O. Hume, Mr Adam, Mr Eardley Norton, Mr J.E. Horward, Mr Phirozeshah Mehta, Mr Surendranath Banerjea, Mr Mano Mohun Ghose, Mr Shurfuddin, Mr R.N. Mudholkar, and Mr W.C. Bonnerjee to represent its views in England and press upon the consideration of the British public the political reform which the Congress had advocated.

A sum of Rs 45,000 be raised for the expenses of the Congress in this country and in England during the ensuing year, and that the different Standing Committees do send their respective appointed amounts to the General Secretary, the one half in three, and the balance in six months.

Charles Bradlaugh was personally present at the 1889 session of the Congress and received a great ovation. He used to avow openly that he was the 'Member for India' and it is said that he obtained the sanction of his constituency for doing so. Bradlaugh prepared a draft bill on the reconstitution of the Government of India and Congress Committees were invited to send suggestions to him for inclusion in his bill. When Bradlaugh actually moved a Bill, the Government of the day felt it necessary to come forward with a Bill of their own. The first official delegation of the Congress visited England in 1890. Dadabhai Naoroji was living permanently in England, and by this time W.C. Bonnerjee had also practically made England his home. So the two naturally became pillars of the Congress work in that country.

The Congress of 1890 felt that a session of the Congress in England itself would have a great effect and accordingly this resolution (XI) was passed: 'Provisional arrangements to be made to hold a Congress, of not less than 100 delegates, in England, all things being convenient, in 1892, and that the several Standing Congress Committees be directed to report, at the coming Congress, the names of the delegates that it proposes to depute from their respective circles.' The next year, it was decided to postpone the matter, a resolution being passed in the following terms: 'In view of the General Election now impending in England, and in accordance with the recommendations of our British Committee, the provisional arrangements, set on foot in pursuance of the resolution passed at the Calcutta Congress of 1890, for holding, all things being convenient, a Congress of not less than 100 delegates in England, in 1892, be now suspended until after such General Election.' In the Congress of 1892, it was resolved that because of the political situation in

England, the idea of holding a session of the Congress there be suspended until after the session of 1893. Perhaps the defeat of the Liberal Party in the General Election of 1895 discouraged the Congress from pursuing this idea for the subject was not referred to again.

The Congress deputed Dinshaw Edulji Wacha, Surendranath Banerjea, and Gopal Krishna Gokhale to give evidence before the Royal Commission on Expenditure in the mid-1890s. The Congress of 1899 (fifteenth session at Lucknow) resolved that an agency be appointed in England for the purpose of organizing, in concert with the British Congress Committee, public meetings for the dissemination of information on Indian matters. Gokhale and Lala Lajpat Rai were deputed to England for publicity work in 1904. Gokhale was sent the next year also. The Congress of 1904 resolved that, because a General Election was coming in England, representatives should be sent and Rs 30,000 should be raised for this purpose. The Congress of 1903 had pledged support to four would-be candidates — Dadabhai Naoroji, W.C. Bonnerjee, Sir Henry Cotton, and Sir John Jardine. The Congress of 1913 (Karachi) appointed a delegation to visit England to deal with four subjects, namely, Indians in South Africa and other Colonies, the Press Act, Reform of the Indian Councils, and separation of Judiciary and Executive functions, and 'other important questions', and the delegates were thanked at the next Congress. Year after year, money was voted for the British Committee and its journal *India* and a resolution thanking the members of the British Committee was adopted in every session.

The publication of *India* was started in 1890. It was first managed by William Digby and subsequently H.E.A. Cotton took over this work. Ambica Charan Majumdar's *Indian National Evolution* first came out in 1915 and an enlarged edition was published in 1917, and this is how the author, the president of the historic session of the Congress held at Lucknow in 1916, evaluated the work of the British Committee in Chapter XII, styled 'The Work in England':

> An act of oppression in a tea garden, a gross insult offered to an Indian gentleman in a railway carriage, the malpractices of the police and the bunglings of the Executive, though these scarcely find a remedy, now all find their way into Parliament, and indirectly exercise a chastening influence upon the Indian administration.

After remarking that the questions agitated by the Congress are familiar to the enlightened British public, he commented that 'India now finds a greater notice in the British press', and that 'all this has been the work of the British Committee and its organ *India*'.

Two MPs, Sir William Wedderburn and H.S. Caine, succeeded in setting up the 'Indian Parliamentary Committee' in 1893, and as many as

100 members of the House of Commons and the Lords came forward to become members. When Hume went back for permanent stay in England, he started working with zeal for both the British Committee of the Congress and the Indian Parliamentary Committee. The Conservatives were in power during 1895-1905 and so the Indian Parliamentary Committee was not able to achieve any thing positive in the shape of constitutional or administrative reform during this period. When the Liberals won the General Elections of 1906, Wedderburn reactivated the Parliamentary Committee and nearly 200 members of the two Houses started taking an interest in the Indian questions as publicized by this body. The thirty-first Congress (Lucknow, 1916) decided that a delegation would be sent to England when the war ended to plead the case for granting of self-government to India. At the next Congress (Calcutta, 1917), the decision was that such a delegation would be sent if considered necessary. The thirty-third Congress (Delhi, 1918) did appoint a delegation and the delegates were thanked at the next Congress.

The Constitution of the Congress had declared in 1908 that the British Committee of the Congress was a component part of the Indian National Congress organization and a resolution of the 1918 Congress stated that the Constitution should be amended 'to bring the work of the British Congress Committee into co-ordination with that of the other component parts of the Congress organization'. Another resolution at the same session was that the journal *India* should be made more attractive and an Indian should be associated in editorial management. A resolution of the 1919 Congress was that a permanent mission should be maintained in England (Resolution XXII).

6. Proposed Congress Constitution

A proposal that a constitution be drawn up for the Indian National Congress was moved as early as at the third session. Trailokya Nath Mitra, a lawyer from Calcutta, with a doctorate in law, moved that 'a committee be appointed consisting of the following gentlemen to consider what rules, if any, may now be usefully formed in regard to the constitution and working of the Congress, with instructions to report thereon to the Congress on the 30th instant.' The inauguration had taken place on 27 December 1887, and this was the first resolution moved, and accepted, when the business session started on the following day. His arguments were:

> We ought to have some sort of constitution for this great assembly . . . some rules as to who our delegates are to be, how they are to be elected, and how certified too. We ought to have some rules as to the procedure to be followed in this assembly, and as to other similar matters. The rules must

of course at the beginning, be very simple indeed, embodying the existing practice as far as possible, and giving as it were, the force of law to custom. They must not be hard and fast rules that will prematurely bind us down to any special scheme; ours is a young and growing institution, and if our constitution is really to fit us, it must grow with us; but there must be some very simple temporary rules to fit the selection of delegates and as to the working of the Congress. That is all I think, we ought at this early stage of our career, to attempt. . .

A committee of thirty-five was appointed and its report was placed before the Congress by Hume on the 30th. The report, he said,

includes a long series of tentative rules . . . you will take it as read . . . These rules, must, we think, stand over for the consideration of the next Congress; but in the meantime they ought to be circulated to all the standing committees to reconsider, at their leisure and see how far they are workable. Next year, they will be brought up again for final consideration together with all such amendations and additions as may have, in the meantime, suggested themselves to the several standing committees. The rules, as they stand, practically embody the existing practice, if not throughout the country, in one province or another; but an additional year's experience will enable all to judge better how far that practice should be accepted and how far it may advantageously be modified.

Dr Trailokya Mitra supported the motion:

The Rules drafted by the Committee appointed under Resolution I stand over for consideration till next Congress, but in the meantime copies be circulated to all Standing Congress Committees, with the request that they will during the coming year act in accordance with these rules so far as this may seem to them possible and desirable and report thereon to the next Congress with such further suggestions as to them may seem meet.

The resolution was passed.

The recommendations of the drafting committee were not printed in the Report of the Third Congress and the following quotation is from Appendix A of A.C. Mazumdar's *Indian National Evolution* (2nd ed. 1917):

Tentative Rules in regard to certain matters connected with the National Congress (framed by the Committee appointed by Resolution I of 1887).

I

There shall be yearly, during the last fortnight of each calendar year a meeting of the delegates of the people of India which shall bear the name of *The Indian National Congress.*

II

It shall from year to year assemble at such places and on such dates as shall have been resolved on by the last preceding Congress; it being, however, left open to the Reception Committee (Rule XII) (should any real necessity for this arise) to change, in consultation with the several Standing Congress Committees (Rule III), the place fixed by the Congress for some other locality.

III

There shall be, as resolved at the 2nd National Congress (XIII of 1886), Standing Congress Committees at all important centres. These committees are at present as in Appendix I, but the Congress may at any sitting add to or diminish the number of these Committees, or alter their jurisdiction. The delegates from any jurisdiction attending a Congress shall form the Standing Committee for that jurisdiction for the ensuing year and they shall have power to add to their number and appoint their own executive. There is at present a General Secretary holding office at the pleasure of the several Congress Committees but henceforth a General Secretary shall be elected at each Congress for the ensuing year.

IV

It shall be the primary duty of all Standing Congress Committees to promote the political education of the people of their several jurisdictions *throughout the year*, and to endeavour, by the circulation of brief and simple tracts and catechisms written in the vernacular of that people, by the holding of public meetings at important centres and by sending competent men round to lecture and explain these subjects, and by all other open and laudable means, to imbue the intelligent and respectable classes everywhere with a healthy sense of their duties and rights as good citizens. Care has to be especially taken to impress the people with a conviction, first, of the immense benefits that the country has derived from British rule, and of the sincere desire that pervades the British nation to do the very best they can for the people of India; secondly, with the same idea, of the more important shortcomings of that rule, due partly to the unavoidable ignorance of the rulers of the real condition of the ruled, and partly to the failure of these latter to make known in a definite and intelligible form their wants and wishes; and thirdly, with the knowledge that all defects in the existing form of the administration may surely, though perhaps slowly, be amended, if the people will only unite in loyal, temperate and persistent demands for the redress of grievances through such persons as they may choose as exponents of their views.

V

To enable the several Committees to carry out this work successfully, they are empowered to create as many sub-committees, (to each of whom a definite sphere of action be assigned), within their jurisdictions, as may be necessary and possible, and they are further empowered to associate themselves with any existing Association and work with them and through their various branches and sub-committees.

VI

Each year, each Standing Congress Committee shall report fully the work that it has done during the year, accompanying the same, as far as may be practicable, by English translations of all the tracts, leaflets and the like that it may have issued during the year; such reports shall be in English, and shall be so despatched as to reach the Secretary of the Reception Committee (Rule XII) on or before the 15th of December, and shall be laid before the Congress and duly considered thereat.

VII

It shall be the duty of all Standing Congress Committees, in consultation with their sub-committee, and as many of the leading men resident therein as may be possible, to divide their several jurisdictions into such electoral circles as may to them seem to be most likely in the existing state of the country to secure a fair representation of the intelligent portion of the community, without distinction of creed, caste, race or colour. Such circles may be territorial, or where local circumstances require this, may each include one or more castes or professions or Associations of any kind. Except in the case of Associations, all delegates shall be elected at Public Meetings held for the purpose. In the case of Associations, delegates shall be elected at General Meetings specially convened in that behalf.

VIII

Delegates may be of any creed, caste or nationality, but must be resident in India and not less than 25 years of age.

IX

It shall be the duty of all Standing Congress Committees to send out, three months before the date fixed for the Congress, special notices to each of their electoral divisions calling upon each to elect the number of delegates assigned under their scheme to such division, as also one or more provisional delegates who will, in case of the death or inability to attend to any of the elected delegates, take the places of these without further election, and to forward to them — the Congress Committee — a full list of such delegates with all particulars in the form given in Appendix II. It will be the duty of the Standing Congress Committee not only to issue such notices, but see that they are acted upon, deputations from their number proceeding, where necessary, to the centres of the divisions, Provided that in case any electoral division fails to elect the required delegates, the Committee is empowered to cancel such division and create in its place another division more ready to do its duty. Each Standing Congress Committee shall forward a complete list (in the form given in Appendix III) of all delegates and provisional delegates elected for their entire jurisdiction to the Reception Committee, so that the same may reach the latter on or before the 15th of December, and it shall be the duty of the Reception Committee to remind the Standing Committee that they are due, and failing to receive these lists to telegraph for them persistently and to bring to the notice of the Congress any serious neglect of this rule.

X

It shall be the duty of each Standing Congress Committee, at least one month before the date fixed for the Congress, to ascertain the cheapest and best routes and modes of conveyance by which the several delegates of their jurisdiction can reach the Congress, the time that will be occupied in transit, and the cost of the journey by both 1st and 2nd class, single and return, and to notify the same to each of the delegates and provisional delegates elected within their jurisdiction.

XI

It shall be the duty of each Standing Congress Committee to notify, so that such notification shall reach the Reception Committee on or before the 1st of November, the subjects that the people of their several jurisdiction desire to see discussed, provided that such subjects shall be of a national character, that is to say, of a nature affecting the whole country, and not provincial, and that in regard to each subject the exact resolution which it is desired to pass be also transmitted, along with, whenever the latter is practicable, the names of the gentlemen who are prepared to propose or support such resolutions.

XII

The Standing Congress Committee of the jurisdiction in which the Congress is to be held shall, not less than six months before the date fixed for the Congress, associate with itself all the leading inhabitants of the place where the Congress is to be held, who may be willing to take part in the proceedings, and with them constitute itself a Reception Committee.

XIII

It shall be the duty of the Reception Committee *(a)* to notify to all the Standing Committees their appointment, and to invite them to proceed to call for delegates and to send in before the appointed date the list of the subjects which the people of their jurisdiction desire should be discussed as required by Rule XI; *(b)* to collect and provide the funds necessary for the entertainment of the delegates and other purposes essential to the holding of the Congress, to arrange for a suitable Meeting Hall; for the suitable lodgement of the delegates of other jurisdictions; for the food of the delegates during their stay, due regard being had to the customs, local or religious, of each, and generally to arrange for everything necessary for their convenience and comfort, and *(c)* to maintain a constant correspondence with all the Standing Congress Committees, and generally, so far as may be, assure themselves that the necessary work is duly proceeding in all jurisdictions.

XIV

It shall be the duty of the Reception Committee to *obtain* from the several Standing Committees the list of subjects referred to in Statute XI, reminding them and giving them ample warning that lists not received by the 1st of November cannot be attended to, and on the 1st of November to proceed to consider such lists and after eliminating all subjects (if there be any such) of a clearly provincial character, or unsupported by definite resolutions intended to be proposed in regard to them, to compile the rest into one list in the form given in Appendix IV, and print and despatch the same by the 15th of November in sufficient numbers to the several Standing Committees to enable these to distribute copies to each delegate and provisional delegate, and the several Standing Committees shall be responsible for their immediate distribution accordingly.

XV

It shall be the duty of the Reception Committee, as soon as possible after its constitution, to select and communicate to the several Standing Congress Committees the names of those gentlemen whom it considers eligible for the office of the President, and in correspondence with them to settle who shall be invited to fill that office, and thereafter when an agreement thereon has been come to, to communicate with the gentleman finally approved by all, or a considerable majority of the Standing Committees, and generally to do all that may be necessary to settle the question of the presidentship at least one month before the Congress meets.

XVI

Of the subjects circulated under Rule XIV, for information only those shall be brought forward and discussed at the Congress which shall be finally approved by a committee (to be called the Subjects Committee) consisting of the President elect, and one or more representatives of each jurisdiction (selected by all delegates who may be then present at the Congress station) which shall meet on the day previous to the inaugural sitting of the Congress. Provided also that this Committee shall be empowered to add any subjects to those included in this list that may for any reasons appear to them specially deserving of discussion, framing at the same time the resolutions that they desire to see proposed in regard to them, and further, to modify as may appear to them necessary, any of the resolutions propounded in regard to the subjects included in the list which they have accepted for discussion. Provided further, that the Committee shall at the same time settle, so far as may be possible, those gentlemen who are to be invited to propose, second and support the Resolutions, and shall put themselves into communication with them, and that they shall at once frame a list of the approved subjects and resolutions in the form given in Appendix V and shall print the same so that a copy may, if possible, be placed in the hands of each delegate at the inaugural sitting of the Congress.

XVII

It shall be the duty of the Chairman of the Reception Committee to preside at the commencement of the inaugural sitting of the Congress, and after delivering such address as he and the Reception Committee may consider necessary, to call upon the assembled delegates to elect a President and after such election to instal the said President in the chair of office.

From and after the installation of the President, he shall direct and guide the entire proceedings of the assembly, he being empowered in all cases, except as hereinafter provided, in which difference of opinion arise or doubts occur, either himself, to rule what course should be taken when his ruling shall be final, or to take a vote from the assembly, when the decision of the majority shall be final.

Until the subjects and resolutions approved by the Subjects Committee have been discussed (and this in such order as the President may direct) and disposed of by the adoption, rejection or modification of such resolutions, no other business shall be brought before the Congress. But after this, if there be time for this, any delegate who shall have given notice in writing at the commencement of the sitting to the President, of his desire to have a particular subject discussed and definite resolution, which he sets forth, proposed, shall have a *right* and a delegate who at *any* time previous to rising shall have given such notice *may,* with the permission of the President rise and ask the President to take the sense of the assembly as to whether such subject shall be discussed. No speaking at this stage shall be allowed. The President shall simply read out the subject and the proposed resolution and make any such remarks as he considers essential and take the vote of the assembly as to whether the subject shall or shall not be discussed. If the vote is in the affirmative the proposer shall then set forth the subject and the resolutions he therein proposes with such explanations as he considers necessary and then, after due discussion, the question shall be disposed of in the usual way. If the vote is in the negative, the subject shall be at once dropped.

Appendix A of Mazumdar's book does not end here for some addenda follow. The several appendices referred to in the Rules are not there and it is not improbable that the drafting committee had not had the time to design the contemplated forms. It is likely however that the addenda were included in the report of the drafting committee submitted to the Congress. The addenda contain some additional matters for *Rule XII,* a revised version of *Rule XVI,* an elaborate *Rule XVII* on procedure at a session and an equally elaborate *Rule XIX* on amendments to resolutions proposed. Then there are detailed suggestions for the Standing Congress Committee with a footnote that 'the suggestions are the result of practical experience gained in working out the electoral system in Madras'. Some sentences from the paragraphs numbered (1), (2) and (3) of the suggestions are quoted below:

(1) The Standing Congress Committee must, under the Tentative Rules, consist in the first instance of all those delegates who attended the last Congress, and these should associate with themselves all those gentlemen who attended as delegates at any previous Congress and all other leading members of Circle who sympathize in the movement. Of course the large body thus formed cannot be expected to work at details. The majority of the members have not the time to attend to a huge series of these. If any matter of great importance arises, they must of course assist with advice, and if required money also, but the regular routine

work, of which there will necessarily be a good deal, must be done by a small number of real workers whom the committee must appoint: men whose circumstances permit them to give a fair share of time and attention to the work, and who are so really and earnestly interested in this that they will not grudge either.

(2) The first point, then for Standing Congress Committee, as soon as it is constituted, is to appoint a Secretary or Secretaries and a *small,* strong Executive Committee — all of them men of the class just referred to — with instructions to hold a meeting *without fail,* one every *week,* on a fixed *day,* at a fixed *hour,* at a fixed *place,* two to form a quorum. All work pertaining to the Standing Congress Committee to be disposed of by those weekly meetings, by such members of the Executive Committee as are present . . .

(3) The most important work of the Executive Committee is to create (if this has not already been done) and consolidate the electoral divisions. The electoral divisions must be so arranged as to cover every portion of the Circle and include every section of the community. One main object in elaborating them is to insure that delegates shall fairly represent every creed, class, race, and section of the community inhabiting the Circle. This can only be achieved in most circles by constituting electoral divisions of two classes, viz. first, territorial, . . . and second, sectional, each to include a special community or an association, or groups of either of these . . .

Paragraph (8) drew attention to the need for creating a Permanent Congress Fund on a future date.

The draft constitution does not appear to have been placed for consideration at the next Congress, namely, the fourth, held at Allahabad in 1888. A resolution [XIII (C)] on the subject was adopted at the Fifth Congress (Bombay, 1889) in the following terms:

> The tentative rules for the constitution and working of the Congress which were first considered at Madras and in regard to which various addenda have from time to time been circulated, be thoroughly considered by the several Congress Committees and definitely dealt with by the Congress at its next session.

However, the subject of having a set of rules adopted in relation to the running of the Congress as an organization was not brought again till the Tenth Congress (Madras, 1894). *Resolution XXVII* of that session ran as follows:

> This Congress is of opinion that the time has come when the constitution of the Congress should be settled, and rules and regulations laid down as to

number of delegates, their qualifications, the localities for assemblage, and the like, and with this view, the Congress requests the Standing Congress Committee of Poona to draw up draft rules and circulate them among the different Standing Congress Committees for their report; these reports together with the draft rules and the Report thereon to be laid before the next Congress for its consideration.

When the Congress next met in December of 1895 in Poona, it was found that the Standing Committee of Poona had not circulated drafts among the other Standing Committees. In this background, the following was passed as Resolution No. I in that session (eleventh):

> The draft rules in regard to the constitution and the working of the Indian National Congress, as framed by the Poona Congress Committee in accordance with the resolution, in that behalf, of the last Congress, be circulated by the Poona Committee to all the Standing Congress Committees, with instructions to report to the General Secretary and the Standing Counsel at least three months before the next Congress. [W.C. Bonnerjee, Pherozeshah Mehta and Ananda Charlu had been appointed 'Standing Counsel' in 1889.]

The resolution was moved by Janaki Nath Ghoshal. A little earlier he had placed the rules of business before the Congress and said in that connection that he had always to assist in framing rules for the conduct of business — these are going to be referred to soon). As to the need for a constitution, his view was that 'the time has hardly arrived when we should fetter the Congress with hard and fast rules'. He added that the British Constitution was guided more by unwritten than written laws, and stated that, in his view, 'that is the ideal constitution'. The justification for referring to Ghoshal's speech is that the point of view expressed by him certainly prevailed till 1899, and was not completely abandoned even then. The one innovative rule of 1899, namely that the affairs of the Congress would be managed by an elected committee of 45 members, was not implemented in practice. But this is anticipating future events.

The rules of business adopted at the Poona Congress of 1895 were as follows: (1) On a point of order, the President's decision will be final. (2) Only a delegate can address the Congress and vote. (3) Delegates are to address the house from the speaker's platform. (4) Proposers, seconders, and supporters for resolutions will be selected by the Subjects Committee. (5) The President will allot time to the speakers. (6) A delegate who has not been selected to speak but who wants to speak, shall send his name and the name of his Circle to the President. (7) One wishing to propose an amendment shall send his name and the seconder's name, together with the names of their Circles, to the President. (8) One who wishes to propose a new subject, must give previous notice at the commencement of the session to the President. (9) No other business shall be brought forward till subjects and resolutions approved by the Subjects Committee are disposed of. (10) Afterwards, if time permits, new subjects for which notice had been given, will be mentioned and if the sense of the assembly be for discussion, then the proposer will be permitted to move his resolution and the matter disposed of.

Similar rules of business used to be adopted at the commencement of each session till a formal constitution came into force in 1908. At the Fourteenth Congress (Madras, 1898), the Reception Committee circulated a draft constitution and a committee was appointed by *Resolution XIX (c)* 'to consider the draft constitution circulated by the Reception Committee of Madras and submit a definite scheme to the next Congress, and this to form first subject of discussion at the next sitting of the Congress'. The Fifteenth Congress (Lucknow, 1899) adopted 11 basic rules and they are quoted below:

Resolved that this Congress adopts the following rules regarding the Constitution of the Congress:

1. The object of the Indian National Congress shall be to promote by constitutional means the interests and the well-being of the people of the Indian Empire.
2. It shall ordinarily meet once a year at such time and in such place as shall have been resolved on by the last preceding Congress. Provided that the Indian Congress Committee, as hereinafter provided for, may in case of necessity, change the place or time of the meeting of the Congress; provided also that in case of emergency the Indian Congress Committee may convene an extraordinary session of the Congress at such time and place as may be determined by them.
3. It shall consist of delegates elected by political associations for other bodies, and by public meetings.
4. Its affairs shall be managed by a Committee, styled the Indian Congress Committee, consisting of 45 members elected by the Congress, 40 of whom shall be elected upon the recommendation, of the different Provincial Congress Committees, and in the absence of such Committees, by the delegates of the respective Provinces in Congress assembled, in the manner hereinbelow laid down, that is to say:

For Bengal including Assam	8
For Bombay including Sind	8
For Madras including Secunderabad	8
For North-Western Provinces including Oudh	6
For Punjab	4
For Berar	3
For Central Provinces	3

The term of office of the members of the Committee shall be the period intervening between two ordinary meetings of the Congress.

5. The Indian Congress Committee shall meet at least three times a year, once immediately after the Congress, once during the year between the months of June and October, as may be determined upon by the Committee, and once immediately before the Congress, at such place as the Committee may find convenient.

6. The Indian Congress Committee shall have an Honorary Secretary and a paid Assistant Secretary, with suitable office staff, for which a sum of Rs 5,000 shall be granted annually, one half of which shall be provided by the Reception Committee of the place where the last Congress is held, and the other half by the Reception Committee of the place where the next succeeding Congress is to be held.

   The Secretary to the Indian National Congress shall be the Honorary Secretary of the Committee.

7. Provincial Congress Committees shall be organized at the capitals of the different Presidencies and Provinces of India for the purpose of carrying on the work of political education, on lines of general appreciation of British rule and of constitutional action for the removal of its defects, throughout the year, by organizing Standing Congress Committees, holding Provincial Conferences, and by such other means as they may deem proper, in consultation with the Indian Congress Committee, for furthering the objects of the Congress. They shall be the responsible agents of the Indian Congress Committee for their respective Provinces, and shall submit annual reports of their work to that Committee.

8. The nomination of the President, the drafting of Resolutions', and all other business in connection with the Congress, shall be done by the Indian Congress Committee. It shall also, subject to the approval of the Congress, frame rules for the election of delegates, the election of speakers, and the conduct of the proceedings of the Congress.

9. Rules and bye-laws shall be framed by the Provincial Congress Committees for the election of members, the conduct of their own proceedings, and other matters appertaining to their business. All such rules and bye-laws shall be subject to the approval of the Indian Congress Committee.

10. A Committee styled the British Congress Committee, shall be maintained in England, which shall represent there the interests of the Indian National Congress. The amount requisite for the expenses of the said Committee shall be determined and voted by the Congress, and the amount so voted shall be raised by the Indian Congress Committee in such manner as may be determined upon by the body from time to time.

11. The Indian Congress Committee shall take such steps as they may deem fit to raise a permanent fund for carrying on the work of the

> Indian National Congress; and such fund shall be invested in the name of 7 trustees, one from each Province in India, to be appointed by the Congress.

Rule 4 on the Indian Congress Committee was amended at the next session, the sixteenth, held at Lahore in 1900, making room for some ex-officio members and slightly altering the composition. The Indian Congress Committee was constituted both at the Congress of 1899 and 1900, but there is no record however that this Committee ever met. The rule was that it should meet three times a year. One of the Rules had provided that this Committee would draft resolutions — but a Subjects Committee was elected as usual every year and the resolutions as always were drafted by the Subjects Committee. From 1901, there is no reference even to the election of the Indian Congress Committee in the Reports of the sessions. Wacha was in charge of the secretariat and it functioned from Bombay, and during this period, Pherozeshah Mehta and Gopal Krishna Gokhale virtually guided the affairs of the Congress.

A committee of 21 members was appointed at the Twentieth Session held in 1904 in Bombay for a report on the 'question of the constitution of the Congress'. At the next Congress (twenty-first, Benares, 1905), a Standing Committee of 21 members was appointed 'to promote the object of the Congress and to take such steps during the year as may be necessary to give effect to the Resolutions of the Congress'. This Committee made some recommendations and the Twenty-second Session of the Congress (Calcutta, 1906) passed an important resolution, but 'tentatively for one year'. The text of *Resolution XVI* of 1906 was as follows:

> Resolved that this Congress adopts tentatively for one year the following recommendations of the Standing Committee of the Congress appointed at Benares last year:
>
> 1. Provincial Congress Committees
>
>   (a) The Committee recommends that each Province should organize at its capital, a Provincial Congress Committee in such manner as may be determined at a meeting or the Provincial Conference, or at a special meeting, held for the purpose, of representatives of different Districts of the Province.
>
>   (b) The Provincial Congress Committee should act for the Province in all Congress matters and it should be its special care to organize District Associations throughout the Province for sustained and continuous political work in the Province.
>
> 2. Central Congress Committee
>
>   The Committee recommends that the Congress should appoint every year a Central Standing Committee for all India, to carry out the Resolutions of the Congress, and to deal with urgent questions that

may arise and which may require to be disposed of in the name of the Congress, and that this Committee should consist of

12 members from Bengal, Bihar, Assam and Burma
8 members from Madras
8 members from Bombay
6 members from the U.P.
6 members from the Punjab
4 members from the C.P.
2 members from Berar

the President of the year and the General Secretaries being ex-officio members in addition.

3. Selection of President

In the matter of the selection of President in future years, the Committee recommends that the following scheme should be adopted:

The Provincial Congress Committee of the Province in which the Congress is to be held should organize a Reception Committee in such manner as it deems proper for making arrangements for the Congress session, and the choice of the President should, in the first instance, rest with the Reception Committee, if after consulting Provincial Congress Committees, the Reception Committee is able to make the choice, by a majority of at least three-fourths of its members. If, however, no such majority can be obtained to support the nomination of any person, the question should be referred to the Central Standing Committee of the Congress, and the decision of the Committee shall be final.

4. Subjects Committee

The Committee recommends that Subjects Committee appointed at each session of the Congress to settle its programmes of work, should consist of

25 representatives of Bengal, Bihar, Assam and Burma
15 representatives of Madras
15 representatives of Bombay
10 representatives of the United Provinces
10 representatives of the Punjab
6 representatives of the Central Provinces
4 representatives of Berar

and 10 additional members for the Province in which the Congress is held, elected by the delegates attending the Congress, from the respective Provinces in such manner as they deem proper and that the President of the year, all ex-Presidents, and all ex-Chairmen of Reception Committee who may be present at the Congress, and the local Secretaries of the Congress for the year, should in addition be ex-officio members of the Subjects Committee.

7. Adoption of a Constitution (1908)

A formal, and more or less, comprehensive, constitution for the Congress was an outcome of the disruption of the twenty-third session of 1907 which met at Surat. The events indicated that between the two groups whom historians have named Moderates and Extremists — though Bal Gangadhar Tilak, the leader of the latter, preferred to call them Nationalists — differences existed both as to goals and methods. There was also a clash of personalities between Tilak on one side and Mehta and Gokhale on the other. The creed of the Moderates was spelt out when they called a Convention of delegates on 28 December 1907, the day following the suspension of the Congress session *sine die*. It was laid down in the letter of announcement which they circulated and it was also stated at the convention, that only those delegates who accepted the following ideology should attend the convention:

(1) That the attainment by India of self-government similar to that enjoyed by the self-governing members of the British Empire and participation by her in the rights and responsibilities of the Empire on equal terms with those members is the goal of our political aspirations.

(2) That the advance towards this goal is to be by strictly constitutional means by bringing about steady reform of the existing system of administration and by promoting national unity, fostering public spirit, and improving the condition of the mass of our people.

Meeting on 28 December, the convention appointed a committee to draft a constitution of the Congress in accordance with this creed, and Gopal Krishna Gokhale and Dinshaw Edulji Wacha were appointed Joint Secretaries of the Committee. The Committee met at Allahabad on 18 and 19 April 1908 and drew up a detailed constitution. The Congress of 1908, also numbered as the twenty-third, the same number as for the disrupted Congress of the previous year, was called in accordance with the rules of this constitution and as laid down in its Article XXXI named 'Transitory Provisions'. The constitution was laid on the table at the Congress of 1908 which met at Madras, but no formal resolution was actually passed adopting this constitution. Nonetheless, this constitution was followed, and by Resoluion XVIII of this session, members were appointed to the All-India Congress Committee, a body set up by this constitution. The XXXI Articles and 31 Rules of this comprehensive Constitution are set out in full at the end of this chapter [See Appendix].

Some minor amendments were made in 1911 and 1912, but only two significant amendments, one made in 1915 and the other in 1917, need be noticed. An amendment of Article XX made in 1915 laid down that as many as 15 delegates could be elected at a public meeting convened by an association provided certain conditions were satisfied. One condition was that the Association should accept Article I of the Congress Constitution by a special resolution. An explanation was added to this Article dealing with election of delegates stating that 'no person elected as a delegate need be a member of any Congress Committee if he is otherwise qualified'. The importance of this amendment lies in the fact that thereby Tilak and his followers could join a session of the Congress as delegates without becoming formally members of any Congress Committee. They had remained outside the Congress ever since the split in 1907. Tilak himself was in detention till 1914. Negotiations started after he was released. After this amendment, he and his followers came as delegates to the 1916 Congress held at Lucknow and that Congress was busy with a momentous matter, namely, drawing up of agreed proposals by the Congress and the Muslim League on the future constitutional set-up. The other important amendment was made at the Thirty-second Congress held at Calcutta in 1917, when the Telegu Districts of the Presidency of Madras, Sind in Bombay Presidency, and Delhi with Ajmer-Merwara and 'British Rajputana' were constituted into separate Congress Provinces. By this act, the Congress may be said to have accepted the linguistic principle as the basis for the formation of Provinces.

In conclusion, the question may be asked: Why was it that for years the leaders of the Congress declined to adopt a defined constitution? How was it that the Congress could function well without a regular membership, and even go on gathering strength as the years rolled by and at the same time, allowing almost anybody to attend a session as a delegate and play a role in the decision-making process? Why was it that formal membership was not insisted upon nor conditions of membership laid down? No doubt these are unusual phenomena for a political party. The clue is not altogether difficult to find. The growth of the early Congress was basically along the lines that Hume had thought of during the seminal months in 1885. That he chose initially a name like 'the Indian National Union' suggests that his aim was to bring about a union of the forces that wanted constitutional and administrative reforms, and with the system prevailing in England as the model, but without the merger of these separate bodies into another organization. Apparently he was not thinking on the lines of a traditional political party with defined rules of membership as also of functioning. He talked about the 'linking in' of the 'Progressive forces' all over the country but wanted that each such organization should maintain its own identity and go on doing its work in its own way. Neither before nor after the first session in Bombay was it demanded of the 'representatives' that they sign any membership form to join this organization. Far from constituting themselves into a separate body, the 'representatives' decided that their 'resolutions be communicated to the Political Association in each province' and 'these Associations be requested . . . to adopt such measures as they may consider calculated to advance the settlement of the various questions dealt with in these resolutions'. Their strategy was not for conducting a movement with themselves organized into a separate body, but to encourage the existing organizations to take up appropriate actions to achieve the goals indicated by the Congress in its several resolutions.

Hume's idea seems to have been that the 'Indian National Conference' should be rather a platform than a party. The 'representatives' assembled in the First Congress endorsed this view. And this point of view continued for many years, and as not a few critics say, till the time independence was achieved. It appears that in the early years nobody felt that the Congress would stand to gain by becoming an exclusive organization with defined political creed and set rules about membership and functioning. Ordinarily a loose organization like that the Congress had in that early period would ill serve a political party as we conceive one. However, the Congress was not strictly a party at this time, or if considered to be one, was a party of a rather special nature. In the political situation in India of the time the stance taken by the early leaders gave the Congress great strength. After all, the Indian educated classes entertained common ideas on some of the basic questions, as for instance, more Indian members in the legislative councils, greater opportunities for qualified young men to get into the higher cadres of Government services, in particular, the I.C.S., reduction of expenditure in some departments of the government like the army, separation of the judiciary from the executive. These were not demands based on abstract principles, not even the one mentioned last. That class of Indians was used to seeing instances of highhandedness on the part of the police and the magistrates and expected that these would end if the judiciary could be made totally independent of the executive. At this time, the legislative councils did not have any elected element and so no question arose of fighting an election with a party manifesto. With the intelligentsia entertaining the same views on basic constitutional and administrative issues, a well-defined party creed would not have been necessary even if elections were to be held.

The Second National Conference that met in Calcutta in the same week as the first Congress in Bombay passed almost identical resolutions as the Congress, and those who had been behind that conference joined the Congress with enthusiasm when the second Congress drew near. The different political and other associations all over the country welcomed as a body the news of the first Congress spread by the newspapers and affirmed their support to the resolutions when these were formally sent to them. When the time came for electing delegates to the second Congress they responded with eagerness. The pattern continued for two and a half decades. The Indian press gave unstinted support to the Congress unasked, as the points of view were basically the same on the main issues. The Congress enjoyed the support of heterogenous organizations in addition to the newspapers of many hues. This perhaps would not have happened had the Congress started with a defined political goal and with rules laid down in black and white about membership, hierarchy of power, etc. In that case, it would have become just one more of the numerous associations that existed then. Instead, the aim of the Congress was to speak with one voice on behalf of the whole country. On the one hand, the path to becoming a delegate and taking part in the decision-making process was kept open for everyone who had such a desire. On the other hand, only national issues and, further, only such of these issues on which there was a national consensus, were accepted for inclusion in the agenda of a session, and, with this end in view, social questions were left severely alone. The combination of the two made the Congress a truly national platform. Admittedly, the 'nation' in this context meant the educated classes who formed, in the language of Governor General Dufferin, 'a microscopic minority' of the total population. But it is that small number of people who counted. It is also true that the followers of Sir Syed Ahmed Khan remained aloof from the Congress and they were a 'microscopic' part of the above 'microscopic minority'. The message of the Congress percolated down to the common man's level because, to the extent the common man understood politics, he found that the Congress was speaking his mind, and more so when the Congress leader addressed public meetings in his own language.

What interest did the small or big organizations have in sending delegates to the Congress sessions and in becoming 'linked in'? The obvious inducement seems to have been that thereby they could cherish much stronger hopes of achieving the demands that they were making in their own way and in isolation from one another. By becoming associated with the Congress they made their own causes a part of the common cause of the whole country. And there was nothing to lose — the Congress did not demand even that they become affiliated in any formal way, not to speak of merging their own separate identities in the Congress. By not defining its specific aims and not laying down rigid rules about membership, the Congress could stay 'open, flexible, and pragmatic'. And this policy gave it great strength. The Congress remained 'linked to a great variety of other political and social organizations' in different parts of the country and 'through them built up its wide and heterogenous support'. It so happened that in the case of the Congress, 'the whole was greater than the parts'. With hindsight, we can say that the early leaders had not been unwise in omitting to lay down a constitution.

When in the sixteenth year of its existence, the Congress did define its goals, it did so in broad general terms, namely, 'to promote by constitutional means the interest and well-being of the people of the Indian Empire'. In the set of basic rules on the Constitution adopted in 1899, no provision was considered necessary for membership of the Congress as an organization. The Congress as a conference was to 'consist of delegates elected by political associations or other bodies, and by public meetings'. The 1908 constitution did not abandon the principle of keeping political associations or public bodies associated with the Congress, only they were required to accept formally the Congress goal which now became attainment of self-government within the British Empire by constitutional means.

APPENDIX 9.1

Constitution of the Indian National Congress Organization, 1908

Objects

ARTICLE I

The objects of the Indian National Congress are the attainment by the people of India of a system of government similar to that enjoyed by the self-governing Members of the British Empire and participation by them in the rights and responsibilities of the Empire on equal terms with those Members. These objects are to be achieved by constitutional means by bringing about a steady reform of the existing system of administration and by promoting national unity, fostering public spirit and developing and organizing the intellectual, moral economic and industrial resources of the country.

ARTICLE II

Every Delegate to the Indian National Congress shall express in writing his acceptance of the Objects of the Congress as laid down in Article I of this Constitution and his willingness to abide by this Constitution and by the Rules of the Congress hereto appended.

Sessions of the Congress

ARTICLE III

(*a*) The Indian National Congress shall ordinarily meet once every year during Christmas holidays at such town as may have been decided upon at the previous session of the Congress.

(*b*) If no such decision has been arrived at, the All India Congress Committee shall decide the matter.

(*c*) An extraordinary session of the Congress may be summoned by the All-India Congress Committee, either of its own motion or on the requisition of a majority of the Provincial Congress Committees, wherever and whenever it may deem it advisable to hold such session.

(*d*) It shall be open to the All-India Congress Committee to change the venue of the Congress to some other town, when such change is deemed by it to be necessary or desirable owing to serious or unforeseen difficulties or other contingencies of a like nature.

Component Parts of the Organization

ARTICLE IV

The Indian National Congress Organization will consist of:

(*a*) The Indian National Congress;

(*b*) The Provincial Congress Committees;

(*c*) District Congress Committees or Associations affiliated to the Provincial Congress Committees;

(*d*) Sub-Divisional or Taluka Congress Committees affiliated to the District Congress Committees or Associations;

(*e*) Political Associations or Public Bodies recognized as Electorates in accordance with clause (3) of Article XX;

(*f*) The All-India Congress Committee;

(*g*) The British Committee of the Congress; and

(*h*) Bodies formed or organized periodically by a Provincial Congress Committee, such as the Provincial or District Conferences or the Reception Committee of the Congress or Conference for the year.

ARTICLE V

No person shall be eligible to be a member of any of the Provincial or District or other Congress Committees or Associations or Bodies mentioned in clauses (*b*), (*c*), (*d*) and (*h*) of Article IV, unless he has attained the age of twenty-one and expresses in writing his acceptance of the Objects of the Congress as laid down in Article I of this Constitution and his willingness to abide by this Constitution and by the Rules of the Congress hereto appended.

Provincial Congress Committees

ARTICLE VI

(*a*) To act for the Province in Congress matters and for organizing Provincial or District Conferences in such manner as it may deem proper, there shall be a Provincial Congress Committee with its headquarters at the chief town of the Province in each of the following nine Provinces:

(1) Madras; (2) Bombay; (3) United Bengal; (4) United Provinces; (5) Punjab (including North West Frontier Province); (6) Central Provinces; (7) Bihar; (8) Berar and (9) Burma.

(*b*) The Provincial Sub-Committees of the Convention shall, in the first instance, form themselves into Provincial Congress Committees.

(*c*) The Secretaries of the Convention Committees shall take steps to form separate Provincial Congress Committees for Central Provinces, Bihar and Burma.

ARTICLE VII

Every Provincial Congress Committee so formed will add to its number

(*a*) Representatives elected in accordance with its term of affiliation by every affiliated District Congress Committee or Association referred to in clause (*c*) of Article IV.

(*b*) As many representatives of recognized Political Associations or Public Bodies referred to in clause (*e*) of Article IV as each Provincial Congress Committee may think fit to determine.

(*c*) Such other persons in the Province as may have attended as many sessions of the Congress as delegates as may be determined by each Provincial Congress Committee for its own Province.

(*d*) All such ex-Presidents of the Congress or ex-Chairmen of Reception Committees of the Congress as ordinarily reside within the jurisdiction of the Provincial Congress Committee and may not have been enrolled as members of the said Committee in accordance with clause (*b*) of Article VI or by virtue of the provisions contained in any of the foregoing clauses of this Article.

(*e*) The Joint Secretary or Secretaries of the Congress ordinarily residing within the jurisdiction of the Provincial Congress Committee, such Joint Secretary or Secretaries being added as ex-officio member or members of the said Committee.

ARTICLE VIII

Every member of the Provincial Congress Committee shall pay an annual subscription of not less than Rs 5.

District or other Congress Committees or Associations

ARTICLE IX

The Provincial Congress Committee shall have affiliated to itself a District Congress Committee or Association for each District, wherever possible, or for such other areas in the Province as it deems proper, subject to such conditions or terms of affiliation as it may deem expedient or necessary. It will be the duty of the District Congress Committee or Association to act for the District in Congress matters with the co-operation of any Sub-divisional or Taluka Congress Committees which may be organized and affiliated to it, subject in all cases to the general control and approval of the Provincial Congress Committee.

ARTICLE X

Every member of the District Congress Committee or Association shall either be a resident of the District or shall have a substantial interest in the District and shall pay an annual subscription of not less than one Rupee.

ARTICLE XI

No District Congress Committee or Association or Public Body referred to in clause (*c*) and (*e*) of Article IV shall be entitled to return representatives to the Provincial Congress Committee or Delegates to the Congress or to the Provincial Conference unless it contributes to the Provincial Congress Committee such annual subscription as may be determined by the latter.

ARTICLE XII

Each Provincial Congress Committee shall frame its own Rules not inconsistent with the Constitution and Rules of the Congress. No district or other Congress Committee or Association mentioned in Article IX shall frame any Rules inconsistent with those framed by the Provincial Congress Committee to which it is affiliated.

The All-India Congress Committee

ARTICLE XIII

The All-India Congress Committee shall, as far as possible, be constituted as hereinbelow laid down:

	15	Representatives of	Madras;
	15	"	Bombay;
	20	"	United Bengal;
	15	"	United Provinces;
	13	"	Punjab (including N.W. Frontier Province);
	7	"	Central Provinces;
	5	"	Bihar;
	5	"	Berar;
and	2	"	Burma;

Provided as far as possible that one-fifth of the total number of representatives shall be Mahomedans.

All ex-Presidents of the Congress, residing or present in India and the General Secretaries of the Congress, who shall also be ex-officio General Secretaries of the All-India Congress Committee, shall be ex-officio members in addition.

ARTICLE XIV

The representatives of each Province shall be elected by its Provincial Congress Committee at a meeting held, as far as possible, before the 30th of November for each year. If any Provincial Congress Committee fails to elect its representatives, the said representatives shall be elected by the Delegates for that Province present at the ensuing Congress. In either case the representatives of each Province shall be elected from among the members of its Provincial Congress Committee, and the election shall be made, as far as possible, with due regard to the proviso in Article XIII.

ARTICLE XV

The names of the representatives so elected by the different Provinces shall be communicated to the General Secretaries. These together with the names of the ex-officio members shall be announced at the Congress.

ARTICLE XVI

The President of the Congress at which the All-India Congress Committee comes into existence shall, if he ordinarily resides in India, be ex-officio President of the All-India Congress Committee. In his absence the members of the All-India Congress Committee may elect their own President.

ARTICLE XVII

(*a*) The All-India Congress Committee so constituted shall hold office from the dissolution of the Congress at which it comes into existence till the dissolution of the following Congress.

(*b*) If any vacancy arises by death, resignation or otherwise, the remaining members of the Province in respect of which the vacancy has arisen shall be competent to fill it up for the remaining period.

ARTICLE XVIII

(*a*) It will be the duty of the All-India Congress Committee to take such steps as it may deem expedient and practicable to carry on the work and propaganda of the Congress, and it shall have the power to deal with all such matters of great importance or urgency as may require to be disposed of in the name of and for the purpose of the Congress, in addition to matters specified in this Constitution as falling within its powers or functions.

(*b*) The decision of the All-India Congress Committee shall, in every case above referred to, be final and binding on the Congress and on the

Reception Committee or the Provincial Congress Committee, as the case may be, that may be affected by it.

ARTICLE XIX

On the requisition in writing of not less than 20 of its members, the General Secretaries shall convene a meeting of the All-India Congress Committee at the earliest possible time.

Electorates and Delegates

ARTICLE XX

The right of electing Delegates to the Indian National Congress shall vest exclusively in (1) the British Committee of the Congress; (2) Provincial or District or other Congress Committees or Associations formed or affiliated as hereinabove laid down; and (3) such Political Associations or Public Bodies of more than three years' standing as may be recognized in that behalf by the Provincial Congress Committee of the Province to which the Political Association or Public Body belongs, provide that no such Political Association or Public Body shall be recognized unless the said Political Association or Public Body, by a Resolution at a General Meeting of its members, express its acceptance of the principles embodied in Article I of this Constitution and makes the acceptance of the same a condition precedent to new membership.

ARTICLE XXI

All Delegates to the Indian National Congress shall pay a fee of Rs. 20 each and shall be not less than twenty-one years at the date of election.

Reception Committee of the Congress

ARTICLE XXII

(*a*) The Provincial Congress Committee of the Province in which the Congress is to be held shall take steps to form a Reception Committee for the Congress. Every one, who ordinarily resides in the Province, fulfils the conditions laid down in Article V of this Constitution and pays a minimum contribution of Rs 25, shall be eligible as a member of the Reception Committee.

(*b*) No one who is only a member of the Reception Committee, but not a delegate, shall be allowed to vote or take part in the debate at the Congress.

(*c*) The Reception Committee shall be bound to provide the necessary funds for meeting all the expenses of the Congress as also the cost of preparing, printing, publishing and distributing the Report of the Congress.

Election of the President

ARTICLE XXIII

(*a*) In the month of June, the Reception Committee shall consult the several Provincial Congress Committees as to the selection of the President for the year's Congress. The Provincial Congress Committees shall make their recommendations by the end of July; and in the month of August the Reception Committee shall meet to consider the recommendations. If a person be recommended by a majority of the members of the Reception Committee present at a special meeting called for the purpose, that person shall be the President of the next Congress. If however, the Reception Committee is unable to elect the President in the manner mentioned above, the matter shall forthwith be referred by it to the All-India Congress Committee, whose decision shall be arrived at, as far as possible, before the end of September. In either case, the election shall be final.

Provided that in no case shall the person so elected President, belong to the Province in which the Congress is to be held.

(*b*) There shall be no formal election of the President by or in the Congress, but merely the adoption (in accordance with the provisions in that behalf laid down in Rule 3, clause (*b*) of the "Rules" hereto appended) of a formal Resolution requesting the President, already elected in the manner hereinabove laid down, to take the chair.

Subjects Committee

ARTICLE XXIV

The Subjects Committee to be appointed at each session of the Congress to settle its programme of business to be transacted shall, as far as possible, consist of:

Not more than	15	representatives of	Madras
"	15	"	Bombay
"	20	"	United Bengal
"	15	"	United Provinces
"	13	"	Punjab (including N.W. Frontier Province)
"	7	"	Central Provinces
"	5	"	Bihar
"	5	"	Berar
"	2	"	Burma
"	5	"	British Committee of the Congress

and additional 10 representatives of the Province in which the Congress is held.

All the above-mentioned representatives being elected, in accordance with Rule 9 of the "Rules" hereto appended, by the Delegates attending the Congress from the respective Provinces.

The President of the Congress for the year, the Chairman of the Reception Committee of the year, all ex-Presidents and ex-Chairmen of Reception Committees, the General Secretaries of the Congress, the local Secretaries of the Congress for the year, not exceeding six in number, and all the members of the All-India Congress Committee for the year, shall, in addition be ex-officio members of the Subjects Committee.

ARTICLE XXV

The President of the Congress for the year shall be ex-officio Chairman of the Subjects Committee.

Contentious Subjects and Interest of Minorities

ARTICLE XXVI

(*a*) No subject shall be passed for discussion by the Subjects Committee or allowed to be discussed at any Congress by the President thereof, to the introduction of which the Hindu or Mahomedan Delegates, as a body, object by a majority of three-fourths of their numbers; and if, after the discussion it shall appear that the Hindu or Mahomedan Delegates, as a body, are, by a majority of three-fourths of their number, opposed to the Resolution which it is proposed to pass thereon, such Resolution shall be dropped.

(*b*) The President of the Congress for the year may nominate five delegates to the Subjects Committee to represent minorities or to make up such deficiencies as he may think necessary.

(*c*) In any representations which the Congress may make or in any demands which it may put forward for the larger association of the people of India with the administration of the country, the interests of minorities shall be duly safeguarded.

Voting at the Congress

ARTICLE XXVII

Ordinarily, all questions shall be decided by a majority of votes as laid down in Rule 21 of the "Rules" hereto appended but in cases falling under Article XXX of this Constitution or whenever a division is duly asked for in accordance with Rule 22 of the "Rules" hereto appended, the voting at the Congress shall be by Provinces only. In cases falling under clause (1) of Article XXX, each Province shall have one vote, to be given as determined by a majority of its Delegates present at the

Congress. In all other cases of voting by Provinces, the vote of each Province, determined as aforesaid, shall be equivalent to the number of representatives assigned to the Province in constituting the All-India Congress Committee.

The British Committee of the Congress

ARTICLE XXVIII

The Reception Committee of the Province in which the Congress is held shall remit to the British Committee of the Congress, through the General Secretaries of the Congress, half the amount of the fees received by it from Delegates.

General Secretaries

ARTICLE XXIX

(*a*) The Indian National Congress shall have two General Secretaries who shall be annually elected by the Congress. They shall be responsible for the preparation, publication and distribution of the Report of the Congress. They shall also be responsible for the preparation and circulation of Draft Resolutions of the Congress, which they must send to the Provincial Congress Committee at the latest in the first week of December.

(*b*) The All-India Congress Committee shall make adequate provision for the expenses of the work devolving on the General Secretaries, either out of the surplus at the disposal of the Reception Committee or by calling upon the Provincial Congress Committee to make such contributions as it may deem fit to apportion among them.

Changes in the Constitution or Rules

ARTICLE XXX

No addition, alteration or amendment shall be made (1) in Article I of this Constitution except by a unanimous vote of all the Provinces, and (2) in the rest of this Constitution or in the "Rules" hereto appended except by a majority of not less than two-thirds of the votes of the Provinces, provided in either case, that no motion for any such addition, alteration or amendment shall be brought before the Congress unless it has been previously accepted by the Subjects Committee of the Congress for the year.

Transitory Provisions

ARTICLE XXXI

(*a*) The Committee appointed by the Convention at Surat on 28 December, 1907 for drawing up a Constitution for the Congress shall exercise all the powers of the All-India Congress Committee till the formation of the latter at the next session of the Congress.

(*b*) The Secretaries of the said Convention Committee shall discharge the duties of the General Secretaries of the Congress till the dissolution of the next session of the Congress.

(*c*) The President and Secretaries of the Convention Committee should, in consultation with the Secretaries of the several Provincial Sub-Committees, arrange for the holding of a Session of the Congress during Christmas next in accordance with this Constitution.

(*d*) For the year 1908, the Reception Committee may, in electing the President, consult the Provincial Congress Committees in the beginning of October, before the end of which month, the Provincial Congress Committees, on being so consulted, shall make their recommendations, and the rest of the procedure prescribed in Article XXIII should be followed and completed as far as possible before the end of November.

Rules for the Conduct and Regulation of the Indian National Congress Meetings

1. The Indian National Congress shall ordinarily hold an Annual Session at such place as may have been decided upon in accordance with Article III of the Constitution and on such days during Christmas week as may be fixed by the Reception Committee. An extraordinary session of the Congress shall be held at such town and on such days as the All-India Congress Committee may determine.

2. Each Congress session shall open with a meeting of the Delegates at such time and place as may be notified by the Reception Committee. The time and place of subsequent sittings of the session be fixed and announced by the President of the Congress.

3. The proceedings of the opening day and at the first sitting of each Congress session shall, as far as possible, consist of:

(*a*) The Chairman of the Reception Committee's inaugural address of welcome to the delegates.

(*b*) The adoption of a formal Resolution, to be moved, seconded and supported by such Delegates as the Chairman of the Reception Committee invites or permits, requesting the President elected by the Reception Committee or the All-India Congress Committee, as the case may be, to take the chair, no opposition by way of a motion for amendment, adjournment or otherwise being allowed to postpone or prevent the carrying out of the said Resolution.

(*c*) The President's taking the chair and his inaugural address.

(*d*) Reading or distribution of the Report, if any, of the All-India Congress Committee and any statement that the General Secretaries may have to make.

(*e*) Any formal motions of thanks, congratulations, condolences, etc., as the President of the Congress may choose to move from the chair.

(*f*) The adjournment of the Congress for the appointment of the Subjects Committee and the announcement by the President of the time and place of the meetings of the Delegates of the different Provinces for the election of the members of the Subjects Committee, and also of the first meeting of the Subjects Committee.

4. No other business or motions in any form shall be allowed at the opening sitting of the Congress Session.

5. The Chairman of the Reception Committee shall preside over the assembly at the first sitting until the President takes the chair. The President of the Congress shall preside at all sittings of the Congress session as well as at all meetings of the Subjects Committee. In case of his absence and during such absence, any ex-President of the Congress present, who may be nominated by the President, and in case no ex-President is available, the Chairman of the Reception Committee shall preside at the Congress sitting; provided that the Subjects Committee may in such cases choose its own Chairman.

6. The President or the Chairman shall have, at all votings, one vote in his individual capacity and also a casting vote in case of equality of votes.

7. The President or Chairman shall decide all points of order and procedure summarily and his decision shall be final and binding.

8. The President or Chairman shall have the power, in cases of grave disorder or for any other legitimate reason, to adjourn the Congress either to a definite time or *sine die*.

9. The election of the members of the Subjects Committee shall take place at meetings of the Delegates of different Provinces held at such place and time as may be announced by the President. Each such meeting, in case of contest, shall have a Chairman who will first receive nominations, each nomination being made by at least five delegates, and then after announcing all the nominations he may ask each Delegate to give in a list of the members he votes for, and he may put the nominated names to the vote in such order as he pleases, or if there are only two rival lists, he shall take votes on these lists and announce the result of the election and forthwith communicate the same to the General Secretaries of the Congress.

10. The Subjects Committee shall deliberate upon and prepare the

agenda paper for the business to be transacted at the next Congress sitting. The General Secretaries shall, as far as practicable distribute among the Delegates a printed copy of the agenda paper for each sitting before the sitting commences.

11. At each sitting of the Congress, the order in which business shall be transacted shall be as follows:

(*a*) The resolution recommended for adoption by the Subjects Committee.

(*b*) Any substantive motion not included in (*a*) but which does not fall under Article XXX of Constitution and which 25 Delegates request the President in writing, before the commencement of the day's sitting, to be allowed to place before the Congress; provided however, that no such motion shall be allowed unless it has been previously discussed at a meeting of the Subjects Committee and has received the support of at least a third of the members then present.

12. Nothing in the foregoing rule shall prevent the President from changing the order of the Resolutions mentioned in Rule 11 (*a*) or from himself moving from the chair formal motions of thanks, congratulations, condolences or the like.

13. The proposers, seconders and supporters of the Resolution recommended for adoption by the Subjects Committee shall be Delegates and shall be selected by the said Committee. The President may allow other Delegates to speak on the Resolutions at his discretion and may allow any distinguished visitor to address the Congress. Nothing in the foregoing, however, shall prevent the President from moving from the chair such Resolutions as he may be authorized to do by the Subjects Committee.

14. An amendment may be moved to any motion provided that the same is relevant to the question at issue, that it does not raise a question already decided or anticipate any question embraced in a resolution on the agenda paper for the day and that it is couched in proper language and is not antagonistic to the fundamental principles of the Congress. Every amendment must be in the form of a proposition complete in itself.

15. When amendments are moved to a motion, they shall be put to the vote in the reverse order to that in which they have been moved.

16. A motion for an adjournment of the debate on a proposition may be made at any time and so also, with the consent of the President or Chairman, a motion for the adjournment of the House. The President or Chairman shall have the power to decline to put to vote any motion for adjournment if he considers it to be vexatious or obstructive or an abuse of the rules and regulations.

17. All motions, substantive or by way of amendment, adjournment, etc., shall have to be seconded, failing which they shall fail. No motions, whether those coming under Rule 11 (*b*) or for amendment, adjournment, closure etc. shall be allowed to be moved unless timely intimation thereof is sent to the President with the motion clearly stated in writing over the signatures of the proposer and seconder with the name of the Province from which they have been elected as Delegates.

18. No one who has taken part in the debate in the Congress on a resolution, shall be allowed to move or second a motion for adjournment or amendment in the course of the debate on that Resolution. If a motion for adjournment of the debate on any proposition is carried, the debate on the said proposition shall then cease and may be resumed only after the business on the agenda paper for the day is finished. A motion for adjournment of the House shall state definitely the time when the House is to resume business.

19. A motion for a closure of the debate on a proposition may be moved at any time after the lapse of half-an-hour from the time the proposition was moved; and if such motion for closure is carried, all discussion upon the original proposition or amendments proposed to it, shall at once stop and the President shall proceed to take votes.

20. No mention for a closure of the debate shall be moved whilst a speaker is duly in possession of the House.

21. All questions shall be decided by a majority of votes, subject, however, to the provisions of Article XXVII and XXX of the Constitution. Votes shall ordinarily be taken by a show of hands or by the Delegates for or against standing up in their places in turn to have the numbers counted.

22. In cases not falling under Article XXX of the Constitution, any twenty members of a Congress sitting may demand a division within five minutes of the declaration of the result of the voting by the President and such division shall be granted. Thereupon the Delegates of each Province shall meet at such time and place as the President may direct and the Chairman of each such meeting shall notify to the President the vote of the Province within the time specified by the President.

23. Every member of a sitting of the Congress or of the Subjects Committee shall be bound (*a*) to occupy a seat in the block allotted to his province, save as provided for in Rule 30, (*b*) to maintain silence when the President rises to speak or when another member is in possession of the House, (*c*) to refrain from hisses or interruptions of any kind or indulgence in improper and unparliamentary language, (*d*) to obey the Chair, (*e*) to withdraw when his own conduct is under debate, after he has heard the charge and been heard thereon, and (*f*) generally to conduct himself with propriety and decorum.

24. No member shall have the right at a Congress sitting to speak more than once on any motion except for a personal explanation or for raising a point or order. But the mover of a substantive motion (not one for amendment or adjournment) shall have the right of reply. A person who has taken part in a debate may speak upon an amendment or motion for adjournment moved after he had spoken. The President or Chairman shall have the right to fix a time-limit upon all speakers, as also to call to order or stop any speaker from further continuing his speech even before the time-limit expires, if he is guilty of tedious repetitions, improper expressions, irrelevant remarks, etc. and persists in them in spite of the warning from the President.

25. If a person does not obey the President's or the Chairman's orders or if he is guilty of disorderly conduct, the President shall have the right, with a warning in the first instance, and without a warning in case of contumacious disregard of his authority, to ask such member to leave the precincts of the House, and on such requisition the member so ordered shall be bound to withdraw and shall be suspended from his functions as a member during the day's sitting.

26. If the President considers that the punishment he can inflict according to the foregoing section is not sufficient, he may, in addition to it, ask the House to award such punishment as the House deems proper. The Congress shall have the power in such cases of expelling the member from the entire Congress Session.

27. The Reception Committee shall organize a body of such persons as it may deem fit for the purpose of keeping order during the meeting of the Congress or of its Subjects Committee or at divisions. There shall be a Captain at the head of this body and he shall carry out the orders of the President or the Chairman.

28. Visitors may be allowed at the sitting of the Congress on such terms and conditions as the Reception Committee determines. They may, at any time, be asked to withdraw by the President. They shall be liable to be summarily ejected from the House if they disobey the Chair, or if they are guilty of disturbance or obstruction, or if they are in anywise disorderly in their behaviour.

29. The meetings of the Subjects Committee shall be open only to the members of that Committee and the meetings of the Delegates of each Province at divisions shall be open to the Delegates of that Province only, subject in either case to the Provisions of Rule 27.

30. The Chairman of the Reception Committee and the President, as well as the Secretaries may, at their discretion, accommodate on the Presidential platform, (1) Leading members of the Congress,

(2) Distinguished Visitors, (3) Members of the Reception Committee and (4) Ladies, whether Delegates or visitors.

31. The foregoing Rules shall apply, *mutatis mutandis* to the Provincial or District Conference organized by the Provincial Congress Committees as provided for in Article VI of the Constitution.

Index

The Town Hall, Calcutta, where a mammoth meeting was held in support of the Ilbert Bill on 28 February 1883.

Delegates at the First Session of the Indian National Congress in Bombay, 28 December 1885.

W.C. Bonnerjee, *who presided over the Congress Sessions of 1885 and 1892.*

Dadabhai Naoroji, who presided over the Congress Sessions of 1886, 1893 and 1906.

Badruddin Tyabji, President of the Congress, 1887.

George Yule, President of the Congress, 1888.

William Wedderburn, who presided over the Congress Sessions of 1889 and 1910.

Pherozeshah Mehta, President of the Congress, 1890.

P. Ananda Charlu, President of the Congress, 1891.

Alfred Webb, President of the Congress, 1894.

Surendranath Banerjea, who presided over the Congress Sessions of 1895 and 1902.

Rahimtulla M. Sayani, President of the Congress, 1896.

C. Sankaran Nair, President of the Congress, 1897.

Anand Mohan Bose, President of the Congress, 1898.

R.C. Dutt, President of the Congress, 1899.

N.G. Chandavarkar, President of the Congress, 1900.

Dinshaw E. Wacha, President of the Congress, 1901.

Lal Mohan Ghose, President of the Congress, 1903.

Henry Cotton, President of the Congress, 1904.

G.K. Gokhale, President of the Congress, 1905.

Delegates at the Allahabad Congress Session, 1888.

A.O. Hume, a British civilian who was active in the affairs of the Indian National Congress.

M.G. Ranade, a distinguished Maharashtrian nationalist.

वन्देमातरम्

सुजलां सुफलां मलयज शीतलां
शस्यश्यामलां मातरम् ।
शुभ्र ज्योत्स्ना-पुलकित यामिनीम्
फुल्लकुसुमित-द्रुमदलशोभिनीम्,
सुहासिनीं सुमधुर भाषिणीम्
सुखदां वरदां मातरम् ॥
सप्तकोटिकण्ठ-कलकल-निनाद कराले
द्विसप्तकोटिभुजैर्धृतखरकरवाले,
अबला केन मा एत बले ।
बहुबलधारिणीं नमामि तारिणीम्
रिपुदल वारिणीं मातरं ॥
तुमि विद्या तुमि धर्म्म,
तुमि हृदि तुमि मर्म्म,
त्वं हि प्राणाः शरीरे ।
बाहुते तुमि मा शक्ति,
हृदये तुमि मा भक्ति,
तोमारइ प्रतिमा गड़ि मन्दिरे मन्दिरे ।
त्वं हिं दुर्गा दशप्रहरणधारिणी
कमला कमल-दल-विहारिणी
वाणी विद्यादायिनी नमामि त्वां
नमामि कमलां अमलां अतुलाम्
सुजलां सुफलां मातरम्,
वन्दे मातरम्
श्यामलां सरलां सुस्मितां भूषिताम्
धरणीं भरणीम् मातरम् ॥

'Bande Mataram' a poem by Bankim Chandra Chatterji which became a symbol of the Swadeshi Movement.

K.T. Telang, a distinguished social reformer and nationalist from Bombay.

Manmohan Ghosh, a prominent Bengali nationalist.

Swami Vivekananda, whose interpretation of Hinduism inspired many Indian nationalists.

Bankim Chandra Chatterji, whose writings promoted the spread of national consciousness.

Bal Gangadhar Tilak, 1881.

THE

Mahratta

WITH WHICH IS INCORPORATED THE

DECCAN STAR.

New Series. } POONA :—SUNDAY, JANUARY 2, 1881. { Vol. I. No. I.

OURSELVES.

The inevitable tendency of progress that has been marked to exist in all countries, communities and ages makes us see the mind of the people ready for a new sort of relation to its writers, and the signs of the time prove to be the key-note of the future good that is calculated to result from the labors of periodical and journal writers of the day. We, therefore, cannot be said to be a day too early in the field. The historical associations that are connected with the charming name we have assumed for ourselves, at once lead the untrained mind to suppose that we shall in time descend on the possessions of the elder and less careful contemporaries; but these are after all the apprehensions of an unsound and weak mind. From the present times it appears likely that a general reconciliation would put an end to all quarrels between the ruler and the ruled, quarrels which under stubborn and thoughtless governors have weakened and disgraced for a time the good Government of Her Imperial Majesty in India. The instant dangers of Her Majesty's Indian Empire have well induced many men of patriotic spirit and feeling to forget private animosities and attempts are being made in every direction to co-operate heartily for the general good. Thus in Bengal, Madras, Punjab and the N.W. Provinces political associations have been formed to represent the wants and wishes of the people and newspapers and periodicals are being published for the purpose of creating a healthy public opinion on all points that concern the longevity of the benign British Rule. At such a time the Deccan was badly in want of an organ which would try its best to effectively represent the Deccanees and bring about a right understanding between the subject and their rulers on this side of the country. The *Mahratta* was, therefore, a *desideratum*. Let us by the bye here mention that because we have taken only a limited region for observations, because we have assumed for ourselves a name that applies only to a limited community, or because the *Mahratta* is in the hands of a few educated Brahmins of Poona, we see no reason why we should make the *Mahratta* a sectarian journal. We assure our readers that not only that the *Mahratta* will not be a sectarian journal, but that it will from time to time extend its sphere of observation even to alien communities and would always without partiality or prejudice weigh questions in the even balances of a clear conscience.

In the next place, it is worth observing here, that though we may deservedly ceremony, the time has not, we are sure, yet come when we can do without a ceremony. We, therefore, embrace this opportunity of bidding a good morrow to our readers by stating in brief what the Policy of the *Mahratta* will be. It has by this time been too wellknown to want any special mention at our hands that the duties of an Indian Journal are two-fold. Our true and primary duty will be to *interpret* and *petition* and *instruct* and advocacy may be said to form the second part of our real work. Having thus defined what our duty will be, we now proceed to discuss what will fall within the scope of interpreting and petitioning and instructing as well as that of advocating. The pages of History are full of evidence to show that since foreigners are not likely to know exactly what the wants and wishes of the ruled are, they are not expected to be the best governors, however benevolent their intentions might be. It may, therefore, be concluded that a foreign rule is almost an impossibility and that foreigners as rulers can only see, do and manage so as to make the yoke as little pressing as possible; it will thus be our first aim to point out to our rulers in a clear and out-spoken manner how best they can manage to make the yoke press as little as possible. To make this more intelligible we shall here string together the multifarious evils that we have been subject to, so that the line of our working may at once be clear and marked. The blessings of the British Rule to India were so many flagrant evils about the times of Sir Thomas Munro that he is reported to have said "it would be more desirable that we should be expelled from the country altogether, than that the result of our system of Government be such an abasement of a whole people." Such writings in good time produced a healthy effect on the minds of the Governors and an act was afterwards passed which is called an "Act for the better Government of India." But the working of this act has not been satisfactory, and we are yet laboring under the pressure of a number of evils which sooner or later England must remove. The first evil that has been forced upon us is the Ryotwari system, which, notwithstanding the vehement opposition of Lord Elphinstone was laid upon us after it had completely ruined Madras; and the result of the system has been that agriculturists are beggared. The next evil in turn is that of heavy transit duties that have broken manufactures, decayed towns and demoralised the people of India. The third evil is the destruction of our municipal institutions which had, according to Mr. Elphinstone, "preserved the people of India through all ... ment of a great portion of freedom and independence." The destruction of our ancient traditional municipal institutions does not stop here. The reformed Governors have forced upon us new municipal institutions which have broken the back of all rate-payers until the hand of destruction is ... in all towns and cities, nay villages. The next evil is the grinding taxation and constant drain upon our resources in the form of a costly machinery of Government, Home charges &c. &c. The next in turn is the wanton destruction of the native Aristocracy who always furnished consumers for the articles of commerce, who stimulated the production of laborers, who were the patrons of arts and manufactures, and lastly the promoters of agricultural improvements. Next in the same category of evils comes the exotic system of English Law, which has most painfully checked the growth of Native Society. Lastly comes the destruction or absorption of Native States. These and many more of the kind have been the evils we have been heir to, and it will be the constant endeavour of the *Mahratta* to impress upon the minds of the benign British Rulers the necessity of eradicating those evils, which they from their stand-point see not but which have spread discontent throughout the length and breadth of this valuable dependency and cast a slur on the benign rule of Britain. In doing this duty of interpreting what the native community says on these points and petitioning the rulers on behalf of the natives of India, the Policy of the *Mahratta* will be that of an unbiased, independent, frank and out-spoken journal, without giving way to despondency if our petitions are not heard, and without in the least fearing the chameleon-like-changing colours of Anglo-Indian Policy. With reference to Native States our policy will always be for the uninterfered continuance of such States. History will bear us out when we say that the decline of a Native State commences from the moment the English come in close contact with it; for it has been observed that the decline arises chiefly from the inordinate influence the Politicals are allowed to exercise. Our attempts, therefore, will always be directed at shielding the native Princes from the uncalled-for interference on the part of the Politicals and exposing the latter to the public gaze. These principles of our policy with regard to Native States have been founded upon the experience of many a statesman, like the Duke of Wellington, Sir Thomas Munro, Sir John Malcolm *et hoc genus omne*. We believe we have defined our policy at sufficient length ...

Title page of Mahratta, *January 2, 1881, founded and edited by Tilak.*

Aurobindo Ghose, 1893.

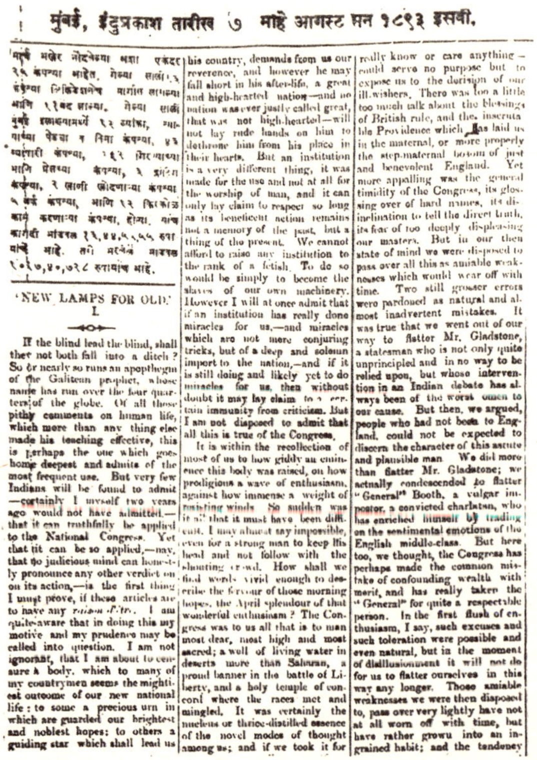

मुंबई, इंदुप्रकाश तारीख ७ माहे आगस्ट सन १८९३ इसवी.

'NEW LAMPS FOR OLD.'

I.

If the blind lead the blind, shall they not both fall into a ditch? So or nearly so runs an apopthegm of the Galilean prophet, whose name has run over the four quarters of the globe. Of all those pithy comments on human life, which more than any thing else made his teaching effective, this is perhaps the one which goes home deepest and admits of the most frequent use. But very few Indians will be found to admit—certainly I myself two years ago would not have admitted,—that it can truthfully be applied to the National Congress. Yet that it can be so applied,—nay, that no judicious mind can honestly pronounce any other verdict on on its action,—is the first thing I must prove, if these articles are to have any *raison d'être*. I am quite aware that in doing this my motive and my prudence may be called into question. I am not ignorant, that I am about to censure a body, which to many of my countrymen seems the mightiest outcome of our new national life: to some a precious urn in which are guarded our brightest and noblest hopes; to others a guiding star which shall lead us his country, demands from us our reverence, and however he may fall short in his after-life, a great and high-hearted nation—and no nation was ever justly called great, that was not high-hearted—will not lay rude hands on him to dethrone him from his place in their hearts. But an institution is a very different thing, it was made for the use and not at all for the worship of man, and it can only lay claim to respect so long as its beneficent action remains not a memory of the past, but a thing of the present. We cannot afford to raise any institution to the rank of a fetish. To do so would be simply to become the slaves of our own machinery. However I will at once admit that if an institution has really done miracles for us,—and miracles which are not mere conjuring tricks, but of a deep and solemn import to the nation,—and if it is still doing and likely yet to do miracles for us, then without doubt it may lay claim to a certain immunity from criticism. But I am not disposed to admit that all this is true of the Congress.

It is within the recollection of most of us to how giddy an eminence this body was raised, on how prodigious a wave of enthusiasm, against how immense a weight of resisting winds. So sudden was it all that it must have been difficult, I may almost say impossible, even for a strong man to keep his head and not follow with the shouting crowd. How shall we find words vivid enough to describe the fervour of those morning hopes, the April splendour of that wonderful enthusiasm? The Congress was to us all that is to man most dear, most high and most sacred; a well of living water in deserts more than Saharan, a proud banner in the battle of Liberty, and a holy temple of concord where the races met and mingled. It was certainly the nucleus or thrice-distilled essence of the novel modes of thought among us; and if we took it for really know or care anything—could serve no purpose but to expose us to the derision of our ill-wishers. There was too a little too much talk about the blessings of British rule, and the inscrutable Providence which has laid us in the maternal, or more properly the step-maternal bosom of just and benevolent England. Yet more appalling was the general timidity of the Congress, its glossing over of hard names, its disinclination to tell the direct truth, its fear of too deeply displeasing our masters. But in our then state of mind we were disposed to pass over all this as amiable weaknesses which would wear off with time. Two still grosser errors were pardoned as natural and almost inadvertent mistakes. It was true that we went out of our way to flatter Mr. Gladstone, a statesman who is not only quite unprincipled and in no way to be relied upon, but whose intervention in an Indian debate has always been of the worst omen to our cause. But then, we argued, people who had not been to England, could not be expected to discern the character of this astute and plausible man. We did more than flatter Mr. Gladstone; we actually condescended to flatter "General" Booth, a vulgar impostor, a convicted charlatan, who has enriched himself by trading on the sentimental emotions of the English middle-class. But here too, we thought, the Congress has perhaps made the common mistake of confounding wealth with merit, and has really taken the "General" for quite a respectable person. In the first flush of enthusiasm, I say, such excuses and such toleration were possible and even natural, but in the moment of disillusionment it will not do for us to flatter ourselves in this way any longer. Those amiable weaknesses we were then disposed to, pass over very lightly have not at all worn off with time, but have rather grown into an ingrained habit; and the tendency

Facsimile of New Lamps For Old, *an article written by Aurobindo Ghose, from the* Indu Parkash, *August 7, 1893.*

Delegates at the Bombay Congress Session, 1904.

V.V.S. Aiyer, a revolutionary nationalist from Tamil Nadu.

C. Vijayaraghavachariar, a prominent nationalist from Tamil Nadu.

Maharaja Lakshmishwar Singh of Dharbanga, an aristocrat who supported the cause of nationalism.

Sister Nivedita, a prominent disciple of Swami Vivekananda who supported the national movement.

Pramathanath Mitra, a revolutionary nationalist from Bengal.

Sarla Devi Choudharani, a prominent nationalist of the period.

'Poor Indian Ryot', a cartoon from Hindi Punch, *December 1904.*

'The Gourmand', a cartoon from Hindi Punch, *December 1904.*

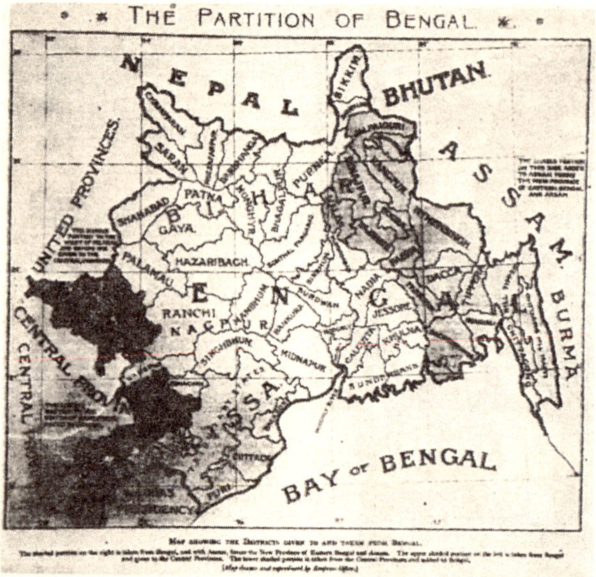

Map showing the partition of Bengal, and districts given to and taken from Bengal, 1905.

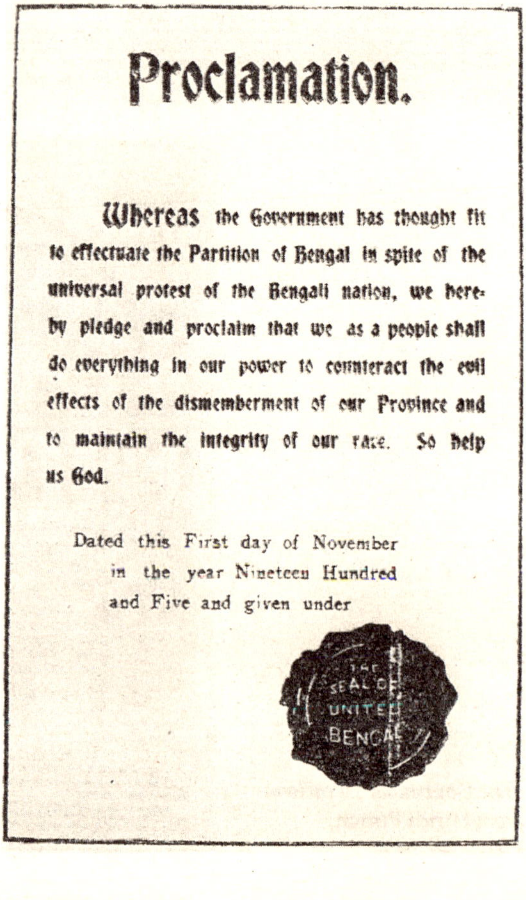

Proclamation.

Whereas the Government has thought fit to effectuate the Partition of Bengal in spite of the universal protest of the Bengali nation, we hereby pledge and proclaim that we as a people shall do everything in our power to counteract the evil effects of the dismemberment of our Province and to maintain the integrity of our race. So help us God.

Dated this First day of November in the year Nineteen Hundred and Five and given under

'The National Proclamation' which used to be read at meetings during the anti-partition struggle in Bengal.

Rabindranath Tagore during the Swadeshi Movement.

Aswini Kumar Dutta, a prominent leader of the Swadeshi Movement.

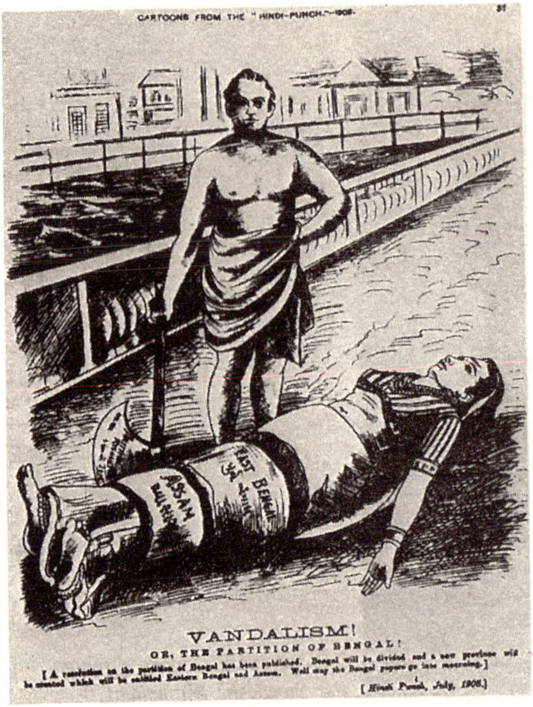

'Vandalism' or partition of Bengal, a cartoon from Hindi Punch, *July 1905.*

'Swadeshism: The Prabhat of the New Year', a cartoon from Hindi Punch, *October 1905.*

Rash Behari Ghose, who presided over the Congress Sessions of 1907 and 1908.

Madan Mohan Malaviya, who presided over the Congress Sessions of 1909 and 1918.

Bishan Narain Dar, President of the Congress, 1911.

R.N. Mudholkar, President of the Congress, 1912.

Nawab Syed Mohammad, President of the Congress, 1913.

Bhupendra Nath Basu, President of the Congress, 1914.

Satyendra P. Sinha, President of the Congress, 1915.

A.G. Muzumdar, President of the Congress, 1916.

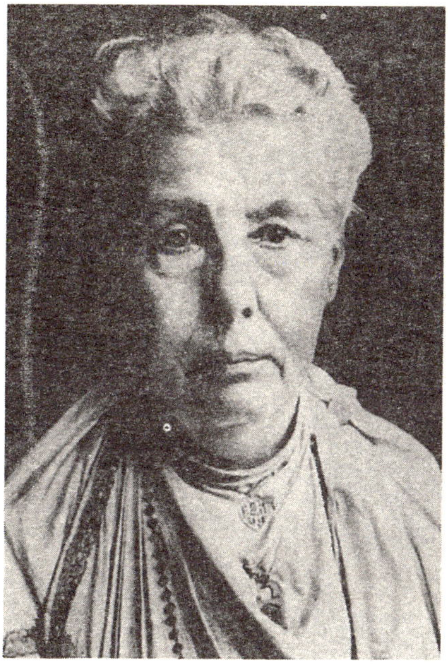

Dr Annie Besant, President of the Congress, 1917.

Syed Hassan Imam, President of the Congress, 1918.

Motilal Nehru, President of the Congress, 1919.

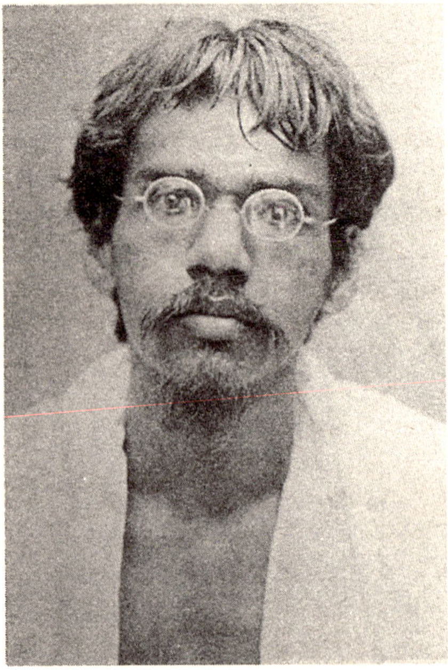

Barindra Kumar Ghose.

B.C. Pal.

First page of Bande Mataram, *September 1907.*

Bande Mataram

Weekly Edition.

PUBLISHED EVERY SUNDAY.

VOL. I. | CALCUTTA, SUNDAY, SEPTEMBER 29, 1907.

OUR PICTURE GALLERY.

SJT. AUROBINDO GHOSE.

Aurobindo after his arrest in 1908.

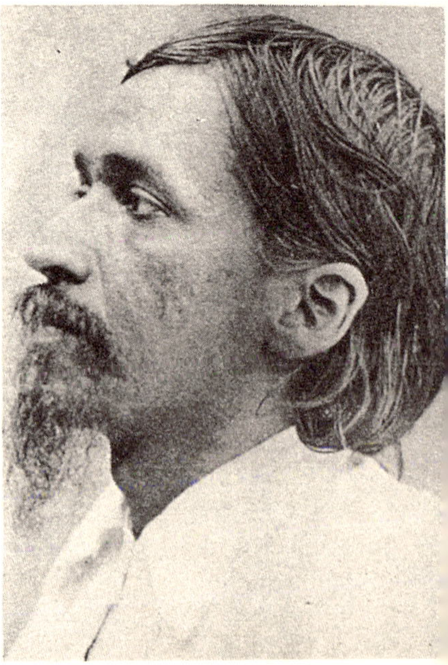

Muraripukur Garden House where the revolutionaries manufactured bombs during the struggle against the partition of Bengal.

The cell where Aurobindo Ghose was kept in solitary confinement during the Alipur Conspiracy Case.

Aurobindo presiding over a meeting of delegates to the Congress Session at Surat, 1907.

Aurobindo, Tilak, Ajit Singh and G.S. Khaparde at a meeting of the extremists.

B.C. Pal with Aurobindo Ghose and other leaders at the Uttarpara meeting, 1908.

Lala Lajpat Rai, B.G. Tilak and B.C. Pal, the three great leaders of the Swadeshi Movement.

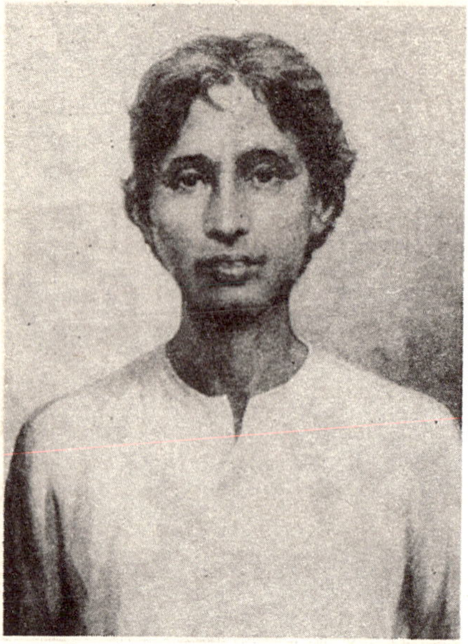

Khudiram Bose, a martyr in the cause of Indian freedom.

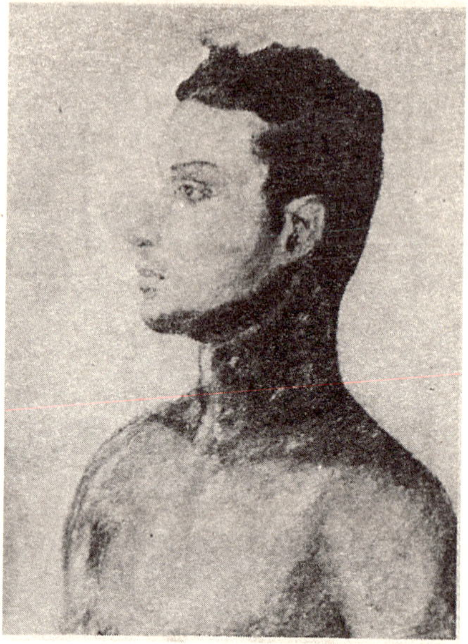

Prafulla Chaki, a prominent revolutionary nationalist.

Some of the revolutionaries accused in the Alipur Conspiracy Case.

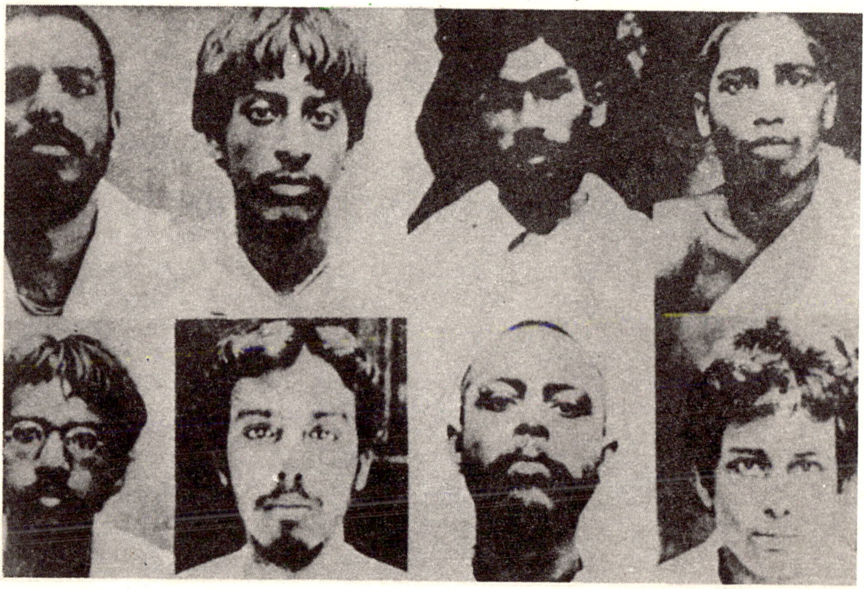

Ajit Singh, a distinguished Sikh nationalist leader of the Punjab.

Shamji Krishna Varma, an eminent revolutionary nationalist who fought for Indian freedom from Europe.

V.G. Pingle, a revolutionary nationalist from Maharashtra.

Veer Savarkar, one of the most eminent revolutionary nationalists of India.

A view of Lucknow Congress Session, 1916.

N.C. Kelkar, a distinguished associate of Tilak.

B.G. Tilak, 1916.

The members of Home Rule League.

Mrs Annie Besant with G.S. Arundale and B.P. Wadia.

The Home Rule League deputation in London.

G.S. Khaparde and B.S. Moonje.

Joseph Baptista.

Gandhiji & Kasturba on their return to India, 1915.

Gandhiji & Kasturba with social workers during his tour of Gujarat, 1916.

Gandhiji being taken in procession by the citizens of Karachi, 1916.

Sabarmati Ashram founded by Gandhiji in 1917 on the bank of the river in Ahmedabad.

Lala Lajpat Rai, the eminent Punjabi nationalist.

C.R. Das, the distinguished Bengali leader.

Maulana Abul Kalam Azad, a pioneer of the Pan-Islamic Movement in India.

Hakim Ajmal Khan, the distinguished Muslim nationalist leader from Delhi.

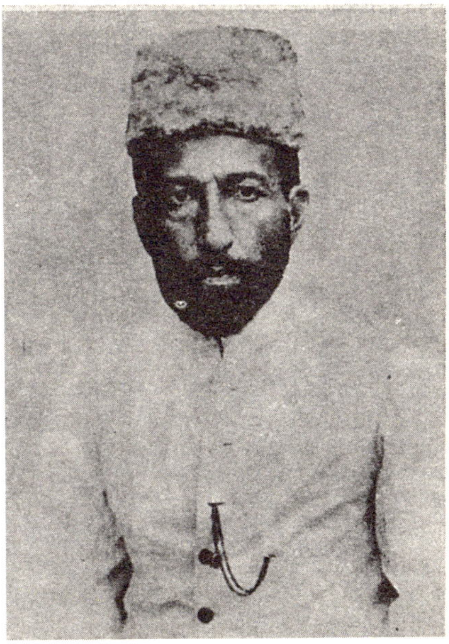

Motilal Nehru who presided over the Amritsar Congress.

M.K. Gandhi at the time of the Amritsar Congress.

Delegates at the Amritsar Congress Session, 1919.